Paul Portner, Claudia Maienborn and Klaus von Heusinger (Eds.)
Semantics – Sentence and Information Structure

This volume is part of a larger set of handbooks to Semantics

1	**Semantics: Foundations, History and Methods**	
	Klaus von Heusinger, Claudia Maienborn, Paul Portner (eds.)	
2	**Semantics: Lexical Structures and Adjectives**	
	Claudia Maienborn, Klaus von Heusinger, Paul Portner (eds.)	
3	**Semantics: Theories**	
	Claudia Maienborn, Klaus von Heusinger, Paul Portner (eds.)	
4	**Semantics: Noun Phrases and Verb Phrases**	
	Paul Portner, Klaus von Heusinger, Claudia Maienborn (eds.)	
5	**Semantics: Sentence and Information Structure**	
	Paul Portner, Claudia Maienborn, Klaus von Heusinger (eds.)	
6	**Semantics: Interfaces**	
	Claudia Maienborn, Klaus von Heusinger, Paul Portner (eds.)	
7	**Semantics: Typology, Diachrony and Processing**	
	Klaus von Heusinger, Claudia Maienborn, Paul Portner (eds.)	

Semantics
Sentence and Information Structure

Edited by
Paul Portner
Claudia Maienborn
Klaus von Heusinger

DE GRUYTER
MOUTON

ISBN 978-3-11-058722-7
e-ISBN (PDF) 978-3-11-058986-3
e-ISBN (EPUB) 978-3-11-058731-9

Library of Congress Cataloging-in-Publication Data
Names: Portner, Paul, editor. | Maienborn, Claudia, editor. | Heusinger,
  Klaus von, editor.
Title: Semantics : foundations, history and methods / edited by Paul Portner,
  Claudia Maienborn, Klaus von Heusinger.
Description: Berlin ; Boston : De Gruyter, [2019] | Series: Mouton reader |
  Includes bibliographical references and index.
Identifiers: LCCN 2018031290 (print) | LCCN 2018045977 (ebook) | ISBN
  9783110589863 (electronic Portable Document Format (pdf) | ISBN
  9783110587227 (print : alk. paper) | ISBN 9783110589863 (e-book pdf) |
  ISBN 9783110587319 (e-book epub)
Subjects: LCSH: Semantics.
Classification: LCC P325 (ebook) | LCC P325 .S37997 2019 (print) | DDC
  401/.43--dc23
LC record available at https://lccn.loc.gov/2018031290

Bibliographic information published by the Deutsche Nationalbibliothek
The Deutsche Nationalbibliothek lists this publication in the Deutsche Nationalbibliografie;
detailed bibliographic data are available in the Internet at http://dnb.dnb.de.

© 2019 Walter de Gruyter GmbH, Berlin/Boston
Cover image: anyaivanova / Getty Images Plus
Typesetting: Integra Software Services Pvt. Ltd.
Printing and binding: CPI books GmbH, Leck

www.degruyter.com

Contents

	Anna Szabolcsi	
1	**Scope and binding** —— 1	

	Elena Herburger	
2	**Negation** —— 46	

	Anastasia Giannakidou	
3	**Negative and positive polarity items** —— 69	

	Roberto Zamparelli	
4	**Coordination** —— 135	

	Manfred Krifka	
5	**Questions** —— 171	

	Chung-hye Han	
6	**Imperatives** —— 225	

	Line Mikkelsen	
7	**Copular clauses** —— 250	

	Louise McNally	
8	**Existential sentences** —— 281	

	Ingo Reich	
9	**Ellipsis** —— 306	

	Stefan Hinterwimmer	
10	**Information structure and truth conditional semantics** —— 339	

	Craige Roberts	
11	**Topics** —— 381	

	Gregory Ward and Betty J. Birner	
12	**Discourse effects of word order variation** —— 413	

Andrew Kehler
13   Cohesion and coherence —— 450

Bart Geurts
14   Accessibility and anaphora —— 481

Malte Zimmermann
15   Discourse particles —— 511

Index —— 545

Anna Szabolcsi
1 Scope and binding

1. Introduction to the core notion of scope —— 2
2. Generalized quantifiers and their elements: operators and their scopes —— 4
3. Scope and constituent structure —— 6
4. Quantifier phrases do not directly bind pronouns —— 15
5. Variable-ful and variable-free binding —— 18
6. No scope for scope? —— 24
7. Scope judgments —— 26
8. Existential versus distributive scope —— 27
9. Counting quantifiers —— 35
10. Clause internal scope behavior —— 36
11. Internal structure —— 38
12. Pronouns as definite descriptions and co-variation with situations —— 38
13. Conclusion —— 41
14. References —— 42

Abstract: The first part of this article (Sections 1–5) focuses on the classical notions of scope and binding and their formal foundations. It argues that once their semantic core is properly understood, it can be implemented in various different ways: with or without movement, with or without variables.

The second part (Sections 6–12) takes up the empirical issues that have redrawn the map in the past two decades. It turns out that scope is not a primitive. Existential scope and distributive scope have to be distinguished, leaving few if any run-of-the-mill quantifiers. Scope behavior is also not uniform. At least three classes of expressions emerge: indefinites, distributive universals, and counters. Likewise, the bound variable interpretation of pronouns is joined by co-variation with situations. As a result, the classical notions of scope and binding are likely to end up as building blocks in the varied mechanisms at work in "scope phenomena" and "binding phenomena", and not as self-contained analyses of those phenomena.

Anna Szabolcsi, New York, USA

1 Introduction to the core notion of scope

The core notion of scope in natural language is the same as in logic. The scope of an operator is that part of the formula (expression, sentence, text) on which the operator performs its characteristic action. If one operator is within the scope of another, their relative scope determines their order of operation. To illustrate, consider the following example from predicate logic, where scope is indicated by brackets and parentheses. (See Gamut (1991) for predicate logic, type theory, and other logical notions not explained in this text.)

(1) $\neg(\forall x[f(x)] \wedge h(x)) \vee k(a)$

The characteristic action of negation is to reverse the truth-value of its scope. In (1) the scope of $\neg$ is $\forall x[f(x)] \wedge h(x)$, so this is the part on which it performs its action; it does not affect $k(a)$. By the same token, $\forall$ and $\wedge$ perform their action earlier than $\neg$ ("earlier" in the sense that their outputs feed $\neg$) and $\vee$ operates after $\neg$ (the output of $\neg$ feeds $\vee$). Similarly, the characteristic action of $\forall$ is to check all possible assignments of values to the variables within its scope that are "linked" to it. In (1) the scope of $\forall x$ is $f(x)$. $\forall x$ does not operate on the x of $h(x)$, because it is not within its scope.

The bracketing in (1) reflects constituent structure: it records the steps in which the formula is built from its subformulae. The scope of an operator is simply the constituent that it is attached to; in linguistic terminology, its sister node. All properties of absolute and relative scope follow from this.

We may immediately add a caveat. In logics with a nimbler syntax it is possible to "arrest" the action of operators and thereby dissociate the chronological order in which they enter the formula from the order of their actual operation. This possibility is relevant to us because, technical details aside (see (26)–(27)), it is reminiscent of the possibility in natural language for operators to take action earlier or later than what the constituent structure produced by some simple syntax might predict. Therefore in talking about natural language one has to distinguish between semantic scope and syntactic domain. The syntactic domain of an expression is defined with reference to c-command, maximal projections, feature inheritance, or similar notions. Many linguists entertain the following hypothesis:

(2) Hypothesis about Scope and Domain:
The semantic scope of a linguistic operator coincides with its domain in some syntactic representation that the operator is part of.

This hypothesis goes back to Reinhart's (1979, 1983) pioneering work on what she called syntactic domains for semantic rules. Reinhart's specific assumption was that the only relevant syntactic representation is surface structure, but the key idea is the more general one, namely, that syntactic structure determines semantic scope and does so in a very particular way. This is not the only possible view: for example, Farkas (1997) puts forth a non-structural theory of scope. So one important task for work on the syntax/semantics interface is to determine whether (2) is correct and if yes, exactly what kind of syntactic representations and notion of domain bear it out.

Another important task is due to the fact that it is not immediately obvious what linguistic expressions are operators. We illustrate this with a classical example. (3) can be paraphrased roughly as (4):

(3) Dogs barked everywhere.

(4) $\forall x[\text{relevant chunk of space}(x)] [\exists y[\text{dog}'(y) \land \text{barked}'(\text{at } x)(y)]]$

It may seem straightforward that $\forall$ is contributed by *everywhere* and $\exists$ by *dogs*. However, Carlson (1977) argued convincingly that bare plurals are not existentially quantified phrases. For example, the quantifier that a bare plural supposedly contributes takes only the narrowest possible scope, unlike quantifiers contributed by overt morphemes. Carlson proposed that bare plurals denote kinds. The existential import associated with the bare plural is contributed by the predicate. *Bark* says that there exist barking realizations of the kind denoted by the subject. The narrowest scope observation then follows, because $\exists$ is buried in the interpretation of the verb and cannot enjoy the relative scopal freedom of freestanding operators.

This example highlights the fact that identifying the truth conditions of a sentence and detecting the work of some operator in it does not immediately tell us which expression, if any, contributes that operator. If Carlson's analysis is correct, any talk about the scope of a bare plural is incoherent – a bare plural is not an operator, nor does it contain one. An alternative analysis leads to the same conclusion. According to van Geenhoven (1998), bare plurals enter the sentence via predicate modification, and existential import is not the contribution of any lexical item but of a default operation known as "existential closure".

Although this article does not discuss bare plurals any further, it is going to discuss other "scope(-like)" phenomena where it is not obvious if there is a scope-taking operator in the sentence and if yes, where it comes from. Indefinites like *some dog* and *two dogs* are a prime case in point.

2 Generalized quantifiers and their elements: operators and their scopes

In many logics, operators are introduced syncategorematically. They are not expressions of the logical language; the syntax only specifies how they combine with expressions to yield new expressions and what their semantic effect is. They function like diacritics in the phonetic alphabet: ' is not a character of the IPA but attaching it to a consonant symbol indicates that the sound is palatal (e.g., [t']). In line with most of the literature we are going to assume that operators embodied by morphemes or phrases are never syncategorematic. But if *every dog* is an ordinary expression that belongs to a syntactic category (say, DP) then it must have a self-contained interpretation. This contrasts with the situation in predicate logic. In (5) the contribution of *every dog* is scattered all over the formula without being a subexpression of it. Everything in (5) other than *bark'* comes from *every dog*.

(5) $\forall x[dog'(x) \rightarrow bark'(x)]$

One of Montague's (1974) most important innovations was to provide a self-contained and uniform kind of denotation for all DPs in the form of generalized quantifiers. The name is due to the fact that it generalizes from the first order logical $\forall$ and $\exists$ and their direct descendants *every dog* and *some dog* to the whole gamut, *less than five dogs*, *at least one dog*, *more dogs than sheep*, *the dog*, etc., even including proper names like *Spot*. (Terminology: we refer to syntactic units like *every dog* as quantifier phrases, noun phrases, or DPs. The label NP is reserved for the complement of the determiner, as in the schematic form *every NP*.)

Some DPs, especially names, are also individual denoters. Therefore they are scopeless in the sense that the different scopes we may attribute to them are truth-conditionally equivalent (Zimmermann 1993), although in other ways it is semantically profitable to subsume them under the rubric of generalized quantifiers. Such treatment makes semantic properties like monotonicity applicable to names, and makes it easy to explain how names conjoin with quantificational DPs. Because we are concerned specifically with scope, in the first half of this article we use DPs that cannot by any stretch of imagination denote individuals. (The theories reviewed here allow one to assign scope vacuously to names, but Fox (2000) proposes the principle of Scope Economy, which requires covert scope-shifting operations like Quantifier Raising to make a truth conditional difference. This makes interesting empirical predictions for VP-ellipsis and other phenomena.)

A generalized quantifier is a set of properties. In the examples below the generalized quantifiers are defined using English and, equivalently, in the language of set theory and in a simplified Montagovian notation, to highlight the fact that they do not have an inherent connection to any particular logical notation. The main simplification is that we present generalized quantifiers extensionally. Therefore each property is traded for the set of individuals that have the property (rather than the intensional analogue, a function from worlds to such sets of individuals), but the term "property" is retained, as customary, to evoke the relevant intuition.

(6) a. *More than one dog* denotes the set of properties that more than one dog has. If more than one dog is hungry, then the property of being hungry is an element of this set.
b. *More than one dog* denotes {P: |dog'∩P|>1}. If more than one dog is hungry, then {a: a∈hungry'}∈{P: |dog'∩P|>1}.
c. *More than one dog* denotes λP∃x∃y[x≠y ∧ dog'(x) ∧ dog'(y) ∧ P(x) ∧ P(y)]. If more than one dog is hungry, then λP∃x∃y[x≠y ∧ dog'(x) ∧ dog'(y) ∧ P(x) ∧ P(y)](hungry') yields the value True.

(7) a. *Every man* denotes the set of properties that every man has. If every man is hungry, then the property of being hungry is an element of this set.
b. *Every man* denotes {P: man' ⊆P}. If every man is hungry, then {a: a∈hungry'}∈{P: man' ⊆P}.
c. *Every man* denotes λP∀x[man'(x) → P(x)]. If every man is hungry, then λP∀x[man'(x) → P(x)](hungry') yields the value True.

The property *(is) hungry'* mentioned above has a simple description, but that is an accident. Properties might have arbitrarily complex descriptions:

(8) If every prof drinks or gambles, then the property of being an individual such that he/she/it drinks or he/she/it gambles is in the set of properties every prof has.

(9) If there is more than one dog that bit every man, then the property of being an individual such that he/she/it bit every man is an element of the set of properties more than one dog has.

(10) If every man was bitten by more than one dog, then the property of being an individual such that there is more than one dog that bit him/her/it is an element of the set of properties every man has.

Properties with simple descriptions and ones with complex descriptions are entirely on a par. We are not adding anything to the idea of generalized quantifiers by allowing properties of the latter kind. But once the possibility is recognized, quantifier scope is taken care of, as we'll now see.

In each case above, some operation is buried in the description of the property that is asserted to be an element of the generalized quantifier. In (8) the buried operation is disjunction; thus (8) describes a configuration in which universal quantification scopes over disjunction. (9) and (10) correspond to the subject wide scope, S>O and the object wide scope, O>S readings of the sentence *More than one dog bit every man*. In (9) the main assertion is about the properties shared by more than one dog, thus the existential quantifier in subject position is taking wide scope. In (10) the main assertion is about the properties shared by every man, thus the universal quantifier in object position is taking wide scope.

This is all there is to it:

(11) The scope of a quantificational DP, on a given analysis of the sentence, is that part of the sentence which denotes a property that is asserted to be an element of the generalized quantifier denoted by DP on that analysis.

3 Scope and constituent structure

3.1 The basic idea

On this view the readings in (8), (9) and (10) correspond to the semantic constituent structures (12), (13) and (14), respectively:

(12)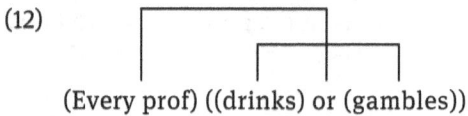
(Every prof) ((drinks) or (gambles))

(13)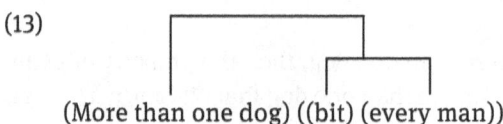
(More than one dog) ((bit) (every man))

(14)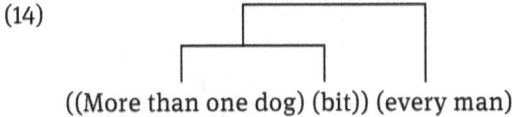

((More than one dog) (bit)) (every man)

Given the hypothesis in (2) we have to ask how well these semantic constituents match up with syntactic constituents. Initial encouragement that a good match can be found comes from observing that wh-fronting creates coherent constituents similar to those we need:

(15) Who drinks or gambles?

(16) Who bit every man?

(17) Who did more than one dog bite?

In this section we consider three ways to implement the above ideas concerning scope. The Montague/May approach produces the above constituent structures in abstract syntax, whether or not there is independent purely syntactic evidence for it. The Hendriks approach dissociates scope from pure syntax in that it allows one to maintain whatever constituent structure seems independently motivated and it still delivers all imaginable scope relations. The proof theoretical perspective in Jäger (2005) and Barker (2007) offers a way to move between the above two as desired. The goals of this discussion are twofold. One is to introduce some fundamental technologies. Another is to show that there is no deep semantic necessity to opt for one technology or the other; the choices can be tailored to what one finds insightful and what the empirical considerations dictate.

3.2 The (first) proper treatment of quantification

We consider two derivations of *More than one dog bit every man* in an extensionalized version of Montague's PTQ (1974). Montague used a syntax inspired by but not identical to a categorial grammar and built sentences "bottom up". This was very unusual at the time when linguists used "top down" phrase structure rules, but today, in the era of Merge in Minimalism, it will look entirely natural.

We assume our verbs to denote functions of individuals (entities of type e). Because quantifier phrases do not denote individuals, they cannot serve as arguments of such verbs. In line with the reasoning above, quantifier phrases combine with expressions that denote properties, and the semantic effect of the combination is to assert that the property is an element of the generalized quantifier. The subject being the highest i.e., last argument of the verb, inflected verb phrases will denote a property anyway, so a subject quantifier phrase can enter the sentence without further ado. If the quantifier phrase is not the last argument, the derivation must ensure that a property-denoting expression is formed for its sake in one way or another; a point made very lucidly in Heim & Kratzer (1998: Ch. 7).

Montague's PTQ offers several ways to build the subject wide scope, S>O and the object wide scope, O>S readings of a sentence. Those chosen below will make the relation between Montague's, May's, and Hendriks's methods the most transparent. We start by applying the verb to placeholder arguments and building a sentence. Placeholders are interpreted as individual variables. Montague employed indexed pronouns as place-holders; we employ indexed empty categories *ec*. Properties (of type <e,t>) are then formed from this sentence by abstracting over the placeholders one by one. Abstraction is achieved by lambda-binding the placeholder variable. (If α is an expression, λx[α] is an expression. λx[α] denotes a function of type <b,a>, where *b* is the type of the variable *x* and *a* is the type of function value α. When applied to some argument β, the value of the function is computed by replacing every occurrence of *x* bound by λx in α by β. E.g., $\lambda x[x^2](3) = 3^2$.)

Each time a property is formed, a quantifier can be introduced. The later a quantifier is introduced, the wider its scope: other operators may already be buried in the definition of the property that it combines with. Montague's PTQ collapsed the two steps of lambda-binding a free variable and applying a generalized quantifier to the property so formed into a single rule of quantifying-in. To make the derivation more transparent, we disentangle the two steps, as do Heim & Kratzer (1998), who construe lambda abstraction as the reflex of the movement of the index on the placeholder. We follow PTQ in replacing the placeholder with the quantifier phrase in the surface string. This feature is syntactically unsophisticated and need not be taken too seriously; see May and Hendriks below.

The derivation of the reading where the subject existential scopes over the direct object universal produces the following last step. The cardinality quantifier *more than one* will be abbreviated using $\exists_{>1}$.

(18) $\lambda P \exists_{>1} z[\text{dog}'(z) \wedge P(z)] \; (\lambda x_2 \forall y[\text{man}'(y) \rightarrow \text{bit}'(y)(x_2)]) =$
$\exists_{>1} z[\text{dog}'(z) \wedge \lambda x_2 \forall y[\text{man}'(y) \rightarrow \text{bit}'(y)(x_2)] \; (z)] =$
$\exists_{>1} z[\text{dog}'(z) \wedge \forall y[\text{man}'(y) \rightarrow \text{bit}'(y)(z)]]$

Recall that the derivations are to be read bottom-up!

(19) Subject > Object reading

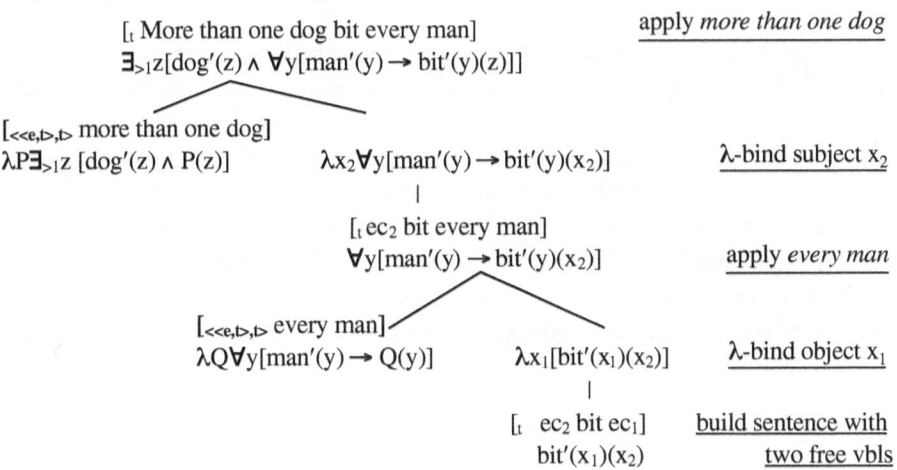

The derivation of the reading where the direct object universal scopes over the subject existential differs from the above in just one respect: properties are formed by λ-binding the subject variable first and the direct object variable second, which reverses the order of introducing the two quantifier phrases. The last step that introduces the universal is this:

(20) λQ∀y[man'(y) → Q(y)](λx₃∃₋₁z[dog'(z) ∧ bit'(x₃)(z)]) =
∀y[man'(y) → λx₃∃₋₁z[dog'(z) ∧ bit'(x₃)(z)](y)] =
∀y[man'(y) → ∃₋₁z[dog'(z) ∧ bit'(y)(z)]]

(21) Object > Subject reading

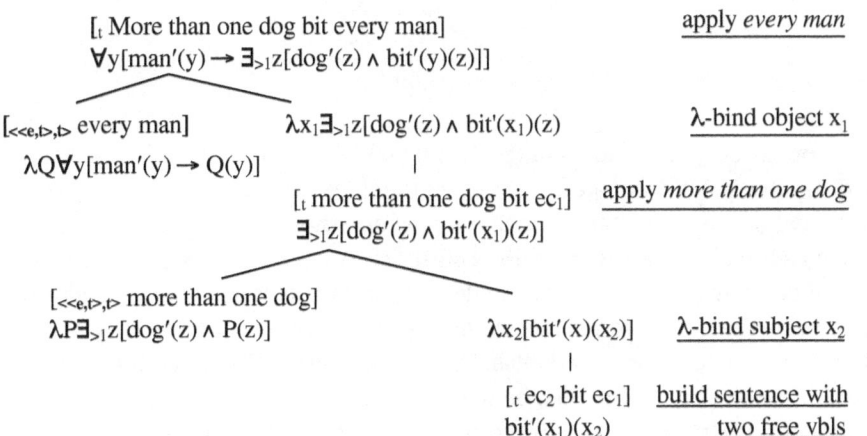

3.3 Quantifier Raising

Within generative syntax May (1977, 1985) first derives a syntactic structure leading to the surface string with quantifier phrases in argument positions. This structure is input to further syntactic rules whose operation feeds only semantic interpretation (Logical Form). Such a rule is Quantifier Raising (QR), which adjoins quantifier phrases to VP or to S (TP in more recent terminology). The scope of the adjoined quantifier phrase is its c-command domain. The definition of c-command is crucial for the details but for the bird's eye view we are taking here we simply assume that a phrase c-commands its sister relative to the first branching node above it. Crucial is the consequence that the higher a quantifier is adjoined, the wider scope it takes.

(22) 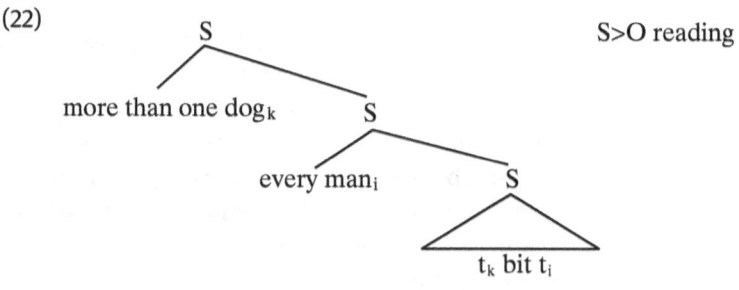 S>O reading

(23) 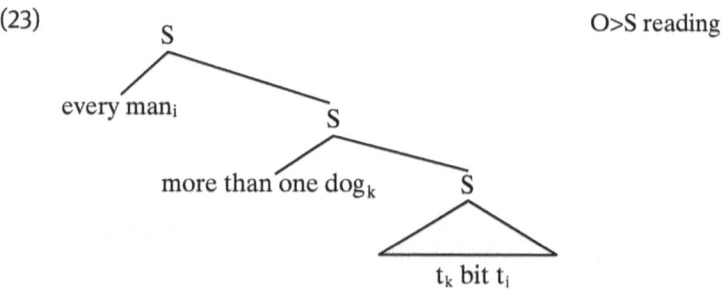 O>S reading

(22) is obviously parallel to Montague's (19) and (23) to Montague's (21). A syntactic difference is that Montague intersperses the steps that disambiguate scope with those that create the surface string, and May does not. A difference more important to us is that while May treats the phrases *every man* and *more than one dog* as normal categorematic expressions in deriving surface syntax, at LF these phrases behave like the syncategorematic operators of the predicate calculus: they directly bind traces that function as variables. This can be remedied by imagining that there is a lambda-binding step hidden between building an S and adjoining a quantifier phrase to it. With that, the parallelism between the two pairs of derivations is essen-

tially complete. Reversing historical order we might look at Montague's grammar as one that builds the output of May's compositionally, without invoking movement. Heim & Kratzer (1998) show that a compositional strategy may even include movement, and within the copy theory of movement Fox (2002) reinterprets the lowest copy of QR as a parametrized definite description.

3.4 All the scopes, but a simple syntax

What emerges from the above is that any representation of the S>O and the O>S readings will have to boil down to the schemas in (24)–(25); similarly for any other pair of quantifiers. $P(x)(y)$ is forced by the assumption that the natural language predicates at hand take individuals as arguments. The lambda-binding (predicate abstraction) steps are forced by the assumption that quantifier phrases denote generalized quantifiers. The two schemas differ as to which argument slot is lambda-bound first and which second.

(24) $QP_a(\lambda y[QP_b(\lambda x[P(x)(y)])])$ S>O

(25) $QP_a(\lambda x[QP_b(\lambda y[P(x)(y)])])$ O>S

One of the key insights in Hendriks (1993) is that it is possible to abstract these interpretive schemas away from the specific quantifier phrases QP_a and QP_b. This in turn allows one to dissociate the interpretive schema from the syntactic constituent structure of the sentence.

Replace QP_a and QP_b with variables A and B of the same type as generalized quantifiers (<<e,t>,t>) and abstract over them with λ operators. Because the variables A, B are not individual variables but are of the generalized quantifier type, the lambda expressions in (26)–(27) take quantifier phrases as arguments, rather than the other way around. The order in which the λA and λB prefixes appear determines the order in which the verb picks up its arguments, but it does not affect their scope, so it can be dictated by independent syntactic considerations; for example we may assume an invariant (S (V O)) structure. In both (26) and (27) the first quantifier phrase the lambda-expression applies to will be the direct object. The relative scope of the quantifier phrases replacing A and B is determined by their relative order within the underlined portions of (26)–(27):

(26) λBλA[A(λy[B(λx[P(x)(y)])])]   schema of S>O

(27) λBλA[B(λx[A(λy[P(x)(y)])])]   schema of O>S

This is the "nimbler logic" hinted at in Section 1 that allows one to arrest the action of a quantifier at the point it enters the formula and to release it where desired. The quantifier's action is released where it actually applies to an expression that denotes a property.

But where are these schemas coming from, if they do not simply record the phrase-by-phrase assembly of the material of the sentence? Hendriks proposes to assign flexible types to verbs, so that two versions of *bite* for example anticipate two different scope relations between the subject and the object. (26) and (27) are two interpretations for the same transitive verb P. Below is a constituent-by-constituent derivation of the O>S reading. The verb combines with both the direct object and the subject by functional application:

(28) bit': $\lambda B \lambda A [B(\lambda z [A(\lambda v [bit'(z)(v)])])]$
      $every\ man'$: $\lambda Q \forall y [man'(y) \rightarrow Q(y)]$
      $bit\ every\ man'$: $\lambda B \lambda A [B(\lambda z [A(\lambda v [bit(z)(v)])])] (\lambda Q \forall y [man'(y) \rightarrow Q(y)]) =$
      $\lambda A [\forall y [man'(y) \rightarrow A(\lambda v [bit'(y)(v)])]]$
      $more\ than\ one\ dog'$: $\lambda P \exists_{>1} z [dog'(z) \land P(z)]$
      $more\ than\ one\ dog\ bit\ every\ man'$:
      $\lambda A [\forall y [man'(y) \rightarrow A(\lambda v [bit'(y)(v)])]] (\lambda P \exists_{>1} z [dog'(z) \land P(z)]) =$
      $\forall y [man'(y) \rightarrow \exists_{>1} z [dog'(z) \land bit'(y)(z)]]$

This is the gist of Hendriks's proposal. More generally, he shows two important things. First, the different interpretations for the verb can be obtained systematically by so-called type-change rules, in this case, by two applications of Argument Raising, see (29). (26)–(27) are due to two different orders in which the subject and the object slots are raised, cf. the underlined segments. Second, all the logically possible scope relations in an arbitrarily multi-clausal sentence, including extensional–intensional ambiguities, can be anticipated by the use of three type-change rules: Argument Raising, Value Raising, and Argument Lowering. We ignore the last one, which is required for certain intensional phenomena. Below are extensionalized Argument Raising and Value Raising. The simplified version of Value Raising is nothing else than the good old type-raising rule that turns proper names into generalized quantifiers.

(29) Argument Raising:
      If α' is the translation of α, and α' is of type $<A,<b,<C,d>>$, then $\lambda x_A \lambda w_{<<b,d>,d>} \lambda y_C [w(\lambda z_b [\alpha'(x)(z)(y)])]$, which is of type $<A,<<b,d>,d>,<C,d>>$, is also a translation of α, where A and C stand for possibly empty sequences of types such that if g is a type, $<A,g>$ and $<C,g>$ represent the types $<a_1, <... <a_n, g>...>>$ and $<c_1, <... <c_n, g> ...>>$.

Simplified by taking A and C to be empty:
If α' is the translation of α, and α' is of type <b,d>, then $\lambda w_{<<b,d>,d>}[w(\lambda z_b[\alpha'(z)])]$, which is of type <<<b,d>,d>,d>, is also a translation of α.

(30) Value Raising:
If α' is the translation of α, and α' is of type <A,b>, then $\lambda x_A \lambda u_{<b,d>}[u(\alpha'(x))]$, which is of type <A,<<b,d>,d>>, is also a translation of α, where A and C stand for possibly empty sequences of types such that if g is a type, <A,g> and <C,g> represent the types <a1, <... <a_n,g>...>> and <c_1, <... <c_n,g> ...>>.

Simplified by taking A to be empty:
If α' is the translation of α, and α' is of type b, then $\lambda u_{<b,d>}[u(\alpha')]$, which is of type <<b,d>,d>, is also a translation of α.

Let us mention two other cases that involve the dissociation of the chronological order of introducing operators into the syntactic structure from the scope they take, and have been handled using very like-minded pieces of logical machinery. Cresti (1995) analyzes "scope reconstruction" using a combination of generalized quantifier type variables and individual type variables, to an effect very much like that of Argument Raising:

(31) How many people do you think I should talk to?
    (i) 'for what number n, you think it should be the case that there are n-many people that I talk to'
    (narrow scope, amount reading of *how many people*)
    (ii) 'for what number n, there are n-many people x such that you think I should talk to x'
    (wide scope, individual reading of *how many people*)

"Reconstruction" is so called because in (i) *n-many people* is "put back" into a lower position for interpretation. Cresti derives the two readings without actual reconstruction. In the derivations below, x is a trace of type e (individuals), and X is a trace of the same type as *n-many people* (intensionalized generalized quantifiers). Working bottom-up, each trace is bound by a λ operator to allow the next trace or the moved phrase itself to enter the chain. The lowest position of the chain is always occupied by a trace x of the individual type, but intermediate traces (underlined) may make one switch to the higher type X. The scope difference with respect to the intensional operator *should* is due to the fact that in (32) the switch from x to X takes place within the scope of *should*, whereas in (33) *should* has no X in its scope. Note that the direction of functional application is type-driven, i.e., in X λX.φ the second expression is applied to the first, whereas in X λx.φ the first is applied to the second.

(32) narrow scope:
 [$_{CP}$ how many people λX[$_{IP}$ ... think [$_{CP}$ X̲ λX[$_{IP}$ ... should [$_{VP}$ X̲ λx[$_{VP}$ ...x...]]]]]]

(33) wide scope:
 [$_{CP}$ how many people λX[$_{IP}$ X̲ λx[$_{IP}$ ... think [$_{CP}$ x̲ λx[$_{IP}$ ... should [$_{VP}$ ...x...]]]]]]

Moltmann & Szabolcsi (1994) use an idea very much like Value Raising to account for the surprising 'librarians vary with students' reading of (34):

(34) Some librarian or other found out which book every student needed.
 √'for every student x, there is some librarian or other who found out which book x needed'

Every student in the complement clause can apparently make the matrix subject referentially dependent; but under normal circumstances *every NP* is known not to scope out of its own clause. Moltmann & Szabolcsi argue that there is no need to assume that here, either. Instead, the complement of *found out, which book every student needed* receives a pair-list reading, 'for every student, which book did he need' and as a whole scopes over the subject of *found out*, which is its clause mate. The result is logically equivalent to scoping *every student* out on its own.

While these works do not use flexible types for verbs, they illustrate the naturalness of the logical tools that Hendriks employs. Inspired by computer science, Barker & Shan (2006) associate linguistic expressions with their possible continuations. A continuation is the skeleton of a syntactico-semantic structure that the expression anticipates participating in. Continuized types are similar to Hendriks's raised types and to context change potentials in dynamic semantics.

3.5 Have your cake and eat it too

The general lesson is this. Once we assign a generalized quantifier denotation to quantifier phrases and understand the simple scenarios of their interaction, there are many different ways to implement those scenarios. They may be acted out in the syntactic derivation of the sentence, but they may as well be squeezed into the flexible types of the participating expressions. Consequently, we may create abstract constituents by movement, but we may alternatively stick to some independently motivated constituent structure. We may bind syntactic variables (placeholders, traces), but we may alternatively do without them and go "variable free". Notably, Hendriks's scope grammar is directly compositional, a property advocated in Jacobson (2002). Direct Compositionality means that each constituent built by the independently motivated syntax is immediately assigned its final and explicit interpretation.

The fact that one can take either approach is good news. But having to choose between them may not be so good, since both approaches offer their own insights. Barker (2007) makes the very important claim that it is in fact not necessary to choose. Building directly on Jäger's (2005) proof theoretical proposal Barker points out that a grammar can deliver "direct compositionality on demand". Here the long-distance (Montague/May/Heim & Kratzer style) and the local (Hendriks style) analyses arise from one and the same set of rules, none of which are redundant.

4 Quantifier phrases do not directly bind pronouns

We have seen that a linguistic theory may link quantifier phrases to variable-like syntactic expressions (traces), although this is not crucial. But predicate logical quantifiers do not only bind variables that might correspond to their traces in the syntactician's sense. (35), which can be seen to translate one reading of (36), contains three bound occurrences of the variable x, of which the one in $room\text{-}of'(x)$ corresponds to the pronoun *his*.

(35) $\forall x[boy'(x) \rightarrow in'(room\text{-}of'(x))(x)]$

(36) Every boy is in his room.

Is the relation between *every boy* and *his* a case of binding in the same sense as the relation between $\forall x$ and the x of $room\text{-}of'(x)$ is, as has often been assumed? There is serious indication that the two at least have something in common. As observed in Reinhart (1983) contrasts like (36) versus (37) show that a quantifier phrase binds a pronoun if the pronoun is within its c-command domain and, therefore, scope (although see Barker & Shan 2008). Coreference between a name or other referring expression and a pronoun is different: it does not require c-command, see (38)–(39).

(37) That every boy was hungry surprised his mother.
    #'for every boy, that he was hungry surprised his own mother'

(38) Jeroen is in his room.

(39) That Jeroen was hungry surprised his mother.

Thus, inducing a bound variable reading in pronouns seems like one of the basic "scope actions" of quantifiers. But nothing in our account of the scope behavior of quantifier phrases interpreted as generalized quantifiers explains how they bind pronouns.

This is good news, because the bound reading of the pronoun in (36) does not come about in the same way as the binding of the x's in (35). In (35) the three variables are all directly bound by $\forall x$ because, in addition to being within its scope, they happen to have the same letter as the quantifier prefix. In contrast, pronouns are not directly bound by quantifier phrases in natural language. In the well-known parlance of syntactic Binding Theory, pronouns have to be co-indexed with a c-commanding item in argument position (subject, object, possessor, etc.), not with one in operator position (the landing site of wh-movement or the adjoined position created by Quantifier Raising). The claim that syntactic binding is a relation between argument positions is grounded primarily in data about reflexives but it is thought to extend to pronouns and offers a simple account of strong and weak crossover. To see WCO in action, consider singular *a different NP*. Because it is not a pronominal, it helps exhibit the full range of scope effects (see Beghelli & Stowell 1997). (40) shows that the prepositional object *every girl* can scope over both the subject and the direct object.

(40) a. A different person sent a gift to every girl.
     b. Vlad sent a different gift to every girl.

But none of the pronouns in (41) can be interpreted as linked to *every girl*:

(41) a. She sent a gift to every girl.
     b. Her aunt sent a gift to every girl.
     c. Vlad sent her gift to every girl.

Bach & Partee's (1984) explanation is that there is simply no syntactic binding in (41), regardless of scope, because the argument position of the quantifier does not c-command the pronoun.

If the pronoun is directly linked to the c-commanding argument position and not to the quantifier itself, what is the actual operator that binds it? The operator that identifies the pronoun with a c-commanding argument position. The technologies for achieving "identification" are varied, but the interpretive result is always the same. (42) presents three equivalent metalinguistic descriptions of the bound pronoun reading of the VP *saw his/her/its own father*:

(42) a. be an individual such that he/she/it saw his/her/its own father
 b. {a: a saw a's father}
 c. λx[x saw x's father]

So the operator that binds the pronoun is the abstraction operator λ. Therefore in this article the quantifier phrase will be neutrally called the antecedent of the pronoun and will not be accorded the false title of the binder.

Once the property described in (42) is derived, it combines with a noun phrase denotation as other properties do, see (6) through (10), and the antecedent is specified:

(43) If every girl saw her own father, then the property of being an individual such that he/she/it saw his/her/its own father is an element of the set of properties shared by every girl.

Proof that the crucial factor in the bound variable reading of pronouns is not the presence of a quantifier phrase comes from the so-called sloppy identity reading of pronouns in ellipsis in coordination (Reinhart 1983). The interpretation of elided VPs matches that of the full VP, but it can do so in two ways. In the so-called sloppy identity reading, the "pronoun in the elided VP" is linked to the subject of the same, elided VP. Crucial to us is the fact that in (44)–(45) *did* can receive the bound variable pronoun reading (42), regardless of whether the subject of the full VP is *every boy* or *Kim*. This in turn shows that the full VP itself can have the (42) reading even if its subject is not a quantifier.

(44) Every boy saw his father, and every girl did too.
 √ '...and every girl saw her own father' (sloppy)

(45) Kim saw his father, and every girl did too.
 √ '...and every girl saw her own father' (sloppy)

In the so-called strict identity reading, the "pronoun in the elided VP" is linked to the subject of the full VP. (44) has no strict reading; on the strict reading of (45), every girl saw Kim's father. (The strict reading itself is not restricted to referential antecedents. It is available with quantificational antecedents too, if those c-command the ellipsis site, as in *Every boy discovered his mistakes before the teacher did [discover that boy's mistakes]*, see Gawron & Peters (1990), Szabolcsi (1992).)

For lack of space this article cannot dwell on the Binding Theory; see Reinhart (2006) for a recent and comprehensive discussion.

5 Variable-ful and variable-free binding

5.1 Pronouns that start out as free variables

In most theories, Montague (1974), May (1977, 1985), Heim & Kratzer (1998), Büring (2005) among them, the derivation of (42) starts out with the pronoun interpreted as a free variable, i.e., one that is assigned an individual in the model by the current assignment. The exact shape of the next step depends on whether a placeholder (trace) is posited in the position that the pronoun should be linked to, or we simply have an as yet unsaturated argument of a function. If there is a placeholder, then the precondition for binding is that the variable translating the pronoun be identical to the one translating the placeholder; if there is simply an unsaturated argument slot, the pronoun's variable needs to bear an index identical to that of the prospective saturator of that argument slot. Then an abstraction operator binds both the placeholder/argument slot and the pronoun in one fell swoop and creates an assignment-independent (closed) expression. In Heim & Kratzer's (1998) and Büring's (2005) formulation these are written as (46)–(47). In syntax the Binder rule inserts the β binding prefix and transfers or copies the index 2 to β from the phrase that is slated to be the subject. (47) spells out the working of the Binder Index Evaluation rule. g is the current assignment of values to variables. $g(2)$ is the individual that g assigns to the variable 2. $g[2{\rightarrow}x]$ is an assignment that differs from g in that it assigns the individual x to variable 2.

(46) $|[\text{saw his}_2 \text{ father}]|^{M,g} = \lambda y[y \text{ saw } g(2)\text{'s father}]$

(47) $|[\beta_2(\text{saw his}_2 \text{ father})]|^{M,g} = \lambda x[\lambda y[y \text{ saw } g[2{\rightarrow}x](2)\text{'s father}](x)]$
    $= \lambda x[x \text{ saw } g[2{\rightarrow}x](2)\text{'s father}] = \lambda x[x \text{ saw } x\text{'s father}]$

See article 1 [Semantics: Noun Phrases and Verb Phrases] (Büring) *Pronouns* for further details.

5.2 Pronouns that grab antecedents for themselves

Crucial to the binding technology just reviewed is that (i) operators manipulate assignments, (ii) pronouns and all other noun phrases come with indices, and

(iii) pronouns start out as free (assignment dependent) variables and become bound (assignment independent) in the course of the derivation – a transition whose compositionality is dubious. Are these features necessary? Just as in the case of quantifier scope, once we understand the semantic core of the phenomenon it is easy to see that it can be implemented in more than one way. We sketch two different ways of building interpretations like (42) without the above features.

Reinhart (1983) argues that reflexives and bound pronouns are essentially the same thing: both receive bound variable interpretations strictly within the c-command domain (scope) of the binder and differ only as to locality. Szabolcsi (1987/1989, 1992) uses reflexives as a stepping-stone for a general theory that captures Reinhart's intuition with very different logical tools. The case of reflexives is striking, because reflexives are ungrammatical if they do not get bound. Therefore assigning them a free variable interpretation in the lexicon amounts to deliberately misinterpreting them in a way that has to be straightened out by syntax. The null hypothesis is that expressions start out with correct interpretations. Szabolcsi proposes to place all the action into the interpretation of the reflexive. *Himself* in (48) is interpreted as an operation on functions that says, 'I saturate the first argument of an (at least) two-place function, and its next argument will bind me'. The "next argument" part ensures that the antecedent c-commands the reflexive. As (49) shows, *saw himself* comes out as denoting a property parallel to (42).

(48)   himself' = $\lambda f \lambda x[f(x)(x)]$, where f is a variable of type <e,<e,t>>

(49)   saw himself' = $\lambda f \lambda x[f(x)(x)](saw') = \lambda x[saw'(x)(x)]$

Operations on functions as in (48) are known as combinators; this specific one is called a duplicator, because its entity argument appears twice in the description of the function value. Combinatory logic has the same expressive power as the lambda calculus, but builds the same meanings differently (Curry & Feys 1958; Quine 1960). Relevant to us is the fact that free variables in combinatory logic are name-like: they never get bound, because no operators manipulate assignments. If desired, a pronoun that is intended to remain free (deictic) can be interpreted as a free variable, and English *he* can be treated as ambiguous between the distinct variables *x, y, z*. To account for bound pronouns in the spirit of Reinhart, Szabolcsi assigns *he* a further lexical interpretation, one that is similar to that of reflexives. On this view the only important difference between *himself* and he_{bound} is that the latter ensures that the c-commanding antecedent is an argument of a higher predicate, cf. Principle B of the Binding Theory that prohibits pronouns from being bound within their local domain.

(50) $he_{bound}/him_{bound}' = \lambda h \lambda f \lambda x[f(hx)(x)]$, where h is a variable of type <e,t> and f is a variable of type <t,<e,t>>

(51) (that) he_{bound} won' = $\lambda h \lambda f \lambda x[f(hx)(x)](won')$ =
$\lambda f \lambda x[f(won'(x))(x)]$

The clause *that he$_{bound}$ won* acts like one big reflexive: the subject of the matrix verb will be interpreted as the antecedent of *he$_{bound}$*. In other words, *he$_{bound}$* is a pied piper: its duplicatorhood "percolates" up to the clause (or other appropriate phrase) that contains *he$_{bound}$* and so anti-locality is ensured, because the pronoun cannot grab an antecedent within that clause. (We ignore the intensionality of *think*.)

(52) thought that he_{bound} won' = $\lambda f \lambda x[f(won'(x))(x)](thought')$ =
$\lambda x[thought'(won'(x))(x)]$

(53) Every boy thought that he_{bound} won' =
$\lambda P \forall z[boy'(z) \rightarrow P(z)]$ $(\lambda x[thought'(won'(x))(x)])$ =
$\forall z[boy'(z) \rightarrow thought'(won'(z))(z)]$

The derivation of *saw his$_{bound}$ father* would proceed analogously, with *his$_{bound}$* having arguments whose types are a bit different from those of *he/him$_{bound}$*; compare the discussion in 5.3.

(54) $his_{bound}' = \lambda h \lambda f \lambda x[f(hx)(x)]$, where h is a variable of type <<e,t>, e> and f is a variable of type <e,<α,t>>

5.3 Pronouns as identity maps

One feature of the duplicator theory of reflexives and bound pronouns is that it avoids turning an assignment dependent expression into an assignment independent one. But there are other ways to achieve this. One is to treat free variables not as dependent on a chosen assignment but as functions from assignments (Sternefeld 2001, among others):

(55) $|[x]|^M = \lambda g[g(x)]$, where g is a variable over assignments

A formula with a free variable inherits this property, i.e., it is also a function from assignments: $\lambda g[f(g(x))]$. Quantifiers continue to manipulate assignments.

Another option is intuitively similar but it even eliminates the manipulation of assignments. It involves trading variables for identity functions, $\lambda x[x]$, for x of any type. Formulas with what used to be a free variable are traded for predicates: $\lambda x[f(x)]$.

This is the proposal adopted by Hepple (1990) and by Jacobson in a series of papers starting with 1992; see especially Jacobson (1999, 2000). Jacobson is dissatisfied with that feature of Szabolcsi's proposal that it retains the standard ambiguity of free pronouns (*he* ambiguously represents the distinct variables *x*, *y*, *z*, ...) and even increases it (*he* versus he_{bound}). In Jacobson's version of variable-free semantics pronouns are identity maps, and this interpretation underlies all their uses.

(56) $he' = \lambda x[x]$, where x is a variable of type e

Sentences with *n* deictic pronouns come out as *n*-place predicates to be applied to some *n*-tuple of contextually salient entities, so the ambiguity of free pronouns is replaced by the contextual dependence of salience. The same identity map interpretation, aided by a combinator that Jacobson names **z**, participates in bound readings. Jacobson's **z** performs the same action that Szabolcsi builds into bound pronouns, compare (50)–(54) with (57), but **z** is a silent operator on verb meanings: a type-shifter. (Hepple interprets both reflexives and pronouns as identity maps. Jacobson does not say how she proposes to treat reflexives.)

(57) $\mathbf{z} = \lambda f \lambda h \lambda x[f(hx)(x)]$

(58) $\mathbf{z}\text{-saw}' = \lambda f \lambda h \lambda x[f(hx)(x)](saw') = \lambda h \lambda x[saw'(hx)(x)]$

Applied to *his father*, interpreted as $\lambda y[\text{father-of}'(y)]$ (we shall see shortly how this comes about), (58) delivers the desired bound reading for the pronoun:

(59) $\mathbf{z}\text{-saw(his father)}' = \lambda h \lambda x[saw'(hx)(x)](\lambda y[\text{father-of}'(y)])$
       $= \lambda x[saw'(\text{father-of}'(x))(x)]$

One straightforward difference between Szabolcsi's and Jacobson's proposals is that only the latter can create duplicated readings in the absence of a reflexive or pronoun. Functional questions are one example where this is relevant. (60) employs *z-chase*' plus a new type <<e,e>,t> interpretation for *what*:

(60) What does no dog chase? Its muzzle.
      For which function f, no-dog' $(\lambda x[\text{chase}'(fx)(x)])$?
      $\lambda z[\text{muzzle-of}'(z)]$.

Dowty (2007: 95–97) notes that the question-answer pair could acquire the same interpretation on Szabolcsi's approach if *what* was given the same <<e,<e,t>>,<e,t>> type as *its muzzle*, interpreted as a duplicator, cf. (50)–(54).

(61) For which Q, no dog'(Q(chase'))?
 λfλx[f(muzzle-of'(x))(x)].

In Dowty's (61) the question itself is not functional, but it expects the answer quantifier to take narrow scope; the pronoun in the answer is responsible for duplication. So function talk may not be strictly necessary here, but it seems crucial elsewhere, e.g., in paycheck pronouns.

Another difference is that whereas both proposals can be easily extended to antecedent-contained deletion as in (62), analyzing it essentially as transitive verb phrase ellipsis (i.e., duplication), only Jacobson's will cover (63) as well:

(62) No dog obeyed every boy who Goldy did.

(63) No dog obeyed every boy who wanted it to.

In (62) the elided part is *obeyed*, whereas in (63) it is *obey him*. To see why this difference is critical we must fill a gap regarding what happens in Jacobson's theory when a pronoun first merges with an argument-taking predicate.

Let us start with *his father*. The relational noun *father* expects an argument of type e, but *he/his* being interpreted as λx[x] is of type <e,e>. Therefore *father* cannot apply to the pronoun. If we wish to maintain that merging expressions is always interpreted as functional application, the type of *father* has to be shifted from <e,α> to <<e,e>,<e,α>>. This shift is performed by the Geach rule, i.e., Jacobson's combinator **g**. In (64) X/Y is the category of functors (syntactic functions) that expect an argument of category Y from the right and return a value of category X: X/Y · Y = X. The category X^Y is mapped to the same type as X/Y, but functors of this category are syntactically inert. X^Y does not apply to arguments of category Y, it only serves as an argument of other functors that look for X^Y. Pronouns interpreted as identity maps have such "domain in the exponent" categories: *he* never applies to *Bill* but can be the argument of **g**(*father-of'*), for example.

(64) If f is an expression of category A/B, then **g**(f) is an expression of category A^C/B^C, where **g** = λhλkλy[h(ky)].

(65) **g**(father-of') = λkλy[father-of'(ky)]

(66) his father' = **g**(father-of')(he') = λkλy[father-of'(ky)](λx[x]) = λy[father-of'(y)]

Likewise, predicates that take *him* or *his father* as an argument do so after undergoing a similar **g**-shift. **z**-*saw* is an exception because **z** incorporates **g**. However, if the pronoun had not been slated to be anteceded by the subject of *saw*, **g**(*saw*) would have been used:

(67) **g**(saw′) = λkλy[λx[saw′(ky)(x)]]

(68) saw him′ = (**g**(saw′))(him′) = λyλx[saw′(y)(x)]

To pave the way back to (63), notice that *his father* is interpreted the same as the function *father-of*, and *saw him* is interpreted the same as *saw*. These, in turn, are semantically the same as if the DP and the VP contained extraction gaps in their internal argument positions. Therefore, in Jacobson's theory there is no semantic difference between the elided phrases in (62) and (63). But Szabolcsi's theory does not produce an *obey him* interpretation for the elided phrase.

The identity function interpretation of pronouns gives rise to a problem that is not satisfactorily solved as of date. As Caroline Heycock has observed, (69) and (70) are logically equivalent. Therefore the theory predicts, incorrectly, that (71) has a reading that can be paraphrased as (72).

(69) λx[mother-of′(x)] = λx[friend-of′(x)]

(70) ∀x[mother-of′(x) = friend-of′(x)]

(71) His mother is his friend.

(72) For every (male) person, his mother is his friend.

One line of attack might be to require expressions containing free pronouns to be predicated of contextually salient entities, and to allow the functional use only as a last resort to avoid a type clash. But it is not obvious how to formulate this efficiently.

Jacobson offers elegant analyses for many hard nuts in binding theory, such as paycheck pronouns, i-within-i effects, copular connectivity, weak crossover, contrastive stress on bound pronouns, and compares them with variable-ful alternatives. See Jacobson (1999, 2000), Kruijff & Oehrle (2003), Barker & Jacobson (2007), and references therein for related work.

A particularly interesting development of this line of research is Jäger (2005), who proposes a proof theoretic implementation of Jacobson's ideas. For LFG's "glue semantics" using linear logic, see Dalrymple (2001).

6 No scope for scope?

In the first part we discussed the classical notions of scope and binding, stressing their semantic core and the freedom in its grammatical implementation. What we did not ask is how well the predictions of the classical theory match up with the data.

This section borrows the title of Hintikka (1997). Our data and the conclusions overlap with but are not identical to Hintikka's.

One feature of the classical theory is that it treats all quantifier phrases alike. Thus, as soon as two expressions are deemed to be quantifier phrases they are predicted to exhibit the same scope behavior. Also, nothing but a stipulation prevents quantifier phrases from scoping out of their clauses, and the stipulation makes all of them clause-bounded. Another feature of the classical theory is that binding requires the argument position of the antecedent to c-command the pronoun. Unfortunately, these predictions are not borne out. The following small sample of data will drive this home.

In (73)–(74) *every show* easily scopes over the subject, but *more than one show* does not:

(73) More than one soprano sings in every show.

(74) Every soprano sings in more than one show.

In (75) *a famous soprano* appears to scope out of its clause, even an island, but in (76)–(77) *more than one soprano* and *every soprano* do not:

(75) Two reporters heard the rumor that a famous soprano owns a tiger.

(76) Two reporters heard the rumor that more than one famous soprano owns a tiger.

(77) Two reporters heard the rumor that every famous soprano owns a tiger.

In (78)–(79) the possessors *every soprano* and *no soprano* can both antecede the pronouns:

(78) Every soprano's keys are in her purse.

(79) No soprano's keys are in her purse.

In (80) *a problem* that is buried in a relative clause and is scopally dependent on *every soprano* can nevertheless antecede the singular pronoun. In (81) *more than one problem* can likewise support a co-varying reading, although a plural pronoun is perhaps preferred.

(80) Every soprano who had a problem wanted to solve it.
 √'for every soprano and her problem, she wanted to solve it'

(81) Every soprano who had more than one problem wanted to solve them/?it.
 √'for every soprano and her more than one problem, she wanted to solve them'

Scope and pronominal anaphora also present their joint surprises for the classical theory. In (82) *a great soprano* appears to both scope in the matrix clause and antecede the singular pronoun in the second conjunct, but in (83)–(84) *more than one soprano* and *every great soprano* do not:

(82) Taro thinks that a great soprano applied and wants to hire her.

(83) Taro thinks that more than one great soprano applied and wants to hire her. (Hire who?)

(84) Taro thinks that every great soprano applied and wants to hire her. (Hire who?)

Many of the developments of the past decades have been based on observations like these. Focusing on noun phrases, below we show that scope is not a primitive (existential scope, distributive scope, and the scope of the descriptive condition need to be factored out) and not a unitary phenomenon (at least bare indefinites, counting quantifiers, and distributive universals have to be distinguished). Likewise, binding relations are due to more than one mechanism (ones based on individuals, situations, and worlds, possibly also agreement). The upshot is not that the classical theory of scope and binding is simply wrong. Instead, it seems that there are few "scope phenomena" and "binding phenomena" that exemplify the classical notions in a pure form. The classical machinery retains its general significance more by offering building blocks for the differentiated theory or theories than by offering self-contained accounts of the particular empirical cases.

The issues reviewed here constitute part of a bigger picture. The articles in Szabolcsi (1997b) and much further work demonstrate that whatever quantificational phenomenon one looks at – branching readings, interaction with negation, distributivity vs. collectivity, intervention effects in extraction and negative polarity licensing (weak islands), event-related readings, pair-list questions, functional readings, and so on – one finds that certain DPs participate and others do not. This suggests that "scope taking", "quantification", and "binding" involve a variety of distinct mechanisms. Each kind of expression participates in those that suit its syntactic structure and its semantics. Szabolcsi (1997a) proposed the following heuristic principle; see the papers in Szabolcsi (1997b) for detailed discussion:

(85) What range of expressions actually participates in a given process is suggestive of exactly what that process consists in.

7 Scope judgments

Scope judgments are held to be notoriously difficult. Part of the difficulty may be an artifact of the classical theory: if one expects all quantifiers to behave uniformly, it is bewildering to find that they do not. Another reason may be that scope independent readings blur the picture, see Hintikka & Sandu (1997), Schein (1993) and Landman (2000). But it is indeed important to proceed carefully when obtaining judgments, now that we see that the diversity of scope behaviors may have theoretical significance.

Where there is a potential ambiguity, one of the readings is typically easy. This tends to be the one where the scopal order of quantifiers and other operators matches their linear order or surface c-command hierarchy. What is often difficult to tell is whether inverse scopal orders are possible. To investigate this it is useful to shut out the easy reading and, to borrow Ruys' (1992) slogan, to let the difficult one shine. For example, the easy, subject wide scope readings of the sentences below are implausible in view of encyclopedic knowledge:

(86) A pink vase graced every table.
A guard is posted in front of every building.

The fact that the sentences nevertheless make perfect sense indicates that the object wide scope readings are fine. At the same time, the fact that the variants below are less natural or even nonsensical confirms that the method still has some discriminating power:

(87) A pink vase graced all / none of the tables.
A guard is posted in front of all / none of the buildings.

Unfortunately, the easy reading can only be shut out if the difficult reading can be true without it. If the difficult reading entails the easy one, there is no shutting it out. In that case one tries to exploit some linguistic phenomenon, such as cross-sentential anaphora, that is contingent on a reading that the grammar produces, not just on what is entailed to be true. In (88), *it* cannot refer back to the unique missing marble whose existence can be inferred from the first sentence.

(88) I dropped ten marbles and found nine of them. #It must be under the sofa.

In this spirit, suppose we want to find out whether *two NP* and *two or more NP* are capable of taking inverse scope over *every NP* – but here the inverse readings entail the easy, linear ones. So, imagine two schools. In the parent-friendly school a teacher is fired if any parent complains. In the teacher-friendly school a teacher is fired only if every parent complains. The following is reported:

(89) Every parent complained about two teachers. They were fired.

(90) Every parent complained about two or more teachers. They were fired.

Can we be in the teacher-friendly school? Speakers usually find it easy to judge that only (89) may describe an incident in the teacher-friendly school. Notice that the choice depends solely on whether *they* in the second sentence can be understood to refer to those teachers who every parent complained about. This in turn depends solely on whether the first sentence has the reading 'there were two (two or more) teachers such that every parent complained about them'. In sum, this scenario seems to test just the scope judgment we are interested in; but the involvement of anaphora and the non-metalinguistic question make the task easier and more natural than it is to judge paraphrases or truth-values.

8 Existential versus distributive scope

8.1 The critical data

The following contrast may be taken to suggest that the scope of *every NP* is clause bounded, which is what May (1977) stipulates for all phrases that undergo Quantifier Raising, but that of *two NP* is not. (91) does not allow firemen to vary with buildings, but (92) allows the two buildings to be chosen independently of the firemen.

(91) Some fireman or other thought that **every building** was unsafe.
      #'for every building, there is a potentially different fireman who thought it was unsafe'

(92) Every fireman thought that **two buildings** were unsafe.
   (i) √'there are two buildings such that every fireman thought that they were unsafe'
   (ii) √'for every fireman, there is a potentially different pair of buildings that he thought was unsafe'

Consider, however, the following. Although (93) allows revolving doors to vary with buildings (so *two buildings* supports a distributive reading), (94) does not allow firemen to vary with buildings. In that respect (94) is like (91).

(93) **Two buildings** have a revolving door.
   √'for each of two buildings, there is a separate revolving door...'

(94) Some fireman or other thought that **two buildings** were unsafe.
   #'for each of two buildings, there is a separate fireman...'

And conversely, (95), just as (92), has two readings. (i) is true in a scenario where sets of apples vary with children: say, each child gets three apples to eat (this possibility was first observed in Kuroda 1982). On reading (ii) the set of apples is chosen independently: a single contextually relevant set of apples is evaluated by all the children. (This under the assumption that *every* requires the NP-set to be non-empty. See Heim & Kratzer (1998: Ch. 6) for discussion. For context dependence, see Stanley & Szabó (2000).)

(95) Every child tasted **every apple**.
   (i) √'every child had his/her own apples and tasted each of them'
   (ii) √'there is a set of apples such that every child tasted each of its members'

The above observations were made more or less independently in Beghelli, Ben-Shalom & Szabolcsi (1997), Beghelli & Stowell (1997), Farkas (1997), Kratzer (1998), Reinhart (1997), Ruys (1992), and Szabolcsi (1997a), among others.

The comparisons indicate that *every NP* and *two NP* are parallel in their behavior, contrary to first impressions. Both support distributive readings, but only within their own clause, and both can be referentially dependent or, even clause-externally, independent. But **what** is their scope? The answer cannot be given using the classical notion of scope. The reason is that the classical theory talks about "the" scope of a quantifier phrase. But (91) through (95) suggest that *every NP* and *two NP* share one scopal property that is clause-bounded and another one that is not. Preliminarily, we may say that both phrases have clause-bounded "distributive scope" and unbounded "existential scope". Distributive scope corresponds to the domain within which the quantifier phrase can make indefinites referentially dependent; existential scope corresponds to the domain within which the set of individuals that the quantifier phrase talks about can be fixed.

Do all quantifier phrases have unbounded existential scope? The answer is No: for example, *two or more buildings* does not.

(96) Every fireman thought that **two or more buildings** were unsafe.
#'there are two or more buildings such that every fireman thought that they were unsafe'

Likewise, distributive scope is not always clause-bounded: *each NP* provides solid counterexamples:

(97) A timeline poster should list the different ages/periods (Triassic, Jurassic, etc.) and some of the dinosaurs or other animals/bacteria that lived in **each**. (Google)
√'for each period, some of the dinosaurs that lived in it'

(98) Determine whether **every number in the list** is even or odd.
#'for every number, determine whether it is even or odd'

(99) Determine whether **each number in the list** is even or odd.
√'for each number, determine whether it is even or odd'

Farkas (1997) observes that there is a third kind of scope to reckon with; she calls it the scope of the descriptive condition. The denotation of NP in *every NP* and *two NP* may be indexed to the world of any superordinate subject or to that of the speaker:

(100) Some boy imagined that **every violinist** had one arm.
    (i) √'a boy imagined of every actual violinist that he/she had one arm'
    (ii) √'a boy thought up an all-one-armed-violinists world'

(101) Some boy imagined that **two violinists** had one arm.

The scope of the descriptive condition cannot be equated with existential scope. This is shown by upward monotonic *two or more NP* and downward monotonic *no violinist*. Neither has unbounded existential scope, but their descriptive conditions can be indexed with the world of the speaker or of a superordinate subject.

(102) Some boy imagined that **two or more violinists** had one arm.

(103) Some boy imagined that **no violinist** had one arm.

The scope of the descriptive condition will not be discussed further here, but article 17 [Semantics: Noun Phrases and Verb Phrases] (Schlenker) *Indexicality and de se* should be relevant.

8.2 Inducing and exhibiting referential variation

Why did it initially seem that *every NP* has clause-bounded scope but indefinites (*some NP, two NP*) unbounded scope? The reason is that different questions were asked in diagnosing their scopes. In connection with universals the question was within what domain they can make other expressions referentially dependent (i.e., distributive scope). In connection with indefinites, the question was within what domains they can remain referentially independent of other operators (i.e., existential scope).

To take a closer look at the ability of one expression to induce referential dependency in another, consider the following diagram that depicts a situation where the S>O reading of *Every man saw some dog* is true (assume that there are altogether three men). The notion of a witness set will be useful in talking about it. A witness of a generalized quantifier (GQ) is a set of individuals that is an element of the GQ and is also a subset of the determiner's restriction set (Barwise & Cooper 1981). Any set of individuals that contains two dogs and no non-dogs is a witness of the GQ denoted by *two dogs*. The unique witness of *every apple* is the set of apples. The unique witness of *no dog* is the empty set. See Beghelli, Ben-Shalom & Szabolcsi (1997) for the discussion of referential variation in these terms.

Fig. 1.1 shows a witness set of the wide scope quantifier *every man'*; each element of this witness is connected by the *see'*-relation to some witness or other of the narrow scope quantifier *some dog'*.

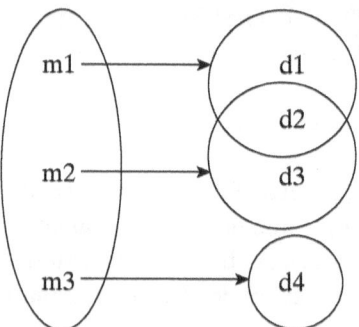

Fig. 1.1: *Scope and witness sets*

A quantifier phrase can induce referential variation only if it has a minimal witness with more than one element – otherwise there is nothing to vary with, and it can exhibit referential variation only if it has more than one witness – otherwise it has no way to vary. The indefinite traditionally considered in the literature was singular *some NP*, whose minimal witnesses are singletons, and thus cannot induce referential variation. On the other hand, the fixed-reference universals that linguistic literature traditionally considered have unique witnesses, and thus cannot exhibit variation. These choices, probably influenced by first order logic, may explain why only one aspect of each was recognized. Plural indefinites and variable-reference universals (as in (96i)) thus play an important role in forcing the conceptual shift.

The position we are taking here, with Beghelli & Stowell (1997) on English, Szabolcsi (1997a) on Hungarian, and work building on these (Lin 1998; Matthewson 2001) is stronger than the position taken in much of the literature that follows Reinhart (1997). We do not only make the existential and distributive scope distinction in the case of indefinites (and definites, to which the arguments seem to carry over) but also in the case of *every NP* type universals. We do not group the latter together with the so-called counting quantifiers such as *two or more NP*, *less than five NP*, etc. The motivation comes in part from the data described in Section 8.1, and is further discussed in 8.3–4. On the other hand, we are not aware of reasons to make the existential versus distributive scope distinction for *each NP* and for counting quantifiers. (*Most (of the)* and *the most* are the least well-studied from this perspective.)

The distinction between existential and distributive scope can be accommodated if we associate two different operators with the noun phrase, an existential and a universal one. We examine these in turn.

8.3 Existential scope, specificity, and Skolem functions

Fodor & Sag (1982) noticed that singular indefinites may have unbounded, island-free scope; in fact, they argued that if an indefinite escapes its own clause it takes maximal scope. Given this and the fact that this reading is best available with specific indefinites, i.e., those modified by a partitive (*a student of mine*), a relative clause (*a director that I know*) or the adjective *certain* (*a certain book*), they proposed that such indefinites are referential. Farkas (1981) countered this by observing that intermediate readings are possible; see Abusch (1994) for further examples.

(104) Each student has to hunt down every paper which shows that some condition proposed by Chomsky is wrong.
 √'each student > some condition > every paper'

Reinhart (1997) captures the possibility of both maximal and intermediate scopes by using the structure-building rule of existential closure of choice function variables. Each choice function picks out an element of the set it applies to. E.g., it may be that $f_1(dog') =$ Spot and $f_2(dog') =$ King; or, if it applies to a set of sets of individuals, it may be that $f_1(two'(dogs')) = \{$Spot,King$\}$ and $f_2(two'(dogs')) = \{$Spot,Fido$\}$. The intermediate reading of (104) will be explicated roughly as follows:

(105) $\forall x[student'(x) \rightarrow \exists f \forall y[(paper'(y) \land$ shows-to-be-wrong$'(f(condition'))(y))$ $\rightarrow$ hunt-down$'(y)(x)]]$

In words: For every student x there is a choice function f such that for every y that is a paper and shows the element that f picks from the set of conditions [proposed by Chomsky] to be wrong, x hunts down y. Here conditions vary only with students, not with papers.

Choice functions were first employed for interpreting specific indefinites by Egli & von Heusinger (1992). In motivating the use of choice functions Reinhart (1997) shows that existential quantification over individual variables would make the truth conditions of sentences involving material implication too weak. (Other problems caused by material implication are not solved by choice functions.) Existential quantification over witness set variables has the same effect as using choice functions, because choice functions pick out witnesses of the indefinites (Szabolcsi 1997a).

Kratzer (1998) argues against non-maximal scope existential quantification over choice functions. She suggests that intermediate readings are only felicitous when there is a contextually salient way of picking elements of the NP-set of the indefinite and pairing them with the individuals the wider-scoping quantifier ranges over. In the case of (104) this would be the way the professor assigned conditions to students. Many examples with intermediate readings in the literature even contain a pronoun within the indefinite's NP that is linked to the wider-scoping quantifier, e.g.,

(106) Each professor rewarded every student who read a certain book that he wrote.
√'each prof$_i$ > a certain book he$_i$ wrote > every student'

Therefore, Kratzer proposes to use parametrized choice functions to interpret indefinites. These are Skolem functions that have both set and individual arguments. On her view the function itself is always contextually given, much like the reference of Fodor and Sag's maximal scope indefinites. Parametrization captures the possible dependence on some quantifier of how the function picks elements from the indefinite's NP-set. (104) will now be explicated as (107). The relevant change from (105) is in the underlined part of (107). The new x is bound by $\forall x$, and $\exists f$ has disappeared; if it were to be spelled out, it would be assigned widest scope.

(107) $\forall x[\text{student}'(x) \rightarrow \forall y[(\text{paper}'(y) \wedge \text{shows-to-be-wrong}'(\underline{f(x)(\text{condition}')})(y)) \rightarrow \text{hunt-down}'(y)(x)]]$

Winter (2004) makes a connection between the analyses of the wide existential scope of indefinites and of functional readings of copular sentences:

(108) The (only) woman that every man loves is his mother.

(109) The (only) function in the set {f: f maps every man to a woman he loves} is the function that maps every man to his mother.

He unifies Kratzer's (1998) and Jacobson's (1994) approaches in terms of Skolem functions of arbitrary arity. Steedman (2000) treats scope alternation and donkey anaphora using Skolem functions.

In Section 8.2 we argued that the existential versus distributive scope distinction extends to universals like *every NP*. This approach may allow for a unification of the context dependence of indefinite interpretation as in Kratzer (1998) with quantifier domain restriction as in Stanley & Szabó (2000). Stanley & Szabó argue that the domain of quantifiers is always contextually restricted, that this restriction may contain a variable linked to another quantifier, and that this restriction is specifically located in the NP, not the determiner. The similarity to indefinite interpretation is captured if in (110) *every child* is interpreted as $f(Pow(child'))$ and *every apple* as $f(x)(Pow(apple'))$. The choice function f applied to the powersets of *child'* and *apple'* picks out the contextually relevant sets of children/apples (cf. the excursion), and the parameter x ensures that sets of apples vary with children:

(110) Every child ate every apple.
'every child [who was at the excursion] ate every apple [that was given to her for that excursion]'

See below on the distributivity of *every NP*.

The issues concerning existentially closed versus contextually given choice functions, Skolemization, and the possibility to unify the treatment of indefinites and quantifiers are vigorously debated in recent literature. See Matthewson (1999, 2001), von Fintel (1999), Chierchia (2001), Schwarzschild (2002), Breheny (2003), and Schlenker (2006), among others.

8.4 Distributive scope

We have observed that distributive scope is clause-bounded, save for the case of *each NP*. (May (1985) attributes the extra-clausal distributive scope of *each NP* to focus.) Barwise & Cooper (1981) build distributivity into the interpretation of all noun phrases, but this does not seem useful even clause-internally. (111) shows that collective and distributive predicates can be coordinated when the subject is a definite or indefinite plural. This suggests interpretation (112), where P is a variable over sets of individuals and distributivity (indicated by **each**) is a property of the second predicate.

(111) Six friends watched a movie together and had a glass of wine.

(112) λP[watched-a-movie-together'(P) ∧ had-a-glass-of-wine-**each**'(P)] (f(six' (friends')))

See further article 7 [Semantics: Noun Phrases and Verb Phrases] (Lasersohn) *Mass nouns and plurals*.

Consider now *every NP* on the analysis proposed above. What accounts for the fact that *every NP* typically participates in distributive readings? Beghelli & Stowell (1997) argue that in those cases *every NP* appears in the specifier of a distributive functional head *Dist*. *Dist* universally quantifies over a subset of the NP-set that is picked out by the (parametrized) choice function discussed in 8.3.

Suggestive evidence that the distributive operator does not originate in the lexical meaning of *every* but is contributed by a functional head in syntax is offered by Hungarian (Szabolcsi 1997a). DPs belonging to different quantifier classes occupy different surface syntactic positions in Hungarian. Some DPs can occur in more than one position and their behavior varies accordingly. Specifically the comparative quantifier *több, mint n gyerek* 'more than *n* children' can occur in the position where *minden gyerek* 'every child' canonically occurs, and if it does, its interpretation parallels that of *minden gyerek*: it has unbounded existential scope and it is exclusively distributive.

(113) In Spec, DistP:
Több, mint hat gyerek felemelte az asztalt.
more than six child up-lifted the table.acc
'More than six children each/*together lifted up the table'

It can also occur in another position where counting quantifiers canonically occur, and there it behaves like one of those: it has no unbounded existential scope and distributivity is not forced:

(114) In Spec, CountP:
Több, mint hat gyerek emelte fel az asztalt.
more than six child lifted up the table.acc
'More than six children each/together lifted up the table'

According to Beghelli & Stowell the fact that both silent *each* and *Dist* are heads explains why the distributive scope of definites, indefinites, and *every NP* is clause-bounded. See also Cecchetto (2004).

Not all universals are alike. *All the NP* is basically a definite plural, whereas *each NP* is more strongly distributive that *every NP* (again, see Beghelli & Stowell).

Important issues not explored here are the connection between distributivity and the singular feature, and the presence of event quantifiers in the immediate scope of distributive operators (Schein 1993; Beghelli & Stowell 1997).

9 Counting quantifiers

The existential versus distributive scope distinction does not extend to so-called counters, and to some of them it could not possibly extend. Recall that the value of, say, $f(five'(men'))$ is some set of five men. This way existential quantification over choice functions is basically the same as existential quantification over sets of a given cardinality. This only yields a truth-conditionally correct result if the determiner is upward monotonic in its scope argument.

(115) Five men walk = There is a set that contains five men and its elements walk.

(116) Fewer than five men walk ≠ There is a set that contains fewer than five men and its elements walk.

(117) Exactly five men walk ≠ There is a set that contains exactly five men and its elements walk.

Counters include *few(er than five) NP, many NP, more than five NP, more than n% of the NPs, at least/most five NP, five or more NP, more NP_1 than NP_2, exactly five NP*, and some others. In view of the above, only the upward monotonic among them could in principle have a separate existential scope component to their interpretation. But if the lack of extra-wide scope is any indication, (76) shows that even those do not have such a component.

Computing with definites, indefinites, and universals involves an individual or set of individuals serving as the logical subject of collective/distributive predication. In the case of counters, no set of individuals serves as a logical subject of predication. (114) basically means that there was an event of table lifting by children and the agent of this event, or each of its subevents, had cardinality greater than six. The intuition that counting is indeed the characteristic action of these quantifiers is corroborated by the grammaticality contrasts between *more than 50% of the NP*, a counter and *most of the NP*, not a counter (Szabolcsi 1997a) and by pyscholinguistic experiments (Hackl 2009).

(118)   They read more than 50% of the books each.

(119)   # They read most of the books each.

(120)   There'll be more than 50% of the kids in the yard.

(121)   # There'll be most of the kids in the yard.

Probably counters come closest to exemplifying generalized quantifiers in the classical sense (but see Hackl (2000) on comparative determiners and Hackl (2009) on *most*).

10 Clause internal scope behavior

Roughly three main classes of DPs have emerged from the foregoing discussion. The first two classes both have unbounded existential scope, but the distributive vs. collective readings of (in)definites depend on the predicate, whereas *every NP* associates with a special functional head, *Dist*. The third class is counters, possibly denoting run-of-the-mill generalized quantifiers.

The three main classes also differ clause-internally. In languages like English, where quantifier scope is rarely disambiguated by word order and intonation, this manifests itself in differences in the ability to take inverse scope. *Every NP* is an excellent inverse scope taker, see (122): it is the poster child for Montague/May/Hendriks style theories. Counters on the other hand do not take inverse scope over *every NP*, although they may over another counter, see (123)–(124):

(122)   More than one soprano sings in every show.
         $\sqrt{}$'every NP > more than one NP'

(123) Every soprano sings in more than one show.
#'more than one NP > every NP'

(124) At least two sopranos sing in more than one show.
?'more than one NP > at least two NP'

Downward monotonic DPs are especially reluctant to take inverse scope. Why this is so is not well-understood, but the fact explains an otherwise mysterious constraint on negative polarity item licensing, namely, that the licensor must c-command the NPI in overt syntax. See article 3 [this volume] (Giannakidou) *Polarity items*.

(125) *He has ever missed no meal.

(126) No meal has he ever missed.

Definites and indefinites can take inverse distributive scope but not nearly as readily as *every NP*. The reasons are debated. They may lie in the semantics of predicates, or in the burden such sentences place on working memory (Reinhart 2006: 2.7.3).

(127) More than one soprano sings in those (six) shows.
?'more than one soprano each'

In Hungarian, where quantifier scope is disambiguated by word order and intonation, the members of the three classes of DPs occupy three distinct regions of the preverbal field; a remarkable cross-linguistic correlation:

(128) (In)definites > Distributives > Counters > Verb > ... [same operator sequence reiterates]

Left-to-right order also determines scope order, therefore a preverbal counter may only outscope a distributive or an (in)definite if the latter occurs in the postverbal field. For details, see Beghelli & Stowell (1997); Szabolcsi (1997a); Brody & Szabolcsi (2003).

Since Hungarian quantifier phrases do not remain in their argument positions in surface structure, they call for a syntax that directly reflects scope assignment. On the other hand, as we have just seen, they do not simply line up in the desired scopal order but occur in designated positions reflecting a semantically flavored classification. Thus these positions are more like the landing sites of *wh*-movement than the adjoined positions created by Quantifier Raising. This explains that quantifier phrase movement in Hungarian is not subject to Scope Economy (Fox 2000): it happens regardless whether it has a disambiguating effect.

German, Japanese, and Mandarin are sometimes called scope freezing languages because (at least on the canonical Subject precedes Object order) they do not allow inverse scope. See Pafel (2006), Hoji (1985), Aoun & Li (1993), and Liu (1997). Unfortunately, not all descriptions take into account the diverse scope behavior of DPs.

Kayne (1998) argues that quantifier scope in English is also assigned in overt syntax, much like it is in Hungarian, but further leftward movements mask the results. Williams (2003) offers an alternative proposal concerning the cross-linguistic variation in how languages use overt syntax to express either case or scope relations.

11 Internal structure

Although the external scope behavior of DPs is very well studied, work on their internal structure and how it determines external behavior has not kept up with the new developments.

Because the choice function variable is of type <<e,t>, <<e,t>,t>> (or some generalization thereof), Reinhart (1997) suggests that it is essentially nothing but the determiner of the indefinite. In view of our argument concerning *every NP* and the larger class of expressions that pattern with it in Hungarian, the same should carry over to these. Then *some, a(n), every*, etc. are not determiners. They may have different semantic roles or, in the spirit of Beghelli & Stowell, they may simply carry features that send the DP to the specifiers of particular functional heads. Winter's (2001) flexible DP hypothesis aims to explain what noun phrases play predicative or quantificational roles; it combines Reinhart's idea with type shifting principles (Partee 1986).

Zamparelli (1995), Krifka (1999), Hackl (2000), Nakanishi (2004), and Takahashi (2006) are pioneering proposals to tie together the compositional semantics and the external behavior of various kinds of noun phrases.

12 Pronouns as definite descriptions and co-variation with situations

12.1 Cross-sentential anaphora

Sections 4–5 were concerned with the classical theory of how DPs antecede ("bind") pronouns within their domain, typically defined with reference to c-command. The claims were illustrated using *every NP*, one of the few good citizens for the classical theory. We now turn to cases without c-command. The most extreme case is cross-sentential anaphora.

Quantifier phrases typically support cross-sentential anaphora by plural pronouns. Kamp & Reyle (1993) and Kadmon (1993) interpret *they* in both (129) and (130) as referring essentially to all the boys who were sad (maximal reference anaphora):

(129) Every boy was sad. They cried.

(130) More than one boy was sad. They cried.

The interesting cases are those where the anaphoric pronoun is grammatically singular and/or it does not have maximal reference in the above sense. Relevant from the perspective of this article is the fact that indefinites support such anaphora:

(131) A boy hid in the corner. He cried.

(132) Two boys hid in the corner. They cried.

Crucially, (131)–(132) are appropriate even if three boys hid in the corner but only one/two of them cried. This fact has been used to support the claim that indefinites are not quantificational, i.e., that the "indefinite determiners" are not existential quantifiers (Heim 1982; Kamp & Reyle 1993); or that they are quantificational but externally dynamic, in the sense that their binding scope extends over the incoming discourse (Groenendijk & Stokhof 1990). See articles 11 [Semantics: Theories] (Kamp & Reyle) *Discourse Representation Theory* and 12 [Semantics: Theories] (Dekker) *Dynamic semantics*.

In the case of *every NP* maximal and non-maximal reference coincide. *More than one NP* in English does not support non-maximal anaphora, but the Hungarian version that occurs in [Spec, DistP] does.

12.2 Co-variation with situations

Sometimes a pronoun receives a co-varying reading within the distributive scope of a quantifier phrase, but (the argument position of) the antecedent does not c-command the pronoun. This constellation is of particular interest to us. If the theory of binding as presented in the first part is correct, such co-varying readings cannot be bound ones.

The relevant reading of (133) is where donkeys vary with farmers and the pronoun's reference co-varies with the donkeys. A comparable reading with cross-sentential anaphora, where the pronoun falls outside the universal's domain, is not available; see (134):

(133)   Every farmer who owns a donkey beats it.

(134)   Every farmer owns a donkey. #It gets beaten.

Similar to (133) is (135), with an adverb of quantification or the antecedent-consequent relation replacing the determiner *every*:

(135)   Always if a farmer owns a donkey, he beats it.

The classical approach to "donkey anaphora" as conceived by Lewis (1975), Kamp (1981/2002) and Heim (1982) takes (135) to be the paradigm case. On this view the adverb of quantification unselectively binds tuples (here: farmer–donkey pairs). The *if*-clause serves as the restriction and the main clause as the scope of the quantifier. Unselective binding means that exactly what variables the operator captures is not a design feature of the operator, it is determined in the course of the derivation of the given sentence. The indefinites introduce free variables and the pronouns co-refer with them. Furthermore (133) is assimilated to (135): the determiner *every* is essentially reanalyzed as *always*. The most striking problem with unselective binding as a general solution for donkey anaphora is known as the proportion problem. Although (133) and (135) have the same truth conditions, (136) and (137) do not. The determiner *most* counts donkey-owning farmers, never farmer–donkey pairs:

(136)   Most farmers who own a donkey beat it.

(137)   Usually/For the most part, if a farmer owns a donkey, he beats it.

So unselective binding should be restricted to adverbs of quantification. De Swart (1993) argues that even there generalized quantification over events is preferable.

The main alternative is to analyze "donkey pronouns" as definite descriptions, dubbed "E-type" or "D-type" pronouns (Evans 1980; Neale 1990b). Singular *it* is interpreted as 'the donkey so owned'. This unfortunately introduces a uniqueness presupposition, unless this pronoun is construed, exceptionally, as number-neutral. Following Berman (1987), Heim (1990) uses situation semantics to eliminate the problem. Elbourne (2005) develops this proposal; on his account (133) is interpreted as (138):

(138) Every minimal situation involving a farmer owning a donkey extends to one where the unique farmer in the situation beats the unique donkey in the situation.

More generally, Elbourne argues that all pronouns are definite descriptions, and the descriptive content is retrieved from the context in the manner of interpreting elided NPs; Fox (2002) applies this strategy to the interpretation of "traces" of movement. See article 1 [Semantics: Noun Phrases and Verb Phrases] (Büring) *Pronouns*.

Büring (2004) shows that the interpretation of the pronoun in (139)–(140) shares all the defining characteristics of donkey pronouns and extends Elbourne's analysis to them:

(139) Every farmer's donkey hates him.

(140) Two sisters of every farmer hate him.

Is co-variance with situations limited to cases where c-command fails? Kratzer (2009) argues that it is not; her position is compatible with Elbourne's.

In sum, the initial expectation seems to be borne out. Donkey pronouns are not interpreted as bound variables, or as containing bound variables, linked either to *a donkey* or to *every farmer*; their reference simply co-varies with the relevant situations. But Barker & Shan (2008) argue for a novel approach to donkey anaphora. This relies on the decomposition of p → q into ¬(p ∧ ¬q) and on the ability of indefinites to take extra-clausal scope. These afford an analysis where *a donkey* scopes over both the restriction and the scope of the universal but under the outermost negation. In plain first-order notation:

(141) $\forall x \neg \exists y[(\text{farmer}'(x) \wedge \text{donkey}'(y) \wedge \text{own}'(y)(x)) \wedge \neg \text{beat}(y)(x)]$

Thus the pronoun finds itself within the scope of the indefinite and can be bound by it, while the correct truth conditions are preserved. This proposal, if generally tenable, eliminates the need for co-variation with situations and re-evaluates the role of c-command in bound readings.

13 Conclusion

An important insight of the last two decades has been that both scope and binding phenomena are decomposable and descriptively diverse. To deal with the new facts the classical technologies have been supplemented with new ones, varieties of choice functions and situation semantics, among other things. We have probably accumulated a bigger toolkit than would be desirable, so enhancing theoretical coherence and technical parsimony is one task. Another is the syntax/semantics interface task of developing seriously compositional analyses not only on the sentence level but also inside quantifier phrases and even quantifier words.

14 References

Abusch, Dorit 1994. The scope of indefinites. *Natural Language Semantics* 2, 83–135.
Aoun, Joseph & Audrey Li 1993. *The Syntax of Scope*. Cambridge, MA: The MIT Press.
Bach, Emmon & Barbara Partee 1984. Quantification, pronouns, and VP-anaphora. In: J. Groenendijk, T. Janssen & M. Stokhof (eds.). *Truth, Interpretation, and Information*. Dordrecht: Foris, 99–130.
Barker, Chris 2007. Direct compositionality on demand. In: C. Barker & P. Jacobson (eds.). *Direct Compositionality*. Oxford: Oxford University Press, 102–131.
Barker, Chris & Pauline Jacobson (eds.). *Direct Compositionality*. Oxford: Oxford University Press.
Barker, Chris & Chung-chieh Shan 2006. Explaining crossover and superiority as left-to-right evaluation. *Linguistics & Philosophy* 29, 91–134.
Barker, Chris & Chung-chieh Shan 2008. Donkey anaphora is in-scope binding. *Semantics and Pragmatics* 1, 1–42, doi: 10.3765/sp.
Barwise, Jon & Robin Cooper 1981. Generalized quantifiers and natural language. *Linguistics & Philosophy* 4, 159–219.
Beghelli, Filippo, Dorit Ben-Shalom & Anna Szabolcsi 1997. Variation, distributivity, and the illusion of branching. In: A. Szabolcsi (ed.). *Ways of Scope Taking*. Dordrecht: Kluwer, 29–70.
Beghelli, Filippo & Timothy Stowell 1997. Distributivity and negation: The syntax of *each* and *every*. In: A. Szabolcsi (ed.). *Ways of Scope Taking*. Dordrecht: Kluwer, 71–108.
Berman, Stephen 1987. Situation-based semantics for adverbs of quantification. In: J. Blevins & A. Vainikka (ed.). *Studies in Semantics* (= University of Massachusetts Occasional Papers 12). Amherst, MA: GLSA, University of Massachusetts, 46–68.
Breheny, Richard 2003. Exceptional-scope indefinites and domain restriction. In: M. Weisgerber (ed.). *Proceedings of Sinn und Bedeutung (= SuB) 7*. Konstanz: University of Konstanz, 38–52.
Brody, Michael & Anna Szabolcsi 2003. Overt scope in Hungarian. *Syntax* 6, 19–51.
Büring, Daniel 2004. Crossover situations. *Natural Language Semantics* 12, 23–62.
Büring, Daniel 2005. *Binding Theory*. Cambridge: Cambridge University Press.
Carlson, Gregory 1977. A unified analysis of the English bare plural. *Linguistics & Philosophy* 1, 413–457.
Cecchetto, Carlo 2004. Explaining the locality conditions of QR: Consequences for the theory of phases. *Natural Language Semantics* 12, 345–397.
Chierchia, Gennaro 2001. A puzzle about indefinites. In: C. Cecchetto, G. Chierchia & M. Guasti (eds.). *Semantic Interfaces*. Stanford, CA: CSLI Publications, 51–90.
Cresti, Diana 1995. Extraction and reconstruction. *Natural Language Semantics* 3, 79–122.

Curry, Haskell & Richard Feys 1958. *Combinatory Logic*. Amsterdam: North-Holland.
Dalrymple, Mary 2001. *Lexical Functional Grammar*. New York: Academic Press.
Dowty, David 2007. Compositionality as an empirical problem. In: C. Barker & P. Jacobson (eds.). *Direct Compositionality*. Oxford: Oxford University Press, 23–102.
Egli, Urs & Klaus von Heusinger 1991. Epsilon-Operator und E-Typ-Pronomen. In: U. Egli & K. von Heusinger (eds.). *Zwei Aufsätze zur definiten Kennzeichnung* (Arbeitspapiere des Fachbereichs Sprachwissenschaft 27). Konstanz: University of Konstanz. English translation in: U. Egli et al. (eds.). *Lexical Knowledge and the Organisation of Language*. Amsterdam: Benjamins, 1995, 121–141.
Elbourne, Paul 2005. *Situations and Individuals*. Cambridge, MA: The MIT Press.
Evans, Gareth 1980. Pronouns. *Linguistic Inquiry* 11, 337–362.
Farkas, Donka 1981. Quantifier scope and syntactic islands. In: R. A. Hendrick, C. S. Masek & M. F. Miller (eds.). *Papers from the Regional Meeting of the Chicago Linguistic Society (= CLS) 17*. Chicago, IL: Chicago Linguistic Society, 59–66.
Farkas, Donka 1997. Evaluation indices and scope. In: A. Szabolcsi (ed.). *Ways of Scope Taking*. Dordrecht: Kluwer, 183–217.
von Fintel, Kai 1999. Quantifier domain selection and pseudo-scope. Paper presented at the *Context-Dependence Conference*, March 26–28, 1999, Cornell University, Ithaka, NY.
Fodor, Janet & Ivan Sag 1982. Referential and quantificational indefinites. *Linguistics & Philosophy* 5, 355–398.
Fox, Danny 2000. *Economy and Semantic Interpretation*. Cambridge, MA: The MIT Press.
Fox, Danny 2002. On logical form. In: R. Hendrick (ed.). *Minimalist Syntax*. Oxford: Blackwell, 82–124.
Gamut, L. T. F. 1991. *Logic, Language, and Meaning*. Chicago, IL: The University of Chicago Press.
Gawron, Mark & Stanley Peters 1990. *Anaphora and Quantification in Situation Semantics*. Stanford, CA: CSLI Publications.
van Geenhoven, Veerle 1998. *Semantic Incorporation and Indefinite Descriptions*. Stanford, CA: CSLI Publications.
Groenendijk, Jeroen & Martin Stokhof 1990. Dynamic predicate logic. *Linguistics & Philosophy* 14, 39–100.
Hackl, Martin 2000. *Comparative Determiners*. Ph.D. dissertation. MIT, Cambridge, MA.
Hackl, Martin 2009. On the grammar and processing of proportional quantifiers: *most* versus *more than half*. *Natural Language Semantics* 17, 63–98.
Heim, Irene 1982. *The Semantics of Definite and Indefinite Noun Phrases in English*. Ph.D. dissertation. University of Massachusetts, Amherst, MA. Reprinted: Ann Arbor, MI: University Microfilms.
Heim, Irene 1990. E-Type pronouns and donkey anaphora. *Linguistics & Philosophy* 13, 37–177.
Heim, Irene & Angelika Kratzer 1998. *Semantics in Generative Grammar*. Oxford: Blackwell.
Hendriks, Herman 1993. *Studied Flexibility: Categories and Types in Syntax and Semantics*. Doctoral dissertation. University of Amsterdam.
Hepple, Mark 1990. *The Grammar and Processing of Order and Dependency: A Categorial Approach*. Ph.D. dissertation, University of Edinburgh.
Hintikka, Jaakko 1997. No scope for scope? *Linguistics & Philosophy* 20, 515–544.
Hintikka, Jaakko & Gabriel Sandu 1997. Game-theoretical semantics. In: J. van Benthem & A. ter Meulen (eds.). *Handbook of Logic and Language*. Amsterdam: Elsevier, 361–410.
Hoji, Hajime 1985. *Logical Form Constraints and Configurational Structures in Japanese*. Ph.D. dissertation. University of Washington, Seattle, WA.

Jacobson, Pauline 1992. Antecedent contained deletion in variable-free semantics. In: C. Barker & D. Dowty (eds.). *Proceedings of Semantics and Linguistic Theory (= SALT)* II, Columbus, OH., 193–214.
Jacobson, Pauline 1999. Towards a variable-free semantics. *Linguistics & Philosophy* 22, 117–184.
Jacobson, Pauline 2000. Paycheck pronouns, Bach-Peters sentences, and variable-free semantics. *Natural Language Semantics* 8, 77–155.
Jacobson, Pauline 2002. The (Dis)organization of grammar. *Linguistics & Philosophy* 25, 601–626.
Jäger, Gerhard 2005. *Anaphora and Type-Logical Grammar*. Dordrecht: Springer.
Kadmon, Nirit 1993. *On Unique and Non-Unique Reference and Asymmetric Quantification*. New York: Garland.
Kamp, Hans 1981. A theory of truth and semantic representation. In: J. Groenendijk, Th. Janssen & M. Stokhof (eds.). *Formal Methods in the Study of Language*. Amsterdam: Mathematical Centre, 277–322. Reprinted in: P. Portner & B. H. Partee (eds.). *Formal Semantics: The Essential Readings*. Oxford: Blackwell, 2002, 189–223.
Kamp, Hans & Uwe Reyle 1993. *From Discourse to Logic*. Dordrecht: Kluwer.
Kayne, Richard 1998. Overt vs. covert movement. *Syntax* 1, 128–191.
Krifka, Manfred 1999. At least some determiners aren't determiners. In: K. Turner (ed.). *The Semantics/Pragmatics Interface from Different Points of View*. Amsterdam: Elsevier, 257–291.
Kratzer, Angelika 1998. Scope or pseudo-scope? Are there wide scope indefinites? In: S. Rothstein (ed.). *Events and Grammar*. Dordrecht: Kluwer, 163–196.
Kratzer, Angelika 2009. Making a pronoun: fake indexicals as windows into the properties of pronouns. *Linguistic Inquiry* 40, 187–237.
Kruijff, Geert-Jan & Richard Oehrle (eds.) 2003. *Resource-Sensitivity, Binding, and Anaphora*. Dordrecht: Kluwer.
Kuroda, Yuki 1982. Indexed predicate calculus. *Journal of Semantics* 1, 43–59
Landman, Fred 2000. *Events and Plurality: The Jerusalem Lectures*. Dordrecht: Kluwer.
Lewis, David 1975. Adverbs of quantification. In: E. L. Keenan (ed.). *Formal Semantics of Natural Language*. Cambridge: Cambridge University Press, 3–15.
Lin, Jo-wang 1998. Distributivity in Chinese and its implications. *Natural Language Semantics* 6, 201–243.
Liu, Feng-hsi 1997. *Specificity and Scope*. Amsterdam: Benjamins.
Matthewson, Lisa 1999. On the interpretation of wide scope indefinites. *Natural Language Semantics* 7, 79–134.
Matthewson, Lisa 2001. Quantification and the nature of cross-linguistic variation. *Natural Language Semantics* 9, 145–189.
May, Robert 1977. *The Grammar of Quantification*, Ph.D. dissertation. MIT. Cambridge, MA. Reprinted: Bloomington, IN: Indiana University Linguistics Club, 1982.
May, Robert 1985. *Logical Form: Its Structure and Derivation*. Cambridge, MA: The MIT Press.
Moltmann, Friederike & Anna Szabolcsi 1994. Scope interactions with pair-list quantifiers. In: M. González (ed.). *Proceedings of the North Eastern Linguistic Society (=NELS) 24*. Amherst, MA: GLSA, University of Massachusetts, 381–395.
Montague, Richard 1974. The proper treatment of quantification in ordinary English. In: R. Thomason (ed.). *Formal Philosophy. Selected Papers of Richard Montague*. New Haven, CT: Yale University Press, 247–271.
Nakanishi, Kimiko 2004. *Domains of Measurement*. Ph.D. dissertation. University of Pennsylvania. Philadelphia, PA.

Neale, Stephen 1990a. Descriptive pronouns and donkey anaphora. *Journal of Philosophy* 87, 113–150.
Neale, Stephen 1990b. *Descriptions*. Cambridge, MA: The MIT Press.
Pafel, Jürgen 2006. *Quantifier Scope in German*. Amsterdam: Benjamins.
Partee, Barbara 1986. Noun phrase interpretation and type-shifting principles. In: J. Groenendijk, D. de Jong & M. Stokhof (eds.). *Studies in Discourse Representation Theory and the Theory of Generalized Quantifiers*. Dordrecht: Foris, 115–143.
Quine, Willard van Orman 1960. Variables explained away. *Proceedings of the American Philosophical Society* 104, 343–347.
Reinhart, Tanya 1979. Syntactic domains for semantic rules. In: F. Günthner & S. Schmidt (eds.). *Formal Semantics and Pragmatics for Natural Languages*. Dordrecht: Reidel, 107–130.
Reinhart, Tanya 1983. *Anaphora and Semantic Interpretation*. London: Croom Helm.
Reinhart, Tanya 1997. Quantifier scope: How labor is divided between QR and choice functions. *Linguistics & Philosophy* 20, 335–397.
Reinhart, Tanya 2006. *Interface Strategies*. Cambridge, MA: The MIT Press.
Ruys, Eddy 1992. *The Scope of Indefinites*. Ph.D dissertation. Utrecht University.
Schein, Barry 1993. *Plurals and Events*. Cambridge, MA: The MIT Press.
Schlenker, Philippe 2006. Scopal independence: A note on branching and wide scope readings of indefinites and disjunctions. *Journal of Semantics* 23, 281–314.
Schwarzschild, Roger 2002. Singleton indefinites. *Journal of Semantics* 19, 289–314.
Sportiche, Dominique 2006. Reconstruction, binding, and scope. In: M. Everaert & H. van Riemsdijk (eds.). *The Blackwell Companion to Syntax, vol. 4*. Oxford: Blackwell, 35–93.
Stanley, Jason & Zoltán G. Szabó 2000. On quantifier domain restriction. *Mind & Language* 15, 219–261.
Steedman, Mark 2000. *The Syntactic Process*. Cambridge, MA: The MIT Press.
Sternefeld, Wolfgang 2001. Semantic vs. syntactic reconstruction. In: H. Kamp, A. Rossdeutscher & C. Rohrer (eds.). *Linguistic Form and its Computation*. Stanford, CA: CSLI Publications, 145–182.
de Swart, Henriëtte 1993. *Adverbs of Quantification: A Generalized Quantifier Approach*. New York: Garland.
Szabolcsi, Anna 1987. Bound variables in syntax: Are there any? In: J. Groenendijk, D. de Jongh & M. Stokhof (eds.). *Proceedings of the 6th Amsterdam Colloquium*. Amsterdam: ILLC, 331–350. Reprinted in: R. Bartsch, J. van Benthem & P. van Emde Boas (eds.). *Semantics and Contextual Expression*. Dordrecht: Foris, 1989, 295–318.
Szabolcsi, Anna 1992. Combinatory grammar and projection from the lexicon. In: I. Sag & A. Szabolcsi (eds.). *Lexical Matters*. Stanford, CA: CSLI Publications, 241–269.
Szabolcsi, Anna 1997a. Strategies for scope taking. In: A. Szabolcsi (ed.). *Ways of Scope Taking*. Dordrecht: Kluwer, 109–154.
Szabolcsi, Anna (ed.) 1997b. *Ways of Scope Taking*. Dordrecht: Kluwer.
Takahashi, Soichi 2006. More than two quantifiers. *Natural Language Semantics* 17, 57–101.
Williams, Edwin 2003. *Representation Theory*. Cambridge, MA: The MIT Press.
Winter, Yoad 2001. *Flexibility Principles in Boolean Semantics*. Cambridge, MA: The MIT Press.
Winter, Yoad 2004. Functional quantification. *Research on Language and Computation* 2, 331–363.
Zamparelli, Roberto 1995. *Layers in the Determiner Phrase*. Ph.D. dissertation. University of Rochester, Rochester, NY.
Zimmermann, Thomas E. 1993. Scopeless quantifiers and operators. *Journal of Philosophical Logic* 22, 545–561.

Elena Herburger
2 Negation

1   Negation and contradiction —— 46
2   Negation and logical entailment: Scalar implicatures —— 54
3   Negation and logical entailment: NPIs —— 59
4   References —— 67

Abstract: This paper deals with some general issues regarding the interpretation of negation, including the relation between negation and presupposition and its relation with scalar implicature. As Horn (1989) documents in humbling detail, thinking about these matters goes back many centuries and has taken many different twists and turns. Needless to say, I cannot even attempt to do justice to the history of the study of negation here. My more limited goal is to present some basic questions regarding the semantics of negation and address how they relate to (i) the status of presuppositions, (ii) where and how scalar implicatures are derived and (iii) whether scalar implicature can be exploited to explain why certain expressions (Negative Polarity Items) are only licit in negative contexts. (On the topic of Negative Polarity Items see article 3 [this volume] (Giannakidou) Polarity items.)

1 Negation and contradiction

1.1 Contradiction and contrariness

One of the first words children learn–or so it seems to their parents–is *no*, and it is clear why: it is a semantically very useful word, one which helps us voice our disagreement in a simple and unmistakable way. The little child's initial *no* may be a general, all-purpose one, but very soon we become proficient at using negation at several levels. Whereas *no* operates on a high, speech act level, as an answer to a question or as a disagreement with the content of a previous utterance, *not* takes lower scope, either over sentences (sentential negation, as in (1)) or over parts of sentences (constituent negation) as in (2):

Elena Herburger, Washington, DC, USA

https://doi.org/10.1515/9783110589863-002

(1) Sandra didn't call.

(2) I didn't hear this from Simon but from Paul.

There are also morphological means of negating individual words by creating their negated counterparts, e.g., *illegal* vs. *legal, unhappy* vs. *happy*. In addition, antonyms can be argued to be related to each other by some sort of semantic negation relation, even if it is one that is not morphologically reflected, cf. *hot* vs. *cold, young* vs. *old, few* vs. *many*. (See Horn 1989 for details and qualifications.)

Obviously, a negated element and its nonnegative counterpart can not both hold true simultaneously. Standing in opposition to each other, they are subject to the Law of Contradiction, which states that a sentence p and its negation (symbolized in propositional logic as ¬p) do not both hold at the same time.

Not all opposition is the same though. If the negated element and its positive counterpart exhaust the possibilities, the opposition is contradictory. If, however, there exits a third option where neither the negation nor its non-negated counterpart hold, the opposition is merely contrary. The adjectives *inanimate* and *animate*, for example, can be argued to stand to each other in contradictory opposition, for a given thing either satisfies one or it satisfies the other and there seems to be no third option. In contrast, *expensive* or *inexpensive* stand in contrary opposition given that many things do not carry a price tag.

Whether the English sentential negation *not* creates an instance of contradictory or contrary negation has been a matter of considerable debate. Note that the negation operator ¬ in propositional logic gives rise to a contradictory opposition, having the semantics given in the truth table in (3). According to (3), p is true whenever its negation ¬p is false and p is false its negation ¬p is true. In other words, ¬ obeys the Law of the Excluded Middle, which states that either p or its negation holds (p ∨ ¬p):

Tab. 2.1: Truth table

p	¬p
T	F
F	T

It is not immediately obvious, however, that the English word *not* gives rise to a contradictory negation as well and that it should be thought of as equivalent to ¬. The difficulty of assimilating the semantics of *not* to that of ¬ has to do with the fact that sentences in natural language are often understood in a way that certain information is (in a naïve, pre-theoretic sense) presupposed. Depending on how this presupposed information is analyzed, negation will result in a contrary or a contradictory opposition. Though the issue is quite general, it was first noted in connection with the semantics of definite descriptions (*the present king of France, the essay Susan wrote last night*). Going down a well-trodden path, I will also begin discussing it in this context (section 1.2). I will subsequently offer some concrete suggestions as to how this discussion can be carried to the clausal level (section 1.3).

1.2 (Definite) descriptions, presupposition and negation

When definite descriptions fail to pick out anything, what happens to the sentences they appear in? Are sentences like (3), (4) or (5) actually false if the speaker did not bike to school, if France is a republic or if Susan failed to write an essay last night?

(3) The bicycle I came to school with has a flat tire.

(4) The present king of France is bald.

(5) Susan brought the essay she wrote last night.

Or do these sentences involve a failure of presupposition, where this failure results in their not expressing any assertion at all or in their not having a truth value at all? Different philosophers, and, following them, different linguists have judged the matter differently.

For Frege (1892), and in a somewhat different form Strawson (1950), definite descriptions are not quantificational but referring expressions and can thus serve directly as arguments of predicates of individuals, e.g., *bald*:

(6) Bald(the-present-king-of-France)

Importantly, on this view definite descriptions are said to presuppose the existence of a referent in the following sense: if they fail to refer, (an utterance of) a sentence containing them will neither be evaluated as true nor as false. Given that meaning is derived compositionally, this holds not only of (4) and (5) but also of their negated versions. Thus (7) comes out as lacking a truth-value if France is a republic:

(7) The present king of France isn't bald.

On a Fregean view then, a sentence and its negation both entail their presuppositions; both (4) and (7) presuppose and entail that France has one and exactly one king. When the presupposition does not hold, semantic composition comes to a halt and neither the sentence nor its negation are assigned a truth value. Since a sentence and its negation only stand in the true-false relation to each other to the extent that their presuppositions are satisfied, sentential negation on this view creates a merely contrary opposition.

Not so for those who analyze definite descriptions not as referring expressions but rather as quantifiers with existential import (e.g., Russell 1905; Neale 1990). When the definite descriptions in (4) and (5) fail to describe anything, the sentences containing them come out as false rather than as lacking a truth value. Furthermore, if definite descriptions are quantifiers, it should be possible for them to scopally interact with other scope bearing expressions, including negation; on a quantificational, non-presuppositional view of definite description, (7), for instance, can be analyzed as ambiguous between (8) and (9):

(8) [The x: Present-king-of-France(x)] ¬ Bald(x)

(9) ¬ [The x: Present-king-of-France(x)] Bald(x)

When (4) is true, its negated version (7) is false both on the wide scope interpretation in (8) and on the narrow scope interpretation in (9). When (4) is false because there is no king of France, (7) is false on the reading in (8), which entails the existence of such a king, but actually true on the reading in (9). Finally, when (4) is false because the French monarch is blessed with beautiful locks, (7) is true under (8) as well as (9). As these examples illustrate, on a Russellian view, 'failure of reference' of a definite description does not result in a lack of truth value. Since any third option asides from 'true' and 'false' is excluded in such instances, the opposition created by negation is one of contradiction.

As is well-known, neither the Fregean nor the Russellian view on definite descriptions is without problems. On a Fregean take it is not easy to explain why a sentence like (7) can actually be true when France has no king--a reading that obtains, for instance, when the sentence is continued by ...*because there is no present king of France*. While a Russellian analysis can attribute this to the wide scope of the negation (cf. (9)), a Fregean approach would require positing a special negation which applies to presupposition ('external' negation). Doing so, however, seems unappealing, both in light of Ockham's razor and because languages do not seem to morphologically distinguish between internal and external negation (Horn 1989).

Another issue the Fregean view has to contend with is the fact that when the presuppositions of a sentence fail, semantic composition does not seem to come to halt altogether. After all, speakers do seem able to assign truth conditions to such sentences; they can clearly say for instance what the world would have to be like for (4) to be true. As a possible way out, instead of positing a halt of semantic composition and the attendant truth value gap, one can give up a two-valued logic and posit a third truth value, along with 'true' and 'false', namely 'valueless' (van Fraasen 1968; Boër & Lycan 1976). Given the premium we put on keeping the logic simple and two-valued, that is, as only recognizing the values 'true' and 'false', this, however, may appear unappealing.

In contrast with the Fregean account, the Russellian one manages to maintain a two-valued logic, an analysis of *not* along the lines of ¬, and is also able to capture that *The present king of France isn't bald* can be true when the definite description fails to describe anyone, cf. (9). The problem of the Russellian account lies elsewhere: it is not complete. Unless we supplement it, it offers no account of a central fact the Fregean approach easily captures, namely the fact that *normally* (4) is taken to be false when the French monarch has hair, not when France is no longer a monarchy. Similarly, *normally* (5) is understood to be false in a context where Susan forgot to bring the essay she wrote the previous night, not when she did not write an essay that night to begin with.

1.3 Negation and backgrounded quantifier restrictions

Fortunately, the problem just noted for a Russellian analysis can be addressed, and the idea that negation gives rise to a contradictory opposition maintained, if instead of distinguishing between two truth values for not being true (false and value-less) one distinguishes pragmatically between two *reasons* why a sentence is false. This has been effectively advocated in Atlas (1993) and Horn (2006) (cf. his notion of 'assertoric inertia'). On this view, a sentence can be false in what we may call a forthright way, namely when the part of it that counts as the foregrounded part ('assertion') is incorrect. Or it can be false in a less direct, pragmatically more manipulative way. This happens when the information which is backgrounded is not correct. (4), for instance, is false in a forthright way when the king of France is not bald, and false in an indirect way when there is no longer a king of France. But on either scenario it is false. Analogously, (5) is false in a direct way when Susan left the essay at home, and false in an indirect way when she did not write it to begin with.

The pragmatic effect of backgrounding seems to be that when we interpret a sentence with the backgrounded material B and foregrounded material F, B seems to tell us what the sentence is about. When we evaluate under what conditions we would judge the sentence true, our attention seems initially to be drawn to the foregrounded material and only at a second glance, so to speak, do we take into account the truth-conditional contributions of the backgrounded material.

The preferred ways of evaluating (4) and (5) now follow if the restrictions of the definite descriptions, denoted by *present king of France* and *essay she wrote last night*, respectively, are systematically backgrounded.

The idea that the restrictions of quantifiers are pragmatically backgrounded finds support in the observation that quantificational restrictions 'set the scene'. Even the restrictions of quantifiers whose restriction and scope are semantically interchangeable, namely symmetrical determiners like *some*, are felt to have a special, scene-setting status, which we can attribute to their being backgrounded (Herburger 2000). (10), for example, is (modulo focus) felt to be about the children and not about those who like spinach, even though switching the restriction and scope as in (11a) vs. (11b) would have no semantic (i.e., truth-conditional) consequences.

(10) Some children like spinach.

(11) a. [Some x: Child (x)] Like-spinach (x)
b. [Some x: Like-spinach (x)] Child (x)

Assuming then that restrictions of quantifiers are backgrounded in the way just described, on a view where *not* gives rise to a contradictory opposition, we can explain why (3) is normally taken to be false in a context where the king is bald: denoting a restriction to a quantifier, 'present king of France' is backgrounded. Given the pragmatics of backgrounded information, however, the preferred conditions where the sentence is false are those that make it false in a direct rather than indirect manner, that is, in a way where the falsity does not lie in the backgrounded material.

Our reward for this detour through the pragmatics of backgrounding is a semantics where sentential negation, at least in as far as sentences with definite descriptions are concerned, creates a contradictory rather than just contrary opposition and which, at same time, is able to do justice to pragmatically preferred ways of interpreting these kinds of sentences.

It is perhaps worth noting at this point that saying that the restrictions of quantifiers are backgrounded is similar but not equivalent to saying that they are presupposed. Apart from the general issues regarding the notion of presupposition discussed above, one difference lies in the fact that on a presuppositional view a restricted quantifier of the form [Q x: F(x)], where F(x) represents the restriction, presupposes that there are some things that are F. A backgrounding approach makes no such existential commitment.

One argument for the presuppositional view seems to come from the interpretation of *every*. Though the universal quantifier in predicate calculus lacks existential import, in many instances *every* seems strange when nothing satisfies its restriction. It seems bizarre, for instance, for a salesman to say (12) when there are no bicycles in the store:

(12) Every bicycle in the store is on sale.

On a presuppositional view this would be attributed to a failure of the presumed presupposition that there are bicycles in the store. As a result (12) should neither be true nor false (cf. Heim & Kratzer 1998). But, arguably, it is not the case that the question whether (12) is true or false does not even arise—for (12) seems false. This, however, suggest that *every* has existential import (cf. Moravcsik 1991). This Aristotelian view of *every* is compatible with the truth of (13a) and the falsity of (13b), which are due to Heim & Kratzer (1998). It is compatible if we assume that the sentences are embedded under a mythology operator or that the sentence quantify over possible (mythological) individuals (Herburger 2000):

(13) a. Every unicorn has exactly one horn.
b. Every unicorn has exactly two horns.

1.4 A quantificational analysis of negated sentences

The discussion on the relation between backgrounded information and negation has concentrated on definite descriptions, mainly because I was retracing history for expository reasons. An analogous argument can be made at the sentential level, I believe, if one considers how intonational focus affects the interpretation of a sentence (Herburger 2000). The basic idea has two parts. First, even sentences without overt adverbs of quantification involve quantification in their semantic interpretation. Second, the non-focused part of the sentence functions as a quantificational restrictor (cf. Rooth 1985 e.g.) and is pragmatically backgrounded. Negation then interacts with the quantifier restricted by the non-focused part much like it does with definite descriptions on the kind of analysis described above; it can take scope over the entire sentence or below the quantifier. Only if negation takes scope below the restricted quantifier does the sentence entail what is said in the backgrounded, non-focused part.

A classic way of saying that even sentences without overt adverbial quantifiers are instances of quantification is to say that sentences are descriptions of events (Davidson 1967; Parsons 1990; Schein 1993 a.o.). Assuming this, we can say that focus structures this quantification: in a simple sentence the non-focused part of a sentence comes to restrict the event quantifier whereas the focus only contributes to the scope of the quantifier. On this view, a sentence like (14) is interpreted as meaning that some contextually relevant visit to the movie theater by Helen was one where Alex was the companion. (14) thus has the logical form in (15):

(14) Helen went to the movies WITH ALEX.

(15) [Some e: C(e) & Went(e) & To(e, *the movies*)] WITH(e, ALEX)

The informational asymmetry between the non-focused and the focused part follows from the backgrounding of the non-focused material, which ends up restricting the event quantifier. The focused material contributes only to the scope and is, as a result, in the fore-rather than background.

When negation enters the picture, we find that on the most salient reading the negation takes scope over the focus, i.e., the scope of the event quantifier (cf. (8) above):

(16) Helen didn't go to the movie WITH ALEX.

(17) [Some e: C(e) & Went(e) & To(e, *the movies*)]¬ WITH(e, ALEX)

The logical forms in (16) and (17) capture that (14) and (15) are both about Helen's going to the movies. They also capture that (14) and (16) on its preferred interpretation both entail that such an event took place.

Just as we saw in connection with definite descriptions above, we can also observe that the sentence also has a less salient reading, where the negation takes wide scope over everything, but where focus still structures the quantification of events. On this interpretation, the sentence is still about Helen going to see a film, but it does not entail that such an event took place:

(18) Helen didn't go to the movies WITH ALEX (because she didn't go to the movies WITH ANYONE. She stayed at home and...).

(19) ¬ [Some e: C(e) & Went(e) & To(e, *the movies*)] WITH(e, ALEX)

This reading is exactly parallel to the second reading of the *The present king of France isn't bald* discussed above, the reading that proved difficult to explain on the Fregean approach, but finds a natural explanation on a supplemented Russellian approach.

Regarding aboutness, it has been analyzed in detail in Portner & Yabushita (1998). On the view argued for here, every quantificational restriction encodes what the sentence is about at the point where the quantifier is interpreted. This holds not only of noun phrase quantifiers, but also of others, including in particular event or adverbial quantifiers, which themselves can include quantifiers either in the restriction or the scope. This results in various, at times nested instances of aboutness. Possibly, the various layers of aboutness are gathered together in a system similar to Potts' (2005) computation of conventional implicature. (See also article 17 [Semantics: Interfaces] (Potts) *Conventional implicature and expressive content*.) I will leave this for consideration elsewhere.

Recapitulating, if we adopt the view that definite descriptions and sentences are quantificational expressions—for instance, a Russellian account for definite descriptions and a Davidsonian account for sentences—and if we further adopt the notion of semantically normal but pragmatically backgrounded information, we can say that sentential negation creates a contradictory rather than just a contrary opposition. This is a welcome result because it allows us to remain logically austere. Of course, there is more one could and probably should say about the relation between negation and presupposition. I have said nothing, for instance, about the behavior of presuppositions like those triggered by *again*. My reticence is not only due to limitations of space but also has to do with the real possibility that 'presupposition' is but a mere catch-all for a series of similar but ultimately separate phenomena, which require separate analyses, see Boër & Lycan (1976). For details on the study of presupposition see article 14 [Semantics: Interfaces] (Beaver & Geurts) *Presupposition*.

2 Negation and logical entailment: Scalar implicatures

Having argued that if a sentence is not true it is false, I now want to turn to a basic semantic fact about negation, one which turns out to have interesting linguistic consequences: negation reverses the direction of logical entailment. If a sentence p asymmetrically entails another sentence q, then the negation of q, ¬q, asymmetrically entails the negation of p, ¬p. For example, if (20) is true, so is (21):

(20) Mariana called both Monica and Michelle.

(21) Mariana called Michelle.

In the scope of negation, however, the conjunctive statement ceases to be the stronger one and becomes the weaker one instead, as the one-way entailment from (22) to (23) shows:

(22) Mariana didn't call Michelle.

(23) Mariana didn't call both Monica and Michelle.

Negation is not alone in reversing the direction of entailment, other elements do too, namely all those that create downward entailing contexts (e.g., Fauconnier 1975; Ladusaw 1980). Though (24) entails (25), when we replace *some* with *every*, which is downward entailing in its restriction, the direction of entailment reverses and we get an inference from the superset case (girl in the school) 'downward' to the subset case (girl in second grade).

(24) Some girls in second grade wanted to be Hermione.

(25) Some girls in the school wanted to be Hermione.

If we do the same in the scope of the quantifier rather than the restriction, we find that both the determiners *some* and *every* behave alike in that both license an upward inference from a subset case to a superset case, as shown by the entailment from (26) to (27):

(26) Every/some girl in second grade owns a blond and blue-eyed Barbie doll.

(27) Every/some girl in second grade owns a Barbie doll.

Direction of entailment matters in a number of linguistically relevant ways (see article 10 [Semantics: Interfaces] (Chierchia, Fox & Spector) *Grammatical view of scalar implicatures*). It matters, for instance, in the derivation of scalar implicatures.

A speaker is not lying, in the proper sense of lying, when she utters (28) in a context where she is fully aware that Gabriel can in fact recite the name of every single player on the team.

(28) Gabriel knows the names of some of the players on the Wizards team.

But in saying what she said, the speaker can be accused of having been misleading, of not having played by the rules of the discourse game, one of which demands that she speak the whole truth (cf. Grice's 1975 Maxim of Quantity). As this example illustrates, when a speaker utters p, where p is entailed by q, the speaker often does so with the intention of conveying to the hearer that she has no grounds for believing that the stronger statement q holds. This invites the inference that the speaker knows that $\neg q$ is true. This inference is available to the extent that one is willing to assume that 'it is not certain that q' is equivalent to 'it is certain that not q', a move which seems relatively benign (in fact an instance of a relevance based implicature, cf. Horn 1989), but which, strictly speaking, discards the possibility that the speaker remains agnostic as to whether q is true. This additional inference is dubbed the 'epistemic' step in Sauerland (2004). It will become relevant in an interesting way later.

Let us next consider more closely one of the defining characteristics of scalar implicatures, namely the way in which they are defeasible (Horn 1972):

(29) Gabriel knows the names of some of the players on the team—in fact, he knows the names of all of them.

That scalar implicatures should be so easily suspended is not surprising if they are not part of the literal meaning of the sentence and are not entailed by it either, but are merely part of what the sentence is taken to mean over and above what it literally states, given a particular discourse context and an implicit set of rules of co-operative behavior.

Another property that is typical of scalar implicatures (but perhaps not indispensable, see below) is that they are generated relative to lexically encoded stronger alternatives for the scalar terms. Examples of such 'Horn scales' are given in (28) (Horn 1972, 1989):

(30) a. boiling>hot>very warm>warm
 b. beautiful>pretty>attractive
 c. must>should>may
 d. terrible>bad>mediocre
 e. and>or
 f. every>most>many>some

In a non-negative context, a statement with a scalar term always entails an alternative statement where, keeping everything else the same, the scalar term is replaced by one to its right. In negative contexts it is the other way around. (Note that hot>very warm>warm>lukewarm>cold>freezing does not qualify as a scale. Note also that the fact that *some* seems to be a member of the same scale as *every* provides another argument for saying that *every* has existential import, as was argued above.)

Since negation and other elements that create negative contexts reverse the direction of entailment, we actually expect that if a scalar expression is embedded in a negative context, this embedding will affect the implicatures the scalar expression generates. After all, scalar implicatures are generated by negating stronger alternative sentences which logically entail the original sentence and what counts as the stronger alternative depends on whether we are dealing with a negative context or not. As we saw, if p entails q, then, if someone utters q, we take her to implicate (but not assert) that she is committed to the truth of ¬p (see above). As we also saw, if p entails q, then ¬q entails ¬p. Therefore, by neo-Gricean reasoning, if someone utters ¬p, she is to be taken to implicate a commitment to the negation of the stronger statement, namely ¬¬q, which is equivalent to q. The prediction this reasoning makes when combined with the entailment reversing property of negation seems correct. Much in the same way that (28) above (*Gabriel knows the name of some of the players*) implicates that he does not know the names of all of the players, we can now observe that (31) implicates that it is not the case that he does not know the name of some of the players, which is the same as saying as that he knows the names of some of them. (Throughout I am abstracting away from uses of negations as in *He is not smart, he is brilliant*. These examples, already discussed in Jespersen 1917, are held to involve a special, meta-linguistic use of negation, Horn 1989).

(31)   Gabriel does not know the name of all of the players.

In an analogous fashion, a Gricean analysis when applied to negative contexts also explains why *or* is felt to be exclusive in some contexts but not in others, thus supporting the 'inclusive' treatment of *or* analogous to the sentential operator from propositional logic. A conjunctive sentence like (32) unilaterally entails its disjunctive version in (33):

(32)   Janet consulted with Paul and Vera.

(33)   Janet consulted with Paul or Vera.

Uttering the latter therefore implicates the negation of the former: when someone says (32) we can take him to implicate that it is not the case that Janet consulted with both Paul and Vera. The exclusive reading of *or* thus reduces to a scalar implicature, and *or* itself retains its inclusive propositional calculus meaning, where the disjunction is true if at least one of its disjuncts is.

Negative contexts again invert everything. The disjunctive statement (34) is now the stronger of the two, entailing the conjunctive statement in (35):

(34)   Janet didn't consult with Paul or Vera.

(35)   Janet didn't consult with Paul and Vera.

Since there is no stronger statement for (32) that could be generated using a Horn scale, no scalar implicature is derived and *or* is merely interpreted in terms of its literal meaning in the same way as propositional operator, as an inclusive *or* ('at least one of the two').

Interestingly, the full force of the neo-Gricean prediction for negative or downward entailing contexts seems to have only been recognized rather recently (Levinson 2000; cf. also Horn 1989, 2005; Sauerland 2004; article 10 [Semantics: Interfaces] (Chierchia, Fox & Spector) *Grammatical view of scalar implicatures)*. Moreover, not everyone seems to agree. Chierchia (2004) cites scalar implicatures in negative contexts as one of several reasons to give up the neo-Gricean view of how semantics and pragmatics interact. Contrary to the popular view, he argues that the pragmatics gets to see parts of the sentence not only once the syntactic and semantic derivations are complete, but as soon as these parts are derived. One of the arguments he gives for the local derivation of scalar implicatures derives from sentences that contain a scalar term in the scope of disjunction (Chierchia 2004: 46):

(36) Mary is either working on her paper or seeing some of her students.

The problem with (36) is this: if one considers the scalar implicatures generated by *some* relative to the entire sentence, one predicts that (36) implicates that it is not the case that [either Mary is working on her paper or she is seeing all of her students]. This, however, entails that Mary is not working on her paper, which is certainly not an implicature the sentence has. Chierchia takes (36) to indicate that one should derive the implicatures of a scalar term (in this case *some*) as soon as the scalar term enters the picture and not at the end of the sentence. The resulting locally generated implicature is then projected and the semantic interpretation continues until the next scalar term, in this case *or*, is interpreted, when a second implicature is generated, namely that either Mary worked on her paper or that she saw some (but not all) of her students, but that she did not do both.

Returning to negative contexts now, Chierchia (2004) argues that negative contexts block the projection of regular scalar implicatures (e.g., 'some but not all') and, moreover, that they lead to the 'recalibration' of scalar implicatures. As a result of this locally stated recalibration, (31) (*Gabriel doesn't know the names of all of the players*) is predicted to implicate that he knows the names of some. As we saw, however, this result is also available on a neo-Gricean account. The question is then whether disjunctive examples like (36) can also be explained on the classical conception of how semantics and pragmatics interact.

The challenge is taken up in Sauerland (2004), who proposes to calculate the implicatures of sentences containing various scalar terms with the help of a two-tier system containing provisional ('primary') implicatures, some of which are then allowed to turn strengthened into definitive ('secondary') implicatures. An important ingredient of Sauerland's analysis consists of the novel scalar alternatives that he posits for disjunction. Whereas, as we noted above, on a traditional neo-Gricean view scalar alternatives are generated by replacing one scalar expression with the next lexicalized stronger one and keeping the rest of the sentence the same, on Sauerland's account a disjunction of the form 'A or B' is said to have as scalar alternative not only 'A and B', as one might expect given an and>or Horn scale (see above), but also the individual disjuncts 'A' and 'B'. This idea is also used in article 10 [Semantics: Interfaces] (Chierchia, Fox & Spector) *Grammatical view of scalar implicatures*, and Fox (2006) and the reader is invited to consult these papers for the relevant details, which would take me too far afield here. My goal here is not to determine where implicatures are generated, locally or globally. This is a big, hotly debated question. My point is merely to reiterate what has been noted in the literature at various times (see above), namely that though there may perhaps be reason to abandon the Gricean picture of how implicatures are generated, they are independent of negation; negative environments are consistent with a Gricean conception of how implicatures are generated.

3 Negation and logical entailment: NPIs

The entailment reversing property of negative contexts is not only relevant for the generation of scalar implicatures, it also seems to play a role in accounting for the distribution of NPIs (see also article 3 [this volume] (Giannakidou) *Polarity items*). As noted in Fauconnier (1975), NPIs like *any, ever, budge an inch* etc. seem to occur in those contexts where the scales are inverted, or where the direction of entailment on a particular scale is inverted (Ladusaw 1980). These contexts, Ladusaw (1980) shows, are downward entailing, licensing inferences from a superset to a subset case, as briefly discussed in connection with the determiners *every, no* and *some* above. (I am simplifying matters here. Not all NPIs are licensed in all downward entailing context (Zwarts 1998; van der Wouden 1997). And not all contexts that license NPIs are downward entailing in an obvious way. Not so obvious cases include licensing by *only, if,* adversative predicates, *barely, most, exactly n* (where n is a small number) (e.g., Linebarger 1987). I will set these cases aside assuming that careful analysis has shown, or will show, that they involve (some sort of) downward entailment after all, cf. e.g., von Fintel (1999) on most of them, Herburger (2000) on *only*, Ludlow (2002) on *most*, Schein (2001) on *if* and Horn (2006) on *barely*. See also article 3 [this volume] (Giannakidou) *Polarity items*.)

The generalization that NPIs are licensed in negative contexts raises a number of questions, the most intriguing of which is perhaps the licensing question. Why should this generalization hold? What is it about negation that explains why in language after language we find lexical items that are restricted to negative contexts and why do these tend to be semantically similar?

The fact that NPIs and scalar implicatures are sensitive to the entailment reversing property of negative contexts makes one wonder if there is a connection between the licensing of NPIs and the generation of scalar implicature. A direct link would, however, be rather remarkable, for the failure to license an NPI seems to lead not just to oddness, but to something stronger, arguably to *, suggesting that NPI licensing is a grammatical phenomenon. In contrast, the generation of implicatures is traditionally considered a purely pragmatic phenomenon (cf. however Chierchia 2004 and article 10 [Semantics: Interfaces] (Chierchia, Fox & Spector) *Grammatical view of scalar implicatures*); sentences with odd implicatures are pragmatically bizarre, but not just because of that ill-formed. In what follows I review a family of approaches that aim to bridge this gap between pragmatics and grammar in order to find a solution to the licensing puzzle. These proposals have in common that they all suggest that NPIs give rise to scalar implicatures that are only felicitous in negative or downward entailing contexts. The discussion in this section summarizes some of the conclusions reached in Herburger & Mauck (2007, 2009).

One analysis that directly aims to exploit the internal semantics of NPIs to explain their distribution is Lahiri's (1998) account of Hindi NPIs. It departs from the observation that Hindi NPIs are made up of an instance of 'even' (*bhii*) and a low scalar element, which is focused and with which *bhii* associates. (Other languages that have similar 'even' NPIs are discussed in Lee & Horn 1994).

(37) ek bhii   'any, even one'
      ek   'one'
      koii bhii   'anyone, any (count)
      koii   'someone'
      kuch bhii   'anything, any'(mass)
      kuch   'something, a little'
      zaraa bhii   'even a little'
      zaraa   'a little'
      kabhii bhii   'anytime, ever'
      kabhii   'sometime'
      kahiiN bhii   'anywhere'
      kahiiN   'somewhere'

Lahiri (1998) takes the presence of *bhii* to trigger two implicatures, analogous to the implicatures that Kartunnen & Peters (1979) posit for English *even*: the existential implicature (some alternative to the focused element makes the sentence true) and the scalar implicature: the element that *bhii* associates with constitutes the least likely among the relevant scalar alternatives to make the sentence true. This offers an elegant solution to the licensing puzzle.

If p entails q, then p is semantically stronger than q and p is less likely than q. Assuming that *bhii* has the 'least likely' meaning described above and that it necessarily takes wide scope over elements responsible for negative contexts, the combination of *bhii* and the focused low scalar elements (e.g., *one, a bit*) predicts that the relevant expressions are only felicitous in those contexts where a low scalar elements will result in the least likely, semantically strongest among the alternative statements. This happens to be the case in negative or downward entailing contexts; (38) will be stronger than (39) only when embedded in a negative context, as the entailment from (40) to (41) shows:

(38) One person arrived.

(39) Two persons arrived.

(40) It is not the case that one person arrived.

(41) It is not the case that two persons arrived.

An account in some ways similar to Lahiri's is proposed in Krifka (1995). Krifka assumes that an NPI like *anything* has the semantics of a low scalar expression and posits that it triggers stronger alternatives involving specific things, e.g., book or pencil (rather than higher scalar terms, e.g., one thing>two things>three things...). In addition, he postulates two operators 'Scal.Assert' and 'Emphatic. Assert'. The first one takes scope over sentences containing weak NPIs like *anything, ever*. The second one takes scope over sentences with strong NPIs like stressed *any*, and *at all*, which have a narrower distribution than weak NPIs. These operators in combination with the basic meaning of the NPIs and the particular alternatives they are assumed to trigger give rise to scalar implicatures which only make sense in negative environments. Thus, Scal.Assert generates the implicature that all statements involving a more specific alternative would lead to falsity. This results in a contradiction for (42): its truth conditions require that Mary saw some thing. Yet, the implicature generated by Scal.Assert and the more specific alternatives require that there be no specific thing that she saw.

(42) *Mary saw anything.

It is to this contradiction that Krifka attributes the unacceptability of the NPI in non-negative contexts like the one at hand. (42) of course contrasts with (43):

(43) Mary didn't see anything.

(43) asserts that there is nothing that Mary saw and, via Scal.Assert and the more specific alternatives, implicates that there is no specific thing that Mary saw. No contradiction ensues, and the sentence is acceptable.

Simplifying somewhat, Emphatic.Assert, which takes scope over sentences with strong NPIs, generates the implicature that the sentence containing the NPI entails the alternative statements that would be generated by replacing the NPI with stronger, more specific alternatives. In relevant respects this part of the analysis works similarly to Lahiri's: since NPIs like *ANY* and *at all* are assumed to have the semantics of low scalar elements, similar to existential quantifiers, they will only lead to the strongest statements when compared to more specific alternatives (and be thus compatible with Emphatic.Assert) when they appear in negative contexts.

A third analysis that tries to explain the licensing puzzle in terms of implicatures generated by NPIs is developed in Chierchia (2006). Chierchia holds that NPIs like *anything* denote low scalar elements and adopts the claim that they induce widening of the domain of quantification (cf. Kadmon & Landman 1993). Given his localist analysis of implicatures (see above), he posits that *any* bears an uninterpretable feature [+σ], which needs to be checked by an operator σ, whose purpose is to lock in the pragmatic implicatures at the point in the derivation at which the operator appears. Chierchia claims that NPIs like *any* create alternative domains that are smaller than the domain of *any*, and, moreover, he assumes that NPIs trigger the presence of a covert 'even' operator, E_c. This operator requires that the proposition the sentence expresses entail all alternative propositions derived with the help of the smaller alternative domains.

On this view, a sentence like **I saw anyone* when interpreted relative to a domain consisting of {a, b, c} will have to entail *I saw someone* relative to all of the following smaller alternative domains {a, b}, {a, c}, and {b, c}. It clearly will not, for the sentence could be true if the speaker saw c, in which case the alternatives involving the set {a, b} would be false. Of course, as soon as the sentence is embedded in a downward entailing context, the inferences from big context set to small context sets will go through. In other words, positing E_c and making certain suppositions about the domain of alternatives, Chierchia (2006) predicts that NPIs are restricted to negative environments.

On a general level, the three approaches just summarized have a great deal in common. They tie together two phenomena which we know are sensitive to negation, namely the licensing of NPIs and the generation of scalar implicatures. This offers an exciting prospect of progress on the licensing question. It also raises a number of questions, however, which may not all have a satisfactory answer. Perhaps the licensing puzzle is not entirely solved yet.

One general issue any analysis that purports to explain the licensing question in terms of scalar implicatures licensed by (components of) NPIs has to contend with is the fact that unlicensed NPIs do not seem to result so much in pragmatic infelicity as in ungrammaticality. Unlike the pragmatically bizarre but nonetheless grammatical sentence (44) *Mary saw anything*, clearly feels like an ill-formed sentence, irrespective of its pragmatics.

(44) Even Dick Cheney wanted to invade Iraq.

A second worry is that several NPIs seem to have synonymous non-NPI counterparts, e.g., *some* and *any* both can be argued to denote an existential quantifier with equivalent domains of quantification. Though Kadmon & Landman (1993) argue that *any* differs from *some* in requiring a widened domain of quantification, this is probably only true for stressed *any* (Krifka 1995; Lahiri 1998). Note, for instance, that the contrast between (45) and (46) seems rather similar to that between (47) and (48) and therefore most likely due to the presence of a determiner as opposed to a bare plural, rather than 'domain widening':

(45) I don't have potatoes.

(46) I don't have any potatoes.

(47) I have potatoes.

(48) I have some potatoes.

Similarly, *ever* and *sometime* seem synonymous, but *ever* is an NPI and *sometime* is not.

If there are NPIs with synonyms that are not restricted to downward entailing contexts, no complete answer to the licensing puzzle will be found just by looking at the semantics of NPIs themselves. But if the semantics of NPIs is not enough to derive their distribution and something must be stipulated in addition, on top of the operators and lexically triggered alternatives Krifka and Chierchia (but not Lahiri) already invoke, then we do not really have an analysis that derives the distribution of NPIs from their semantics after all. Rather we have an analysis that accounts for the licensing puzzle with certain additional suppositions. And how good any such analysis is depends on its empirical coverage, its internal elegance and on how plausible the additional suppositions are.

Thirdly, the analyses surveyed here also face a descriptive limitation. As Israel (1996) points out, not all NPIs are low scalar expressions and not all NPIs are thus suitable for making the strongest claim in a negative context, a claim, that is, that entails all alternative claims using higher scalar alternatives, as the 'even' analyses demand. In fact, some NPIs denote elements that occupy relatively high rungs on a Horn scale, for instance the NPI *much* in (49) or the NPI *all that* in (50):

(49) He didn't like it much.

(50) Jane may not be all that smart.

It is not obvious how to explain the distribution of these 'understating' NPIs by invoking an 'even' of some form. In fact, it seems impossible because the 'even' accounts exploit a low scalar semantics which these elements seem to lack.

Finally, there is also a technical issue concerning the scope of *bhii*, Scal. Assert, Emphatic.Assert and E_c. The way the analyses just summarized work, it is essential that the relevant operators take scope over the element responsible for the downward entailing context, rather than under it. This seems to violate the lexical integrity of NPIs that contain an instance of 'even', which speakers do not seem to intuitively decompose semantically (Lahiri 1998). In addition, it also requires a very specific and high scope for the operator (Rullmann 1997; Herburger 2003), which effectively amounts to saying that it behaves as a PPI. This arguably just pushes the problem elsewhere.

If the skepticisms just voiced are justified, then we are still faced with the mysterious generalization that NPIs are licensed in negative contexts. But while it is not easy to make sense out of this pattern, it may not be impossible either. I think it may be useful to take into account what happens pragmatically when negation combines with a low scalar element.

It seems no accident that so many NPIs are low scalar elements. In fact, the analyses we just considered heavily rely on this (though too heavily, as we saw, as they ignore the existence of understating NPIs). If the low scalar property is a typical property of NPIs but not a defining one, how do we explain it? As essentially already noted in Jespersen (1917), and more recently in Israel (1996) (and many others as well), low scalar expressions are pragmatically useful in negative contexts, making a negation more 'emphatic'. Compare, for instance (51) with (52):

(51) I don't know.

(52) I don't have the faintest idea.

While both sentences deny that the speaker knows anything, the latter rules it out more categorically by explicitly eliminating the possibility that the speaker knows a bit about the matter. In light of the pragmatic usefulness of low scalar elements in negative contexts, one can hypothesize that *some* of them come to be so frequently used in negative contexts that they over the course of time come to be restricted to such contexts. Which low scalar expressions take this route is in the end an arbitrary matter. If so, it would no longer be surprising that two low scalar expressions in one language or across languages may share their meaning but not their distribution, i.e., that one but not the other is restricted to negative contexts. It would furthermore explain why one and the same lexical item may function as an NPI at one point of its history but not at another (see Herburger & Mauck 2007 for examples).

In more modern terms, we can say that those low scale elements that are only possible in negative contexts have acquired a morphological, uninterpretative feature [u neg] (cf. Klima 1964; Chierchia 2004). This feature lacks semantic content (in distinction to Israel's 1996 i-value) and needs to be checked syntactically in order for the NPI to be licensed. (Contra Chierchia 2004, however, for the reasons spelled out above, I do not assume that it is checked by a silent operator σ that freezes scalar implicatures.)

What about understating NPIs, which, as we saw, occupy a high rung on a Horn scale rather than a low one? Understating expressions are also useful pragmatically (Israel 1996).

As we saw in the previous section, (53) can and is normally taken to be true when Gwen purchased some prints. But, if we suspend the scalar implicature, the sentence can also be considered true when she bought none:

(53) Gwen didn't buy many prints at the antiques shop.

Though it is often useful to make very strong claims to ensure one is really being understood, at times it seems preferable to understate matters. It can save one from pronouncing negative and unpleasant things (cf. *They weren't very enthusiastic about your proposal.*) Vagueness and understatement are also rhetorically interesting and the basis of some subtle jokes. We can now speculate that to the extent that relatively high scalar expressions come to be restricted to negative contexts, i.e., acquire the feature [u neg], the suspension of the scalar implicature is conventionalized and they acquire their purely understating interpretation. As a result, speakers of English know that *I didn't like it much* really means that the speaker did not like it, not that she liked it a bit. We can further speculate that understating NPIs are relatively scarcer than low scalar ones because it may be generally pragmatically more important to be emphatic and clear than to be understating and potentially vague (cf. Israel 1996).

If NPIs are semantically predisposed scalar expressions that have acquired a feature that grammatically forces them to appear only in a negative context, we might also have the beginning of an explanation of why sentences with unlicensed NPIs are judged ungrammatical rather than pragmatically bizarre: the +NPI feature ([u neg]) is simply not checked in non-negative contexts. I say beginning of an explanation because a complete account of course requires explaining how exactly the NPI feature is checked in negative contexts. And this, it turns out, is more of a challenge than one might initially think.

To just briefly show some of the issues involved, some of the syntactic literature assumes that NPIs can be simply licensed by an 'affective' element that c-commands them (Klima 1964 and many others since). But, as Ladusaw (1980) shows, this cannot be right--at least not on standard assumptions about the syntax. As briefly noted above, determiners differ in their entailment properties. *Some*, for instance, is neither downward entailing in its restriction or its scope, but in fact upward entailing in both. *Every*, on the other hand, is downward entailing in its restriction but upward entailing in its scope, and *no* is downward entailing in both its restriction and scope. *Some* is easy to explain on a simple minded syntactic account: it is simply not +affective. *Every* can also be made sense out of: it is affective and, via c-command, licenses an NPI in the part that it c-commands, namely the restriction. But *no* poses a problem, for it licenses NPIs both in the restriction and the scope but only c-commands the former.

The upshot of this is that a simple minded syntactic account will not do. But hopefully a sophisticated one will. One possible solution to consider is Ludlow's (2002) proposal. While I cannot fully explain this analysis here—it is quite involved—I want to sketch some of its major features.

Ludlow first argues for adopting a particular logic as the metalanguage (L*). L* has a semantics for quantifiers which makes it possible to tell from the logical form of a sentence if a variable is in a downward entailing context or not: it is only when it appears in the scope of an even number of negations. He then makes a number of minimalist assumptions regarding the syntax-semantics interface (positing a great many functional projections), which make it possible to not only tell semantically if we are dealing with a downward entailing context, but also syntactically, since it is reflected by the local c-command of a negation. While the result is very interesting if one wants to argue that NPIs are syntactically licensed, as I am doing here, one can easily sense that the analysis is intricate. Given the limited scope of the present paper, I leave at these rather general level of descriptions and refer the interested reader for details to Ludlow (2002), and also Herburger & Mauck (2007) for a summary.

My conclusion regarding the licensing puzzle posed by NPIs is then limited to this: though it is clearly important to investigate the semantics of NPIs in order to better understand why they are restricted to negative contexts, the attempts we canvassed that rely on the presence of an *even*-like component are attractive but also raise a number of non-trivial questions. I take this to suggest that it may be worth to also consider alternative explanations of the licensing puzzle. In this context, I considered the more traditional view that NPIs are expressions that are pragmatically useful in negative contexts, leading to very strong or rather understated claims. I argued that what distinguishes NPIs from synonymous expressions that are not restricted to negative contexts is a feature which needs to be checked syntactically. How this is done exactly is an important matter an account of which I leave for consideration elsewhere.

4 References

Atlas, Jay David 1993. The importance of being 'Only': Testing the neo-Gricean versus neo-entailment paradigms. *Journal of Semantics* 10, 301–318.
Boër, Steven & William Lycan 1976. The myth of semantic presupposition. In: A. Zwicky (ed.). *Papers in Nonphonology* (OSU Working Papers in Linguistics 21). Columbus, OH: Ohio State University, 1–90.
Chierchia, Gennaro 2004. Scalar implicatures, polarity phenomena and the syntax/pragmatics interface. In: A. Belletti (ed.). *Structures and Beyond*. Oxford: Oxford University Press.
Chierchia, Gennaro 2006. Broaden your views: Implicatures of domain widening and the "logicality" of language. *Linguistic Inquiry* 37, 535–590.
Davidson, Donald 1967. The logical form of action sentences. In: N. Rescher (ed.). *The Logic of Decision and Action*. Pittsburgh, PA: University of Pittsburgh Press, 216–234.
Fauconnier, Gilles 1975. Pragmatic scales and logical structure. *Linguistic Inquiry* 6, 353–375.
von Fintel, Kai 1999. NPI-licensing, Strawson-entailment, and context-dependency. *Journal of Semantics* 16, 97–148.
Fox, Danny 2006. *Free Choice Disjunction and the Theory of Scalar Implicature*. Ms. Cambridge, MA, MIT.
van Fraasen, Bas C. 1968. Presuppositions, implication, and self-reference. *Journal of Philosophy* 65, 136–157.
Frege, Gottlob 1892. Über Sinn und Bedeutung. *Zeitschrift für Philosophie und philosophische Kritik* 100, 25–50.
Grice, H. Paul 1975. Logic and conversation. In: P. Cole & J. Morgan (eds.). *Syntax and Semantics 3: Speech Acts*. New York: Academic Press, 41–58.
Herburger, Elena 2000. *What Counts: Focus and Quantification*. Cambridge, MA: The MIT Press.
Herburger, Elena 2003. A note on Spanish *ni siquiera*, 'even', and the analysis of NPIs. *Probus* 15, 237–258.
Herburger, Elena & Simon Mauck 2007. *On 'Even' NPIs*. Ms. Washington, DC, Georgetown University.
Herburger, Elena & Simon Mauck 2009. NPIs pragmatically. In: *Proceedings of the Annual Meeting of the Berkeley Linguistics Society (= BLS) 35, Parasession on Negation*. Berkeley, CA: Berkeley Linguistics Society.
Heim, Irene & Angelika Kratzer 1998. *Semantics in Generative Grammar*. Malden, MA: Blackwell.
Horn, Laurence 1972. *On the Semantic Properties of Logical Operators in English*. Ph.D. dissertation. University of California, Los Angeles, CA. Reprinted: Bloomington, IN: Indiana University Linguistics Club, 1976.

Horn, Laurence 1989. *A Natural History of Negation*. Chicago, IL: The University of Chicago Press.
Horn, Laurence 2006. The border wars. In: K. Turner & K. von Heusinger (eds.). *Where Semantics Meets Pragmatics*. Amsterdam: Elsevier, 21–48.
Horn, Laurence 2006. *ONLY Connect: How to Unpack an Exclusive Proposition*. Ms. New Haven, CT, Yale University.
Israel, Michael 1996. Polarity sensitivity as lexical semantics. *Linguistics & Philosophy* 19, 619–666.
Jespersen, Otto 1917. *Negation in English and other Languages*. Copenhagen: A.F. Host.
Kadmon, Nirit & Fred Landman 1993. Any. *Linguistics & Philosophy* 16, 353–422.
Kartunnen, Lauri & Stanley Peters 1979. Conventional implicature. In: C.-Y. Oh & D. Dinneen (eds.). *Syntax and Semantics 11: Presupposition*. New York: Academic Press, 1–56.
Klima, Edward S. 1964. Negation in English. In: J.A. Fodor & J.J. Katz (eds.). *The Structure of Language*. Englewood Cliffs, NJ: Prentice Hall, 246–323.
Krifka, Manfred 1995. The semantics and pragmatics of polarity items. *Linguistic Analysis* 35, 209–257.
Ladusaw, William A. 1980. *Polarity Sensitive as Inherent Scope Relations*. New York: Garland.
Lahiri, Utpal 1998. Focus and negative polarity in Hindi. *Natural Language Semantics* 6, 57–123.
Lee, Young-Suk & Laurence R. Horn 1994. *'Any' as an Indefinite plus 'Even'*. Ms. New Haven, CT, Yale University.
Levinson, Stephen 2000. *Presumptive Meanings: The History of Generalized Conversational Implicature*. Cambridge, MA: The MIT Press.
Linebarger, Marcia 1987. Negative polarity and grammatical representation. *Linguistics & Philosophy* 10, 325–387.
Ludlow, Peter 2002. LF and natural logic. In: G. Preyer & G. Peter (eds.). *Logical Form and Language*. Oxford: Oxford University Press, 132–168.
Moravcsik, Julius 1991. "All A's are B's": Form and content. *Journal of Pragmatics* 16, 427–441.
Neale, Stephen 1990. *Descriptions*. Cambridge, MA: The MIT Press.
Parsons, Terrence 1990. *Events in the Semantics of English: A Study in Subatomic Semantics*. Cambridge, MA: The MIT Press.
Portner, Paul & Katshuhiko Yabushita 1998. Specific indefinites and the information structure theory of focus. *Journal of Semantics* 18, 271–297.
Potts, Christopher 2005. *The Logic of Conversational Implicatures*. Oxford: Oxford University Press.
Rullmann, Hotze 1997. Even, polarity, and scope. In: M. Gibson, G. Wiebe & G. Libben (eds.). *Papers in Experimental and Theoretical Linguistics 4*. Edmonton, AB: PETL, Department of Linguistics, University of Alberta, 40–64.
Russell, Bertrand 1905. On Denoting. *Mind* 14, 479–493.
Sauerland, Uli 2004. Scalar implicatures in complex sentences. *Linguistics & Philosophy* 27, 367–391.
Schein, Barry 1993. *Plurals and Events*. Cambridge, MA: The MIT Press.
Schein, Barry 2001. Adverbial, descriptive reciprocals. In: R. Hastings, B. Jackson & Z. Zvolenksy (eds.). *Proceedings of Semantics and Linguistic Theory (= SALT) XI*. Ithaca, NY: Cornell University, 404–430.
Strawson, Peter 1950. On referring. *Mind* 59, 320–340.
van der Wouden, Ton 1997. *Negative Contexts: Collocation, Polarity and Multiple Negation*. London: Routledge.
Zwarts, Frans 1998. Three types of polarity. In: F. Hamm & E. W. Hinrichs (eds.). *Plurality and Quantification*. Dordrecht: Kluwer, 177–238.

Anastasia Giannakidou
3 Negative and positive polarity items

1   Introduction: common paradigms of polarity items and basic terminology —— 70
2   Core questions about polarity: sanctioning, variation, and sensitivity —— 76
3   NPI-licensing and downward entailment —— 79
4   NPI-licensers as a natural class: from downward entailment to nonveridicality —— 87
5   Strong NPIs: only licensed by antiveridicality —— 93
6   NPIs in veridical contexts: licensing versus *rescuing* —— 99
7   The scalar approach to polarity —— 103
8   The other side of polarity: non-deictic variables and referential deficiency —— 112
9   Positive polarity items —— 116
10   Main conclusions —— 125
11   References —— 127

Abstract: In this chapter, we discuss the distribution and lexical properties of common varieties of negative polarity items (NPIs) and positive polarity items (PPIs). We establish first that NPIs can be licensed in negative, downward entailing, and nonveridical environments, and within the NPI class we distinguish two main distributional patterns: an NPI with a broad distribution in the environments just mentioned, and a more narrow NPI appearing only in negative contexts. We also note that within the broad class there are scalar and non-scalar NPIs. We examine to what extent the scalarity approach (originating in Kadmon & Landman 1993) can explain the basic patterns, and conclude that this approach, by reducing all polarity phenomena to one source, fails to capture that a significant number of NPIs and PPIs are not scalar, and that there is variation within the scalar class between broader (*any*) and narrow NPIs (either, minimizers). Another fundamental problem with pure scalarity is that it predicts weaker effects (contradictions, presupposition failures) with ill-formed NPIs than is actually the case. We then consider the variation approach pursued by Giannakidou (1998 and sequel) which posits two possible lexical

Anastasia Giannakidou, Chicago, USA

sources of polarity: (a) scalarity (Giannakidou 2007a), which mostly yields weaker ill-formedness, and (b) referential deficiency of expressions that end up becoming NPIs. The variation approach is more consistent with the diversity of NPIs, and extends easily to PPIs, which, as a class, appear to be non-scalar (Szabolcsi 2004; Ernst 2009).

1 Introduction: common paradigms of polarity items and basic terminology

Polarity phenomena in natural language are pervasive. In this chapter, we study the properties of two of the most famous classes: 'negative polarity items' (NPIs) and 'positive polarity items' (PPIs). This first section offers the background necessary for our discussion, and introduces the terminology that will help identify NPIs and PPIs as distinct among other PI-paradigms.

1.1 Negative polarity items

NPIs are typologically very common (Haspelmath 1997 reports data from forty languages), and seem to exist in virtually every language we consider. Their hallmark property is exclusion from positive assertions with simple past (i.e., episodic sentences that make reference to a single positive event; Giannakidou 1997). English *any, ever*, Greek *tipota* 'anything', and Dutch *ook maar iets* 'anything' are well-known NPIs:

(1) a. Bill didn't buy *any* books.
    b. *Bill bought any books.   (versus: Bill bought {*War and Peace*/two books}).

(2) a. *Bill has *ever* read *War and Peace*.
    b. Bill hasn't ever read *War and Peace*.

(3) a. Dhen idhe *tipota* o   Janis.   Greek
       not   saw anything the John
       John didn't see anything.
    b. *Idhe tipota o Janis.
       *John saw anything.

(4) a. Niemand heeft *ook maar iets* gezien.   Dutch
       nobody   has   even something seen
       Nobody saw anything.

    b. *Jan heeft ook maar iets gezien.
       *John saw anything.

Any, ever, ook maar iets, and *tipota* are ill-formed in positive episodic sentences, but become fine with negation (and their distribution is in fact much broader, as we see later). Importantly, *any, ever* and *ook maar iets* are scalar in the sense that they invoke a ordered domain of quantification, or may contain *even* (*ook maar* translates as *even*, as we see in the gloss above). Statements with scalar NPIs are usually strong, emphatic statements. Greek *tipota* is not scalar; a negative statement with *tipota* is weak (as opposed to an emphatic variant that we review later, and which is always emphatic; see Giannakidou 1994 and sequel).

The non-scalar NPI is a weak indefinite in that it always gets interpreted with narrow scope, and can never be used if the speaker has a specific object in mind (Giannakidou 1997, 1998; Giannakidou & Quer 2010). Such indefinites are said to have "low" referentiality (Partee 2008), and are labeled also *epistemically non-specific* (Haspelmath 1997), *extremely non-specific* (Farkas 2002), or *referentially vague* (Giannakidou & Quer 2010). They are sensitive to 'knowledge of the speaker' and can only be used when the speaker does not know what their referent is. Such indefinites are referentially deficient also in that they are unable to introduce discourse referents on their own, as indefinites normally do (Giannakidou 1998). Referentially deficient NPIs are common crosslinguistically; besides Greek NPIs, similar distributions with NPIs are observed in Romanian (*vreun*; Farkas 2002; Falaus 2009), Salish (*ku*; Matthewson 1998), Navajo (*h... da*; Fernald & Perkins 2006), N-of-N structures in some Southern dialects of Dutch (van Craenenbrook 2008), and Korean *nwuku-(ila)to* NPIs (Yoon 2008). Scalar NPIs and non-scalar referentially deficient NPIs are the two main types that we find, and these will be the main object of study in this chapter.

NPIs belong to various syntactic categories: there are nominal NPIs, as the ones above, but also NPI adverbs (*ever*, Dutch *ooit;* Hoeksema 1999), NPI verbs (*hoeven, brauchen* in Dutch and German; van der Wouden 1994), NPI focus particles such as EVEN (Greek *oute*, Giannakidou 2007a; Spanish *nisiquiera* Herburger 2003, English *either*); and a class known as *minimizers* because they contain expressions of minimal amount (the earliest reference is Fauconnier 1975):

(5) a. Bill isn't here yet.
    b. *Bill is here yet.

(6) a. I haven't seen Bill in years.
    b. *I saw Bill in years.

(7) a. Bill doesn't like pasta either.
    b. *Bill likes pasta either.

(8) a. Je   hoeft niet te komen.   (Dutch)
       you   need not to come
       You need not come.

    b. *Je hoeft te komen.

(9) a. Dhen theli   na dhi   *oute*   to idhio tou to pedi.   (Greek)
       not want3sg to see.3sg   even.NPI   the self   his the child
       He doesn't want to see even his own child.

    b. *Theli na dhi *oute* to idhio tou to pedi.
       #He wants to see even his own child.

(10) a. Bill didn't lift *a finger* to help me.
     b. She didn't say *a word* all night.

NPIs are said to be *licensed* (or *triggered*; Ladusaw 1980) by negation. Licensing normally says that the NPI must be in the scope of negation, and scope often translates into overt c-command:

(11) a. ¬∃x. book (x) ∧ bought (bill, x)
     b. ∃x. book (x) ∧ ¬ bought (bill, x)

(12) a. *Any books Bill didn't buy.
     b. Bill didn't buy any books.

Any books can only be interpreted inside the scope of negation, as in (11a) — the scoping in 11b is impossible. Furthermore, appearance to the left of negation, in a position where *any* is not c-commanded by negation, is prohibited, though logically *any books* may still be in the scope of negation. Not all NPIs must be overtly c-commanded by their licenser, and language specific conditions can play a role, but this is certainly a strong tendency for (a subset of) NPIs. In this paper, our focus is on the semantics, and details of syntactic questions like overt c-command are put aside (see Giannakidou (1998: 232–242) for a semantic explanation for this tendency, by attributing it to the fact that NPIs cannot be topical: construals like (12a) are not possible because *any* would have to be interpreted as a topic, but it can't). For an attempt to reanalyze overt c-command as LF licensing, see Uribe-Etxeberria (1994).

1.2 Free choice items

Free choice items (FCIs) are often thought of in relation to NPIs. Because of *any*, which exhibits both NPI and FCIs usage, attempts have been made to attribute NPIs and FCIs to a common source (Chierchia 2006). This dual usage, however, does not characterize all NPIs, certainly not the non-scalar ones; hence attempts at unification are bound to face a number of empirical challenges, as we will see in the paper.

FCIs express what Vendler (1967) called *freedom of choice*, a property manifested in the typical FCI use of *any* in generic sentences and with modal verbs:

(13) *Opjadhipote* ghata kinigai pondikia.   (Greek)
      Any   cat   hunts mice.   (English)

(14) *Opjosdhipote* fititis bori na   lisi afto to provlima. (Greek)
      Any   student can subj   solve this   problem.   (English)

In Greek the FCI *opjadhipote* is distinct lexically from NPI *tipota* (Giannakidou 1998 gives the full paradigms). These sentences with FCIs are not about specific cats, so in this sense FCIs are also non-referential expressions. However, FCIs are usually scalar-marked, and require exhaustive variation (Giannakidou 2001) — properties also described as *domain widening* (Kadmon & Landman 1993), *indifference* (von Fintel 2000; Horn 2000a, 2000b), *domain vagueness* (Dayal 1998), *non-individuation* (Jayez & Tovena 2005). Free choice is usually marked with special morphology — e.g., Greek *–dhipote*, and many languages follow the pattern of Greek with distinct lexicalizations of NPIs and FCIs (see Giannakidou & Cheng 2006; C. Lee 1997; Quer 1998, 1999; Vlachou 2007; Menéndez-Benito 2010 among others).

Importantly, FCIs are bad in both positive *and* negative episodic sentences:

(15) a. *Idha   opjondhipote.   (Greek; Giannakidou 2001)
        saw.perf.1sg FC-person
        *I saw anybody.

     b. *Dhen idha   opjondhipote.
         not saw.perf.1sg FC-person
         Intended: I didn't see anybody.

Unlike NPIs, FCIs remain bad with negation in an episodic (simple past) context. Giannakidou (1998, 2001) and Giannakidou & Cheng (2006) show that this fact characterizes FCIs in many languages, e.g., Spanish, Catalan, French, Chinese:

(16) *(Non) Expulsaron del partido a *cualquier* disidente. (Spanish; Quer 1999)
  not expel.3pl from-the party ACC FC dissident
  Intended: *They expelled any dissident from the party.
  Intended: They didn't expel any dissident from the party.

(17) *(No) Li   va   comprar *qualsevol* ram.   (Catalan; Quer 1998)
  not her/him aux.3sg to.buy   FC   bouquet
  Intended: *S/he bought him/her any bouquet.
  Intended: S/he did't buy him/her any bouquet.

But not all FCIs are polarity sensitive; e.g., German *irgendein* (Kratzer & Shimoyama 2002) is fine in positive episodic contexts, and so is English *wh-ever* (Horn 2000a, 2005):

(18) a. *Irgendjemand*   hat angerufen.   (Kratzer & Shimoyama 2002: (6))
       irgend-one   has called

   b. *Opjosdhipote tilefonise.   (Greek)

(19) a. Bill bought *whichever* book he liked.
   b. *Bill bought whichever book.

Indeed, looking across languages, one finds variation in FCIs with respect to their status as polarity items — though the majority does seem to exhibit polarity sensitivity. I am not going to discuss how FCIs come to be polarity sensitive (see Giannakidou 2001; Giannakidou & Cheng 2006); rather, we consider FCIs only in order to compare them to NPIs when it comes to assessing the idea that they are due to the same source (in particular, widening or scalarity). Given that FCIs remain bad with negation, we must hypothesize that NPIs and FCIs, as classes, cannot be sensitive to the same thing.

1.3 Positive polarity items

Affirmative PIs, or positive PIs (PPIs) are expressions that are 'repelled' by negation and tend to escape its scope. PPIs were first identified as a class in Baker

(1970), and are discussed more recently in Szabolcsi (2004), Nilsen (2003), and Ernst (2009). Expressions like *some, already, would rather,* and speaker oriented adverbs have been identified as PPIs in the literature:

(20) a. Bill didn't buy some books.
b. ∃x. book (x) ∧ ¬ bought (b, x)

(21) a. Bill would rather be in Montpellier.
b. #Bill wouldn't rather be in Montpellier.

(22) a. John is here already.
b. #John isn't here already.

(23) a. Unfortunately, John died.
b. #John didn't unfortunately die.

As we see, *some books* exhibits the scope outside negation that *any* lacks, and only that. *Would rather* and *already* are also odd with negation, and likewise *unfortunately*. (Only metalinguistic denial — which is *not* regular negation (Horn 1989) — can rectify them, and see Ernst 2009 for discussion.) This contrasting behavior of NPIs and PPIs prompted analyses of PPIs as *anti-licensed* by negation (Giannakidou 1997, 1998; Progovac 1994; also Ladusaw 1980), but recently attempts have been made to reformulate anti-licensing as a positive condition (Szabolcsi 2004; Giannakidou 2006a).

1.4 Roadmap

Polarity phenomena are significant because they provide a case of well-formedness that is not fully determined by syntax: the distribution of NPIs is not predicted by their syntactic category alone, and they seem to be sensitive to semantic factors of the sentence (roughly at this stage, the presence or not of negation). This sensitivity addresses the fundamental relation between syntactic and semantic well-formedness, and polarity thus provides a uniquely complex domain to investigate the relation between syntax and semantics, and the nature of semantic knowledge broadly understood.

In this chapter, we examine the distribution and meaning of NPIs and PPIs, in the light of the issues that have determined the research in the past 30 years: distributional variation (within and across languages), mode of sanctioning (licensing, anti-licensing), and how the lexical semantics of the PI relates to its limited distribution. These foundational issues are presented in section 2. In section 3, we examine the basic distribution patterns of NPIs and see that NPIs are licensed in negative, downward entailing and nonveridical contexts (which may be upward entailing). In section 4, we discuss the notion of nonveridicality in more detail and show a correlation between mood and NPI licensing that concerns both scalar and non-scalar NPIs. In section 5 further we single out a class within NPIs that is licensed more narrowly in negative contexts. In section 6, we revisit the broad NPI class that appears in nonveridical contexts, and show that within this class, there is an NPI type, notably illustrated by English *any* and minimizers, that can appear in *veridical and non-DE* contexts. We propose that this NPI is not actually licensed in these cases, but *rescued* by a global negative inference. In section 7 we discuss the scalarity approach to NPIs, and conclude that it is inadequate empirically and conceptually as a general theory of NPIs. In section 8, we identify low referentiality as a possible lexical source of NPIs, and define a class of NPIs that contain variables that cannot be used deictically. This is a widely attested class crosslinguistically. In section 9, finally, we examine PPIs. We follow Ernst (2009) in acknowledging that the scalar approaches face problems when it comes to characterizing PPIs and PPI-variation. An approach based on veridicality and speaker commitment is argued to be more successful in this respect.

2 Core questions about polarity: sanctioning, variation, and sensitivity

NPI licensing has been a central issue in linguistic theory, and indeed one that has received considerable attention since Klima's (1964) seminal work on English negation. In the earlier works, the focus was on English NPIs, but recent crosslinguistic studies extended the empirical domain of polarity, and made obvious a complexity that in the earlier works went unnoticed.

The central theoretical task in most theories of polarity in the past 30 years has been to delimit the set of potential NPI-licensers. This is known as the *licensing* question (Ladusaw 1996). In order to be able to predict if an expression can act as a licenser or not, we have come to expect a coherent characterization of the set of expressions that can *possibly* allow PIs within and across languages. There have been two main approaches to the licensing question: a pragmatic one based on negation, and a semantic one. The pragmatic approach, best represented by Baker (1970) and Linebarger (1980, 1987, 1991) claims that *all* licensing is done by negation, either by entailment (with negation), or (conventional or conversational) implicature, when there is no negation in the sentence. Linebarger also proposes that NPIs must be in the *direct* scope of negation (Linebarger 1987), excluding PIs when "harmful" material intervenes between negation and PI; these cases are known as *intervention* phenomena and will not be discussed in the present paper for reasons of space (see Jackson 1994, however, for a good overview).

The semantic approach originates in Ladusaw (1980), and is further developed in Zwarts (1995), von Fintel (1999), and Giannakidou (1994, 1995, 1997, 1998, 1999, 2001, 2002, 2006a). It maintains that the set of possible NPI licensers must include expressions that are negative, downward entailing (DE, Ladusaw; or Strawson DE; von Fintel 1999), or simply nonveridical — in this case without being negative or DE (Giannakidou, Zwarts). In sections 3 and 4 we define these terms precisely.

A second important question concerns the *status* of illicit NPIs. Polarity, as mentioned earlier, raises the question of well-formedness that is not purely determined by syntax. If not purely syntactic, then what is the nature of polarity ill-formedness? Since Ladusaw, the intuition has been that sentences with failed NPIs, e.g., *Bill brought any presents, *Bill talked to John either, are unacceptable in a sense stronger than mere lexical anomaly, or presupposition failure.

(24) a. #The king of France arrived yesterday.
  b. #Jason has a population of 3 million.

Here we have a presupposition failure and a category mistake (people cannot have populations), and the sentences are perceived as odd, though we can almost figure out what they mean (e.g., *If Jason were a city, then it would have the population of 3 million*, and likewise, *If France had a King then that person could have arrived yesterday*). Ill-formed *any, tipota, ook maar*, and similar NPIs, on the other hand, are odd in a qualitatively different way. But how exactly?

In the more than thirty years of research on polarity, with a few exceptions (Ladusaw 1996; Giannakidou 1998, 2001), scholars were eager to ignore the status question. Ladusaw in his dissertation certainly thought that *any* failures are not mere pragmatic oddities, and presented polarity conditions as cases of grammatical *semantic well-formedness* (see also Ladusaw 1983). Recently, on the other hand, the tendency has been to view NPI ill-formedness as pragmatic infelicity or, as Chierchia puts it, 'logical failure' (Lahiri 1998; Krifka 1995; Chierchia 2006; van Rooy 2003). In these approaches, NPI failures are typically reduced to presupposition failures or contradictions. However, recent processing evidence suggests that polarity failures have stronger psychological status mere lexical anomalies (Saddy at al. 2004; Drenhaus et al. 2006; Drenhaus, Blaszczak & Schütte 2010). This research finds a biphasic N400/P600 pattern with violating conditions of NPIs, suggesting that the processing of NPIs is linked to syntactic and semantic factors: roughly, the N400s reflect the attempts to integrate the NPI semantically, and the P600 manifests the processing cost relating to syntax. These results, though to some extent inconclusive, challenge the idea that NPI failures are mere presupposition failures or contradictions, and at any rate call for caution when it comes to deciding what kind of explanation for the NPI-distribution one must look for. We will come back to the questions of status when we discuss the pragmatic theories later in section 7.

Finally, a third important question concerns compositionality: for a given PI-paradigm, what exactly is responsible for the limited distribution we see? This question prompts a close examination of the lexical contribution of individual classes of NPIs, but in the earlier days polarity conditions were postulated as global, composition external filters on sentences (or grammatical representations), without recourse to the lexical meaning of the NPI. (Another case of such global filtering were the principles of binding theory). For instance, *semantic filtering* (Ladusaw 1983) claims that a syntactically well-formed structure with *any* will be filtered out semantically, because *any* is subject to a semantic licensing condition (it requires negation), and this condition is not satisfied if there is no negation. Why *any* is subject to this condition is not explained, but is merely stipulated.

In current theorizing, the idea of global semantic filtering is unsatisfactory. Instead, we want lexical motivation for the observed licensing rules; we want to understand how the lexical or morphological content of a given PI is responsible for its limited distribution. In the new agenda, the polarity status is no longer stipulated but follows from compositional processes, and PIs are no longer "special" or mysterious, but manifestations of properties and phenomena whose existence is independently motivated in the grammar. Recent examples of theories inspired by this goal are: Kadmon & Landman (1993), Lee & Horn (1994), Krifka (1995), Israel (1996, 2004), Lahiri (1998), Tovena (1998), Giannakidou (1998, 2000, 2001, 2007), Chierchia (2006). A view of sensitivity has emerged where PIs are 'deficient' because they contain, or lack, components in their meanings, thereby creating more demands on the environments of occurrence.

Having outlined these important foundational issues, we now go back to *any* and the Greek and Dutch NPIs we introduced earlier, and take a closer look at their distribution.

3 NPI-licensing and downward entailment

There is indeed a class of NPIs (to be discussed in section 5) whose distribution is limited to mainly negative contexts. The distribution of *any*, however, exceeds negation by far. I proceed to show this incrementally. First, *any* is fine in the scope of *few* (the IP c-commanded by *few professors*), and in the NP argument (i.e., the restriction) of the universal quantifier *every*:

(25) a. Every [student who saw anything] contacted the police.
b. {Few professors/*Many professors} invited any students.

The restriction of *every*, especially, makes a remarkable case against negation being the key factor in the appearance of *any*. *Any* also appears in questions, and in *if*-clauses:

(26) a. If you say anything about this, I'll be very upset.
b. Did you see anybody?

Klima (1964) coined the term "affective" to unify descriptively negation, questions, and the other environments where *any* occurs, but "affective" remains merely a descriptive label in Klima. Real progress beyond that was made with Ladusaw (1980) who argued that there is an underlying semantic property characterizing all affective contexts: downward entailment (DE).

3.1 Downward entailment, and degrees of negativity

Ladusaw proposed the following licensing condition for NPIs:

(27) *Ladusaw's (1980) licensing condition*
α is a trigger for negative polarity items in its scope iff α is downward entailing.

Trigger is the expression in the sentence that is needed to make the NPI legitimate, i.e., the *licenser* of the NPI. Unlike upward entailing (UE) functions, which are order preserving and closed under supersets, DE functions are order reversing and closed under subsets. Both are illustrated below (the definitions rely on Zwarts 1986; Giannakidou 1998):

(28) A function f is upward entailing iff for every X,Y: if X⊆Y, then $f(X) \subseteq f(Y)$

(29) A function f is downward entailing iff for every X,Y: if X⊆Y, then $f(Y) \subseteq f(X)$

UE functions support inference from sets to supersets, and DE functions support inference from sets to subsets. In DE contexts, expressions denoting sets can be substituted for expressions denoting subsets *salva veritate*. Negation, *few students* and the restriction of *every* are DE:

(30) a. Lucy does not like linguistics.
⟦syntax⟧ ⊆ ⟦linguistics⟧
───────────────────────
∴ Lucy does not like syntax.

b. Few students like linguistics.
⟦syntax⟧ ⊆ ⟦linguistics⟧
───────────────────────
∴ Few students like syntax.

(31) Every [student who likes linguistics] came to the party.
⟦student who likes syntax⟧ ⊆ ⟦student who likes linguistics⟧
───
∴ Every student who likes syntax came to the party.

DE thus appears to capture the occurrence of NPIs with negation and in the restriction of *every*. This was a remarkable result, and DE initiated a fruitful research program for semanticists (Hoeksema 1986; Zwarts 1986, 1993; van der Wouden 1994; Kas 1993; Dowty 1994; among many others); one also finds references to licensing environments as non-UE (Postal 2000; Progovac 1994).

Zwarts (1993), further, conceptualized DE contexts as *minimally* negative in that they satisfy the first and fourth of de Morgan relations, and he defined within this class more *strongly* negative functions: antiadditive and antimorphic ones. Antiadditive functions satisfy the first de Morgan biconditional. Antimorphic functions, on the other hand, convey *classical* negation in Zwarts's terminology and satisfy all four of the de Morgan relations; sentence negation is thus antimorphic:

(32) Downward entailment
    (a) $f(X \cup Y) \rightarrow f(X) \cap f(Y)$
    (b) $f(X) \cup f(Y) \rightarrow f(X \cap Y)$

Antiadditivity
    (a) $f(X \cup Y) \leftrightarrow f(X) \cap f(Y)$
    (b) $f(X) \cup f(Y) \rightarrow f(X \cap Y)$

Antimorphicity
    (a) $f(X \cup Y) \leftrightarrow f(X) \cap f(Y)$
    (b) $f(X) \cup f(Y) \leftrightarrow f(X \cap Y)$

Antiadditive functions are a subset of the DE, and antimorphic functions are a subset of the anti-additive. A DE quantifier like *few* is not antiadditive, but *nobody* is. Depending on whether they are licensed by DE, antiadditive or antimorphic expressions, Zwarts distinguishes between *weak*, *strong*, and *superstrong* NPIs. *Any* is weak in this system because it is licensed by *few*, but the Dutch *ook maar iets* (that we saw at the beginning of the chapter) is strong: it is not licensed by *weinig* 'few' and needs *niemand* 'nobody':

(33) a. **Weinig* mensen hebben   ook maar iets gezien.   (Zwarts 1981)
few   people   have.3pl anything   seen
Few people saw anything.

b. *Niemand* heeft   ook maar iets gezien.
nobody   have.3pl anything   seen
Nobody saw anything.

Van der Wouden (1994) further mentions a class of collocations that require antimorphic negation, i.e., idioms like *voor de poes* in Dutch, which can only occur in with negation: *niet voor de poes zijn* "to not be considered lightly". In this tradition, the shared enthusiasm has been that we can characterize semantically the class of NPI-licensers, and that within that class we can neatly establish varying degrees of sensitivity to stronger or weaker forms of negation. The facts, however, are not as neat because, as we see next, not all environments where NPIs appear can be described as DE.

3.2 Problems with DE: NPIs appear in non-DE contexts

Critiques of DE are to be found in numerous places in the literature starting with Linebarger (1980); I will mention here also Zwarts (1995), Giannakidou (1997, 1998, 2006a), and van Rooy (2003). Linebarger's criticism aimed to show that an entailment based approach to NPIs is simply untenable (see Giannakidou 2006a for addressing some of Linebarger's concerns). From our current perspective, the main conceptual problem with both the old-style Ladusaw and the refined Zwarts style DE-condition is, as mentioned earlier, that they are merely stipulated as global, composition external filters on representations that contain PIs; why NPIs are subject to DE-based licensing rules remains a mystery. Most accounts within this earlier tradition limit their analytical goal to simply positing licensing conditions.

In this section we focus on the main empirical problem: DE does not predict the correct set of licensing environments in English or crosslinguistically, and it is not flexible enough to capture the variation attested.

3.2.1 Non-uniform and unexpected licensing in the restrictions quantifiers

Though DE appears to explain nicely the occurrence of NPIs in the restriction of *every*, the distribution of NPIs in the restrictions of quantifiers is factually more complex. First, we find a contrast between the restriction of *every*, which allows *any*, and the restriction of *each* and *both*, which doesn't (Giannakidou 1997, 1998); for earlier notes see also Horn (1972), Seuren (1984):

(34) {Every student/the students} who saw anything reported to the police.

(35) a. */??Each student who saw anything reported to the police.
b. */??Both students who saw anything should report to the police.

(Greek NPIs behave exactly the same.) This asymmetry is problematic for DE which predicts uniform licensing in universal restrictions, and Giannakidou (1997, 1998, 1999) argued that the contrast follows if we consider that *each* and *both*, but not *every*, are presuppositional. Presuppositional determiners can only be defined in non-empty domains. *Every* has no such restriction and can be used in a context that allows an empty domain (for more details see Giannakidou 1998, 1999). The non-sanctioning with *each/both* then suggests that, for NPIs, it is not DE that matters, but whether or not there exists a nonempty domain.

Israel (2004) further observes (and see Sailer 2009 for more recent discussion) the following data, supporting again the correlation between NPIs in the restriction and (non)existence:

(36) a. *Most* children with *any sense* steal candy.
b. *Most* people who would *lift a finger* to help Bill now are either very foolish or very well-paid.

We see here that *most* too can license an NPI in its restriction — despite that it is not DE. For *most* to license NPIs, it must be used generically — these are law-like contexts where the existential commitment of *most* gets suspended. These data support what we just observed about *every* versus *each/both*, and are problematic if we assume that DE is all that we need to account for NPIs in restrictions of determiners. Giannakidou (1998: Ch. 3) finally discusses certain specificity effects that can be understood as pointing in the same direction, and see also Hoeksema 2008, 2010 for data from Dutch suggesting the role of non-existence in the restriction.

3.2.2 NPIs in questions

DE cannot explain the occurrence of NPIs in questions. It is very hard to establish monotonicity patterns in questions, and to my knowledge, there has been no successful attempt to do this, a difficulty noted already by Ladusaw (see also Guerzoni & Sharvit 2007). This is a serious empirical problem, as NPIs are very common in questions: in virtually every language that can be identified to have an NPI with distribution that exceeds negation, the minimal extension is questions. I illustrate below with Greek and Dutch:

(37) a. Heb   je   ook maar iets gezien?   (Dutch)
        have.2sg you anything   seen
        Did you see anything?

    b. Idhes   tipota?   (Greek)
       saw.2sg   anything
       Did you see anything?

The Dutch *ook maar iets*, and the Greek *tipota* are fine in information questions (and with no negative bias), while *not* being licensed by the equivalents of *few*:

(38) a. */??Liji anthropi idhan tipota.   (Greek)
        few people   saw.3pl anything
        Few people saw anything.

    b. * To poli 5   anthropi idhan tipota.
         At most five people   saw   anything.

    c. *Weinig mensen hebben ook maar iets gezien.
        Few people saw anything.

The non-occurrence of *ook maar iets* and *tipota* with a DE quantifier, and their improvement with questions, challenges the assumption that these items are sensitive to DE, and the attempt to render them strong NPIs fails: a strong NPI, according to Zwarts, is expected to occur in antiadditive environments only, but questions are not DE, let alone antiadditive. Things become worse next, when we consider modal and other non-DE contexts.

3.2.3 Modal and other non-DE enviroments for NPIs

NPIs appear in imperatives, with modal verbs, subjunctive complements of propositional attitudes, habituals, and disjunctions (Giannakidou 1994, 1995, 1998, 1999, 2006a). I illustrate with Greek and English *any* in order to keep things simple, but similar observations are reported for NPIs in Salish (Matthewson 1998), Chinese (Lin 1996), Navajo (Fernald & Perkins 2006), Russian (Haspemath 1997; Pereltsvaig 2000), Ossetic (Haspelmath 1997), Hindi NPIs (Lahiri 1998), N-of-N NPIs in southern Dutch dialects (van Craenenbrok 2008), and Romanian *vreun* NPIs (Farkas 2002; Falaus 2009), to mention just some of the paradigms.

(39) a. Patise   {kanena/opjodhipote} pliktro.
       press.imperative any key
       Press any key.

   b. O Janis bori na milisi me {kanenan/opjondipote}.
      the John may subj talk.3sg with anybody
      John may talk to anybody.

   c. O Janis ine prothimos na milisi me {kanenan/opjondipote}
      the John is willing   subj talk.3sg with anybody
      John is willing to talk to anybody.

Modal environments are known to be non-monotone. We talk more about the licensing of NPIs with propositional attitudes in section 4, but notice here that in Greek both the non-scalar NPI and the FCI are good in modal contexts. In other words, it is not just FCIs that we find in imperatives, with modals verbs and propositional attitudes.

Another problematic case for DE is the conditional. I illustrate below with *any* as well as the Greek NPIs and FCIs, to make clear that it is not just a free choice effect that we observe:

(40) An kimithis me {opjondhipote/kanenan} tha se skotoso.
     if sleep.2sg with FCI-person/NPI-person FUT you kill.1sg
     'If you sleep with anybody, I'll kill you.'

Heim (1984) noted the problem with classic DE in conditionals. If the set of situations where one *goes to Spain and has a car accident* is a subset of the set of situations where one *goes to Spain*, it becomes problematic to infer from *If you go to Spain you will have a good time* that *If you go to Spain and have a car accident you will have a good time*. Heim herself suggested that we can maintain DE if we strengthen pragmatically the antecedent, and the line of pragmatically restoring DE is later taken on in von Fintel (1999). However, Giannakidou (2006a) shows that if we allow pragmatic reasoning to determine DE, we make too broad predictions—and we lose one of the most appealing features of the Ladusaw-Zwarts approach: that NPIs are sensitive to semantic properties of the environment of occurrence.

Another non-negative and non-DE NPI-environments is the habitual. Giannakidou (1995) noted that Greek NPIs and FCIs appear in habitual sentences with Q-adverbs of varying force (meaning *often, rarely, sometimes, never*). In Greek, the habitual sentence Greek contains imperfective aspect:

(41) I   Eleni dhiavaze   sinithos {kanena} periodhiko (otan variotane).
       the Ellen read.imperf.3sg usually   NPI/   magazine
       Ellen used to read {some magazine or other} when she was bored.

The ambiguity of the English simple past, which allows perfective and habitual readings, may help improve *any*, if speakers understand the sentence as habitual, as indicated above. And we also see here that the NPI appears in the scope (the main VP) of the clause, not the restriction.

Finally, NPIs occur in disjunctions (Giannakidou 1998):

(42) a. I   bike mesa kanenas   i   afisame to fos anameno. (disjunction)
        either entered.3sg NPI   OR   left.1pl   the light on
        (??/#Either anybody came in OR we left the light on.)

   b. *Bike mesa kanenas   ke   afisame to fos anameno.   (conjunction)
      *Anybody came in AND we left the light on.

(Notice here the asymmetry with *any*, discussed in Giannakidou 1999, 2006a.) The occurrence of NPIs in disjunctions but not conjunctions is very unexpected from the point of view of negation or DE, and suggests a role of veridicality for NPI-licensing: disjunctions are nonveridical, but conjunction is veridical (it requires that both conjuncts be true; Zwarts 1995).

I summarize below the broad distribution of NPIs, *any* and FCs, some of which I illustrated here. The Tab. 3.1 relies on Giannakidou 2001.

Rows 1–17 are the core polarity data an adequate theory of polarity must explain. Notice that, of these environments, only the restriction of universal quantifiers, DE quantifiers (which are *not* licensers in Greek), and negation are DE, the rest are not.

Tab. 3.1: Comparative distribution of broad NPI, FCI and 'any' sanctioning environments

Environments	any	Broad NPI	Free choice item
1. Episodic negation	OK	OK	*/#
2. Episodic yes/no question	OK	OK	*/#
3. Conditional (*if*-clause)	OK	OK	OK
4. Restriction of *every/all*	OK	OK	OK
5. (Non-antiadditive) Downward entailing Q	OK	*	*
6. Modal verbs	OK	OK	OK
7. Directive attitudes (e.g., *want, insist, suggest, allow*)	OK	OK	OK
8. Imperatives	OK	OK	OK
9. Habituals	OK	OK	OK
10. Disjunctions	*	OK	OK
11. *isos/perhaps*	*	OK	OK
12. Stative verbs	OK	*	OK
13. *prin/before* clauses	OK	OK	OK
14. NP Comparatives	OK	*	OK
15. *monon/only*	OK	*	*
16. Emotive factive verbs	OK	*	*
17. Episodic past sentences	*	*	*
18. Positive existential structures	*	*	*
19. Epistemic attitudes (e.g., *believe, imagine, dream, say*)	*	*	*
20. Progressives	*	*	*
21. Non-emotive factives (e.g., *know, remember*)	*	*	*

Before moving on to nonveridicality, let me again emphasize that the broader distribution of the Greek NPI is not a peculiarity of Greek and English *any*, but is found in various languages. In many cases we are dealing with non-scalar NPIs that belong to the decreased referentiality class that we mentioned at the beginning (especially in Greek, Salish, Navajo, Chinese, Romanian; but not in Hindi, English). Now we move on to nonveridicality as the property unifying negation and these non-negative, non-DE licensing environments as a natural class.

4 NPI-licensers as a natural class: from downward entailment to nonveridicality

In philosophy, the term *veridicality* is related to truth and sometimes existence (as in Montague 1969). Giannakidou (1994 and sequel) and Zwarts (1995) propose that the main distributional fact about NPIs is that they are excluded from veridical sentences and are allowed in nonveridical ones, and define the notion in terms of truth.

4.1 Main definitions

Veridicality is a property of sentence embedding functions: such a function F is veridical if Fp entails or presupposes the truth of p. If inference to the truth of p under F is not possible, F is nonveridical. More specifically, veridical operators express certainty and an individual's commitment to the truth of a proposition, but nonveridical expressions express uncertainty and lack of commitment. Within the class of the nonveridical expressions, negation is identified as ANTI-VERIDICAL in that $NOT\ p$ entails that p is false.

The intuitive idea behind veridicality and nonveridicality is very simple: a linguistic item L is veridical if it expresses certainty about, or commitment to, the truth of a sentence; and L is nonveridical if it doesn't express commitment. For example, if *We know that Bill left* then *Bill left* is true — in fact *Bill left* is not simply entailed *under the verb* know, but presupposed to be true, i.e., it is part of the context's common ground. Hence all factive verbs are veridical. But if it is true that I have a desire that *Bill leaves*, I am not committed to the truth of *Bill leaves*. From this intuitive description, we see immediately that veridicality and nonveridicality correlate with the two basic categories of the indicative selecting verbs (factives), and the subjunctive ones (volitionals). In Giannakidou (1998) and (1999) I developed a formal system that described these distinctions, and I will reproduce part of that discussion here.

The notion of veridicality and nonveridicality that I employ here is one of epistemic assessment, and epistemic assessment itself relies on an *individual* assessing whether the proposition denoted by a sentence is true or false. This individual is the *individual anchor* (Farkas 1992; Giannakidou 1998, 1999), and I made the assumption that *every sentence*, embedded or not, is true or false with respect to an individual. An unembedded sentence will be assessed as true or false with respect to the speaker. With propositional attitudes (which are propositional operators, a treatment originating in Hintikka 1962), we have two possible individual anchors for truth assessment: the speaker, as in the unembedded sentence, and the attitude subject; and the complement sentence may be true or false depending on whose perspective we take.

In my earlier work, I added to the context 'models of individuals'. These models represent the doxastic state of individuals, as in the philosophical tradition where belief and knowledge states are modeled as sets of possible worlds in terms of accessibility functions relative to individuals (see Hintikka 1962 and Heim 1992, among many others).

(43) *DF*1: Model of an individual (Giannakidou 1999: (44))
Let c= <cg(c), W(c), M, s, h, w_0, f,...> be a context.
A model M(x) ∈ M is a set of worlds associated with an individual x; x is the individual anchor.

The context assumed in this definition is Stalnakerian. It is a tuple consisting of a common ground (cg(c)), a context set W(c), i.e., the set of worlds in which all the propositions in the cg(c) are true (i.e., it is the set of worlds compatible with that is believed to be true by the agents of the conversation prior to any assertion), an assignment function *f*, and a number of what Condoravdi calls *Kaplanian* (Condoravdi 1994) parameters such as the speaker *s*, the hearer *h*, the actual world w_0, and possibly other parameters. Models are construed as collections of worlds in *c*, corresponding essentially to the accessibility functions what we know from the treatment of attitudes in modal logic and possible world semantics.

In the simplest case, i.e., for an unembedded assertion, and for sentences embedded under epistemic verbs as we shall see later, M(x) stands for an individual's belief state: it represents the doxastic status of that individual, and it includes worlds compatible with what x believes in the actual world. This is captured in the definition below, where M(x) is indexed with B:

(44) *DF* 2: Belief model of an individual (Giannakidou 1999: (45))
Let c= <cg(c), W(c), M, *s*, *h*, w_0, *f*,...> be a context.
A model $M_B(x)$ ∈ M is a set of worlds associated with an individual x representing worlds compatible with what x believes.

The proposition *p* of an unembedded assertion will be evaluated with respect to the speaker's model, naturally:

(45) a. John won the race.
      b. [[John won the race]] = 1 iff
         $\forall w \, [w \in M_B(s) \rightarrow w \in \lambda w'. \text{John wins the race in } w']$

This tells us that if the speaker decides in a context to truthfully assert the sentence *John won the race*, (s)he must believe that John won the race, which means that all worlds in his model $M_B(s)$ are *John-won-the race* worlds. Hence: $M_B(x) \subseteq p$:

(46) DF3: Truth in an epistemic model
      A proposition p is true in an epistemic model $M_B(x)$ iff:
      $\forall w \, [w \in M_B(x) \rightarrow w \in \lambda w'. p(w')]$

So, unembedded assertions express the speaker's doxastic (or broadly, epistemic) commitment. This is formalized in some recent works (e.g., Alonso-Ovalle & Menendez-Benito 2010) by introducing an implicit assert operator in the syntax that brings in the $M_B(x)$, but in Giannakidou (1998, 1999), $M_B(x)$ remain a parameter of evaluation that need not syntactically present. The question of whether $M_B(x)$ needs to be syntactically present or not parallels the debate about whether the *judge* (Lasersohn 2005), i.e., the individual anchor for predicates of personal taste, must be represented syntactically as a covert pronoun (as in Stephenson 2007) or not. The debate is not central to what we discuss here though, so I leave it aside.

Unembedded positive assertions in the simple past, then, like *John won the race*, are veridical. We are now ready to define the notion:

(47) DF4. (Non)veridicality for propositional operators (following Giannakidou 2006a)
      i. A propositional operator *F* is veridical iff *Fp* entails or presupposes that *p* is true in some individual's model $M(x)$; p is true in $M(x)$, if $M(x) \subset p$.
      ii. If (i) is not the case, *F* is nonveridical.
      iii. A nonveridical operator *F* is *anti*veridical iff *Fp* entails *not p* in some individual's model: iff $M(x) \cap p = \emptyset$

Given that a proposition *p* is true in a model $M(x)$ iff it is true in all worlds in $M(x)$, *DF4* says that an expression *F* will be veridical if the proposition F embeds is universally true in all worlds in $M(x)$. So veridical operators express an individual's doxastic or epistemic commitment to the truth of a proposition. When this is the case, no NPIs will be licensed.

Nonveridical expressions, on the other hand, lack truth commitment: it is not the case that all worlds w in $M(x)$ are p-worlds. This is typically what we get with volitional and future oriented predicates, questions, disjunctions, modal verbs, subjunctive taking verbs—all licensing environments for NPIs.

Within the class of the nonveridical functions, negation is identified as ANTI-VERIDICAL: assertion of *NOT p* requires that the set of worlds in M_B(speaker) and the p worlds are disjoint:

(48) *Antiveridicality* of negative assertion
⟦not p⟧ is true in M_B(speaker) iff M_B(speaker) ∩ p = ∅

Negation, a prototypical NPI-licenser is antiveridical. Giannakidou (1998) used the term *averidical* (with Greek *a-* meaning *without*) for non-assertive sentences such as imperatives and questions because for their assessment we do not use the concepts or truth or falsity, hence they lack veridicality by definition. Since then, I am using the term nonveridical to include the nonveridical and averidical cases, because the latter too, strictly speaking, do not require satisfaction of clause (i), i.e., truth in a speaker's model.

I showed in my earlier work that nonveridicality is relevant for NPIs, FCIs, as well as mood choice (at least in Greek). I should mention also that Quer's (1998, 2001) account of mood in Spanish and Catalan implements the notion of model that I define here, and suggests that the availability of multiple models is the key to explaining mood shifts in Romance. An interesting case where we see the workings of nonveridicality is the interaction between NPI licensing and propositional attitudes. It will be helpful to consider the main facts here because they tend to not be discussed much.

4.2 Propositional attitudes and NPI licensing

Giannakidou (1995, 1998, 1999) observes a correlation between mood choice and NPI licensing in Greek: NPIs appear in subjunctive complements (*na*) of propositional attitude verbs that are *directive* (meaning *want, ask, suggest* and the like), but are excluded from the indicative (*oti*), complements of epistemic, factive, and similar verbs:

(49) I Ariaδni epemine na afiso {opjonδipote/kanenan} na perasi
the Ariadne insisted.3sg subj let.1sg FC-person/NPI-person subj come.3sg
mesa.
in
'Ariadne insisted that I allow anyone in.'

(50) I   Ariaδni   θa   iθele   na   milisi   me {opjonδipote/kanenan}
    the Ariadne would like.3sg subj talk.1sg with FC- /NPI-
    fititi.
    student
    'Ariadne would like to talk to any student.'

(51) a. *O   Pavlos   pistevi   oti   idhe   {kanenan/opjonδipote}.
        the   Paul   believe.3sg   that   saw.3sg   NPI/FCI
        *Paul believes that he saw anybody.

    b. *Kseri   oti   ayorasa   {kanena/opjoδipote} aftokinito.
        know.3sg   that   bought.1sg   NPI/FCI   car
        *He knows that I bought any car.

This correlation is found in most of the languages that possess this type of broad NPI, even if there is no formal subjunctive-indicative distinction; and notice that *any* too is fine in the (infinitival) complements of *would like, insist*, while it is out in *that* clauses of epistemic and factive verbs.

(52) a. John would like to invite any student.
    b. John asked us to invite any student.
    c. John is willing to invite any student.
    d. I insist that you allow anyone in.

(53) a. *John believes that we invited any student.
    b. *John dreamt that we invited any student.

Giannakidou (1998, 1999) argues that epistemic and factive attitudes are veridical. For *x believes that p* to be true, it must be the case that *x*, the main clause subject, is committed to the truth of the embedded proposition *p*. Though the speaker might disagree, a prerequisite for the sentence to be true is that Jacob's epistemic model (i.e., the set of worlds compatible with what Jacob believes) be a subset of the worlds where *p* is true: $M_B(Jacob) \subseteq p$. The speaker may believe or even know that what Jacob believes is false, but this is irrelevant for Jacob's beliefs.

(54) $[\![$Jacob believes that Ariadne loves Paul$]\!]_c = 1$ iff
    $\forall w\,[w \in M_B(Jacob) \to w \in \lambda w'. \text{Ariadne loves Paul in } w']$

(See also Tancredi 2007 for a very similar formulation.) Since all worlds in the model $M_B(Jacob)$ are *p*-worlds, *believe* is veridical: $[\![pistevo(x, p)]\!]_c = 1 \to [\![p]\!]_{MB(x)} = 1$; likewise, other epistemic verbs such as *think,* and *imagine,* and fiction verbs (*dream*). Factives are *strongly* veridical: the worlds in the speaker's model too are *p*-words, consistent with the observation that factive complements are presupposed to be true (see Giannakidou 1998, 1999 for more discussion).

The directive class, on the other hand, does not require an individual's commitment to the truth of the embedded proposition, and thus express a weaker relation between the speaker and the embedded proposition. Consider *thelo* 'want'. Intuitively, "wanting something is preferring it to certain relevant alternatives, the relevant alternatives being those possibilities that the agent believes will be realized if he does not get what he wants." (Stalnaker 1979: 89; see also Heim 1992). This simply requires that the intersection between $M_B(x)$ and *p* be nonempty:

(55) ⟦Jacob wants that Ariadne leave⟧$_c$ =1 if
$\exists w\ [w \in M_B\ (Jacob) \land w \in \lambda w'. Ariadne\ leave\ in\ w']$

X wants p is true in case there is a world in $M_B(x)$ that is also *p*-world. We can thus envision $M_B(x)$ as partitioned into two sets, W_1 and W_2. W_1 is the part that intersects with *p*. W_2, is the part containing non-*p* worlds: therefore $W_2 \cap p = \varnothing$. The worlds in W_1 are more desired alternatives than the worlds in W_2, but from *want (x, p)* we cannot infer that *p* is true in $M_B(x)$. Giannakidou 1998 extends this analysis to modal verbs (which also allow NPIs).

Nonveridicality thus makes the right predictions as to where NPIs may appear and captures the distribution of the broad type of NPI. (Other labels for this NPI have been "affective PI", Giannakidou (1997), nonveridical PI; Giannakidou (1998). Here I adopt the NPI label, following the tradition.) Within the broad NPI class, further, we need to distinguish between the Greek type NPI which is licensed only in nonveridical contexts, and the *any*-like NPIs which exhibit a more liberal distribution and can appear even in veridical contexts under certain conditions. This discussion continues further in section 6.

I will close by summarizing the main tenets of what I call here the nonveridicality theory of polarity, a label that refers to a number of works inspired by the notion (Giannakidou 1997, 1998, 1999, 2001, 2006a, 2007, 2009; Giannakidou & Cheng 2006; Giannakidou & Zwarts 1999; Giannakidou & Yoon 2010; Zwarts 1995; Lin 1996 for "non-existence"; a (non)veridicality calculus in a categorial type logic for PI-licensing has been proposed for Italian by Bernardi 2002). The nonveridicality theory represents the most detailed, crosslinguistically oriented program for FCIs and NPIs to date, and its starting point is that PIs across languages and paradigms have varied, but predictable, distributions in nonveridical contexts. The main tenets can be summarized as follows:

(56) **The Nonveridicality theory of Polarity**
   A. *Licensing Property*
   PIs appear in nonveridical contexts. Nonveridical contexts include modal, intensional, generic, downward entailing contexts, disjunctions, and non-assertive contexts (questions, imperatives, and the protasis of conditionals).

   B. *Varied distribution due to lexical composition*
   For each PI paradigm, its lexical semantic properties and its morphosyntactic features will determine where precisely, within the licensing space, the PI will appear. Crucially, there are TWO lexical semantic sources for polarity: *scalarity* and *referential deficiency*.
   i. Referentially deficiency covers NPIs that are dependent indefinites (unable to be text-level existentially closed), referentially vague indefinites (indicating uncertainty), two kinds of FCIs (definite or indefinite, both containing a dependent world variable), and the subjunctive mood (which is a non-deictic tense; Giannakidou 2009).
   ii. Scalarity handles NPIs whose meaning includes an EVEN-like component (Giannakidou 2003, 2007; C.-M. Lee 1999; Yoshimura 2007: J.-H. Lee 2010; Yoon 2008).

   C. *Two modes of sanctioning*:
   NPIs can be *licensed* or *rescued* (Giannakidou 2006a). Licensing happens in the scope of an operator that has the licensing property. Rescuing happens in an otherwise non-licit context due to global semantic-pragmatic reasoning (rescuing accounts for the alleged 'Strawson DE' cases). Rescuing is a secondary option: there are no PIs that are rescued but not licensed.

These three clauses define a flexible framework where various NPI and FCI paradigms can be studied and understood. We examine in this paper the main patterns we find, starting the class of stricter NPIs — those that are only sensitive to negative and antiveridical contexts.

5 Strong NPIs: only licensed by antiveridicality

Within the class of of nonveridical functions, antiveridical ones are those entailing the negation of p. This category helps make sense of a very common pattern crosslinguistically: NPIs that are licensed very narrowly and appear only with negation and the antiveridical connective *without* (Giannakidou 1997, 1998, 1999). These NPIs are often labelled "strong" or "strict", as opposed the broad NPIs which are thought of as *weak*. Strict NPIs do not appear in nonveridical environments that are not negative.

5.1 *Either*

Either is known to be an NPI with very narrow distribution (Nathan 1999; Rullman 2003; Giannakidou 2006a):

(57) a. John didn't come either.
     b. John left without talking to Bill either.
     c. * Did John come either?
     d. * I want John to come either.
     e. * Pick this up either!

There is some variation in the reported data, but all sources agree that *either* is licensed mainly by negative and negative-like expressions.

5.2 Minimizers in Greek, Japanese and Korean

Minimizers in Greek, Japanese and Korean also show very narrow distribution (in contrast to the corresponding class in English, which is very liberal, as we see in section 6). They are only allowed with negation and antiveridical *without*. I give here some of the relevant data (for Greek, see Giannakidou 1998, 1999):

(58) *Dhen dhino dhekara jia to ti th' apojinis.*
     not give.1sg damn about the what will happen.2sg
     I don't give a damn about what will happen to you!

(59) Kathotan eki *xoris na lei leksi*!
     He just stood there without saying a word.

(60) * Dhinis dhekara ja to ti tha apojino?
       Do you give a dam about what will happen to me?

(61) * An dhinis dhekara, tha me akousis.
(If you dive a damn, you'll listen).

(62) a. Watasi-wa   gakusei-o   {dare-mo / hito-ri-mo}   mi-nakat-ta.
I-TOP   student-ACC {who-MO / one-CL-MO}   see-NEG-PAST
'I didn't see any students.'

b. *Gakusei-o   {dare-mo / hito-ri-mo}   mita-ra   siras-ero.
student-ACC {who-MO / one-CL-MO}   see-if   inform-IMP
'If you see any student, inform me.'

(For more Japanese data, see Nakanishi 2007; Yoshimura 2007.) Yoshimura (2007) argues that –mo lexicalizes as an item with ONE and the wh-indeterminate *dare*, and gets special intonation, in agreement with other strict NPIs crosslinguistically (e.g., Greek minimizers, and n-words; we review these in a minute). Japanese –mo is an additive focus particle that means *also* and in this context *even*. (Japanese also has an unambiguously EVEN item: -*sae*; see Yoshimura 2007 for extensive discussion.)

Minimizers are also strict NPIs in Korean (J.-H. Lee 2010; C. Lee 1999, 2003), and in this language, a particle meaning exclusively EVEN is used: -*to*.

(63) Ku-nun   pamsay   *hanmati-to*   ha-ci   an-ess-ta.
he-Top   all night   a word-NPI-even   say-Comp   Neg-Pst-Decl
He didn't say a word all night.

(64) a. *Ku-nun   pamsay   hanmati-to   ha-ess-ta.
he-Top   all night   a word-NPI-even   say-Pst-Decl
*He said a word all night.

b. *Ku-nun   pamsay   hanmati-to   ha-ess-ni?
he-Top   all night   a word-NPI-even   say-Pst-Q
Did he say a word all night?

c. *ne-ka   hanmati-to   ha-myen, nay-ka ne-lul
cwukyeperi-keyss-ta.
you-Nom a word-NPI-even   say-if   I-Nom   you-Acc
kill-Fut-Decl
If you say a word, I'll kill you.

-*To* is itself an NPI-even, used with negation and *without* (unlike –*mo*)—and is also to be found in the Korean n-word (*anwu-to*), producing again a strict NPI (C.

Lee 1999, 2003). So, in Korean and Japanese we find NPI-EVEN based NPIs that have this stricter distribution.

5.3 NPI-EVEN

NPI-EVEN is observed, in addition to Korean, in many languages: e.g., Spanish (Herburger 2003), German (*einmal*; König 2003, and Greek (*oute*; Giannakidou 2007). I give below examples form Greek:

(65) a. Dhen theli   na   dhi   oute   to   idhio tou to pedi.
         not want3sg subj see.3sg even.NPI the self   his the child
         He doesn't want to see even his own child.

   b. ...xoris na theli na dhi oute to idhio tou to pedhi.
      Without wanting to see even his own child

   c. *Theli na dhi oute to idhio tou to pedi.
      He wants to see even his own child.

   d. *Idhe oute to idio tou to pedi?
      Did he see even his own child?

Rooth (1985) claims that there is an NPI-*even* in English, and for more extensive recent discussion of the relation between EVEN meanings and polarity see Giannakidou (2007). The connection between strict minimizers and *even* is clear when one looks at languages like Korean, as we saw, and Greek (*oute* can be added to the minimizers).

Lahiri (1998) pursues an analysis of Hindi NPIs that relies on EVEN but, crucially, his Hindi NPIs exhibit broad distribution, not the narrow one observed typically when a language lexicalizes an NPI-EVEN. Likewise, NPIs that have been claimed to contain *even* in English, i.e., minimizers as we see in section 6, exhibit broader distribution than the strict minimizer NPIs observed here in Greek, Japanese, and Korean. It seems reasonable then to assume that, when it comes to using a lexical item meaning EVEN as the basis for an NPI, we must acknowledge at least two different EVENs: one that serves as the basis for strict NPI, and one that produces a broader variety. The former, according to Giannakidou (2007) following Rooth, expresses high likelihood, but the latter low likelihood, and may also be more flexible in the kind of scale it depicts (for this, see also Hoeksema & Rullmann 2001).

5.4 N-words in strict negative concord

N-words (Laka 1990) in 'strict' negative concord languages (Giannakidou 1998, 2000, 2006a) can also be thought of as strong NPIs: they cannot appear without negation in the clause:

(66) a. *(Dhen) theli na dhi KANENAN.   Greek
not want.3sg subj. see.1sg n-person
He doesn't want to see anybody.

b. *(Non) ho visto nessuno.   Italian (Zanuttini 1991)
He didn't see anybody.

(67) a. *Idhe KANENAN?
Did he see anybody?

b. *Ho visto nessuno?
Did he see anybody?

The Japanese *dare-mo* and Korean *anwu-to* fall into this category too. The fact that n-words also provide negative fragment answers does not threaten their status as NPIs in strict negative concord, if we assume that fragment answers involve ellipsis of a negated IP (Giannakidou 1998, 2000, 2006a; Merchant 2004). Space prevents me from expanding here; see Giannakidou 2006b and Zeijlstra 2004 for more comprehensive recent discussions.

Importantly, n-words come often with emphatic intonation, as indicated above with upper case. In my earlier work, I took the emphatic NPI paradigm in Greek to be lexically distinct from the non-emphatic NPI—which is deaccented, has much broader distribution, and is still licensed with negation. The version *(Dhen) theli na dhi kanenan* 'It is not the case that she wants to see somebody" is really a weaker, non-emphatic negation, compared to the emphatic n-word version above (see also Suranyi 2006 for two variants of n-words with negation in Hungarian, and empahtic and nonemphatic negative sentences with NPIs in Chinese, Cheng & Giannakidou 2011). It is important to keep in mind that the stronger NPI classes (including EVEN-containing NPIs) show correlation with emphatic intonation. The broader classes (including *any*) are not emphatic. So, clearly, negative sentences with NPIs are not always emphatic, it depends on what kind of NPI they contain.

Besides negation, strict NPIs appear also in the scope of negative particles such as *without* and its equivalents, as we saw. *Without p* entails *not p*, hence *without*, just like negation, is antiveridical (Giannakidou 1997, 1998). Crucially, the stricter NPI class is *not* licensed with weak DE quantifiers (*at most n, few N*), since these are not antiveridical:

(68) a. *To poli pende fitites dhiavasan oute ena arthro.
    At most 5 students read even one article.

b. *To poli pende fitites dhiavasan KANENA arthro.
    At most 5 students read any article.

(For the relevant data in Japanese and Korean see Yoshimura 2007, Yoon 2008.) Besides their severely restricted distribution in antiveridical contexts, strict NPI classes, including n-words, are also distinct from the broader NPIs in that they obey syntactic locality restrictions: their licenser must usually be a clausemate. This is emphasized in Giannakidou (1998, 2000, and especially 2006a), where examples are given with minimizers and n-words from numerous languages including Greek, Slavic, Hungarian, Romance (for the original data see also Progovac 1994; Zannuttini 1991; Przepiorkopski & Kupc 1997; and others); in Giannakidou (2007) it is further shown that NPI-*oute* is also licensed within a clause.

(69) a. *Dhen ipa oti o Janis diavase *oute* tis *Sindaktikes Dhomes*.
        I didn't say that John read even *Syntactic Structures*.

b. *O Janis dhen ipe oti idhe KANENAN.
    John didn't say that he say anybody.

c. *O Janis dhen ipe oti dini dhekara.
    ?John didn't say that he gives a damn.

(70) * John didn't say that Bill came either.

Notice the contrast with the broader NPIs *any* and *kanenas*, which can be licensed long distance even through syntactic islands (see Giannakidou & Quer 1995, 1997 for data on Greek, Spanish, and Catalan, Giannakidou 1998, 2000; Yoshimura 2007 on Japanese):

(71) a. Dhen tou ipan oti o Bill milise me kanenan.
        They didn't tell him that Bill talked to anybody.

b. Dhen prodose mistika pou eksethesan kanenan. (relative clause)
    He didn't reveal secrets that exposed anybody.

The impossibility of long-distance licensing of strict NPIs, and the fact that it is observed systematically in a number of (often unrelated) languages, suggests that, with this class, licensing is not merely a question of semantic compatibility with a certain context, but rather, perhaps primarily, a question of syntax. The locality has been implemented as QR (Giannakidou 1998, 2000; an idea extended further to Japanese by Shimoyama 2003; Yoshimura 2007; and Hungarian, Suranyi 2006), and in other analyses as a form of agreement (as was originally suggested by Haegeman & Zannuttini 1981 in the *Neg-criterion;* more recent discussions in Progovac 2005; Zeijlstra 2004; Watanabe 2004; Herburger & Mauck 2006; Giannakidou 2007). In both QR and agreement accounts, the NPI actually moves to a position higher than negation, in violation of c-command, thus allowing for a definition of PI-hood that does not necessarily map into a syntactic scope (see especially Giannakidou 1998, 2000).

To sum up, we have seen in the last two sections that the notion of nonveridicality allows us to unify the polarity environments as a natural class, and predicts that NPIs may appear in contexts that are unrelated to negation or DE as long as they are nonveridical: with modalities, directive propositional attitudes, disjunctions, and questions. Antiveridicality, on the other hand, is the notion we need as a criterion for the stricter NPI classes that are licensed narrowly by more 'negative' licensers. For this class, which is often emphatic, a growing body of literature suggests that we must view licensing also as a syntactic, and not merely a semantic (NPI-EVEN based), relation. Such a conclusion appears to weaken the view that *all* polarity phenomena as purely semantic — and suggests that a more realistic view of polarity is appropriate, where polarity is a landscape of phenomena, some of which may depend on syntax more than others.

6 NPIs in veridical contexts: licensing versus *rescuing*

In this section, we review unexpected occurrences of *any* in veridical contexts, such as sentences with *only,* emotive factive verbs, *hardly, barely,* and *most*. These cases were used by Linebarger as an argument against the attempt to characterize semantically the class of NPI licensers. I start with the NPIs known as minimizers, and which, as we mentioned at the beginning, can be thought of as containing expressions of minimal amount. In Greek, Korean and Japanese, as we just saw, minimizers are strict NPIs, occurring only with antiveridical expressions. In English, on the other hand, minimizers behave more liberally:

(72) a. Ruth didn't *lift a finger* to help me.
  b. Ruth doesn't *give a damn* about what I think.
  c. Did Ruth *lift a finger* to help?
  d. If you *you give a damn*, you'll listen.

English minimizers are also fine with directive propositional attitudes, as is shown in the following data, retrieved with Google, 10/17/2006; *gratia* Jason Merchant:

(73) She's still funny and cute and smart and *I wish she gave a damn* that we aren't friends anymore. I miss Candice. www.xanga.com/betweenIDs

(74) "I just *wish you gave a damn* about something besides your television set." Mr. Smith threw the remote control across the room stomped out of the room ... www.deadmule.com/content/word.of.mule.php?content_id=952

(75) till the pianist finished, we left, and I dropped off tom and went home. Now *I wish I had said a word*. It would have come out lame though, I just know it. everything2.com/index.pl?node_id=1166781

English minimizers must therefore be thought of as *broad or, weak* NPIs, despite the fact that scholars often refer to them as *strong*. The reason why people label them strong NPIs does not have to do with their distribution, obviously, but with the fact that minimizers (in all languages) trigger negative bias in questions (an observation that goes back to Borkin 1971). Negative bias is the expectation (*not* a presupposition see Guerzoni 2004; Giannakidou 2007) of a negative answer to the question containing the minimizer.

(76) Do you give a damn about me?
  Expected answer: No you don't.
  Less expected, though possible answer: In fact, I do!

In more recent accounts, negative bias is either supposed to be triggered by a negative feature on the minimizer (Postal 2003), or is attributed to the presence of a silent or overt *even* (Linebarger 1980; Heim 1984) in English, and crosslinguistically (Giannakidou 2007). The *even* meaning responsible for bias, crucially, cannot be NPI-EVEN, since NPI-EVEN was shown earlier to be ungrammatical in questions.

English minimizers and *any* are broad NPIs that have an additional peculiarity when we compare them to the Greek style broad NPI *kanenas:* they can appear in the scope of *only*, and in the complement clauses of emotive factive verbs.

(77) a. I am glad he said a word!
b. I'm glad we got any tickets.   (from Kadmon & Landman 1993)
c. Mary regrets that she lifted a finger.
d. Only Mary {gives a damn/said anything}.

These data are well known (see Atlas 1993, 1996, and Horn 1996), and pose a puzzle for both DE and nonveridicality, since factives and *only* are veridical and not DE:

(78) Only Bill left   →   Bill left.

(79) Only Larry ate a vegetable   -/→ Only Larry ate broccoli.
Larry may have eaten spinach.

(80) Larry regrets that I bought a car. -/→ Larry regrets that I bought a Honda.
Because, in fact, I bought a Ferrari, and Larry might not regret this at all.

Von Fintel (1999) and Hoeksema (1986) propose weaker versions of DE to deal with the problem, by allowing the inference to the subset to be part of the common ground. For instance, if we know in the context that John ate spinach, then from *Only John ate a vegetable* we can infer that *Only John ate spinach*. By making this move, however, i.e., by allowing context knowledge to influence reasoning, weak DE overgenerates (Atlas 1993; Giannakidou 2006a); it predicts, for instance, that NPIs may occur also in positive sentences: if I know that John ate spinach, then upon hearing *John ate a vegetable* I can infer that *John ate spinach*—yet this will not be sufficient for allowing me to use *any*. Weakening DE in this way therefore fails to provide a true explanation and predicts a flexibility of judgement that is not observed (see Atlas 1993 and Giannakidou 2006a for discussion of more specific problems).

Greek-style broad and narrow NPIs, we must note, are excluded from *only* and factives (Giannakidou 1998), and Giannakidou (2006a) gives examples illustrating the same for Spanish minimizer NPIs:

(81) a. *Xerome pou   {dhinis dhekara/ipes tipota}.
        I am glad   {you give a damn/you said anything}.

b. *Mono i Maria   {dhini dhekara/ipe tipota}.
   Only Mary   {gives a damn/said anything}.

c. *I Maria metaniose pou kounise to daktilaki tis.
   Only literal interpretation: Mary regrets that she lifted her finger.

(82) a. *María se arrepintió de haber movido (ni) un dedo.
    Mary regrets that she lifted a finger.

b. *María se arrepintió de haber gastado (ni) un duro.
    María regrets having spent a red cent.

Greek and Spanish broad NPIs and minimizers are well behaved NPIs, and are ungrammatical with *only* and factives, as expected. The absence of DE in *only* and emotive factives (and some other cases including *long after, hardly, barely*; all impossible in Greek, at least, Giannakidou 2006a), were used by Linebarger as challenges for a semantic explanation for NPI-licensing. However, given the Greek and Spanish facts we see here, we must admit that this unexpected NPI-sanctioning of *any* and English minimizers is not a general phenomenon, but specific to the English type of NPI.

To account for the Linebarger challenge, Giannakidou (2006a) suggests that *any* and minimizers instantiate a class of NPIs that can not only be licensed—in the traditional sense of being in the scope of nonveridical expression at LF—but also *tolerated* in a context if that context gives rise globally to a nonveridical inference. In this case, the NPIs are *rescued*:

(83) *Rescuing by nonveridicality*   (Giannakidou 2006a)
    A PI α can be rescued in the scope of a veridical expression β in a sentence S, if (a) **the global context C** of S makes a proposition S' available which contains a nonveridical expression β; and (b) α can be associated with β in S'.

"Association with a nonveridical proposition" means "be in the scope of a nonveridical expression at a level other than LF", however we are to define it, perhaps at the expressive layer (suggested in Yoshimura 2007; Park 2009, building on Potts 2005). The global context C of S is the set of propositions that arise from S without necessarily being *entailed* by it. C thus contains the assertion (entailments), presuppositions, and implicatures. The negative proposition that is responsible for rescuing will be conventionally contributed by some expression in the sentence. In the case of *only*, it is the non-cancelable conjunct *no x other than y P*; with a negative factive, e.g., *regret*, it is the counterfactual *I wish that not p* that is conventionally contributed by it. With *barely* and *hardly* the NPIs are rescued via association with a background negative proposition (whose precise status is still a matter of debate, see Horn 2002), while their veridical or non-DE component becomes, according to Horn (2002), *assertorically inert*.

Rescuing builds on what I called *indirect licensing* in earlier work (Giannakidou 1998, 1999), and happens in violation of scope at LF. Horn (2002) discusses these phenomena in the context of assertoric inertia, intended to capture the state of affairs where an NPI appears in the syntactic scope of an expression that does not have the *semantic* potential to license it. The idea, roughly, of assertoric inertia is that when conflicting inferences arise — e.g., as with *only*, the prejacent is veridical but the exclusive inference is nonveridical — one of the inferences becomes assertorically inert, in the case of *only* the veridical prejacent, thus allowing *any* to be licensed. The contrast between the Greek-style NPIs and English-type *any*/minimizers (see Beaver & Clark 2003 for some data from Dutch) shows that we must allow this kind of rescuing/indirect licensing as an option in the grammar, but only as a secondary one: to my knowledge, there are no reports of NPIs that appear to be rescued but not licensed (such NPIs would have to be fine with *only* and emotive factives, for instance, but unacceptable with negation).

Given that the option of rescuing exists, languages may exploit it to a varying degree for the various items. English seems to be more liberal than Greek in this respect. Ideally, one would like to know why a particular type of NPI favors rescuing, or why a given language X exploits the rescuing strategy more liberally than a language Y, but I will leave this to future research. One obvious avenue to explore is that the NPI itself contributes to the rescuing effect, as suggested by Ladusaw's idea of "auto-licensing' in earlier work.

We move on now to the compositionality question.

7 The scalar approach to polarity

In the following two sections, we address the question of compositionality: why do PIs appear the contexts they appear in? What is it about negative and nonveridical environments that makes them appropriate environments for NPIs? Why are some NPIs more narrow, and some more broad? Addressing these questions is extremely important, as I said at the beginning, because in answering them we gain a better understanding of what NPIs mean, and how — and to what extent — their meaning restricts their distribution.

There have been two approaches to compositionality. The first claims that there is only one source of ill-formedness in polarity — *scalarity*, which in some form or other, is supposed to be the culprit of *all* polarity phenomena (Kadmon & Landman 1993; Krifka 1995; Chierchia 2006; Lee & Horn 1994; Lahiri 1998). This position has been very influential, so we need to assess very carefully what it says and how far it can go. The second approach within the nonveridicality theory of polarity that we mentioned earlier (Giannakidou 1998, 2001, 2006a, 2007) is a variation or, diversity position. It claims that there are *two* main sources of lexical sensitivity: (a) scalarity, which in most cases contains some sort of morphological marking via e.g., a focus particle such as EVEN (Giannakidou 2007); and (b) referential deficiency, i.e., a difficulty in the NPI to refer to an object in the usual ways existential quantifiers do (Giannakidou 1998). Referentially deficient NPIs are in fact quite common, and referential deficiency comes in many forms, e.g., non-deictic (or dependent reference, as we will see below), free choice, referential vagueness (Giannakidou & Quer 2010).

In what follows, I address the scalarity approach. In the next section we examine the referential deficiency approach.

7.1 Domain widening

Kadmon & Landman's (1993) influential paper on *any* proposed a unified theory for NPI and FCI *any* by appealing to the notion of domain widening:

(84) Meaning of *any* (Kadmon & Landman 1993)
      any CN= the corresponding indefinite NP or CN with the additional semantic/pragmatic characteristics (widening, strengthening) contributed by *any*.

(85) Widening of *any* (Kadmon & Landman 1993)
      In an NP of the form *any CN*, *any* widens the interpretation of the common noun phrase along some contextual dimension.

Domain widening says that the use of *any* widens the quantificational domain. *Any* is thus unlike other quantifiers—whose domain must be typically narrowed down. Widening is felicitous only if it produces *strengthening*:

(86) Licensing condition for *any*: Strengthening
      Any is licensed only if the widening that it induces creates a stronger statement, i.e., only if the statement on the wide interpretation entails the statement on the narrow interpretation.

The idea is that widening must have a purpose, and this is to make a stronger statement (see also Krifka 1995). So, the driving idea is that statements with *any* are always strong, emphatic—recall however, that NPIs as a class are *not* strong in the sense of emphatic. Greek broad NPIs, and similar NPIs crosslinguistically typically produce weak statements — as opposed to their emphatic variants that are indeed emphatic but have much narrower distribution. And, apart from the Greek type, it is helpful to note Israel's (1998) *attenuating* NPIs ("long", "much", "yet", "in weeks") which do not yield a stronger negative assertion, but a weakened one.

Strengthening is said to be satisfied in a negative context, but not in a positive one:

(87) a. I didn't see any book on the table.
b. *I saw any book on the table.

The positive sentence is out because, in Chierchia's words, "domain widening is pointless" (Chierchia 2006: 557) in a positive sentence. If it is true that I saw a book in the narrower domain, it is also true that that I saw one in the wider domain, thus the widened statement is too weak, and for this reason not very informative. Strengthening, however, is satisfied with negation and DE quantifiers. Here lies the essence of all widening/scalarity based accounts.

Chierchia (2006) further pursues a unitary analysis for FCI and NPI *any* via domain widening — implemented in a system where implicatures project in a syntax-like manner. Chierchia excludes *any* in the positive sentence in the following way. First, the NPI introduces alternative smaller domains, indicated by the index *i*, which refers to numbers between 1 and the maximum number (in this arbitrary case *three*) that we take our largest domain to consist of:

(88) a. *I saw any boy. (Chierchia's (47))
b. Meaning
$\exists w' \exists x \in D_{w'} [boy_{w'}(x) \wedge saw_w(I, x)]$ D= {a,b,c}

c. Alternatives
$\exists w' \exists x \in D_{w'} [boy_{i,w'}(x) \wedge saw_w(I, x)]$, where $1 \leq i \leq 3$

In a domain that consists of three boys, *any boy* quantifies over domains that contain one boy, two boys, and all three boys. These alternatives are active with a word like *any*, and must be used to enrich plain meaning, according to Chierchia. The domain of individuals is not ordered, but in choosing among alternatives, speakers tend to go for the strongest one they have evidence for. In the case above, we end up saying that even the most broad choice of D makes the sentence true: "in other words, the base meaning will acquire an *even*-like flavor" (Chierchia 2006: 556).

The positive sentence also gives rise to the following implicature (Chierchia's (48)):

(48) Implicature
∃w'∃x∈$D_{w'}$ [boy$_{w'}$ (x) ∧ saw$_w$ (I, x)] ⊆$_c$
∃w'∃x∈$D_{w'}$ [boy$_{i,w'}$ (x) ∧ saw$_w$ (I, x)], where 1 ≤ i ≤ 3, and
p ⊆$_c$ q means: p is stronger (hence, less likely) than q relative to the common ground c.

Chierchia claims that "given the way domains are chosen, (48) is logically false: all of the alternatives are logically stronger than the statement in *b*; therefore, the latter statement cannot be less likely than its alternatives. The positive sentence enriched by implicature (48) is inconsistent, whence its deviance." (Chierchia 2006: 556).

7.2 Problems with domain widening and scalarity

Here I will take widening theories to task and see how far they can go in explaining (at least some of) the core facts we saw in this chapter, and how successful they are in being compositional, in the sense that they derive the restricted distribution by meaning alone.

In all widening approaches (Kadmon & Landman, Krifka, Chierchia), the failure of *any* in a positive veridical sentence follows from informational strength. Sentences with unlicensed *any* are claimed to be impossible because the use of *any* renders them too weak to be informative (Kadmon & Landman, Krifka), or inconsistent (Chierchia) after implicature enrichment. The first, rather obvious, problem lies precisely here: the ill-formedness that such a type of explanation predicts is weak (Giannakidou 1998, 2001): sentences with failed *any* must have the same psychological status as uninformative or contradictory sentences. But this is not true. Speakers generally perceive, with failed NPIs, an effect stronger than mere infelicity, which is what characterizes uninformative sentences. Contradictions, tautologies (*The morning star is the morning star*), presupposition failures (*The king of France is my brother*), lexical anomalies (*The green ideas sleep furiously*) are never judged ungrammatical. The grammar generates them, and speakers have an intuition that they can produce them; they can even figure out ways to render them felicitous in certain contexts. Pragmatically odd sentences as thus perhaps non-sensical without context, but certainly repairable and grammatically possible.

Deciding that polarity ill-formedness is psychologically equivalent to mere "logical failure" (to borrow the term from Chierchia) is not a trivial question. Certainly, Ladusaw did not think they were equivalent, and Giannakidou made repeatedly the same point in discussions about various kinds of NPIs. Both Ladusaw (especially Ladusaw 1983) and Giannakidou view NPIs as a case for semantic well-formedness being a *grammatical* constraint, not merely a pragmatic one. And since Chomsky (1957, 1964), the field has generally (and I think correctly) accepted that speakers' reactions to, and intuitions about, "odd" and "ungrammatical" sentences differ. Thus, unless we have an independent (e.g., *psychological*) metric that *shows* that NPIs failures and contradictions or uninformative sentences are the same, the scalarity approach simply predicts too weak a result.

Giannakidou (2007) shows that in the EVEN-NPI domain in Greek, there are NPIs that are ungrammatical (NPI-EVEN), and NPIs that are indeed only merely odd. For negative concord phenomena — where n-words are subject to much stricter licensing conditions and for which speakers have an even clearer intuition that the NPIs (n-words) are not simply odd but ungrammatical — it is unavoidable to posit further syntactic constraints. So, the informativity based scalar accounts can only go a small distance, but have gained prominence because a lot of the variation and distribution nuance is often "abstracted away" in the descriptions.

Chierchia does acknowledge the insufficiency of the purely pragmatic account as the following passage shows: "So why is a sentence like (47a) (an NPI-licensing violation) ungrammatical? There is an impasse here between the way domain widening explains the distribution of NPIs (using Gricean principles) and the way such principles are typically taken to work...." (Chierchia 2006: 557). And later on, he posits a lexical entry for *any* (his (51)) where, in addition to widening, *any* is claimed to have an uninterpretable feature [+σ] (Chierchia 2006: 559), ensuring that *any* will be in the scope of some operator. It is checking of this feature that renders *any* grammatical, and this is a clear withdrawal from the purely pragmatic position.

One could still view the pragmatic principle of widening as *motivating* the grammatical constraint (perhaps historically, perhaps synchronically). (Thanks to Paul Portner for the suggestion.) Widening and strengthening may not be the explanation for NPI ungrammaticality, but rather a description of how the grammatical constraint emerged. (In the literature on the definiteness effect similar reasoning has sometimes been pursued.) However, the research in the widening account is not satisfied with such a modest goal. Their goal, as clearly stated in Kadmon & Landman, Krifka, and Chierchia, is a more ambitious one: to explain the distribution of *any* directly, and only, via widening and strengthening. Chierchia's [+σ] feature, then, is a withdrawal from this purely pragmatic position, since widening alone cannot rule out correctly NPIs in positive episodic sentences (Giannakidou 2001).

Another problem lies with the very claim that *any* induces widening: widening is not always present with *any*, NPIs or FCIs (as noted in Krifka 1995, who actually accepts an emphatic and a non-emphatic variant of *any*, and more recently Duffley & Larivée 2010). Consider the examples below:

(89) Pick any one of *these 5 cards*.

(90) Consider any arbitrary number.

Here *any* extends over a very specific domain of the five cards in the context supplied by the partitive. We cannot talk about domain widening in this case. Likewise, the set of numbers is infinite, so it is hard to see what domain extension would yield in *any arbitrary number*.

Duffley and Larivée point out as problematic for widening the case of questions:

(91) Did you hear any noise?

"Contrary to questions with end-point scalars, such sentences usually do have the force of neutral information-seeking questions. Since information questions do not normally bear on scalar end-points, a scalar analysis of *any* is highly problematic in this environment." (Duffley & Larivée 210: 6). And they continue: "Besides the interrogative above, the scalar paraphrase by means of 'even the least/even a single' also encounters difficulties in its application to other common uses of *any* in standard polarity contexts. Three such cases are given below:

(15) If you find any typos in this text, please let us know.

(16) You can pull out of the driveway. I don't see any cars coming.

(17) We checked the wiring before we made any changes to the electrical box."
(Duffley & Larivée 2010: 7)

In these contexts, *any* is interpreted indeed very weakly, unlike scalar, EVEN containing items which typically give rise to stronger statements. It should be thus clear that widening is not empirically motivated always, not even for *any*, the item for which it was designed.

Another problem, when one considers the generality of the widening approach — and recall that the approach has indeed been conceived of as a general theory of NPIs — has to do with the fact that not all NPIs are scalar. *Kanenas*, as mentioned earlier, is not:

(92) Fere   kanena gliko.
     Bring some   cake.
     (Context: No need for something specific; it doesn't matter what you bring really).

Kanena is a non-scalar existential, and statements with it are typically weak and nonemphatic. The *kanenas*-type of NPI seems to require not a wide or even ordered domain, but some variation in the domain because it is referntially vague — as Giannakidou & Quer (2010) suggest. Such NPIs are non-scalar, but are still unacceptable in the veridical positive sentence, just like the scalar ones. For these NPIs, which are in fact more common than we think, domain widening is simply not a plausible starting point.

Now, even when it comes to scalar items, recall that not all such PIs improve with negation: *any* improves, but FCIs, in many languages (Greek, Spanish, Catalan, Romanian, Chinese), remain unacceptable with negation:

(93) a. *Idha   opjondhipote.   (Greek; Giannakidou 2001)
         saw.perf.1sg FC-person
         *I saw anybody.

   b. *Dhen idha   opjondhipote.
         not saw.perf.1sg FC-person
         Intended: 'I didn't see anybody.'

The problem posed by these data is twofold. First, the non-improvement of FCIs with negation undermines the idea that NPI and FCI are due to the same source (*pace* Chierchia 2006). Clearly, this cannot be the case, or at least it cannot *generally* be the case. Second, the scalarity based account predicts improvement with negation for *all* scalar items; there is no way to distinguish between the scalar NPI and the scalar FCI. The ill-formedness of FCI *opjondhipote* suggests, again, that there is something other than widening that further reduces the distribution of FCIs. Giannakidou (2001) argues that this additional dimension in FCIs is intensionality, and regardless of whether one accepts this analysis, it is simply not true that all scalar items improve with negation.

The asymmetry within the class of NPIs and FCIs in terms of polarity poses an equally challenging problem. Take *any* and *whoever* as the contrastive pair here. Both involve domain widening (Jacobson 1995; Horn 2002; Giannakidou & Cheng 2006), but only *any* is polarity sensitive:

(94) a. Whoever saw a fly in his soup complained to the manager.
     b. Irgendeiner hat angerufen.
     c. * Anyone complained to the manager.

Likewise, *irgendein* in German patterns with *whoever* and not with *any*, despite its domain widening (Kratzer & Shimoyama 2002). This variation leads to a conclusion similar to the one we just reached regarding the variation with negation: there must be something other than widening that further reduces the distribution of some scalar items, but not others.

The final puzzle for domain widening is posed by the fact that items like *any*, as we saw earlier, are admitted in a large set of contexts not related to negation and DE: modal verbs, imperatives, questions, nonveridical propositional attitudes, generic and habitual sentences and disjunctions. It is not obvious how widening and strength invoked by Kadmon & Landman, Krifka and Chierchia can be extended to explain why *any* is licit in these contexts. Consider, for example, the generic and habitual case:

(95) a. Any cat hunts mice.
 b. Opjadhipote ghata kinigai pondikia.

(I am not using the *kanenas* paradigm here since it does not involve widening.) Here *any cat*, which is an NPI/FCI and gets widened interpretation, does *not* entail the more narrow one, since there are exceptions to generic generalizations (Krifka et al. 1995). Hence *any* should be unacceptable in this context. But it is not; rather, genericity is a very common context for supposedly widened items.

Consider also NPIs in questions. I noted earlier that there is no successful analysis of questions as DE, and in the informativity based theories that we are discussing this fact has been recognized (see especially van Rooy 2003, Guerzoni & Sharvit 2007). The strategy is to assume that NPIs are allowed in (non-rhetorical) questions either because they make the question more *general* than the corresponding one without the NPI (Krifka), or because a question turns a settled issue into an unsettled one (Kadmon & Landman). But why should a general question be preferred to a more specific one, as these theorists pose? And how, and why, should this notion of generality be seen as a special case of strength in questions?

Van Rooy (2003) proposes that strength in questions must be reduced to *entropy*. Entropy is the measure of the informativity value of a question. The informative value of question Q is maximal just in case the answers to Q are all equally likely to be true. The value becomes less than maximal when an NPI occurs (resulting in biased readings). In van Rooy's words: "The NPI weakens the satisfaction conditions for the positive answer, q, and strengthens the satisfaction conditions for the negative answer ¬q." (van Rooy 2003: 263). It is further proposed that entropy can replace strength also in assertions, so it allegedly provides the unifying notion of strength.

This type of explanation should make us pause. First of all, the use of an NPI in questions generally does *not* yield bias in polar questions — only the use of a certain type of NPIs does, and is due to a particular kind of EVEN that it contains (Giannakidou 2007). Secondly, the entropy and strength explanation is analytically too weak: as mentioned already, less informative sentences do not become less grammatical. Van Rooy takes it for granted that informativity impacts grammaticality directly, and as we saw with widening, this is not a sound assumption—or at least, it should be one argued for, not just taken for granted.

The purely pragmatic route thus produces liberal theories that predict more fluid judgment than we have with NPIs. Even *any*, an NPI of the more liberal kind as we noted, cannot occur just as freely as van Rooy's reasoning predicts. In fact, in questions, free choice *any*, and FCIs generally, are systematically out. The diagnostic is the ability to modify *any* by *almost* (only FCI-*any* accepts this modification, Davison 1981):

(96) a. *Did you see almost anybody?
 b. *Idhes sxedhon opjondhipote? (Greek)

FCIs are prototypical scalar items, but they fail to be licensed in questions (see also Quer 1998 for Spanish, Catalan data). This robust empirical fact is a surprise for van Rooy's unifying negation and questions account, and remains a surprise for all strengthening theories: FCIs, involving domain widening, are *not* admitted in the alleged unified environments of strength: negation and questions; and non-scalar weak NPIs, on the other hand, like *kanenas*, do appear in negation and questions. This suggests (a) that widening does not necessarily correlate with strength, and (b) that widening and strengthening (in whatever version) do not predict the right kind of polarity sensitivity, a dooming conclusion in both cases. It must be admitted that we still need other factors (syntactic or semantic) besides pure informativity for accurately restricting NPI and FCI distribution, and distinguish correctly between the two.

Finally, regarding other nonveridical NPI environments, it is unclear how informativity as entropy would apply, e.g., in directive, but not epistemic, propositional attitudes. I know of no research that has actually defined strength in this domain, and this is probably because if we want to have strength for these cases, the notion itself becomes too weak to be useful.

To summarize, then, we saw in this section that a purely pragmatic theory of domain widening, by appealing exclusively to scalarity and conversational principles such as informativity and strength, does not predict the correct distribution of various kinds of NPIs or FCIs; nor does it predict the correct effect of illicit

NPIs. Domain widening also misses the fact that scalar and non-scalar NPIs are equally sensitive to negation, questions, and other nonveridical environments, and is unable to account for variation with respect to negation (negation does *not* save all widened items: FCIs remain bad), or within scalar items as regards their polarity status or not (some FCIs are polarity sensitive, and some others aren't). In the end, it becomes obvious that even though widening may indeed be a lexical property of some NPIs (though recall the difficulties with *any*), when it comes to working out the details of the explanation, it becomes impossible to make the argument that it is widening alone that restricts the distribution of these NPIs. Chierchia admits this point by adding a syntactic feature [+σ] to *any*. But by doing that, the purely pragmatic argument loses its appeal, and NPIs can no longer be offered as a case illustrating a direct impact of pragmatic principles on sentence grammar. This conclusion carries over to Lahiri's (1998) account based on the overt presence of EVEN in Hindi broad NPIs, and I will refer here to Giannakidou (2007) for detailed consideration and counterarguments.

8 The other side of polarity: non-deictic variables and referential deficiency

As we noted already, one of the empirical limitations of the scalarity approaches is that they tend to lump together all polarity phenomena as scalar, thus assigning priviledged status to scalarity as the basis for explanation. Non-scalar NPI indefinites of the *kanenas* type were noted early in Haspelmath's, Giannakidou's, Lin's, and Matthewson's work, but research tended to place these in the margins, despite the fact that they are common crosslinguistically. In this section we focus on these NPIs, and show that they instantiate a very important aspect of negative polarity that has to do with what I call broadly *referential deficiency*.

By 'referential deficiency', I mean to refer to obligatorily narrow scope phenomena that have been known to semanticists for many years—e.g., incorporated nominals in Greenlandic Eskimo (Bittner 1987; van Geenhoven 1998), accusative-partitive alternation in Finnish (Kiparsky 1998) and related phenomena in Turkish (Enç 1991; de Hoop 1992), the genitive of negation in Russian (Partee 2008; Borschev et al. 2008), English bare plurals always taking scope inside negation (Carlson 1977), narrow scope indefinites that must be bound by higher quantifiers (*egy-egy* indefinites in Hungarian, Farkas 1998, and similar items in Russian, Basque, and other languages; Pereltsvaig 2008). Almost all analyses of obligatorily narrow scope expressions assume a notion of 'low ', or decreased (to use Partee's 2008 word) referentiality to capture narrow scope — as opposed to 'higher' referentiality, or specificity, that characterizes indefinites that tend to take wide scope (i.e., indefinites with specificity markers, or accusative marked indefinites in Finish and Turkish, as observed in the accusative-partitive alternation). Scales of referentiality have also been proposed (Anagnostopoulou & Giannakidou 1995), and referentially low expressions occupy the bottom end of those scales.

The referential deficiency approach says that NPIs of this kind cannot refer in the normal way. In Giannakidou (1998: 70–71, 139–140) I suggested that the *kanenas* type of NPI must be seen as referentially deficient. By making this move, we capture the need to be 'licensed' as a need to be in the scope of an operator — negation being one such operator along with the rest of the other nonveridical ones. In this context, no special status is given to licensing per se, and I used the label 'dependent' existential to capture the *kanenas* NPI:

(97) An existential quantifier $\exists x_d$ is dependent iff the variable x_d it contributes does not introduce a discourse referent in the main context. (based on: Giannakidou 1998: 70)

A dependent existential in this sense is an existential that cannot assert existence in a default context. This is formalized by using a designated variable: "x_d" (in Giannakidou 1998 originally "x_{ni}" 'for 'no introduction'). In the indefinite theory of existentials, we would have to say that dependent indefinites contain variables that cannot be closed under Heim's (1982) *text level* existential closure (Giannakidou 1997, 1998); i.e., they cannot receive values from the context. Such variables will not be able to be used in unembedded veridical sentences because they cannot receive a value. Under negation, happily, they will not be forced to refer, and likewise in embedded contexts (see Giannakidou 1998: Ch. 3 for details).

(98) 〚kanenas〛 = **person** (x_d)

(99) a. *Idha   kanenan.
         saw.1sg   anybody

   b. Dhen idha   kanenan.
      not   saw.1sg anybody

(100) a. # $\exists x_d$ **person** $(x_d) \wedge$ **saw** (I, x_d)
    b. $\neg \exists x_d$ [**person** $(x_d) \wedge$ **saw** (I, x_d)

Under negation, ∃-closure of x_d will be fine because x_d will not introduce a discourse referent. Generally, then, dependent variables of this kind will be fine in the scope of nonveridical operators, because these ensure that x_d will not be forced to introduce, or be associate with, a discourse referent in the main context. Den Dikken & Giannakidou (2002) analyze further *any*, and *wh-the-hell* phrases as NPIs of this kind.

The intuition that some quantifiers cannot assert existence is also found in Matthewson's (1998) claim that the NPI *ku...a* and *kwel...a* determiners in St'at'imcet Salish "represent the notion of 'non-assertion of existence'" (Matthewson 1998: 179). (The Salish determiners appear to be a bit broader in their distribution than the Greek *kanenas*—but it is important to note the parallel). Matthewson further argues that such determiners do not entail non-existence of an entity, rather they "merely fail to positively assert the existence of an entity" (Matthewson 1998: 179). Giannakidou (1998) likewise notes that dependent reference does not imply lack of reference:

(101) An dhis kanenan$_i$, pes tu$_i$ na me perimeni.
    If you see anybody, tell him to wait for me.

Here *kanenan* does introduce a discourse referent, which is subsequently the antecedent to the pronoun *tu*. Yet the introduction of the referent is done not in the main context but in an embedded one (the protasis of the conditional). Dependent existentials thus receive values only in embedded domains; their 'deficiency' is that the assignment function *g* cannot give them a value in a main context. In other words, dependent indefinites of the *kanenas* type cannot be interpreted *deictically*. As a technical aside here, we assume that multiple domains are available in a sentence when there is embedding (Giannakidou 1998; Tancredi 2007a, 2007b), just like there are multiple models; recall our discussion of propositional attitudes. In fact, we can define (following Tancredi) a conversion function that would assign a distinct domain to each model. We can then rephrase the dependency of the *kanenas* indefinite as a claim that it cannot receive a value in the main domain.

The dependent reference that yields polarity sensitive expressions, then, applies to variables that cannot be interpreted in the context as free variables. It will thus be helpful to think of the NPI-variables as 'non-deictic' variables — as suggested to me by Barbara Partee — instead of merely 'dependent' ones — since the term 'dependent' has also been used, e.g., by Farkas (1998), to refer to variables that simply need to co-vary with a quantifier, and which do not yield NPIs. Farkas's choice of "dependent" seems to be a misnomer, however. The so-called dependent indefinites that she studied seem to be distributive object NPs, that are, crucially, reduplicated, e.g., *egy-egy* in Hungarian. Reduplication is a hallmark property of distributive NPs in many languages, Greek included (Giannakidou 2011). In the case of distributive NPs, it should be clear that we are not talking about referential dependency in the sense of not being able to introduce a discourse referent; rather we are dealing with a different kind of co-variation constraint that characterizes lexically distributitive QPs.

I define the notion of non-deictic variable below:

(102) *Non-deictic variables*
A variable x is non-deictic iff x cannot be interpreted as a free variable.

A non-deictic variable is thus one whose assignment function is constrained in this particular way — and perhaps an easy way to think of this is as a presupposition on the assignment function g, e.g., on a par with constraints on g that we have with definites, or anaphoric pronouns.

In Giannakidou (1998, 2001), the referential deficiency variable analysis is extended to FCIs which are argued to contain a non-deictic *world* variable w_d. This variable cannot become licit just by being existentially closed in the scope of some operator (after all, there *is* no text-level existential closure of a world variable). Rather it can only become licit via binding by a Q-operator that can bind a world variable. In an episodic context (positive *and* negative) there is no such operator, the variable remains unbound, and the FCI becomes illicit. We can thus explain the empirical contrast between FCIs and NPI *vis a vis* negation, and why FCIs need adverbial quantification contexts: they contain a dependent variable of type s which, because of its nature, needs to be bound, and can't be simply existentially closed in the scope of a nonverdical operator.

A non-deictic variable will create a lexical item that will be a good candidate for becoming an NPI of the broad variety — though from this it does not necessarily follow that all NPIs that contain non-deictic variables will *synchronically* show the same distribution. The path from being a non-deictic variable to being grammaticalized as an NPI may be longer or shorter for various items across languages, and other factors in grammar and, especially, use are expected to play a role. For example, Romanian *vreun* is a non-deictic NPI that appears in non-veridical contexts, but still not in directive propositional attitudes or direct scope of negation (Farkas 2002, Falaus 2009). Given the broad array of nonveridical contexts, grammaticalization can start from any one of these environments — and spread gradually across. It does not follow from the nature of non-deictic reference that negation or propositional attitudes must be the priviledged starting points. Licit contexts can spread over time — and they can also shrink (as Hoeksema 2010 shows to be the case for Dutch *enig*). Becoming an NPI is a fluid process — and the deictic variable idea must be understood primarily as a possible lexical source for NPIs pointing to particular distribution (nonveridical contexts), not as a predictor that *all* non-deictic variable NPIs will have synchronically identical distributions.

Another important thing to consider is that the NPI that contains a non-deictic variable, like *any*, may also contain other lexical properties that will put in place additional factors in determining its distribution. This is where scalarity may become relevant. If you are a non-deictic indefinite *and* have, e.g., a scalar implicature, you are bound to show distribution similar to that of *any*. There may also be tension between the two lexical properties — referential deficiency and scalarity — that may result in dominance, over different stages in time, of one property (and thus distribution) over the other. Viewing lexical sensitivity flexibly indeed affords a unitary analysis of *any* and for the apparent NPI-FCI variety of item generally — a welcome result. It can also explain why there are nonveridical contexts where this type of NPI does not appear — e.g., disjunctions, or why *any* may favor negation more than *kanenas*.

Space prevents me from elaborating more in this paper, but it is important to emphasize that NPI-lexicalization must be viewed as a dynamic process, not a static one, and diachronic work will be instrumental in helping us understand the basic tenets and shifts across language and NPI types. It is also quite plausible that we discover, for instance, that there are NPIs that favor negation and modal contexts only, or just modal contexts, or just intensional contexts, or just questions. These sensitivities to subsets of the nonveridical are all to be expected, and the task will then be to determine what further lexical properties are out there in the world's languages that can possibly narrow down the distribution of NPIs.

9 Positive polarity items

Positive polarity items (PPIs) are thought to have "the boring property that they cannot scope below negation" (Szabolcsi 2004: 409). In this section, we consider two representative members of the class — the indefinite *some* PPIs, and speaker oriented adverbs (Nilsen 2003; Ernst 2009). As with NPIs, we see that at least one instance of PPIs (*some*) concerns the referntiality properties of expressions — and another (speaker oriented adverbs) has to do with speaker commitment to the truth of a proposition. In both cases, PPIs will need to be situated in a veridical context — because in nonveridical contexts and negation neither referentiality nor truth commitment are satisfied. Crucially, as Szabolcsi and Ernst both emphasize, scalarity is not a factor in PPIs: PPI *some* and speaker oriented adverbs are non-scalar.

We will also uncover a particular intonational pattern for *some*, from which only stressed SOME emerges as a PPI. Unstressed *some*, crucially, is just a non-PI indefinite, as we shall see. The accenting that we find signals scoping above negation, a pattern agreeing with what we find with some NPIs that need to be raised above negation in other languages as we mentioned in section 5. Importantly, as I said, the study of the PPIs discussed here shows that scalarity plays no role in PPI distribution.

9.1 Two kinds of *some* indefinites: emphatic and non-emphatic *some*

Ever since Jespersen, *some* has been thought of as a PPI in that it must scope above negation:

(103)   You didn't see something.

This sentence cannot mean that you *didn't see anything*, where an existential quantifier scopes below negation. Scoping above negation is the defining property of a PPI, and it is indeed observed with equivalent items across many languages, e.g., Serbocroatian (Progovac 1994, 2005), Dutch (van der Wouden 1994), Greek (Giannakidou 1997, 1998), Hungarian (Szabolsci 2004), among others. It has gone unnoticed, however, that this scoping has a particular intonation: *some* is accented (uppercase henceforth), and negation is de-accented:

(104)   You didn't see SOMETHING.

The reverse pattern, when *some* is de-accented, allows, and perhaps even favors, a narrow scope reading under negation. In this case, negation is accented (*emphatic denial*). PPIs like *some* are thought to be "allergic" to negation, and this allergy was formulated as *anti-licensing* by negation (Progovac, Giannakidou, Ladusaw) in the sense that *some* must raise structurally in a position above negation (plausibly via QR). PPIs in this context are the reverse of NPIs, and scholars thought of them as contrasting pairs; van der Wouden (1994) further identifies a class of so-called *bipolar* items: these are claimed to require a decreasing licensor (an NPI-property) but cannot occur under a local antimorphic item (a PPI-property). Van der Wouden argues that NPI-hood and PPI-hood are two primitive properties and may therefore coexist in one item, but it is hard to assess this claim empirically first because this alleged category is very rare, and second, because the NPI and PPI "features" are not lexically but only distributionally defined.

Apart from clausemate negation, *some* is excluded also from the immediate scope of a negative quantifier, and *without*:

(105) a. John didn't call SOMEONE.   # not > some
 b. Nobody called SOMEONE.   # no one > some
 c. John came to the party without SOMEONE.   # without > some

So we can generalize that emphatic SOME must scope above antiveridical elements. However, *some*-PPIs have been notorious for scoping *below* non-local negation (Progovac 1994; Szabolcsi 2004):

(106) Bill didn't say that you saw something.   not > say > some

This narrow scoping wrt negation is peculiar for items that must escape the scope of negation in the first place. To make things worse, narrow scoping of *some* is observed even with local negation, if *negation + some* is found under an NPI-trigger — a fact noted in Jespersen, Baker and Postal, and emphasized by Szabolsci. I give below data from Szabolcsi (2004: (33)–(40)):

(33) I don't think that John *didn't call someone*.   √ not > not > some

(34) No one thinks that John *didn't call someone*.   √ no one > not > some

(35) I am surprised that John *didn't call someone*.   √ surprise > not > some

(36) I regret that John *didn't call someone*.   √ regret > not > some

(37) If we *don't call someone*, we are doomed.   √ if (not > some)

(38) Every boy who *didn't call someone* ...   √ every (not > some)

(39) Only John *didn't call someone*.   √ only > not > some

(40) Few boys *didn't call someone*.   √ few > not > some

Why would a PPI under negation become legitimate in NPI contexts? Szabolsci suggests that this is so because PPI plus negation is an NPI itself. PPIs are claimed to "have two NPI-features. One is a strong-NPI feature like that of *yet* and *squat*: it requires a clausemate antiadditive licensor, according to Szabolcsi, without intervention. The other is a weak-NPI feature like that of *ever*: it requires a Strawson-decreasing licensor (not necessarily clausemate but without intervention). I propose that these two features are normally 'dormant'. A context that can license the strong-NPI feature 'activates' and, in the same breath, licenses that feature. What we have seen indicates, however, that the other, weak-NPI feature also gets activated at the same time — activated, but not licensed. Therefore, the emergent constellation is illegitimate, unless a licensor for the weak-NPI feature is provided. In other words, PPIs do not detest antiadditives; they have a latent craving for antiadditives. That they appear to detest them is due to the fact that the satisfaction of this craving activates another, which needs to be satisfied independently." (Szabolcsi 2004: 429).

In such an account, a negative condition (anti-licensing) is reduced to a positive one (licensing), and an underlying NPI source is posited in both NPIs and PPIs. The exact nature of the commonality needs to be refined, but the appeal of the reasoning here cannot go unnoticed. However, there are reasons to be cautious. One obvious shortcoming is that this account envisions NPI and PPI licensing in terms of syntactic features purely — negations, in particular — and gives us little insight into the lexical semantics of *some* itself.

Szabolcsi is correct to point out that *some* is not scalar, or strictly referential: clearly, in the cases above it takes narrow scope. However, Szabolcsi treats *some* as ¬¬∃, with the two negations canceling each other out, and it is difficult to see this as more than mere stipulation. What is the evidence for the two negations? And why do we never see overt realizations of them in *some* crosslinguistically? This is typologically quite surprising, because negation in languages is never "forgotten" to be marked, if there (Horn 1989). Ultimately, why would a language bother to implement two negations on an expression just in order to cancel them out?

In assessing Szabolci's data, it is important to note two things. First, the narrow scope *some* we just observed is non-emphatic; reproducing the examples with emphatic SOME is odd:

(107) a. # I don't think that John didn't call SOMEONE.
      b. # No one thinks that John didn't call SOMEONE.
      c. # I am surprised that John didn't call SOMEONE.
      d. # Every boy who didn't call SOMEONE ...
      e. # Only John didn't call SOMEONE.
      f. # Few boys didn't call SOMEONE.

The judgments here are from a total of five native speakers, and obviously a more large scale inquiry is needed to establish the conditions on the availability of the two intonational patters for *some*. Two things are important here: first, the narrow scope correlates with non-emphatic intonation, and second, nonemphatic intonation is *not* the intonation observed with clausemate negation. Based on this contrast, it becomes plausible to argue that the narrow scope *some* is a different species from the PPI emphatic *SOME* under negation. Intonation has been shown to distinguish NPI paradigms in various langages (Greek,

Japanese, Korean, just to mention some of the cases we saw earler) — and it can be understood as a morphological feature. The emphatic member of the pair is the one that outscopes negation, just like, e.g., the emphatic member of *kanenas/KANENAS* outscopes negation in the analysis of Giannakidou (1998, 2000). Emphatic SOME, then, becomes part of this general interaction between negation, scope and intonation.

Notice that SOME is also odd when negation is long distance:

(108) a. *John didn't {say/claim/know} that Bill talked to SOMEONE.
b. No one {said/claimed/knew} that Bill talked to SOMEONE.

If SOME has to undergo QR to adjoin to the main IP to get scope higher than negation and *no one,* then the impossibility of SOME can be explained, since QR is not allowed through a tensed clause. Likewise, emphatic NPIs that undergo QR were shown not to be licensed long distance for exactly the same reason (see Giannakidou 1998, 2000 for discussion).

Secondly, to go back to Szabolcsi's observation, lower negation is in fact *not* necessary for narrow scope non-emphatic *some*: this *some* is "licensed" without it:

(109) a. I don't think that John called someone.
b. No one thinks that John called someone.
c. I am surprised that John called someone.
d. I regret that I called someone.
e. If we call someone, we'll get help.
f. Most boys who called someone ...
g. Some boys called someone.
h. Few boys called someone.

Nonemphatic *some* thus appears freely in any context, regardless of veridicality or monotonicity, and it behaves in all respects like a "regular" indefinite (*a NP*) which can be specific (wide scope) or non-specific (narrow scope) depending on the context. There seems to be nothing more interesting to non-emphatic *some*. In other words, there seem to be two varieties of *some* indefinites, an emphatic and a non-emphatic version, and only emphatic SOME is a PPI.

Why does emphatic SOME need to scope above negation? In my view, the most profitable avenue will be to think of SOME as an indefinite that conveys 'high' referentiality, to go back to Partee's terminology we employed in our examination of the 'low' referentiality NPIs in section 8. SOME is in contrast to those non-deictic indefinites, and can never be interpreted deictically. If high referentiality relates to specificity — since specific indefinites are also forced to scope above negation and intentional operators, as is well known — then the use of SOME can be seen as some kind of specificity marking on the NP, akin to using, e.g., *certain*, or *particular*. Notice their parallel wide scope with negation:

(110) a. Sue didn't talk to a certain Norwegian — his name is Otto.
b. Sue didn't talk to a particular Norwegian — his name is Otto.
c. Sue didn't talk to SOME Norwegian — his name is Otto.

A certain, a particular, and *SOME* all want to escape negation, and a next task may be to examine whether SOME and *a certain/a particular* also pattern alike in other cases where wide scope is forced for the specific indefinites: with intensional contexts, and interaction with other quantifiers.

(111) Every student visited SOME museum.   (a specific museum only)

Inverse scope seems indeed to be favored with SOME here, according to the judgment of the five native speakers I checked with. Yet more precise work is needed to establish the extent of the parallelism between emphatic SOME and specific indefinites like *a certain*. (With intensional verbs, for instance, forced specificity is less obvious: *The committee wants to hire SOME candidate* is a bit odd to begin with; but this could also be due to blocking by *a certain*, or additional dimensions in the meaning of SOME.) At any rate, I think it is fair to say that the idea that emphatic SOME is a highly referential or specific expression helps us understand better its PPI property: i.e., why it needs to be interpreted with wide scope with respect to negation.

9.2 Speaker oriented adverbs as PPIs

Speaker oriented adverbs have been analyzed recently as polarity items by Nilsen (2003) and Ernst (2009). The main observation here too is that these adverbs are incompatible with the scope of local negation, as illustrated below with *unfortunately*, which Ernst calls strong *evaluative*, and the epistemic modal adverb *possibly*:

(112) a. Unfortunately, John disappeared.
b. #John didn't unfortunately disappear.

(113) a. John possibly left the country.
b. #John didn't possibly leave the country.

The positive sentence says that John disappeared and that this is unfortunate for the speaker. The negation of this sentence ought to express truth reversal: John did not disappear and this is not unfortunate. Rather than saying this, however, the negative sentence comes out odd. Similarly with *possibly*.

Evaluative adverbs like *unfortunately, luckily, possibly* are PPIs, Ernst argues, because they expresses subjectivity. He distinguishes three types of speaker oriented adverbs, two of which are subjective and thus PPIs (Ernst 2009: (61)):

(114) *Strong PPIs*: Subjective. Blocked in all nonveridical contexts. Indirect licensing disallowed.
Weak PPIs: subjective or objective. Blocked in antiveridical contexts, allowed sometimes in nonveridical non-negative contexts. Indirect licensing allowed.
Non-PPIs: Objective. Allowed in all nonveridical contexs.

We see here the correlation between subjectivity and PPI status. Upon uttering (112a), the speaker is committed to the truth of John's disappearing, and further asserts that this *fact* is unfortunate. I am giving below the formulations from Ernst (2009 (62)):

(115) Subjectivity (for speaker orientation) (Ernst 2009: (62))
Where a speaker asserts Q= ADV(p) (thus Q is in $M_E(s)$),
(a) ADV is subjective iff all the worlds by which Q is evaluated are consistent with respect to $M_E(s)$ at the time of utterance; otherwise ADV is objective.
(b) Consistency: a set of worlds (q-worlds) is consistent with a belief state M if the proposition q is true both in q-worlds and in all the worlds in M.

Subjectivity thus formulated renders evaluative adverbs veridical; recall that factive expressions (e.g., verbs) are veridical too.

(116) $[\![$John has unfortunately disappeared$]\!]_c = 1$ iff
$\forall w\ [w \in M_B\ (speaker) \rightarrow w \in \lambda w'. John\ disappeared\ in\ w']$

Every world in the speaker's belief model is a world where John disappeared. From this, incompatibility with negation follows: negation would require that the proposition be false in all the worlds, and this leads to a contradiction. This type of reasoning predicts oddity and not ungrammaticality, and this is precisely the status of (112b) with illicit *unfortunately*, as indicated. The truth condition for epistemic speaker oriented adverbs like *possibly* also requires truth commitment to the main proposition but not in in M_E(speaker); rather, in the hearer's epistemic model (Ernst 2009: 30).

In Ernst's analysis, nonveridical sentences — questions, conditionals, etc. — will be problematic for *unfortunately* and generally adverbs of this category:

(117) a. #Has he unfortunately disappeared?
      b. #If he has unfortunately disappeared…

Nonveridical contexts allow some worlds in M_B (speaker) to not be *p*-worlds, and this again conflicts with the truth condition (116) of the strong PPI *unfortunately*. Factive adverbs like *unfortunately*, then, are veridical and will only be usable in veridical contexts.

Ernst further shows that there is variation within the adverb PPI class — *unfortunately* is excluded from all nonveridical contexts, but epistemic modal adverbials (*possibly*), and what he calls *weak evaluatives* (*mysteriously*) can appear in questions and the antecedent of conditionals given certain conditions. Below, I give Ernst's chart which summarizes the variation, and some examples from his paper to illustrate:

(118) *Ernst (2009):*

Tab. 1

Adverb type	Regular negation	Questions/ conditionals	Negative questions	Negative counter-factuals	Low-tone denial MN	Other metalinguistic negation (MN)
a. Strong evaluatives (*unfortunately, luckily*)	*	*	*	*	*	OK
b. Weak evaluatives (*mysteriously, conveniently*)	*	*/OK	OK	OK	OK	OK
c. Modals (*probably, possibly*)	*	*/OK	?/OK	*/OK	OK	OK
d. Evidentials (*clearly, obviously*)	OK	OK	OK	OK	OK	OK

(119) a. Are they *probably* going to be invited to the meeting?
      b. Where have they *probably* put the loot?
      c. #Are they *unbelievably* going to be invited to the meeting?

(120) a. If, as you say, they're *probably* in line for an award, maybe we should get tickets for the ceremony as soon as we can.
      b. If they have *conveniently* decided to withdraw, the competition will go better for us.
      c. #If they have *luckily* decided to withdraw, the competition will go better for us.

Notice that strong evaluatives remain consistently odd in questions, conditionals. This contrast and variation, unnoticed in Nilsen (2003), suggests that not all speaker oriented adverbs express full speaker commitment; *mysteriously, probably* can be seen as expressing partial commitment, hence the truth of *p* does not hold in all worlds in M_B (speaker), but in a subset of this model (a view, I think, consistent with Ernst's). This predicts incompatibility with negation, but greater flexibility with respect to nonveridical operators. Evidential adverbs, on the other hand, are objective: they rely on evidence for the truth of *p* outside the speaker's beliefs. If speaker commitment is the source of PPI-status, we thus capture nicely the fact that evidential adverbs are *not* PPIs (and are fine with negation):

(121) John didn't *clearly* express his desires.

Space prevents me from elaborating more on these very interesting ideas (see Ernst's paper for more details). The two important things to emphasize is that variation in the PPI domain, and speaker commitment are the keys to understanding the incompatibility of speaker oriented adverbial PPIs with negation and other nonveridical operators.

One final point worth highlighting is that scalarity is not relevant for speaker oriented adverbs — see Ernst's extensive arguments (Ernst 2009: 528–532 against Nilsen's *domain narrowing* analysis). Ernst's main objections are that there is no evidence that the adverbial itself contains a scalar component in its meaning. Additionally, Nilsen discusses only *possibly*, and it is not obvious how his approach would extend to the larger and more varied class of adverbs we observe generally. In the end, the scalar approach would fail even with the epistemic ones like *possibly*, as this type of adverbial is actually OK in the scope of DE operators:

(122) One often hears the term "responsible pharmacist" but few *probably* take time to explore its meaning. (Ernst 2009: (87a)).

(123) * One often hears the term "responsible pharmacist" but few *strangely* take time to explore its meaning. (Ernst 2009: (88a)).

Notice the contrast with the evaluative *strangely* which remains odd in the scope of the non-veridical DE *few*. Regarding *probably*, the question is, if it is scalarity that rules out this type of adverb with negation, why is *few* ok?

10 Main conclusions

In this paper, we reviewed a number of classical patterns of NPIs and PPIs, and the main conclusions to be drawn from our discussion are the following. First, polarity patterns within and across languages reveal two main kinds of sensitivity: (a) a more narrow sensitivity to negation and antiveridicality, and (b) a broader sensitivity to nonveridicality. The former characterizes a class of NPIs and PPIs that have very strict distribution, and is often realized also as a syntactic dependency (agreement or QR) in the case of NPIs. Sensitivity to negation also explains the incompatibility of referential PPIs (emphatic SOME) with negation, and the strongly evaluative (thus subjective) speaker oriented adverbs that need, as a class, to avoid the scope of negation.

Importantly, we saw that mere downward entailment is only a very weak NPI licenser, and often, hardly a licenser (Greek, Salish, Chinese and Korean NPIs, Dutch *ook maar*, and similar items). For PPIs, mere DE plays no role (Szabolcsi 2004; Ernst 2009). In this case, referentiality and (speaker) commitment to the truth of the embedded proposition were shown to be the decisive lexical properties of PPIs — those that make them resist the scope of negation (emphatic SOME), and other nonveridical operators (speaker oriented adverbs).

We also found that the scalarity based approaches to NPIs cannot provide a conceptually or analytically secure foundation for a unifying explanation of why NPIs, including *any*, appear in nonveridical contexts generally. At most, they predict a sensitivity to negation for those NPIs that can be seen as scalar, but even in these cases, we saw that distribution exceeds negation and DE considerably (recall *any*, English minimizers, and Lahiri's Hindi NPIs the distribution of which ranges through modalities, questions, propositional attitudes and other nonveridical contexts). We also saw that it is not even clear that *any* itself is a scalar NPI — recall the objections voiced in Duffley & Larivée (2010) (along with similar objections in various places in the earlier literature). At the same time, purely pragmatic approaches, in all varieties — widening and strengthening, EVEN based, entropy based — predict illicit NPIs to be merely uninformative or contradictory, when, in fact, they are ungrammatical. These approaches are also unable to capture why some scalar expressions are good with negation (NPIs), but some others are not (FCIs).

Finally, the scalar approach does not seem to be a plausible theory for NPIs that are not scalar, or for scalar NPIs, like Israel's 2004 *attenuating* NPIs ("long", "much", "yet", "in weeks") which do not yield a stronger negative assertion, as expected by strengthening/widening in all forms, but a weakened one. The existence of such paradigms renders any attempt to unify all NPI phenomena under scalarity and strength simply untenable.

I suggested, following my earlier work, that it is empirically and analytically more attractive to think of polarity phenomena as a family of dependencies to nonveridicality (negation and DE included), with two possible lexical sources for NPIs: scalarity, and referential deficiency. Scalar NPIs sometimes contain EVEN, and we need a refined enough theory that will allow distinct and varied distributions of NPIs containing EVEN expressions (Giannakidou 2007). At the same time, expressions can become NPIs because of some sort of referential defficiency they contain. I argued that NPIs like *kanenas, any, ku,* and similar items, are variable contributing expressions that are "special" in that they cannot introduce a discourse referent in the main context, they cannot assert existence of an object. One way to capture this is to say that their variable is non-deictic, and can therefore *not* be interpreted as a free variable receiving a contextual value. FCIs contain a similar non-deictic world variable, and the subjunctive mood is a non-deictic tense in exactly the same way (Giannakidou 2009). This inability to introduce a discourse referent in the main context renders the expressions that contain non-deictic variables unusable in veridical contexts.

Conceptually, the existence of expressions that have an inherent inability to refer should not come as a surprise. Certainly, anaphoric pronouns are expressions that cannot refer without an antecedent; and so are bare nominals (singulars, in particular) in many languages, and other, case marked, narrow scope NPs (in Finish, Turkish, the genitive of negation in Russian, see Borschev et al. 2008, Partee & Borschev 2004 and earlier work by Paducheva cited there). What I suggested in Giannakidou (1998), and reiterate here, is that a central portion of polarity phenomena has to do with this difficulty, or uncertainty, in referring. With elements like *any*, deficient reference may also combine with a scalar component (maybe an implicature, because it is certainly not present in all contexts).

I would like to close with a word of caution. The process on NPI creation and use must be seen as a dynamic one, as patterns do not remain stable over time (Hoeksema 2010), and distributions of the same NPI classes are synchronically rarely completely identical across languages. Nonveridicality, scalarity, and non-deictic reference must thus be seen as predictors of where NPI *could* occur, not as rigid preconditions that NPIs *must* occur in *all* nonveridical environments.

Acknowledgment: I would like to thank the editors of the volume for giving me the opportunity to write this article, and Paul Portner in particular for his extremely helpful and generous comments. In the year and a half I have been working on this paper, materials were presented at the *Zentrum für Allgemeine Sprachwissenschaft* (ZAS) Berlin, UMass Amherst *Linguistics Colloquium*, the *Semantics Research Seminar* at Keio University in Tokyo, Japan, and the DIP Colloquium at the University of Amsterdam. I am thankful to the audiences of those venues for their very useful feedback. In my more recent thinking about polarity, I also benefited enormously from discussions with Maria Aloni, Jay Atlas, Tom Ernst, Jack Hoeksema, Larry Horn, Makoto Kanazawa, Angelika Kratzer, Manfred Krifka, Jason Merchant, Josep Quer, Barbara Partee, Paul Postal, Chris Potts, Rob van Rooy, Anna Szabolcsi, Chris Tancredi, Yoad Winter, and Frans Zwarts. Many thanks to all for the very stimulating comments. There is still a lot of work left to be done, and it is my hope that, when it comes to identifying new polarity phenomena or rethinking about the old ones, this article will prove a helpful guiding resource.

11 References

Alonso-Ovalle, Luis & Paula Menéndez-Benito 2010. Modal indefinites. *Natural Language Semantics* 18, 1–31.
Anagnostopoulou, Elena & Anastasia Giannakidou 1995. Clitics and prominence; or why specificity is not enough. In: A. Dainora et al. (eds.). *Proceedings of the Annual Meeting of the Chicago Linguistic Society (= CLS) 31*. Chicago, IL: Chicago Linguistic Society, 132–150.
Atlas, Jay D. 1993. The importance of being only: Testing the neo-gricean versus neo-entailment paradigms. *Journal of Semantics* 10, 301–318.
Atlas, Jay D. 1996. *Only* noun phrases, pseudo-negative quantifiers, negative polarity items, and monotonicity. *Journal of Semantics* 13, 265–328.
Baker, Carl L. 1970. Double negatives, *Linguistic Inquiry* 1, 169–186.
Beaver, David & Brady Clark 2003. *Always* and *only*: Why not all focus sensitive operators are alike. *Natural Language Semantics* 11, 323–362.
Bernardi, Raffaella 2002. *Reasoning with Polarity in Categorial Type Logic*. Ph.D. dissertation. University of Utrecht.
Bittner, Maria 1987. On the semantics of Greenlandic antipassive and related constructions. *International Journal of American Linguistics* 53, 194–231.

Borkin, Ann 1971. Polarity items in questions. In: *Proceedings of the Annual Meeting of the Chicago Linguistic Society (= CLS) 7*. Chicago, IL: Chicago Linguistic Society, 53–62.

Borschev, Vladimir, Elena V. Paducheva, Barbara H. Partee, Yakov G. Testelets & Igor Yanovich 2008. Russian genitives, non-referentiality, and the property-type hypothesis. In: A. Antonenko J. F. Bailyn & Ch. Bethin (eds.). *Proceedings of the Formal Approaches to Slavic Linguistics: The Stony Brook Meeting 2007 (= FASL) 16*. Ann Arbor, MI: Michigan Slavic Publishers, 48–67.

Carlson, Greg 1977. *Reference to Kinds in English*. Ph.D. dissertation. University of Massachusetts, Amherst, MA.

Cheng, Lisa L.-Ch. & Anastasia Giannakidou 2011. The non-uniformity of wh-indeterminates with polarity and free choice in Chinese. In: K.-H. Gil & G. Tsoulas (eds.). *Crosslinguistic Patterns of Quantification*. New York: Oxford University Press.

Chierchia, Gennaro 2006. Broaden your views. Implicatures of domain widening and the "Logicality" of language. *Linguistic Inquiry* 37, 535–590.

Condoravdi, Cleo 1994. *Descriptions in Context*. Ph.D. dissertation. Yale University, New Haven, CT.

van Craenenbroeck, Jeroen 2008. About something. Towards a syntactic decomposition of polarity. Paper presented at the *CUNY Syntax Supper*, CUNY Graduate Center at the City University of New York, November 25, 2008.

Davison, Alice 1981. *Any* as universal or existential. In: J. van der Auwera (ed.). *The Semantics of Determiners*. London: Croom Helm, 11–34.

Dayal, Veneeta 1998. *Any* as inherently modal. *Linguistics & Philosophy* 21, 433–476.

den Dikken, Marcel & Anastasia Giannakidou 2002. From *hell* to polarity: Aggressively non-d-linked wh-phrases as polarity items. *Linguistic Inquiry* 33, 31–61.

Dowty, David 1994. The role of negative polarity and concord marking in natural language reasoning. In: M. Harvey & L. Santelmann (eds.). *Proceedings of Semantics and Linguistic Theory (= SALT) IV*. Ithaca, NY: Cornell University, 114–145.

Drenhaus, Heiner, Peter beim Graben, Stefan Frisch, Douglas Saddy 2006. Diagnosis and repair of negative polarity constructions in the light of symbolic resonance analysis. *Brain & Language* 96, 255–268.

Drenhaus, Heiner, Joanna Blaszczak & Juliane Schütte 2010. *An ERP Study on the Strength of Licensers in Negative Polarity Constructions*. Ms. Potsdam, University of Potsdam.

Duffley, Patrick & Pierre Larivée 2010. Anyone for non-scalarity? *English Language and Linguistics* 14, 1–17.

Enç, Mürvet 1991. The semantics of specificity. *Linguistic Inquiry* 22, 1–25.

Ernst, Thomas 2009. Speaker oriented adverbs. *Natural Language and Linguistic Theory* 27, 497–544.

Falaus, Anamaria 2009. *Polarity Items and Dependent Indefinites in Romanian*. Ph.D. dissertation. Université de Nantes.

Farkas, Donka F. 1992. On the semantics of subjunctive complements. In: P. Hirschbühler (ed.). *Romance Languages and Modern Linguistic Theory*. Amsterdam: Benjamins, 69–105.

Farkas, Donka F. 1998. Dependent indefinites. In: F. Corblin, D. Goddard & J.-M. Marandin (eds.). *Empirical Issues in Formal Syntax and Semantics*. Frankfurt/M.: Peter Lang, 243–267.

Farkas, Donka F. 2002. Extreme non-specificity in Romanian In: C. Beyssade et al. (eds.). *Romance Languages and Linguistic Theory 2000*. Amsterdam: Benjamins, 127–151.

Fauconnier, Gilles 1975. Pragmatic scales and logical structure. *Linguistic Inquiry* 6, 353–375.

Fernald, Theodore B. & Ellavina Perkins 2006. Negative polarity items in Navajo. In: A. Berez, S. Gessner & S. Tuttle (eds.). *Proceedings of the Dene (Athabaskan) Languages Conference (= ALC) 2006* (Alaska Native Language Center Working Papers 7). Fairbanks, AK: ANLC Publications, 19–48.
von Fintel, Kai 1999. NPI-licensing, Strawson-entailment, and context-dependency. *Journal of Semantics* 16, 97–148.
von Fintel, Kai 2000. Whatever. In: B. Jackson & T. Matthews (eds.). *Proceedings of Semantics and Linguistic Theory (= SALT) X*. Ithaca, NY : Cornell University, 27–40.
van Geenhoven, Veerle 1998. *Semantic Incorporation and Indefinite Descriptions: Semantic and Syntactic Aspects of Noun Incorporation in West Greenlandic*. Doctoral dissertation. University of Tübingen. Reprinted: Stanford, CA: CSLI Publications.
Giannakidou, Anastasia 1994. The semantic licensing of NPIs and the Modern Greek subjunctive. *Language and Cognition* 4, 55–68.
Giannakidou, Anastasia 1995. Subjunctive, habituality and negative polarity. In: M. Simons & T. Galloway (eds.). *Proceedings of Semantics and Linguistic Theory (= SALT) V*. Ithaka, NY: Cornell University, 132–150.
Giannakidou, Anastasia 1997. *The Landscape of Polarity Items*. Ph.D. dissertation. University of Groningen.
Giannakidou, Anastasia 1998. *Polarity Sensitivity as (Non)veridical Dependency*. Amsterdam: Benjamins.
Giannakidou, Anastasia 1999. Affective dependencies. *Linguistics & Philosophy* 22, 367–421.
Giannakidou, Anastasia 2000. Negative ... Concord? *Natural Language and Linguistic Theory* 18, 457–523.
Giannakidou, Anastasia 2001. The meaning of free choice. *Linguistics & Philosophy* 24, 659–735.
Giannakidou, Anastasia 2002. Licensing and sensitivity in polarity items: From downward entailment to nonveridicality. In: M. Andronis, A. Pycha & K. Yoshimura (eds.). *Proceedings of the Annual Meeting of the Chicago Linguistic Society (= CLS) 38*. Chicago, IL: Chicago Linguistic Society, 29–53.
Giannakidou, Anastasia 2006a. *Only*, emotive factive verbs, and the dual nature of polarity dependency. *Language* 82, 575–603.
Giannakidou, Anastasia 2006b. N-words and negative concord. In: M. Everaert et al. (eds.) *The Blackwell Companion to Syntax, vol III*, 327–391. Wiley-Blackwell.
Giannakidou, Anastasia 2007. The landscape of EVEN. *Natural Language and Linguistic Theory* 25, 39–81.
Giannakidou, Anastasia 2009. The dependency of the subjunctive revisited: Temporal semantics and polarity. *Lingua* (special issue on *Mood*) 119, 1883–1908.
Giannakidou, Anastasia 2011. Greek quantifiers. In: E. L. Keenan & D. Paperno (eds.). *Handbook of Quantifiers in Natural Language*. Dordrecht: Springer.
Giannakidou, Anastasia & Lisa Cheng 2006. (In)definiteness, polarity, and the role of wh-morphology in free choice. *Journal of Semantics* 23, 135–183.
Giannakidou, Anastasia & Josep Quer 1995. Two mechanisms for the licensing of negative indefinites. In: L. Gabriele, D. Hardison & R. Westmoreland (eds.). *Proceedings of the Annual Meeting of the Formal Linguistics Society of Mid-America (= FLSM) 6, vol. 2: Syntax II & Semantics/Pragmatics*. Bloomington, IN: IULC Publications, 103–114.
Giannakidou, Anastasia & Josep Quer 1997. Long distance licensing of negative indefinites. In: D. Forget et al. (eds.). *Negation and Polarity, Syntax and Semantics*. Amsterdam: Benjamins. 95–113.

Giannakidou, Anastasia & Josep Quer 2010. What we gain, and what we lose, with a Hamblin semantics for free choice: From free choice to referential vagueness. Paper presented at the *Workshop on Alternative-Based Semantics*, University of Nantes, October 29–30, 2010.

Giannakidou, Anastasia & Suwon Yoon 2010. No NPI licensing in comparatives. Paper presented at the *Annual Meeting of the Chicago Linguistic Society (= CLS) 46*, April 8–10, 2010.

Guerzoni, Elena 2004. EVEN-NPIs in questions. *Natural Language Semantics* 12, 319–343.

Guerzoni, Elena & Yael Sharvit 2007. A question of strength: On NPIs in interrogative clauses. *Linguistics & Philosophy* 30, 361–391.

Haegeman, Liliane & Rafaella Zanuttini 1981. Neg-heads and the neg-criterion. *The Linguistic Review* 8, 233–251.

Haspelmath, Martin 1997. *Indefinite Pronouns*. Oxford: Oxford University Press.

Heim, Irene 1982. *The Semantics of Definite and Indefinite Noun Phrases*. Ph.D. dissertation. University of Massachussetts, Amherst, MA. Reprinted: Ann Arbor, MI: University Microfilms.

Heim 1984. A note on negative polarity and downward entailingness. In: C. Jones & P. Sells (eds.). *Proceedings of the North Eastern Linguistic Society (=NELS) 14*. Amherst, MA: GLSA, University of Massachusetts, 98–107.

Herburger, Elena 2003. A note on Spanish *ni siquiera*, 'even', and the analysis of NPIs. *Probus* 15, 237–256.

Herburger, Elena & Simon Mauck 2006. NPIs are low Scalar Items +F. Ms. Washington, DC, Georgetown University.

Hintikka, Jaakko 1962. *Knowledge and Belief: An Introduction to the Logic of the Two Notions*. Ithaka, NY: Cornell University Press.

Hoeksema, Jacob 1986. Monotonie en superlatieven. In: C. Hoppenbrouwers et al. (eds.). *Proeven van taalwetenschap*. Groningen: Instituut RUG, 38–49.

Hoeksema, Jacob 1994. On the grammaticalization of negative polarity items. In: S. Gahl, A. Dolbey & C. Johnson (eds.). *Proceedings of the Annual Meeting of the Berkeley Linguistics Society (= BLS) 20*. Berkeley, CA: Berkeley Linguistics Society, 273–282.

Hoeksema, Jacob 1999. Aantekeningen bij *ooit*, deel 2: De opkomst van niet polair ooit. *Tabu* 29, 147–172.

Hoeksema, Jacob 2008. There is no number effect in the licensing of negative polarity items: a reply to Guerzoni and Sharvit. *Linguistics & Philosophy* 31, 397–407.

Hoeksema, Jacob 2010. Dutch ENIG: From nonveridicality to downward entailment. *Natural Language and Linguistic Theory* 28, 837–859.

Hoeksema, Jacob & Hotze Rullmann 2001. Scalarity and polarity: A study of scalar adverbs as polarity items. In: J. Hoeksema et al. (eds.). *Perspectives on Negation and Polarity Items*. Amsterdam: Benjamins, 129–171.

de Hoop, Helen 1992. *Case Configuration and Noun Phrase Interpretation*. Ph.D. dissertation. University of Groningen.

Horn, Laurence 1972. *On the Semantic Properties of Logical Operators in English*. Ph.D. dissertation. University of California, Los Angeles, CA.

Horn, Laurence R. 1989. *A Natural History of Negation*. Chicago, IL: The University of Chicago Press.

Horn, Laurence R. 1996. Exclusive company: *Only* and the dynamics of vertical inference. *Journal of Semantics* 13, 1–40.

Horn, Laurence R. 2000a. *Any* and *(–)ever*: Free choice and free relatives. In: A. Z. Wyner (ed.). *Proceedings of the Annual Meeting of the Israel Association for Theoretical Linguistics (= IATL) 15*. Jerusalem: Akademon, 71–111.

Horn, Laurence R. 2000b. Pick a theory: Not just any theory. In: L. Horn & Y. Kato (eds.). *Negation and Polarity: Syntactic and Semantic Perspectives*. Oxford: Oxford University Press, 147–192.
Horn, Laurence R. 2002. Assertoric inertia and NPI-licensing. In: M. Andronis et al. (eds.). *Proceedings of the Annual Meeting of the Chicago Linguistic Society (= CLS) 38, Parasession on Negation and Polarity*. Chicago, IL: Chicago Linguistic Society, 55–82.
Horn, Laurence R. 2005. Airport '86 revisited: Toward a unified indefinite *any*. In: G. Carlson & F. J. Pelletier (eds.). *The Partee Effect*. Stanford, CA: CSLI Publications, 179–205.
Horn, Laurence R. 2006. The boarder wars: A neo-Gricean perspective. In: K. von Heusinger & K. Turner (eds.). *Where Semantics Meets Pragmatics*. Amsterdam: Elsevier, 21–48.
Israel, Michael 1996. Polarity sensitivity as lexical semantics. *Linguistics & Philosophy* 19, 619–666.
Israel, Michael 2004. The pragmatics of polarity. In: L. Horn & G. Ward (eds.). *The Handbook of Pragmatics*. Oxford: Blackwell, 701–723.
Jackson, Eric. 1994. *Negative Polarity, Definites under Quantification and General Statements*. Ph.D. dissertation. Stanford University, Stanford, CA.
Jacobson, Pauline 1995. On the quantificational force of the English free relative. In: A. Kratzer et al. (eds.). *Quantification in Natural Language, Vol. 2*. Dordrecht: Kluwer, 451–487.
Jayez, Jacques & Lucia Tovena 2005. Free choiceness and non-individuation. *Linguistics & Philosophy* 28, 1–71.
Jespersen, Otto 1909–1949. *A Modern English Grammar on Historical Principles*. London: George Allen and Unwin Ltd.
Kadmon, Nirit & Fred Landman 1993. Any. *Linguistics & Philosophy* 16, 353–422.
Kas, Mark 1993. *Essays on Boolean Semantics and Negative Polarity*. Ph.D. dissertation. University of Groningen.
Kiparsky, Paul 1998. Partitive case and aspect. In: M. Butt & W. Geuder (eds.). *The Projection of Arguments: Lexical and Compositional Factors*. Stanford, CA: CSLI Publications, 265–307.
Klima, Edward 1964. Negation in English. In: J. Fodor & J. Katz (eds.). *The Structure of Language*. Englewood Cliffs, NJ: Prentice Hall, 246–323.
König, Ekkehard 2003. *The Meaning of Focus Particles: A Comparative Perspective*. London: Routledge.
Kratzer, Angelika & Shimoyama, Junko 2002. Indeterminate pronouns: The view from Japanese. In: Y. Otsu (ed.). *Proceedings of the Tokyo Conference on Psycholinguistics 3*. Tokyo: Hituzi Syobo, 1–25.
Krifka, Manfred 1995. The semantics and pragmatics of polarity items in assertion. *Linguistic Analysis* 15, 209–257.
Krifka, Manfred, Francis J. Pelletier, Greg Carlson, Alice ter Meulen, Gennaro Chierchia & Godehard Link 1995. Genericity: An introduction. In: G. Carlson & F. J. Pelletier (eds.). *The Generic Book*. Chicago, IL: The University of Chicago Press, 1–124.
Ladusaw, William 1980. *Polarity Sensitivity as Inherent Scope Relations*. New York: Garland.
Ladusaw, William 1983. Logical form and conditions on grammaticality. *Linguistics & Philosophy* 6, 373–392.
Ladusaw, William 1996. Negation and polarity items. In: S. Lappin (ed.). *The Handbook of Contemporary Semantic Theory*. Oxford: Blackwell, 321–341.
Lahiri, Utpal 1998. Focus and negative polarity in Hindi. *Natural Language Semantics* 6, 57–123.
Laka, Itziar 1990. *Negation in Syntax: On the Nature of Functional Categories and Projections*. Ph.D. dissertation. MIT, Cambridge, MA.

Lee, Chungmin 1997. Negative polarity and free choice: Where do they come from? In: P. Dekker, M. Stokhof & Y. Venema (eds.). *Proceedings of the Amsterdam Colloquium 11*. Amsterdam: ILLC, 217–222.

Lee, Chungmin 1999. Types of NPIs and nonveridicality in Korean and other languages. In: G. Storto (ed.). *Syntax at Sunset 2* (UCLA Working Papers in Linguistics 3). Los Angeles, CA: University of California, 96–132.

Lee, Chungmin 2003. Negative polarity items and free choice in Korean and Japanese: A contrastive study. *Korean Society of Bilingualism* 22.

Lee, Jung-Hyuck 2010. Nonveridical dependency: Korean and Japanese focus particles. *Japanese/Korean Linguistics* 17, 231–245.

Lee, Young-Suk & Laurence R. Horn 1994. *Any as an Indefinite plus even*. Ms. New Haven, CT, Yale University.

Lin, Jo-Wang 1996. *Polarity Licensing and Wh-Phrase Quantification in Chinese*. Ph.D. dissertation. University of Massachusetts, Amherst, MA.

Linebarger, Marcia 1980. *The Grammar of Negative Polarity*. Ph.D. dissertation. MIT, Cambridge, MA.

Linebarger, Marcia 1987. Negative polarity and grammatical representation. *Linguistics & Philosophy* 10, 325–387.

Linebarger, Marcia 1991. Negative polarity as linguistic evidence. In: L. M. Dobrin, L. Nichols & R. Rodriguez (eds.). *Proceedings of the Annual Meeting of the Chicago Linguistic Society (= CLS) 27, Part Two: The Parasession on Negation*. Chicago, IL: Chicago Linguistic Society, 165–188.

Matthewson, Lisa 1998. *Determiner Systems and Quantificational Strategies. Evidence from Salish*. The Hague: Holland Academic Graphics.

Menéndez-Benito, Paula 2010. On universal free choice items. *Natural Language Semantics* 18, 33–64.

Merchant, Jason 2004. Fragments and ellipsis. *Linguistics & Philosophy* 27, 661–738.

Montague, Richard 1969. On the nature of certain philosophical entities. *The Monist* 53, 159–194.

Nakanishi, Kimiko 2007. Presentation at the *Annual Meeting of the Linguistic Society of America (= LSA), Workshop on Semantic/Pragmatic Perspectives on Negative Polarity Items*, January 4–7, 2007.

Nathan, Lance 1999. *Either: Negative Polarity Meets Focus Sensitivity*. Honors Thesis. Brown University, Providence, RI.

Nilsen, Oystein 2003. *Eliminating Positions*. Ph.D. dissertation. University of Utrecht.

Park, Eun-Hae. 2009. Free choice and wh-indeterminates in Korean: Definiteness, indefinites, and expressive content. Ph.D. dissertation. University of Chicago, Chicago, IL.

Partee, Barbara H. 2008. Negation, intensionality, and aspect: Interaction with NP semantics. In: S. Rothstein (ed.). *Theoretical and Crosslinguistic Approaches to the Semantics of Aspect*. Amsterdam: Benjamins, 291–317.

Partee, Barbara H. & Vladimir Borschev 2004. The semantics of Russian genitive of negation: The role and nature of perspectival structure. In: K. Watanabe & Robert B. Young (eds.). *Proceedings of Semantics and Linguistic Theory (= SALT) XIV*. Ithaca, NY: Cornell University, 212–234.

Pereltsvaig, Asya 2000. Monotonicity-based versus veridicality-based approaches to negative polarity: Evidence from Russian. In: T. Halloway King & I. A. Sekerina (eds.). *Formal*

Approaches to Slavic Linguistics: The Philadelphia Meeting 1999. Ann Arbor, MI: Michigan Slavic Publishers, 328–346.

Pereltsvaig, Asya 2008. Russian *nibud'*-series as markers of co-variation. In: N. Abner & J. Bishop (eds.). *Proceedings of the West Coast Conference on Formal Linguistics (= WCCFL) 27*. Somerville, MA: Cascadilla Proceedings Project, 370–378.

Postal, Paul M. 2000. *The Ohio Lectures on squat*. Ms. New York, New York University.

Postal, Paul M. 2003. *Skeptical Linguistic Essays*. Oxford: Oxford University Press.

Potts, Christopher 2005. *The Logic of Conventional Implicatures*. Oxford: Oxford University Press.

Progovac, Ljiljana 1994. *Positive and Negative polarity: A binding approach*. Cambridge: Cambridge University Press.

Progovac, Ljiljana 2005. Negative and positive feature checking and the distribution of polarity items. In: S. Brown & A. Przepiorkowski (eds.). *Negation in Slavic*. Bloomington, IN: Slavica Publishers, 179–217.

Przepiórkowski, Adam & Anna Kupc 1997. Eventuality negation and negative concord in Polish and Italian. In: R. D. Borsley & Adam Przepiórkowski (eds.). *Slavic in Head-Driven Phrase Structure Grammar*. Stanford, CA: CSLI Publications, 211–246.

Quer, Josep 1998. *Mood at the Interface*. Ph.D. dissertation. University of Utrecht.

Quer, Josep 1999. *The Quantificational Force of Free Choice Items*. Ms. Amsterdam, University of Amsterdam.

Rooth, Mats 1985. *Association with Focus*. Ph.D. dissertation. University of Massachusetts, Amherst, MA.

van Rooy, Robert 2003. Negative polarity items in questions: Strength as relevance. *Journal of Semantics* 20, 239–273.

Rullmann, Hotze 2003. Additive particles and polarity. *Journal of Semantics* 20, 329–401.

Saddy, Douglas, Heiner Drenhaus & Stefan Frisch 2004. Processing polarity items: Contrastive licensing costs. *Brain & Language* 90, 405–502.

Sailer, Manfred 2009. On reading-dependent licensing of strong negative polarity items. In: A. Riester & T. Solstad (eds.). *Proceedings of Sinn and Bedeutung (= SuB) 13*. Stuttgart: University of Stuttgart, 455–468.

Seuren, Pieter 1984. The comparative revisited. *Journal of Semantics* 3, 109–141.

Shimoyama, Junko 2003. *Wide Scope Universals in Japanese*. Ms. Montreal, McGill University.

Stalnaker, Robert 1979. Assertion. In: P. Cole (ed.). *Syntax and Semantics 9: Pragmatics*. New York: Academic Press, 315–332.

Suranyi, Balazs 2006. Quantification and focus in negative concord. *Lingua* 116, 272–313.

Szabolcsi, Anna 2004. Positive polarity – negative polarity. *Natural Language and Linguistic Theory* 22, 409–452.

Tancredi, Christopher 2007a. *A Multi-Model Modal Theory of I-Semantics, Part I: Modals*. Ms. Tokyo, University of Tokyo.

Tancredi, Christopher 2007b. *A Multi-Model Modal Theory of I-Semantics, Part II: Identity and Attitudes*. Ms. Tokyo, University of Tokyo.

Tovena, Lucia 1998. *The Fine Structure of Polarity Items*. New York: Garland.

Uribe-Etxebarria, Miriam 1994. *Interface Licensing Conditions on Negative Polarity Licensing: A Theory of Polarity and Tense Interactions*. Ph.D. dissertation. University of Connecticut, Storrs, CT.

Vendler, Zeno 1967. *Linguistics in Philosophy*. Ithaka, NY: Cornell University Press.

Vlachou, Evangelia 2007. *Free Choice Items In and Out of Context*. Ph.D. dissertation. University of Utrecht.

van der Wouden, Ton. 1994. *Negative Contexts*. Ph.D. dissertation. University of Groningen.
Yoon, Suwon 2008. *From Non-Specificity to Polarity: Korean N-Words*. Ms. Chicago, IL, University of Chicago.
Yoshimura, Keiko 2007. *Focus and Polarity in Japanese*. Ph.D. dissertation. University of Chicago, Chicago, IL.
Zanuttini, Raffaella 1991. *Syntactic Properties of Sentential Negation. A Comparative Study of Romance Languages*. Ph.D. dissertation. University of Pennsylvania, Philadelphia, PA.
Zwarts, Frans 1981. Negatief polaire uitdrukkingen I. *Glot International* 4, 35–132.
Zwarts, Frans 1986. *Categoriale Grammatica en Algebraische Semantiek. Een studie naar negatie en polariteit in het Nederlands*. Ph.D. dissertation. University of Groningen.
Zwarts, Frans 1993. *Three Types of Polarity*. Ms. Groningen, University of Groningen. Reprinted in: F. Hamm & E. Hinrichs (eds.). *Plural Quantification*. Dordrecht: Kluwer, 1998, 177–238.
Zwarts, Frans 1995. Nonveridical contexts. *Linguistic Analysis* 25, 286–312.

Roberto Zamparelli
4 Coordination

1 Introduction —— 135
2 Coordination vs. subordination —— 137
3 Syntactic and semantic relations among coordinands —— 143
4 Semantics —— 153
5 Conclusions —— 168
6 References —— 168

Abstract: The behavior of coordination, the operation which links together linguistic material by means of "and" and "or", is different from that of any other linguistic operation, and can only be understood in terms of the combination of syntactic and semantic processes. The article presents the key features of this phenomenon, from old syntactic puzzles (the parallelism requirement, the Coordinate Structure Constraint, the ellipsis patterns), to semantic facts such as the difference between Boolean and non-Boolean conjunction, the cumulativity/distributivity pattern, the possibility of "nested" pluralities and the scopal behavior of "and" and "or". The article reviews the main theories that have been put forth to explain these facts, with an eye on their interrelations and on the way syntax and semantics can sometimes compete for a solution.

1 Introduction

The term "coordination" refers to a linguistic operation that combines two or more constituents, typically of the same semantic and syntactic type, into a larger unit of that semantic and syntactic type, by means of one or more linking elements. In English, linking elements are the conjunction *and*, the disjunction *or* and the adversative linker *but*, collectively called COORDINATORS. The units that are coordinated will be called COORDINANDS in this article (CONJUNCTS, when linked by conjunction, DISJUNCTS, when linked by the disjunctive connector).

Any syntactic unit can be conjoined or disjoined: sentences (1a), phrases (1b,c), words (1d):

Roberto Zamparelli, Trento, Italy

(1) a. [John had a beer], [Mary watched a film] and
  [Sue made popcorn]. *conjunction of Ss*
 b. Martin will [fly to Venice] or [drive to Milan] *disjunction of VPs*
 c. John [wanted a beer] but [got a martini]. *adversative conjunction of tensed VPs*
 d. Jacky [loathes] and [despises] his boss. *conjunction of Vs*

Coordination has a special status among linguistic operations. Typologically, it is probably a universal of human language (Haspelmath 2007). Syntactically, coordination differs from other syntactic processes in at least four respects. First, it can target constituents of any kind. Second, it shows a discrepancy between a syntactic and a semantic notion of 'head'; as syntactic heads, *and*, *or* and *but* are nearly invisible: no noun or verb selects for complements obligatorily containing these words; the syntactic category of the coordination is copied from the category of its coordinands; on the other hand, the semantic relation among the coordinands is determined by the coordinator, which thus acts as a purely semantic head. Third, the structural status of the coordinands (specifiers, adjuncts, or objects in some special 'tridimensional' structural position) is unclear. Finally, coordinate structures allow a pattern of ellipsis and long distance dependencies which is different from the one found in other syntactic structures.

Semantically, conjunction and disjunction of declarative sentences are naturally mapped onto the standard Boolean connectives of propositional calculus, $\wedge$ and $\vee$, but coordination in natural language can join many syntactic categories that cannot be directly mapped onto truth values. In distributive cases like (2a), a conjunction of noun phrases ("Determiner Phrases", DP, in the rest of this article) is equivalent to the sentential conjunction in (2b), interpreted as (2c). However, in the presence of cumulative predicates this equivalence does not hold (3).

(2) a. Matt spoke with Sue and Karl *distributive*
 b. $\equiv$ Matt spoke with Sue and Matt spoke with Karl
 c. *speak-with'(Matt',Sue') $\wedge$ speak-with'(Matt',Karl')*

(3) a. Matt and Sue are a happy couple *cumulative*
 b. $\neq$ Matt is a happy couple and Sue is a happy couple.

Many proposals have tried to derive (2a) from (2b) by means of 'reduction rules' at the level of syntactic and/or phonetic forms (CONJUNCTION REDUCTION). The same effect can be obtained semantically, assigning to *and*, *or* and *but* a more general semantics, from which the analysis of (2a) as (2c) can be made to follow without assuming a level at which the syntactic structure in (2b) is realized. Neither route is trivial, since conjunction can trigger the scopal and distributivity ambiguities found in non-coordinated plural noun phrases, with the additional complexity given by the possibility of embedded coordinations (e.g. conjuncts inside disjuncts, disjuncts inside conjuncts).

In the analysis of coordination the interplay between syntax and semantics is crucial, with a trade off between syntactic and semantic complexity: to the extent a syntactic derivation of (2a) from (2b) can be motivated, the semantics of distributive coordination becomes simpler, at the expense of the complexity of the reduction system. The existence of cases where some material in the coordinands seems indisputably to be missing (especially gapping, see below, and article 12 [this volume] (Ward & Birner) *Discourse and word order*) increases the motivations for reduction approaches. Considering these facts, the present article will address many issues that span syntax and semantics.

The general structure is as follows. First, I will list some properties which distinguish *coordination* from *subordination*. On the bases of these properties, a core set of "coordinators" will be introduced and discussed in Section 2.2. Section 3. will discuss various issues concerning the syntactic and semantic relations between coordinands: the parallelism requirement, the Coordinate Structure Constraint (Section 3.2.), the potential role of ellipsis in "conjunction reduction" (Section 3.3.) and gapping (Section 3.4.). Sections 4.1. and 4.2. discuss the semantics of "Boolean" and "non-Boolean" *and*, Section 4.3. addresses cumulativity and distributivity effects, 4.4., the debate between 'flat' and 'nested' pluralities and Section 4.5. some issues concerning the scope of coordination.

2 Coordination vs. subordination

We begin by spelling out some differences between COORDINATION and (clausal) SUBORDINATION. The latter is found in sentential arguments (subjects, objects (4)) and in modification (5), and is introduced by a vast range of subordinating conjunctions with different meanings (e.g. *because, since, when, after* etc.), or by positional and morphological markers such as gerunds or participles.

(4) a. [That Luna Rossa lost] is a pity.
    b. Father said [that he will give me a car.]

(5) a. Father gave us a car [because/after we got a driving license.]
    b. [Having obtained a driving license] I was keen to get a car.

2.1 Some properties of coordination and subordination

[A] Pretheoretically, in coordination all the coordinands have the same status and contribute equally to the global meaning of the coordination, mediated by the meaning of the coordinator. This contrasts with subordination, which presents an asymmetry between a main and a subordinate element. The latter is syntactically and semantically dependent on the main element: if the main element is removed the rest becomes ill-formed. A corollary is that coordinands can be reshuffled without major meaning changes (see Section 4.1. for some exceptions), and can often be omitted preserving grammaticality.

(6) Marco studies in Caracas and Luis works in Madrid. ≡ Luis works in Madrid and Marco studies in Caracas.

(7) a. I met {Sam ((, Graham) and Jeff) / Graham ((, Jeff) and Sam) / Jeff ((, Graham) and Sam)}
    b. I will take {a cab (or a bus) / a bus (or a cab)}

In subordination the order $[S_1$ sub-conj $S_2]$ cannot be swapped around the conjunction without a strong meaning change (though the group [sub-conj S_2] can sometimes be anteposed to S_1: *when Mary came, John left*)

[B] A single conjunction or disjunction can contain an indefinite amount of coordinands (8a), any of which can in turn be a full coordination (8b). This is one of the most pervasive cases of direct recursion in natural language.

(8) a. [Alice, Matt, Bruce, Jack and Jim] all joined the project in its first year.
    b. [[Alice and Bruce] or Matt] will pick you up.

Syntactic theories that only allow binary branching typically decompose (8a) into a sequence of nested binary coordinations ((9) for VO languages, where ANDP and &P are possibly distinct categories and & can be realized as 'comma intonation' alone). In a structure of this sort, every coordinand C-commands the following ones (recall that a node A C-commands a node B in a tree iff A does not dominate B but every node that dominates A also dominates B). Since C-command is generally believed to affect pronoun binding, the possibility of forward variable binding among coordinands is evidence for an asymmetrical structure like (9) (see (10a), contrasted with (10b), which inverts linear order, and (10c), where the linear order is preserved but the binder *every* is embedded in a position from which it does not C-commands *her*).

(9) a. [&P Alice & [&P Matt & [&P Bruce & [ANDP Jack and Jim]]]]

(10) a. [The school board], [every girl]$_i$ or/and [her$_i$ mother]
 b. * [Her$_i$ mother] and/or [every girl]$_i$
 c. ??either [the school board and [every girl]$_i$] or [her$_i$ mother]

Subordination is often claimed not to allow iteration. Whether this is true depends on the precise definition of "iteration" and "subordination" (relative clauses are syntactically subordinate, yet allow stacking). If this criterion is regarded as a definitory property, the status of *but*, traditionally counted among coordinators, becomes problematic, since this adversative contrasts only weakly with *because* in nested clauses (11). However, it is quite possible that iteration might also be conditioned by processing factors.

(11) a. ? John was attacked but fortunately he had a gun but unfortunately it was not loaded but fortunately he had bullets but unfortunately they were blanks.
 b. ??John arrived late because he was caught in a traffic jam because it was already rush hour when he left because he was blocked by a long phone call.

[C] Subordinating conjunctions are very specific with respect to the syntactic categories they introduce (e.g. *because*+S/*of*-PP, *after*+S/DP), while, as mentioned above, *and/or* can target any category (12), and even lexical heads (13) (but see Section 3.4.).

(12) a. [John] and [Mary] are coming.   DP&DP
 b. We still need the [bat] and [ball].   NP&NP
 c. [In London] and [in Berlin] it is still cold.   PP&PP
 d. the [red] and [blue] flag   Adj(P)&Adj(P)
 e. Mary has [left] and [gone to India]   VP&VP
 f. I would know if [Mary left] and [Peter returned]   IP&IP

(13) a. I [can] and [will] visit her.   Modal&Modal
 b. [under] or [beside] the bed.   P&P

In the X-bar structural framework of Jackendoff (1977), coordination seems able to apply at X' level. If the structural relation between a V/Aux and an adjacent subject/wh-element is head-specifier (of IP or CP), some coordinations must target I' (14) or C' (15):

(14) a. John [has left] and [will return]
b. It would be unfortunate for him [to leave] and [to fail to return]

(15) a. Who [has Mary invited] and [does Bill want to see]?
b. Liebt [Julia Romeo] und [Kleopatra Cäsar?]   *German*
    loves Juliet Romeo and Cleopatra Caesar?

[D] Coordination licenses reduced forms of the coordinands that subordination does not license (Ross 1967; see also article 9 [this volume] (Reich) *Ellipsis*). In VO languages, these are the absence of sentence-medial material in non-initial coordinands (GAPPING); the absence of final material in non-final coordinands (RIGHT-PERIPHERAL DELETION, RPD or "Right Node Raising") and possibly, the absence of initial material in non-initial coordinands (LEFT-PERIPHERAL DELETION, LPD, or "Initial Forward Ellipsis").

Gapping always erases the main V/Aux, possibly plus additional material (see (16); I use overstrike to mark material which is semantically active but not pronounced). RPD usually applies to direct objects (17), but can be extended to other cases (see (72) below).

(16) [Father gave us a car] {and / *because / *when} [mother, ~~gave us~~ a house]

(17) Mary illustrated ~~a long book about lizards~~ {and / *because / *after} Jack edited [a long book about lizards].

The third and most controversial type of coordination ellipsis, LPD, consists in the absence of initial material in the non-initial coordinands ((18), with the bracketing indicated).

(18) Mr. Sing [VP [V wrote] his grandfather a letter] {and / *because / *when} [VP ~~wrote~~ his grandmother a postcard.]

Note that positing LPD in these cases is unnecessary in theories willing to give the group IO+DO the status of a constituent (e.g. Larson 1987).

[E] Coordination is a strong island for long-distance dependencies ("extraction", in the terminology of movement-based grammars, which I adopt here) (19), a fact termed COORDINATE STRUCTURE CONSTRAINT (CSC) in Ross (1967). An element can be extracted from a coordinand only if it is extracted from all other coordinands in the same coordination (in "ACROSS-THE-BOARD" fashion, ATB, in the terminology of Williams 1978).

(19) a. *Who did you see [Mary] and [a friend of t_i]?   *CSC violations*
 b. *Who did Fay [send a letter to t_i] and [forgot all about it]?
 c. *the apples$_i$ that [I cooked t_i] and [Fred ate them].

(20) a. the apples$_i$ that [I cooked t_i] and [Fred ate t]   *ATB extractions*
 b. [Which cat]$_i$ does [Mary hate t_i] and [Fred love t_i]?

In subordination, it is not a problem to extract from the main element only (21a), provided subjacency is respected, while as a general rule subordinated modifiers block extraction (21b). ATB-extraction is not possible in subordinating structures (22) (modulo "parasitic gap" cases, e.g. *which part$_i$ did your attempt to fix t_i actually damage t_i?*. According to Munn 1993, ATB-extractions should be assimilated to parastic gaps).

(21) a. Who do you think [t_i saw Jean alive] after [Jack had visited her]?
 b. *Who do you think [Matt saw Jean alive] after [t_i had visited her]?

(22) a. Tell me [which ice-cream taste]$_i$ [you hated t_i] {and / *because} [your mum always bought t_i]?
 b. *[Which man]$_i$ did you like [the description of t_i] before [seeing a portrait of t_i]?

2.2 What counts as a "coordinator"?

The properties just presented are not only a testbed for any syntactic and semantic theory of coordination, but also a way to define what should really count as a "coordinating element". *And* and *or* give the clearest contrasts with canonical subordinators such as *because*, and will be taken as 'prototypical' coordinators. In English, *and* and *or* can be modified by *both* and *either* respectively, before the first coordinand. *Both/and* and *either/or* pairs will be termed CORRELATIVE COORDINATORS. In other languages, correlative coordinations use repeated forms (Dutch *of/of*, French *ou/ou*, cf. English *either/or*) or coordinators different from the non-correlative *and* (Italian *sia/che* lit. 'be/that', "both/and").

(23) a. *Both* Marc *and* Lucy love opera.
 b. I will meet *either* Carl *or* Susy

Correlative coordination behaves like normal coordination with respect to the equality and invertibility of coordinands (Property [A]), the ellipsis facts ([D]), and extraction ([E]). *Both/and* conjunction, on the other hand, differs with respect to [B] (being limited to two coordinands) and [C], since it cannot apply equally well to all syntactic categories (see e.g. (24), (25)). In addition, *both/and* does not have a cumulative meaning, see Section 4.3.

(24) a. ??Both [Mary is here] and [John is in the office]   *both* IP *and* IP
     b. ??Both [Carl left] and [Mary returned]

(25) a. ??Mary both [has arrived] and [is getting dressed]   *both* I' *and* I'
     b. ??Mary both [had done it] and [would gladly do it again]

The status of *but* in less clear. Contrastive coordination with *but* is restricted: non-sentential adversative clauses with more than two elements are out (**John was tall but slim but strong*); *but* can apply to certain categories only with the help of a support element, *also*, (26). Moreover, adversatives are not symmetrical: (27a) and (27b) are not equivalent in meaning.

(26) a. Matt is slim but (also) strong.
     b. Matt is a clerk but *(also) a friend.
     c. Jerry left early but (*also) Mary stayed in till late.

(27) a. He is ugly, but he is rich.
     b. He is rich, but he is ugly.

These facts place adversatives at the periphery of the coordination proper, or at least of the part which can be analyzed by sentential semantics: the meaning of *but* seems rather to involve pragmatics and discourse. In broad terms, A *but* B could be described as the negation of the expectation of an inference: A leads to expect or infer R, B entails ¬R, and B is in some sense 'more important' than A. However, the notions of 'expectation' and 'importance' can be spelled out in a variety of ways, leading to a range of discourse relations which cannot be examined here (see the notion of "Contrast" in article 13 [Semantics: Theories] (Zeevat) *Rhetorical relations*, Section 3, Steube & Umbach 2001, and especially Winter & Rimon 1994). In the rest of this article, I will mostly concentrate on *and* and *or*.

    Correlative coordinations are often negated in special ways: English *neither/nor*, German *weder/noch*, Italian *né/né*. Given De Morgan's law, *neither/nor* can be seen as a conjunction of negations, with the conjunctor taking wide scope (28b), or a negated disjunction (28c).

(28) a. Leo ate neither the rice nor the carrots. ≡
     b. [Leo did not eat the rice] and [Leo did not eat the carrots]   [¬R] ∧ [¬C]
     c. It is not the case that [[Leo ate the carrots] or [he ate the rice]].   ¬[R∨C]

But can also be associated with negation. In (29), negation associates with that part of the first sentential conjunct which corresponds to the second conjunct (here, the DP *Sue*); the rest is presupposed:

(29) a. Matt didn't call Linda, but Sue
     b. PRESUPPOSITION: ∃x[Matt called x]
        ASSERTION: [x≠Linda] ∧ [x=Sue]

ASYNDESIS, the lack of any overt coordinator in coordination is a common way to connect categories, though typologically it is more used for conjunction than for disjunction. In English, asyndesis is found with sentences and, in some cases, attributive adjectives, but not noun phrases:

(30) a. Theories come, theories go, data stay.
     b. Where do you go? How long will you be away?
     c. He was a tall, slim, pale, goofy-looking boy.
     d. ??Alex played with teddy bears, logo blocks.

It would be an error to think that all cases of sentence juxtaposition are forms of asyndesis: many cases cannot be connected by *and* or *or*, and allow *but* only to the extent the juxtaposed elements can be perceived as contrasting (31).

(31) a. Carla is not a clerk { ; / *and / *or / ?but} she is a nurse.
     b. What are you doing? {*and / *or / *but} stop it!

3 Syntactic and semantic relations among coordinands

3.1 Parallelism

Coordinands have a special relation both with their sentential context and with each other. It can be summarizes in two rules:

(32) All coordinands in a coordination must be able to occur individually in the sentential context in which the whole coordination occurs.

(33) Each coordinand must be formally similar to all other coordinands (William's 1978 "Law of Coordination of Likes")

The main exception to (32) is number agreement: the conjunction of singular DP arguments can trigger plural agreement in the predicate. This is not true of many sentential subjects (34), of nominal conjuncts denoting the same individual (*John and only John was able to answer*), of conjuncts with singular quantifiers (especially *no*: *No plant and no animal was harmed in the production of this film*), and of cases where the conjunction is interpreted as mereological sum (*[Beer and lemonade] is my favorite summer drink*).

(34) [That Karl arrived late] and [that his stay was so short] was/*were quite surprising.

The main issue with respect to (33) is what counts as 'formally similar'. One immediate possibility is that that formal similarity amounts to identity of syntactic categories (Chomsky 1957). This turns out to be neither a necessary nor a sufficient condition: (35) illustrate acceptable cases where two conjuncts have different syntactic status, (36) cases where different categories, which should all apparently satisfy (32), cannot be conjoined, (37) cases where categorial identity is not sufficient, given the different semantic functions of the conjuncts (most examples from Schachter 1977, Sag et al. 1985).

(35) a. [Jack] and [every other student] protested. [PN&DP]
  b. He spoke [fluently] and [with ease]. [Adv&PP]
  c. Jack is [a republican], and [proud of it]. [DP&AdjP]
  d. Pat has been [healthy] and [of sound mind]. [Adj&PP]
  e. That was [a rude remark] and [in very bad taste]. [DP&PP]
  f. Sandy is either [a lunatic] or [under the influence of drugs] [DP or PP]
  g. I am [hoping to get an invitation] and [optimistic about my chances]. [VProg&Adj]
  h. I am neither [an authority on this subject] nor [trying to portray myself as one] [DP&VProg]

(36) a. * [Running] and [to overeat] may be unhealthy. [VPart&AuxP]
  b. ??It's odd [for John to be busy] and [that Helen is idle now] [NonFinCP&FinCP]
  c. * John sang [beautifully] and [a carol]. [Adv&DP]

(37) a. * Mary makes [very little money] and [her own clothes]   [DP&DP]
    b. * John ate with [his mother] and [good appetite].   [DP&DP]
    c. ??John ate [with his mother] and [with good appetite].   [PP&PP]
    d. * [Why do you keep pacing up and down] and [please try to relax]
                                                                 [CP&CP/IP]

Most potential conjunctions of unlike categories (e.g. PP&CP) are ruled out simply because it is impossible to find a single, identical sentential context which can accommodate either category; in this sense, the effect of (33) can often be derived from (32). Cases like (36c) or (37a) can also be excluded via (32) if we assume that *a carol*, unlike *beautifully*, must be selected by a transitive *sing*, and that the *make* of *make money* is lexically different from the *make* of *make clothes*. In the same spirit, (37b) might justify the existence of two *with*s (comitative and manner). The remaining ill-formed cases can be categorized into two classes: syntactic mismatches, like (36a) (and perhaps (37d), if ±DECLARATIVE is among the features that must be formally similar across coordinands; see however (49) below), and semantic mismatches, where the coordinated modifiers do not have the same semantic 'function' ((37c) and (38)), in a sense yet to be formalized.

(38) a. ??He wrote his novel [in Rome] and [in 1980]
    b. ??He wrote [carefully] and [in the metro]

Unlike syntactic mismatches, semantic ones can often be improved by giving the conjuncts the semantics of interrogative elements (39), or simply changing the coordinator (40) and providing a suitable context. In some cases, e.g. (41), sentential coordinations seem to be ruled out at a purely pragmatic level, as a failure to sustain a common discourse topic, possibly in violation of the Gricean maxim of Relevance (see article 15 [Semantics: Interfaces] (Simons) *Implicature*).

(39) a. [Where] and [when] did he write his novel?   *cf. (38a)*
    b. [How] and [where] did he work?   *cf. (38b)*

(40) a. Since in 1980 he lived in New York, he must have written it either [in Rome] or [in 1980].
    b. I can work {either [carefully] or [in the metro] / [in the metro], but also [carefully]}

(41) ??[I have brown hair] and [land mines can kill moles]

Since many cases of coordination of unlike categories are found in predicative position, Sag et al. (1985) propose that (33) can be satisfied by giving the conjoinable categories the feature [+PREDICATIVE], and making the similarity requirement sensitive to this feature. One open question is how this approach fares with non-copular verbs such as *remember* (in *He remembered [the appointment] and [that it was important to be on-time]*).

The notion of formal similarity can be approached in model-theoretic semantics by requiring identity of semantic types among the coordinands. In a flexible type system like that of Partee & Rooth (1983), Partee (1987), a proper name, natively of type *e*, must be lifted to the type of generalized quantifiers (<*et*>*t*, the set of all the properties that apply to the individual named) in order to be able to appear in coordinations such as (42) (on Type-Shifting, see article 8 [Semantics: Interfaces] (de Hoop) *Type shifting*). The license to coordinate predicates advocated by Sag et al. (1985) would translate in this system as a license to coordinate *et*-type elements (modulo satisfying (32), an additional condition still needed to rule out, e.g. **the [man$_{<et>}$] and [tall$_{<et>}$]*).

(42) [John]$_{e \Rightarrow <et>t}$ and [every other student]$_{<et>t}$ left the room.

A second semantic constraint on DP coordinands has to do with *monotonicity*. Recall that a determiner is upward/downward monotonic on one of its arguments (the *restrictor* or the *main predicate*) if it supports inferences from the denotation of the original argument to, respectively, a *generalization* or a *specification* of that denotation (see the article 4 [Semantics: Noun Phrases and Verb Phrases] (Keenan) *Quantifiers*, on Generalized Quantifiers, GQ). For instance, *at least 3* is upward but not downward monotonic because it validates the inference in (43a), but not that in (43b). *No* and *fewer than three* has the opposite pattern. Given these properties, holds (cf. Barwise & Cooper 1981, 4.10).

(43) a. At-least-3 (R,P∩Q) ⇒ At-least-3 (R,P):
   "At least three people walk" ⇒ "At least three people move"
   b. At-least-3 (R,P) ⇏ At-least-3 (R,P∩Q):
   "At least three people move" ⇏ "At least three people walk"

(44) Two DPs can be coordinated with *and/or* iff they have the same direction of monotonicity (upward or downward) over their predicate. They can (usually) be coordinated with *but* iff their monotonicity is mixed.

(45) and (46) illustrate. The monotonicity on the restrictor (R in (43)) is irrelevant: for instance, *at least 3* and *all* are upward and downward entailing in their first arguments.

(45) a. [All the children] {and/??but} [at least three women] attended
the meeting. ⇑,⇑
b. [No children] {and / ??but} [less then three women] attended the
meeting. ⇓,⇓

(46) a. [All the teachers] {??and / but} [no students] attended the meeting. ⇑, ⇓
b. [Few students] {??and / but} [every teacher] attended the meeting. ⇓, ⇑

Note, however, that proper names and simple indefinites are upward monotonic just like *more than three*, yet *but* cannot take these DPs as its second argument in (47).

(47) Less than three students but (also) {*John / *a friend / more than three professors} attended the meeting.

Specific and non-specific indefinites can often coordinate, suggesting that they have (or can be type-shifted to) the same semantic type.

(48) a. I am looking for [a pen my mother gave me] and [some sheets of paper to
take a few notes]. *a specific pen, any old sheet.*
b. To build this tower, all I need is [metal] and [the project I wrote last year].

Interrogative and declarative sentences cannot usually be coordinated (see (37d)), but counterexamples exist, with restricted orders (49), (50), suggesting that this might be a semantic more than a syntactic problem.

(49) a. [The guy finally comes back] and [who do you think he meets in the
street on his very first day]?
b. *[Who do you think the guy meets in the street on his first day] and [he
had finally come back]

(50) [I heard a noise], but [what was it?]

Imperatives and declaratives (in this order) can also be coordinated, but with a semantics closely resembling *if/then* clauses (48). These SEMANTICALLY ASYM-METRIC COORDINATION have been shown by Culicover & Jackendoff (1997) to have mixed properties of coordination and modification, including the impossibility of more than two coordinands within a single coordination of this type (52).

(51) a. (Take) another step, and I shoot.
       "If you take another step, I shoot"
    b. Come out slowly, or you are dead.
       "If you don't come out slowly, you are dead"

(52) a. You drink another beer, and I am leaving.   *conditional semantics OK*
    b. You drink another beer, Bill eats more pretzels, and I am leaving.
                                                        conditional semantics ??

The most extreme case of asymmetric coordination is of course SINGLE-CONJUNCT COORDINATION, which is restricted to sentential material ((53), (54)). Since the missing coordinand is always initial this structure is strong evidence for an asymmetric structure for coordination, but its formal semantics and its discourse properties are largely unexplored.

(53) a. And so it was that [...] I saw no more of it than this sort of luminous panel
       ... *Marcel Proust*
    b. And the winners are: ...

(54) A: So I took the money and ran.
    B: {But / And} how were you thinking to get away with it?

A final property of coordination is the possibility to modify even non-sentential conjuncts (mostly, non-initial ones) with adverbials such as *maybe, probably, possibly*, which normally apply at sentence-level (55). This has been taken as evidence for a conjunction reduction analysis of coordination (Camacho 2004), but these modifiers can appear equally well in the subjects of *cumulative* predicates (56), the least likely candidates for reduction analyzes.

(55) I will call Luis, Matt and {maybe / possibly / probably} Jorge.

(56) a. Cases [A], [B] and [probably C] will all be identical.
    b. Sue, Matt and probably Bill will get together for lunch.

3.2 The Coordinate Structure Constraint

The Coordinate Structure Constrain (CSC) (Ross 1967) and the possibility of Across-the-Board (ATB) extraction have received a great deal of attention in the syntactic literature, also in relation to the phenomenon of parasitic gaps, which seem to behave in certain respects in ATB-fashion (Chomsky 1986, Munn 1993). The constraints can be stated as in (57).

(57) In a coordinate structure
    a. no conjunct may be moved;
    b. nor may any element contained in a conjunct be moved out of that conjunct.

A possible approach is to derive the CSC from the requirement of syntactic and semantic identity of the coordinands, i.e. (33). The intuition is that a coordinand containing a gap is not of the same semantic/syntactic category as one with no gap; this mismatch would block coordination. This solution is already sketched in Schachter (1977), but finds a natural implementation in theories where the presence of a gap changes the category of the coordinand in which it appears. One example is Combinatorial Categorial Grammar (CCG, Steedman 1990, 2000), which extends standard Categorial Grammar by adding to the main rule of function application some rules of *function composition* and *type raising*, e.g. (58). The rule for coordination (slightly simplified) is (59).

(58) a. FORWARD COMPOSITION ($>B$)
       $X/Y\ Y/Z \Rightarrow_B X/Z$
   b. SUBJECT TYPE RAISING ($>T$)
       $NP \Rightarrow_T S/(S\backslash NP)$

(59) *and* := $(X''\backslash X)/X'$

X, X' and X'' are variables over functions of the same type. $(X''\backslash X)/X'$ is a function that takes an expression on the right (forward slash) of the *and* and returns a function that takes a expression on the left (backward slash) of *and* to return a third expression of the same category. In this framework, an ATB extraction like *apples that I cook and you eat* is analyzed by type-raising the subject to a Generalized Quantifier meaning (see (60a)), then use (59) to compose subject and verb, giving (60b).

(60) a. apples   that   I   cook   and   you
       N   (N\N)/(S/NP) S/(S\NP) (S\NP)/NP ((S/NP)\(S/NP))/(S/NP) S/(S\NP)
       eat
       (S\NP)/NP

b. apples that   [I cook]   and   [you eat]
   N   (N\N)/(S/NP) S/NP   ((S/NP)\(S/NP))/(S/NP)   S/NP

When an object is present in one of the conjuncts, it combines with the verb, blocking the possibility for the subject and verb to compose. This leads to a bracketing like (61), where *and* can no longer apply. Essentially the same analysis has been put forth in Phillips (2003), in a processing-based model of grammar.

(61) *apples that [I cook]$_{<S/NP>}$ and [you [eat them]]$_S$

The relation between the possibility of ATB extractions and the categorial identity of the extraction sites is reinforced by the observation that ATB extraction is possible also in *equative* copular constructions:

(62) Which city$_i$ is [your opinion of t_i] [my opinion of t_i]?   (Heycock & Kroch 1999)

Vice-versa, exceptions to the ATB have been reported in cases where the semantics of coordination seems less symmetrical, closer to temporal/causal subordination, e.g. (63):

(63) What did you [go out] and [say *t*]   *cf.* "*what did you go out to say?*"

A balanced solution to the CSC problem should also cover the partial acceptability of other cases, e.g. (64), and take into account the potential role of ellipsis, discussed in the next sections.

(64) A document [of which]$_i$ he already knows [the content *t*], and [whether it could be useful for him].

3.3 Parallelism and Conjunction Reduction

The issue of parallelism among coordinands has obviously strong connections with the possibility for some material inside the conjuncts to be missing. For instance, if LPD is possible, many of the apparent coordinations of unlike categories seen in (35) can be reduced to coordinations of likes plus ellipsis under identity (65). The ellipsis must be possible only under strict identity of lexical meaning and argument structure, or cases like (66) would be licensed.

(65) a. Jack [$_{I'}$ is a republican], and [$_{I'}$ ~~is~~ proud of it]
 b. Pat has [$_{VP}$ been healthy] and [$_{VP}$ ~~been~~ of sound mind].
 c. [$_{IP}$ I am hoping to get an invitation] and [$_{IP}$ ~~I am~~ optimistic about my chances].

(66) John [ate with his mother] and {*[~~ate~~ a sandwich] / ??[~~ate~~ with good appetite]}.

Extending this approach, it is possible to use ellipsis to obtain the effect of full Conjunction Reduction:

(67) a. John saw Mary and ~~John saw~~ Jill   LPD
 b. John ~~saw Mary~~ and Bill saw Mary   RPD
 c. John saw ~~Mary~~ and ~~John~~ greeted Mary.   RPD+LPD

A radical version of this approach holds that coordination applies *only* at the level of the sentences: any apparent coordination of smaller constituents would be the result of reduction rules, either syntactic (particularly in early generative grammar: Chomsky 1957, Gleitman 1965, Lakoff & Peters 1969, but see more recent applications in van Oirsouw 1987, Camacho 2004) or at some level of "logical forms" (Schein 1997). This approach makes sense of the sentential adverbs in (55), (56) above, but requires agreement and other processes to apply after the reduction rules, to get the correct form of verbs, reflexives, etc. Note that restricting coordination to IP/CP still does not allow us to treat conjunction as the $\wedge_{\langle t,t \rangle}$ connective of propositional logic, since imperative and interrogative IP/CPs, whose meaning is only indirectly based on truth values, can also be coordinated. Cumulative predicates remain a problem in this solution, but can be tackled by less radical ellipsis-based theories (e.g. Wilder 1994, 1997), according to which coordination can take place only at "major categories", minimally argumental DPs and IPs. In this view, (12a) above would not involve reduction, but (12b), (12d), (12e) and (13) would. Agreement is not a problem in this approach, but scope is, since *a rich man's friends and relatives often fight* derives from *[[a rich man]$_i$'s friends] and [[a rich man]$_j$'s relatives]* ..., where the indefinites would normally be associated to distinct discourse referents, unlike in the reduced clause. I will return to this point in Section 4.5.

All the variants of the reduction idea can be implemented in the so-called TRIDIMENSIONAL approach (Goodall 1987, Muadz 1991, Moltmann 1992), in which the coordinands are represented as different, parallel syntactic "planes" (sets of phrase markers), which are linearized at PF. In this system, (68a) is one of the possible linearizations of the set of planes (68b), if planes span the whole main clause. Adverbs like *respectively* can be seen as filters on the set of admissible planes.

(68) a. John and Mary met Bill and Sue.

    b. Plane 1: John met Bill   *Planes 1+2 form the "respectively" reading*
       Plane 2: Mary met Sue
       Plane 3: John met Sue
       Plane 4: Mary met Bill

3.4 Gapping, RPD and LPD

The correct treatment of Gapping, RPD and LPD also depends on the role of reduction. If coordination is always at sentence level, a gapped structure like (69) must be the conjunction of two full sentences with one verb unpronounced. In a 3D approach with parallel planes, the gap is generated by the procedure that linearizes the planes ((69) would come from Planes 3 and 4 in (68b)).

(69) John met Sue and Mary, Bill.

Systems in which constituents smaller than clauses can be coordinated see the missing elements in gapping or RPD as constituents that have been syntactically 'factored' by means of movement rules or equivalent devices (sometimes in partial violation of the ATB requirement, see Johnson 1994), and which are thus shared across all coordinands. To illustrate, in CCG an RPD like *Harry found and I cooked the mushrooms* is obtained type-raising the two subjects via the rule in (58b), then combining each of them with their unsaturated verbs via Forward Composition, in (58a). The result is conjoined and applied to the common object (70). One positive aspect of this approach, in contrast to ellipsis, is its potential to capture cases where an anaphor in the shared object is linked to material in each coordinand (71).

(70) [[[$_{<s/np>}$ Harry found] and [$_{<s/np>}$ I cooked]][the mushrooms]]
(71) [Sue$_i$ took] and [Tim$_j$ framed] [two astonishing pictures of themselves$_{i+j}$]

One problem for this analysis (and indeed, for any non ellipsis-based analysis) is that the missing material in the left coordinand can be a subpart of a morphologically complex word (72a), and needs not be a constituent (72b).

(72) a. [Pre-~~processing~~] and [post-processing]
     b. [a [positively ~~charged~~ ~~electrode~~] and [a [negatively charged] electrode]

Gapping is obtained in CCG by type raising the subject in the right conjunct and combining it with the conjunction, first, then with the remnant (73). The resulting category is an object which is missing a transitive verb ((S\NP)/NP) to become a sentence.

(73) Harry eats beans, [[and Barry,] rice]$_{S\backslash((S\backslash NP)/NP)}$

The first conjunct, a sentence, is then decomposed by means of a new rule, which factors it in a transitive verb plus a function that takes this verb to become a sentence (74). This latter part can then be coordinated with the gapped conjunct, using a conjunction rule slightly more complex than (59). The system works with more than two coordinands, but the way the coordinator is combined with the pre-gap element in (73) could be problematic when the gap is more deeply embedded (see (75), or (72b)).

(74) Harry eats beans$_{(S\backslash NP)/NP\ S\backslash((S\backslash NP)/NP))}$ [[and Barry,] rice]$_{S\backslash((S\backslash NP)/NP)}$.

(75) Either [Sue bought all the wine] or [[Jill ~~bought~~ the red one] and [Matt ~~bought~~ the white one]].

4 Semantics

In many languages, including all the European ones, the same lexical operator is used to coordinate IPs, CPs, VPs, DPs, AdjPs and PPs. In other languages, different words are used for the conjunction of DPs and 'eventive' categories (IP, VP), but disjunction tends to be quite uniform, and finer distinctions in conjunction are extremely rare (Payne 1985, Haspelmath 2007). Thus, an important goal in a semantic theory that assumes the possibility of coordinating non-sentential material without reduction is to define meanings for *and* and *or* that are sufficiently uniform across categories, or have at least a uniform core which can be extended in special cases.

4.1 Propositional coordination

Propositional logic offers a model for the meaning of a binary coordination of propositions, elements with an extension in D_t ({t,f}, the set of truth values). Starting from the truth value of propositions P and Q, the truth value of P COORD

Q can be derived from Tab. 4.1, with $and_{t<tt>}$ mapped to $\wedge$, $or_{t<tt>}$ to $\vee$ or to $\neq$ ("exclusive or", XOR), and *neither/nor* to $\downarrow$ (NAND, Quine's *dagger*). Coordinations with more then two members can be reduced to binary coordinations, either assuming the syntax in (9), or a flat syntactic structure plus a process of semantic interpretation that involves semantic 'Currying' (see Winter 2007).

Tab. 4.1: Truth table for binary logical connectives

P	Q	P∧Q	P∨Q	P≠Q	P↓Q
0	0	0	0	0	1
0	1	0	1	1	0
1	0	0	1	1	0
1	1	1	1	0	0

Alternatively, in an intensional framework in which propositions are treated as sets of possible worlds, conjunction and disjunction can be treated as *intersection* and *union*, respectively, over the sets of worlds denoted by each conjunct. While quite intuitive, this approach is not free of problems; see the discussion in Section 4.5.

(76) a. ⟦John left⟧ = {w : John left at world w}
 b. ⟦Mary stayed⟧ = {w : Mary stayed at world w}
 c. ⟦John left and Mary stayed⟧ = {w : John left at world w} ∩ {w : Mary stayed at world w}
 d. ⟦John left or Mary stayed⟧ = {w : John left at world w} ∪ {w : Mary stayed at world w}

The mapping between coordinators and logical connectors is by no means biunique: non restrictive relatives such as *Jack, who is British, likes anchovies* lack the word *and* but logically entail sentential conjunctions (*Jack is British and he likes anchovies*). Conversely, sentential *but* (and subordinating conjunctions like *since, because, though*, etc.) have the logical meaning of $\wedge$, but add elements of meaning of their own, at the level of presuppositions, discourse inferences, etc. Even the sentential conjunctor *and* has more to its meaning than pure $\wedge$: it reduces to the logical meaning in (77a), but in a conjunction of events like (77b) it adds a temporal dependence of the n-th conjunct from the previous ones which can imply a causal link (so *Bill shot and Calvin died* is interpreted differently from *Calvin died and Bill shot*).

(77) a. [Bill is a doctor] and [Jack is a lawyer].
 b. [Martha arrived] and [Bertha left]

The *or* of natural language is frequently interpreted *exclusively*, i.e. as ≠ in Tab. (4.1). *John will come to pick you up, or Jack will* suggests that John and Jack will not come together. This tendency is strengthened by the use of *either/or*: *either P or Q* seems to mean (P∨Q)∧¬(P∧Q). However, this effect does not require that *or* be logically interpreted as ≠, but can be attributed to the effect of pragmatic scales, and ultimately to the Grician principles of cooperation (see article 15 [Semantics: Interfaces] (Simons) *Implicature*, and Levinson 2000). Let's assume that *or* is inclusive, i.e. that it is mapped onto ∨. Since in upward monotonic contexts P∧Q entails P∨Q, if a speaker knows that P is true and Q is true it would be more informative for him or her to say *P and Q* rather than *P or Q*. It follows that an addressee who hears *P or Q* and has no reason to think that the speaker is not cooperative will assume that the speaker has not uttered *P and Q* because he or she has no evidence that P∧Q, or has evidence to the contrary. The hearer concludes that P∨Q is true but P∧Q might not be, whence the impression that *or* is exclusive. In downward entailing linguistic environments such as the scope of negation or the antecedent of conditionals, the implication from *and* to *or* no longer holds. In these environments, the intuition that *(either/)or* is exclusive vanishes: (78), for instance, does in no way suggest that if you win with both dice and roulette the casino will be any less watchful.

(78) If you always win either at dice or roulette the casino will keep a watchful eye on you.

The idea that *or* is logically exclusive is also incompatible with a binary branching analysis of multiple disjunctions. Suppose that the coordinands $C_1, \ldots, C_n$ are all true. If C_1 *or* ...*or* C_{n-1} *or* C_n has the nested structure in (79), interpreted as a sequence of binary exclusive disjunctions, the resulting global disjunction will be true if n is odd and false if n is even. This sensitivity to parity is not only unknown in other syntactic and semantic phenomena, but also in contrast with the intuition that multiple disjunctions should be true if at least one disjunct is true.

(79) [C_1 or [...or [C_{n-1} or C_n]...]]

4.2 Coordination of non-propositional categories

The coordination of constituents that do not have a denotation in D_t cannot be carried out with the tools of propositional logic. If the extension of a predicate is of type *et* (a subset of the domain of entities, D), *and* and *or* in (80a) and (80b) must denote *set intersection* and *set union*, respectively, much as in the propositional case (76c) and (76d) This correctly renders (80) as (81).

(80) a. Martha is [short and dark]
     b. Roger is [in the kitchen] or [in the bathroom]

(81) a. *Marta'* ∈ [⟦short⟧ ∩ ⟦dark⟧]
     b. *Roger'* ∈ [⟦in_kitchen⟧ ∪ ⟦in_bathroom⟧]

But this method won't do in (82a) and (b): names denote members of D, and union and intersection only apply to sets.

(82) a. Martha and Roger had dinner.
     b. Martha or Roger will pick you up.

However, if proper names are treated as the set of their properties at a given index (i.e. ⟦John⟧ = λP.P(*John'*)), namely as generalized quantifiers, the intersection and union approach can be retained (83), and indeed generalized to the coordination of any element of 't-*conjoinable*' semantic type, defined in (84) (cf. Partee & Rooth 1983. Intuitively, these are the types that end in a truth value).

(83) a. *have_dinner'* ∈ [λP.P(*Martha'*)] ∩ [λQ.Q(*Roger'*)]
     b. *pick_you_up'* ∈ [λP.P(*Martha'*)] ∪ [λQ.Q(*Roger'*)]

(84) a. t is a conjoinable type
     b. if β is a conjoinable type, then for all α, αβ is a conjoinable type.

Generalized conjunction and disjunction are defined recursively in (85) and (86), where τ is a t-conjoinable type, and X⊓Y, X⊔Y are shorthands for two binary composition operations (i.e. (⊓Y(X))(Y) and (⊔Y(X))(Y)). ⊓ and ⊔ can also be considered as the *meet* and *join* operators of a Boolean algebra ⟨D_τ, ⊓, ⊔, ¬⟩ (where ¬_{<ττ>} is the complementation operator defined in a way analogous to (85), (86)), hence the name of *Boolean* conjunction/disjunction for these operators (Keenan & Faltz 1985, Winter 2001).

(85) ⊓_{τ(ττ)} =
     a. ∧_{t<tt>}   if τ = t
     b. λX_τ λY_τ λZ_α [X(Z) ⊓_{β<ββ>} Y(Z)]   if τ = αβ

(86) $\sqcup_{\tau(\tau\tau)} =$
  a. $V_{t<tt>}$ if $\tau = t$
  b. $\lambda X_\tau \lambda Y_\tau \lambda Z_\alpha [X(Z) \sqcup_{\beta<\beta\beta>} Y(Z)]$ if $\tau = \alpha\beta$

The definitions above yield full distributivity for cases such as (82a), which receives the analysis in (87).

(87) $[\lambda P.P(Martha') \sqcap \lambda Q.Q(Roger')](have\_dinner') = have\_dinner'(Martha') \wedge have\_dinner'(Roger')$

This might seems a way to replicate Full Conjunction Reduction semantically, but important differences exist. For instance, conjunction reduction would tend to derive the expressions on the left in (88a) and (88b) from those on the right, despite the fact that the two are not equivalent. In GQ-theory, however, a quantificational DP takes its predicate as an argument: (88b), with generalized conjunction of the predicates on the left side, is translated as (89), which λ-conversion reduces to the correct meaning.

(88) a. Not every woman sang and danced ≠ not every woman sang and not every woman danced.
  b. Some woman sang and danced ≠ [some woman]$_i$ sang and [some woman]$_i$ danced.

(89) $\lambda P \exists y[woman'(y) \wedge P(y)](\lambda x[sing'(x) \wedge dance'(x)]) = \exists y[woman'(y) \wedge sing'(y) \wedge dance'(y)]$

However, the meaning of *Martha and Roger are a couple* is not obtained in this analysis, and requires further extensions.

4.3 Cumulative and distributive readings

The problem posed by cumulative predicates was know at least since Medieval times (in the work of Peter of Spain, *Summulae Logicales*, William of Ockham *Summa Logica* and others, see Lasersohn 1995). In the modern tradition of logical semantics it is customary to distinguish three types of predicates over plural arguments (conjunctions, or simple plural DPs): CUMULATIVE, that always apply to their argument as a 'plurality' (or 'bunch' or 'collection': the names vary considerably in the literature) (90a); DISTRIBUTIVE, that directly apply to the atomic individuals (or *atoms*) that are members of the plurality (90b); and MIXED, that can apply to either (90c) (on these, see article 7 [Semantics: Noun Phrases and Verb Phrases] (Lasersohn) *Mass nouns and plurals*). Mixed predicates give rise to a semantic ambiguity: (90c) can mean that the individual salary of John and Mary is $5000 or that their global salary is $5000.

(90) {John and Mary / My two guests}
    a. ...are a couple/live together/met in Paris.
    b. ...are teachers/live in Paris/were born in 1972.
    c. ...lifted a piano/earn $5000 per month/weigh 140 kg.

Boolean $and_{\tau<\tau\tau>}$ is perfectly adequate for the arguments of distributive predicates and for the distributive reading of mixed ones, but inadequate for cumulative readings, which seem to require a different operator, frequently referred to as NON-BOOLEAN *and*. A minimal requirement for this *and* (written and^{bunch} here) is that when applied to *e*-type arguments it takes two individuals and returns a plurality that has just those individuals as members: $and^{bunch}_{e<ee>} = \lambda x \lambda y. x \oplus y$ (here I use $\oplus$, from Link 1983, for the operation that combines two plural or singular individuals into a plural one. I also assume that $a \oplus b = a$ iff $a = b$, and that the pluralization of an *et*-type predicate is the closure under $\oplus$).

A simple account for (90) is that cumulative predicates (or readings of predicates) require their conjoined arguments to contain and^{bunch}, while distributive predicates (or readings) require and^{bool}. The existence of a link between the type of coordinator used and the distributivity pattern is confirmed by the fact that correlative coordinators such as *both/and* or *as well as* can only occur with distributive predicates:

(91) a. *Both Uta and Frida are a couple/live together/met in Paris.
    b. *Martha as well as Sue are a couple/live together/met in Paris.

In general, however, the cumulative/distributive distinction cannot be reduced to an ambiguity of *and*, since its effects are replicated with simple plural DPs: the distributive reading of *approximately 2 million Italians weigh over 100Kg* simply cannot be reduced, syntactically or semantically, to *Ugo weighs over 100Kg, Marco weighs over 100 kg.*, ... On the contrary, any solution that applies to plurals should carry over to simple *and* cases, provided such cases are able to form pluralities, as and^{bunch} does. Unfortunately, the application of and^{bunch} to more complex conjunctions is not straightforward. In (92), and^{bunch} can apply only if *or* takes scope over *and*, giving (92b) (see Section 4.5.).

(92) a. [Mary] and [[the postman] or [the milkman]] met. *(see Winter 2001, 31)*
     b. [Mary and^{bunch} the postman] or [Mary and^{bunch} the milkman] met.

Moreover, some cumulative predicates may apply to conjunctions of GQs as well (93), so either *and^{bunch}* must be extended to the GQ domain or some operation must derive individuals from these DPs before and$_{e<ee>}$ is applied.

(93) a. [Some women] and [some men] met.
     b. [Less than four women] and [less than five men] met.

Hoeksema (1988) argues for the second solution. *Every boy and every girl met* would undergo quantifier raising to give (94). Apart from syntactic concerns (the CSC is violated), this approach has been shown to overgenerate.

(94) [every boy *x* [every girl *y* [*x* and$_{e<ee>}$ *y* met]]]

Pursuing the first route, Hoeksema (1983) derives (93a) by extracting *minimal properties* from each GQ and joining them. This is problematic for (93b) and other downward-entailing GQ, which have no minimal elements. A possible solution might be to assume that the GQs in (93b) do have a (pragmatically derived) bottom (so (93b) is interpreted as *some but <4 women and some but <5 men met*). Note that when a bottom is excluded, as in (95a), *and* seems to be obligatorily interpreted as *and^{bool}*: the predicate distributes over the conjunct, if possible (95a), and is ill-formed, otherwise (95b).

(95) a. [No boys] and [no girls] met ≡ [No boys] met and^{bool} [no girls] met
     b. *[No boy] and [no girl] met.

Extensions of non-Boolean *and* have been used also for those predicate conjunctions in which an analysis in terms of intersection or union/bunch-formation does not work (Krifka 1990). (96) illustrates the case with DP restrictions, (97) with primary predicates and modifiers.

(96) a. An ill-matched [man] and [woman] always fight together.
     b. Twenty [linguists] and [philosophers] came to the party.

(97) a. (As the shot was heard), the ducks [dived] and [flew away].
     b. The guests were [in the kitchen] and [in the swimming pool]
     c. "A" and "B" are [a vowel] and [a consonant].
     d. A [red] and [green] flag

The conjunction in (96a) (possible only in some languages, see Heycock & Zamparelli 2005) denotes a set of man-woman couples; (96b) seems to refer to a group of 20 people containing at least one linguist, at least one philosopher, and possibly people who are both (the real intersective reading salient in *Chomsky, the famous linguist and philosopher*). The incompatible predicates in (97a–c) apply to different subsets of the denotation of the subject; *red* and *green* in (97d) apply to different parts of the flag. Link (1983) incorporates this notion of 'part', or 'subset' in the semantics of predicate non-Boolean conjunction, and proposes (98). This gives to (97c) the meaning in (99).

(98) P_{et} and^{bunch} Q_{et} = $\lambda x \exists y, k[x = y \oplus k \wedge P(y) \wedge Q(k)]$

(99) $\exists x,y[\text{``A''} \oplus \text{``B''} = x \oplus y \wedge vowel'(x) \wedge consonant'(y)]$

Krifka (1990) attempts to generalize (98) into (100), which is however not a biconditional.

(100) $\alpha_{\sigma t}(\beta_\sigma) \wedge \alpha'_{\sigma t}(\beta'_\sigma) \rightarrow \alpha_{\sigma t} \oplus \alpha'_{\sigma t}(\beta_\sigma \oplus \beta'_\sigma)$.

The strength of the generalization expressed by (99)/(100) and its empirical base have been criticized by Winter (2001) and others. Without further constraints (e.g. a pragmatic requirement that the choice of parts must be independent of the properties predicated of them), (100) ends up supporting the truth of e.g. *The house is small and large* (i.e. a small part of it is small, the rest is large). Moreover, the class of predicates that are judged non contradictory when substituted for *red* and *green* in (97d) seems extremely small, perhaps restricted to adjectives that can double as nominals (Lasersohn 1995). However, the empirical problem remains in full force for primary predicates.

It is important to stress at this point that, regardless its exact formulation, the idea of two versions of *and* is far from ideal. Typologically, there do not seem to be languages that lexically distinguish a Boolean and a bunch-forming *and* (Payne 1985); second, the putative ambiguity does not affect verb agreement, nor the possibility of inserting sentential adverbials, as seen in (56) above; third, if the choice of *and* within the subject depends on the predicate, conjoined predicates like those in (101a) pose a dilemma: *meet* should select *and*^{bunch}, *have a beer each* the Boolean *and*. A conjunction reduction analysis as in (101b) cannot help, since in such an analysis elements can be elided or 'unified' only under strict lexical identity (so as not to allow (37)/(66)), a condition that does not obtain here due to the two *ands*.

(101) a. John and Mary [met at the bar] and [had a beer each].
b. John and^{bunch} Mary [met at the bar] and$_{t<tt>}$ ~~John and^{bool} Mary~~ [had a beer each].

One way to obtain the facts in (96) and (97) with a single *and* might be to make its basic definition more general and appeal to syntactic or semantic filters to exclude unwanted meanings. Heycock & Zamparelli (2005) propose a definition for *and* as SET-PRODUCT (102) (similar to Krifka's):

(102) P_{et} and^{sp} Q_{et} = SP(P,Q) = $\lambda x \forall y, k[y \in P \land k \in Q \rightarrow x = y \oplus k]$

This definition has the following properties: given two sets of atoms P and Q and a set K = SP(P,Q), the set of atoms in K is P∩Q; if K is pluralized, we obtain the correct denotation for conjunctions like (96b), (97b); if applied to two *e*-type individuals lifted to the corresponding singleton properties, and then down again (i.e. $j \Rightarrow \{j\}$, $m \Rightarrow \{m\}$, SP($\{j\},\{m\}$) = $\{j \oplus m\} \Rightarrow j \oplus m$) SP constructs a plurality, much as *and*$_{e<ee>}$; if extended to t-conjoinable type and applied to upward entailing GQ, it returns their intersection. Thus, a single operation plus a set of type-shifting rules and filters can perform the main operations attributed to Boolean and non-Boolean *and*.

A similar attempt for a unified, non-Boolean semantics of conjunction has been done within an *event-based* framework in Lasersohn (1995). Here, sentences are taken to denote not truth values but the sets of EVENTUALITIES which the sentences describe, while predicates denote functions from eventualities to the sets of groups/individuals that satisfy the predicate in that eventuality. This leads to the definition in (103):

(103) $e \in [\![\text{[DP VP]}]\!]$ iff $[\![\text{DP}]\!] \in [\![\text{VP}]\!](e)$

In this system, the conjunction of two individuals a and b is {a, b} (corresponding to the plurality a⊕b), so *and* is set formation, while the conjunction of sentences S^1 and S^2, true of eventualities e_1 and e_2, is $\{e^1, e^2\}$. Working with eventualities gives Lasersohn the possibility to analyze sentence-final *together* (as in *John and Mary lifted a piano together*, as well as complex temporal cases like *The air was alternately cold and wet*.

Another approach that makes use of eventualities and thematic roles but assumes full Conjunction Reduction at the level of Logical Forms is described in Schein (1997). This is one of the few semantic systems in which even cumulative semantic predicates are treated, in a sense, distributively: *Mary and John met* is rendered (informally) as:

(104) There is a meeting event *e* such that Mary is an agent of *e* and John is an agent of *e*.

As in in other systems that use theta roles in the logical representation, two problems arise: how the compositional construction of the meaning representation is performed, and how, in the case of multiple eventualities, the right theta role is connected to the right eventuality. On the other hand, it is fair to say that the use of both individuals and events gives to these theory an expressive power which might turn out to be necessary for any theory of coordination that attempts to tackle times and events.

On a completely different route, Winter (1996, 2001) proposes a theory of Boolean conjunction tightly integrated with general plurality, distributivity and scope. His claim is that a single, Boolean meaning for *and* and *or* (in (85) and (86)), is sufficient for all types of coordination, once cumulativity effects are handled by a set of "type-shifting" and "type-fitting" operators (the former applying freely, the latter, only to resolve type mismatches in the derivation).

4.4 Embedded coordinations

The fact that a DP conjunction can have among its conjuncts a plural DP, including another conjunction, raises the question whether the semantics of structures like (105) is 'flat', as in (105a) or rather 'nested', as in (105b) (assume that ⟦cows⟧ = {$Lilly'$, $Brown'$}, ⟦pigs⟧ = {$Rosy'$, $Babe'$} and that ⟦the cows⟧ = ⟦Lilly and Brown⟧ = $Lilly' \oplus Brown'$). If plurals are rendered as sets, (105a) would correspond to a treatment of and^{bunch} as set union, and the denotation of a plural count DP would always be a set of atoms; (105b) would correspond to a treatment of and^{bunch} as set formation, with the result that plural denotations could include both atoms and pluralities. In the 'union/flat' view, *and* is associative (since $\{a\} \cup (\{b\} \cup \{c\}) = (\{a\} \cup \{b\}) \cup \{c\}$), in the 'set-formation/nesting' view, it isn't (since $\{a,\{b,c\}\} \neq \{\{a,b\},c\}$).

(105) The cows and the pigs
 a. $Lilly' \oplus Brown'' \oplus Rosy' \oplus Babe'$ flat structure (equivalent to set union)
 b. $(Lilly' \oplus Brown') \oplus (Rosy' \oplus Babe')$ nested structure (equivalent to set formation)

Nested pluralities are introduced in the grammar by *and* (and possibly by the pluralization of group nouns, e.g. *committees*, if group nouns in the singular denote a sort of plurality), but their presence has widespread consequences for the denotation of all predicates and modifiers, and expands the list of semantic types needed by the grammar. This additional complexity pays for empirical coverage, since nested structures can easily distinguish between (106a) (historically false) and (106b) (true, in the bracketing indicated) (Hoeksema 1983).

(106) a. Blücher, Wellington and Napoleon fought against each other near Waterloo.

b. [[Blücher] and [Wellington]] and [Napoleon]] fought against each other near Waterloo.

Notice that the fact that (106a) might have the 'nested' syntactic structure shown above in (9) does not give rise to a nested semantics (see Winter 2007): (106a) can only be interpreted distributively to the level of individuals, namely as a battle with three mutual enemies. On the other hand, the syntactic bracketing of (106b) does correspond to semantic nesting. The 'nested' view is challenged in Schwarzschild (1996), who points out that although a verb like *separate* seems to cut along the line provided by the two plural denotation in the nested theory (so that (107a), from Landman 1989a, is not equivalent to (107b)), this effect is merely a pragmatic implicature which can be reversed by means of modifiers: (108a) and (b) are equivalent, and each entails the corresponding sentence in (107).

(107) a. The cards below seven and the cards from seven up were separated.
b. The cards below ten and the cards from ten up were separated.

(108) a. The cards <7 and the cards ≥7 were separated *by color*
b. The cards <10 and the cards ≥10 were separated *by color*

On the basis of this and similar examples, Schwarzschild argues for a 'flat' account supplemented by the creation of pragmatic partitions, sensitive (among other things) to the syntax of the coordination. This pragmatic process drives the choice of a *cover* (109) which is used for the interpretation.

(109) Let A be a set. $C \subseteq (\wp(A)\text{-}\emptyset)$ is a *cover* for A iff $\cup C = A$

However, a cover-based analysis of distributivity can overgenerate. (110), for instance, should be true in case each of John, Mary and Bill is paid $14,000 (the distributive reading), or if $14,000 is the total sum of their incomes, but not if each earns $7,000 (so the sum of *two* incomes is $14,000), a possibility which is predicted by the cover, since {John⊕Mary, John⊕Bill, Bill⊕Mary} is in the extension of the predicate.

(110) John, Mary and Bill were paid exactly $14,000 last year.

Finally, a flat structure has trouble with overlapping sets, as in (111): the DP would just denote {S,V}, and it is not clear how pragmatics should be able to extract {S, V⊕S}.

(111) [Serena and [Serena and Venus]] will play in the first single and the first double tonight.

4.5 The scope of coordination

One of the problems for Conjunction Reduction was precisely the fact that coordination within an argument was expected to take wide scope over any other argument: *a man saw Clark and Sue* was automatically interpreted as *a man saw Clark and a man saw Sue*, with different referents for *a man*. This meaning is probably unobtainable, in contrast with other cases of ellipsis (e.g. *Jack killed a deer and Bill did, too*). There are, however, cases in which coordination does seem able to take either wide or narrow scope (WS/NS): in (112), for instance, a reading involving distinct persons/bullets is quite natural. For most speakers, the presence of an overt or implicit modal operator is essential for WS. It should be noted that these readings have different prosodic patterns, which, if properly taken into account, might make coordination scopally unambiguous, after all.

(112) a. Someone important must have been born in that house and (in) that castle. ∧ >SOMEONE
b. A 9mm bullet killed both the first and the last victim. ∧ > A

Conjunction can take either scope with respect to external negation (in some languages, WS seems to be even obligatory, Szabolcsi & Haddican 2004):

(113) Here you are not allowed to [sing] and [stamp your feet]
a. ... but you are allowed to do one without the other   NS "and": ¬ > ∧
b. ≡ you are not allowed to sing and you are not allowed to stump your feet   WS "and": ∧ > ¬

Note that unlike nominal quantifiers, which might shift scope by moving covertly to different C-commanding positions, in ways not dissimilar from overt Wh-movement (see e.g. QR/Q-construal in Heim 1982, Beghelli & Stowell 1997), the wide scope of *and* in e.g. (113) cannot be obtained simply by raising *and* to the left periphery of the sentence: the conjuncts themselves have to be 'expanded' up to sentence-size (once again, in a way symmetrical to 'conjunction reduction').

Disjunction can also participate in scope interactions. (114) illustrates the two scopes with intensional verbs (Partee & Rooth 1983), (115), with negation:

(114) The waiter is looking for (either) forks or spoons.
    a. ≡ The waiter is looking for pieces of silverware which might be forks or spoons.   LOOK-FOR> ∨, *de dicto*
    b. ≡ Either he is looking for forks or for spoons (–I don't know which one)
                                                                ∨ >LOOK-FOR

(115) Mary didn't take (either) algebra or logic
    a. ≡ she took neither algebra not logic   ¬ > ∨
    b. ≡ either she didn't take algebra, or she didn't take logic.   ∨ > ¬

Despite these similarities, the scopal behavior of *and* and *or* is not symmetrical, and in general the scope of disjunction is freer. One contrast is between *either/or* and *both/and* coordinations. Larson (1985) observes that when *either* is absent, or present but adjacent to the first disjunct, as in (115), the disjunction can take multiple scopes, whereas when *either* appears dislocated from the first disjunct, as in (116), the only scope possibility must be the one corresponding to the overt position of *either*: not wider (116a) and not narrower (116b).

(116) John thinks that either Mary is looking for a maid or for a cook.
    a. Either John thinks that Mary is looking for a maid, or that she is looking for a cook.   *impossible reading*
    b. John thinks that Mary is looking for one person who is either a maid or a cook.   *impossible reading*

The solution proposes by Larson for *or* is that the position of *either* always marks the scope of disjunction, but *either* can move to its final scope-marking position, overtly, as in (116), or covertly, at Logical Forms (LF). The WS/NS readings of (115) would correspond to different LF positions of *either*. Schwarz (1999) takes issue with this analysis, pointing out that the apparent dislocated positions for *either* might just be ellipsis of the beginning of the second conjunct (i.e. LPD, cf. (117)). Unlike Larson's, this solution explains the contrast between (118a) and (118b); the scope variability of (114)/(115), on the other hand, should now be explained without resorting to covert movement.

(117) John is either looking for forks or ~~looking for~~ spoons.

(118)   a.   They will lock either me or you up.
        b. ??Either they will lock me or ~~they will lock~~ you up.

One limit of ellipsis-based derivations, of course, is that no differences between *both/and* and *either/or* are expected. *Both* doesn't have the same distribution as *either*: dislocated positions for *both* are possible, but very limited ((119a) but not (119b)). This contrasts with (114b).

(119) a. The waiter is both looking for forks and spoons.
b. *Both the waiter is looking for forks and spoons.

Note, however, that some of the missing positions for *both* could just be attributed to the fact that *both/and* cannot conjoin certain categories (e.g. not IP/I' – see (24) above).

Larson's proposal entails that possible scopes of disjunction would be just those corresponding to the syntactic positions *either* can move to. This generalization has been challenged by proposals that compare disjunction to an indefinite in Discourse Representation Theory. Just like indefinites, disjunction would provide a free variable which can be unselectively bound even across islands (Rooth & Partee 1982). It should be noted, however, that unlike the island-free scope of indefinites, the putative island-escaping behavior of disjunctive scope rests on judgements that are rather delicate. For instance, it seems that if Jack is *the man who met Sue* and Nick is *the man who met Matt* (120) does not have the WS reading *either Jack or Nick will come (but I don't know who)*.

(120) The man who met Sue or Matt will come tomorrow.

Winter (2000) suggests that in (121a) *or* can take scope outside the conditional. It is however quite difficult to distinguish this reading (impossible given Larson's generalization, since *either* cannot appear before *if*) from the one in (121b), where *or* takes WS, but remains inside the antecedent.

(121) a. If Bill praises Mary or Sue, John will be happy (but I don't remember which one)
b. If (either) [Bill praises Mary] or [Bill praises Sue], John will be happy (but I don't know which is the case)

In (122), on the other hand, the embedded disjunction appears to take wide scope from inside a conjunction island which remains under the negation (i.e. HEAR> $\vee > \neg > \wedge$)

(122) I heard one should not take [alcohol] and [[piridroxina] or [fromizol]] (but I don't remember which one).

However, the island violation could be avoided: syntactically, by assuming an elided *alcohol and* right before *fromizol*, semantically, assuming that the semantic equivalence (A ∧ (P∨F)) ↔ (A∧P) ∨ (A∧F) is computed before scope taking. Either way, *or* is no longer embedded.

At the other end of the scope spectrum we encounter cases where an element takes scope outside the coordination despite being, apparently, within the first conjunct. In the case of negation, a gap in the second conjunct is crucial to get the effect (Siegel 1987), while this is not necessary for *either/both* in English (124).

(123) Ward *can*'t eat caviar and Sue, __ eat beans.   ¬ > ∧

(124) a. Mary *either* is driving to the airport or she is taking a cab
       b. Mary is *both* going to the wedding and she is attending the reception afterward.

The analyzes for these cases have tried to keep the problematic element outside the coordinand, either allowing a coordination between a VP and S (under restricted circumstances, see Larson 1985), or having a more complex structural analysis for gapping (Johnson 1994).

A final problem due to the interaction of multiple operators obtains when disjunction, treated as union of propositions (see Section 4.1.), is combined with counterfactuals or modal operators. For instance, the standard possible-world semantics for a sentence such as *Sarah can leave* uttered at world w is that there is at least one world w' accessible from w where things go according to permissions, and Sarah leaves at w'. Thus, one would expect that the reading of (125) where *or* takes scope below *can* should mean that *both* worlds where Sarah leaves and worlds where Sarah stays are represented among the w-accessible deontically ideal worlds.

(125) Sarah can stay or leave.

But in fact, if the disjunction is the union of the propositions that Sarah stays and that Sarah leaves, nothing rules out that one of the disjuncts brings no contribution at all: (125) should be compatible with the continuation *in fact, she must leave*, which seems contradictory. The problem, first noted in Wright (1968) and Kamp (1973), can be addressed by giving a different semantics for disjunction (Zimmerman 2001), or in terms of scalar implicatures (the key idea is that if one of the conjuncts was known to be irrelevant it would have been more informative for the speaker to omit it; a technical implementation in a Hamblin semantics is in Alonso-Ovalle 2006).

5 Conclusions

After more than fifty years of linguistic research, coordination continues to stand out as a major puzzle in linguistics. Among other language puzzles, however, it is one of the most methodologically fertile, since—as I have tried to show in this article—the phenomenon requires an unparalleled level of integration and interplay between syntax and semantics.

The existence of conjunction reduction even in limited forms would simplify the semantics, at least in non-cumulative cases, but would also force us to re-evaluate much of what we know about constituent structure, deletion, and 'unpronounced material' in general. Vice-versa, under the assumption that no hidden syntactic structures should be postulated, the semantic mechanisms needed to deal with cases such as *Marta or Luis, Ann and possibly Sue and Jack will each drink a beer and then play cards together* might require a serious departure from the idea that semantics is 'read off' syntax. Future studies should try to establish whether the properties of coordination so extensively studied for Germanic and Romance languages are robustly attested in other language groups, and whether empirical evidence obtained with corpus-based, psycholinguistic and functional neuroimaging techniques can help us understand where the line between syntactic and semantic analysis should be drawn.

6 References

Alonso-Ovalle, Luis 2006. *Disjunction in Alternative Semantics*. Ph.D. dissertation. University of Massachusetts, Amherst, MA.
Barwise, Jon & Robin Cooper 1981. Generalized quantifiers and natural language. *Linguistics & Philosophy* 4, 159–219.
Bayer, Samuel 1996. The coordination of unlike categories. *Language* 72, 579–616.
Beghelli, Filippo & Tim Stowell 1997. Distributivity and negation. In: A. Szabolcsi (ed.). *Ways of Scope Taking*. Dordrecht: Kluwer, 71–107.
Camacho, José 2004. *The Structure of Coordination: Conjunction and Agreement Phenomena in Spanish and Other Languages*. Dordrecht: Kluwer.
Chomsky, Noam 1957. *Syntactic Structures*. The Hague: Mouton.
Chomsky, Noam 1986. *Barriers*. Cambridge, MA: The MIT Press.
Culicover, Peter & Ray Jackendoff 1997. Semantic subordination despite syntactic coordination. *Linguistic Inquiry* 28, 195–217.
Dowty, David 1988. Type raising, functional composition, and non-constituent conjunction. In: R. Oehrle, E. Bach & D. Wheeler (eds.). *Categorial Grammars and Natural Language Structures*. Dordrecht: Reidel, 153–197.
Gleitman, Lila 1965. Coordinating constructions in English. *Language* 41, 260–293.

Goodall, Grant 1987. *Parallel Structures in Syntax: Coordination, Causatives and Restructuring.* Cambridge: Cambridge University Press.
Haspelmath, Martin 2007. Coordination. In: T. Shopen (ed.). *Language Typology and Syntactic Description*, vol. II. 2nd ed. Cambridge: Cambridge University Press, 1–51.
Heim, Irene 1982. *The Semantics of Definite and Indefinite Noun Phrases.* Ph. D. dissertation. University of Massachusetts, Amherst, MA.
Heycock, Caroline & Anthony Kroch 1999. Pseudocleft connectivity: Implications for the LF interface level. *Linguistic Inquiry* 30, 365–397.
Heycock, Caroline & Roberto Zamparelli 2005. Friends and colleagues: Plurality, coordination, and the structure of DP. *Natural Language Semantics* 13, 201–270.
Hoeksema, Jack 1983. Plurality and conjunction. In: A. ter Meulen (ed.). *Studies in Modeltheoretic Semantics.* Dordrecht: Foris, 63–84.
Hoeksema, Jack 1988. The semantics of non-Boolean 'and'. *Journal of Semantics* 6, 19–40.
Jackendoff, Ray 1977. *X'-Syntax: A Study of Phrase Structure.* Cambridge, MA: The MIT Press.
Johnson, Kyle 1994. Bridging the gap. In: K. Johnson. *In search of the English Middle Field.* Ms. Amherst, MA, University of Massachusetts.
Kamp, Hans 1973. Free choice permission. *Proceedings of the Aristotelian Society* 74, 57–74.
Keenan, Edward L. & Leonard M. Faltz 1985. *Boolean Semantics for Natural Languages.* Dordrecht: Kluwer.
Krifka, Manfred 1990. Boolean and non-Boolean 'and'. In: L. Kálmán & L. Pólos (eds.). *Papers from the Second Symposium on Logic and Language.* Budapest: Akadémiai Kiadó, 161–188.
Lakoff, George & Stanley Peters 1969. Phrasal conjunction and symmetric predicates. In: D. Reibel & S. Schane (eds.). *Modern Studies in English: Readings in Transformational Grammar.* Englewood Cliffs, NJ: Prentice Hall, 113–142.
Landman, Fred 1989a. Groups, I. *Linguistics & Philosophy* 12, 559–605.
Landman, Fred 1989b. Groups, II. *Linguistics & Philosophy* 12, 723–744.
Larson, Richard 1985. On the syntax of disjunctive scope. *Natural Language and Linguistic Theory* 3, 217–264.
Larson, Richard 1987. On the double object construction. *Linguistic Inquiry* 18, 335–392.
Lasersohn, Peter 1995. *Plurality, Conjunction and Events.* Dordrecht: Kluwer.
Levinson, Steven 2000. *Presumptive Meanings.* Cambridge, MA: The MIT Press.
Link, Godehard 1983. The logical analysis of plurals and mass terms: A lattice-theoretical approach. In: R. Bäuerle, Ch. Schwarze & A. von Stechow (eds.). *Meaning, Use, and the Interpretation of Language.* Berlin: de Gruyter, 302–323.
Moltmann, Friederike 1992. *Coordination and Comparatives.* Ph. D. dissertation. MIT, Cambridge, MA.
Muadz, Husni 1991. *Coordinate Structures: A Planar Representation.* Ph. D. dissertation. University of Arizona, Tucson, AZ.
Munn, Alan 1993. *Topics in the Syntax and Semantics of Coordinate Structures.* Ph. D. dissertation. University of Maryland, College Park, MD.
van Oirsouw, Robert R. 1987. *The Syntax of Coordination.* London: Croom Helm.
Partee, Barbara 1987. Noun phrase interpretation and type-shifting principles. In: J. Groenendijk, D. de Jongh & M. Stokhof (eds.). *Studies in Discourse Representation Theory and the Theory of Generalized Quantifiers.* Dordrecht: Foris, 115–143.
Partee, Barbara & Mats Rooth 1983. Generalized conjunction and type ambiguity. In: R. Bäuerle, Ch. Schwarze & A. von Stechow (eds.). *Meaning, Use, and Interpretation of Language.* Berlin: de Gruyter, 361–383.

Payne, John 1985. Complex phrases and complex sentences. In: T. Shopen (ed.). *Language Typology and Syntactic Description*. Cambridge: Cambridge University Press, 3–41.
Phillips, Colin 2003. Linear order and constituency. *Linguistic Inquiry* 34, 37–90.
Rooth, Mats & Barbara Partee 1982. Conjunction, type ambiguity and wide scope *phor*. In: D. Flickinger, M. Macken & N. Wiegand (eds.). *Proceedings of the First West Coast Conference on Formal Linguistics (=WCCFL)*. Stanford, CA: Stanford Linguistics Association, 353–362.
Ross, John R. 1967. *Constraints on Variables in Syntax*. Ph. D. dissertation. MIT, Cambridge, MA. Reprinted: Bloomington, IL: Indiana University Linguistics Club.
Sag, Ivan, Gerald Gazdar, Thomas Wasow & Steven Weisler 1985. Coordination and how to distinguish categories. *Natural Language and Linguistic Theory* 3, 117–171.
Schachter, Paul 1977. Constraints on coordination. *Language* 53, 86–103.
Schein, Barry 2017. *Conjunction Reduction Redux, MIT Press*. Ms. Los Angeles, CA, University of Southern California. A revised version appeared as Barry Schein 'And' Conjunction Reduction Redux, MIT Press, 2017
Schwarz, Bernhard 1999. On the syntax of *either...or*. *Natural Language and Linguistic Theory* 17, 339–370.
Schwarzschild, Roger S. 1996. *Pluralities*. Dordrecht: Kluwer.
Siegel, Muffy E. A. 1987. Compositionality, case, and the scope of auxiliaries. *Linguistics & Philosophy* 10, 53–76.
Steedman, Mark 1985. Dependency and coordination in the grammar of Dutch and English. *Language* 6, 523–568.
Steedman, Mark 1990. Gapping as constituent coordination. *Linguistics & Philosophy* 13, 207–264.
Steedman, Mark 2000. *The Syntactic Process*. Cambridge, MA: The MIT Press.
Steube, Anita & Carla Umbach (eds.) 2001. *Kontrast: Lexikalisch, semantisch, phonologisch* (Linguistische Arbeitsberichte 77). Leipzig: University of Leipzig.
Szabolcsi, Anna & Bill Haddican 2004. Conjunction meets negation: A study in cross-linguistic variation. *Journal of Semantics* 21, 219–249.
von Wright, Georg Henrik (1968). *An Essay in Deontic Logic and the General Theory of Action with a Bibliography of Deontic and Imperative Logic*. Amsterdam: North-Holland.
Wilder, Chris 1994. Coordination, ATB and ellipsis. In: J.-W. Zwart (ed.). *Minimalism and Kayne's Antisymmetry Hypothesis*. Groningen: University of Groningen, 291–331.
Wilder, Chris 1997. Some properties of ellipsis in coordination. In: A. Alexiadou & T. A. Hall (eds.). *Studies on Universal Grammar and Typological Variation*. Amsterdam: Benjamins, 59–107.
Williams, Edwin 1978. Across-the-board rule application. *Linguistic Inquiry* 9, 31–43.
Winter, Yoad 1996. A unified semantic treatment of singular NP coordination. *Linguistics & Philosophy* 19, 337–391.
Winter, Yoad 2000. On some scopal asymmetries of coordination. In: H. Bennis, M. Everaert & E. Reuland (eds.). *Interface Strategies*. Amsterdam: Royal Netherlands Academy of Arts and Sciences, 387–406.
Winter, Yoad 2001. *Flexible Principles in Boolean Semantics*. Cambridge, MA: The MIT Press.
Winter, Yoad 2007. *Multiple Coordination: Meaning Composition vs. the Syntax-Semantics Interface*. Ms. Utrecht, University of Utrecht.
Winter, Yoad & Rimon, Mori 1996. Contrast and implication in natural language. *Journal of Semantics* 11, 365–406.
Zimmermann, Thomas E. 2001. Free choice disjunction and epistemic possibility. *Natural Language Semantics* 8, 255–290.

Manfred Krifka
5 Questions

1 Questions as speech acts and as semantic objects —— 171
2 Types of questions —— 173
3 Answers to questions —— 181
4 Modeling question meanings —— 184
5 Further topics —— 207
6 Conclusion —— 220
7 References —— 221

Abstract: Questioning is a basic type of speech act essential for human communication, and questions form a distinct sentence type in every language. The article first gives a survey of different uses of questions, as speech acts and as embedded clauses. It then lists the various types of questions and characterizes the notion of congruent answer. It gives an introduction to the principal semantic approaches to questions, including the functional approach, the proposition set approach and the partitional approach, and discusses how question meanings can be constructed from given syntactic structures. The last section takes up a number of supplementary topics, like the relation between indefinite NPs and interrogative pronouns, the nature of question-embedding predicates, biased questions and focus within questions, and the role of questions in structuring discourse.

> *There are four ways of answering questions. Which four? There are questions that should be answered categorically. There are questions that should be answered with an analytical answer, defining or redefining the terms. There are questions that should be answered with a counter-question. There are questions that should be put aside.*
> (Pañha Sutta, translated from the Pali by Thanissaro Bhikkhu)

1 Questions as speech acts and as semantic objects

We will be concerned with the most pedestrian type of questions here that the Enlightened One mentioned, the questions that should be answered categorically by *yes* or *no, this* or *that*. Yet even then questions are a highly interesting linguistic

---

Manfred Krifka, Berlin, Germany

https://doi.org/10.1515/9783110589863-005

phenomenon that continues to inspire developments in syntax, semantics, and pragmatics.

In the classification of speech acts by Searle (1975), questions form a subtype of directives, one of the major five classes, together with commands and requests. This is because questions try to make the addressee do something, namely, provide a particular piece of information. While this is certainly the prototypical function of questions, one should be aware that not every request for information is expressed by a question – consider, e.g., commands like *Tell me the time!* Also, an assertion like *You want coffee* whose truth value is only known by the addressee may be used to express a question; if not true, the addressee can be expected to reject it. It has been claimed that Yélî Dnye, a Papuan language, does not distinguish between assertions and polar (yes-no) questions at all (cf. Mitterer & Stivers 2006).

On the other hand, not every sentence with question form expresses a request for information. There are exam questions like *Rome was founded when?* in which the questioner knows the answer but wants to check the ability of the addressee to supply it. There are rhetorical questions like *Did you ever lift a finger to help me?*, which amounts to a strong assertion that you never lifted a finger to help me. There are reflective questions that do not oblige the addressee to answer but express the speaker's interest in an issue, such as German *Ob es wohl regnen wird?*, lit. 'whether it will rain?' There are deliberative questions that do not ask for facts but inquire what should be done, as in *What should I do?*, and whose answers, consequently, are directives, e.g., *Read this article!* There are questions that express conditions, as in *Are you easily tired? XYZ will help you.* Questions are also used to seek confirmation in cases in which the speaker is not sure, as in question tags, cf. *He will come, won't he?*, or to utter commands, as in *Could you open the window?* And there are embedded questions (sometimes called "indirect questions") like *Bill knows who will come*, which do not express information requests either.

Nevertheless, the various uses of unembedded or root questions can be reduced to one basic pragmatic function, namely, expressing lack of information of a specified type. We will see how the wide variety of question uses can be derived from this core meaning. Embedded questions, on the other hand, do not imply lack of information. Yet there are properties that questions as speech acts and questions as constituents of clauses have in common.

Stenius (1967) has argued that utterances used to perform speech acts like assertions, commands, and questions can be partitioned into a sentence radical denoting a semantic object, like a proposition, and a sentence mood indicator or illocutionary operator that turns this semantic object into a communicative act. While Stenius considered only simple yes/no-questions, which may have the same sentence radical as assertions, we can assume that the sentence radical of questions in general is a proposition that is partly unspecified. Such open propositions can be used to perform speech acts that express that the speaker lacks information, as specified by the gaps in the sentence radical. For example, the question *Who will come?* contains a sentence radical COME(x), where "x" identifies the information lacking. Either this incomplete semantic form is understood in itself as requesting completion, or it is combined with an illocutionary operator QUEST that formally expresses a request to the addressee to specify the lacking pieces of information in such a way that the resulting closed proposition is true. Embedded questions, as in *Bill knows who will come*, presumably contain the sentence radical only, as in KNOW(COME(x))(BILL), which says that Bill knows for which entities the sentence radical COME(x) will lead to a true proposition. That is, root questions and embedded questions are both built on interrogative sentence radicals:

(1) *Who will come?*
    QUEST(COME(x))

(2) *Bill knows who will come.*
    ASSERT(KNOW(COME(x))(BILL)).

The semantics of questions deals with the interrogative sentence radicals that occur in root questions or as dependent clauses; the pragmatics of questions is concerned with the various roles that questions serve in communication. While the main focus of this article is on semantics, the meaning of interrogative sentence radicals, we also have to consider different uses of questions, as the proposed semantics should ultimately lead to an explanation of how questions function in communication. As questions often request answers, the linguistic form of answers will also constrain possible theories of questions, and hence, interrogative sentence radicals. The semantics of interrogative sentence radicals should furthermore provide for an explanation of the distribution of embedded questions – which predicates allow for indirect questions, and why.

2 Types of questions

We can distinguish three types of interrogative sentence radicals, and correspondingly, of questions, according to the type of the lacking information: constituent questions, polarity questions and alternative questions.

2.1 Constituent questions

Constituent questions create an open proposition by leaving parts of the description of the proposition unspecified. Languages apply interrogative pro-forms for this purpose. In English, these pro-forms have an initial *wh-* (going back to Indo-European $^+k^w$); hence terms like "*wh*-questions" or "*wh*-pronoun". A better term might be "completion question", reflecting the German term *Ergänzungsfrage*.

In English, constituents that can be questioned include all arguments and adjuncts that are part of the description of a proposition:

(3) a. *What did John read?*
    b. *Who read this book?*
    c. *When did John read this book?*
    d. *Where did John read this book?*
    e. *Why did John read this book?*

Questioning a constituent that includes the finite verb requires a higher-order verb, as in *What did John do?*. But there are languages that have interrogative pro-verbs; e.g., Kiribati (Austronesian) has seven pro-verbs expressing meanings like 'to do what', 'to be where', or 'to do how':

(4) *Kam na aera?*
    you.PL FUT do.what
    'What will you do?'

It is also possible to question subconstituents, as e.g., [*Whose book*] *did John read?* Again there are differences between languages. English lacks a way to question ordinals, which German has:

(5) *Den wie-viel-t-en Geburtstag feiert Maria?*
    lit. 'The how-many-th birthday does Maria celebrate?'

It has been suggested (Gil 2001) that only open-class items can be questioned; this excludes pro-forms for prepositions or determiners (other than number words). There are languages with a very small inventory of question constituents, like Asháninca (Arawakan, Peru) with possibly a single such constituent that is further specified by various light verbs (cf. Cysouw 2007). It should be mentioned that constituent questions can also be expressed without any interrogative pro-form (cf. Gretsch 2000) (rising intonation is crucial).

(6) *Sie sind geboren am_?*
    you are born   at_
    'When are you born?'

Constituents that are not part of the descriptive sentence radical cannot be questioned. This holds, in particular, for constructions that specify the nature of the speech act, but also for constituents expressing speaker attitudes, as the initial adverbials in the following examples:

(7) a. Frankly, *I don't like you.*
    b. Luckily, *the train was late.*

Languages differ not only in the types of interrogative pro-forms, but also in where they are realized within a sentence. While many place them sentence-initally, as in English, many others leave them *in situ* (cf. Dryer 2005a). Some languages move interrogative pro-forms into a dedicated focus position, such as the preverbal position in Hungarian (cf. Szabolcsi 1981), or to a postverbal position in Western Bade (Chadic; cf. Tuller 1992), which corresponds to the preferred focus position in these languages. Many exhibit both strategies: English allows for in situ in echo questions, which request the repetition of linguistic material that was not understood properly or about which the speaker is incredulous, and in exam questions. In general, in situ interrogative pro-forms appear to be marked intonationally (indicated by accent):

(8) a. *You are leaving whén?*
    b. *Napoleon died whích year?*

It is possible to use more than one interrogative pro-form per clause, resulting in so-called "multiple questions". In English, only one pro-form undergoes movement, the others remain in situ and are accented. In Slavic languages and in Romanian, all interrogative pro-forms can move (cf. Comorovski 1996). In the following examples, movement is indicated by coindexed traces.

(9) Who will t_1 read what?

(10) *Cine$_1$ ce$_2$ [t$_1$ ti-a   spus t$_2$]*
     who what you-AUX told
     'Who has told you what?'

We will see that there are at least two subtypes of multiple questions, "matching" questions that are supposed to be answered by more than one answer, and non-matching questions for which there is no such restriction.

Movement of interrogative pro-forms is restricted by syntactic island constraints, (cf. 11). Ungrammaticality can be avoided by the in situ strategy (cf. 12) or by moving the whole syntactic island (so-called pied piping, cf. 13).

(11) *[Which author]$_i$ did Bill read [a book by t$_i$]?

(12) *Bill read [a book by which author]?*

(13) *[A book by which author] did John read?*

Answers to such questions do not consist just of the *which*-phrase, but must correspond to the syntactic island. For example, (12) and (13) cannot be answered by *Jane Austen*, but need more complex phrases like *a book by Jane Austen*. Such data have led to the idea that even in situ structures like (12) involve syntactic movement, at the level of logical form (cf. Nishigauchi 1990; von Stechow 1996).

Constituent questions also occur in embedded structures:

(14) *John knows what Bill will read.*

(15) *John knows who will read what.*

The syntactic structure of embedded questions often differs from root questions. In English root questions, there must be a verbal head preceding the subject (cf. 16), which must be an auxiliary – different from German (cf. 17). When questioning the subject itself, this requirement does not obtain, arguably because the subject itself has already undergone movement, and the verbal head precedes the subject trace (cf. 18):

(16) *What will / does Bill read?*

(17) **What reads Bill? / Was liest Bill?*

(18) *Who$_i$ read t$_i$ 'War and Peace'?*

In questions embedded by verbs like *know*, the requirement that the verbal head precedes the subject does not obtain:

(19) *John knows what Bill will read. / *what will Bill read.*

(20) *John weiß, was Bill liest. / *was liest Bill.*

This suggests that the filling of a pre-subject position by a verbal head is a feature of root clauses. If we assume, as suggested in (1/2), that verbs like *know* embed the sentence radical of a question, whereas root questions arise by applying the illocutionary operator QUEST, we can assume that it is the QUEST operator that triggers movement of the wh-expression and the pre-subject verbal head requirement (cf. Baker 1968 for ideas along these lines).

As we have seen, there are two strategies of forming questions. The in situ strategy does not require, and in fact does not allow, a pre-subject verbal head:

(21) *Does / *Will Bill read whát?

(22) *Liest Bill wás?

In situ questions express the illocutionary force by non-syntactic, purely prosodic means, for example by rising tone on the interrogative pro-forms. In this case, it seems that no interrogative sentence radical is formed, as these questions do not occur as embedded questions:

(23) a. *John knows what Bill read.*
 b. **John knows (that) Bill read whát.*

However, languages that only have the in situ strategy, like Japanese, use such questions also in embedded structures, as in the following example:

(24) Naoya-wa [Mari-ga nani-o nomiya-de nonda ka] imademo oboeteru
 Naoya-TOP Mari-NOM what-ACC bar-LOC drank Q even.now remember
 'Naoya still remembers what Mary drank at the bar.'

Ishihara (2004) has shown that the embedded wh-word is prosodically prominent and leads to deaccenting of the rest of the embedded sentence up to the interrogative marker *ka* that it is associated with.

2.2 Polarity questions

The second type of questions, which are also called "Yes/No-Questions" (German *Entscheidungsfrage*, 'decision question'), request an answer that specifies whether the proposition expressed by their sentence radical holds or does not hold, rather than closing a proposition with an open parameter.

(25) *Will Bill read 'War and Peace'?*

(26) *Does Bill understand the task?*

In these realizations of polarity questions we find pre-subject verbal heads, just as in constituent questions, but there is no additional *wh*-movement, as there is no inter-rogative pro-form. Just as with constituent questions, this requirement is absent in embedded questions, where a special complementizer, in English *whether* or *if*, must be present:

(27) *John knows whether/if Bill read 'War and Peace'.*

(28) **John knows (whether/if) did Bill read 'War and Peace'.*

Just as with constituent questions, there is a way to form questions without a pre-subject verbal head, by modulating a sentence with indicative word order by a strong final rise (cf. Gunlogson 2003). Again similar to constituent questions, polarity questions marked in this way cannot be embedded by verbs like *know*.

(29) *Bill read 'War and Peace'?*

(30) **John knows Bill read 'War and Peace'?*

The strategy of marking polarity questions by interrogative word order is typologically rare but happens to be widespread in European languages, in particular in Germanic languages (cf. Siemund 2001; Dryer 2005b). The second strategy, rising intonation, is very frequent, but not universal; for example, it is reported to be non-existent in Quechua, Greenlandic and Yelí Dnye (isolate, Rossel Island, Papua New Guinea).

Another way of marking polarity questions is by question particles. They often occur at the periphery of the sentence, e.g., sentence-finally as in Japanese (31), or sentence-initially in Swahili (32).

(31) kono hon wa omoshiroi desu ka
    this book TOP interesting COP Q
    'Is this book interesting?'

(32) je, a-li-kwenda shule-ni?
    Q 3SG-PST-go school-LOC
    'Did (s)he go to school?'

Peripheral realization is to be expected for illocutionary operators, which take the whole sentence radical in their scope. But we find question particles also in other positions, e.g., preverbally in Georgian and cliticized to the first constituent in Latin:

(33) čai xom ginda?
      tea Q you.want
      'Do you want tea?'

(34) Puer-ne bonus est?
      boy-Q good is
      'Is the boy good?'

Many languages have question-specific modal particles, which are not obligatory and often express additional meaning components, like a bias towards a positive or negative answer. For example, in German the particle *denn* expresses expectation of a negative answer.

Another type of marking is by verbal morphology, as in Greenlandic:

(35) Iga-va.
      cook-INTER.3SG,
      'Do you cook?'

The last marking strategy is particularly important for understanding the semantics of polarity questions, to be dealt with below; it consists of disjunctive constructions as in Chinese:

(36) nǐ   hē   pijiǔ bu hē   pijiǔ
      2SG drink beer NEG drink beer
      'Do you drink beer?'

2.3 Alternative questions

The third type of questions is semantically related to constituent questions, as they request information to close an open proposition.

(37) Did Bill read 'War and Peáce' or 'Anna Karénina'?

(38) John knows whether Bill read 'War and Peáce' or 'Anna Karénina'.

It is crucial that the first alternative receives a strong rising accent, and the final a strong falling accent. Without this, the sentence would be interpreted as a yes/no question with a disjunctive term in its descriptive part ('Is it true that Bill read W&P or AK?').

Alternative questions differ from constituent questions as they mention the possible completions explicitly. But this can also be done with constituent questions:

(39) What did Bill read, 'War and Peáce' or 'Anna Karénina'?

(40) John knows what Bill read, 'War and Peáce' or 'Anna Karénina'.

In contrast to constituent questions, finite verbs, prepositions and quantifiers can be questioned, for which no wh-forms exist in English:

(41) Did Bill búy or bórrow this book?

(42) Did the plane fly abóve or belów the clouds?

(43) Did you drink móst or áll of the whiskey?

Alternative questions also differ from constituent questions as they do not show *wh*-movement, which seems to be triggered by a specific feature expressed by *wh*-constituents.

(44) *'War and Peace' or 'Anna Karenina' did Bill read?

We find the same island restrictions in interpretation as in *wh*-in situ cases:

(45) A: *Did Bill read a book by Jane Austen or by Charlotte Brontë?*

(46) **Jane Austen. / A book by Jane Austen.*

As standard examples show (cf. 37), alternative questions have pre-subject verbal heads, which indicate the presence of the QUEST operator, as argued for above. As there is no overt movement of a question constituent, they appear syntactically as a subtype of polarity questions, yet the meaning they express is similar to constituent questions.

3 Answers to questions

3.1 The question/answer relation and the semantics of questions

In their prototypical use, questions are requests for answers. Consequently, any theory of questions will have to take into account the discourse relation between question and answer. As we have seen in the motto of this article, the Pañha Sutta already used this very relation to classify questions. In more recent times, this research strategy was attractive because answers are assertions, and there are well-developed semantic theories of assertions.

Now, naturalistic reactions to questions come in a wide variety, including *I don't know* or *Go and ask someone else*, or by various strategies of telling more, less, or something different than what a speaker has asked for. Such reactions are important for the pragmatics of the questions/answer-relation. The answers that are of particular interest for the semantics of questions are so-called "congruent" answers (cf. von Stechow 1990).

(47) Q: *Who will go where tomorrow?*
    A1: *Fritz will drive to Potsdam tomorrow.*
    A2: *Fritz will go to Potsdam tomorrow.*
    A3: *Fritz will go to the townhall of Potsdam tomorrow.*
    A4: *Fritz will go somewhere tomorrow.*

Among the three reaction to Q's question, the congruent answers are A2 and A3; they satisfy the informational need expressed by the question, depending on the granularity level of the conversational background of the question in specifying the person and place variable. In contrast, A1 gives more information than is required, and A4 gives less information, as it does not specify the place variable. As stated, the semantics of questions is formulated in terms of possible congruent answers like the following (assuming the granularity level requires cities):

(48) *Fritz will go to Potsdam tomorrow.*
    Fritz will go to Berlin tomorrow.
    Franz will go to Potsdam tomorrow.
    Franz will go to Berlin tomorrow.
    ...

But is it justified to give assertions this privileged role in semantics? Perhaps we can develop a semantics for assertions in terms of a semantics for questions, instead of the other way round? In fact, in the current setup, which distinguishes between the meaning of sentence radicals and speech acts, we do neither. Rather, both questions and assertions are based on sentence radicals, where the sentence radical of an assertion that is a congruent answer specifies the open parameters of the sentence radical of the question:

(49) QUEST [x WILL GO TO y TOMORROW]
      ASSERT [FRITZ WILL GO TO POTSDAM TOMORROW]

The relation between QUEST and ASSERT belongs to pragmatics; an utterance based on QUEST expresses an informational need, a request to specify information of a particular type, and a congruent answer based on ASSERT satisfies this information need. The systematic relation between the sentence radical [x WILL GO TO y TOMORROW] and the sentence radical [FRITZ WILL GO TO POTSDAM TOMORROW] belongs to semantics, and in the section on modeling question meanings we will discuss various ways how this relation can be captured.

3.2 Marking answer congruence

Often, a fully specified sentence radical can answer more than just one question. For example, the assertion *Fritz will go to Potsdam tomorrow* is a congruent answer to at least the following questions:

(50) a. *What happened?*
      b. *What will happen tomorrow?*
      c. *What will Fritz do tomorrow?*
      d. *Where will Fritz go tomorrow?*
      e. *When will Fritz go to Potsdam?*
      f. *Who will go to Potsdam tomorrow?*
      g. *Who will go where tomorrow?*
      h. *Who will go where when?*

But notice that the answer indicates the type of question by its focus. We understand focus here as a feature of syntax that has repercussions in semantic interpretation and in phonological realization, as expressed by sentence accent. The importance of sentence accent in answering questions was first observed by Paul (1880). In the following, focus is indicated by an F subscript, and sentence accent by accented letters. Notice that the realization of (51a–d) is the same, an instance of focus ambiguity.

(51) a. [Fritz will go to Pótsdam tomorrow]$_F$
b. [Fritz will go to Pótsdam]$_F$ tomorrow.
c. Fritz will [go to Pótsdam]$_F$ tomorrow.
d. Fritz will go [to Pótsdam]$_F$ tomorrow.
e. Fritz will go to Potsdam [tomórrow]$_F$.
f. [Frítz]$_F$ will go to Potsdam tomorrow.
g. [Frítz]$_F$ will go to [Pótsdam]$_F$ tomorrow.
h. [Frítz]$_F$ will go to [Pótsdam]$_F$ [tomórrow]$_F$.

While the truth conditions of all the answers in (51) are the same, they differ in signaling which question they answer. Focus is thought to indicate alternative meanings; focus in answers indicates that the alternatives are all congruent possible answers to the question. It should be added that languages do not generally mark question/answer coherence by focus. For example, Zerbian (2006) points out that Northern Sotho (Bantu) lacks focus marking except for subjects.

Most of the answers in (51) have a pedantic ring to them as they rephrase much of the material of the question. In real life, speakers tend to omit parts that are present in the question and give elliptical answers, also called "term answers":

(52) b. *Fritz will go to Pótsdam.*
c. *Go to Pótsdam.*
d. *To Pótsdam.*
e. *Tomórrow.*
f. *Frítz.*
g. *Frítz, to Pótsdam.*

Parts belonging to the focus obviously cannot be elided. Hence elliptical answers provide a test to determine the focus of non-elliptical answers: If an elliptical paraphrase of a focused sentence necessarily contains some constituent α then α must be part of the focus.

4 Modeling question meanings

4.1 Preliminaries

In this section we will turn to the ways in which the meaning of interrogative sentence radicals, the sentences that embed them, and the questions that are formed with them, can be represented in model-theoretic, truth-conditional semantics. There are three established approaches, which will be called the functional representation, the proposition set representation, and the partition representation. We will also discuss an approach recently developed, Inquisitive Semantics.

In the development of these representation frameworks, embedded questions have played an important role, as they are constituents of indicative sentences, and indicatives can be investigated in familiar truth-conditional theories. In particular, semantic theories of questions have tried to reconstruct logical inference patterns like the following:

(53) *John knows what Bill read.*
Bill read 'War and Peace'.
Hence: *John knows that Bill read 'War and Peace'.*

But notice that this inference holds only under a total (exhaustive) understanding of the embedded question, which is not always the most natural one. For example, from *John knows where one can buy a Chinese newspaper in Berlin* and *One can buy a Chinese newspaper in the Asia Shop at Potsdamer Straße* it does not follow that *John knows that one can buy a Chinese newspaper in the Asia Shop at Potsdamer Straße*, as the first sentence may be considered true already if John knows some place or other where one can buy a Chinese newspaper.

For root questions, it is crucial to consider congruent answers to questions (see above). We find elliptical or term answers and non-elliptical answers, where the focus of the answer corresponds to the interrogative pro-form of the question.

(54) A: *Who read 'War and Peace'?*
B: [$_F$ *Bill*].
C: [$_F$ *Bill*] *read 'War and Peace'.*

As with embedded interrogatives, we find that answers can be understood exhaustively or non-exhaustively, in which case they specify one or a few instances, but not necessarily all of them.

For each of the four approaches to the meaning of questions, we will consider how they treat embedded questions, and what they have to say about pairs of questions and congruent answers, in particular, about the focus of non-elliptical answers.

4.2 The functional (or categorial) approach

The idea that interrogative sentence radicals denote open propositions suggests that they should be reconstructed as functions that map the missing piece of the proposition to the whole proposition. We call this the functional representation; it is the same as what Groenendijk & Stokhof (1997) call the "categorial" representation. For a simple interrogative like *which novel Bill read*, we initially have the following options:

(55) *which novel Bill read*
   a. $\lambda x[\text{NOVEL}(x) \wedge \text{READ}(x)(\text{BILL})]$
   b. $\lambda x \in \text{NOVEL}[\text{READ}(x)(\text{BILL})]$

(55a) is a total function; it maps every entity x to truth iff x is a novel and Bill read x. This representation treats the descriptive content of the interrogative constituent *which novel* and the remainder of the sentence the same. Yet there is an important difference: Answering (55) by naming a non-novel that Bill actually did read (e.g., *the New York Times*) should be just inappropriate, not false. The analysis in (55a) does not capture this. In contrast, (55b) is a partial function that is only defined for novels. In this case, the answer *the New York Times* is inappropriate because the question meaning cannot even be applied to this entity, as it is not in the domain of this function. Hence we will follow the representation (55b).

Both question representations in (55) are extensional, but can be turned into intensional representations. Assuming a framework with explicit quantification over possible worlds i, in which the proposition 'Bill read 'War and Peace'' is rendered by $\lambda i[\text{READ}_i(\text{W\&P})(\text{BILL})]$, we have the choice between two formats:

(56) a. $\lambda x \in \text{NOVEL} \lambda i[\text{READ}_i(x)(\text{BILL})]$
   b. $\lambda i \lambda x \in \text{NOVEL}_i[\text{READ}_i(x)(\text{BILL})]$

(56a) appears to be most straightforward, as it proposes a function from novels (to propositions). However, in this representation we cannot make the predicate NOVEL dependent on the index i. There are cases where we would like to do that. For example, assume that Bill read 'War and Peace', then *Mary knows which novel Bill read* entails in one reading not only that Mary knows that Bill read 'War and Peace', but also that 'War and Peace' is a novel. Hence (56b) seems more appropriate, a function from indices i to a function from novels at i to truth values, in particular to Truth iff Bill read x in i. Hence we will follow this representation. Consider the following examples:

(57) *which novel Bill read*
 $\lambda i \lambda x \in \text{NOVEL}_i[\text{READ}_i(x)(\text{BILL})]$

(58) *who read 'War and Peace'*
 $\lambda i \lambda x \in \text{PERSON}_i[\text{READ}_i(\text{W\&P})(x)]$

(59) *when Bill read 'War and Peace'*
 $\lambda i \lambda R \in \text{TEMPORAL\_SPECIFICATION}_i[R(\lambda i[\text{READ}_i(\text{W\&P})(\text{BILL})])(i)]$

(60) *who read which novel?*
 $\lambda i \lambda x \in \text{PERSON}_i \lambda y \in \text{NOVEL}_i[\text{READ}_i(y)(x)]$

For (59), the function ranges over the meanings of temporal specifications that apply to propositions, like *in 1998*. If indices i are considered to have a world and time component, $i = \langle w,t \rangle$, then this temporal modifier meaning could be rendered by $\lambda \langle w,t \rangle \lambda p[p(\langle w,1998 \rangle)]$. The multiple question (60) denotes a function from pairs x,y of persons and things to the proposition that x read y.

Alternative questions are treated in a similar way, where the alternatives specify the domain of the function:

(61) *whether Bill read 'War and Peace' or 'Anna Karenina'*
 $\lambda i \ \lambda x \in \{\text{W\&P, AK}\} \ [\text{READ}_i(x)(\text{BILL})]$

For polarity questions, we can assume a function that has two functions in its domain, the identity function and the negation for truth values, cf. (62). This is reminiscent of the Chinese way of forming such questions, cf. (36). The operators $\lambda t.t$ and $\lambda t.\neg t$ correspond to the possible answers *yes* and *no*.

(62) *whether Bill read 'War and Peace'*
 $\lambda i \lambda f \in \{\lambda t.t, \lambda t.\neg t\}[f(\text{READ}_i(\text{W\&P})(\text{BILL}))]$

Interrogative sentence radicals can be used to form questions, which then express an interest of the speaker in finding out the "Werteverlauf", or value-range, of the indicated function, i.e., for which arguments the value is Truth. Take the following example:

(63) *Which novels by Tolstoy did Bill read?*
QUEST($\lambda i \lambda x \in$NOVELS BY TOLSTOY$_i$[READ$_i$(x)(BILL)])

> 'Speaker tries to get Addressee to specify for which arguments the function $\lambda x \in$NOVELS BY TOLSTOY$_{i_0}$[READ$_{i_0}$(x)(BILL)] yields Truth for the world of evaluation i_0.'

The domain restriction of the function and the description of the argument serve quite different purposes. As for the first, it restricts the function to novels by Tolstoy; an answer like *Crime and Punishment* is sorted out as inappropriate. As for the argument description, it describes the conditions under which an argument counts as a true answer; if the answer is *Anna Karenina and War and Peace*, denoting the sum individual AK+W&P, the addressee effectively asserts the proposition READ(AK+W&P)(BILL). As stated above, the information inherent in a question is partitioned into a description of the domain and a description of the values. This is important, as the answer presupposes (and does not assert) that *Anna Karenina* and *War and Peace* are novels by Tolstoy; it asserts – given that the presupposition is satisfied – that Bill read these novels.

In many cases the description of the value of a question function can be seen as suggesting that there is an argument to which the function can truthfully be applied. A question like *What did you just steal from my pocket?* could very well lead to a law suit, as an innocent addressee can rightly feel to be accused of theft. Besides existence, questions also suggest uniqueness of the argument to which they can be truthfully applied. A question like *Which novel by Tolstoy did Bill read?* suggests that Bill read exactly one novel by Tolstoy, whereas the original question (63) suggests that Bill read more than one. We can express such presuppositions by the iota operator that identifies the unique or maximal individual for which the descriptive part is true:

(64) *Which novel by Tolstoy did Bill read?*
QUEST($\lambda i \lambda x \in$NOVEL BY TOLSTOY$_i$[READ$_i$(x)(BILL)])
'Speaker asks Addressee to identify the unique/maximal object $\iota x \in$NOVEL BY TOLSTOY$_{i_0}$[READ$_{i_0}$(x)(BILL)] for the world of evaluation i_0.'

However, on closer inspection existence, uniqueness and maximality occur too inconsistently to be captured by a presuppositional analysis. In the literature, there is a debate between analyses that take such meaning effects seriously, e.g., Higginbotham & May (1981), and others that downplay these effects, such as Groenendijk & Stokhof (1997). In any case, there are questions that do not come with existential import (e.g., *Who can solve this problem?*). Existence and – as we have seen already – exhaustivity can be cancelled:

(65) *Which novel by Tolstoy did Bill read, if any?*

(66) *I need a Chinese newspaper. Where can I buy one?*

We now turn to the issue of how the answerhood relation can be treated under the functional analysis of questions. This is straightforward for elliptical or term answers. A question and its term answer determine a proposition when we apply the question meaning to the meaning of the term answer:

(67) A: *Which book did Bill read?*
  QUEST($\lambda i \lambda x \in BOOK_i$ [READ$_i$(x)(BILL)])

  B: *'War and Peace'*.
  ANSW(λi.W&P)
  Question radical Q applied to answer radical A, $\lambda i[Q(i)(A(i))]$:
  $\lambda i[\lambda x \in BOOK_i[READ_i(x)(BILL)](W\&P)]$
  = $\lambda i[READ_i(W\&P)(BILL)]$.

Non-elliptical answers like *Bill read War and Peace* show a more indirect relation to the question under the functional theory. But notice that the answer $\lambda i[READ_i(W\&P)(BILL)]$ specifies the argument(s) for which the question meaning $\lambda i \lambda x \in BOOK_i[READ_i(x)(BILL)]$ is mapped to a true proposition, namely W&P. This is facilitated by the focus feature of the answer, which naturally can be taken to indicate a partition between a focus part and a background part, where the background part corresponds to the question meaning. (This is the so-called structured meaning account of focus developed by Szabolcsi 1981; von Stechow 1981, 1990 and Jacobs 1983).

(68) *Bill read [$_F$'War & Peace'].*
  ASSERT($\lambda i \lambda x[READ_i(x)(BILL)]$, W&P)

The pre-theoretical notion of congruent answers can be explicated in the functional approach as follows: If F is the focus and B is the background of the answer, and Q is the question radical, then the answer is congruent iff for every index i, Q(i) ⊆ B(i), and Q(i)(F) is defined. This is satisfied in our example (67–68), as $\lambda x \in BOOK_i[READ_i(x)(BILL)]$ is a subset of $\lambda x[READ_i(x)(BILL)]$, and W&P is an element of BOOK$_i$. In this way, we can also capture answers to polarity questions like *yes* and *no*, which are interpreted as functions from truth values to truth values:

(69) A: *Did Bill read 'War and Peace'?*
  QUEST($\lambda i \lambda f \in \{\lambda t.t, \lambda t \neg t\}[f(READ_i(W\&P)(BILL))]$)

B: *No.*
ANSW(λt.¬t)

Question radical applied to answer radical:
λi[λf∈{λt.t, λt.¬t}[f(READ$_i$(W&P)(BILL))](λt.¬t)]
= λi¬[READ$_i$(W&P)(BILL)

Turning to embedded questions, the functional theory offers analyses like the following:

(70) *John knows which book Bill read.*
KNOW(λiλx∈BOOK$_i$[READ$_i$(x)(BILL)])(JOHN)

This can be understood in such a way that John knows the value-range of the embedded function for the index of evaluation i. That is, John knows for each x in the domain of the function whether its value is Truth or Falsity. This explains why the inference (53) holds, for the exhaustive interpretation of KNOW. We can capture the question-embedding reading of *know* as follows, by reducing it to the proposition-embedding *know*:

(71) KNOW$_{i0}$(Q)(x) iff
   a. $\forall$y[Q(i$_0$)(y) $\rightarrow$ KNOW$_{i0}$(λi[[Q(i)(y)](x)]]
   b. $\exists$y[Q(i$_0$)(y) $\land$ KNOW$_{i0}$(λi[[Q(i)(y)](x)]]

Here, (a) represents the exhaustive interpretation: x knows Q iff or every true answer y, it holds that x knows that Q(y). (b) represents the non-exhaustive interpretation, which just requires that x knows for some true answer y that Q(y).

While the basic idea of the functional analysis appears quite natural, it has been criticized as it entails that questions have different logical types (cf. Groenendijk & Stokhof 1982). This is problematic considering the fact that embedded interrogatives of different types can easily be conjoined. For example, (72) combines a question of type $\langle$e, st$\rangle$ and a question of type $\langle\langle$st, st$\rangle$, st$\rangle$.

(72) *Mary knows what Bill read and whether he fell asleep.*

However, notice that (72) is truth-conditionally equivalent to (73), which suggests that the conjunction of the two embedded questions in (72) can be interpreted as in (74), which is based on a natural operation in a semantics with lifted Boolean operators (cf. Keenan & Faltz 1985).

(73) *Mary knows what Bill read and knows whether he fell asleep.*

(74) *what Bill read and whether he fell asleep.*
  $\lambda F[F(\lambda x \in \text{THING}[\text{READ}(x)(\text{BILL})] \wedge F(\lambda f \in \{\lambda t.t, \lambda t.\neg t\}[f(\text{FELLASLEEP}(\text{BILL}))])]$

We conclude this presentation of the functional approach to questions with a few words about its history. It was proposed in various forms by a variety of authors. Cohen (1929) can be seen as an early example; he suggested that interrogative pronouns have the role of variables in mathematical equations. Jespersen (1940) coined the term "x-question" that expresses a similar idea. Other versions were proposed by Hull (1975) and, using the lambda calculus, by Belnap & Steel (1976), Tichy (1978), Hausser & Zaefferer (1979) and Hausser (1983). The way in which functional questions have been treated here has not followed any particular framework but has tried to work out the essence of this approach. Put simply and in the most general terms, it assumes that interrogatives are "incomplete" propositions where the positions at which they are incomplete and the type of meanings that would make them complete are specified by the *wh*-constituents.

4.3 The proposition set approach

The proposition set approach models the meaning of questions by the set of propositions that are answers to the question. In contrast to the functional approach, it takes full, propositional answers as basic, not term answers.

(75) *who read 'War and Peace'*
  $\{\lambda i[\text{READ}_i(\text{W\&P})(x)] \mid x \in \text{PERSON}\}$,

(76) *when Bill read 'War and Peace'*
  $\{\lambda i[\text{AT}_i(t)(\lambda i[\text{READ}_i(\text{W\&P})(\text{BILL})]] \mid t \in \text{TIME}\}$,

(77) *who read which novel*
  $\{\lambda i[\text{READ}_i(y)(x)] \mid y \in \text{NOVEL}, x \in \text{PERSON}\}$

For example, (75) is the set of propositions $\lambda i[\text{READ}_i(\text{W\&P})(X)]$, where x varies over persons, $\{\lambda i[\text{READ}_i(\text{W\&P})(\text{BILL})], \lambda i[\text{READ}_i(\text{W\&P})(\text{MARY})], ...\}$.

This is the set of propositions that would be expressed by congruent answers, *Bill read War and Peace, Mary read War and Peace* etc. In the formulation given in (75) the predicate PERSON is not in a position to be evaluated at the index i of the proposition. This can, however, be achieved as follows:

(78) $\lambda p \exists x[p = \lambda i[\text{PERSON}_i(x) \wedge \text{READ}_i(\text{W\&P})(x)]]$

Alternative questions can be expressed as propositions restricted by the alternative phrase:

(79) *whether Bill or Mary read 'War and Peace'*
 $\{\lambda i[\text{READ}_i(\text{W\&P})(x)] \mid x=\text{BILL} \vee x=\text{MARY}\}$
 $= \{\lambda i[\text{READ}_i(\text{W\&P})(\text{BILL})], \lambda i[\text{READ}_i(\text{W\&P})(\text{MARY})]\}$

The simplest way of dealing with polarity questions is to assume that they combine a proposition and its negation:

(80) *whether Bill read 'War and Peace'*
 $\{\lambda i[\text{READ}_i(\text{W\&P})(\text{BILL})], \lambda i\neg[\text{READ}_i(\text{W\&P})(\text{BILL})]\}$

The treatment of non-elliptical, full answers is straightforward:

(81) A: *Which novel by Tolstoy did Bill read?*
 $\text{QUEST}(\{\lambda i[\text{READ}_i(x)(\text{BILL})] \mid x \in \text{NOVEL BY TOLSTOY}\})$

 B: *Bill read 'War and Peace'*
 $\text{ASSERT}(\lambda i[\text{READ}_i(\text{W\&P})(\text{BILL})])$

This answer is congruent, as the answer proposition is an element of the set of propositions specified by the question.

Elliptical answers like *'War and Peace'* could be modeled as the remnants of full answers, where parts that were mentioned in the question are suppressed: ~~Bill read~~ *'War and Peace'*. As far as polarity questions are concerned, the simple answers *yes* and *no* cannot be captured in a straightforward way. What we can derive are full answers like *Bill read 'War and Peace'*, meaning $\lambda i[\text{READ}_i(\text{W\&P})(\text{BILL})]$, which is an element of the polarity question meaning (80).

How can we express the relation between the question and the focus in the answer? Notice that any solution to this problem will also account for elliptical answers, as they can be understood as specifying the focus only. The most natural way is to employ Alternative Semantics for the representation of focus (Rooth 1992), which assumes that expressions have two semantic representations, a standard meaning and a set of alternatives induced by the item in focus:

(82) *Bill read [*'War and Peace'*]$_F$.*
 Meaning: $\lambda i[\text{READ}_i(\text{W\&P})(\text{BILL})]$
 Alternatives: $\{\lambda i[\text{READ}_i(x)(\text{BILL})] \mid x \in \text{ALT}(\text{W\&P})\}$

A declarative sentence containing focus is assumed to be a congruent answer to a question iff its set of alternatives A corresponds to the question meaning Q, a condition that is interpreted by Rooth (1992) in the sense that Q ⊆ A. This condition obtains for questions like (81A) and answers like (82).

Focus also helps to explain a certain distinction between infelicitous answers. The assertion *Bill read 'Crime and Punishment'* is infelicitous as an answer to (81), as 'Crime and Punishment' is not a novel by Tolstoy. The answer *It is raining* is also infelicitous, but more severely so. The original theory does not account for this difference. The refined theory, which factors in the focus in answers, does: The first infelicitous answer is bad because it is not an element of Q, but at least it holds that Q is a subset of the set of alternatives of the answer (provided that focus is on *Crime and Punishment*, and the alternatives are all novels).

(83) $\{\lambda i[\text{READ}_i(x)(\text{BILL})] | x \in \text{NOVEL BY TOLSTOY}\} \subseteq \{\lambda i[\text{READ}_i(x)(\text{BILL})] | x \in \text{ALT}(\text{C\&P})\}$

For the second infelicitous answer, *it is raining*, it does not even hold that the answer alternatives contain the question meaning. Hence it violates the criterion for congruent questions more severely.

Embedded interrogatives consist in applying a question-embedding verb to a set of propositions (84). As before, question-embedding *know* can be reduced to proposition-embedding *know* (85), which says that for all propositions in the question meaning p, Mary knows that p.

(84) *Mary knows which novel by Tolstoy Bill read.*
$\text{KNOW}_{i0}(\{\lambda i[\text{READ}_i(x)(\text{BILL})] | x \in \text{NOVEL BY TOLSTOY}\})(\text{Mary})$

(85) $\forall p \in \{\lambda i[\text{READ}_i(x)(\text{BILL})] | x \in \text{NOVEL BY TOLSTOY}\}[p(i_0) \rightarrow \text{KNOW}_i(p)(\text{MARY})]$

The proposition set theory proposes the same semantic type of questions – sets of propositions – no matter how they are formed. This allows for the conjunction of different types of questions, which can be represented in a straightforward way by set union.

(86) *Mary knows what Bill read and whether he fell asleep.*
$\text{KNOW}_{i0}(\{\lambda i[\text{READ}_i(x)(\text{BILL})] | x \in \text{THING}\} \cup$
$\{\lambda i[\text{FELL\_ASLEEP}_i(\text{BILL})], \lambda i \neg [\text{FELL ASLEEP}_i(\text{BILL})]\})(\text{MARY})$

Interpreted exhaustively, this means that Mary knows every true proposition in this set, which gives us the right result. However, it is questionable that the conjunction is interpreted by set union, as normally it is understood as intersection.

The proposition set theory of questions goes back to Hamblin (1973). In the version of Karttunen (1977) the meaning of a question is the set of answers that are true. This makes it slightly simpler to express the relation between question-embedding *know* and declarative-embedding *know*:

(87) *which novel by Tolstoy Bill read* (in world i_0):
$\{p \mid \exists x \in \text{NOVEL BY TOLSTOY}[p = \lambda i[\text{READ}_i(x)(\text{BILL})] \wedge p(i_0)]\}$

(88) *Mary knows which novel by Tolstoy Bill read.*
$\forall p \in \{p \mid \exists x \in \text{NOVEL BY TOLSTOY}[p = \lambda i[\text{READ}_i(x)(\text{BILL})] \wedge p(i_0)]\}$
$[\text{KNOWS}_{i_0}(p)(\text{MARY})]$

It should be pointed out that the functional analysis of questions is more fine-grained than the proposition set analysis. It is possible to turn a functional representation into a propositional one, following the recipe (89), but not the other way round.

(89) If F is a functional representation of a question, then $\{F(X) \mid X \in \text{DOMAIN}(F)\}$ is its proposition set representation.

Following a general methodology rule that strives for the weakest representation of a phenomenon possible, propositional representations of questions are to be preferred if they capture all the linguistic phenomena. But do they? Krifka (2001b) points out several shortcomings. There is the problem that straightforward answers to polarity questions like *yes* and *no* cannot be captured directly; we can only model full answers. Another problem is that the proposition set theory cannot distinguish between polarity questions and a certain type of alternative question. Both the questions of (90) and (91) will be represented by (92), even though the answer patterns are different, as the alternative question excludes the answer *Yes*.

(90) A: *Did Bill leave?*
B: *Yes. / He did (leave).*

(91) A: *Did Bill leave, or not?*
B: **Yes. / He did (leave).*

(92) $\{\lambda i[\text{LEFT}_i(\text{BILL})], \lambda i \neg[\text{LEFT}_i(\text{BILL})]\}$

In the functional theory we can express the meanings of the two questions in distinct ways that invite the distinct answer patterns:

(93) $\lambda i \lambda f \in \{\lambda t.t, \lambda t.\neg t\}][f(\text{LEFT}_i(\text{BILL}))]$

(94) $\lambda i \lambda p \in \{\lambda i[\text{LEFT}_i(\text{BILL})], \lambda i \neg [\text{LEFT}_i(\text{BILL})]\}[p(i)]$

While (93) asks for the proposition modifier that yields a true proposition when applied to the proposition 'Bill left', (94) asks which of the two propositions 'Bill left', 'Bill didn't leave' is true. Answers like *yes* and *no* that specify preposition modifiers are impossible in (94), whereas full answers are possible for (93), just as full answers are possible as a more complex answering strategy in the functional analysis in general.

Another problem appears when we look at the focus pattern of answers (cf. Krifka 2001b, 2004). Recall that the focus of answers was explained by the requirement that the question meaning is a subset of focus-induced alternatives of the answers, $Q \subseteq A$. This does not exclude over-focused answers such as the following:

(95) A: *What did Bill read?*
$\{\lambda i[\text{READ}_i(x)(\text{BILL})] \mid x \in \text{NOVEL}\}$

B: $[Bill]_F$ read [*'War and Peáce'*]$_F$
Meaning: $\lambda i[\text{READ}_i(\text{W\&P})(\text{BILL})]$
Alternatives: $\{\lambda i[\text{READ}_i(x)(y)] \mid x \in \text{ALT}(\text{W\&P}), y \in \text{ALT}(\text{BILL})\}$

The focus pattern of B's answer is not the one of a congruent answer, yet the meaning of the question is a subset of its alternatives. One can exclude such cases by a pragmatic rule for alternatives, a rule that Schwarzschild (1999) introduced for contrastive focus, which prefers the minimal focus pattern that satisfies the context requirements. In (95), focus on *'War and Peace'* would be sufficient. But the preference for minimal focus marking does not exclude focus marking that is too broad, as in the following answer to A's question in (95):

(96) B: *Bill [read 'War and PEACE']*$_F$.
Meaning: $\lambda i[\text{READ}_i(\text{W\&P})(\text{BILL})]$
Alternatives: $\{\lambda i[P_i(\text{BILL})] \mid P \in \text{ALT}(\lambda i \lambda x[\text{READ}_i(\text{W\&P})(x)])\}$

In (96) we have incorrect focus assignment, yet the requirement $Q \subseteq A$ is satisfied. We would have to supplement Schwarzschild's rule that selects for the least specific focalization to exclude unwarranted multiple focus by one that selects for the most specific focus to exclude unwarranted broad focus.

4.4 The partitional approach

We now turn to the third type of question representation, which was proposed by Higginbotham & May (1981) and in much greater detail by Groenendijk & Stokhof (1982, 1984). In a sense, it incorporates features of both the functional approach and the proposition set approach. In Groenendijk & Stokhof's theory, question meanings are constructed in two steps. First, a functional representation FR is built, as in (97a). In a second step, a relation between indices is constructed using the rule in (97b).

(97) *which novel Bill read*
   a. $\lambda i \lambda x[\text{NOVEL}_i(x) \land \text{READ}_i(x)(\text{BILL})] = \text{FR}$
   b. $\lambda j \lambda i[\text{FR}(i) = \text{FR}(j)]$
       $= \lambda j \lambda i[\lambda x[\text{NOVEL}_i(x) \land \text{READ}_i(x)(\text{BILL})] = \lambda x[\text{NOVEL}_j(x) \land \text{READ}_j(x)(\text{BILL})]]$

This results in an equivalence relation between indices that holds between index j and i iff the novels that Bill read in j and the novels that Bill read at i are the same. The indices i, j are indistinguishable as far as the interrogative *which novel Bill read* is concerned. As equivalence relations generally do, this creates a partition of the set of indices (hence the term for this type of question theory used here). Let ER be the representation of a question meaning by an equivalence relation, as in (97b), then the corresponding partition is defined as follows:

(98) $\{p \mid \forall i \forall j[i,j \in p \text{ iff } \text{ER}(j)(i)]\}$

A partition of the set of indices is a set of propositions – hence the similarity to the proposition set theory – but the propositions are non-overlapping and exhaust the set of all indices.

It is perhaps best to compare the proposition set theory and the partitional theory with the help of an example. Assume that there are two readable things, 'War and Peace' and 'Crime and Punishment'. In this model, the question *What did Bill read?* is interpreted in the proposition set theory as involving two propositions (99), and in the partitional theory as involving four propositions (100):

(99) Proposition set representation of *what Bill read*

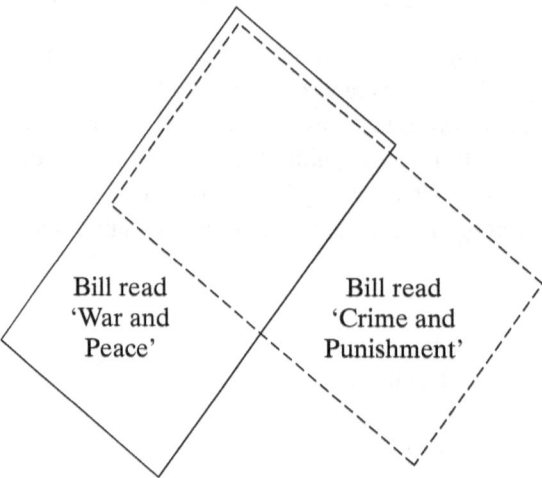

(100) Partitional representation of *what Bill read*

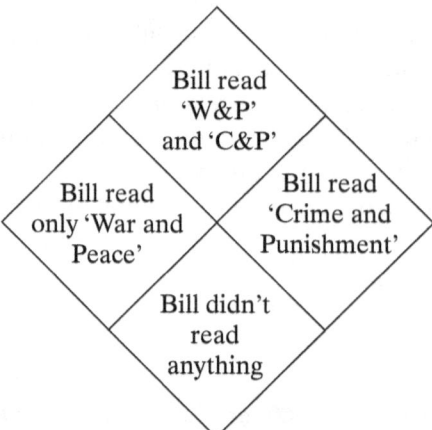

While the proposition set representation contains overlapping propositions and does not cover every index, the partition representation consists of mutually non-overlapping propositions that together cover all indices. Consequently, the partition approach takes the exhaustive interpretation of questions as basic. An answer like *Bill read 'War and Peace'* is to be interpreted as *Bill read only 'War and Peace'*, if it is to be understood as a congruent answer. Groenendijk & Stokhof assume an operator with the semantics of *only* that creates exhaustive interpretations (see below). Furthermore, negative answers like *Bill didn't read anything* are answers just like other answers. In the propositional theory such answers are peculiar as they do not correspond to any proposition in the question set.

The formation rule for equivalence relations illustrated in (97) is flexible enough to capture different types of questions. This is illustrated with a VP question and with a multiple question:

(101) *what Bill did*
 $\lambda j \lambda i [\lambda P[\text{ACTION}_i(P) \wedge P_i(\text{BILL})] = \lambda P[\text{ACTION}_j(P) \wedge P_j(\text{BILL})]]$

(102) *who read which novel*
 $\lambda j \lambda i [\lambda x \lambda y [\text{PERSON}_i(x) \wedge \text{NOVEL}_i(y) \wedge \text{READ}_i(y)(x)] =$
 $\lambda x \lambda y [\text{PERSON}_j(x) \wedge \text{NOVEL}_j(y) \wedge \text{READ}_j(y)(x)]]$

For example, (102) describes the equivalence relation that holds between two indices iff the same persons read the same novels in them.

When comparing the functional approach and the proposition set approach we observed that the question constituent and the other parts of the question play distinct roles in answers, as the question constituent contributes presupposed information (cf. 63). This is not captured in the usual representations of the partitional theory. As a consequence, representations like (97) do not indicate that the question presupposes that Bill read only one novel, in contrast to questions like *Which novels did Bill read?*, or questions based on number-indifferent question words like *who* and *what*. We can introduce this presuppositional component and at the same time regain the insight that negative answers like *nobody* are special by a variant of the partitional theory in which the construction of partitions is based on the following rule instead of (97b), where ι maps sets to the maximal element in the set, if defined.

(103) $\lambda j \lambda i [\iota(FR(i)) = \iota(FR(j))]$

We could easily generalize ι to various types. In the simple case that FR is of type $\langle s, \langle e, t \rangle \rangle$ we get the following interpretation, given by way of example (97a):

(104) *which novel Bill read*
 a. $\lambda i \lambda x [\text{NOVEL}_i(x) \wedge \text{READ}_i(x)(\text{BILL})]$, = FR
 b. $\lambda j \lambda i [\iota x [\text{NOVEL}_i(x) \wedge \text{READ}_i(x)(\text{BILL})] = \iota x [\text{NOVEL}_j(x) \wedge \text{READ}_j(x)(\text{BILL})]]$

This presupposes that Bill read exactly one novel. If presuppositions are taken to select admissible common grounds, then the set of indices to be partitioned is reduced, as it cannot include indices in which Bill read more than one novel, or no novel at all. Returning to our example where there are just two novels, the partition can be depicted as follows:

(105) *which novel Bill read*

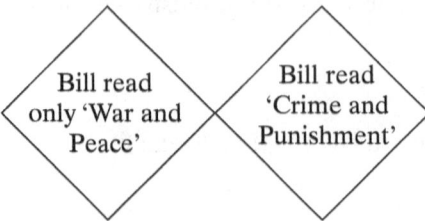

Let us return to the standard representations of questions in the partitional account. For alternative questions we can assume that the restriction is expressed by a disjunction:

(106) *whether Bill read 'War and Peace' or 'Crime and Punishment'*
$\lambda j \lambda i [\lambda x [[x=\text{W\&P} \lor x=\text{C\&P}] \land \text{READ}_i(x)(\text{BILL})] =$
$\lambda x [[x=\text{W\&P} \lor x=\text{C\&P}] \land \text{READ}_j(x)(\text{BILL})]]$

This creates the partition illustrated in (100). While this gives us essentially the right result, the problem remains that alternative questions presuppose that two of the mentioned alternatives do not hold at the same time, a meaning component not expressed by (106).

For polarity questions the suggested representation is one in which no constituent is identified by a lambda-abstraction:

(107) *whether Bill read 'War and Peace'*
$\lambda j \lambda i [\text{READ}_i(\text{W\&P})(\text{BILL})] = \text{READ}_j(\text{W\&P})(\text{BILL})]$

This yields an equivalence relation that sorts indices into two sets, one in which Bill read 'War and Peace', and another one in which he didn't. Note that this is the same representation that the proposition set analysis would assign to this question. It also runs into the same problem as that analysis, namely that it leads to the same interpretation as the alternative question *whether Bill read 'War and Peace' or not* (cf. discussion of 91 and 92).

One attractive feature of the partitional theory of questions is that it can explain properties of embedded questions in an elegant way. Question-embedding predicates like *know* apply to the extension of a question meaning (that is, the question meaning applied to the index of evaluation, i_0). As a result, the inference from knowing-who to knowing-that follows straightforwardly:

(108) Mary knows who came.
 $\text{KNOW}_{i_0}(\lambda j\lambda i[\lambda x[\text{CAME}_i(x)] = \lambda x[\text{CAME}_j(x)]](i_0))(\text{MARY})$
 $= \text{KNOW}_{i_0}(\lambda i[\lambda x[\text{CAME}_i(x)] = \lambda x[\text{CAME}_{i_0}(x)]])(\text{MARY})$
 $= \text{KNOW}_{i_0}(\lambda i[\text{CAME}_i(\text{BILL}) \wedge \text{CAME}_i(\text{JOHN})])(\text{MARY})$
 iff Bill and John are the only ones who came at i_0

This means that *Mary knows who came* has the same truth conditions as *Mary knows that Bill came and John came* in case Bill and John are the only ones who came. Similarly, if no one came, (108) means the same as *Mary knows that no one came*. This is because the equation in the extensional question meaning states that the entities that come in i are the same as the entities that came in the real world. In addition to extensional question predicates like *know*, there are predicates like *wonder* for which such inferences do not hold – notice that *wonder* does not even embed *that*-clauses. Groenendijk & Stokhof take *wonder* to be a predicate that takes question intensions, which have a type different from the meanings of *that*-clauses:

(109) Mary wonders who came.
 $\text{WONDER}_{i_0}(\lambda j\lambda i[\lambda x[\text{CAME}_i(x)] = \lambda x[\text{CAME}_j(x)]])(\text{MARY})$

We can capture the meaning roughly by saying that Mary would like to know in which cell of the partition defined by the embedded questions the real world i_0 is.

Like the proposition set analysis, the partitional analysis assigns the same semantic type to all questions – functions from indices to functions from indices to truth values (i.e., relations between indices) for intensional questions, and functions from indices to truth values for extensional questions. This predicts that questions can be combined by the Boolean operator *and*. In contrast to the proposition set analysis, we can now apply the usual intersective semantics of *and*: If the two questions Q_1 and Q_2 induce the partitions $P(Q_1)$ and $P(Q_2)$, the question Q_1 and Q_2 will induce the partition $P(Q_1) \cap P(Q_2)$. This is illustrated in the following example:

(110) who came and who left
 $= \lambda j\lambda i[\lambda x[\text{CAME}_i(x)] = \lambda x[\text{CAME}_j(x)]] \cap \lambda j\lambda i[\lambda x[\text{LEFT}_i(x)] = \lambda x[\text{LEFT}_j(x)]]$
 $= \lambda j\lambda i[\lambda x[\text{CAME}_i(x)] = \lambda x[\text{CAME}_j(x)] \wedge \lambda x[\text{LEFT}_i(x)] = \lambda x[\text{LEFT}_j(x)]]$

If there are two persons, Bill and Mary, then this intersection can be graphically represented as follows. Observe that the result is a partition, hence a proper question meaning.

(111)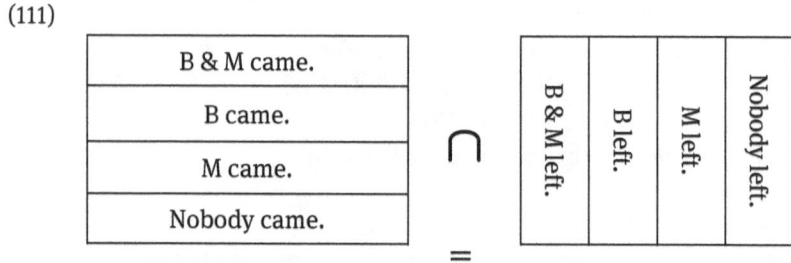

B & M came. B & M left.	B & M came. B left.	B & M came. M left.	B & M came. Nobody left.
B came. B & M left.	B came. B left.	B came. M left.	B came. Nobody left.
M came. B & M left.	M came. B left.	M came. M left.	M came. Nobody left.
Nobody came. B & M left.	Nobody came. B left.	Nobody came. M left.	Nobody came. Nobody left.

We have already mentioned that the partitional theory takes the exhaustive interpretation of questions as basic. The role of focus in answers is to indicate where exhaustification has to be applied. In the partitional approach no specific theory of focus has been developed, but as long as we assume that focus indicates alternatives, any focus theory should do. Groenendijk & Stokhof (1984) consider the structured meaning approach of Szabolcsi (1981). Consider the following interchange:

(112) Who read 'War and Peace'?
 Bill$_F$ read 'War and Peace'.
 ⟨λiλx[READ$_i$(W&P)(x)], BILL⟩

Focus on *Bill* introduces a structured meaning, as indicated. This can be used to form an exhaustive interpretation, based on an operator that has the meaning of *only* (Groenendijk & Stokhof actually present a more general version of the exhaustivity operator).

(113) $\lambda\langle B,F\rangle \lambda i[B(i)(F) \wedge \forall X[B(i)(X) \rightarrow X = F]]$
 Applied to (112) this operator derives the following meaning:

(114) $\lambda i[\text{READ}_i(\text{W\&P})(\text{BILL}) \wedge \forall x[\text{READ}_i(\text{W\&P})(x) \rightarrow x = \text{BILL}]]$

4.5 Inquisitive semantics

The last framework we will consider here is currently being developed by Groenendijk and others (cf. Groenendijk & Roelofsen 2009). Its point of origin is the partitional representation, but it leads to a representation that is closely related to the proposition set representation. It provides a framework in which coordinations of interrogative and indicative sentences can be treated, and which is also well suited to capture the role of questions in conversation, a point to which we will return below.

Inquisitive semantics assumes relations between indices that are reflexive and symmetric, but not necessarily transitive, and hence do not form partitions of indices; such relations are called "states" (of conversation). If two indices stand in such a relation, their difference in factual content is not at issue at the current point in conversation.

The point of departure is the total relation s_0 that distinguishes between none of the indices: $s_0 = I \times I$, the so-called "ignorant" state. An assertion like *It is raining* reduces the input state to a state s_1 so that it applies only to those index pairs $\langle i,j \rangle$ such that it is raining in i and raining in j. We write s[p] for the "update" of a state s by a proposition p. States s for which it holds that if $\langle i,i \rangle \in s$ and $\langle j,j \rangle \in s$ then $\langle i,j \rangle \in s$ are called "indifferent"; notice that s_1 is indifferent. As the sentence *it is raining* results in a reduction of the initial state s_0, it is called "informative". In the following graphical representations, states are represented by sets of sets of indices, with representative indices indicated by dots and the relation between them; if s is a state, then s is represented by the set of all the largest sets of indices S such that for all i,j∈S: $\langle i,j \rangle \in S$. For indifferent states this is a singleton set:

(115) s_0: ignorance   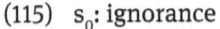$s_1 = s_0[p]$.

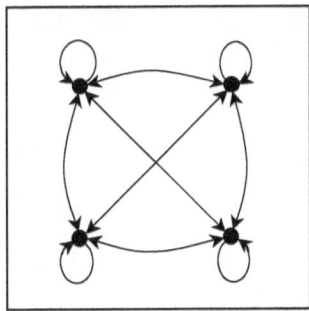 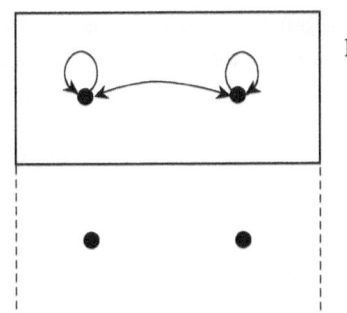

Disjunction plays a crucial role in Inquisitive Semantics; it is treated as the source of inquisitiveness, as it introduces alternatives. A question like *Is it raining?* is interpreted as a disjunction of the form [p ∨ ¬p], and an alternative question like *Is it raining or snowing?* leads to a disjunction of the form p ∨ q. Disjunction is not interpreted as a Boolean operation, but leads to the formation of a set of "possibilities". More specifically, we have that $s[p \vee q] = s[p] \cup s[q]$, as illustrated in (116). Notice that s_2 is not indifferent, and that s_3 is neither indifferent nor transitive. We say that states like s_2 and s_3 have two "possibilities".

(116) $s_2 = s_0[?p]$ $\qquad\qquad\qquad s_3 = s_0[p \vee q]$
$\quad\quad\;\; = s_0[p \vee \neg p]$

This representation is reminiscent of Hamblin's but actually it is weaker: In Hamblin's theory questions like *Did John come, or did John and Bill come?* would lead to a set of two propositions, one a subset of the other. This is not a possible configuration in Inquisitive Semantics, as $[p \vee [p \wedge q]]$ would have the same meaning as p.

Disjunctions can also occur in assertions, of course, as in *it is raining or it is snowing*. For this Groenendijk proposes an operation of "indifferentiation" that amounts to Euclidian closure, or the union formation over possiblities. In the language of inquisitive logic, this is handled by an "assertive closure" operator !. In the following example, s_5 is again a state of indifference.

(117) $s_5 = s_0[![p \vee q]]$

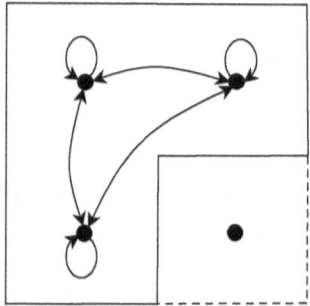

Negation is defined in such a way that s[¬φ] applies to all index pairs ⟨i,j⟩ ∈ s such that ⟨i,i⟩ ∉ s[φ] and ⟨j,j⟩ ∉ s[φ]. It is applicable to indifferent states and to inquisitive states, and leads to indifferent states. Assertive closure can be defined by double negation: !p := ¬¬p. The left-hand side of (118) illustrates that the negation of the inquisitive state after [p ∨ q] and of the indifferent state after ![p ∨ q] has the same result.

(118) $s_6 = s_0[¬![p ∨ q]]$ $s_7 = s_0[?[p ∨ q]]$
       $ = s_0[¬[p ∨ q]]$

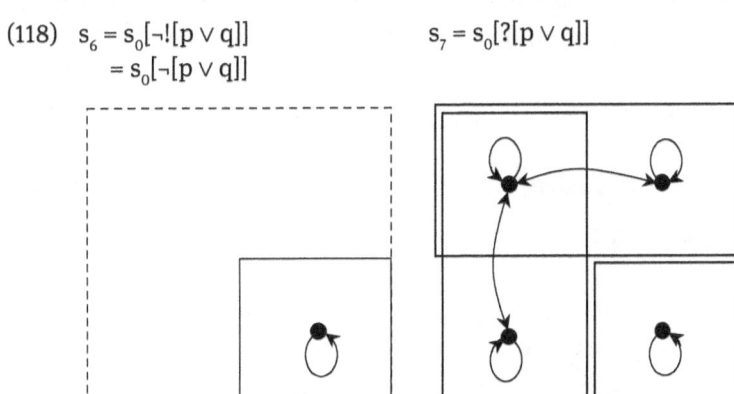

The right-hand side of (118) illustrates the meaning of the question ?[p ∨ q], short for [p ∨ q] ∨ ¬[p ∨ q]. Notice that this is distinct from the question [p ∨ q], as it includes the possibility that neither p nor q are hold. This captures the fact that question like *Did John come or did Bill come, or did neither of them come?* does not presuppose that anyone came, in contrast to the alternative question *Did Jóhn come or did Bíll come?*

Inquisitive Logic allows for the coordination of questions, as in *(John knows) whether it is raining and whether the newspaper will be delivered*, and for the coordination of questions and assertions like *(John knows) that it is raining and whether the newspaper will be delivered*. Coordination is dynamic, incremental update: s[p & q] = s[p][q], which leads to interpretations like the following:

(119) $s_5 = s_0+[?p \ \& \ ?q]$ $s_6 = s_0+[p \ \& \ ?q]$

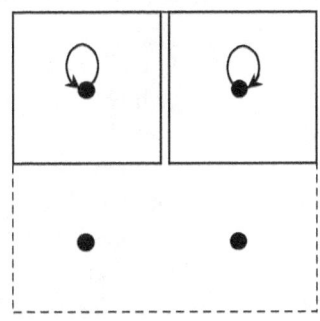

While inquisitive semantics has not been extended beyond polarity and alternative questions in published work so far, this can be done in natural ways (cf. Kratzer & Shimoyama 2002 for a related proposal within the proposition set account). Constituent questions can be seen as generalized disjunctions. A question like *Who came?*, where Mary, Sue and Bill are the alternatives, amounts to the disjoined question *Did Mary come or did Sue come or did Bill come?* More generally, we can render the meaning of constituent questions as follows:

(120) *Who came?*

$$\bigvee_{x \,\in\, \text{PERSON}} \text{CAME}(x)$$

We will return to Inquisitive Semantics below. Next we will turn to the issue how question meanings are constructed.

4.6 The construction of question meanings

Question meanings, like meanings of complex expressions in general, should be derived compositionally, and we should ask how the four approaches to question interpretation can work with what syntactic theories offer for the syntactic structure of questions. We have seen that there are two syntactic strategies for question constituents: they either move to a dedicated position ("*wh*-movement"), or they remain in situ, in which case they typically carry some sort of intonational marker. There are also mixed strategies, like movement languages that leave question constituents of certain questions like echo questions in place, or that move only one question constituent in multiple questions. Then there is the phenomenon of partial wh-movement in which one *wh*-element marks the scope of the question, and another one stays in a more local position, as in the following German example:

(121) Was₁ denkst du, [wen₁ ich t₁ gesehen habe].
       what thinks you who I   seen   have
       'Who do you think I saw?'

See Sabel (2006) for an overview of wh-movement types. In alternative questions, the alternative construction never moves, but is always marked intonationally.

Marking questions by movement or an equivalent syntactic operation (see Ginzburg & Sag 2001 for an HPSG account) is suggestive of the functional representation of question meanings. Movement can be seen as a syntactic operation that identifies positions in the description of a proposition, which provides the blueprint for the construction of a functional meaning. The *wh*-feature in the question constituent triggers movement, the content of the question constituent defines the domain of the function, and the trace identifies the position abstracted over:

(122) a. [[*which novel*]$_1$ [*Bill* [*read* t$_1$]]]
 b. $\lambda x_1 \in$ NOVEL [READ(x_1)(BILL)]

Marking questions by in situ question constituents is suggestive of the proposition set theory. Hamblin (1973) has proposed that question words are interpreted as sets of meanings, leading to sets of meanings when combined with other meanings:

(123) *which novel*: {x|x is a novel}
 read: $\lambda y \lambda x$[x read y]
 read which novel: {λx[x read y] | y is a novel}
 Bill: BILL
 Bill read which novel: {Bill read y | y is a novel}

No movement is required. The intonational marking of question constituents *in situ* can be seen as focus marking, where focus indicates the presence of alternatives.

The partitional theory makes crucial use of lambda abstraction, which suggests that questions are constructed by movement. Inquisitive Semantics leads to representations that are somewhat similar to the proposition set theory, and similarly does not require *wh*-movement in general.

In spite of these natural affinities between syntactic realizations of questions and approaches to their semantics, it should be stressed that different ways of question marking do not presuppose one or the other semantic representation. We have seen in (89) that propositional representations can be derived from functional representations (which can be constructed from syntactic structures containing *wh*-movement). And we can derive functional representations from structures without overt *wh*-marking if we assume *wh*-movement (or some equivalent process) on logical form. Considering the fact that many languages show mixed strategies (e.g., the movement strategy of one question constituent only, or the in situ strategy for certain types of questions only) one could also envision mixed semantic representations. Furthermore, there are syntactic considerations that argue for one or the other type of process. For example, the island restrictions discussed above square well with a movement (or coindexation) account, as do the so-called "intervention effects" (Beck 2006) that prohibit certain operators like negation between the interpretation site of a *wh*-element and its trace, as in the following German example where *niemandem* 'to nobody' intervenes between was_2 and its trace t_2 at LF.

(124) *Wer_1 hat t_1 niemandem was gegeben?
   LF: Wer_1 was_2 [hat t_1 niemandem t_2 gegeben?]
   'Who didn't give what to nobody?'

4.7 A comparison of question theories

After having discussed four distinct approaches to question meanings, a comparison is in order.

First, we should consider the complexity of the question representations. The functional representation takes a privileged role here, as we can derive the propositional representation from it (cf. 89), but not vice versa. Functional representations also form the basis of the partitional theory, as it uses functional abstracts to construct the equivalence relation that then defines the partition (cf. 97, 98). This is how Groenendijk & Stokhof derive partitional representations. Furthermore, example (120) illustrates how a functional representation can be turned into a representation of Inquisitive Semantics. None of these construction rules are reversible. With this, we can draw the following map for the syntactic marking of questions and the logical expressiveness of semantic question representations.

(125)

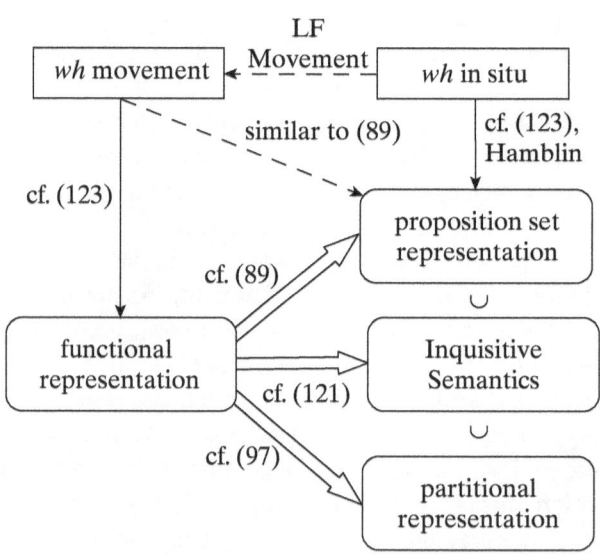

The functional representation is the most finely articulate one from which all the others can be derived. Among the non-functional representations, the representations of Inquisitive Semantics are a proper subset of the general proposition set representations (it disallows two propositions where one is the subset of the other). And partitional representations form a proper subset of the representations of Inquisitive Semantics (the propositions do not overlap, and are exhaustive).

5 Further topics

5.1 Indefinites and interrogatives

Interrogative pronouns like *when* and *where* can be decomposed into two parts: one expressing interrogativity (*wh-*), the other expressing the type or sort of entities that are asked (e.g., *-en* for time, which also occurs in *th-en*; *-ere* for place, which also occurs in *th-ere*). In most languages, this combination appears to be at least partially transparent, and we find completely transparent systems in Pidgin and Creole languages (cf. Muysken & Smith 1990).

In many languages, interrogative pro-forms are related to indefinite pro-forms, as in English *how* and *somehow*, or German *wer* and *irgendwer* (cf. Haspelmath 1997). In languages that have segmentally identical forms, the two readings differ either in prosody or in syntax. In German, the interrogative form receives special accent or is moved to a dedicated position, as examples (127a, b) show:

(126) *Bill hat was gelesen.*
   'Bill has read something.'

(127) a. *Bill hat wás gelesen?*
   b. *Was/Wás hat Bill gelesen?*
   'What did Bill read?'

In Lhakota, the presence of an interrogative particle turns an indefinite into a *wh*-term; again, the indefinite has to be focused (cf. van Valin & LaPolla 1997).

(128) *šúka ki táku yaxtáka he*
   dog DEF something bite QU
   'What did the dog bite?'

(129) šúka ki táku yaxtáka
 dog DEF something bite
 'The dog bit something.'

The similarity between indefinite and interrogative pronouns is well-motivated at an intuitive level: these two forms have in common that semantic information is left unspecified. How can this intuition be captured by the different frameworks of question representations? As for the proposition set representation, notice that it can be rendered in a format in which the *wh*-constituent is represented by an existential indefinite:

(130) who read 'War and Peace'
 $\lambda p \exists x[\text{PERSON}(x) \wedge p=\lambda i[\text{READ}_i(\text{W\&P})(x)]]$

For the partitional account, Haida (2008) has proposed a variety that works with dynamic existential quantifiers that are natural meanings of indefinites, italicized in (131). The biconditional expresses that the context-change potential of the two formulas is exactly the same, which amounts the same truth conditions as in the original approach by Groenendijk & Stokhof.

(131) who read 'War and Peace'
 $\lambda j[\exists x[\text{PERSON}_j(x) \wedge \text{READ}_j(\text{W\&P})(x)] \leftrightarrow \exists x[\text{PERSON}_i(x) \wedge \text{READ}_i(\text{W\&P})(x)]]$

No proposal exists so far for the functional account that would explain the relationship between indefinites and *wh*-words. However, the idea can be implemented in a number of ways; one just has to make sure that the semantic contribution of the indefinite is used to restrict the question function. If we assume a standard analysis of indefinites as Generalized Quantifiers Q that undergo LF-movement, then this can be done by reference to the witness set W(Q):

(132) Who did Mary meet?
 QUEST [*someone*$_1$ [Mary met t$_1$]]
 QUEST($\lambda P \exists x[\text{PERSON}(x) \wedge P(x)]$) ($\lambda x_1[\text{MET}(x_1)(\text{MARY})]$)
 = $\lambda x \in W(\lambda P \exists x[\text{PERSON}(x) \wedge P(x)])$ [$\lambda x_1[\text{MET}(x_1)(\text{MARY})]$]

The indefinite character of *wh*-words also explains why they can be antecedents to anaphora, as in *Who wrote 'War and Peace' (hint: his name starts with 'T')*, a fact that can be captured in dynamic theories like the one of Haida.

One surprising fact is that the indefinite interpretation almost always appears to be derived from the interrogative interpretation, if there is any morphological relation at all (cf. English *where – somewhere*. Bhat (2000) has called this the "Interrogative-Indefinite Puzzle." It can be explained by pointing out that the basic form *where* itself is not an interrogative yet, but just a variable; it becomes one only by association with an interrogative operator by movement or focus. Forms like *somewhere*, or German *irgendwann*, consist of an indefinite quantifier *some* that binds this variable.

A particularly natural explanation of Bhat's observation can be obtained in Inquisitive Semantics. In (120) we have analyzed constituent questions as generalized disjunctions. Now, indefinites, as existentials, are generalized disjunctions. In Inquisitive Semantics, the basic meaning of the disjunction is inquisitive; only by assertive closure do we get a non-inquisitive, indifferent meaning. We can interpret the additional marking of indefinites as the assertive closure operator. This is illustrated with German *wer* and *irgendwer*.

(133) *wer*: *irgendwer*:

$\lambda P \bigvee_{x \in \text{PERSON}} P(x)$ $\lambda P\,! \bigvee_{x \in \text{PERSON}} P(x)$

5.2 Question-embedding predicates

Right from the beginning we have treated questions in their double role, as speech acts and as part of other sentences. In this section we will turn to some of the semantic properties of the predicates that embed questions.

We have assumed that root questions and embedded questions have in common that they both involve a sentence radical:

(134) *Which novel did Bill read?*
 QUEST($\lambda i \lambda x \in \text{THING}_i[\text{READ}_i(x)(\text{BILL})]$)

(135) *Mary told Jane which novel Bill read.*
 $\lambda i[\text{TELL}_i(\lambda i \lambda x \in \text{THING}_i[\text{READ}_i(x)(\text{BILL})])(\text{JANE})(\text{MARY})]$

As we have observed, root questions have an additional feature insofar as they require an auxiliary verb in second position. Now, notice that certain verbs allow for embedded "root" questions:

(136) *Which novel did she have to read, Mary wondered / asked / is curious about.*

Embedded root questions are limited in Standard English but readily occur in varieties such as Irish English (cf. McCloskey 2005, a quote from Joyce's *Dubliners*):

(137) *The baritone was asked what did he think of Mr. Kearsey's conduct*

Embedded root questions only occur under predicates like *ask, wonder,* or *want to know* that express an inquisitive interest – all predicates that do not embed *that*-clauses. Hence, in the framework of Groenendijk & Stokhof they require question intensions as their complements (cf. 109 above). However, in this account it is not explained why we find root clause features in precisely those embedded questions. Krifka (2001a) proposed a theory in which this is explained by the assumption that these verbs actually embed question speech acts, not sentence radicals.

(138) *Mary wondered which novel did Bill read*
  λi[WONDER$_i$(QUEST(λiλx∈NOVEL$_i$[READ$_i$(x)(BILL)])(MARY)]

This says: Mary has an interest in the information that would be satisfied by answers to the indicated question.

Beyond the class of inquisitive verbs, there are further subclasses of question-embedding verbs, and different classifications have been proposed (cf. Baker 1968; Wunderlich 1976; Karttunen 1977; Dipper 1997). Several of the nine classes that Karttunen lists have to do with acquiring, retaining, or communicating knowledge (e.g., *discover, remember, disclose*). They all allow for expressing this knowledge by a *that*-clause, but also by an interrogative clause that generally stands for the true answer of this question. We have seen how the various approaches to question semantics explain this meaning (e.g., 71, 85, 108). In all theories, the *that*-clauses that specify the answer are necessarily understood as factive, that is, they are presupposed to be true. Indeed, question-embedding predicates receive a factive interpretation even if their non-interrogative variant is not factive (cf. Karttunen 1977):

(139) a. *Mary told John that Bill is coming.*
  b. *Mary told John whether Bill is coming.*

In (139a) it is left open whether or not Bill is in fact coming, but (b) presupposes that Mary told John the truth. This factivity effect of embedded questions is the reason why verbs that differ from others only because they lack factivity do not embed questions, such as *believe*:

(140) *Mary knows whether Bill is coming.*

*Mary believes whether Bill is coming.

In addition to verbs expressing relations to knowledge, Karttunen lists verbs that express matters of relevance or of dependency, such as *be important* or *care*, and *depend on* and *be related to*. Again, these cases are to be interpreted with respect to the instances that truly satisfy the sentence radical. Consider the case of *depend on*:

(141) *What you get depends on what you ask for.*
 DEPEND ON$_{10}$($\lambda i\lambda x$[GET$_i$(x)(YOU)])($\lambda i\lambda x$[ASK FOR$_i$(x)(YOU)])
 iff $\forall i,j \in R_{10}$[ιx[ASK FOR$_i$(x)(YOU)] $\neq \iota x$[ASK FOR$_j$(x)(YOU)]
  $\rightarrow \iota x$[GET$_i$(x)(YOU) $\neq$ GET$_j$(x)(YOU)]]

This is a modal statement; it says that for all accessible worlds i, j, iff they differ in what you ask for, then they differ in what you get. Notice that *depend on* is an intensional predicate in terms of Groenendijk & Stokhof, yet it is different from *wonder* as it does not allow for root clause syntax of the embedded question.

We conclude this section by mentioning two additional types of embedded question-like constructions. One concerns so-called "concealed questions" (Baker 1968, Heim 1979), which are of a different syntactic type, the type of determiner phrases, but are interpreted like questions:

(142) *Bill asked / knew the time.*

This means the same as *Bill asked / knew what the time was*, whose embedded questions would be interpreted as:

(143) $\lambda i\lambda x$[x = TIME$_i$]

The concealed questions in (142) can be seen as a different way of constructing the meaning (143), by invoking the standard operation of type lifting of a meaning of type e to a meaning of type $\langle e,t \rangle$ (cf. Partee 1987). In the case at hand, the standard meaning of *the time*, λi[TIME$_i$] of type $\langle s,e \rangle$, which yields the time of the index i, is lifted to $\lambda i\lambda x$[x = TIME$_i$], which is a regular question meaning that maps for each index i a variable x to Truth iff it is the time of i.

The second type of question-like meanings that should be mentioned here are embedded exclamatives, as in the following examples:

(144) *Bill was amazed about how (very) tall she was*

(145) *Bill was amazed about who (all) came to the party.*

Exclamatives of this type show the familiar question syntax (cf. e.g., Zanuttini & Portner 2003). Like questions, they denote a set of alternatives (however specified, e.g., by a function or by a proposition set). But in addition, these alternatives are ordered, e.g., in (144) along the degree scale. In the proposition set analysis this order can be expressed as follows: $\{\langle \lambda i[\text{TALL}_i(\text{SHE})(d)], \lambda i[\text{TALL}_i(\text{SHE})(d')]\rangle \mid d < d'\}$

Exclamative clauses then come with a presupposition that the actual index i_a is contained in a proposition that is ordered higher than expected (called "factivitiy" by Grimshaw 1979). In the following, P is the set of propositions typical for questions, and < is the order relation characteristic for exclamatives.

(146) $\text{EXCL}(\langle P, <\rangle)$ presupp: $\exists p \in P[i_0 \in p \wedge \exists p' < p[\text{EXPECT}(s, i_0 \in p')]$

From this it follows that exclamative clauses are formed over a variable that ranges over degrees, like tallness in (144) or cardinality and noteworthiness in (145). In German, there is a specialized *wh*-determiner *welch* which is restricted to degrees denoted by adjectives or certain nouns, and consequently only occurs in exclamatives:

(147) *Welch kluger   Schachzug dies ist!*
       'What a clever move   this is!'

(148) *Welch ein Idiot ich bin!*
       'What an idiot I   am!'

5.3 Multiple questions

All semantic representations of questions mentioned above can deal with multiple constituent questions, in the sense that the way they deal with questions with one constituent can be generalized to questions with two or more constituents. But multiple questions show interesting properties that do not follow in a straightforward way from the basic treatment.

First, multiple questions come in at least two distinct types. One comprises multiple echo questions and quiz questions:

(149) A: *Esmeralda needs a bandoneon.*
       B: *Whó needs whát?*

(150) *Which Turkish singer won the Eurovision Song contest in which year?*

In the examples above we expect one answer due to special properties of context in which the question is uttered. In contrast, the second type, also called "matching questions", presupposes that there is more than one group of satisfying instances:

(151) *I don't have proper records about the assignments in the literature class. Which student is supposed to present which novel?*

(152) *When did Bill spend his vacation where?*

One difference between the two types of multiple constituent questions is that in the case of quiz questions the *wh*-elements can be conjoined in case they are adverbials, cf. (153). (In languages with multiple *wh*-movement such as Romanian, this even holds for arguments, cf. Comorovski 1996.)

(153) *When and where did Bill spend his vacation?*

The first type of multiple constituent questions, quiz questions, can be captured easily, as we have seen. In the functional representation, for example, it can be rendered as follows:

(154) *Which student presented which novel?*
  QUEST($\lambda i \lambda x \in $STUDENT$_i \lambda y \in $NOVEL$_i$[PRESENTED$_i$(y)(x)])

The uniqueness assumption can be enforced in a similar way as with singular constituent questions (cf. 64), i.e., QUEST is understood to ask to identify, relative to the actual index i_0, the unique x that is a student at i_0 and the unique y that is a novel at i_0 such that x presented y at i_0. But why do matching questions lack this uniqueness requirement? The answer given by Higginbotham & May (1981) is that such questions lead to a construction of a function, which in turn satisfies the uniqueness requirement. The idea is that the logical form of (154), given in (155a) or alternatively its semantic representation, repeated in (155b), is turned into a question radical over a function that maps elements of the set STUDENT$_i$ to elements of the set NOVEL$_i$, as given in (155c). This rule, which combines two (or more) question constituents is called "absorption"; it is a rule that violates compositionality in the strict sense.

(155) a. [*which* student]$_1$ [*which* novel]$_2$ [t$_1$ *presented* t$_2$]
  b. $\lambda i \lambda x \in $STUDENT$_i \lambda y \in $NOVEL$_i$[PRESENTED$_i$(y)(x)]
  c. $\lambda i \lambda f$[STUDENT$_i \rightarrow $NOVEL$_i$] $\forall x$[PRESENTED$_i$(f(x))(x)]

If (155c) serves as sentence radical of a question, then the question, as usual, asks for the unique function that satisfies the description. In our case, it asks for the unique function f from the set of students to the set of novels such that for each student x, f(x) is a novel that x read. Notice that this enforces that each student read a unique novel, otherwise there would be more than one such function. This is the case in situation (156a), where there are two functions from students to novels, $\{\langle s_1,n_1\rangle, \langle s_2,n_2\rangle, \langle s_3,n_4\rangle, \langle s_4,n_4\rangle\}$ and $\{\langle s_1,n_1\rangle, \langle s_2,n_3\rangle, \langle s_3,n_4\rangle, \langle s_4,n_4\rangle\}$.

(156) a.   b.

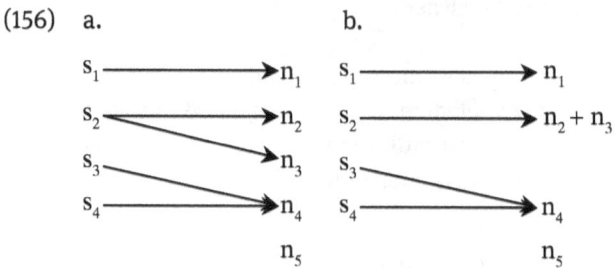

In situations of this type, it is more appropriate to use plurals, as in *which student presented which novels*. Plurals can apply to sum individuals as well as to single individuals, and this allows for the construction of a unique function $\{\langle s_1,n_1\rangle, \langle s_2,n_2+n_3\rangle, \langle s_3,n_4\rangle, \langle s_4,n_4\rangle\}$, as illustrated in (156b).

The domain of the function is typically specified in the sense that it is given in discourse (a phenomenon called D-linking, cf. Comorovski 1985, 1996 and Pesetsky 1987). The domain is specified by the question constituent that is first in surface order. Often, this question constituent c-commands the others in the underlying order as well, which is the basis of the so-called "superiority" effect (cf. Chomsky 1973), according to which sentences like *What did who see?* are ungrammatical.

5.4 Quantifying into questions

Matching questions sometimes have a communicative effect similar to questions containing a quantifier:

(157) *Which novel did every student present?*

In addition to a reading which asks for the unique novel x for which it holds that every student presented x, there is a reading equivalent to (154), which becomes prominent when *every student* is deaccented. For this reading, the universal quantifier has to scope out of the question. In the partition approach we get the following representation:

(158) $\lambda j \lambda i [\forall x \in \text{STUDENT}_j \rightarrow$
$[\lambda y[\text{NOVEL}_i(y) \land \text{PRESENTED}_i(y)] = \lambda y[\text{NOVEL}_j(y) \land \text{PRESENTED}_j(y)]]$

It turns out that this is a well-behaved question meaning, as it is an equivalence relation. It holds between indices j,i iff for every student x in j, the novels that x read in j and the novels that x read in i are indistinguishable. Interestingly, with quantifiers other than universal quantifiers, the result fails to be an equivalence relation, and this correctly predicts that such cases do not allow for a reading of the type of matching questions easily (cf. e.g., *which novel did several students present?*)

Cases like (157), and their restriction to universal quantifiers, have been taken by Krifka (2001a) as evidence that semantic operators can scope out of speech acts:

(159) $\forall x[\text{STUDENT}_{i0}(x) \rightarrow \text{QUEST}(\lambda i \lambda y \in \text{NOVEL}_i[\text{PRESENTED}_i(y)(x)])]$

More specifically, the universal quantifier is understood as a generalization of conjunction of question speech acts. That is, the question asks *which novel did Bill present*, *which novel did Mary present*, etc.

We can identify a different type of quantification over questions when we look at embedded questions, as in the following example:

(160) *Bill knows, for the most part, who cheated on the exam.*

This type of quantification is not possible for questions embedded under verbs like *wonder*. One explanation is that the quantifier modifies the quantifier that we have assumed for the reduction of question-embedding *know* to declarative-embedding *know*.

(161) $\text{MOST}(\lambda x[\text{CHEATED}_{i0}(x)]) (\lambda i \lambda x[\text{KNOW}_{i0}(\lambda i[\text{CHEATED}_i(x)])(\text{BILL})])$

This says that for most x such that x cheated, Bill knows that x cheated. See Berman (1989) and Lahiri (1991) for studies of quantifications over embedded questions.

5.5 Biased questions

The various semantic representation formats for questions all have the property that they do not distinguish an expected answer from other possible answers. However, speakers can impose a certain bias within the answers. This is most evident with polarity questions. A question with declarative syntax as in (162) suggests that the speaker considers it likely that the underlying proposition, here 'You are born in Texas', is true. This bias can be strengthened with a question tag.

(162) *You are born in Texas (aren't you?)*

Similarly, an embedded question with the complementizer *if* sometimes suggests a bias towards the underlying proposition, whereas *whether* indicates neutrality. For this reason, (163b) is strange in contrast to (a), as it suggests that Bill does not favor the proposition that Jill would marry him over the other (cf. Bolinger 1978). However, no such contrast is apparend with the embedding verb *wonder*.

(163) a. *Bill asked Jill if she would marry him.*
       b. *Bill asked Jill whether she would marry him.*

Gunlogson (2003) proposed that sentences like (162) are declaratives without the characteristic falling intonation, which indicates the lack of speaker commitment that is normally required for assertions. But such sentences can also be understood as questions if we capture their bias by representing them by only one proposition (in the proposition set theory), or by a function that only allows for a positive answer (in the functional theory):

(164) $\{\lambda i[\text{MARRY}_i(\text{BILL})(\text{JILL})]\}$

(165) $\lambda f \in \{\lambda p.p\}[f(\lambda i[\text{MARRY}_i(\text{BILL})(\text{JILL})])]$

As before, questions ask the addressee to provide the information in which property the real world is, or which sentence operator provides for a true proposition. But as there is no choice in the case at hand, the speaker strongly suggests that the real world is indeed in the selected proposition. Still this is not an assertion; the addressee is required to do something, and saying *no* will result in rejecting the proposition.

We have to distinguish from examples like (162) cases in which a strong rising intonation expresses incredulity (here expressed by two question marks). Under this contour, example (166a) expresses that the speaker did not believe that you were born in Texas. The same holds for the positive question (167b), whereas the negative question (167c) expresses that the speaker believed that you were born in Texas.

(166) a. *You are born in Texas??*
b. *Are you born in Texas??*
c. *Aren't you born in Texas??*

Romero & Han (2002) analyze such questions as involving a VERUM element that expresses that a proposition is true against contrary evidence. Examples (166a,b) then have the representation (167a), whereas example (166c) has the representation (167b), with CERTAIN as the "verum" element.

(167) a. $\{\lambda i\text{CERTAIN}(\text{BORN\_IN\_TEXAS}_i(\text{YOU})),$
$\lambda i\neg\text{CERTAIN}(\text{BORN\_IN\_TEXAS}_i(\text{YOU}))]\}$

b. $\{\lambda i\text{CERTAIN}(\neg\text{BORN\_IN\_TEXAS}_i(\text{YOU})),$
$\lambda i\neg\text{CERTAIN}(\neg\text{BORN\_IN\_TEXAS}_i(\text{YOU}))\}$

A point in favor of this analysis is that we can form questions like *Are you INDEED born in Texas?* which contain a VERUM element. However, there is nothing in the questions in (166) that seems to identify VERUM. Rather, the special intonation contour can be associated with a subtype of the question force operator expressing incredulity in a positive answer. This seems to suggest that we would have to assume that the alternatives that questions raised are, in addition, endowed with a preference relation among them.

5.6 Fine-grainedness of alternatives

Imagine you are a tourist in Zanzibar City and got lost in the maze of streets of the Old Town. You might ask a local: *Where am I?* The answer, *In Zanzibar*, might be true, but it is not very helpful. Why? Obviously, the question was not understood as fine-grained enough. In the situation just described, alternatives like *Zanzibar* and *Daressalaam* don't help; it is given that the speaker is in Zanzibar, and more fine-grained alternatives are required.

Imagine now you give a lecture in an institute that you don't know well. You ask the director, *Who will be in the audience?*, and you get a list of names. This is less helpful if you don't know the people than an answer like *several anthropologists, a neuro-scientist, and a historical linguist*.

Such differences have been addressed by Ginzburg (1995) under the notion of "resolvedness", which specifies that the addressee of an answer has particular goals, and that the choice of one of the alternatives in the answer is supposed to assist the addressee in making a selection between alternatives in achieving this goal.

5.7 Focus and NPIs in questions

We have seen that questions induce alternatives that are taken up by the focus of the answer. But questions can also contain focus themselves, as in the following examples:

(168) a. *Did BILL$_F$ go to the party?*
b. *What did BILL$_F$ bring?*

As usual, focus indicates the presence of alternatives, here of alternative questions. For example, (168) suggests that in addition to the question expressed, alternative questions that can be expressed by *Did x go to the party?* are relevant at the current point of discourse. That is, we have a set of speech acts as alternatives:

(169) $\{\text{QUEST}(\{\lambda i[\text{CAME}_i(x)], \lambda i \neg [\text{CAME}_i(x)]\}) | x \in \text{ALT}(\text{BILL})\}$

Indicating alternative possible speech acts means that the speaker, at the current point in discourse, has reasons to select, out of this set, the one speech act that is actually made. This is quite similar to the role of contrastive topics, which also occur in questions:

(170)   *As for Bill, did he go to the party?*

Another way of introducing alternatives is by the use of negative polarity items (NPIs, see article 3 [this volume] (Giannakidou) *Polarity items*), which also occur in questions (cf. Fauconnier 1980). We find both grammaticalized NPIs like *ever* and idiomatic NPIs like *lift a finger*:

(171) a. *Did you ever smoke marihuana?*
b. *Did you ever lift a finger to help me?*

While (171a) can be understood as a regular question seeking information, (171b) clearly is a rhetorical question, implying that you never lifted a finger to help me.

How can we explain the specific effects of NPIs in questions? The distribution of NPIs in assertions has been explained in various ways, e.g., by downward-entailingness and by non-veridicality, which initially do not seem to be particularly helpful. However, Krifka (1995) and van Rooij (2003) have suggested that the idea that NPIs indicate the presence of alternatives that are ordered along a scale makes sense for questions. For example, *ever* denotes the most general time under consideration, indicating more specific times as its alternatives. Forming a question on a most general proposition indicates an attempt by the speaker to make the possible answers equally likely. For example, *ever* in (171b) indicates that the speaker is so sure that the answer will be negative that he or she tries to increase the likelihood for a positive answer by letting the time index range over all possible times. Thus, (171b) is a question with a very strong negative bias, practically equivalent to a strong assertion. In the information-seeking question (171a), the speaker suggests a common ground in which the immediate informational need would be best satisfied by the answers 'Bill smoked (at some time or other)' and 'Bill didn't smoke (at any time)', which is the case in a common ground lacks any knowledge concerning Bill's smoking at specific times.

5.8 Questions and text structure

Since antiquity questions were seen as structuring devices of texts, and even today journalists learn that newspaper articles should answer six questions: *What? Who? Where? When? How? Why?* Several theories have been developed in recent years that investigate this function of questions in discourse and dialogue. For example, Question Theory (Klein & von Stutterheim 1987) assumes that text genres are structured by typical questions (imagine a description of your last vacation). Van Kuppevelt (1995) and Roberts (1996) have developed discourse theories that work with notions like questions-under-discussion and of question stacks that are answered systematically by the sentences of a text. Büring (2003) has shown how such notions can be used to analyze the type of contrastive topics (CT) that are indicated by a rising intonation pattern; the idea is that CTs indicate (possibly implicit) strategies which break down a complex question into subquestions.

(172)   *I visited my parents last week.*
        (Implicit question: How are they?)
        [*My father*]$_{CT}$ *is doing fine, but* [*my mother*]$_{CT}$ *is in a hospital.*

Inquisitive Semantics (Groenendijk 2008) considers this role of questions in the information flow in conversation as crucial, and has developed a theory of "Inquisitive Dialogue Management". Recall that information states are considered to be reflexive and symmetric relations between situations. Asking an initial question amounts to changing an indifferent state to an inquisitive state, as in (116a,b). Such conversational moves are modeled by stacks of states; here we add to the existing stack of states the new inquisitive state. Dialogue participants follow certain pragmatic rules, e.g., they should maintain a common ground, and they should be compliant, a formal notion that captures various possible continuations of inquisitive states: One of the possibilities offered by inquisitive states can be asserted, or the possibilities can be refined. This amounts to splitting up a question into subquestions can be captured within this framework: If we take (116a) to be the state after the question *Are your parents doing fine?*, then one continuation would be (a) *Yes, my parents are doing fine*, yielding an indifferent state. Another one would be (b) *Is your mother doing fine?*, yielding another inquisitive state, with the suggestion that (116a) cannot be answered directly. If (116b) is continued by *My mother is not doing fine*, then we get the small square in (174b) as a result, which entails the lower rectangle in the original question, (116a).

(173)   Possible continuations of (116a)
        a.   b.

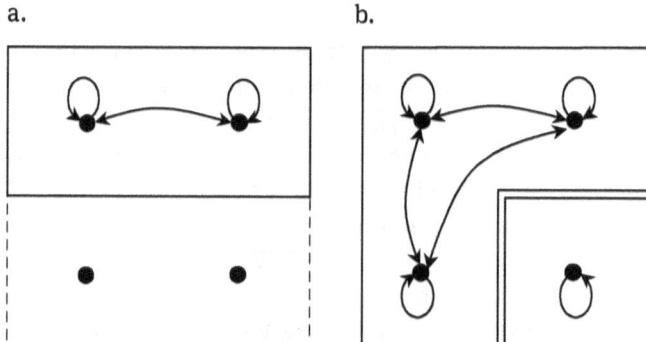

Groenendijk shows how the notion of alternative changes of states can lead to quantity implicatures that may lead to exhaustive interpretations of answers.

6 Conclusion

It has been said that questions are more interesting than answers. Certainly, the point can be made that the semantics of questions is far richer than the semantics of assertions, and as a field of study it is as lively as ever.

Acknowledgment: I would like to thank Andreas Haida, Sophie Repp, Klaus von Heusinger and Paul Portner for very valuable comments on this article. Also, I acknowledge support by the Deutsche Forschungsgemeinschaft (DFG) *Sonderforschungsbereich 637 Information Structure*, and Bundesministerium für Bildung und Forschung (BMBF) (Grant Nr. 01UG0711).

7 References

Baker, Carl 1968. *Indirect Questions in English*. Ph.D. dissertation. University of Illinois, Urbana, IL.
Beck, Sigrid 2006. Intervention effects follow from focus interpretation. *Natural Language Semantics* 14, 1–56.
Belnap, Nuel D. & Thomas B. Steel 1976. *The Logic of Questions and Answers. With Bibliography of the Theory of Questions and Answers by Urs Egli and Hubert Schleichert*. New Haven, CT: Yale University Press.
Berman, Stephen 1989. An analysis of quantificational variability in indirect questions. In: E. Bach, A. Kratzer & B. Partee (eds.). *Papers on Quantification*. Amherst, MA: University of Massachusetts, 19–28.
Bhat, Darbhe N.S. 2000. The indefinite-interrogative puzzle. *Linguistic Typology* 4, 365–400.
Bolinger, Dwight 1978. Yes/no questions are not alternative questions. In: H. Hiz (ed.). *Questions*. Dordrecht: Reidel, 87–105.
Büring, Daniel 2003. On D-trees, beans, and B-accents. *Linguistics & Philosophy* 26, 511–545.
Chomsky, Noam 1973. Conditions on transformations. In: S. Anderson & P. Kiparski (eds.). *A Festschrift for Morris Halle*. New York: Holt, Rinehart & Winston, 232–286.
Cohen, Felix 1929. What is a question? *The Monist* 39, 350–364.
Comorovski, Ileana 1985. Control and obviation in Romanian. In: S. Choi et al. (eds.). *Proceedings of the Second Eastern States Conference on Linguistics (= ESCOL) 2*. Columbus, OH: Ohio State University, 47–56.
Comorovski, Ileana 1996. *Interrogative Phrases and the Syntax-Semantics Interface*. Dordrecht: Kluwer.
Cysouw, Michael 2007. Content interrogatives in Asheninca Campa: Corpus study and typological comparison. *International Journal of American Linguistics* 73, 133–163.
Dipper, Stefanie 1997. *Zur Selektion von Fragesatzkomplementen* (Arbeitspapiere des Sonderforschungsbereichs 340, Bericht Nr. 122). Stuttgart: University of Stuttgart.
Dryer, Matthew S. 2005a. Position of interrogative phrases in content questions. In: M. Haspelmath et al. (eds.). *The World Atlas of Language Structures*. Oxford: Oxford University Press, 378–381.
Dryer, Matthew S. 2005b. Polarity questions. In: M. Haspelmath et al. (eds.). *The World Atlas of Language Structures*. Oxford: Oxford University Press, 470–473.
Fauconnier, Gilles 1980. Pragmatic entailment and questions. In: J.R. Searle, F. Kiefer & M. Bierwisch (eds.). *Speech Act Theory and Pragmatics*. Dordrecht: Reidel, 57–69.
Gil, David 2001. Creoles, complexity, and Riau Indonesian. *Linguistic Typology* 5, 325–371.

Ginzburg, Jonathan 1995. Resolving questions I & II. *Linguistics & Philosophy* 18, 459–527, 597–609.
Ginzburg, Jonathan & Ivan Sag 2001. *Interrogative Investigations*. Stanford, CA: CSLI Publications.
Gretsch, Petra 2000. *Fokale Ellipsen in Erwachsenen- und Kindersprache*. Tübingen: Niemeyer.
Grimshaw, Jane 1979. Complement selection and the lexicon. *Linguistic Inquiry* 10, 279–362.
Groenendijk, Jeroen 2008. Inquisitive semantics: Conditionals, questions, and disjunction. In: T. Friedman & S. Ito (eds.). *Proceedings of Semantics and Linguistics Theory (= SALT) XVIII*, Ithaka, NY: Cornell University, 729–746.
Groenendijk, Jeroen & Floris Roelofsen 2009. *Inquisitive Semantics and Pragmatics*. Ms. Amsterdam, University of Amsterdam, http://www.illc.uva.nl/inquisitive-semantics. April 2, 2011.
Groenendijk, Jeroen & Martin Stokhof 1982. Semantic analysis of WH-complements. *Linguistics & Philosophy* 5, 175–233.
Groenendijk, Jeroen & Martin Stokhof 1984. *Studies on the Semantics of Questions and the Pragmatics of Answers*. Ph.D. dissertation. University of Amsterdam.
Groenendijk, Jeroen & Martin Stokhof 1997. Questions. In: J. van Bentham & A. ter Meulen (eds.). *Handbook of Logic and Language*. Amsterdam: Elsevier, 1055–1124.
Gunlogson, Christine 2003. *True to Form: Rising and Falling Declaratives as Questions in English*. New York: Routledge.
Haida, Andreas 2008. *The Indefiniteness and Focusing of wh-Words*. Doctoral dissertation. Humboldt-Universität zu Berlin.
Hamblin, Charles Leonard 1973. Questions in Montague English. *Foundations of Language* 10, 41–53.
Haspelmath, Martin 1997. *Indefinite Pronouns*. Oxford: Clarendon Press.
Hausser, Roland 1983. On questions. In: F. Kiefer (ed.). *Questions and Answers*. Dordrecht: Reidel, 97–158.
Hausser, Roland & Dietmar Zaefferer 1979. Questions and answers in a context-dependent Montague grammar. In: F. Guenthner & S.J. Schmidt (eds.). *Formal Semantics and Pragmatics for Natural Languages*. Dordrecht: Reidel, 339–358.
Heim, Irene 1979. Concealed questions. In: R. Bäuerle, U. Egli & A. von Stechow (eds.). *Semantics from Different Points of View*. Berlin: Springer, 51–60.
Higginbotham, James & Robert May 1981. Questions, quantifiers, and crossing. *The Linguistic Review* 1, 41–80.
Hull, Robert D. 1975. A semantics for superficial and embedded questions in natural language. In: E. L. Keenan (ed.). *Formal Semantics of Natural Language*. Cambridge: Cambridge University Press, 33–45.
Ishihara, Shinichiro 2004. Prosody by phase: Evidence from focus intonation–wh-scope correspondence in Japanese. In: S. Ishihara, M. Schmitz & A. Schwarz (eds.). *Interdisciplinary Studies on Information Structure (ISIS) 1* (Working Papers of the SFB 632). Potsdam: Universitätsverlag Potsdam, 77–119.
Jacobs, Joachim 1983. *Fokus und Skalen. Zur Syntax und Semantik der Gradpartikeln im Deutschen*. Tübingen: Niemeyer.
Jespersen, Otto 1940. *A Modern English Grammar on Historical Principles*. Copenhagen: Munksgaard.

Karttunen, Lauri 1977. Syntax and semantics of questions. *Linguistics & Philosophy* 1, 3–44.
Keenan, Edward L. & Leonard M. Faltz 1985. *Boolean Semantics for Natural Language*. Dordrecht: Reidel.
Klein, Wolfgang & Christiane von Stutterheim 1987. Quaestio und referentielle Bewegung in Erzählungen. *Linguistische Berichte* 109, 163–183.
Kratzer, Angelika & Junko Shimoyama 2002. Indeterminate pronouns: The view from Japanese. In: Y. Otsu (ed.). *Proceedings of the Tokyo Conference on Psycholinguistics (=TCP) 3,* Tokyo: Hituzi Syobo, 1–25.
Krifka, Manfred 1995. The semantics and pragmatics of polarity items. *Linguistic Analysis* 25, 209–257.
Krifka, Manfred 2001a. Quantifying into question acts. *Natural Language Semantics* 9, 1–40.
Krifka, Manfred 2001b. For a structured account of questions and answers. In: C. Féry & W. Sternefeld (eds.). *Audiatur vox sapientiae. A Festschrift for Arnim von Stechow*. Berlin: Akademie Verlag, 287–319.
Krifka, Manfred 2004. The semantics of questions and the focusation of answers. In: C. Lee, M. Gordon & D. Büring (eds.). *Topic and Focus: A Cross-Linguistic Perspective*. Dordrecht: Kluwer, 139–151.
van Kuppevelt, Jan 1995. Discourse structure, topicality, and questioning. *Journal of Linguistics* 31, 109–147.
Lahiri, Utpal 1991. *Embedded Interrogatives and Predicates that Embed Them*. Ph.D. dissertation. MIT, Amherst, MA.
McCloskey, James 2005. Questions and questioning in a local English. In: R. Zanuttini et al. (eds.). *Crosslinguistic Research in Syntax and Semantics*. Washington, DC: Georgetown University Press, 87–126.
Mitterer, Holger & Tanya Stivers (eds.) 2006. *Annual Report 2006*. Technical Report. Nijmegen, Max Planck Institute of Psycholinguistics.
Muysken, Pieter & Norval Smith 1990. Question words in Pidgin and Creole languages. *Linguistics* 28, 889–903.
Nishigauchi, Taisuke 1990. *Quantification in the Theory of Grammar*. Dordrecht: Kluwer.
Partee, Barbara 1987. Noun phrase interpretation and type-shifting principles. In: J. Groenendijk (ed.). *Studies in Discourse Representation Theory and the Theory of Generalized Quantifiers*. Dordrecht: Foris, 115–143.
Paul, Hermann 1880. *Prinzipien der Sprachgeschichte*. Leipzig: Niemeyer.
Pesetsky, David 1987. Wh-in situ: Movement and unselective binding. In: E. Reuland & A. ter Meulen (eds.). *The Representation of (In)definiteness*. Cambridge, MA: The MIT Press, 98–129.
Roberts, Craige 1996. Information structure in discourse: Towards an integrated formal theory of pragmatics. In: J.H. Yoon & A. Kathol (eds.). *Papers in Semantics* (OSU Working Papers in Linguistics 49). Columbus, OH: Ohio State University, 91–136.
Romero, Maribel & Chung-hye Han 2002. Verum focus in negative yes/no questions and Ladd's p/non p ambiguity. In: B. Jackson (ed.). *Proceedings of Semantics and Linguistic Theory (=SALT) XII*, Ithaca, NY: Cornell University, 204–224.
van Rooij, Robert 2003. Negative polarity items in questions: Strength as relevance. *Journal of Semantics* 20, 239–273.
Rooth, Mats 1992. A theory of focus interpretation. *Natural Language Semantics* 1, 75–116.
Sabel, Joachim 2006. Typologie des W-Fragesatzes. *Linguistische Berichte* 206, 147–194.
Schwarzschild, Roger 1999. GIVENness, AvoidF and other constraints on the placement of accent. *Natural Language Semantics* 7, 141–177.

Searle, John 1975. Indirect speech acts. In: P. Cole & J.L. Morgan. *Syntax and Semantics 3: Speech Acts*. New York: Academic Press, 59–82.
Siemund, Peter 2001. Interrogative constructions. In: M. Haspelmath et al. (eds.). *Sprachtypologie und sprachliche Universalien – Language Typology and Language Universals. Ein internationales Handbuch der zeitgenössischen Forschung – An International Handbook of Contemporary Research* (HSK 20). Berlin: de Gruyter Mouton, 1010–1028.
von Stechow, Arnim 1981. Topic, focus, and local relevance. In: W. Klein & W. Levelt (eds.). *Crossing the Boundaries in Linguistics*. Dordrecht: Reidel, 95–130.
von Stechow, Arnim 1990. Focusing and backgrounding operators. In: W. Abraham (ed.). *Discourse Particles*. Amsterdam: Benjamins, 37–84.
von Stechow, Arnim 1996. Against LF pied-piping. *Natural Language Semantics* 4, 57–110.
Stenius, Erik 1967. Mood and language game. *Synthese* 17, 254–274.
Szabolcsi, Anna 1981. Compositionality in focus. *Folia Linguistica* XV, 141–161.
Tichy, Pavel 1978. Questions, answers, and logic. *American Philosophical Quarterly* 15, 275–284.
Tuller, Laurice 1992. The syntax of postverbal focus constructions in Chadic. *Natural Language and Linguistic Theory* 10, 303–334.
van Valin, Robert D. & Randy J. LaPolla 1997. *Syntax: Structure, Meaning and Function*. Cambridge: Cambridge University Press.
Wunderlich, Dieter 1976. *Fragesätze und Fragen. Studien zur Sprechakttheorie*. Frankfurt/M.: Suhrkamp.
Zanuttini, Rafaella & Paul Portner 2003. Exclamative clauses: At the syntax-semantics interface. *Language* 79, 39–81.
Zerbian, Sabine 2006. *Expression of Information Structure in the Bantu Language Northern Sotho*. Doctoral dissertation. Humboldt-Universität zu Berlin.

Chung-hye Han
6 Imperatives

1 Introduction —— 226
2 Issues —— 227
3 Force —— 234
4 Modality —— 238
5 Reference of the covert subject —— 244
6 Conclusion —— 247
7 References —— 247

Abstract: This paper investigates the meaning of imperatives, sentences that have distinctive imperative morphology on the verb and/or distinctive imperative syntax, and are canonically used to express the illocutionary force of directives such as commands and requests. I start the paper with a brief survey of some essential characteristics of imperatives that should be accounted for by any analysis of the meaning of imperatives. I then present a summary of proposals in the literature on the sentential force and modality expressed by imperatives, and how they account for the characteristics of imperatives. I will mainly discuss works of Han (1999, 2000) and Portner (2005, 2007), making reference to other works as necessary (Bolinger 1977, Huntley 1984, Davies 1986, Wilson & Sperber 1988, Potts 2003, Roberts 2004, Mastop 2005, Schwager 2006), as Han and Portner contain extensive discussions on force and modality of imperatives from two contrasting perspectives. Han takes the position that force and modality are formally encoded in the logical form of imperatives, while Portner takes the position that these are not formally represented and are instead derived indirectly on the basis of the semantic object that the imperative denotes. Despite the contrasting positions, they both reach a similar conclusion: the force of the imperative is to add the content of the imperative to a particular discourse component (Plan Set for Han and To-Do List for Portner), and the modality of the imperative is to restrict or update the ordering source associated with deontic modality. The paper ends with a discussion on the syntactic nature of the covert subject in the English imperative, and how it gets to have 2nd person reference (Schmerling 1975, Beukema & Coopmans 1989, Potsdam 1998, Platzack & Rosegren 1997, Han 2000, Rupp 2003, Portner 2005, Pak, Portner & Zanuttini 2007, Zanuttini 2008).

Chung-hye Han, Burnaby, BC, Canada

https://doi.org/10.1515/9783110589863-006

1 Introduction

Imperatives are sentences with distinctive imperative morphology on the verb and/or distinctive imperative syntax. They are canonically used to express the sentential force of directives such as commands and requests. It is important to make a distinction between the imperative as a formal category and the discourse functions of imperatives. For example, all of the sentences in (1) have a similar discourse function in the sense that they all express a directive force. But only (1a) is an imperative because it has a covert subject understood to be 2nd person and a bare verb form, the two main morphosyntactic characteristics of the imperative in English. (1b) and (1d) are formally declaratives, and (1c) is formally an interrogative. This paper is about the meaning of the imperative sentence type exemplified in (1a).

(1) a. Wash your hands!
    b. You will wash your hands.
    c. Will you wash your hands, please?
    d. You should wash your hands.

It is worth noting that defining the formal category of imperatives is sometimes not so straightforward. For example, in many Romance languages, sentences that express polite or negative commands take a different form, such as an indicative, subjunctive, or infinitive verb, perhaps with distinct syntax, from the canonical imperative form. One might argue that these should also be classified as imperatives. Be that as it may, in this paper, we will restrict the discussion to the canonical form with the imperative verb and the imperative syntax.

One of the most prominent issues in the meaning of imperatives is to account for the sentential force of the imperative. How do imperatives get to have a sentential force? Is force formally represented in the logical form of the imperative? Or, is it a derived notion, not formally represented, generated through pragmatic inference? Whether force is formally represented or not, how can it be defined? Another prominent issue in the meaning of imperatives is to account for the modality of the imperative. Many researchers have noted the intuition that the modality of the imperative has something to do with deontic modality. Deontic modality expresses that a proposition is obligatory or permissible according to some normative background such as law, morality, convention, etc. The questions that arise from this intuition are: Is modality formally represented in imperatives or is it a derived notion? Can we give a formal account of the modality of the imperative using a theory of modality independently proposed to account for modals such as *should* or *must*? In this paper, I present the approaches that have been proposed in the literature in addressing these questions. I will mainly discuss works of Han (1999, 2000) and Portner (2005, 2007), making reference to other works as necessary, as Han and Portner contain extensive discussions on the issues pertaining to force and modality of imperatives from two contrasting perspectives.

Han argues that force and modality are directly encoded in the logical form of the imperative. According to Han, the clause structure of the imperative contains an "[imp]" feature in the C domain, which maps onto a force-indicaqting operator *directive*. This *directive* operator takes the propositional type of subjunctive or infinitival, which she represents as *irrealis(p)*. The term *irrealis* is intended to capture the fact that subjunctives and infinitives in general express the modality of unrealized, and *p* stands for the core proposition expressed by the imperative. This produces (2) as the logical form of imperatives. Importantly, for Han, the traditional truth-conditional semantics interprets up to *irrealis(p)* and *directive* is interpreted by pragmatics.

(2) Han's (2000) logical form of imperatives
    directive(irrealis(p))

Portner (2005, 2007), on the other hand, argues that force and modality are not directly encoded in the logical form of the imperative, but instead are derived indirectly on the basis of the semantic object that the imperative denotes. He proposes that imperatives denote properties, not propositions, that can only be true of the addressee. He postulates a covert operator high in the clause structure, that turns the imperatives into properties, through predicate abstraction. And because imperatives are properties, they are restricted to interact with pragmatics in a certain way, ending up with the meaning that they have.

The rest of the paper is organized as follows. In section 2, I present some essential characteristics of imperatives. In sections 3 and 4, I summarize the proposals by Han and Portner pertaining to the force and modality of imperatives, and discuss how each of the proposals accounts for the characteristics presented in section 2. Section 5 contains a discussion on the syntactic nature of the covert subject in the English imperative, and how it gets to have 2nd person reference.

2 Issues

In this section, I list some essential characteristics of imperatives that should be addressed by any analysis of the meaning of imperatives.

2.1 Illocutionary forces of imperatives

Imperatives can express various illocutionary forces. They canonically express directive forces such as order, command, request, suggestion, advice, warning and instruction, as in (3)–(7). But they can also express forces that do not seem to be straightforwardly directives, such as permissions, wishes, threats, and dares, as in (8)–(10).

(3) Order, command
    a. Stand at ease! (a commander in the army to his soldiers)
    b. Take down this poem. (a teacher to her class)
    c. Clean that mess up at once! (a mother to her child)

(4) Request
    a. Please bring me some water.
    b. Open the window, please.

(5) Suggestion, advice
    a. A: Excuse me, I want to get to the station.
       B: Take a number 3 bus. (Wilson & Sperber 1988, (1))
    b. Get some rest. (to a friend who looks tired)

(6) Warning
    a. Do not annoy him, or you'll be sorry.
    b. Be quiet. I am warning you.

(7) Instruction
    Beat two eggs. Put salt and sugar into the beaten eggs. Mix then well. (Cooking instructions)

(8) Permission
    a. Come in. (as a reply to a knock on the door)
    b. A: Can I open the window?
       B: Oh, open it, then. (Wilson & Sperber 1988, (2))

(9) Threat, dare
    a. Go on. Throw the rock. I dare you.
    b. Hit me and you'll be sorry.

(10) Wish
   a. Get well soon.
   b. Please don't rain.
   c. (A is calling B, and mutters to himself:) Answer the phone.

2.2 No embedded imperatives

Many languages do not allow imperatives to be embedded, as observed by Sadock & Zwicky (1985) and Palmer (1986). Instead, languages tend to use subjunctives or infinitivals in the embedded clauses of reported directives. Examples (11) to (16) are from Han (2000). (Note however that it has been pointed out that there are languages that allow embedded imperatives, as in Krifka 2001 and Portner 2005.)

(11) English
   a. Give me the book!
   b. *I demand that give me the book.
   c. I order you to give me the book.
   d. I demand that you give me the book.

(12) Modern Greek
   a. Grapse.
      write-2sg.Imp
      'Write!'

   b. *O Yannis se dietakse   grapse.
      the Yannis you ordered-2sg write-2sg.Imp
      'Yannis ordered you to write.'

   c. O Yannis se dietakse   na grapsis.
      the Yannis you ordered-2nd.sg NA write-2sg.Subj
      'Yannis ordered you to write.'

(13) Spanish
   a. ¡Habla   le!
      talk-2sg.Imp her
      'Talk to her!'

  b. *Pido que habla le.
    ask that talk-2sg.Imp her
    'I ask that you talk to her.'

  c. Pido que le hables.
    ask that her talk-2sg.Subj
    'I ask that you talk to her.'

(14) Italian
  a. Fallo!
    do-2sg.Imp-it
    'Do it!'

  b. *Ti ordino che fallo.
    you order that do-2sg.Imp-it
    'I order you to do it.'

  c. Ti ordino che lo faccia.
    you order that it do-2sg.Subj
    'I order you to do it.'

(15) French
  a. Finis!
    finish-2sg.Imp
    'Finish!'

  b. *J'exige que tu finis.
    I-requires that you finish-2sg.Imp
    'I require that you finish.'

  c. J'exige que tu finisses.
    I-require that you finish-2sg.Subj
    'I require that you finish.'

(16) German
  a. Sei   nicht zu aufdringlich!
    be-2sg.Imp Neg too pushy
    'Don't be too pushy!'

b. *Hans empfiehlt, dass Du nicht zu aufdringlich sei.
   Hans suggests that you not too pushy be-2sg.Imp
   'Hans suggests that you not be too pushy.'

c. Hans empfiehlt, dass Du nicht zu aufdringlich seist.
   Hans suggests that you not too pushy be-2sg.Subj
   'Hans suggests that you not be too pushy.'

2.3 Future orientation

Imperatives across languages are not tensed morphosyntactically (Zanuttini 1991, 1997), and have future orientation in terms of meaning. (Note however that Mastop 2005 argues that Dutch has past tensed imperatives.) This can be shown by the fact that imperatives are compatible with future oriented adverbials, as in (17a), but not with past oriented adverbials, as in (17b).

(17) a. Finish your homework tomorrow.
     b. *Finish your homework yesterday.

In addition, even adverbs that are not necessarily future-oriented can only be future-oriented in imperatives. For instance, *now* and *tonight* can occur in linguistic contexts that are not future-oriented, as shown in (18). In fact, *tonight* can even be past-oriented, as in (18b).

(18) a. John is eating now.
     b. John finished his homework tonight.

But when *now* and *tonight* occur in imperatives, they can only be future-oriented, as in (19) and (20). In particular, *now* in (20) means something similar to *from now on*.

(19) a. Behave yourself when the guests arrive tonight.
     b. Finish your homework tonight.

(20) a. Behave yourself now.
     b. Finish your homework now.

Moreover, as observed by Katz & Postal (1964), imperatives can be followed by tag questions with the auxiliary *will*, as in (21), providing more support for the future orientation of imperatives.

(21) a. Behave yourself, will you?
 b. Behave yourself, won't you?

2.4 Imperative subject

In English, the imperative subject can be overt or covert. When the subject is covert, it is understood to be a 2nd person pronoun. This is supported by the binding examples in (22) and tag-question formation examples in (23).

(22) a. Behave yourself/yourselves.
 b. *Behave himself/myself/ourselves/themselves.

(23) a. Be quiet. Will you?
 b. *Be quiet. Will he/I/they/we?

When the subject is overt, it can be not only a 2nd person pronoun, but also a 3rd person nominal expression, including a quantifier, indefinite, definite, bare noun plural, proper noun, and even 3rd person pronoun. What these nominal expressions share as the imperative subject is that they can all be ascribed an addressee interpretation (Potsdam 1998, Rupp 2003, Zanuttini 2008). This is clearly so in cases where imperatives have overt 2nd person subjects as in (24) or covert subjects that are understood to be 2nd person as in (22a) and (23a). But even in the imperatives with a 3rd person subject, as in (25), the subject referent is in some sense being addressed by the speaker, as pointed out by Stockwell et al. (1973). Examples in (25) are from Rupp (2003) and Potsdam (1998).

(24) a. You behave yourself.
 b. Don't you move!

(25) a. Nobody move.
 b. Everybody get out as quick as he/you can.
 c. Somebody pay the bill.
 d. People interested in the project come and see me afterwards!
 e. The boy in the corner stand up.
 f. Chris stand by the door and Shirley watch the window!
 g. He who carries the machine gun step away from the car!

This intuition is further supported by examples like (26) and (27). The examples in (26) show that the subject in the tag question must be in the 2nd person, even though the subject in the preceding imperative is in the 3rd person. The examples in (27) show that the 3rd person subjects of imperatives are anaphorically related to a 2nd person pronoun in the subsequent sentences.

(26) a. *The boy in the corner stand up, will he?
　　 b. The boy in the corner stand up, will you?

(27) a. Nobody$_i$ move. I am begging you$_i$/*him$_i$/*them$_i$.
　　 b. Somebody$_i$ pay the bill. I am begging you$_i$/*him$_i$/*them$_i$.

2.5 Speaker's belief in the realization of the situation

Speakers believe that the state of affairs described by an imperative is realizable. Hence, it is infelicitous to follow an imperative with a sentence that expresses the speaker's belief that the situation described by the imperative will not be realized.

(28) # Pay the fee! But you won't.

2.6 Agentivity

Imperatives are in principle agentive. That is, the situation described by the imperative presupposes an agent who is responsible for bringing it about (unless the imperative is used to express a wish). That is why imperatives with individual-level predicates are infelicitous as shown in (29): the situation described by an individual-level predicate is not something that an agent can bring about under normal circumstances.

(29) a. # Be tall.
　　 b. # Have blue eyes.

2.7 No truth value

Imperatives cannot be said to be true or false. They do not assert anything about the current world and so it does not make sense to assign a truth value to imperatives.

3 Force

3.1 Adding a proposition to a Plan Set

Many previous studies on the semantics of imperatives propose that the imperative denotes a type of proposition. Bolinger (1977) argues that the imperative is a type of bare infinitival that denotes hypothetical situations. Huntley (1984) and Davies (1986) argue that imperatives denote propositions that specify potential situations. Wilson & Sperber (1988) argue that imperatives denote propositions that specify possible and desirable situations, where the situation is either desirable to the speaker or the hearer. According to all these studies, the imperative becomes a purely pragmatic category, as the force expressed by it is the result of pragmatic reasoning and inference based on discourse contexts.

Han (2000) accepts the idea that imperatives have propositional content, but argues against the approach that the propositional content is all there is to the meaning representation of imperatives. She observes that if the imperative is a pragmatic category, the fact that so many languages have special morphosyntactic forms for the canonical expression of directives remains unexplained. For Han, imperatives are propositions and a little more.

Han argues that the syntax of imperatives contains "[imp]" feature in the C domain, which maps onto a force-indicating operator, labelled as *directive*, in the logical form of imperatives, represented in (2). So, for Han, the fact that imperatives have an illocutionary force is not the result of pragmatic inference, but of direct encoding in their logical forms. And pragmatic reasoning and inference contribute in determining the exact content of the illocutionary force expressed by the imperative. This accounts for the fact that although imperatives canonically express directive force, they can also express non-directive forces such as permissions, wishes, dares and threats depending on the discourse context. Han's proposal is inspired by Frege (1960) and Lewis (1976), who advance that the meaning component of sentences is divided into the force component, whose interpretation is subject to rules of discourse, and the propositional component, whose interpretation is subject to truth-conditional semantics.

Han takes a force-indicating operator to be responsible for allowing a speaker to use a sentence to perform a speech act (Austin 1962, Searle 1969, 1976). She calls this operator in imperatives *directive* because the canonical force of imperatives is directive force. She argues that *directive* is a function that takes a proposition (p) and returns a Directive Action. She proposes that by performing a directive action, the speaker instructs the addressee to update a particular discourse module which she calls the Plan Set. An addressee's Plan Set is a set of propositions that specifies the addressee's intentions which represent the state of affairs s/he intends to bring about. Thus, an imperative is an instruction of the speaker to the addressee to add a proposition to his/her Plan Set. (A similar notion was used by Potts 2003 and Roberts 2004 to explain the discourse function of imperatives.)

For Han, the presence of a force-indicating operator in the logical form of imperatives prohibits them from appearing in embedded clauses, as, by assumption, only matrix clauses contain a force-indicating operator. From the definition of the imperative as an instruction to the addressee to update his/her Plan Set, it follows that the addressee is in effect the planner. This accounts for the intuition that the subject of the imperative represents the addressee. As the notion of plan presupposes that the planner has the ability to carry out the plan, issuing an instruction to the addressee to update his/her Plan Set with p implies that the speaker believes that the address has the ability to bring about the situation described by p. This accounts for the speaker's belief in the realization of the situation described by the imperative. If the addressee updates the Plan Set with p, then s/he makes it presupposed that s/he intends to bring about the situation described by p. This accounts for the agentivity of the imperative. Moreover, the future-orientation of imperatives follows from the intuitive concept of "plan": if you are planning to bring about the situation described by p, then the situation is not yet realized at the time that p is planned and it can be realized in the future. Further, if the speaker tells the addressee to plan to bring about the situation described by p, the implication is that the speaker intends the addressee to bring about the situation described by p, hence giving rise to the directive illocutionary force.

But what about imperatives that have non-directive force, such as permissions, wishes, and threats? Sentences in general can be used by speakers to perform indirect speech acts, by virtue of conversational implicatures arising from Gricean inferences in discourse contexts (Grice 1975, Searle 1975). Interpreting the force-indicating operator *directive* is the job of pragmatics, so the canonical force associated with it can be cancelled and a non-canonical force can be generated depending on the discourse context. In a context in which a person A has expressed the desire and intention to perform p, the implication is that A already has p in his/her Plan Set. For instance, if A knocks on your door, then A is expressing his/her desire and intention to come in. That is, by knocking on your door, A is implying that his/her plan is to come in. By uttering *Come in!* in this context, you are acknowledging A's plan, rather than instructing A to update his/her Plan Set. It may be that if an imperative is uttered in a context in which it is already known that the addressee has p in the Plan Set, then it performs the speech act of permission as an indirect speech act. An imperative such as *Have a nice day!* expresses a wish in general. A person does not usually have control over having a nice day. S/he may have the desire and intention of having a nice day, but bringing about this state of affairs is not completely up to him/her. An imperative can then be used to perform the speech act of wishing as an indirect speech act if it is known that the addressee does not have control over realizing p.

Imperatives that have the force of threats or dares express the opposite of what they literally mean. For instance, in an appropriate context, the second imperative in the sequence *Go ahead. Hit me! (I dare you.)* can be expressing that the speaker is warning the addressee not to hit him/her. This is not specific to imperatives. Declaratives can also express the opposite of their literal meaning when they are used ironically or sarcastically. Imperatives that express threats and dares are comparable to declaratives that express irony and sarcasm. Han's position is that just as we would not want to complicate the literal meaning of declaratives to handle sarcasm and irony, we would not want to complicate the literal meaning of imperatives to handle the threats and dares. Instead, they should be handled by Gricean reasoning and inference.

3.2 Adding a property to a To-Do List

Portner (2005) argues that an imperative denotes a property that can only be true of the addressee. He proposes that the imperative subject contributes a variable, an addressee-oriented logophoric pronoun, and postulates a covert operator high in the clause structure that binds this variable, abstracting over it to make the clause denote a property.

In imperatives with a covert subject pronoun or a 2nd person subject pronoun, the subject argument is the variable that is abstracted over. For example, Portner presents (30b) as the denotation of the imperative in (30a), and (31b) as the denotation of (31a). Here, c represents the context of utterance.

(30) a. Leave!
 b. $\lambda w \lambda x : x = \text{addressee}(c). [x \text{ leaves in } w]$

(31) a. You be quiet!
 b. $\lambda w \lambda x : x = \text{addressee}(c). [x \text{ is quiet in } w]$

In imperatives with a quantified subject, Portner argues that the quantifier contributes a covert domain variable that is abstracted over. Further, in imperatives with a proper noun subject, noting that such imperatives must be embedded in a contrastive structure, Portner argues that the contrastive focus on the subject introduces a variable for a set of addressees for the operator to bind and to abstract over. An example of an imperative with a quantified subject and the corresponding denotation are given in (32), and an example of an imperative with a proper noun subject and the corresponding denotation are given in (33).

(32) a. Everyone sit down!
  b. $\lambda w \lambda x : x = \text{addressee}(c). [\forall y : y \in x . y \text{ sits down in } w]$

(33) a. JOHN stand HERE and MARY stand THERE!
  b. $\lambda w \lambda x : x = \text{addressee}(c). [\text{John} \in x \ \& \ \text{John stands here in } w \ \& \ \text{Mary} \in x \ \& \ \text{Mary stands there in } w]$

Portner proposes that the force of the imperative is to add the imperative denotation to a discourse component, which he labels the To-Do List of the addressee. Portner states that in discourse, there can be several To-Do Lists, such as the To-Do Lists of the speaker, the addressee or other individuals. The type of To-Do List relevant for imperatives is the addressee's To-Do List. He intuitively defines the To-Do List of the addressee as a collection of actions that the addressee should take. This makes the canonical force of imperatives directive. He notes that the way he defines the directive force of the imperative is in parallel to the way assertive force of a declarative is seen as an addition of the declarative denotation (proposition) to the Common Ground (Stalnaker 1978), and the way question force of an interrogative is seen as an addition of a question denotation (a set of propositions, Hamblin 1976, Karttunen 1977) to a Question Set (Ginzburg 1995a, 1995b, Roberts 1998).

Portner makes two assumptions about the Common Ground, the Question Set and the To-Do Lists. First, by definition, the Common Ground is a set of propositions, the Question Set is a set of sets of propositions, and a To-Do List is a set of properties. And second, these three sets are universally available discourse components. Taking the two assumptions together, he derives the fact that declaratives, interrogatives and imperatives are universally available sentence types and concludes that sentential force need not be formally encoded. Even without the formal encoding of a force marker, imperatives are restricted to update the To-Do List of the addressee, and not any other discourse component. Since an imperative denotes a property, it is not suitable for being added to the Common Ground or the Question Set, and so must be added to a To-Do List. Moreover, since an imperative denotes a property which can only be true of the addressee, it must be added to the To-Do List of the addressee, and not to the To-Do List of any other individual. The same reasoning applies to declaratives and interrogatives: declaratives denote propositions, so they are restricted to update the Common Ground, and interrogatives denote sets of propositions, so they are restricted to update the Question Set. Portner thus concludes that force is not directly encoded in the logical form of the imperative, or any other clause type. Instead, it is indirectly derived on the basis that imperatives denote properties which can only be true of the addressee and declaratives denote propositions and interrogatives denote sets of propositions.

As imperatives denote properties, they do not have truth values, and they generally cannot occur as embedded clauses across languages. The intuition that the imperative subject refers to an addressee is captured by the proposal that the variable contributed by the subject is an addressee-oriented logophor. The future-orientedness of imperatives is captured by the fact that To-Do Lists are future-oriented by definition. The agentivity of the imperative and the speaker's belief in the realization of the situation expressed by the imperative are captured by the fact that the To-Do List of the addressee can be thought of as a collection of actions that the addressee should take.

The notion of To-Do List is used in Mastop (2005) as well. For Mastop, imperatives are action terms that are inherently performatives, and expand the To-Do List of an agent, thereby constraining the set of future courses of events. Mastop provides a semantics of imperatives in the framework of dynamic semantics. See Mastop for details.

4 Modality

4.1 Restricting the ordering source

Han (1999) explores the intuition that the modality of the imperative is similar to the deontic modality expressed by modal verbs like *must* and *may*, and proposes a formal account of the modality of the imperative by extending Kratzer's semantics of modality and conditionals (Kratzer 1986, 1991).

Before presenting Han's theory, here, I briefly provide Kratzer's theory on modality as a background (more detailed account can be found in article 14 [Semantics: Noun Phrases and Verb Phrases] (Hacquard) *Modality*). According to Kratzer, an expression of modality is associated with a modal base and an ordering source. The modal base is a set of propositions which constitutes a conversational background. In the case of deontic modality, the modal base can be a subset of relevant facts in the world of evaluation w. The modal base defines a set of worlds in which all the propositions in the modal base are true. This set of worlds is accessible from w. The ordering source is a set of propositions that induces an ordering on the set of all worlds. In the case of deontic modality, these propositions constitute what the law provides in *w*, what is moral in *w*, what is normal in *w*, etc. The ordering source can further restrict the set of accessible worlds to the most ideal worlds according to what is legal, moral, normal, etc. The resulting set of worlds constitutes the domain of quantification in evaluating the truth of modal sentences. For instance, (34a) is true iff *John pays the fee* is true in all the worlds in the domain of quantification, and (34b) is true iff *John pays the fee* is true in at least one world in the domain of quantification. Another way of looking at this is to say that (34a) is true iff the domain of quantification is a subset of the set of worlds in which *John pays the fee*, and (34b) is true iff the intersection of the domain of quantification and the set of worlds in which *John pays the fee* is non-empty.

(34) a. John must pay the fee.
b. John may pay the fee.

In conditionals as in (35), the antecedent is added to the modal base to restrict the set of accessible worlds. The ordering source further restricts the accessible worlds to the set of the most ideal worlds as the domain of quantification. The conditional is true iff *John pays the fee* is true in all these worlds. In other words, (35) is true iff the domain of quantification is a subset of the set of worlds in which *John pays the fee* is true.

(35) If John takes the course, he must pay the fee.

Han (1999) proposes that an imperative defines a non-empty set of worlds as a domain of quantification. This set of worlds is determined by means of the modal base, which is the set of all the facts known to the speaker in *w*, and the ordering source, which is the set of obligations or permissions issued by the speaker. A crucial point for Han is that the ordering source for an imperative includes the corresponding core proposition of the imperative. For example, in (36), the ordering source includes the proposition *You pay the fee*. This makes the set of worlds that an imperative defines the intersection between the set of worlds in which the core proposition is true and the set of worlds that are compatible with all the facts that the speaker knows and are closest to the ideal determined by the obligations and permissions issued by the speaker.

(36) Pay the fee!

For Han, the speaker's belief in the realization of the situation expressed by the imperative is accounted for by the proposal that the modal base of the imperative includes all the facts known to the speaker in the world of evaluation. This is unlike the modal base of deontic modal sentences, which can be a subset of the facts known to the speaker. For instance, the fact that the discourse in (28) (repeated below as (37)) is infelicitous can be explained as follows. Assume that in the discourse, the speaker knows that the addressee never pays fees, which is consistent with the assertion *But you won't*. So, the modal base in this context includes the proposition *You never pay fees*. Then, the intersection between the set of the most ideal worlds compatible with all the facts that the speaker knows and the set of worlds that validates *You pay the fee* returns an empty set, resulting in an incoherent discourse.

(37) #Pay the fee! But you won't.

Further, the fact that imperatives do not have truth values is accounted for by the proposal that semantically, imperatives contribute a domain of quantification, but not a proposition that is evaluated with respect to this domain. Note that the core proposition of the imperative is included in the ordering source, hence it functions to restrict the domain of quantification. Comparing imperatives to deontic modal sentences as in (34a) and (34b) and conditionals as in (35), imperatives take only one argument, the domain of quantification, while deontic modal sentences and conditionals take two arguments, the domain of quantification, and the proposition that is evaluated with respect to this domain. In a way, an imperative is like a defective conditional that only has an *if*-clause, but not the consequent. Both an imperative and an *if*-clause restrict the domain of quantification. The difference is that the *if*-clause restricts the modal base, whereas the imperative restricts the ordering source.

Han notes that, as discussed by Davies (1986) and Clark (1993), when an imperative is conjoined with a modal sentence, the whole sequence is interpreted as a conditional, as in (38). She argues that this can be seen as an instance of modal subordination (Roberts 1989): the imperative defines a domain of quantification and subsequent modal sentences are evaluated with respect to this domain. In (38), the first sentence, the imperative, restricts the set of accessible worlds. The second sentence in (38a) is evaluated in the set of worlds restricted by the imperative, and the second sentence in (38b) is evaluated in the complement of the set of worlds restricted by the imperative, giving the entire sequence a conditional interpretation.

(38) a. Come to the party! And John will be happy.
≈If you come to the party, John will be happy.

b. Come to the party! Or John will be unhappy.
≈If you don't come to the party, John will be unhappy.

A more recent work on examples such as (38a) by Russell (2007) identifies that the first conjunct in the sequence is ambiguous between an imperative and a subjectless declarative. Russell develops a compositional semantic analysis of the sequence with imperatives by combining the semantics of imperatives in Huntley (1984), semantics of speech act conjunction in Krifka (2001), and semantics of modal subordination in Roberts (1989). See Russell for further details.

A comparable analysis of the modality of imperatives to Han's can be found in Schwager (2006). Like Han, Schwager argues that imperatives denote modalized propositions and utilizes Kratzer's theory on modality to develop its semantics. For Schwager, however, imperatives are just like modalized declaratives, the only difference being that while modalized declaratives have descriptive usage and performative usage, imperatives are restricted to performative usage. In Schwager's analysis, the semantics of imperatives have a necessity modal operator and a presuppositional component that restricts their usage to contexts in which a modalized declarative of the form *you must/should* would achieve performative effect. See Schwager (2006) for further details.

4.2 Selecting subsets of the ordering source

Portner (2007) also attempts to integrate his theory on imperatives with Kratzer's (1991) theory on modality by making a connection between the To-Do Lists and the ordering source used in the interpretation of what he calls "priority" modal sentences. Noting that the term "deontic" can be confusing because it can be both broadly construed (to refer to the modality relating to desires, goals, as well as laws, rules, morality and the like), and narrowly construed (to refer only to the modality relating to laws, rules, and morality), he introduces a new term "priority" to refer to the broad class of deontic modality, the one relevant for the modality of imperatives. I will thus use the term priority modality in the discussion of Portner's theory on modality and imperatives.

Portner argues that while the Common Ground helps to determine the modal base, the To-Do Lists help to determine the ordering source for the interpretation of priority modals. So, in a sequence of discourse as in (39), A's utterance of the imperative contributes to the To-Do List of the addressee, and then this To-Do List determines the ordering source which is used in the interpretation of B's utterance of the priority modal sentence.

(39) A: Present this proposal to our bankers!
B: I should take the 7 a.m. flight to New York then.

Portner presents two empirical arguments to support the connection between the To-Do Lists and the ordering source of the priority modality: (i) the directive force of imperatives comes in different flavors, just as the modality of priority modal sentences comes in different flavors; and (ii) the flavor of an imperative affects the flavor of subsequent imperatives and modals, and the flavor of a modal affects the flavor of subsequent modals and imperatives.

First, the fact that imperatives can express different flavors of directive force, such as order, invitation or suggestion, should be seen as parallel to the fact that modal sentences can express different flavors of priority modality, such as obligations, desires or goals. The variety of modal flavors comes from different types of ordering source. (40b) has a deontic ordering source, (41b) has a bouletic ordering source, and (42b) has a teleological ordering source. In a similar fashion, the To-Do List of the addressee can also be classified into different types. The To-Do List of (40a) represents a set of orders, the To-Do list of (41a) represents the addressee's desires, and the To-Do List of (42a) represents the addressee's goals.

(40) a. Sit down right now! (order)
b. Noah should sit down right now (given that he's been ordered to do so).

(41) a. Have a piece of fruit! (invitation)
b. Noah should have a piece of fruit (given that he's hungry).

(42) a. Talk to your advisor more often! (suggestion)
b. Noah should talk to his advisor more often (given that he wants to finish).

Second, once an imperative or a priority modal sentence selects for a particular flavor of meaning, this flavor does not easily change within the local unit of discourse, and determines the flavor of meaning adopted by subsequent imperatives and modal sentences. For example, the sequence in (43) is odd because out of context, (43a) is likely to be an order, but (43b) is likely to be a suggestion. In (44), if (44a) is taken to be an order, then (44b) is likely to be interpreted as an order too, and if (44a) is taken to be a suggestion, then (44b) is likely to be interpreted as a suggestion too. The sequence in (45) is odd because the speaker, A, has just issued a directive to the addressee to pay his/her taxes, perhaps according to the law that applies to the addressee, and the addressee, B, immediately asks if s/he should pay the taxes, according to the law that applies to him/her. It seems that the sequence in (45) is only possible if the addressee was not paying attention to A's utterance.

(43) a. Be there at least two hours early.
b. Then, have a bite to eat.

(44) a. You must be there at least two hours early.
b. Then you must have a bite to eat.

(45) A: Pay your taxes!
B: Ok. #Should I pay my taxes?

Portner attributes this persistence in the flavor of priority modality and directive force to the requirement that the ordering source be stable within the local unit of discourse. So, if an imperative is interpreted with respect to the To-Do List of the addressee that represents a set of orders, then the subsequent imperatives and modal sentences must be interpreted with respect to the To-Do List or the ordering source of the same type. If an imperative is interpreted with respect to the To-Do List of the addressee that represents the addressee's desires, then the subsequent imperatives and modal sentences must be interpreted with respect to the To-Do List or the ordering source of the same type.

Portner formalizes the idea of selecting sub-types of To-Do List and priority ordering source by defining a set of selection functions. Postulating that there is one unified To-Do List (a set of properties) and priority ordering source (a set of propositions) relativized to an individual (for example, the addressee), he proposes that the sub-type of ordering source is determined by a salient selection function. This function takes a world, and a set of propositions and properties, and returns a subset of propositions and properties. This subset is the salient ordering source used to interpret imperatives or priority modal sentences in discourse. For example, if the salient selection function is deontic relativized to an addressee, then it will return a set of propositions and properties that form a deontic ordering source as in (46a), and if the salient selection function is bouletic relativized to an addressee, then it will return a set of propositions and properties that form a bouletic ordering source as in (46b). In fact, there could be many more selection functions than the ones exemplified in (46) used in the discourse.

(46) For any individual x, would w, and set of propositions and properties $\prod$:
   a. $deontic_x(w, \prod) = \{y \in \prod : y$ expresses an obligation of x in $w \vee y(x)$ expresses an obligation of x in $w\}$
   b. $bouletic_x(w, \prod) = \{y \in \prod : y$ expresses a desire of x in $w \vee y(x)$ expresses a desire of x in $w\}$
   c. $teleo_x(w, \prod) = \{y \in \prod : y$ expresses a goal of x in $w \vee y(x)$ expresses a goal of x in $w\}$

In sum, the To-Do List of the addressee is part of the priority ordering source, and the utterance of an imperative selects a coherent subset of the priority ordering source, determining the flavor of the directive force expressed by the imperative. This in turn determines the flavor of the directive force and priority modality of subsequent imperatives and modal sentences.

So far, we have seen how force and modality of imperatives are treated in the literature. Though there are differences, such as whether to formally represent force and modality in the logical form of imperatives and whether the type of imperatives is proposition or property, there seems to be some consensus in the treatment of the force and modality of imperatives. The force in imperatives is to update a particular discourse component, Plan Set for Han, and To-Do List for Portner and Mastop. The modality in imperatives is connected to deontic/necessity modality, and Kratzer's theory on modality is utilized in the analyses by Han, Schwager and Portner. Han however does not provide an account of how the modal component and the force component interact in discourse and falls short of defining the context changing potential of imperatives. Portner on the other hand defines the To-Do List as part of the ordering source and shows how it influences the subsequent discourse. Mastop sees imperative as a context creating function and defines its semantics in dynamic semantic framework. In the next section, I turn to the reference of the covert subject in imperatives and how it relates to the semantics of imperatives.

5 Reference of the covert subject

In English, the imperative subject can be overt or covert. When the subject is covert, it is plausible to posit that the empty subject corresponds to the 2nd person pronoun, based on the evidence from binding and tag-question formation in (22) and (23). In this section, I address the question of what kind of empty category the covert subject is and how it gets to have 2nd person pronoun reference.

According to Schmerling (1975), imperatives are a sentence type in their own right, with certain formal properties peculiar to them, and the covert subject in imperatives is the result of a special deletion rule that is not a subcase of any general phenomenon of the language. Beukema & Coopmans (1989) claim that the covert subject in imperatives is the *wh*-trace of an empty topic operator. Potsdam (1998) and Rupp (2003) argue that it is *pro*. Platzack & Rosengren (1997) propose that imperatives have no true syntactic subject but a null actor argument in [Spec,VP] referred to as *imppro*. Portner (2005) argues that the imperative subject provides a variable which is an addressee-oriented logophoric pronoun that can be covert.

The claim that the covert subject in imperatives is either the trace of an empty topic operator or *pro* entails the conclusion that English allows these empty categories only in imperatives. Likewise, the claim that imperatives have *imppro*, which is not a true syntactic subject, or that the covert subject in imperatives is the result of a special subject deletion rule applying only to imperatives entails the conclusion that English has a fourth empty category that occurs only in imperatives. Moreover, the claim that the imperative subject can be deleted because it is a logophoric pronoun raises the question of why we don't find covert logophoric pronouns in other sentence types in English.

Han (2000) proposes that the syntactic status of the covert subject in the English imperative is PRO, whose reference is determined by the interpretive property of the directive force-indicating operator. Han observes that the English imperative is not tensed, and that English independently has two types of untensed clauses, infinitivals and subjunctives. Further, embedded clauses of directive verbs, such as *order* and *demand*, are infinitivals, as in (47a), or subjunctives as in (47b). In infinitivals, the subject position has a null case and so PRO must occur, controlled by the indirect object of the higher clause. In subjunctives, the subject has nominative case and so must be overt.

(47) a. I order you [PRO to give me the book].
  b. I demand that [you give me the book].

Putting all these observations together, Han concludes that the propositional type of the English imperative can be either the subjunctive or the infinitive type. If it is the subjunctive type, the imperative has an overt subject, and if it is the infinitive type, the imperative has the PRO subject.

In addressing the question of how the reference of PRO is identified as 2nd person, Han adopts the approach that implicit arguments in semantics can identify the reference of PRO (Bhatt & Izvorski 1998). Implicit arguments do not occupy a syntactically projected position and yet are active syntactically to serve as an identifier of PRO (Bhatt & Pancheva 2006). For instance, Bhatt & Izvorski (1998) argue that the matrix predicates in (48) have an implicit argument paraphrasable as *for someone*. This implicit argument is interpreted generically because the entire sentence is generic. This generic implicit argument licenses PRO_{arb}.

(48) a. [PRO_{arb} writing haiku] is fun.
b. Ships are sunk [PRO_{arb} to collect insurance].

Extending this analysis to the domain of imperatives, Han proposes that the directive force-indicating operator provides an implicit addressee argument, and this argument controls the PRO subject, identifying it as 2nd person.

While Han's PRO analysis accounts for the fact that the covert subject in imperatives behaves as 2nd person pronoun syntactically and semantically, through control by the addressee argument, it cannot explain how overt 3rd person subjects in imperatives (as in (25)) must be connected to the addressee as well, as no control is involved in these cases. What is needed in the analysis is that the subject is somehow equated with the addressee argument, whether it is covert or overt and whether it is 2nd person or 3rd person, so that it is the addressee. Moreover, in Han's analysis, although the notion of addressee is also relevant in the force of interrogatives (*I am asking you* ...) and declaratives (*I am telling you* ...), it is not clear why only the addressee argument of the directive force-indicating operator in imperatives is relevant for the reference of the subject.

These issues do not arise in Zanuttini (2008). She proposes that the syntactic representation of imperatives have a functional projection, called Jussive Phrase, that is not present in other clause types. The head of the Jussive Phrase contains 2nd person feature and this feature is shared with the subject, through entering AGREE relation with it. This accounts for the 2nd person pronominal nature of the covert subject in imperatives. In Zanuttini's analysis, the covert subject is *pro* that can only occur in the context of Jussive Phrase. The overt subject *you* is a spell-out of this 2nd person feature. As a pronominal element with 2nd person feature, both the covert and the overt *you* refer to the addressee. For 3rd person subjects, such as bare nouns (as in (25d)), and proper names (25f), noting the fact that these do not have a determiner, Zanuttini argues that the null determiner head of these nominal elements AGREEs with the 2nd person feature of the Jussive Phrase. For quantificational subjects (25a–c), assuming that every quantificational phrase has a null syntactic element that corresponds to its domain restriction, Zanuttini argues that the null domain restriction element and the Jussive Phrase enter the AGREE relation. This way, all imperative subjects are endowed with 2nd person feature, hence being connected to the addressee. In Zanuttini's analysis, the fact that the notion of addressee is only relevant for imperatives is accounted for by the proposal that the presence of Jussive Phrase with 2nd person feature is unique to imperatives. The analysis of the reference of the subject with the postulation of Jussive Phrase is extended to Korean in Pak, Portner & Zanuttini (2007).

6 Conclusion

In this paper, in investigating the meaning of imperatives, I have presented two main approaches in the literature: one, proposed by Han, that force and modality are both formally represented in the logical form of the imperative, and the other, proposed by Portner, that force and modality of the imperative are derived on the basis of the denotation of the imperative as a property. I observed how the two differing approaches can account for the characteristics of imperatives surveyed in section 2. Despite the contrasting perspectives though, both Han and Portner reach a similar conclusion: the force of the imperative is to update a particular discourse component and the modality of the imperative is connected to the ordering source of deontic modality. For Han, this discourse component is called the Plan Set, which is a set of propositions, and for Portner, this is called the To-Do List, a set of properties. Han however does not explicitly make the connection between the Plan Set and the deontic ordering source. Portner, on the other hand, does make this connection, stating that the To-Do List is a subset of the deontic ordering source. Further, Portner's analysis accounts for how the use of the imperative can influence the subsequent discourse, making the theory dynamic in nature. I take the convergence in the approaches to force and modality and the incorporation of dynamic semantics in the account of the meaning of imperatives as a welcome progress, which can form a basis for future work on related topics.

7 References

Austin, J. L. 1962. *How to Do Things with Words*. Oxford: Clarendon Press.
Beukema, Frits & Peter Coopmans 1989. A government-binding perspective on the imperative in English. *Journal of Linguistics* 25, 417–436.
Bhatt, Rajesh & Roumyana Izvorski 1998. Genericity, implicit arguments and control. http://www-bcf.usc.edu/~pancheva/PROarb.ps. December 7, 2010.

Bhatt, Rajesh & Roumyana Pancheva 2006. Implicit arguments. In: M. Everaert & H. van Riemsdijk (eds.). *The Blackwell Companion to Syntax, vol. 2*. Oxford: Blackwell, 554–584.
Bolinger, Dwight 1977. *Meaning and Form*. London: Longman.
Clark, Billy 1993. Relevance and "pseudo-imperatives". *Linguistics & Philosophy* 16, 79–121.
Davies, Eirlys 1986. *The English Imperative*. London: Croom Helm.
Frege, Gottlob 1884/1960. *Die Grundlagen der Arithmetik. Eine logisch-mathematische Untersuchung über den Begriff der Zahl*. Breslau: Koebner. English translation in: G. Frege. *The Foundations of Arithmetic. A Logico-mathematical Enquiry into the Concept of Number*. Translated by J. L. Austin. New York: Harper.
Ginzburg, Jonathan 1995a. Resolving questions, Part I. *Linguistics & Philosophy* 18, 459–527.
Ginzburg, Jonathan 1995b. Resolving questions, Part II. *Linguistics & Philosophy* 18, 567–609.
Grice, H. Paul 1975. Logic and conversation. In: P. Cole & J. L. Morgan (eds.). *Syntax and Semantics 3: Speech Acts*. New York: Academic Press, 41–58.
Hamblin, Charles L. 1976. Questions in Montague English. In: B. H. Partee (ed.). *Montague Grammar*. New York: Academic Press, 247–259.
Han, Chung-hye 1999. Deontic modality, lexical aspect and the semantics of imperatives. In: The Linguistic Society of Korea (ed.). *Linguistics in the Morning Calm, vol. 4*. Seoul: Hanshin Publications, 479–495.
Han, Chung-hye 2000. *The Structure and Interpretation of Imperatives. Mood and Force in Universal Grammar*. New York: Garland.
Huntley, Martin 1984. The semantics of English imperatives. *Linguistics & Philosophy* 7, 103–134.
Karttunen, Lauri 1977. Syntax and semantics of questions. *Linguistics & Philosophy* 1, 3–44.
Katz, Jerrold & Paul Postal 1964. *Integrated Theory of Linguistic Description*. Cambridge, MA: The MIT Press.
Kratzer, Angelika 1986. Conditionals. In: A. M. Farley, P. Farley & K. E. McCullough (eds.). *Papers from the Parasession on Pragmatics and Grammatical Theory*. Chicago, IL: Chicago Linguistic Society, 1–15.
Kratzer, Angelika 1991. Modality. In: A. von Stechow & D. Wunderlich (eds.). *Semantik – Semantics. Ein internationales Handbuch zeitgenössischer Forschung – An International Handbook of Contemporary Research* (HSK 6). Berlin: de Gruyter, 639–650.
Krifka, Manfred 2001. Quantifying into question acts. *Natural Language Semantics* 9, 1–40.
Lewis, David 1976. General semantics. In: B. H. Partee (ed.). *Montague Grammar*. New York: Academic Press, 1–50.
Mastop, Rosja 2005. *What Can You Do?* Doctoral dissertation. University of Amsterdam.
Pak, Miok, Paul Portner & Raffaella Zanuttini 2007. Agreement and the subjects of jussive clauses in Korean. In: E. Elfner & M. Walkow (eds.). *Proceedings of the North Eastern Linguistic Society (= NELS) 37, vol. 1*. Amherst, MA: GLSA, 127–138.
Palmer, Frank Robert 1986. *Mood and Modality*. Cambridge: Cambridge University Press.
Platzack, Christer & Inger Rosengren 1997. On the subject of imperatives: A minimalist account of the imperative pronoun and negated imperative. *Journal of Comparative Germanic Linguistics* 1, 177–224.
Portner, Paul 2005. The semantics of imperatives within a theory of clause types. In: K. Watanabe & R. B. Young (eds.). *Proceedings of Semantics and Linguistic Theory (= SALT) XIV*. Ithaca, NY: Cornell University. http://semanticsarchive.net/Archive/mJlZGQ4N/PortnerSALT04.pdf. December 7, 2010.
Portner, Paul 2007. Imperatives and modals. *Natural Language Semantics* 15, 351–383.

Potsdam, Eric 1998. *Syntactic Issues in the English Imperative*. New York: Garland.
Potts, Christopher 2003. Keeping world and will apart: A discourse-based semantics for imperatives. Paper presented at at the *NYU Syntax/Semantics Lecture Series*. October 17, 2003.
Roberts, Craige 1989. Modal subordination and pronominal anaphora in discourse. *Linguistics & Philosophy* 12, 683–721.
Roberts, Craige 1998. Information structure in discourse: Towards an integrated formal theory of pragmatics. http://semanticsarchive.net/Archive/WYzOTRkO/InfoStructure.pdf. December 7, 2010. (Revised version of: Roberts, Craige 1996. Information structure in discourse: Towards an integrated formal theory of pragmatics. In: J. H. Yoon & A. Kathol (eds.). *Papers in Semantics* (OSU Working Papers in Linguistics 49). Columbus, OH: The Ohio State University, 91–136.)
Roberts, Craige 2004. Context in dynamic interpretation. In: L. R. Horn & G. Ward (eds.). *The Handbook of Pragmatics*. Oxford: Blackwell, 197–220.
Rupp, Laura 2003. *The Syntax of Imperatives in English and Germanic*. Basingstoke: Palgrave Macmillan.
Russell, Benjamin 2007. Imperatives in conditional conjunction. *Natural Language Semantics* 15, 131–166.
Sadock, Jerrold M. & Arnold M. Zwicky 1985. Speech act distinctions in syntax. In: T. Shopen (ed.). *Language Typology and Syntactic Description, vol. 1*. Cambridge: Cambridge University Press, 155–196.
Schmerling, Susan 1975. Imperative subject deletion and some related matters. *Linguistic Inquiry* 6, 501–511.
Schwager, Magdalena 2006. *Interpreting Imperatives*. Doctoral dissertation. University of Frankfurt.
Searle, John R. 1969. *Speech Acts*. Cambridge: Cambridge University Press.
Searle, John R. 1975. Indirect speech acts. In: P. Cole & J. L. Morgan (eds.). *Syntax and Semantics 3: Speech Acts*. New York: Academic Press, 59–82.
Searle, John R. 1976. The classification of illocutionary acts. *Language in Society* 5, 1–24.
Stalnaker, Robert C. 1978. Assertion. In: P. Cole (ed.). *Syntax and Semantics 9: Pragmatics*. New York: Academic Press, 315–332.
Stockwell, Robert, Paul Schachter & Barbara Partee 1973. *The Major Syntactic Structures of English*. New York: Holt, Rinehart & Winston.
Wilson, Deirdre & Dan Sperber 1988. Mood and the analysis of non-declarative sentences. In: J. Dancy, J. M. E. Moravcsik & C. C. W. Taylor (eds.). *Human Agency. Language, Duty and Value*. Stanford, CA: Stanford University Press, 77–101.
Zanuttini, Raffaella 1991. *Syntactic Properties of Sentential Negation. A Comparative Study of Romance Languages*. Ph.D. dissertation. University of Pennsylvania, Philadelphia, PA.
Zanuttini, Raffaella 1997. *Negation and Clausal Structure. A Comparative Study of Romance Languages*. Oxford: Oxford University Press.
Zanuttini, Raffaella 2008. Encoding the addressee in the syntax. Evidence from English imperative subjects. *Natural Language and Linguistic Theory* 26, 185–218.

Line Mikkelsen
7 Copular clauses

1   Introduction —— 250
2   A taxonomy of copular clauses —— 252
3   The meaning(s) of the copula —— 261
4   Connectivity —— 265
5   Conclusion —— 277
6   References —— 278

Abstract: This article provides an overview of research on copular clauses, focussing on three questions. First, how many types of copular clauses there are, second, what meaning is contributed by the copula, and third, what so-called connectivity effects tell us about the structure of copular clauses.

1 Introduction

Copular clauses are a minor sentence type in which the contentful predicate is not a verb, but some other category like AP, NP or PP. In some languages there is no verbal element at all in these clauses; in other languages there is a verbal copula joining the subject and the non-verbal element. Copular clauses (of the verbal and of the non-verbal kind) come in a great variety of forms and intuitively seem to express different kinds of information. The English examples in (1) provide a first illustration of the range of variation.

(1) a. Emily is a carpenter.
　　b. What Harvey did next was wash himself thoroughly.
　　c. Electronically is usually fastest.　　　　　　　　　(Partee 1986: (5g))
　　d. That's my brother.
　　e. Red is my favorite color.
　　f. My favorite color is red.
　　g. The only thing we couldn't agree on was whether we should go to France first.

Line Mikkelsen, Berkeley, CA, USA

https://doi.org/10.1515/9783110589863-007

This article is structured around three central questions in the investigation of copular clauses. The first question, which I will call the taxonomy question, is how many kinds of copular clauses there are. Intuitively the copular clauses in (1) are different in various respects (and the list could easily be expanded) and the taxonomy question is whether any of these differences are significant enough to posit distinct types of copular clauses and if so, which types exist. I address this question in section 2. by discussing the four-way taxonomy proposed by Higgins (1979).

The second question relates to the copula itself: what is its semantic contribution and is its contribution the same in all copular clauses? I will call this the copula question and various answers to it are discussed in section 3.

The final question concerns CONNECTIVITY EFFECTS, which is the term used in the literature for the unusual distribution of pronouns, R-expressions, negative polarity items and other elements in certain copular clauses. The copular clause in (1b) above provides an example of this: the reflexive pronoun *himself* appears to not be locally c-commanded by its antecedent *Harvey*. The connectivity question is how this unusual distribution is best accounted for. Section 4. reviews the main candidate answers from the literature.

As with any overview article, certain difficult decisions had to be made as to which material to include and which to set aside. In addition to narrowing the thematic scope of the article to the three questions outlined above, I also made the decision to focus on English copular clauses. This is a serious limitation, both because there is significant cross-linguistic variation in the form and properties of copular clauses and because some of the most important work on copular clauses is on languages other than English. However, I found that it was impossible to do justice to this variation and literature within the prescribed scope of this article. Two further limitations deserve mention. Even with the thematic narrowing defined by the three questions, there is more literature than can be included here. Thus I will not be able to discuss several important works on the taxonomy and copula questions, including Halliday (1967), Declerck (1988), and Rothstein (2001). I urge the reader to consult these independently. Finally, I will focus on copular clauses of the form 'NP be NP'. To some extent, this choice reflects a bias in the literature. However, it should be recognized that the copula, at least in many languages, is truly cross-categorial and hence that the real scope of inquiry is 'XP be XP' (or 'XP XP' for languages that lack a copula, though excluding regular verbal predication). The cross-categoriality of the copula is touched upon in section 3.4. English *be* has a variety of other uses, including progressive, passive, and modal uses, which will also not be discussed here. Existential clauses (*There is a cat outside the door*) are discussed in article 8 [this volume] (McNally) *Existential sentences*.

2 A taxonomy of copular clauses

Much work on the syntax and semantics of copular clauses takes as its starting point the taxonomy proposed in Higgins (1979: 204–293), which distinguishes four types of copular clauses:

(2) PREDICATIONAL
   a. The hat is big.
   b. The hat/present/thing I bought for Harvey is big.
   c. What I bought for Harvey is big.

(3) SPECIFICATIONAL
   a. The director of *Anatomy of a Murder* is Otto Preminger.
   b. The only director/person/one I met was Otto Preminger.
   c. Who I met was Otto Preminger.

(4) IDENTIFICATIONAL
   a. That (woman) is Sylvia.
   b. That (stuff) is DDT.

(5) EQUATIVE
   a. Sylvia Obernauer is HER.
   b. Cicero is Tully.

The taxonomy is based on intuitions as well as detailed observations about English copular clauses. The intuition about predicational clauses is that they predicate a property of the subject referent. In this respect they are like non-copular clauses, though they obviously differ from these in that the property is contributed entirely by the post-verbal element (which following Higgins I call the predicate complement). Intuitively, the other three kinds of copular clauses do not involve predication. Equatives, as the name suggests, equate the referents of the two expressions flanking the copula. Neither is predicated of the other. Specificational clauses involve valuing of a variable: the subject expression sets up a variable (the x that directed *Anatomy of a Murder* in (3a)) and the post-copular expression provides the value for that variable. Identificational clauses are different again, in that they typically involve a demonstrative subject and according to Higgins "are typically used for teaching the names of people or of things" (Higgins 1979: 237). Each of these are discussed on more detail in the following four subsections.

A note on terminology: the examples in (2c) and (3c) are pseudoclefts, which are characterized by having a wh-clause as one the terms flanking the copula.

Thus (2c) is a predicational pseudocleft, and (3c) a specificational pseudocleft. The examples in (2b) and (3b) do not involve a wh-clause, but their subjects contain a headed relative clause. As far as I can tell, there is no name for these in the literature, but I draw attention to them here, because at various points in what follows (especially in section 4 on connectivity) it is useful to distinguish these from pseudoclefts, and from "plain" copular clauses, like the ones in (2a), (3a), (4), and (5). While plain copular clauses, pseudoclefts, and copular clauses with a headed relative clause differ in form, there is consensus in the literature from Higgins and onwards that the taxonomy applies to all forms of copular clauses, and that we should seek an analysis of predicational and specificational clauses that generalizes across these form differences.

2.1 Equatives

While equative clauses, especially of the sort in (5b), have been the object of much attention in the philosophical literature, their linguistic status is somewhat murky. Some languages have been argued to lack equative clauses altogether (Adger & Ramchand 2003 make this claim for Scottish Gaelic), and to resort to more elaborate locutions (like *be the same person as* in English) to express what (5b) expresses. Similarly, Geist (2007) argues that there are no monoclausal equatives in Russian. Instead, equation is mediated, syntactically and semantically, by a demonstrative pronoun. Even within English, it must be noted that outside special cases, like *Muhammad Ali is Cassius Clay, Mark Twain is Samuel Clemens*, and (5b), main clause equatives involving two names are difficult to contextualize (try *Sylvia is Louise*). However, embedding under a propositional attitude verb (*Tanya thinks that Sylvia is Louise*) alleviates this for reasons discussed in Berg (1988). Equatives of the form in (5a), where one NP is a pronoun and the other a name, are easier to contextualize: they are natural answers to *Who is who?* in a situation where individuals can be identified both by name and by sight, as is the case for instance at a conference (see Aloni 2001: 13–15 for relevant discussion).

In both kinds of equatives, the issue of non-referential uses of names arises (e.g. Groenendijk, Stokhof & Veltman 1996). One reading of (5b) involves strongly referential use of both names: the speaker and hearer are both acquainted with Tully, under the name *Tully*, and with Cicero, under the name *Cicero*, but the hearer does not know that they are in fact the same individual. In that scenario, (5b) would be informative about the world. In other cases though, equatives seem to provide information about the language, in particular the names of people. In those cases, (5b) is understood roughly as 'the person you know as Cicero is also called Tully'. Similarly, (5a) is informative and natural in a context where the hearer does not know Sylvia Obernauer or does not know her vividly enough in Kaplan's sense. Consistent with these observations, there is a strand of work that argues that no copular clause in any language is truly equative (Moro 1997, den Dikken 2006, Adger & Ramchand 2003) and that even apparently symmetrical clauses like like (5b) are in fact instances of predication.

On the other hand, Heycock & Kroch (1999) argue from examples like (6)–(7) that equatives are a productive clause type, at least in English:

(6) a. Your attitude toward Jones is my attitude toward Davies.
    b. My attitude toward Davies is your attitude toward Jones.

(7) Honest is honest.

They emphasize the symmetry of these clauses and liken them to coordination in that respect (Heycock & Kroch 1999: 378, fn. 9). Like coordination, equatives seem to require two elements of the same type and to allow the two to occur in either order, as in (6).

Other terms used for equatives in the literature include identity clause and equational clause.

2.2 Predicational clauses

The subject of a predicational clauses is typically a referential NP (8), though quantificational expressions are also allowed (9):

(8) Harvey/my brother/the guest of honor/she was happy.

(9) Everyone/noone was happy.

One indication that the subject is referential in (8) is that it pronominalizes with a gendered pronoun, just like a referential subject of a non-copular clause does (the assumption that the pronoun of a tag question is controlled by the subject of the tagged clause is discussed and defended in Mikkelsen 2005: 70–72):

(10) The guest of honor was happy, wasn't she/he/*it?

(11) The guest of honor spoke after dinner, didn't she/he/*it?

Similarly, quantificational subjects pronominalize with *they*, as they do in non-copular clauses:

(12) Everyone was happy, weren't they?

(13) Everyone went to the graduation, didn't they?

The predicate complement can be an AP, as in (8) and (9), or a PP, DP or NP:

(14) Sylvia is [from Seattle].

(15) Sylvia is [an architect].

(16) Sylvia is [the architect on that project].

(17) Sylvia is [my friend].

(18) Sylvia is [mayor of Seattle].

Evidence that these predicate complements are semantically predicative comes from two observations. First, they can be targeted by VP ellipsis:

(19) Sylvia is the architect on that project, but I wish she wasn't.

Second, the elements that flank the copula in predicational clauses can express a proposition without the copula in embedded contexts (as long as the restrictions imposed by the embedding verb or preposition are obeyed):

(20) I consider [Sylvia my best friend].

(21) With [Sylvia absent], there is no point in continuing this discussion.

(22) With [Sylvia the only available candidate], there is no point.

This is not true for other kinds of copular clauses; here the copula is needed (Rothstein 1995):

(23) I consider [my best friend *(to be) Sylvia].   [specificational]

(24) With [the only available candidate *(being) Sylvia], there is no point in continuing this discussion.   [specificational]

(25) I believe [that *(to be) Sylvia].   [identificational]

(26) I believe [her *(to be) Sylvia]. [equative]

Other names for predicational clauses in the literature include ascriptive and ascriptional.

2.3 Specificational clauses

The term specificational derives from the intuition that these clauses are used to specify who (or what) someone (or something) is, rather than to say anything about that person (or entity). Thus (27) is used to say who directed a particular movie, not to say something about that person:

(27) The director of *Anatomy of a Murder* is Otto Preminger.

Intuitively, we can say (with Akmajian 1979) that the subject phrase introduces a variable (the x such that x directed *Anatomy of a Murder*) and the predicate complement provides the value for that variable. In light of the preceding discussion of symmetry and refentiality in equative and predicational clauses, the profile of specificational clauses can be characterized as in (28):

(28)

	NP1	copula	NP2
equative	referential		referential
predicational	referential		non-referential
specificational	non-referential		referential

Evidence from the non-referential status of the subject of specificational clauses comes from pronominalization:

(29) The director of *Anatomy of a Murder* is Otto Preminger, isn't it?

(30) The director of *Anatomy of a Murder*, that's Otto Preminger.

Strikingly, the subject of a specificational clause pronominalizes with the pronouns *it* and *that* as opposed to the gendered pronouns *he* and *she*; compare (29) to (10) above. As argued in Mikkelsen (2005: 64–86), this is evidence that the subject of specificational clauses is non-referential.

I have, deliberately, been using the term "referential" without defining it. There are several proposals in the literature as to what the relevant notion of referentiality is. Some are semantic, some pragmatic. On the semantic side, Mikkelsen (2005) and Geist (2007) propose that the relevant notion of referentiality is that expressed in Partee's (1987) family of NP types. In particular, referential is identified with type e, and non-referential with type $\langle e,t \rangle$ (or $\langle s,\langle e,t \rangle \rangle$). This semantic analysis fits naturally with a syntactic analysis of specificational clauses in which they involve movement of a predicative NP across the copula (the so-called predicate inversion analysis originally proposed by Moro 1997 and defended most recently by den Dikken 2006). Mikkelsen adopts this syntactic analysis for Danish and English and Geist assumes it for Russian, though she rejects it for English. Romero (2005) and Comorovski (2007) agree with Geist and Mikkelsen that the referential post-copular NP is type e (at least for what Romero calls Reading A, which is what is relevant here), but argue that the hallmark of a specificational subject is that it is intensional, in particular that it denotes an individual concept, i.e. a function of type $\langle s,e \rangle$. Comorovski (2007) adds the requirements that the individual concept be non-rigid and indirectly contextually anchored via a referential expression inside the specificational subject. Thus for Romero and Comorovski the asymmetry is one of intensionality, not "predicativity". Intensionality also plays a role in Alexiadou & Giannakidou's (1999) analysis, albeit a different role. They propose (p. 7) that specificational clauses equate co-extensive sets where the set denoted by the subject is given in predicate notation ($\{x|P(x)\}$), i.e. intensionally, and the set denoted by the post-copular phrase in given in list notation ($\{a,b,c\}$), i.e. extensionally. Finally, Müller-Reichau (2007) suggests that specificational subjects denote kinds.

Moving into the domain of pragmatics, several authors have proposed that specificational clauses are like question–answer pairs (Ross 1972, den Dikken, Meinunger & Wilder 2000, Schlenker 2003), with the question-denoting element preceding the copula and its answer following the copula. Schlenker (2003) provides the most thorough implementation of this line of analysis and I discuss it in detail in section 4.1.

There is another strand of work arguing that semantically specificational clauses involve equation of individuals, just like (true) equatives do and that the difference between them is not at the level of semantic types, but rather along some pragmatic dimension. Heycock & Kroch (1999, 2002) suggest that the relevant dimension is an information-structural one: specificational clauses are equatives with a particular information structure, one where the GROUND is constructed entirely from the subject phrase and the focus falls on the post-copular expression (in line with early observations by Akmajian 1979 and Higgins 1979). Heller (2005) agrees with Heycock and Kroch that specificational clauses are pragmatically asymmetric (and semantically symmetric), but she proposes that the relevant pragmatic dimension is DISCRIMINABILITY. Equi-extensional terms may be more or less discriminate: simplifying somewhat, proper names are more discriminate than definite descriptions with contentful nouns, which in turn are more discriminate than definite descriptions with bleached nouns (like *thing, place, person*), which in turn are more discriminate than free relative clauses. Specificational clauses, as opposed to equatives and to predicational clauses, exhibit rising discriminability: the pre-copular expression is less discriminate than the post-copular expression. In the end Heller is unable to provide a definition of discriminability, but her study nonetheless offers valuable insights into the nature of specificational clauses. Heller's work is also important because she draws attention to the relevance of pragmatic factors other than topic and focus, which have dominated the literature since Higgins (1979).

Specificational clauses exhibit other important properties. Probably the most famous one is connectivity and section 4 is devoted to that. Higgins (1979: 298–328) also points out a series of restrictions on specificational pseudoclefts: the focal (i.e. post-copular) item cannot be extracted or deleted; nothing can be moved out of the post-copular element; subject-auxiliary inversion is not possible; the copula must be finite and cannot be gapped; the tense of the copula must agree with the tense of the verb in the wh-clause (tense harmony); sentential adverbials, "straight" negation and tag questions are not allowed. Predicational pseudoclefts are not subject to these restrictions. Most of them do not hold of plain specificational clauses either, which indicates that these restrictions should not be pinned on the notion of specification itself. Perhaps for this reason, these restrictions have received less attention in the subsequent literature, though den Dikken, Meinunger & Wilder (2000) and Sharvit (2003) are important exceptions.

There is one further distinction associated with specificational pseudoclefts that should be mentioned here. In the examples given above, the wh-clause precedes the copula (see e.g. (3c)). However, it is also possible for the wh-clause to follow the copula while maintaining a specificational reading:

(31) Otto Preminger was who I met.

(32) Important to himself is what John is. (den Dikken, Meinunger & Wilder 2000: (2b))

den Dikken, Meinunger & Wilder (2000) argue that such reversed pseudoclefts constitute a separate subtype of specificational clause (their Type B). They show that Type B pseudoclefts exhibit different properties from unreversed pseudoclefts (their Type A) and propose that the two involve different syntactic derivations. Following the literature, I will continue to focus on Type A, that is specificational pseudoclefts where the wh-clause precedes the copula.

Another term for specificational is specifying.

2.4 Identificational clauses

Identificational clauses are characterized by having a demonstrative pronoun or demonstrative phrase in the subject position. Some of Higgins' examples (from Higgins 1979: 237–239, 244) are given in (33). Note that the demonstrative must be understood as having deictic, not anaphoric, reference (Higgins 1979: 220, 224, 245).

(33) a. That (man) is Joe Smith.
  b. That (woman) is the Mayor of Cambridge.
  c. That (place) is Boston.
  d. That's a teacher who has been helping me with my polynomials.

According to Higgins the subject of identificational clauses is referential, while the predicate complement is 'Identificational' (the meaning of the latter term is unclear to me). As regards their function, Higgins (1979: 237) says that these sentences are "typically used for teaching the names of people or of things". This function is easy to contextualize for the examples in (33a–c). Imagine that you are at a party with your friend. You don't know anyone, but your friend does, so she starts filling you in, using (33a) and (33b) together with a discrete nod of her head. Similarly, imagine that you are looking out the window from an airplane and you see a city beneath you which you identify as Boston. Then you can use (33c), together with a pointing motion, to share this piece of information with your travel partner.

Identificational clauses can also be used as responses to questions for more information about an individual. An example is (33d) used as a response to (34).

(34) John? Who's that?

Here we imagine a prior mention of John by the speaker of (33d). The name was not enough to satisfy the speaker of (34), hence the request for more information in (34).

There is another type of copular clauses which Higgins does not discuss, but which might be considered identificational. These are like the clauses in (33), except that the subject is not a demonstrative but the pronoun *it*:

(35) It is Joe Smith/the mayor of Cambridge/Boston.

These are called TRUNCATED CLEFTS by Hedberg (2000: 898) based on their similarity with the *it*-clefts in (36), see also Declerck (1988: 124–139), Büring (1998: 42–47), Mikkelsen (2007) and references cited there.

(36) a. It is Joe Smith/the Mayor of Cambridge who is standing over there.
b. It is Boston that we see underneath us.

Overall, identificational clauses have received less attention in the subsequent literature than the other members of Higgins' taxonomy and when they are discussed it is typically with the aim of showing that they do in fact not form a separate category (Sharvit 2003: 387–391, Heller 2005: 193–199, Mikkelsen 2005: 118–130).

2.5 What is the taxonomy a taxonomy of?

The presentation above mostly relied on the surface characteristics of the different kinds of copular clauses. An important question though, one that Higgins himself struggled with (Higgins 1979: 204–208, 360), is what exactly the taxonomy is a taxonomy of. Higgins' somewhat vague answer was that it is a taxonomy of "functions" of copular clauses. Later research has provided three broad answers to this question. One is that the taxonomy categorizes semantic species of copular clauses: each species is distinguished by the meaning of its pieces and/or their semantic composition. This approach thus posits different meanings for the elements flanking the copula and possibly, though not necessarily, also different meanings for the copula itself. Though quite different from each other, I would include the analyses of Partee (1986), Rothstein (2001), and Schlenker (2003) in this category. Another strand of research, which includes Heggie (1988), Moro (1997), and den Dikken (2006) argues that there is a single, semantically uniform, underlying structure for copular clauses, and that the varieties catalogued by Higgins are different surface realizations of this underlying copular structure. Under this conception the taxonomy classifies surface syntactic configurations. A third position is that the taxonomy is a taxonomy of syntax-semantics alignments which is further conditioned by information structure (Mikkelsen 2005, Geist 2007, and to some extent Heller 2005). This is an issue that deserves further consideration, especially in regards to the notion of construction (Kay & Fillmore 1999).

2.6 Reducing the taxonomy

While Higgins' taxonomy has been the starting point of much work on copular clauses over the past three decades, it has not been universally accepted. Several researches have argued that one or more of the four categories are spurious and should be collapsed with some other category. Heycock & Kroch

(1999) and den Dikken (2006) have argued that the distinction between specificational and equative clauses is spurious, though they differ in which category they take to be real: Heycock and Kroch propose that specificational clauses are a subtype of equatives, whereas den Dikken categorizes both as specificational. Mikkelsen (2005: 118–130) maintains the distinction between specificational and equative clauses, but suggests that the identificational class be eliminated. Her proposal is that identificational clauses with a pronominal subject (like *That/It is Joe Smith*) are in fact specificational, whereas identificational clauses with a phrasal demonstrative subject (*That man is Joe Smith*) are equative. Birner, Kaplan & Ward (2007) take issue with this reclassification and instead group all identificational clauses with equatives. Both of these proposals thus yield a three-way distinction between predicational, specificational, and equative clauses. Heller (2005: 198ff) tentatively proposes to reduce Higgins' taxonomy even further. She suggests, with Heycock & Kroch (1999), that specificational clauses are a subtype of equative, and, in a novel move, that identificational clauses should be grouped with predicational clauses (see also Heller & Wolter 2008). This leaves just two types of copular clauses: predicational clauses and equative clauses.

3 The meaning(s) of the copula

A natural question to ask in the light of Higgins' taxonomy is whether the different kinds of copular clauses involve different copulas. The most extreme positive answer would hold that each of the four clause types involve a different copula; thus there would be a copula of equation, a copula of predication, a copula of specification, and a copula of identification. As far as I know, no one has defended this position, though one could perhaps argue that this position is implicit in Higgins (1979). Weaker positive answers have been defended in the literature, in particular that there are two copulas and that there are three. In opposition to both of these positions there is a substantial body of work arguing that there is only one copula. For ease of reference, I will refer to these positions as the 3-be, 2-be, and 1-be positions, respectively. As will become clear, this division is somewhat artificial since the specific proposals within each category are quite different in spirit and in detail and some proposals do not fall unambiguously into one category. Nonetheless, the division helps structure the material in this section. It should also be noted that this section does not aim to exhaust the literature on the meaning of the copula, though it does aim to convey the range and variety of proposals that have been put forth.

3.1 3-be positions

I do not know of any works that explicitly argue for a 3-be position, but it is implicit in Schlenker (2003), Romero (2005), and Comorovski (2007). These authors posit a specificational copula and argue that it is different from the copula found in equatives. Whereas the equative copula typically equate individuals (though see section 3.4. below), the specificational copula equate propositions (according to Schlenker), or equate an individual with the value of an individual concept applied to the world of evaluation (according to Romero and Comorovski). (See specific denotations in Romero 2005: 715, (67a) and Comorovski 2007: 72, (49).) Since neither the equative nor the specificational copula can reasonably be assumed to be involved in predicational clauses (for reasons made clear by Geach 1962), these analyses effectively entail the existence of three semantically distinct copulas.

3.2 2-be positions

Echoing Russell (1919: 119) 2-be positions draw a distinction between a contentful copula of identity and a essentially meaningless copula of predication. The denotations in (37) and (38) are representative:

(37) $[\![be_{ident}]\!] = \lambda x \lambda y [y = x]$

(38) $[\![be_{pred}]\!] = \lambda P \lambda x [P(x)]$

2-be positions differ, however, in their assumptions about the distribution of these two copulas across the clause types distinguished by Higgins (1979). Mikkelsen (2005) assumes that the copula of identity is found in equatives and that the copula of predication is found in both predicational and specificational clauses. (Recall from section 2.6 above that in that account, Higgins' identificational class is split up and distributed into the equative and specificational classes.) In contrast, Heller (2005) assumes that the identity copula is found in equative and specificational clauses, whereas the copula of predication is used in predicational and identificational clauses.

3.3 1-be positions

The most influential 1-be position is the one put forth in Williams (1983) and further developed in Partee (1986). Williams (1983) proposes that *be* always takes one referential and one predicative element and that the semantic role of *be* is to predicate the latter of the former. What is unusual about *be* is that it may take these two arguments in either order: in a predicational clause the copula combines first with the predicative element to its right and then with the referential element in subject position (39a); in a specificational clause the copula combines first with the referential element to its right and then with the predicative element in subject position (39b).

(39) a. ⟦be⟧ = $\lambda P\lambda x[P(x)]$
   b. ⟦be⟧ = $\lambda x\lambda P[P(x)]$

If equative clauses like *Cicero is Tully* involve two referential elements, neither of the denotations in (39) can be used to compose these clauses. Partee (1986) argues that this type-mismatch is resolved by type-shifting the post-copular NP. In particular, the type-shifter IDENT, a member of the family of type-shifters proposed in Partee (1987), applies to the denotation of *Tully* (represented as t) and derives the predicative denotation $\lambda y[y = t]$. This makes equatives type-identical to predicational clauses and the *be* in (39a) applies straightforwardly. Williams (1983) and Partee (1986) do not discuss identificational clauses, but if these are in fact not a separate category, but rather belong with one (or more) of the other three categories, then they too are covered by Partee's (1986) analysis.

Geist (2007) follows Partee (1986) as far as predicational and specificational clauses are concerned, but suggests (§3.1) that the type-mismatch in equatives are resolved by type-shifting the copula itself. Concretely, Geist proposes that the *be* of predication in (39a) function composes with the identity function $\lambda u\lambda y[y = u]$. This yields a *be* of identity ($\lambda u\lambda x[x = u]$), which then combines with the two referential expressions.

Heycock & Kroch (1999) assume that the two elements flanking the copula form a small clause underlyingly and that the copula combines with this small clause. Thus, in contrast to the analyses of Williams, Partee, and Geist, the pre- and post-copular elements compose semantically without the mediation of the copula. In the case of predicational clauses, the composition of the small clause is straightforward: the type ⟨e,t⟩ element applies to the type e element. In the case of equatives (which they take to include specificational clauses), Heycock & Kroch (1999: 381–382) point to the existence of an equative small clause which, when embedded under a semantically vacuous copula, produces equative copular clauses. Under that view, the identity relation resides in a null functional head of the small clauses.

All three 1-*be* analyses thus assume that (at least some) equatives involve an identity relation, but differ on how the identity relation enters the semantic composition. Geist (2007) is the only one that locates the identity relation in the (type-shifted) copula itself, which is important given the observation that equative readings are typically unavailable in embedded contexts without *be* (though see Heycock & Kroch 1999: 381 for relevant discussion):

(40) *I believe [Cicero Tully]

Geist attributes the ungrammaticality of (40) to the fact that the identity relation is tied to the copula: no copula, no identity relation. Heycock & Kroch (1999) could perhaps appeal to subcategorization: if predicational and equative small clauses are headed by different functional heads, then the embedding verb could subcategorize for the former, but not the latter (see relevant data at the end of section 2.2.). It is less clear to me how Partee's (1986) analysis could be extended to account for the ill-formedness of (40). Note that (40) is well-formed if the embedded clause is a full copular clause: *I believe Cicero to be Tully*.

3.4 Polymorphic *be*

Above I have concentrated on copular clauses of the form 'NP be NP' and the meaning(s) of the copula that have been proposed for such clauses. However, the copula occurs with phrases of other categories, as the examples in (41) illustrate (these are borrowed from Partee 1986: 355; see also Heycock & Kroch's 'AP be AP' example in (7) above).

(41) a. To love is to exult.
 b. From A to B is 600 miles.
 c. Because he was out of money wasn't his only reason.
 d. Outside from one point of view may be inside from another.
 e. Electronically is usually fastest.

This leads Partee (1986) to propose that the copula is polymorphic, in particular that "*be* takes arguments of types X and $\langle X,t \rangle$ for any type X" (Partee 1986: 355). The denotations in (39) instantiate this denotation schema for $X = e$. Most other analyses are not as explicit about the polymorphism of the copula, but it seems to me that most of them can be extended along the lines drawn by Partee. For instance, the analyses of Romero (2005) and Comorovski (2007) could be generalized as follows (more realistic type-assignments would have $\langle s,t \rangle$ in place of t). Equative clauses equate expressions of like types for any type, hence equative *be* is of type $\langle X, \langle X,t \rangle \rangle$. Specificational *be* combines expressions of types X and

⟨s, X⟩ and is of type ⟨X,⟨⟨s, X⟩,t⟩⟩. Finally, predicational *be* combines expressions of types ⟨X,t⟩ and X (as proposed by Partee) and is itself of type ⟨⟨X,t⟩,⟨X,t⟩⟩.

One question that to my knowledge has not received much explicit attention in the literature is whether all four types of copular clauses in Higgins' taxonomy exhibit equal degrees of freedom as regards the syntactic category and semantic type of the elements flanking the copula. This is relevant not only for deepening the understanding of the taxonomy itself, but also for evaluating the proposals regarding the meaning of the copula reviewed above. If the copula is equally polymorphic in all four kinds of copula clauses, that would seem to support a 1-be position. If, on the other hand, there is variation in degree of polymorphism and if that variation lines up with the various subtypes of copular clauses, then that would seem to favor a multiple-be position.

4 Connectivity

Connectivity in copular clauses refers to the phenomenon where an element is present or interpreted in a way that is normally associated with a certain syntactic configuration seemingly without that configuration obtaining. (Higgins 1979 used the term "connectedness", but since Kayne used this term for an unrelated concept, the term "connectivity" has become standard and I will use it throughout.) Four kinds of connectivity effects figure in the literature: binding theory connectivity (for Principles A, B and C), bound variable connectivity, negative polarity item (NPI) connectivity, and opacity connectivity. The first three concern phenomena that are usually assumed to involve c-command, whereas opacity connectivity concerns semantic selection, which is typically taken to require sisterhood. The examples in (42)–(47) illustrate the four kinds of connectivity. In each case, the a. example is a specificational clause exhibiting the relevant type of connectivity, the b. example is a non-copular clause in which the elements under consideration stand in their standard structural relationship (c-command within a certain domain or sisterhood), and the c. example is a non-copular clause in which they do not. (Some speakers find (45c) grammatical, which raises questions about the c-command requirement on variable binding and hence the import of examples like (45a).)

(42) Principle A
 a. What Harvey$_i$ did next was wash himself$_i$ thoroughly.
 b. Harvey$_i$ washed himself$_i$ thoroughly.
 c. *Before Harvey$_i$ left, Miriam washed himself$_i$ thoroughly.

(43) Principle B
 a. *What Harvey$_i$ did next next was wash him$_i$ thoroughly.
 b. *Harvey$_i$ washed him$_i$ thoroughly.
 c. Before Harvey$_i$ left, Miriam washed him$_i$ thoroughly.

(44) Principle C
 a. *What he$_i$ did next was wash Harvey$_i$ thoroughly.
 b. *He$_i$ washed Harvey$_i$ thoroughly.
 c. Before he$_i$ left, Miriam washed Harvey$_i$ thoroughly.

(45) Bound variable connectivity
 a. What [every tennis player]$_i$ loves is his$_i$ racket.
 b. [Every tennis player]$_i$ loves his$_i$ racket.
 c. *After [every tennis player]$_i$ left the court, someone picked up his$_i$ racket.

(46) NPI connectivity
 a. (They found a lot of interesting things at the house, but) what they didn't find was any photos from his childhood.
 b. They didn't find any photos from his childhood.
 c. *Even though they didn't look very hard, they found any photos from his childhood.

(47) Opacity connectivity
 a. What they are looking for is a nanny.
 b. They are looking for a nanny.
 c. The one they are looking for found a nanny.   (no de dicto reading)

While connectivity effects are canonically associated with pseudoclefts, as in the a. examples above, most connectivity effects are also found in specificational clauses where the subject is a headed relative clause, see (48) and (49), and binding connectivity effects are also found when there is no relative clause at all, as in (50).

(48) The thing he$_i$ did next was wash himself$_i$/him$_{*i}$/Harvey$_{*i}$ thoroughly.

(49) The thing we didn't find was any photos from his childhood.

(50) His$_i$ biggest worry is himself$_i$/him$_{*i}$/Harvey$_{*i}$.

There are three broad approaches to explaining connectivity, which I will refer to as the ellipsis approach, the logical form approach, and the semantic approach.

As we will see each of them is associated with a different analysis of specificational clauses. Furthermore, the semantic approach is revisionist (to use Schlenker's 2003 term) in the sense that c-command is rejected as a requirement for NPI licensing and binding, and sisterhood as a requirement for semantic selection, contra mainstream assumptions. The other two approaches maintain the standard theories of binding, NPI licensing, and selection and propose that the relevant syntactic configurations do obtain, though they are not observable at the surface.

4.1 The ellipsis approach

The account of connectivity effects under the ellipsis approach is beautifully simple: the distribution and interpretation of the relevant elements in the post-copular phrase (pronouns, R-expressions, NPIs, and de dicto indefinites) are licensed exactly the way they generally are, but the syntactic licensing relationships are obscured by ellipsis. Thus the example exhibiting Principle A connectivity in (42a) has the structure in (51), where the post-copular expression is a full IP. That IP contains a subject which licenses the reflexive locally, but the subject (and the past tense) are ellided:

(51) What Harvey$_i$ did next was [$_{IP}$ he, PAST wash himself$_i$ thoroughly].

Similarly, principle Principle B connectivity (43a) and Principle C connectivity (44a) arise from the presence of a c-commanding, coindexed subject in the post-copular phrase, illicitly binding the pronoun (52) or R-expression (53):

(52) What Harvey$_i$ did next was [$_{IP}$ he, PAST wash him$_i$ thoroughly].

(53) What he$_i$ did next was [$_{IP}$ he, PAST wash Harvey$_i$ thoroughly].

The analysis extends straightforwardly to bound variable connectivity (54), NPI connectivity (55), and opacity connectivity (56):

(54) What [every tennis player]$_i$ loves is [$_{IP}$ [every tennis player]$_i$ loves his$_i$ racket].

(55) What they didn't find was [$_{IP}$ they didn't find any photos from his childhood].

(56) What they are looking for is [$_{IP}$ they are looking for a nanny].

The challenge for the ellipsis account lies in motivating the semantic and syntactic assumptions necessary for this very simple and attractive account of connectivity effects: (i) that the pre-copular element is a question, at least semantically, (ii) that the post-copular phrase is syntactically a full IP, though part of it goes unpronounced and (iii) that there is a reasonable semantic composition that derives the intended meaning from the three parts. This challenge is taken up by Schlenker (2003) and den Dikken et al. (2000), and though their analyses and arguments differ, I discuss them together here.

Assumption (i) breaks into three cases based on the form of the subject. When the subject is a *wh*-clause (*what Harvey did next*), the assumption is that this is an embedded interrogative as opposed to a free relative clause (see den Dikken, Meinunger & Wilder 2000: 71–81, Schlenker 2003: 168, and Caponigro & Heller 2007: 245–252 for relevant discussion). When the subject contains a headed relative (*the thing Harvey did next*), the assumption is that this NP is the idiosyncratic spell-out of an underlying interrogative structure (den Dikken, Meinunger & Wilder 2000: 82–83, Schlenker 2003: 190). Finally, when the subject is an NP without a relative clause (*Harvey's biggest worry*), the assumption is that this NP is a concealed question: a syntactic NP with the meaning of a question.

The second assumption that must be justified under the ellipsis account of connectivity is that the post-copular element is a full IP underlyingly. The account of connectivity rests entirely on this assumption (see (51)–(56)). Perhaps the most direct evidence for this assumption comes from the possibility (for some speakers for some examples; den Dikken, Meinunger & Wilder 2000: 45–46) of pronouncing the entire IP:

(57)   What I did then was [I called the grocer].   (Ross 1972: (39b))

Indirect evidence for the syntactic presence of a full IP comes from the fact that the post-copular element may vary in "size" and form in just the way a regular answer does. If such fragment answers are derived by ellipsis (Merchant 2004), it is natural to assume that the same ellipsis operations are at work in specificational clauses.

Finally, it must be shown how the copula, subject and predicate complement compose semantically to arrive at a proper meaning for specificational clauses. Schlenker proposes that the copula found in specificational clauses, be_{spec}, equates propositions. Being a declarative IP, the post-copular phrase straightforwardly denotes a proposition. As for the subject, Schlenker adopts the semantics for questions proposed in Groenendijk & Stokhof (1997), according to which the extension of a question is a proposition, namely the unique, exhaustive, true answer to the question in the world of evaluation. The difference, then, between specificational clauses and equatives is that only the former equate propositions, in particular a question and its answer, whereas the latter equate other semantic objects.

4.2 The logical form approach

In a certain derivational sense the logical form account of connectivity is the inverse of the ellipsis account. Where the ellipsis account assumes that the relevant syntactic configuration is established at an early stage of the derivation (and is then later obscured by ellipsis), the logical form account, as developed by Heycock & Kroch (1999: 388–394), posits that the relevant syntactic configuration is created at a very late stage in the derivation, one that Heycock & Kroch dub 'logical form'. This stage is later than regular L(ogical)F(orm) and is derived from it by a special operation of ι-reduction. They illustrate these assumptions by deriving the logical form for the specificational sentence in (58), which does not exhibit any connectivity effects.

(58) What Fiona bought was that ancient dictionary.

Like Schlenker, Heycock & Kroch assume an equative semantics for specificational clauses, but unlike Schlenker, they take the wh-clause to be a free relative clause, and not an embedded question. In (58) the gap in the free relative is type e, and Heycock & Kroch assume that the free relative denotes an element of the same type as the gap, in particular the ι-expression in (59), where y is a variable over individuals and where the ι-operator is defined as in (60).

(59) ιy[Fiona bought y] [= H&K's (65)]

(60) ιy[f(y)] denotes a iff f(a) AND ($\forall z$)(f(z) iff $z \leq a$) [= H&K's (66)]

The post-copular DP straightforwardly denotes an individual, and we thus arrive at (61), which is "a representation of the surface structure of [(58)] considered as a semantically interpreted object and hence [...] the starting point of the derivation of the sentence's logical form" (Heycock & Kroch 1999: 388).

(61) ιy[Fiona bought y] = 'that old dictionary' [= H&K's (67)/(84b)]

ι-reduction applies to (61) to yield (62c). As I understand it, there are three substeps to ι-reduction. First, the ι-operator is eliminated by applying the definition in (60). This yields (62a). Then the focus of the pseudocleft, i.e. the right-hand argument of the identity relation, substitutes for the ι-bound variable, as shown in (62b). This substitution is licensed by the identity relation itself (Heycock & Kroch 1999: 388). Finally, the second clause, which imposes maximality, is dropped. (62c) is the resulting logical form.

(62) a. Fiona bought y AND ($\forall z$) (Fiona bought z iff $z \leq y$) = 'that ancient dictionary'
b. Fiona bought that ancient dictionary AND ($\forall z$) (Fiona bought z iff $z \leq$ 'that ancient dictionary')
c. Fiona bought that ancient dictionary

In essence, what is created at logical form for a specificational pseudocleft is the corresponding simple clause paraphrase. This goes a long way towards accounting for connectivity effects, because in the simple clause paraphrase the expected syntactic licensing relationship does obtain: compare the a. and b. sentences in (42)–(47) above. The final assumption that Heycock and Kroch must make is that logical form is the level relevant for binding, NPI licensing, and semantic selection. In support of this somewhat radical assumption, they point to the existence of connectivity effects in question–answer pairs (63) and other discourse contexts (64).

(63) A: What did Mary$_i$ see?
B: Herself$_i$/Her$_{*i}$ in the mirror.

(64) There is something he$_i$ still wants to commission;
it's a portrait of himself$_i$/him$_{*i}$/John$_{*i}$.

In the example analyzed in (59)–(62) it is individuals that are being equated, but Heycock and Kroch point out that their analysis can be extended to specificational clauses with other types of foci, which is relevant for examples like (42)–(44) and (47) above, by allowing "the type of the ι-bound variable to range over all the semantic types that free relatives can denote" (Heycock & Kroch 1999: 383). Additionally, appropriate definitions of the ι-operator must be provided for each of these types.

Finally, to account for connectivity in specificational clauses that do not contain relative clause, like (65) below and (50) above, Heycock & Kroch (1999: 390) propose that "at the level of interpretation [i.e. LF; LM], a noun phrase like *his claim* in [65] must be represented in the same way as the free relative *what he claimed* [...] so as to be equally subject to ι-reduction".

(65) His$_i$ claim was that John$_i$ was innocent.

4.3 The semantic approach

The semantic approach to connectivity, as developed by Jacobson (1994), Sharvit (1999), Cecchetto (2000), and Heller (2002, 2005), holds that there is no hidden syntactic structure in specificational clauses, nor any post-LF transformations, and that the apparent lack of syntactic licensing (between antecedent and anaphor, between binder and variable, between negation and NPI, and between intensional predicate and de dicto NP) is real. From this they draw the general conclusions that c-command is not a necessary condition for anaphor licensing, variable binding, or NPI licensing, nor is sisterhood required to license de dicto readings of NPs. The task then is to explain why "unlicensed" reflexives, bound variable pronouns, NPIs, and de dicto readings are possible in specificational clauses, but (typically) not in non-specificational clauses.

Jacobson (1994) provides an account of bound variable connectivity in copular clauses, in particular the example in (66) (apart from the subject being a headed relative clause, rather than a wh-phrase, this is like the tennis player example in (45a)):

(66) The woman who every Englishman$_i$ loves is his$_i$ mother.

Her account account is couched in a variable-free semantics with a Categorial Grammar syntax and differs radically from the ones reviewed above: not only is there no c-command at any level of representation between *every Englishman* and *his*, in fact there is no binding relation between these two elements at all. Instead, the effect of binding that we observe in the relevant interpretation of this sentence (that it is true iff every Englishman loves his own mother) is the result of equating functional interpretations of the pre- and post-copular phrases. The relevant functional interpretations will be discussed in detail below, but intuitively (though not quite accurately) they are i) the function f such that for every Englishman x, x loves f(x) and ii) the-mother-of function. Both are functions from individuals to individuals and (66) equates these functions.

The functional reading of *his mother* is derived as follows: the pronoun denotes the identity function on individuals, $\lambda x[x]$, as personal pronouns generally do in Jacobson's system. Ordinarily the common noun *mother* denotes a relation between individuals (type $\langle e,\langle e,t\rangle\rangle$), but in this syntactic context it shifts to a type $\langle e,e\rangle$ meaning, namely the function mapping each individual into their mother: $\lambda x[\iota y[\text{mother}'(x)(y)]]$. The two functions compose and the result is that function that maps each individual into their mother, a.k.a. the-mother-of function:

(67) $\lambda x[\iota y[\text{mother}'(x)(y)]] \circ \lambda x[x] = \lambda x[\iota y[\text{mother}'(x)(y)]]$

The semantic composition of the pre-copular phrase is more involved. Lets first consider the interpretation of the verb in the relative clause. The ordinary meaning of *love* is a relation between individuals (i.e. type ⟨e,⟨e,t⟩⟩), but it can shift to a type ⟨⟨e,e⟩,⟨e,t⟩⟩ meaning by rule z, which is defined in (68):

(68) Let α be an expression with meaning of type ⟨X,⟨e,Y⟩⟩. Then there is a homophonous expression β with meaning of type ⟨⟨e,X⟩,⟨e,Y⟩⟩, where β ′ = z(α′). The definition of z is: For any function g, z(g) = λf[λx[g(f(x))(x)]] (for f a variable of type ⟨e,X⟩).

In (69), rule z is applied to *love*:

(69) z(love′) = λf[λx[love′(f(x))(x)]]

The shifted meaning of *love* is "a relation between individuals and functions from individuals to individuals, such that to z(love) some function f is to be an x who stands in the ordinary *loves*′ relation to f(x)" (Jacobson 1994: 165). This achieves the effect of variable binding in a sentence like *Every Englishman loves his mother*. The object noun phrase *his mother* has the functional interpretation derived in (67) and hence is of the right type (⟨e,e⟩) to combine with z(love′). The resulting VP meaning is a function from individuals to truth values, which yields true for an individual x if x z-loves the-mother-of function, that is, if x loves the mother of x. This VP meaning in turn can serve as the argument for the quantificational subject *every Englishman* and we arrive at the bound variable interpretation, namely that *every Englishman* has the VP property of z-loving the-mother-of function, that is the property of loving ones mother. Rule z thus effects binding by linking the pronoun in the object of *love* to a higher argument position, here the subject. It targets the pronoun inside the lower argument by requiring a functional interpretation for that argument (see the "lift" on the first argument of *love* from X to ⟨e,X⟩ in (68)). Now back to the relative clause in (66). Here there is a gap in the object position of *love*, namely the gap of relative clause extraction. Under Jacobson's Categorial Grammar assumptions such gaps have no meaning at all. Nonetheless, *love* shifts by rule z and, since there is no object to combine with, function composes with the meaning of the subject:

(70) every-Englishman-loves′ = every-Englishman′ o z(love′)
    = λf[every-Englishman′(λx[love′(f(x))(x)])]

The next piece is the meaning of the relative pronoun *who*. In Jacobson's analysis *who* is responsible for combining the relative clause meaning derived in (70) with the meaning of the common noun *woman* and it does so by intersecting the sets denoted by each of these. In the case of (66), the set denoted by the relative clause is a set of functions from individuals to individuals (see (70)). Hence *woman* also needs to denote a set of such functions (otherwise the intersection would be guaranteed to be empty), in particular the set of functions into women:

(71) type $\langle\langle e,e\rangle,t\rangle$ meaning for *woman* = $\lambda g[\forall x[\text{woman}'(g(x))]]$

Relative *who* in turn takes as arguments these two sets of functions and returns their intersection:

(72) who' = $\lambda A[\lambda B[\lambda f[B(f) \wedge A(f)]]]$
(for A and B variables of type $\langle\langle e,e\rangle,t\rangle$ and f a variable of type $\langle e,e\rangle$)

The last piece we need to derive the meaning of the pre-copular phrase is a suitable denotation of for the definite article. Here Jacobson assumes a variant of Partee's (1987) IOTA operator, in particular that *the* maps a set of functions to the unique member of that set. The derivation for the subject of (66) is given in (73) (I have renamed the function variable f in the meaning of *every Englishman loves* h):

(73) a. every-Englishman-loves' = (70)
   b. who' = (72)
   c. who-every-Englishman-loves' = who'(every-Englishman-loves')
      = $\lambda A[\lambda B[\lambda f[B(f) \wedge A(f)]]](\lambda h[\text{every-Englishman}'(\lambda x[\text{love}'(h(x))(x)])])$
      = $\lambda B[\lambda f[B(f) \wedge \lambda h[\text{every-Englishman}'(\lambda x[\text{love}'(h(x))(x)])](f)]]$
      = $\lambda B[\lambda f[B(f) \wedge \text{every-Englishman}'(\lambda x[\text{love}'(f(x))(x)])]]$
   d. woman' = (71)
   e. woman-who-every-Englishman-loves' = who-every-Englishman-loves' (woman')
      = $\lambda B[\lambda f[B(f) \wedge \text{every-Englishman}'(\lambda x[\text{love}'(f(x))(x)])]](\lambda g[\forall x[\text{woman}'(g(x))]])$
      = $\lambda f[\lambda g[\forall x[\text{woman}'(g(x))]](f) \wedge \text{every-Englishman}'(\lambda x[\text{love}'(f(x))(x)])]$
      = $\lambda f[\forall x[\text{woman}'(f(x))] \wedge \text{every-Englishman}'(\lambda x[\text{love}'(f(x))(x)])]$
   f. the-woman-who-every-Englishman-loves'
      = IOTA(woman-who-every-Englishman-loves')
      = $\iota f[\forall x[\text{woman}'(f(x))] \wedge \text{every-Englishman}'(\lambda x[\text{love}'(f(x))(x)])]$

The subject of (66) thus denotes the unique function with the range women such that every Englishman z-loves that function.

With functional interpretations of the pre- and post-copular phrases in place, we can turn to Jacobson's analysis of the copula. In so far as the bound variable connectivity effect observed in (66) is argued to follow from the equating of the two functions denoted by the elements flanking the copula, one might propose a type-suitable equative meaning for the specificational copula, as indeed Sharvit (1999: 306) does (see (77) below). Jacobson, however, pursues a polymorphic 1-be analysis in the vein of Partee (1986) (see sections 3.3. and 3.4.): the copula found in specificational clauses is the copula of predication, though its two arguments are reversed, such that the "predicative" (type $\langle X,t\rangle$) element is to the left and the "referential" (type X) element to the right. In the case of (66), $X = \langle e,e\rangle$ and *be* has the denotation in (75b). In order for the copula to combine with the subject, the subject must shift to a "predicative" meaning, i.e. to a type $\langle\langle e,e\rangle,t\rangle$ meaning. This is done by a functional version of Partee's (1987) IDENT operator which maps a function to the (singleton) set containing that function:

(74) IDENT(f)=λg[g≡f] (where f and g are both type $\langle e,e\rangle$, and ≡ means semantic equivalence)

Hence (66) composes as in (75):

(75) a. his-mother' = (67)
 b. is' = λi[λP [P(i)]]
  (for i a variable of type $\langle e,e\rangle$ and P a variable of type $\langle\langle e,e\rangle,t\rangle$)
 c. is-his-mother' = is'(his-mother')
  = λi[λP [P(i)]](λx[ιy[mother'(x)(y)]])
  = λP [P(λx[ιy[mother'(x)(y)]])]
 d. the-woman-who-every-Englishman-loves'
  = IDENT(the-woman-who-every-Englishman-loves')
  = IDENT((73f))
  = λg[g≡ιf[$\forall$x[woman'(f(x))] $\wedge$ every-Englishman'(λx[love'(f(x))(x)])]]
 e. the-woman-who-every-Englishman-loves-is-his-mother'
  = is-his-mother'(the-woman-who-every-Englishman-loves')
  = λP [P(λx[ιy[mother'(x)(y)]])](λg[g≡ιf[$\forall$x[woman'(f(x))] $\wedge$ every-Englishman'(λx[love'(f(x))(x)])]])
  = λg[g≡ιf[$\forall$x[woman'(f(x))] $\wedge$ every-Englishman'(λx[love'(f(x))(x)])]](λx[ιy[mother'(x)(y)]])
  = λx[ιy[mother'(x)(y)]]≡ιf[$\forall$x[woman'(f(x))] $\wedge$ every-Englishman'(λx[love'(f(x))(x)])]]

To summarize: Jacobson analyzes bound variable connectivity as the result of equating two type $\langle e,e\rangle$ functions. In her system functional interpretations noun phrases arise in two ways: through the presence of a pronoun (as in *his mother*) or through A-bar extraction (as in the relative clause *who every Englishman loves*).

Following Partee (1986), the equative relation is not the direct contribution of the copula, but rather introduced through type-shifting on the subject.

Sharvit (1999) extends the semantic approach to opacity connectivity, NPI connectivity, and Principle A connectivity. She offers tentative proposals for Principles B and C connectivity, which are substantiated by Cecchetto (2000).

Sharvit's account of opacity connectivity relies on Zimmermann's (1993) analysis of intensional predicates, according to which the opaque reading of *They are looking for a nanny* (=47b) arises from *look for* taking a property as its internal argument, here the nanny property. Hence the gap in the relative clause in (76a) (= (47a)) is of type $\langle s,\langle e,t\rangle\rangle$ and the relative clause minus *what* denotes a set of properties, as shown in (76b), where T is a contextually determined variable over plural individuals. In (76c), relative *what* applies to this set and picks out the maximum member of the set, with the result that the meaning of the entire subject phrase is the maximum property in the set of properties that they are looking for, i.e. of type $\langle s,\langle e,t\rangle\rangle$ (see Sharvit 1999: 306 for details).

(76) a. What they are looking for is a nanny.
   b. they-are-looking-for' = $\lambda P_{\langle s,\langle e,t\rangle\rangle}$ [look-for'(T,P)]
   c. what-they-are-looking-for' = what'(they-are-looking-for')
      = Max(they-are-looking-for')
      = Max($\lambda P_{\langle s,\langle e,t\rangle\rangle}$ [look-for'(T,P)])

The key to deriving an opaque, i.e. type $\langle s,\langle e,t\rangle\rangle$, reading of the post-copular phrase is, again, that an identity relation is imposed on the pre- and post-copular elements. Instead of attributing the identity relation to type-shifting (by IDENT) of the pre-copular phrase, Sharvit locates the identity relation in the meaning of the copula itself:

(77) be' = $\lambda X \lambda Y[X = Y]$ (where type(X) = type(Y))

Since (77) requires that the two elements *be* composes with be of the same type, and the subject of (76a) denotes a property (the one given in (76c)), a *nanny* must be property type as well, and that type-requirement is what derives the opaque reading. In that sense, the availability of such a reading (which is the connectivity effect under investigation) is a by-product of the identity meaning of the copula. This copula-regulated type-matching between the gap in the pre-copular phrase and the post-copular element is also at work in Sharvit's (1999) account of NPI connectivity, but for reasons of space I omit the details of that analysis.

Finally Sharvit extends Jacobson's account of bound variable connectivity to binding theory connectivity (examples (42)–(44) above). For Principle A connectivity (*What Harvey$_i$ did next was wash himself$_i$ thoroughly*), the basic idea is that there is no real binding between the two NPs (*Harvey* and *himself*). Instead the reflexive is taken to be an argument-reducing operation on transitive verbs in the spirit of Reinhart & Reuland (1993). Rather than positing a separate rule for the reflexive, Sharvit exploits the tools used in Jacobson's account of bound variable connectivity. wash' shifts by rule z to the meaning in (78) (cf. (68) and (69) above):

(78) $z(wash') = \lambda f[\lambda x[wash'(x,f(x))]]$

Following Jacobson, the reflexive denotes an identity function on individuals ($\lambda y[y]$) which combines with the shifted meaning of the verb to yield the property-meaning in (79):

(79) wash-himself' = $\lambda f[\lambda x[wash'(x, f(x))]](\lambda y[y])$
       = $\lambda x[wash'(x, \lambda y[y](x))]$
       = $\lambda x[wash'(x,x)]$

The VP-gap in the relative clause is also property-type, which results in a property denotation for the entire pre-copular expressions (through derivational steps analogous to (76b) and (76c) above). Thus (42a) composes as in (80), ignoring tense and the adverbials *next* and *thoroughly*, and letting Harvey' = h:

(80) what-Harvey-did-was-wash-himself' = be'(wash-himself')(what-Harvey-did')
       = $\lambda O_{\langle s\langle e,t\rangle\rangle} \lambda P_{\langle s\langle e,t\rangle\rangle} [O = P](\lambda x[wash'(x,x)])(Max(\lambda N_{\langle s,\langle e,t\rangle\rangle} [N(h)]))$
       = $\lambda P_{\langle s\langle e,t\rangle\rangle} [\lambda x[wash'(x, x)] = P](Max(\lambda N_{\langle s,\langle e,t\rangle\rangle} [N(h)]))$
       = $\lambda x[wash'(x, x)] = Max(\lambda N_{\langle s,\langle e,t\rangle\rangle} [N(h)])$
       = 1 iff self-washing is the greatest element in set of properties that hold of Harvey in the world of evaluation.

In this analysis, there is no syntactic licensing of the reflexive by its antecedent in (42a). Rather, the reflexive is possible because a property interpretation is possible (in fact required) for the post-copular phrase. This in turn is the result of two facts: the property-interpretation of the relative clause and the type-matching requirement imposed by the copula. Again, we see that the connectivity effect, here the appearance of a reflexive not c-commanded by its antecedent, is a by-product of the semantic composition of the specificational clause.

4.4 Further issues

Above I focussed on the dominant accounts of the core data associated with the connectivity question. The research cited above (and other research) has raised further issues that are currently under scrutiny. All I can do here is to mention a few of these. First, there is the empirical question of whether different connectivity effects have an equal distribution within a language as well as across languages (see e.g. Sharvit 1999: 321–323, 328–331, den Dikken, Meinunger & Wilder 2000, Heller 2002, and Heller 2005: 9). Secondly, there is evidence of connectivity effects outside the domain of copular clauses, including question–answer pairs and sentences with copula-like predicates like *consist in*. Strikingly, each of the three approaches to connectivity discussed above cites the existence of connectivity effects in question–answer pairs as evidence for their position, though the arguments they offer in support of these claims obviously differ. As far as I can tell, the existence of connectivity effects with copula-like predicates have received less attention. Third, various authors, including Sharvit (1999), den Dikken, Meinunger & Wilder 2000, and Cecchetto (2000), have pointed out the existence of ANTI-CONNECTIVITY EFFECTS, which are like connectivity effects in that the normal licensing conditions are not met in the specificational clause, but unlike the regular connectivity effects examined above, the licensing conditions are also not met in the simple clause paraphrase. This is illustrated for reflexive binding in (81), taken from Schlenker (2003: 203).

(81) a. What John thinks that Mary likes is himself.
    b. *John thinks that Mary likes himself.

Anticonnectivity effects are potentially problematic for the ellipsis approach and the logical form approach, in so far as their account of connectivity relies on the simple paraphrase being part of the derivation of the connectivity sentence and the normal licensing conditions being met in that part of the derivation. See Schlenker (2003: §5) for further data, references, and relevant discussion.

5 Conclusion

In the introduction, I distinguished three questions regarding copular clauses: the taxonomy question (how many types of copular clauses are there and what are their defining properties), the copula question (how many copulas are there and what is their semantic contribution), and the connectivity question (how are connectivity effects best accounted for and what do they tell us about the structure of the clauses they occur in and about the phenomena involved, i.e. binding, NPI licensing, etc.). As the body of the article made clear, there is no consensus on the answers to these questions. That is not to say, of course, that the last three decades of research has not deepened our understanding of copular clauses. I strongly believe that it has. For each question, there is a set of well-articulated and competing proposals, which have led to new questions being asked and old ones being asked in a more precise way. General theoretical tools, such as semantic type theory, have been applied to the study of copular clauses, and, though not reflected in this article, data from a wider range of languages are now part of the debate.

6 References

Adger, David & Gillian Ramchand 2003. Predication and equation. *Linguistic Inquiry* 34, 325–359.
Akmajian, Adrian 1979. *Aspects of the Grammar of Focus in English*. New York: Garland.
Alexiadou, Artemis & Anastasia Giannakidou 1999. Specificational pseudoclefts as lists. In: K. Shahin, S. Blake & E.-S. Kim (eds.). *Proceedings of the West Coast Conference on Formal Linguistics (= WCCFL) 17*. Stanford, CA: CSLI Publications, 1–15.
Aloni, Maria 2001. *Quantification under Conceptual Covers*. Doctoral dissertation. University of Amsterdam.
Berg, Jonathan 1988. The pragmatics of substitutivity. *Linguistics & Philosophy* 11, 355–370.
Birner, Betty J., Jeffrey P. Kaplan & Gregory Ward 2007. Functional compositionality and the interaction of discourse constraints. *Language* 83, 323–349.
Büring, Daniel 1998. Identity, modality and the candidate behind the wall. In: D. Strolovitch & A. Lawson (eds.). *Proceedings of Semantics and Linguistic Theory (= SALT) VIII*. Ithaca, NY: Cornell University, 36–54.
Caponigro, Ivano & Daphna Heller 2007. The non-concealed nature of free relatives. Implications for connectivity crosslinguistically. In: C. Barker & P. Jacobson (eds.). *Direct Compositionality*. Oxford: Oxford University Press, 237–263.
Cecchetto, Carlo 2000. Connectivity and anti-connectivity in pseudoclefts. In: M. Hirotani et al. (eds.). *Proceedings of the North Eastern Linguistic Society (= NELS) 30*. Amherst, MA: GLSA, 137–151.
Comorovski, Ileana 2007. Constituent questions and the copula of specification. In: I. Comorovski & K. von Heusinger (eds.). *Existence. Semantics and Syntax*. Dordrecht: Springer, 49–77.
Declerck, Renaat 1988. *Studies on Copular Sentences, Clefts and Pseudoclefts*. Dordrecht: Foris.
den Dikken, Marcel 2006. *Relators and Linkers. The Syntax of Predication, Predicate Inversion, and Copulas*. Cambridge, MA: The MIT Press.
den Dikken, Marcel, André Meinunger & Chris Wilder 2000. Pseudoclefts and ellipsis. *Studia Linguistica* 54, 41–89.
Geach, Peter Thomas 1962. *Reference and Generality. An Examination of Some Medieval and Modern Theories*. Ithaca, NY: Cornell University Press.

Geist, Ljudmila 2007. Predication and equation in copular sentences. Russian vs. English. In: I. Comorovski & K. von Heusinger (eds.). *Existence. Syntax and Semantics*. Dordrecht: Springer, 79–105.
Groenendijk, Jeroen & Martin Stokhof 1997. Questions. In: J. van Benthem & A. ter Meulen (eds.). *Handbook of Logic and Language*. Cambridge, MA: The MIT Press, 1055–1124.
Groenendijk, Jeroen, Martin Stokhof & Frank Veltman 1996. Coreference and modality. In: S. Lappin (ed.). *The Handbook of Contemporary Semantic Theory*. Oxford: Blackwell, 179–213.
Halliday, Michael A. K. 1967. Notes on transitivity and theme in English (Part 2). *Journal of Linguistics* 3, 199–244.
Hedberg, Nancy 2000. The referential status of clefts. *Language* 76, 891–920.
Heggie, Lorie 1988. *The Syntax of Copular Structures*. Ph.D. dissertation. University of Southern California, Los Angeles, CA.
Heller, Daphna 2002. On the relation of connectivity and specificational pseudoclefts. *Natural Language Semantics* 10, 243–284.
Heller, Daphna 2005. *Identity and Information. Semantic and Pragmatic Aspects of Specificational Sentences*. Ph.D. dissertation. Rutgers University, New Brunswick, NJ.
Heller, Daphna & Lindsey Wolter 2008. That is Rosa. Identificational sentences as intensional predication. In: A. Grønn (ed.). *Proceedings of Sinn und Bedeutung (= SuB) 12*. Oslo: Department of Literature, Area Studies and European Languages, University of Oslo, 226–240.
Heycock, Caroline & Anthony Kroch 1999. Pseudocleft connectedness. Implications for the LF interface level. *Linguistic Inquiry* 30, 365–397.
Heycock, Caroline & Anthony Kroch 2002. Topic, focus, and syntactic representations. In: L. Mikkelsen & C. Potts (eds.). *Proceedings of the West Coast Conference on Formal Linguistics (= WCCFL) 21*. Somerville, MA: Cascadilla Press, 101–125.
Higgins, Roger Francis 1979. *The Pseudo-cleft Construction in English*. New York: Garland.
Jacobson, Pauline 1994. Binding connectivity in copular sentences. In: M. Harvey & L. Santelmann (eds.). *Proceedings of Semantics and Linguistic Theory (= SALT) IV*. Ithaca, NY: Cornell University, 161–178.
Kay, Paul & Charles J. Fillmore 1999. Grammatical constructions and linguistic generalizations. The What's X doing Y? construction. *Language* 75, 1–33.
Merchant, Jason 2004. Fragments and ellipsis. *Linguistics & Philosophy* 27, 661–738.
Mikkelsen, Line 2005. *Copular Clauses. Specification, Predication and Equation*. Amsterdam: Benjamins.
Mikkelsen, Line 2007. On so-called truncated clefts. In: L. Geist & B. Rothstein (eds.). *Kopulaverben und Kopulasätze. Intersprachliche und intrasprachliche Aspekte*. Tübingen: Niemeyer, 47–68.
Moro, Andrea 1997. *The Raising of Predicates. Predicative Noun Phrases and the Theory of Clause Structure*. Cambridge: Cambridge University Press.
Müller-Reichau, Olav 2007. Das Subjekt eines spezifizierenden Satzes als Artterm. In: L. Geist & B. Rothstein (eds.). *Kopulaverben und Kopulasätze. Intersprachliche und intrasprachliche Aspekte*. Tübingen: Niemeyer, 69–90.
Partee, Barbara 1986. Ambiguous pseudoclefts with unambiguous be. In: S. Berman, J. Choe & J. McDonough (eds.). *Proceedings of the North Eastern Linguistic Society (= NELS) 16*. Amherst, MA: GLSA, 354–366.

Partee, Barbara 1987. Noun phrase interpretation and type-shifting principles. In: J. Groenendijk, D. de Jong & M. Stokhof (eds.). *Studies in Discourse Representation Theory and the Theory of Generalized Quantifiers*. Dordrecht: Foris, 115–143.
Reinhart, Tanya & Eric Reuland 1993. Reflexivity. *Linguistic Inquiry* 24, 657–720.
Romero, Maribel 2005. Concealed questions and specificational subjects. *Linguistics & Philosophy* 28, 687–737.
Ross, John Robert 1972. Act. In: D. Davidson & G. Harman (eds.). *Semantics of Natural Language*. Dordrecht: Reidel, 70–126.
Rothstein, Susan 1995. Small clauses and copula constructions. In: A. Cardinaletti & M. T. Guasti (eds.). *Small Clauses*. San Diego, CA: Academic Press, 27–48.
Rothstein, Susan 2001. *Predicates and their Subjects*. Dordrecht: Kluwer.
Russell, Bertrand 1919. *Introduction to Mathematical Philosophy*. London: Allen and Unwin.
Schlenker, Philippe 2003. Clausal equations (A note on the connectivity problem). *Natural Language and Linguistic Theory* 21, 157–214.
Sharvit, Yael 1999. Connectivity in specificational sentences. *Natural Language Semantics* 7, 299–339.
Sharvit, Yael 2003. Tense and identity in copular constructions. *Natural Language Semantics* 11, 363–393.
Williams, Edwin 1983. Semantic vs. syntactic categories. *Linguistics & Philosophy* 6, 423–446.
Zimmermann, Thomas E. 1993. On the proper treatment of opacity in certain verbs. *Natural Language Semantics* 1, 149–179.

Louise McNally
8 Existential sentences

1   What is an existential sentence? —— 281
2   The existential proposition —— 287
3   Analyses of the definiteness restriction —— 293
4   Analyses of the predicate restriction —— 300
5   Conclusion —— 302
6   References —— 302

Abstract: The term 'existential sentence' is used to refer to a specialized or non-canonical construction which expresses a proposition about the existence or the presence of someone or something. Because of their special structural and interpretive characteristics, existential sentences have offered a rich ground on which to test theories concerning the semantics of noun phrases and of predication, as well as theories concerning the role of non-canonical constructions in information packaging. This chapter begins by reviewing the basic structural, semantic and discourse functional properties of existential sentences. Since, across languages, existential sentences resemble copular, possessive and locative sentences, considerable debate has arisen about the extent to which their semantics are similar. The chapter therefore continues with an overview of the different analyses that have been proposed for the core existential proposition. The remainder of the chapter is devoted to two distinctive features of these sentences which have generated substantial discussion in the semantics and pragmatics literature: 1) the so-called definiteness restriction, which limits the ability of definite and quantificational nominals to appear as the 'pivot' of the construction; and, 2) the predicate restriction, which has been claimed to restrict the expressions that can appear as the 'coda' to so-called stage-level predicates.

1 What is an existential sentence?

The term 'existential sentence' is used to refer to a specialized or non-canonical construction which expresses a proposition about the existence or the presence of someone or something. Thus, the sentence in (1a) is considered existential because

Louise McNally, Barcelona, Spain

https://doi.org/10.1515/9783110589863-008

it is specialized (insofar as it has an expletive subject, whose distribution is highly restricted in English) and entails nothing other than the existence of one even prime number. In contrast, (1b) will not be considered existential for the purposes of this article because, even though it entails nothing other than the existence of one even prime number, there is nothing specialized about its syntax: it has the canonical subject-predicate structure used in English. Finally, (1c), though closely related to the construction in (1a), differs from it in syntactic details, in its use in discourse, and in the fact that, thanks to the verb, it entails something more than mere existence or presence. This latter type of sentence, an example of the 'presentational-*there*' construction (see e.g., Aissen 1975), will not concern us further here.

(1) a. There is one even prime number.
     b. One even prime number exists.
     c. There stood in the corner an empty coat rack and umbrella stand.

Existential sentences vary somewhat in structure, semantics, and pragmatics from language to language, though they generally share certain characteristics as well. This article will include examples from a variety of languages, though the discussion of their semantics and pragmatics will be based primarily on English.

1.1 Structural properties

Syntactically, existential sentences typically manifest most or all of the following five characteristics (see Francez 2007 for a particularly clear discussion and examples). First, an expletive subject, like English *there* or French *il* in (2a–b), may be required; however, in languages without expletives no such subject appears, as illustrated by the Catalan and Maori examples in (2c–d). Note that *hi* in (2c) is a locative clitic equivalent to French *y* in (2b):

(2) a. There are bugs eating the corn.

   b. Il y   a   eu   une reunion.
      it LOC has been a   meeting
      'There has been a meeting.'

   c. Hi   ha espai a l'   armari.
      there has space to the closet
      'There is space in the closet.'

d. Āe he taniwha.
      yes a taniwha
      'Yes, there are taniwhas.' (from Bauer 1993, cited in Chung & Ladusaw 1994: 42)

Second, though existential sentences do not always contain a verb (see e.g., (2d)), if there is one it is often homophonous with a verb meaning 'to be' (2a) or 'to have' (2b–c), or with some other verb related to possession (such as *geben* 'give' in German in (3a)) which is 'bleached' of its content; it may also be a special lexical item such as Hebrew *yeS* (3b).

(3) a. Es gab ein Kind in dem Garten.
       it gave a   child in the garden
       'There was a child in the garden.'

   b. yeS harbe tisot   ad   xacot.
      EX   many flights until midnight
      'There are many flights until midnight.' (Francez 2007: 60)

Curiously, the survey in Clark (1978) indicates that the verb in existential sentences is rarely, if ever, homophonous with a verb that literally means 'exist', although in English one does find sentences like (4):

(4)   There exists one even prime number.

However, Aissen (1975), building on Ross (1974), has argued that such sentences, which are also attested with a limited set of verbs including *remain*, *ensue*, and *follow*, do not share all of the properties of existential sentences with *be*, but rather manifest some characteristics of the latter and some of the so-called 'presentational-*there*' construction illustrated in (1c).

Third, in all existential sentences there is a 'pivot' nominal which describes the individual whose existence is under discussion (*bugs* in (2a), *une reunion* in (2b), etc.). The pivot is typically subject to certain semantic restrictions which will be discussed in section 3.

Fourth, in most languages, a 'coda' phrase may appear (such as *eating the corn* in (2a)), which is external to the pivot noun phrase. As with the pivot, only predicates meeting certain semantic conditions are licensed as codas, as will be discussed in sections 1.2 and 4.

Finally, in many, though by no means all, languages, a locative expression appears which may be obligatory and 'bleached' of content (e.g., *there*, *y*, *hi*), though the syntactic role this expression plays in the construction may vary from one language to another. For instance, in English it is the subject, while in French and Catalan it is not. The presence of such a locative expression has resulted in the frequent grouping of existential sentences together with locative constructions (see e.g., Lyons 1967; Kuno 1971; Kimball 1973; Clark 1978; Freeze 1992; Rigau 1997; Zeitoun et al. 1999 and several more recent references cited in Francez 2007), although others (e.g., Milsark 1974) have argued that the similarity between existential and locative sentences is superficial or spurious, at least in some languages.

A crucial and very difficult question is how all of these elements in an existential sentence are related syntactically and semantically. On this point there has been considerable disagreement among linguists. Existential sentences are often truth-conditionally equivalent to copular sentences ascribing a property or location (see article 7 [this volume] (Mikkelsen) *Copular clauses* for more on such sentences). For example, (2a) is synonymous with (5), though it differs in the contexts in which it is used.

(5) Bugs are eating the corn.

For this reason, many analyses have related existential and copular sentences derivationally or have attributed to them the same basic predicational structure, in which the pivot nominal serves as the argument to the coda phrase, which in turn effectively serves as the main predicate for the sentence – this was the intuition behind the '*There*-insertion' transformation in transformational grammars (e.g., Burt 1971; Milsark 1974; see e.g., Stowell 1978; Safir 1985; Pollard & Sag 1994 for related analyses for English).

However, other linguists have treated the similarity between existential and copular sentences as accidental. For example, Barwise & Cooper (1981), Chung (1987) (for Chamorro), and McNally (1992) argue that the pivot is the only complement to the existential predicate. On such analyses the coda either has to be treated as a pivot-internal modifier (as assumed by Barwise & Cooper), or else as some sort of adjunct. McNally (1992) specifically proposes that those codas which cannot be plausibly treated as pivot-internal modifiers should be analyzed as predicative adjuncts similar to the depictive adjunct in (6).

(6) They ate the vegetables steamed.

Finally, Williams (1984, 1994), Hazout (2004), and Francez (2007) all argue that the pivot nominal is in fact the main *predicate* of the existential sentence while the coda serves as a pivot-internal modifier or as an adjunct. What constitutes the subject of the existential predication is a matter of disagreement: Williams and Hazout argue that it is the expletive, though they do not provide an explicit semantics for this predication relation; Francez argues that the pivot denotes a property of an implicit contextual domain (something intuitively similar to a location), whose identity can be restricted by the coda phrase. The variety in the proposals for the basic syntax and argument structure of existential sentences makes it difficult to directly compare the semantic analyses that have been proposed in the literature for what Francez refers to as the 'existential proposition.' Nonetheless, a brief overview and comparison of these analyses is provided in section 2.

1.2 Semantic and discourse functional properties

Although it is unlikely that one single semantics and discourse function can be assigned to existential sentences cross-linguistically, certain semantic and discourse functional properties are consistently associated with these sentences across languages. Perhaps the most important of these is the intuition that existential sentences serve primarily to introduce a novel referent into the discourse – one fitting the description provided by the pivot nominal. This function is, in turn, almost certainly related to two other characteristics commonly attributed to existential sentences. The first of these is the so-called *definiteness restriction* on the pivot nominal (an early exhaustive description of which appears in Milsark 1974), to be discussed in section 3. Though the exact characterization of the facts is complex, as a first approximation the definiteness restriction amounts to a restriction on the acceptability of definite, demonstrative, and necessarily quantificational noun phrases, including proper names and personal pronouns, in the pivot (see Chapter IX for more details on these various kinds of noun phrases):

(7) a. ??There is each/every first-year student present.
    b. ??There are most first-year students in that class.
    c. ??There is the neighbor's dog barking.
    d. ??There is that carpet under the table.
    e. ??There are them / Anna and Bob waiting outside.

As will be discussed in section 4, Milsark related the definiteness restriction to another semantic restriction which is evident in existential sentences in English and other languages. Specifically, the coda has to be what Carlson (1977a) referred to as a stage-level predicate, as exemplified in (8); so-called individual-level predicates are not licensed, as shown in (9). Though the precise definition of what counts as an individual- or stage-level predicate is a difficult matter which cannot be dealt with here, stage-level predicates tend to describe accidental properties, while individual-level predicates tend to describe essential ones.

(8) a. There were many people in line already.
 b. There were a few people waiting for hours.
 c. There was a live pig roasted.
 d. There were no taxis available.

(9) a. ??There were many students anarchists.
 b. ??There were lots of donors generous.
 c. ??There were inmates psychotic.

It is also often claimed of existential sentences that they are *thetic* (term due to the philosophers Brentano and Marty; see Kuroda 1972; Sasse 1995 for modern discussions), purely rhematic, or topicless; or, alternatively, if they are assumed to have a topic-comment or theme-rheme structure, the topic or theme is hypothesized to be a location rather than the referent of the pivot (see e.g., Babby 1980 for Russian; see also Kim 1997, and Leonetti 2008 for Romance and a general survey): Since the only obligatory nominal in an existential sentence is the pivot, and the pivot introduces a novel referent (whether directly or indirectly), there is no other candidate expression except perhaps the coda that can provide the topic of the sentence or serve as the subject of a categorical (logical subject-predicate) or theme-rheme propositional structure. Note that the failure of the pivot to serve as a topic would also follow directly if the pivot were in fact the main predicate of the existential sentence. (See Chapter XV for more on notions such as *theme*, *rheme*, and *topic*.)

These semantic and pragmatic generalizations, though frequent, are not entirely unproblematic, however. For example, Abbott (1992, 1993, 1997) and Ward & Birner (1995) have argued that existential sentences serve not only to introduce novel discourse referents but also to reintroduce or focalize referents that have already been mentioned. Consider, for example, (10) (from the Challenger commission transcripts, cited in Ward & Birner 1995: 727):

(10) I think there was one flight where we had one problem. It wasn't ours, but there was that one flight.

In this example a demonstrative noun phrase appears in the pivot position which is directly anaphoric to an expression that appears in the previous sentence. A more familiar example is provided by the so-called list use of existentials (see e.g., Rando & Napoli 1978), illustrated in (11), in which proper names are often found:

(11) A: Who showed up?
     B: Well, there was Alex.

Such examples raise the question of whether a uniform semantics and discourse function can be given for everything that looks formally like an existential sentence, or whether in reality there are several subtypes of existential sentence, perhaps with distinct semantics and pragmatics.

The claim that the pivot cannot be a topic is similarly questionable. As Leonetti (2008: Fn 21) points out, existential sentences in which the pivot is topicalized are attested; the English, Catalan and Spanish examples in (12a), (12b), and (12c), respectively, illustrate. In the Catalan example, the presence of the partitive clitic *n'* (glossed as 'some') is anaphoric to *pintura* and marks the sentence clearly as a clitic left-dislocation construction. In such constructions the left-dislocated expression has been argued to be topical (see e.g., Vallduví 1992):

(12) a. They told us there was a solution, and indeed a solution, there was.

    b. Pintura, n'   hi   ha dins   l'armari.
       paint   some there has in   the closet
       'Paint, there is in the closet.'

    c. Ardillas, hay en el   bosque.
       squirrels have in the woods
       'Squirrels, there are in the woods.'

Understanding such counterexamples in the face of the strong intuitions concerning the discourse referent introduced by existential sentences and the information structure of these sentences entails first making a decision as to the basic semantics of existential sentences, a difficult issue to which we now turn.

2 The existential proposition

The space of possibilities for the basic semantics of existential sentences includes various options, five of which will be mentioned here. On the first option, proposed in Barwise & Cooper (1981), an existence predicate serves as the main predicate. The pivot is analyzed as a generalized quantifier and thus takes the existence predicate as its argument, as in (13b) for the sentence in (13a) (though one might also consider treating the pivot as non-quantificational when possible and having the existence predicate take it as its argument, as in (13c), where the pivot is analyzed for the purposes of illustration as denoting the value of a choice function, along the lines of Reinhart (1997) or Kratzer (1998); see also Chapter IX).

(13) a. There is one good answer.
 b. (**one**(λx[**answer**(x) $\wedge$ **good**(x)]))(λx[**exist**(x)])
 c. **exist**($f(\lambda x$[**answer**(x) $\wedge$ **good**(x) $\wedge$ $|x| \geq 1$]))

Either way, such an analysis runs into trouble in cases where the coda phrase cannot be plausibly treated as part of the pivot (see Keenan 1987 for arguments that such cases do in fact exist). However, Zucchi (1995) suggests a variant of this analysis on which the coda serves to contextually restrict the domain of quantification of the pivot, eliminating this criticism concerning the syntactic and semantic function of the coda.

The second option involves treating the coda, rather than an existence predicate, as the main predicate. Again, the pivot could in theory be treated either as a generalized quantifier (following e.g., Keenan 1987, see (14b)) or as non-quantificational (14c).

(14) a. There was a room available.
 b. (**a**(λx[**room**(x)])) (λx[**available**(x)])
 c. **available**(f(**room**))

Such an analysis effectively equates existential sentences semantically with copular sentences. However, Keenan (1987) adds the proposal that what makes existential sentences special is the possibility of what he calls an existential reading, formulated as in (15), where '1' is the universal property, that is, a property all individuals have, roughly analogous to the property of existing:

(15) 1 ∈ Det(NP ∩ XP) (Keenan 1987: 301, minor details modified)

Keenan observes that an existential sentence with a logical form like that in (14b) will have an existential reading just in case the determiner in the pivot has the property of being what he calls *existential*. Keenan's notion of an existential determiner will be discussed in section 3, as it plays a role in his account of the definiteness restriction.

Among the criticisms that have been leveled against analyses like that in (14), two stand out. First, there is evidence that the coda is not the main predicate. For example, Williams (1984) argues that if the coda were the main predicate, it should be able to extract like a main predicate. But as the contrast between (16a–b) shows, it does not.

(16) a. How sick were the children?
b. *How sick were there the children?

Such reduced acceptability under extraction is characteristic of adjuncts.

McNally (1992: Ch. 2) offers an additional argument against treating the coda as the main predicate, based on asymmetries between extraction from within complements vs. adjuncts. Huang (1982) showed that extraction of an adjunct from within a complement or main predicate is possible, whereas extraction of an adjunct from within an adjunct is not. (17), which shows the contrast in acceptability in the extraction of a manner adverbial from a main predicate vs. a depictive adjunct, illustrates this asymmetry.

(17) a. How badly was she coughing _?
b. *How badly did you leave the concert hall coughing _?

The impossibility of such extraction out of the coda indicates that it is an adjunct, and not the main predicate.

(18) *How badly were there people coughing _ in the audience?

As yet another argument against treating the coda as the main predicate, Francez (2007: Ch. 4) observes that quantificational expressions within the coda always take scope over the pivot, while quantificational predicates in main clauses need not take wide scope over their subjects; contrast (19a) and (19b):

(19) a. Some drummer I know is in every rock band.
b. There is some drummer I know in every rock band.

While the scope facts follow on Francez' analysis of the coda as a modifier, this argument is weakened by the fact that the pivot can be independently shown to take narrowest scope (see section 3, below).

A second criticism of analyses like that in (14) is that there are a number of types of existential sentences that do not have acceptable copular sentences as counterparts (see e.g., Kimball 1973 and the examples in (20)).

(20)   a. There was space in the room.
      b. ??Space was in the room.
      c. There was a fire in the school.
      d. ??A fire was in the school.

If the compositional semantics for the contrasting pairs in (20) is the same, it is difficult to explain why the existential sentences are acceptable while the copular sentences are not.

A third possible analysis for the existential proposition is that proposed in Milsark (1974, 1977), on which the existential predicate contributes an existential operator; the pivot denotes a property that serves as its restriction (with any determiner that might be present serving as a cardinality predicate); and the coda serves as the scope of the existential quantifier. Milsark's semantic 'E rule' is as follows (1974: 206):

(21)   *there* AUX (*have-en*) *be* Q NP X is interpreted: the class C denoted by NP has at least one member c such that P(c) is true, where P is a predicate and P is the reading of X and the set of such members c is of cardinality Q.

See Landman (2004) for a variant on this property-based analysis of the pivot.

The analysis in McNally (1992), closely related to Milsark's, constitutes a fourth possibility for the existential proposition. This analysis differs from Milsark's on three points. First, the pivot is analyzed not as a property looking to be bound by an existential operator, but rather as the *entity correlate of a property* (Chierchia 1984) – the reification of a property that allows it to serve as the argument to another predicate (just as the nominalization *goodness* of the adjective *good* allows us to say things like *Goodness is a virtue*). Second, and relatedly, the main predicate in the sentence is the property of being *instantiated*, which applies to the pivot's denotation. Though these two aspects of the analysis might appear to be simply notational variants of Milsark's analysis, see McNally (2009) for arguments that they make distinct empirical predictions. Finally, the coda, as mentioned above, is analyzed as a VP-internal adjunct modifier which stands in a control relation to the pivot and which serves to restrict the spatiotemporal index at which the main predicate holds by forcing it to be included in the time the adjunct predicate holds of its argument. The semantics for (14a) on this analysis is sketched in (22), where (i) constitutes the core existential proposition, and (ii) and (iii), the ultimate effect of the adjunct predicate (see McNally 1992: Chapter 4 for a slightly different formulation and further details).

(22) (i) **instantiate**($\cap \lambda x[\textbf{room}(x)]$);
 (ii) the token individual y who supports the truth of (i) at a time t is in the extension of **available** at t'; and
 (iii) $t \leq t'$.

Milsark's and McNally's analyses share the fact that they remove any quantificational force from the pivot. Though both argue that this leads to a natural account of the definiteness restriction (see below), the proposal to treat the pivot as a property can be criticized. For example, the semantics proposed in (21) and (22) initially run into difficulties when the pivot contains a monotone decreasing determiner such as *no*, *few*, or *at most two*, or a non-monotone one like *exactly three* (see article 4 [Semantics: Noun Phrases and Verb Phrases] (Keenan) *Quantifiers*). Take (23) as an example:

(23) There was exactly one cookie left.

If *exactly one* is treated as a cardinality predicate, (21) and (22) predict that (23) will be true not only when there is exactly one cookie left, but also when there is more than one left: (21) and (22) only require finding an individual cookie with a cardinality of exactly one, but fail to make the sentence false if more than one such individual can be found. To solve this problem, McNally (1998) suggests a decompositional analysis for *no* and *few* (equivalent to a sentential negation plus *a* and *many*, respectively), following a proposal in Ladusaw (1992) (see also Chapter XIII); she follows Krifka (1999) in arguing that *at most* and *exactly* should be factored out from the semantics of the pivot and treated as focus-sensitive operators whose semantics is incorporated at the clause level. Francez (2007) points out that such an analysis is inelegant, though he provides no conclusive empirical arguments against it. Francez also observes (as did McNally) that it is difficult on the analysis in (22) to treat the coda as a controlled adjunct predicate in a fully compositional fashion.

Francez's (2007) alternative constitutes a fifth proposal for the existential proposition. Francez argues that the pivot – and not an existence predicate or the coda – should be the main predicate of the existential proposition. However, he also maintains that the pivot should denote a generalized quantifier, that is, a property of sets. This leads him to conclude that the logical subject of the existential proposition must be a set, rather than an individual. Specifically, he proposes that this set is a *contextual domain* – a set of salient entities in the context. Hypothesizing that the subject of the existential proposition is a contextual domain is a way of capturing the intuition that existential sentences are 'about the context.' This domain as its name suggests, is not directly denoted by any specific constituent in the existential sentence; however, the coda can contribute to restricting its identity. Francez's definition of contextual domains appears in (24). It defines this domain as a set of individuals who stand in a contextually specified relation R to another individual α.

(24) For every element α of type τ, let d_α be the contextual domain of α, where
$d_\alpha =_{def} \lambda y_{\tau'}[R_{<\tau',<\tau,t>>}(\alpha,y)]$

Francez's analysis of a sentence like (25a) is thus as in (25b). The pivot contributes the negative existential quantifier, the rest of the sentence contributes nothing else, and thus the quantifier is applied to the contextually-supplied domain d_α.

(25) a. There was no coffee.
b. $\lambda P_{<e,t>}[\mathbf{no}(\lambda x[\mathbf{coffee}(x)],P)](d_\alpha)$

What might d_α be? It must be a set of individuals, in order to serve as the scope of *no coffee*. And by (24) it will have to be a set that stands in contextually-determined relation R to some type of object. Francez (2007: 74–75) suggests for this particular example that α is the spatio-temporal parameters of utterance, and R is the relation of being located within those parameters. Thus, (25b) ends up being equivalent to (26), which can be paraphrased as saying that no coffee has the property of being in the set of things located within the spatiotemporal parameters of the utterance (represented in (26) as st_u).

(26) $\mathbf{no}(\lambda x[\mathbf{coffee}(x)],\lambda y[\mathbf{loc}(st_u,y)])$

When there is an explicit coda, the analysis treats the coda as a modifier which as a rule serves to restrict the relation R.

(25b) has the virtue of treating the pivot as the main predicate in a technical sense, an analysis for which there is increasing syntactic support. However, it is not at all usual for the subject of a predication to be a set and, moreover, to effectively serve as the nuclear scope of a quantifier. It is therefore not clear to what extent this analysis really preserves the spirit of the claim that the pivot is the main predicate. On the other hand, unlike Keenan's analysis it manages to treat the coda as a modifier, and it avoids the criticisms that have been made of property-based analysis of the pivot.

As can be seen, each of these analyses has pros and cons. Given the comparatively little content of existential sentences, it might even be the case that different languages choose different options for expressing the existential proposition (see McNally 2009 for examples and discussion of this possibility).

3 Analyses of the definiteness restriction

The definiteness restriction, illustrated in (7), is the characteristic of existential sentences that has received greatest attention in the semantics and pragmatics literature. In addition to the restrictions on necessarily quantificational noun phrases and certain definite and demonstrative noun phrases (including personal pronouns and proper names), Milsark claimed that there are restrictions on the indefinite noun phrases that are licensed as well, which limit the acceptability of partitives (including covert partitives, identifiable by stress on the determiner) and generically interpreted indefinites, though Hoeksema (1989) observes that the restriction on partitives holds for English only when there is no coda phrase.

(27) a. ??There are five of the prime numbers less than 10. (cf. Five of the prime numbers are less than 10.)
 b. ??There were SOME teachers on strike, but not others.
 c. ??There are dinosaurs extinct. (cf. Dinosaurs are extinct.)

Milsark (1977) referred to the noun phrases/determiners excluded from the pivot position as *strong*, and to those licensed in the position as *weak*. An important aspect in the development of subsequent analyses of the definiteness restriction has been the attempt to arrive at a more precise and empirically adequate characterization of the weak/strong distinction.

A number of different syntactic, semantic and pragmatic analyses of the definiteness restriction have been proposed. Since space precludes reviewing all of these here, only the most representative of these analyses will be reviewed. Strictly syntactic analyses of the restriction will not be discussed, as the facts clearly indicate that even these analyses must ultimately rely on semantic or pragmatic notions. For example, Milsark himself, Woisetschlaeger (1983), Holmback (1984), and others have observed that morphologically definite noun phrases such as those in (28) are perfectly acceptable in existential sentences when they are ostensibly semantically indefinite.

(28) a. There was the most amazing painting in their collection!
　　　b. There was the mother of a student waiting outside.

Thus, no analysis that appeals exclusively to the form of the pivot will account for the definiteness restriction.

To an important extent the divergence in the analyses of the restriction reflect divergence in the starting assumptions concerning the data. These divergences will be introduced as the different analyses are reviewed.

Although Milsark (1974, 1977) did not provide a fully formalized, compositional semantic account of the definiteness restriction, the essence of his proposal was clear. If we posit that the existential predicate contributes an existential operator, we would expect the pivot to license only those expressions whose denotations could combine with such an operator. In other words, the pivot has to denote a property. Pivots containing necessarily quantificational determiners such as *each* and *every* should be excluded because they are already quantificational. The operator contributed by such determiners will bind any variable within the logical form for the pivot. In contrast, Milsark suggested, weak indefinite noun phrases are systematically licensed as pivots because indefinite determiners can be analyzed as cardinality predicates, making the noun phrase amenable to a property-type analysis. Heim (1987: 23) characterizes the restriction in similar, if negatively defined terms:

(29)　*There be x, when x is an individual variable.

(29) would exclude, for example, the bound variables left behind by quantifier raising. Heim also argues that the generalization in (29) can account for another fact that has been related to the definiteness restriction, namely that when the pivot is relativized, only a so-called amount relative reading appears to be available.

Amount relative clauses can be distinguished from ordinary relative clauses both syntactically and semantically. The semantic difference is that the amount relative describes a quantity rather than a specific individual. This is evident in examples like (30), an adaptation of one of Heim's amount relative examples:

(30)　It would take days to drink the champagne they spilled that evening.

The relative clause in (30) refers to the quantity of champagne that was spilled, not to the exact same liquid that was spilled. Turning to syntax, amount relatives are different from ordinary relatives in that they require a definite or universal determiner on the head noun they modify, and can only be introduced by *that* or a null relative pronoun in some dialects of English (see Carlson 1977b). Note that the amount reading of (30) disappears if the determiner is not universal or the relative pronoun is changed to *which*:

(31) a. It would take days to drink some champagne they spilled that evening.
 b. It would take days to drink the champagne which spilled that evening.

Heim observes that relativization of the pivot syntactically resembles amount relativization, as the examples in (32b–c) show:

(32) a. You've eaten every cookie there is in the house.
 b. *You've eaten some/two/many cookies there are in the house.
 c. *You've eaten every cookie which there is in the house.

She argues that the contrast between examples like (32a) and (32b–c) follows if in ordinary relativization of the pivot an individual variable is left behind in the position of the gap; she suggests that in amount relativization, the variable left behind does not correspond to the gap but rather to a subpart of the gap. Thus, the logical forms for the noun phrases containing the amount and restrictive relatives in (32a) and (32c) could be informally represented as in (33a) and (33b), respectively. Heim suggests that the universal quantifier in the amount relative is interpreted as a maximality operator over degrees d:

(33) a. Max d: there were d-many cookies in the house
 b. every x: cookie $x \wedge$ there was x in the house.

Despite the initial appeal of this proposal, there is one important respect in which relativization of the pivot differs from amount relativization: the former imposes an identity of individuals requirement. That is, in order for (34) to be true, it is not enough that I read a quantity of books identical to the quantity on the table in question; I must have read the exact same books that were on the table.

(34) I read all the books there were on the table.

Grosu & Landman (1998) propose a semantics for amount relatives which attempts to account for this fact. However, McNally (2008) argues that there are problems with Grosu & Landman's analysis and that, despite the superficial similarities between amount relatives and relativization of the pivot, we cannot conclude that the latter is necessarily amount relativization. Nonetheless, McNally fails to provide an alternative analysis for all of the facts, and relativization of the pivot remains an understudied and poorly understood phenomenon.

Returning to the definiteness restriction, what exactly Milsark's (or Heim's) basic account of the restriction predicts for proper names, pronouns, definites, and strong (e.g., partitive) indefinites depends on the assumptions one makes about the semantics of these latter expressions. Partee's (1987) theory of noun phrase type shifting leads one to expect that all of these expressions should be able to shift to well-defined and felicitous property-type denotations, for example those in (35):

(35) a. $[[Anna]] = \lambda x[x = \mathbf{a}]$
 b. $[[the\ dog]] = \lambda x[x = \iota y[\mathbf{dog}(y)]]$
 c. $[[them_i]] = \lambda x[x = y_i]$

But if such denotations are available, we might expect these sorts of noun phrases to be acceptable in existential sentences.

In fact, as noted in section 1.2, there is good evidence that true definite noun phrases are indeed acceptable (see, in addition to the references cited elsewhere in this article, Ziv 1982 and Lumsden 1988). But let us maintain for a moment the view that they are not, or at least that such noun phrases are attested only with an alternative kind of interpretation, such as the presentational interpretation illustrated in (1c), or the list interpretation illustrated in (11). Such a view is assumed in both Barwise & Cooper's (1981) and Keenan's (1987, 2003) accounts of the restriction.

Both Barwise & Cooper and Keenan assume that noun phrases as a rule denote generalized quantifiers. They take as their first task a proper semantic characterization of those quantifiers that appear in (English) existential sentences vs. those that do not – in other words, a more precise account of the weak/strong distinction. Barwise & Cooper (1981: 264) begin by defining strong and weak determiners as in (36).

(36) A determiner D is *positive strong* or (*negative strong*, resp.) if for every model $M = \langle E, [[\ ]] \rangle$ and every $A \subseteq E$, if the quantifier $[[D]](A)$ is defined, then $A \in D(A)$ (or $A \notin D(A)$, resp.). If D is not (positive or negative) strong then D is *weak*.

A quantifier is strong if it is headed by a strong determiner. However, other factors may make a quantifier strong. Even though proper names lack a determiner altogether in English, they always behave like quantifiers constructed out of strong determiners; similarly, partitive noun phrases, even though they may contain weak determiners, also behave as if strong. In both cases, this behaviour can be shown to be follow from the existence presupposition associated with the noun phrase.

Barwise & Cooper's explanation of the definiteness restriction is pragmatic: Under the assumption that the existential proposition is of the form in (13b), existential sentences with strong nominals as pivots will be tautologous or contradictory, but never contingent, and thus will be systematically uninformative. However, this account of the restriction falls apart if the coda is external to the pivot, as Keenan (1987) and others have argued: Even if it is not new information that the denotation of the pivot exists, the ascription of the coda property to the pivot's denotation could well be informative.

Keenan's characterization of the class of noun phrases licensed in existential sentences and his account of the definiteness restriction are slightly different. Rather than claiming that definite and universal noun phrases are unacceptable as pivots, he simply assumes that they lack the existential reading in (15), above. Keenan (1987: 291) defines the class of determiners that yield noun phrases with the existential reading as *existential* (see (37a)); Keenan (2003) proves that the existential determiners are equivalent to those defined as *intersective* as in (37b). The intersective determiners, in turn, are just those that are *conservative* on both their first and second arguments (see Barwise & Cooper 1981 on the notion of conservativity; note that Keenan 2003 also generalizes these definitions to $n > 1$-place determiners and Boolean combinations of determiners).

(37) a. A function f from properties to sets of properties is existential iff for all properties $p, q, p \in f(q)$ iff $1 \in f(q \wedge p)$.
b. [A function denoted by a determiner] D from P_E into $GQ_{E,X}$ is intersective iff for all subsets A, A', B, B' of E, if A ∩ B = A' ∩ B' then DAB = DA'B'.

Intuitively, an existential determiner is one whose semantics can be calculated without making a comparison between sets, as is necessary with, for example, proportional determiners such as *most*. To know whether e.g. each student in a given class read *Hard Times* it is necessary to compare the set of students in the class who read *Hard Times* with the set who did not, or with the set of students as a whole. In contrast, in order to determine the truth of a proposition involving an intersective determiner such as *two*, as in *Two students read Hard Times*, we need only identify the set of students who read *Hard Times* and determine its cardinality. This makes the contribution of an intersective determiner more like that of a property than like that of a true quantificational operator.

However, the facts are not so simple. As Lumsden (1988) observes, necessarily quantificational noun phrases are perfectly acceptable in existential sentences when they quantify over kinds, as in (38a), or similar higher-order objects, as in (38b), where what is asserted is the existence of an instance of every one of a set of types of reasons:

(38) a. There was each of the three kinds of chocolate available.
b. There was every reason to believe that it would rain.

Although Wilkinson (1991) suggests accounting for examples like (38a) by reanalyzing noun phrases of the form *D kind of N* as equivalent to *an N of D kind*, McNally (1992) points out various ways in which these two types of noun phrases are not equivalent, thus casting doubt on the viability of such a reanalysis.

Still, the acceptability of the noun phrases in (38) and the intuition that they are somehow 'covertly indefinite' raises the possibility that the definiteness restriction is not semantic but rather pragmatic in nature. Pragmatic analyses of the restriction fall into two general groups. One group (e.g., Prince 1992; Ward & Birner 1995; Abbott 1992, 1993; Zucchi 1995) attribute the restriction to a condition on the discourse status of the referent associated with the pivot. For example, Prince (1992) argues that the referent of the pivot has to be 'hearer-new,' i.e., not part of the common ground at the time of utterance. Ward & Birner (1995) argue that the notion of hearer-newness can be extended to account even for cases of definite noun phrases in pivot position; specifically, such noun phrases are licensed just in case it is possible to construe the referent of the noun phrase as hearer-new in the context (e.g., because it has been forgotten about by the hearer). However, Abbott (1997) contends that it is difficult to maintain that the referent of the pivot is hearer-new particularly in cases where the pivot is anaphoric, such as in (10), above, and suggests that 'it may not be the case that any single discourse-based principle can account for the distribution of NPs in this construction.' (1997: 107).

The second general group of pragmatic approaches to the definiteness restriction builds in one way or another on the non-topical nature of the pivot position, often taking into account that the existential construction in most languages exists in a paradigm with one or more other constructions that are conventionally associated with a different information structure (see Hannay 1985; Borschev & Partee 2002; Mikkelsen 2002; Beaver et al. 2005; Francez 2007; Hu & Pan 2007; Partee & Borschev 2007). The intuition behind these proposals is that indefinite noun phrases often make poor subjects, particularly when there is a strong association between subject and topic in a language, while definite noun phrases make good ones. Existential sentences in many languages serve to get out of subject position a noun phrase which would otherwise have to be expressed as a subject (compare e.g., (20a–b), above). Part of the argument for this view comes from the observation, developed in detail in Beaver et al. (2005), that the cross-linguistic variation in the definiteness restriction is gradient rather than absolute. Beaver et al. present a quantitative study which, rather than dividing noun phrases into two groups (weak vs. strong), orders them on a scale according to how many subject properties they manifest. They argue that this same scale can be used to predict the variation in the definiteness restriction across languages. Existential sentences in different languages may be sensitive to different points on the scale, but it should always be the case that if a language allows a given noun phrase candidate for canonical subject in the pivot position, it should also allow all *worse* candidates for canonical subject to appear as pivots as well. Similarly, if a given noun phrase type is blocked from pivot position, all *better* candidates for canonical subject on the scale should be blocked as well.

Finally, in contrast to the above-mentioned proposals, which offer a unified account for the definiteness restriction, McNally (1992) argues that the restriction is part semantic and part pragmatic in nature. Her analysis is grounded in the claim in (22) that the existential predicate selects for the entity correlate of a property. On this analysis, any noun phrase that can plausibly be treated as an entity correlate of a property *or* as a quantifier over entity correlates of properties is expected to have a well-formed interpretation in the pivot position. If the notion of 'weak' is taken to describe the semantic restriction on the type of the pivot and if the semantics in (22) is recast in set-theoretic terms (as in McNally 1998), the proposal also leads naturally to the definition of 'weak' as 'property denoting' (see Ladusaw 1994 for a development of this idea).

When coupled with Partee's theory of type shifting, McNally's proposal directly accounts for the contrast between examples like (38) and similar examples, such as (7a), which quantify over ordinary token individuals. The latter are excluded because they neither quantify over entity correlates of properties nor are able to type shift felicitously to denote entity correlates of properties (see McNally 1998 for details on which kinds of noun phrases do not have a felicitous property-type denotation and why they do not). However, since definites, demonstratives, partitive indefinites, proper names, and pronouns can all felicitously shift to a property type under Partee's theory and then can shift to the entity correlate of that type, they are predicted to have well-formed interpretations in existential sentences, which, as noted above, they do. To account for the oddness of existential sentences with these kinds of noun phrases (when they are in fact odd), McNally adopts a Prince-style pragmatic account. However, a mixed semantic-pragmatic account of the restriction would also be possible using a Beaver et al.-style analysis of the conditions on definites instead of one based on hearer-newness.

Though a non-unified analysis of the definiteness restriction might seem less attractive than a unified one, McNally argues that it predicts that the patterns of variation found in the restriction cross-linguistically will reflect the split between those noun phrases which are excluded in English for semantic reasons and those which are excluded for pragmatic reasons. This prediction is confirmed, for example, in Catalan, which systematically allows definites, demonstratives, names and pronouns in existential sentences, but allows only necessarily quantificational noun phrases that quantify over kinds or similar higher order objects.

The mixed semantic-pragmatic analysis also predicts an asymmetry in the scopal behavior of the pivot. The great majority of noun phrases in pivot position systematically have only narrowest scope with respect to other operators in an existential sentence (though see Francez 2007 for possible counterexamples). This is seen in e.g., (39a), which is unacceptable because *some* must take wide scope with respect to negation but cannot. The narrowest scope requirement follows if the pivot denotes a (scopeless) entity correlate of a property. However, there is no reason on this analysis to expect that pivots denoting quantifiers like those in (38) should have to take narrowest scope, and indeed they needn't (see (39b)).

(39) a. ??There wasn't some student at the meeting.
     b. There wasn't one particular variety of wine that we expected on the list.

Empirical studies such as Ward & Birner's and Beaver et al.'s make clear that the facts concerning the definiteness restriction are much more complex than what was suggested by earlier studies of the phenomenon, and that additional cross-linguistic research is needed to determine how best to parameterize a theory of the restriction so that it can account for the attested variation while capturing what existential sentences have in common across languages. It seems likely that some kind of gradient or non-unified analysis will be inevitable; what remains to be determined is whether an analysis that is purely pragmatic or one that mixes semantic and pragmatic conditions will prove more insightful.

4 Analyses of the predicate restriction

The second restriction on existential sentences discussed in Milsark (1974) limits the types of predicates that appear in the coda: As illustrated in (9), above, those allowed in the coda correspond to Carlson's (1977a) class of stage-level predicates, while those excluded correspond to his class of individual-level predicates.

The predicate restriction has generated much less discussion in the semantics and pragmatics literature than the definiteness restriction, in part because there is less controversy over the facts. Perhaps the only point of contention has been whether noun phrases are systematically excluded (which would be consistent with the behaviour of nominal predicates under Carlson's classification) or whether temporary state-descriptive nominals are licensed, as Nathan (1978) and Hannay (1985) suggest, using examples such as (40) in support.

(40) ??There was a woman the president.

However, examples such as (40) are not generally considered acceptable in the literature and there seems to be little or no evidence in favor of the claim that noun phrases are licensed as codas.

The analysis of the predicate restriction is deeply bound up with the syntactic analysis of existential sentences and with the nature of the existential proposition. Milsark (1974, 1977) observed a correlation between those predicates which are excluded from the coda and those which disallow weak noun phrases as subjects of copular sentences. This sort of correlation is exactly what is expected if existential sentences express the same propositional structure as copular sentences. In contrast, if the coda is not considered an independent constituent but rather simply a post-nominal modifier, as in Jenkins (1975), Barwise & Cooper (1981) or Williams (1984), a non-stipulative explanation of the coda restriction should follow from independently necessary restrictions on post-nominal modifiers. Finally, those analyses on which the coda is a modifier must derive the restriction from independently motivated restrictions on the kind of modification the coda provides. For example, McNally (1992) proposes that the coda serves to restrict the spatio-temporal parameters within which the referent of the pivot is instantiated; on this view, individual-level predicates are ruled out because they lack the ability to provide the necessary sort of spatio-temporal restriction. Francez (2007) makes a similar claim concerning modification of the contextual domain.

It is obvious that a decision concerning the best analysis of the predicate restriction can only be made by taking into account the syntax and argument structure of existential sentences. It must take into account the analysis of the definiteness restriction as well. For example, a Milsark-style analysis of the predicate restriction predicts that when definite noun phrases are (exceptionally) licensed as pivots, we should find violations of the predicate restriction as well. However, this does not happen, as (41), an adaptation of (10), shows.

(41) I think there was one flight that was a problem. *It wasn't ours, but there was that one flight the problem.

This fact thus serves as another sort of argument, beyond the syntactic, semantic and typological arguments that have been advanced with increasing frequency, against the view that existential sentences and copular sentences have the same propositional structure.

5 Conclusion

Thanks to their special structural and interpretive characteristics, existential sentences have offered and continue to offer a rich ground on which to test theories concerning the semantics of noun phrases and of predication, as well as theories concerning the role of non-canonical constructions in information packaging. Their close relation to locative sentences raises interesting psychological and philosophical questions about the relationship between the notion of presence and that of existence. Finally, the striking similarities and differences in existential sentences across languages present interesting challenges for efforts to develop theories of 'cross-linguistic' semantics.

6 References

Abbott, Barbara 1992. Definiteness, existentials, and the 'list' interpretation. In: C. Barker & D. Dowty (eds.). *Proceedings of Semantics and Linguistic Theory (= SALT) II*, Columbus, OH: The Ohio State University, 1–16.

Abbott, Barbara 1993. A pragmatic account of the definiteness effect in existential sentences. *Journal of Pragmatics* 19, 39–55.

Abbott, Barbara 1997. Definiteness and existentials. *Language* 73, 103–108.

Aissen, Judith 1975. Presentational-*there* insertion: A cyclic root transformation. In: R. E. Grossman, J. L. San & T. J. Vance (eds.). *Papers from the Regional Meeting of the Chicago Linguistic Society (= CLS) 11*. Chicago, IL: Chicago Linguistic Society, 1–14.

Babby, Leonard H. 1980. *Existential Sentences and Negation in Russian*. Ann Arbor, MI: Karoma Publishers.

Barwise, Jon & Robin Cooper 1981. Generalized quantifiers and natural language. *Linguistics & Philosophy* 4, 159–219.

Bauer, Winfried 1993. *Maori*. London: Routledge.

Beaver, David, Itamar Francez & Dmitry Levinson 2005. Bad subject! (Non)-canonicality and NP distribution in existentials. In: E. Georgala & J. Howell (eds.). *Proceedings of Semantics and Linguistic Theory (= SALT) XV*. Ithaca, NY: Cornell University, 19–43.

Borschev, Vladimir & Barbara H. Partee 2002. The Russian genitive of negation in existential sentences: The role of theme-rheme structure reconsidered. In: E. Hajičová et al. (eds.). *Travaux du cercle linguistique de Prague, vol. 4*. Amsterdam: Benjamins, 185–250.

Burt, Marina 1971. *From Deep to Surface Structure*. New York: Harper & Row.

Carlson, Gregory N. 1977a. *Reference to Kinds in English*. Ph.D. dissertation. University of Massachusetts, Amherst, MA. Reprinted: New York: Garland, 1980.
Carlson, Gregory N. 1977b. Amount relatives. *Language* 53, 520–542.
Chierchia, Gennaro 1984. *Topics in the Syntax and Semantics of Infinitives and Gerunds*. Ph.D. dissertation. University of Massachusetts, Amherst, MA. Reprinted: New York: Garland, 1989.
Chung, Sandra 1987. The syntax of Chamorro existential sentences. In: E. Reuland & A. G. B. ter Meulen (eds.). *The Representation of (In)definiteness*. Cambridge, MA: The MIT Press, 191–225.
Chung, Sandra & William A. Ladusaw 2004. *Restriction and Saturation*. Cambridge, MA: The MIT Press.
Clark, Eve 1978. Locationals: Existential, locative and possessive constructions. In: J. Greenberg (ed.). *Universals of Human Language*. Stanford, CA: Stanford University Press, 85–126.
Francez, Itamar 2007. *Existential Propositions*. Ph.D. dissertation. Stanford University, Stanford, CA.
Grosu, Alexander & Fred Landman 1998. Strange relatives of the third kind. *Natural Language Semantics* 6, 125–170.
Freeze, Ray 1992. Existentials and other locatives. *Language* 68, 553–95.
Hannay, Michael 1985. *English Existentials in Functional Grammar*. Dordrecht: Foris.
Hazout, Ilan 2004. The syntax of existential constructions. *Linguistic Inquiry* 35, 393–430.
Heim, Irene 1987. Where does the definiteness restriction apply? Evidence from the definiteness of variables. In: E. Reuland & A. G. B. ter Meulen (eds.). *The Representation of (In)definiteness*. Cambridge, MA: The MIT Press, 21–42.
Hoeksema, Jack 1989. Review of E. Reuland & A. ter Meulen (eds.). *The Representation of (In) definiteness* (Cambridge, MA,1987). *Language* 65, 115–125.
Holmback, Heather 1984. An interpretive solution to the definiteness effect problem. *Linguistic Analysis* 3, 195–215.
Hu, Jianhua & Haihua Pan 2007. Focus and the basic function of Chinese existential *you*-sentences. In: I. Comorovski & K. von Heusinger (eds.). *Existence. Semantics and Syntax*. Dordrecht: Springer, 133–145.
Huang, C. T. James 1982. *Logical Relations in Chinese and the Theory of Grammar*. Ph.D. dissertation. MIT, Cambridge, MA.
Jenkins, Lyle 1975. *The English Existential*. Tübingen: Niemeyer.
Keenan, Edward 1987. A semantic definition of indefinite NP. In: E. Reuland & A. G. B. ter Meulen (eds.). *The Representation of (In)definiteness*. Cambridge, MA: The MIT Press, 286–317.
Keenan, Edward 2003. The definiteness effect: Semantics or pragmatics? *Natural Language Semantics* 11, 187–216.
Kim, Yookyung 1997. *A Situation Semantic Account of Existential Sentences*. Ph.D. dissertation. Stanford University, Stanford, CA.
Kimball, John 1973. The grammar of existence. In: C. Corum, C. T. Smith-Stark & A. Weiser (eds.). *Papers from the Regional Meeting of the Chicago Linguistic Society (= CLS) 9*. Chicago, IL: Chicago Linguistic Society, 262–270.
Kratzer, Angelika 1998. Scope or pseudoscope? Are there wide scope indefinites? In: S. Rothstein (ed.). *Events and Grammar*. Dordrecht: Kluwer, 163–196.
Krifka, Manfred 1999. At least some determiners aren't determiners. In: K. Turner (ed.). *The Semantics/Pragmatics Interface from Different Points of View*. Amsterdam: Elsevier, 257–291.

Kuno, Susumu 1971. The position of locatives in existential sentences. *Linguistic Inquiry* 2, 233–278.

Kuroda, Shige-Yuki 1972. The categorical and the thetic judgment. *Foundations of Language* 9, 153–185.

Ladusaw, William A. 1992. Expressing negation. In: C. Barker & D. Dowty (eds.). *Proceedings of Semantics and Linguistic Theory (= SALT) II*. Columbus, OH: The Ohio State University, 237–260.

Ladusaw, William A. 1994. Thetic and categorical, stage and individual, weak and strong. In: M. Harvey & L. Santelmann (eds.). *Proceedings of Semantics and Linguistic Theory (= SALT) IV*. Ithaca, NY: Cornell University, 220–229.

Landman, Fred 2004. *Indefiniteness and the Type of Sets*. Oxford: Blackwell.

Leonetti, Manuel 2008. Definiteness effects and the role of the coda in existential constructions. In: A. Klinge & H. Hoeg-Muller (eds.). *Essays on Nominal Determination*. Amsterdam: Benjamins, 131–162.

Lumsden, Michael 1988. *Existential Sentences: Their Structure and Meaning*. London: Routledge.

Lyons, John 1967. A note on possessive, existential, and locative sentences. *Foundations of Language* 3, 390–396.

McNally, Louise 1992. *An Interpretation for the English Existential Construction*. Ph.D. dissertation. University of California, Santa Cruz, CA. Reprinted: New York: Garland, 1997.

McNally, Louise 1998. Existential sentences without existential quantification. *Linguistics & Philosophy* 21, 353–392.

McNally, Louise 2008. DP-internal *only*, amount relatives, and relatives out of existential sentences. *Linguistic Inquiry* 39, 161–169.

McNally, Louise 2009. Properties, entity correlates of properties, and existentials. In: A. Giannakidou & M. Rathert (eds.). *Quantification, Definiteness, and Nominalization*. Oxford: Oxford University Press, 163–187.

Mikkelsen, Line 2002. Reanalyzing the definiteness effect: Evidence from Danish. *Working Papers in Scandinavian Syntax* 69, 1–75.

Milsark, Gary 1974. *Existential Sentences in English*. Ph.D. dissertation. MIT, Cambridge, MA. Reprinted: New York: Garland, 1979.

Milsark, Gary 1977. Toward an explanation of certain peculiarities of the existential construction in English. *Linguistic Analysis* 3, 1–29.

Nathan, Geoffrey 1978. *The Syntax and Semantics of the English Existential Construction*. Ph.D. dissertation. University of Hawaii at Manoa, Honolulu, HI.

Partee, Barbara H. 1987. Noun phrase interpretation and type-shifting principles. In: J. Groenendijk, D. de Jongh & M. Stokhof (eds.). *Studies in Discourse Representation Theory and the Theory of Generalized Quantifiers*. Dordrecht: Foris, 115–144.

Partee, Barbara H. & Vladimir Borschev 2007. Existential sentences, BE, and the genitive of negation in Russian. In: I. Comorovski & K. von Heusinger (eds.). *Existence. Semantics and Syntax*. Dordrecht: Springer, 147–190.

Pollard, Carl & Ivan Sag 1994. *Head-Driven Phrase Structure Grammar*. Chicago, IL: The University of Chicago Press.

Prince, Ellen 1992. The ZPG-letter: Subjects, definiteness, and information status. In: W. Mann & S. Thompson (eds.). *Discourse Description: Diverse Linguistic Analyses of a Fund Raising Text*. Amsterdam: Benjamins, 295–325.

Rando, Emily & Donna Jo Napoli 1978. Definites in *there*-sentences. *Language* 54, 300–313.

Reinhart, Tanya 1997. Quantifier scope: How labor is divided between QR and choice functions. *Linguistics & Philosophy* 20, 335–397.
Rigau, Gemma 1997. Locative sentences and related constructions in Catalan: *ésser/haver* alternation. In: A. Mendikoetxea & M. Uribe-Etxebarria (eds.). *Theoretical Issues at the Morphology-Syntax Interface*. Bilbao: Universidad del País Vasco, 395–421.
Ross, John R. 1974. There, there, (there, (there, (there))). In: M. LaGaly, R. Fox & A. Bruck (eds.). *Papers from the Regional Meeting of the Chicago Linguistic Society (= CLS) 10*. Chicago, IL: Chicago Linguistic Society, 569–587.
Safir, Kenneth 1985. *Syntactic Chains*. Cambridge: Cambridge University Press.
Sasse, Hans-Jürgen 1995. 'Theticity' and VS order: A case study. *Sprachtypologie und Universalienforschung* 48, 3–31.
Stowell, Timothy. 1978. What was there before *there* was there? In: D. Farkas, W. M. Jacobsen & K. W. Todrys (eds.). *Papers from the Regional Meeting of the Chicago Linguistic Society (= CLS) 14*. Chicago, IL: Chicago Linguistic Society, 458–471.
Vallduví, Enric 1992. *The Informational Component*. New York: Garland.
Ward, Gregory & Betty Birner 1995. Definiteness and the English existential. *Language* 71, 722–742.
Wilkinson, Karina 1991. *Studies in the Semantics of Generic Noun Phrases*. Ph.D. dissertation. University of Massachusetts, Amherst, MA.
Williams, Edwin 1984. *There*-insertion. *Linguistic Inquiry* 15, 131–153.
Williams, Edwin 1994. *Thematic Structure in Syntax*. Cambridge, MA: The MIT Press.
Woisetschlaeger, Eric 1983. On the question of definiteness in 'an old man's book'. *Linguistic Inquiry* 14, 137–154.
Zeitoun, Elizabeth, Lillian M. Huang, Marie M. Yeh & Anna H. Chang 1999. Existential, possessive, and locative constructions in Formosan languages. *Oceanic Linguistics* 38, 1–42.
Ziv, Yael 1982. Another look at definites in existentials. *Linguistics* 18, 73–88.
Zucchi, Alessandro 1995. The ingredients of definiteness and the definiteness effect. *Natural Language Semantics* 3, 33–78.

Ingo Reich
9 Ellipsis

1   Introduction —— 306
2   S-ellipsis —— 310
3   A-ellipsis —— 313
4   Parallelism —— 325
5   Information structure —— 328
6   Discourse —— 331
7   Psycholinguistics —— 332
8   References —— 334

Abstract: The fact that languages are organized in an economic way is probably most obvious when it comes to ellipsis. Every day we make frequent use of fragmental expressions like "tall decaf cappuccino, please" or "Kathleen a blueberry muffin" to get some message across, relying on the assumption that the addressee is in a position to somehow resolve the missing parts (of information) from the context and common knowledge. The way we drop (supposedly) redundant parts, however, is by no means arbitrary; it is systematically guided by syntactic, semantic, pragmatic and other factors. This article gives a review of the most central elliptical constructions as well as the most prominent approaches to tackling them, with special focus on the semantic, pragmatic and psycholinguistic aspects of the matter.

1 Introduction

When in the movie "You've Got Mail" Kathleen Kelly (Meg Ryan) utters the sentence *I love daisies*, she expresses the thought or proposition that she, Kathleen Kelly, loves daisies. Conversely, anybody who wants to express the thought or proposition that she or he loves daisies seems *a priori* to be forced to utter a full-fledged sentence, for only full-fledged sentences denote semantic objects of the required type (thoughts or propositions). But the fact is that, in a Starbucks, Kathleen Kelly may very well simply utter the string in (1) consisting of two adjectives and a noun to order a tall decaf cappuccino. Similarly, the string *Kathleen*

Ingo Reich, Saarbrücken, Germany

https://doi.org/10.1515/9783110589863-009

a blueberry muffin in (2), a sequence of two noun phrases, conveys the complete thought or proposition that Kathleen orders a blueberry muffin.

(1) Tall decaf cappuccino.

(2) Joe orders a cappuccino, and Kathleen a blueberry muffin.

Data like (1) and (2) thus teach us that non- or subsentential expressions may very well be used to convey a complete thought or proposition, provided that the addressee is (known to be) in a position to somehow resolve the missing parts of information. This phenomenon is generally known under the label "ellipsis" (from greek *élleipsis*, "omission").

1.1 Delimiting ellipsis

The main characteristic of ellipsis thus is that in a given utterance or construction relevant parts (of information) are omitted (by the speaker), and have to be supplemented (by the hearer). Without any further qualifications this coarse characterization of ellipsis covers both the omission of the object *das* ("it") in (3) and the missing (indefinite) object in (4a).

(3) (*Was für ein Handy!*)   *Muss ich unbedingt haben!*
     (what for a cell-phone!)   must I at-all-costs have!
     '(What a cell phone!) I must have it, at all costs!'

(4) a. Sie aß stundenlang. / She ate for hours.
     b. *Er trägt stundenlang. / *He carries for hours.

There are good reasons to draw a line between (3) and (4a), however: In (4a), the possibility of dropping the object hinges on lexical properties of the selecting predicate; cf. (4b). (3), on the other hand, illustrates a more general phenomenon, TOPIC DROP in German (cf. Fries 1988; Cardinaletti 1991). Topic drop systematically targets pronouns within the "prefield" (the position preceding the fronted verb in main clauses) and thus is structurally rather than lexically constrained (cf. (3) to *Ich muss unbedingt haben!*). This strongly suggests that (3) and (4a) in fact illustrate two different phenomena, ellipsis on the one hand and valency (cf. article 4 [Semantics: Lexical Structures and Adjectives] (Levin & Rappaport Hovav) *Lexical Conceptual Structure*) on the other.

(5) illustrates another phenomenon that we may not really want to discuss under the term ellipsis, the systematic omission of adverbial information (but cf. article 11 [Semantics: Interfaces] (Jaszczolt) *Semantics and pragmatics* for relevant discussion): (5a), for example, conveys that it is raining *at some contextually given time and place* though time and place are left implicit. Similarly, an utterance of (5b) typically conveys that the speaker had a large breakfast *today*.

(5) a. It's raining.
    b. I had a large breakfast.

What is special about this data is that – in contrast to (1) and (2) above – we do not really feel (5a) and (5b) to be in any serious way incomplete. This apparently relates to the fact that, syntactically, (5a) and (5b) constitute well-formed sentences. We take this as sufficient reason to exclude such data from the following considerations, and thus (further) restrict our use of the term ellipsis to *prima facie* non- or subsentential expressions.

1.2 Resolving ellipsis

If we confine ourselves in the way outlined above, then (1) and (2) illustrate that there are two prominent ways of reconstructing the relevant information in elliptical constructions.

To see this, first consider (2). What is omitted in the second conjunct in (2) is the verb. Since the first conjunct contains a suitable verb, the verb *orders*, this verb is taken to fill the gap, and the second conjunct is taken to denote the proposition that Kathleen orders a blueberry muffin. In other words, the gap is filled by referring to a suitable linguistic antecedent. What matters here is the observation that in (2) the reference to a linguistic antecedent is in fact indispensable, for the second conjunct seems simply ungrammatical (or senseless) in isolation; cf. (6). Let's call this antecedent-based ellipsis (a-ellipsis).

(6) *(Kathleen standing at the counter, ordering a blueberry muffin)*
    Joe: *Look, Kathleen a blueberry muffin!

In (1), however, there is no linguistic context present at all, and the missing information has to be resolved from non-linguistic context only, i.e., from the information provided by the current situation and world knowledge (cf. Klein 1993 for discussion). (1) differs from (2) in that this is in fact possible. Let's call this SITUATION-BASED ELLIPSIS (s-ellipsis).

1.3 Understanding ellipsis

As is clear from the above, the crucial (and obvious) question to ask when one tries to understand the mechanisms underlying ellipsis is the following: How is ellipsis resolved?

To get a grip on this question, we can try to split it into three subquestions: (i) What do possible (linguistic or non-linguistic) antecedents look like? (ii) What is the nature of the gap itself? And, (iii), how is the relation between the antecedent and the gap to be characterized? If we make the reasonable assumption that the nature of the gap determines to a large extent the nature of possible antecedents as well as the nature of the antecedent-gap relation, then we need to focus on the question of what options we have in analyzing the gap.

Apparently, the answer is, to a considerable extent, theory-dependent. Within the general framework of generative grammar there are *prima facie* the following options: First, the gap could be construed as a trace t. If it is, then the antecedent is a moved constituent, and the antecedent-gap relation is a relation created by movement. This is the MOVEMENT APPROACH to ellipsis, and its perspective on the matter is syntactic.

Alternatively, one could think of the gap as a phonologically null (unpronounced) pronoun *pro*. In that case the antecedent-gap relation is a relation of anaphora, and possible antecedents should be constrained by general constraints on anaphoric relations. The ANAPHORA APPROACH tackles ellipsis from a semantic point of view.

Both options considered so far assume that the relevant non-sentential utterance – like *Kathleen a blueberry muffin* – is in fact, and despite all appearances, a sentential expression of the form "Kathleen t_i a blueberry muffin" or "Kathleen pro_i a blueberry muffin", where the gap is filled by some pronominal element, which is interpreted semantically by relating it to its antecedent *orders* in the first conjunct. Another option – one which still subscribes to the sentential analysis of ellipsis – is to assume that the gap is not filled by some pronominal element, but by the predicate *orders* itself. The basic idea is that *orders* is present syntactically as well as semantically, but that it simply goes unpronounced – the reason being that the second occurrence of *orders* is, in a sense, redundant. Usually, this is represented by crossing out the relevant parts as in "Kathleen ~~orders~~ a blueberry muffin". The notion of redundancy which is at stake here is one of identity, and ellipsis is considered as (phonological) deletion under identity. This is the DELETION APPROACH to ellipsis. Its perspective is syntactic, if the underlying notion of identity is defined on the level of syntax; it is semantic, if it is defined on the level of semantics.

A final option is, of course, to consider non-sentential utterances like *Kathleen a blueberry muffin* as just what they seem to be: non-sentential utterances – in the case at hand a sequence of two noun phrases. Although this approach is probably the most intuitive one, it raises many non-trivial questions: Why is it that a sequence of two noun phrases can be used to convey a proposition? And how is it possible to realize a speech act with non-sententials? Minimally, approaches of this sort have to tell a story about how the information lexically encoded by the two noun phrases is enriched so that a complete thought is understood, a story that could be told on the level of conceptual structure or on the level of pragmatics.

2 S-ellipsis

As it turns out, the last approach – let's call it the FRAGMENTS APPROACH – seems to be the most promising one when it comes to s-ellipsis. This is mainly because the fragments approach predicts one of the key features of s-ellipsis: indeterminacy.

2.1 Indeterminacy

(1), for example, can be paraphrased by *I'd like to have a tall decaf cappuccino* just as well as by *give me a tall decaf cappuccino, please*. In this respect, s-ellipsis seems to behave quite similarly to discourse particles like those in (7).

(7) Hi, Bye, Cheers!, Cheese!

But in contrast to discourse particles, s-ellipsis does not rely on lexically encoded conventions: *Decaf*, for instance, can be used – depending on the context, cf. (8) – as an imperative, as an assertion, or as a question (cf., e.g., Barton 1990; Stanley 2000; Stainton 2004).

(8) Customer: *Decaf!* Barista: *Decaf?* Customer: *Yes, decaf.*

The indeterminacy of utterances like *decaf* thus stems from the fact that the lexical meaning of the participle has to be enriched (on a semantic, conceptual or pragmatic level) by relevant information implicit in the non-linguistic context, until some propositional object results that speech acts can operate on. However, despite being largely determined by context, there are still several ways to express this missing information linguistically.

This is also true of so-called "text type ellipsis", i.e., the use of non-sententials in specific contexts, like headlines (9a), bylines (9b), or road signs (9c).

(9) a. Bush in Germany
 b. By David Pogue.
 c. Stuttgart 14km

But, as far as I can see, there is no compelling reason to think that text type ellipsis works essentially differently from other cases of s-ellipsis, except for the fact that its almost conventionalized form helps a great deal in determining the intended propositional content.

2.2 Structural evidence

Reconsidering the question of what options we have in modeling s-ellipsis, it is quite clear that the movement approach is ruled out, since it necessarily requires a linguistic antecedent. But what about the other approaches? Both the anaphora approach and the deletion approach are, in principle, consistent with the gap not having a linguistic antecedent. Within the anaphora approach, it can be argued that the usual distinction between deictic and anaphoric pronouns carries over to the silent pronouns assumed in ellipsis (cf. Hankamer & Sag 1976), and that in s-ellipsis one or more silent deictic pronouns are at work (cf., e.g., Barton 1990; Schwabe 1994). Proponents of the deletion approach, on the other hand, may adduce that s-ellipsis usually has a paraphrase of the form "deictic pronoun + be/modal + fragment" (*I want a / this is a tall decaf cappuccino*), where the deictic pronoun depends on non-linguistic context anyway, and the predicate is just an auxiliary, not a full verb, and thus easily reconstructable (cf., e.g., Merchant 2004). Bare and *wh*-infinitivals show the same kind of paraphrases with the additional complication that the underlying modal is not uniquely determined: (10b), for example, could mean *Who can I ask for advice?* as well as *Who should I ask for advice?*; cf. Reis (1995; 2003) and Grohmann & Etxepare (2003) for discussion.

(10) a. *Rasen nicht betreten!*
  grass not   walk-on!

 b. *Wen um Rat   fragen?*
  who for advice ask?

Further support for the deletion approach stems from the fact that in languages like German, noun phrases in s-ellipsis show case (11a), and reciprocals are fine, too (11b).

(11) a. *Dem Herrn einen Kaffee.*
 the-DAT guy a-ACC coffee

 b. *Nein, nicht nébeneinander!*
 no, not side-by-side

The corresponding arguments in favor of the deletion approach are based on the following two assumptions: (i) case is assigned by some predicate in syntax; (ii) reciprocals, not being deictic, call for a linguistic antecedent. As far as I can see, though, neither argument is watertight. In a minimalist syntax, for example, linguistic structure is built bottom-up, phase by phase, and each phase is interpreted semantically and phonologically as a single unit. If this approach is on the right track, information about case needs to be present in a noun phrase before the noun phrase combines with the verb. In minimalist terms, case just needs to be 'checked' at a later point in the derivation. But suppose that case only needs to be checked if there *is* a later point in the derivation, the claim being that cases like (11a) are simply sequences of noun phrases. On this view, the primary function of case is to correlate noun phrases with likely thematic roles (e.g., beneficiary, theme), and thus to give additional clues as to what information, accessible from non-linguistic context, is meant to fill the gap (cf. Barton & Progovac 2005). Quite similarly, *each other* denotes a concept that links two objects in a symmetric way, and it seems not altogether inconceivable to provide an analysis of reciprocals which can express the appropriate relation in the absence of a verb.

Another piece of data seemingly supporting the deletion approach is (12).

(12) *Jedem sein Wehwehchen.*
 everybody his little-ailments

In (12) the interpretation of the pronoun *sein* ("his") varies with the interpretation of the quantifier *jedem*; in other words, the pronoun is bound by the quantifier. Binding, however, is usually considered to be a process that involves λ-abstraction over the variable introduced by the pronoun, triggered by a syntactic mechanism that requires movement of the relevant quantifier. Movement, in turn, requires some underlying sentential structure, minimally a position the quantifier can be moved to. On the other hand, examples like (12) are quasi 'idiomatic constructions', and there is no intuition whatsoever as to what the missing parts could actually look like. So chances are good that (12) is simply a sequence of two noun phrases.

An example of a fragment that does not require any completion at all, but rather some kind of restructuring (*the ...that* = *what*) is (13), discussed in Portner & Zanuttini (2005).

(13) The strange things that he says!

(14) der   / die   Angestellte
      the-MASC / the-FEM employee

Lexicalized noun phrase ellipsis as in (14) is not felt to be in any way incomplete either, even though there are good reasons for assuming some covert noun phrase here: In contrast to morphological conversion gender is not fixed and may depend on a hidden noun.

3 A-ellipsis

As we mentioned at the outset, a-ellipsis crucially differs from s-ellipsis in that only the former presupposes the presence of a linguistic antecedent. Even though we will see that this way of partitioning ellipsis phenomena is not as clear cut as may have been suggested, there is certainly something real to this distinction. Within a-ellipsis phenomena we in turn distinguish between CONSTITUENT ELLIPSES as in (15), and *prima facie* cases of NON-CONSTITUENT ELLIPSES as in (16a,b) (omitted constituents are marked with a Δ).

(15) *Joe Fox:* How can you forgive this guy for standing you up and not forgive me for this tiny little thing like putting you out of business. – Oh how I wish you would Δ.

(16) a. Clemens has no younger brothers, and Pettitte Δ no older brothers.
      b. LeBron James and the Cavaliers visit the Garden on Wednesday, and Kobe Bryant and the Los Angeles Lakers Δ Δ on Sunday.

In (15), it is the VP *forgive me for this tiny little thing like putting you out of business* which is dropped, leaving the finite auxiliary *would* stranded. This type of ellipsis is known under the term VP ELLIPSIS. In (16a) and (16b) on the other hand, it is the finite predicate that is lacking in the second (i.e., non-initial) conjunct. This is the crucial characteristic of an ellipsis type called GAPPING since Ross (1967; 1970); cf. Repp (2009) for recent discussion. As (16b) illustrates it is possible to elide other constituents alongside the finite predicate, in this case the object *the*

Garden, which may be argued to not form a constituent with the finite verb *visit*. The following German example is a less controversial case:

(17) Caspar brachte dem Jesuskind Gold dar,   Baltasar Δ Δ Myrrhe Δ
   Caspar gave the infant Jesus gold V-PART, Baltasar Δ Δ myrrh Δ

Gapping is further restricted to coordinations, cf. **Kobe visited the Garden on Sunday, although LeBron on Wednesday*, and thus falls under the label COORDINATE ELLIPSES.

3.1 Coordinate ellipsis

Besides Gapping there are several other instances of coordinate ellipsis. The probably most controversial case in question is RIGHTWARD DELETION (RD), i.e., the supposed deletion of a string right-adjacent to the coordinating conjunction; cf. (18) and (19).

(18) Yao Ming stood tall in the lane and
   Δ made the Knicks look small and woefully inadequate.

(19) [Once I read a story about a butterfly in the subway, and today, I saw one.] It got on at 42nd, and Δ Δ off at 59th, where, I assume it was going to Bloomingdales.

More recent analyses of RD in terms of deletion are put forward in Klein (1993), van Oirsouw (1993) and Wilder (1997). However, as Höhle (1991), Hartmann (2002), and Sternefeld (2006) argue, there are good reasons to believe that Rightward Deletion is just an instance of constituent coordination (or some equivalent structure). To see this, consider (20).

(20) Nobody is 6.5 feet tall and weighs 100 pounds.

It is quite obvious that in (20) *nobody* has wide scope relative to *and*, i.e., (20) is not truth-conditionally equivalent to its presumed source *Nobody is 6.5 feet tall and nobody weighs 100 pounds*. Given an analysis of RD in terms of phonological deletion, this is, however, quite unexpected, since (by definition) deleting the phonological matrix of *nobody* leaves its syntax and semantics untouched (and since we know that *nobody* does not allow for cross-sentential anaphora, an analysis in terms of E-type-anaphora is not an option either).

This property of RD contrasts with the fact that in Gapping the elision of quantified expressions systematically preserves the interpretation of the base structure, i.e., (21a) *is* semantically equivalent to (21b): In either case it is not necessarily (and most probably not) the same book Harry and Hermine gave each other. This shows that if RD is ellipsis at all, it is certainly different from Gapping (and in fact from coordinate ellipsis in general).

(21) a. Hermine gave Harry a book and Harry Δ Hermine Δ
  b. Hermine gave Harry a book and Harry gave Hermine a book

The bottom line is that with great certainty data like (18) is to be treated as constituent (C') coordination. Whether this is also true of data like (19) is not fully clear though.

STRIPPING (BARE ARGUMENT ELLIPSIS), cf. (22), shows striking similarities to Gapping; it is therefore frequently taken to be in fact an instance of Gapping ellipsis.

(22) Hermine is a loyal friend,
  a. and (probably) Ginny, too.
  b. – and (probably) Ginny.
  c. (but) (probably) not Ron.

These examples are tied together by the fact that they all have a paraphrase with the coordinated subjects adjacent to each other, as in *Hermine and Ginny are loyal friends*. This suggests an analysis only relying on (i) DP coordination and (ii) movement of *and Ginny* to the right periphery of the relevant sentence; cf. Reinhart (1991) and McCloskey (1991).

Given that agreement is syntactic (and not phonological), the above agreement facts tell us, however, that (22a) and (22b) are certainly not due to rightward movement. The fact that Stripping is not possible with collective predicates like *meet*, and the fact that the distant conjunct can be modified with adverbials like *probably* point in the same direction. But what about (22c)? (22c) has the peculiar property that its presumed base structure *[...] but not Ron is a loyal friend* is ungrammatical, and the grammatical *[...] but Ron is not a loyal friend* results in the wrong word order. Similar observations hold in German; cf. Culicover & Jackendoff (2005), Winkler & Konietzko (2010), and the contrast in (23).

(23) weder Harry mag Snape noch (?? mag) Ron (*mag) Snape
  neither Harry likes Snape, nor (?? likes) Ron (*likes) Snape

(24) Nobody fears spiders, except Ron.

So (22c) and (23) are good candidates for rightward movement, as is (24) for semantic reasons (cf., e.g., von Fintel 1993 for discussion). This, of course, would entail that adverbials like *not* and *probably* may directly modify DPs, not only VPs. Though this is not unproblematic from a semantic point of view, it is not altogether inconceivable to develop an adequate semantics for DP-modifying adverbials within an event semantics; cf. Schein (1993).

Similar questions can be raised with respect to COMPARATIVE ELLIPSIS as in (25a). The fact that comparatives allow for Gapping-like ellipsis as in (25c) suggests that comparatives are underlyingly coordinate (in some relevant sense), and that (25a) is due to deletion rather than to rightward movement of *(than) Ginny* (from a position adjacent to *more*).

(25) Hermine reads more books
    a. than Ginny
    b. than Ginny does
    c. than Ginny newspapers
    d. than Ginny does newspapers

This is supported by the fact that comparatives also allow for VP ellipsis (25b), and what we may call PARTIAL VP ELLIPSIS (25d); cf. Lechner (2004) for discussion.

All kinds of coordinate ellipsis considered so far fall under the general term of FORWARD ELLIPSIS, i.e., they target non-initial conjuncts. There is one kind of ellipsis in coordinate structures though which is directed backwards, and which is called RIGHT NODE RAISING (RNR) since the work of Ross (1967) and Postal (1974), cf. (26), but which I'd rather call LEFTWARD DELETION (LD) for reasons that will become clear in a minute.

(26) Harry loves Δ and Ron hates pie.

It is a well-known fact that, apart from the direction of ellipsis, LD behaves differently from Gapping in many crucial (though not in all) respects; cf. Wilder (1997) and Hartmann (2002) with focus on German, and Neijt (1979) and Johnson (2006) with focus on English. The most striking difference certainly is that the single remnant of LD – like *Harry hat mit* ("Harry has with") in (27) – does not necessarily form a constituent of its own, whereas each remnant in Gapping – like *Ginny* and *über Ron* ("at Ron") in (28) – does. The latter are in fact to be characterized as "major constituents" (Hankamer 1971), i.e., as XPs directly attaching to the main verbal projection line. This captures the fact that Gapping is not able to cut into PPs, cf. *... *und Ginny über* (*... *and Ginny at*), which is somewhat surprising given (i) that *Ron* is redundant, and (ii) that English allows for preposition stranding.

(27) *Harry hat mit △ △ und Ginny hat über Ron gelacht*
Harry has with △ △ and Ginny has at   Ron laughed

(28) *Harry hat mit   Ron gelacht und Ginny △ über Ron △*
Harry has with Ron laughed and Ginny △ at   Ron △

The most telling property of LD however is that not even the leftward-deleted string Ron gelacht itself generally forms a constituent of its own. Since German knows no preposition stranding at all (neither in leftward nor in rightward movement; cf. *Ginny hat über t_1 gelacht Ron_1), we may safely conclude that there is no way to derive LD in (27) via some kind of "right node raising" as originally proposed in Ross (1967) and Postal (1974) for English. This is also suggested by the fact that LD even cuts into words; cf. *Carly is over- and Will is underpaid*, taken from Johnson (2006). In the latter case, LD is subject to morpho-phonological (rather than syntactic) constraints; cf. Höhle (1982) and Wiese (1996).

Additional support comes from the fact that LD tolerates violations of island constraints (locality constraints) on movement: In (29a) the right-peripheral main verb *empfahl* ("recommended") of the relative clause got elided alongside the right-peripheral participle *gelesen* ("read") of the matrix clause. This violates the complex noun phrase constraint; cf. Neijt (1979). In Gapping, this constraint needs to be respected; cf. (29b).

(29) a. *Harry hat [das Buch [das Ginny △]] △ , und Ron (hat) [das Buch, [das Hermine*
Harry has [the book [that Ginny △]] △ and Ron (has) [the book [that Hermine
empfahl]],   gelesen
recommended]] read

b. **Harry hat [das Buch, [das Hermine empfahl]],   gelesen*
Harry has [the book [that Hermine recommended]] read,
und Ron △ [△ △ [△ Ginny △]] △
and Ron △ [△ △ [△ Ginny △]] △

These observations strongly suggest that LD and Gapping are in fact two essentially different phenomena that both happen to be restricted to coordinate structures. There is one crucial property, however, that LD and Gapping have in common (and which delimits both from RD): Deleted quantifiers are systematically interpreted *in situ*, i.e., they have narrow scope relative to the coordinating conjunction; cf. (21) above and (30): (30a) is truth-conditionally equivalent to (30b), and (30b) = (21b) is, in turn, truth-conditionally equivalent to (21a).

(30) a. Hermine gave Harry ∆ and Harry gave Hermine a book
    b. Hermine gave Harry a book and Harry gave Hermine a book

To account for this and other properties of LD, it has been proposed that LD may call for a multi-dimensional analysis of coordination which allows for sharing constituents in base position; cf. Williams (1978), Erteschik-Shir (1987), Goodall (1987) and others. Recently, this idea has been revived and implemented in multi-dominance grammars that do away with the restriction that a node in a phrase structure tree must not be immediately dominated by two or more different nodes, cf., e.g., Bachrach & Katzir (2007) and Wilder (2007) for details and further references. A simplified example may look roughly as in (31).

(31)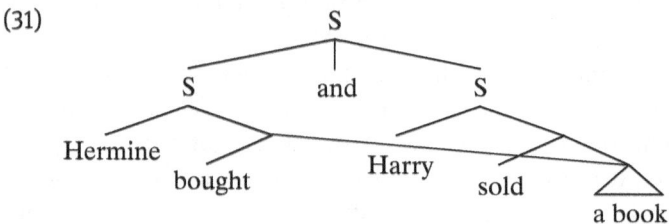

A weak point in the use of multi-dominance grammars is, of course, that they considerably complicate syntax. Moreover, despite adding complexity to the grammar, multi-dominance grammars do not give a straightforward answer to the question of why coordinate ellipsis is restricted to coordinate structures.

The latter does not apply to Johnson's (1996; 2000) analysis of Gapping in terms of ATB-movement, cf. (32) (nor, in fact, to the original multi-dimensional analyses).

(32) some$_1$ ate$_2$ [[t_1 t_2 natto] and [others t_2 rice]]

If Gapping is due to movement (of *ate*), then we may understand why both the gap and the remnants in Gapping respect constraints on movement. And if the relevant movement (of *ate*) is ATB, then we may understand why Gapping is restricted to coordinate structures (simply because ATB movement is; cf. article 4 [this volume] (Zamparelli) *Coordination*).

One may object that this analysis makes use of a somewhat dubious movement process, but, first, similar analyses have been put forward in terms of sideward movement, cf. Zoerner & Agbayani (2000) and Winkler (2005), and, second, a detailed analysis of ATB-movement based exclusively on key concepts of the minimalist approach is provided for in Reich (2009a; 2009b). What seems more problematic to me is the fact that this analysis, as it stands, gives us the wrong word order in German gapped verb final sentences; cf. (33).

(33) * *dass Hermine₁ liebt₂ [[t₁ t₂ Ron] und [Ron t₂ Hermine]]*
      that Hermine loves [[t₁ t₂ Ron] and [Ron t₂ Hermine]]

Multi-dominance as well as ATB-movement approaches make an interesting prediction though: Since it is one and the same node that is multiply dominated/moved ATB, the identity condition on coordinate ellipsis is predicted to be morphosyntactic. This, however, is a rather strong prediction, and it doesn't seem to be borne out; cf. Eisenberg (1973), Bayer (1996), and Wilder (1997). To see this, consider (34). Although *helfen* ("help") und *unterstützen* ("support") select for different case features, dative [D] and accusative [A] respectively, the LD in (34) is perfectly fine.

(34) *Sie helfen einander [D] und sie unterstützen einander-*[A]
      they help each-other-[D] and they support each-other-[A]

This suggests a phonological or semantic rather than a morphosyntactic identity condition on LD. Now consider the contrast in (35), modeled on an example from Eisenberg (1973).

(35) a. ?*weil ich Bier trinke und sie Milch trinken*
         since I beer drink and they milk drink

   b. ??*weil ich Bier trinke und du Milch trinkst*
         since I beer drink and you milk drink

In (35a,b) the deleted *trinke* ("drink") differs from its antecedent (*trinken* and *trinkst*, respectively) not only in person, but also in the phonological realization of this morphosyntactic feature. Still, (35a) is surprisingly good, (35b) is worse, and suppletive forms as in **weil ich alt bin und er jung ist* ("since I old am, and he young is") are completely out.

This shows two things. First, since the person feature on the verb is (usually taken to be) uninterpretable, the contrast cannot be due to semantics, i.e., the relevant identity condition in LD seems to be phonological, as argued in Eisenberg (1973), Klein (1993) and Wilder (1997). But it doesn't seem to be as strict (phonological identity) as these authors suggest: The more antecedent and ellipsis differ in phonological form, the worse the data gets.

Gapping, on the other hand, is far more liberal than LD is: Even suppletive forms as in *weil ich alt bin und er jung ist* ("since I old am, and he young is") are perfectly fine in German. However, as Wilder (1997) observes, the antecedent and the gapped verb must not differ in interpretable features like, for example, tense:

(36) *Beckham spielte gestern   und ich spiele morgen
    Beckham played yesterday, and I play tomorrow

This strongly suggests that Gapping is, in contrast to LD, subject to a semantic identity constraint. But if this is on the right track, then the term "coordinate ellipsis" is just a collective term for all different kinds of ellipsis that share one property: For whatever (and most probably different) reasons, their occurrence is restricted to coordinate structures.

But in fact it isn't evident at all that all kinds of coordinate ellipses discussed so far only occur in coordinate structures in a strict sense. Short answers (37) and corrections (38) share many crucial properties with Gapping like the major constituent constraint, island sensitivity and locality; cf. Neijt (1979) and Reich (2007) for detailed discussion.

(37) a. Who loves whom?
    b. Ron Hermine, and [...]

(38) Hermine loves Harry. No, Ron.

However, short answers and Gapping also show some minor differences which are worth pointing out here. Firstly, as Neijt (1979) observes, short answers seem to behave somewhat differently with respect to the tensed island condition (but cf. Reich 2007). Secondly, they are more liberal with respect to the deletion of "stranded" prepositions; cf. *What did Harry look for? A book.* vs. **Harry looked for a DVD, and Hermine a book.*

If we still pursue the (viable and promising) idea that there is a uniform treatment of short answers and Gapping, and thus drop ATB-movement as an essential ingredient in the analysis, there is still an interesting alternative that predicts crucial properties of both short answers and Gapping. The basic idea is to focus on non-initial conjuncts, cf. (39): First, we move (conjunct-internally) future remnants like *others* and *rice* 'out of the way'; then we (phonologically) delete the emptied constituent $[t_1$ ate $t_2]$ under (semantic) identity.

(39) Some ate natto and [others₁ rice₂ [t̶₁̶ ̶a̶t̶e̶ ̶t̶₂̶]]

This analysis was first proposed in Sag (1976) and Pesetsky (1982), and has been taken up more recently by Depiante (2000) and Merchant (2004), amongst others.

Even though we lose the prediction that Gapping is restricted to coordinate structures, we still account for the fact that remnants in Gapping (and short answers) show properties of moved constituents like being island-sensitive. On the negative side, we have to note that in languages like German, there is absolutely no evidence of multiple movement to the left periphery of V1- and V2-sentences: In overt syntax, the preverbal position is (essentially) restricted to exactly one constituent. Moreover, this kind of analysis forces us to say that all kinds of adverbials, negation and even modal particles (which are known to only occur as VP adjuncts in German) may move across the fronted finite verb in (and only in) the case of Gapping, for they are all possible remnants in German Gapping constructions. This strongly suggests that the traditional in situ analysis of Gapping, see, e.g., Hankamer (1971; 1979), may be quite close to the truth after all (cf. Reich 2007 for a recent proposal).

There is one argument though which is always held against the traditional in situ analysis: Suppose this analysis is essentially correct; then Gapping and short answers are in fact an instance of real non-constituent deletion. But, so the argument goes, all (relevant) syntactic processes systematically target constituents. Therefore an in situ approach cannot be on the right track. The flaw in the argument is, of course, that it does not take into account the possibility that Gapping may not be driven syntactically (but semantically). Moreover, from an empirical point of view, it is far from clear whether it is in fact desirable to try to reduce Gapping to some kind of constituent ellipsis (like VP ellipsis or Sluicing).

3.2 Constituent ellipsis

In clear cases of CONSTITUENT ELLIPSIS the relevant gap (Δ) systematically correlates with a maximal constituent: an NP in (40), a VP in (41), and a TP or IP in (42).

(40) *Ron kaufte ein neues Auto, bevor das alte Δ verkauft war*
 Ron bought a   new   car, before the old   sold   was

(41) a. I won a car, before you did Δ.
 b. I won a nice car yesterday, and you did Δ today.

(42) Someone wins. Guess who Δ!

With the exception of SLUICING in (42) (a term due to Ross 1967 referring to stranded *wh*-phrases) these ellipsis phenomena are usually named after the dropped XP, i.e., we have a case of NP ELLIPSIS in (40), and a case of VP ELLIPSIS in (41). Constituent ellipses differ from LD and Gapping in that they are not systematically restricted to coordinate structures; cf. (41a). The fact that the dropped XP alternates with a pronominal realization in the case of NP and VP ellipsis (*the old one*; [...] *and you did so, too*) suggests that the gap could be construed as a covert pronominal "*e*" which is of syntactic type NP, VP or TP, respectively, and which anaphorically refers to some corresponding linguistic antecedent.

As Lobeck (1995) and Williams (1995), amongst others, point out, there is good reason to believe that something along these lines is on the right track, for VP ellipsis is ungrammatical (just) if anaphorical relationships are blocked; cf. (43).

(43) a. *Anyone can e_i who wants to [see the doctor]$_i$
 b. *Anyone can turn *it*$_i$ in to me now who has written his [term paper]$_i$

And (44a) (cf. Lobeck 1995) illustrates that in VP ellipsis the antecedent gap relation may even cross a complex noun phrase boundary – again paralleling anaphora; cf. (44b).

(44) a. The man who [likes meat]$_i$ met the woman who doesn't e_i.
 b. (*Billy really likes [his new car]$_i$*.)
 I think that the fact that it$_i$ is an antique was a big selling point.

Suppose then that the relevant gap is in fact some covert pronominal. In this case it is also to be expected that the gap may refer back to "split" antecedents (45), that it may pick up nominal antecedents (46), and that it is insensitive to voice mismatches (45c). As the following data taken from Lobeck (1995) and Kehler (1993) show, this seems to be correct.

(45) a. I can [walk]$_i$, and I can [chew gum]$_j$.
 Garry can $e_{i \oplus j}$ too, but not at the same time.

 b. Meanwhile, they sense a drop in visitors to the city.
 Those who do *e*, they say, are not taking cabs.

 c. A lot of this material can be presented in a fairly informal fashion, and often I do *e*. (Noam Chomsky, The Generative Enterprise)

And what is more, Chao (1987) argues that VP ellipsis can in fact be used deictically (which, of course, questions our classification of VP ellipsis as a-ellipsis); cf. (46).

(46) a. You shouldn't have *e*!
 b. I will *e* if you do *e*.

The German advertisement in (47) suggests that this is also true for Sluicing.

(47) Sie wissen wohin, wir wissen wie. Die Bahn.
 you know where-to, we know how. German Railway.

Examples like (48) (cf. Hankamer & Sag 1976: 392) show that this does not generalize to all instances of VP ellipsis, however. Why it is that deictic use is licit in some cases, but illicit in others, is still unclear (but cf. Pullum 2001, Merchant 2006 for discussion).

(48) *(Hankamer attempts to stuff a 9-inch ball through a 6-inch hoop)*
 Sag: It's not clear that you'll be able to *(do it).

Fully worked-out semantic analyses which build on the idea that in constituent ellipsis there is only some kind of semantic and anaphoric relationship to be established, can be found, for example, in Dalrymple, Shieber & Pereira (1991), Shieber, Pereira & Dalrymple (1999) and Hardt (1993; 1999) for VP ellipsis, and in Chung, Ladusaw & McCloskey (1995) for Sluicing. But there are also good arguments pointing in another direction. First of all, note that constituent ellipsis, in contrast to corresponding cases of anaphora, allows for binding into the ellipsis site; cf. (49), discussed in Johnson (2001).

(49) a. This is the book of which Bill approves,
 and this is the one of which he doesn't Δ.

 b. *This is the book which O.J. Berman reviewed,
 and this is the one which Fred won't do it.

Secondly, there are examples which show that VP ellipsis is not necessarily insensitive to a change in voice; cf. (50a), taken from Kehler (2002). In Sluicing voice mismatches are in fact systematically out; cf. (50b), taken from Merchant (2001).

(50) a. *This problem was looked into by John, and Bob did Δ, too.
 b. *Someone murdered Joe, but we don't know who by Δ.

Thirdly, overt extraction out of the ellipsis site seems to be sensitive to the violation of island constraints, at least in the case of VP ellipsis; cf. (51a) (discussed in Kennedy 2003). With Sluicing, on the other hand, this doesn't seem to be a problem; cf. (51b).

(51) a. *Dogs, I understand, but cats, I don't know [a single person [who does Δ]].
 b. They want to hire [someone [who knows a Balkan language]], but I don't know which Δ.

Last but not least, VP ellipsis seems to be sensitive to the violation of binding conditions, cf. (52) from Fiengo & May (1994), which is unexpected in semantic approaches.

(52) *John embarrassed $Bill_i$, and he_i did ~~embarrass $Bill_i$~~, too.

Given a deletion approach, (52) can be accounted for as a violation of binding condition C (a pronominal mustn't bind a coreferential R-expression). However, Fiengo & May (1994) also cite grammatical examples of this sort, cf. (53), and further examples that illustrate that VP ellipsis may obliterate binding conditions (cf. also Williams 1995):

(53) a. Mary voted for Ben_i, and he_i did ~~vote for *Ben_i/$himself_i$~~, too.
 b. Mary thinks that Ben will win, and he_i does ~~think that *Ben_i/he_i will win~~, too.
 c. Ben_i voted for $himself_i$, and Mary did ~~vote for *$himself_i$/him_i~~, too.

If we stick to the deletion approach, (53) shows that the identity condition on VP ellipsis can not be syntactic in a strict sense, but requires VEHICLE CHANGE, the switching from a name or a pronominal representation to some (other) pronominal representation.

Hence, the identity condition on VP ellipsis is either semantic or it operates on a level of syntax which interfaces with semantic interpretation. Within generative grammar the only level fulfilling this requirement is logical form (LF), the level where scopal ambiguities are resolved by covertly raising quantifiers (QR). That LF may in fact be the relevant level on which identity conditions on constituent ellipsis operate is also suggested by (54), which illustrates a phenomenon called ANTECEDENT CONTAINED DELETION (cf. May 1985).

(54) Sandy hit everyone that Bill did Δ.

In (54) the elided VP Δ is buried within the quantificational object DP, which is, in turn, contained in the matrix-VP. In other words: the elided VP is, in overt syntax, part of its antecedent VP. As a consequence, there is no (straightforward) way of copying the antecedent VP into Δ without ending up in an infinite regress. On LF, however, the quantifier *everyone that Bill did* Δ is, for independent reasons, covertly raised to a position above (say, to the right of) the matrix-VP, leaving a trace t_1 behind; cf. (55).

(55) Sandy [$_{VP}$ [$_{VP}$ hit t_1] [everyone that Bill did Δ]$_1$]

This movement thus destroys the nested structure, and generates a possible antecedent, namely *[VP hit t_1]*. This is probably one of the strongest arguments in favor of an LF analysis, but cf. Baltin (1987), Larson & May (1990), and Wilder (2003) for discussion.

4 Parallelism

Additional support is provided by the important observation that all kinds of a-ellipsis show parallelism effects. To see this, consider the "chicken"-argument (56), which goes back to John Ross and George Lakoff, and is discussed in quite some detail in Sag (1976).

(56) a. The chickens are ready to eat
      b. and the children are Δ, too.

Considered in isolation, (56a) has two readings, the "the chickens eat" and the "the chickens are being eaten" reading. Similarly, the sentence *the children are ready to eat* has, in principle, two corresponding readings. Therefore, what one expects is that the sequence (56a)–(56b) has two times two, i.e., four readings. What we observe, however, is that whatever reading we go for in (56a), the VP ellipsis in (56b) is understood in exactly the same way. Thus, in fact, (56) is only two ways ambiguous, and the relevant readings are parallel.

The same is true of quantifier scope; cf. (57), cited in Sag (1976). Considered in isolation, (57a) allows for a wide scope reading of *someone* (someone has the property of having hit everyone) as well as a narrow scope reading (everyone was hit by some person).

(57) a. Someone hit everyone,
      b. and then Bill did Δ.

Within the sequence (57a)–(57b), however, there is only a wide scope reading of *someone* available, the reason most probably being that *Bill*, a referential expression, necessarily has 'wide scope' relative to the deleted quantifier *everyone* (cf. Fox 2000). This observation thus can be taken as good evidence that the identity condition on VP ellipsis does in fact operate on LF, and that it furthermore requires strict syntactic identity of the elided VP and its antecedent.

At first sight, this seems to be contradicted by the following observation: While the pronoun in (58a) has only two readings, one deictic (referring to, say, Felix), the other anaphoric (referring back to John), (58b) allows for three readings, one deictic (referring to Felix), and two anaphoric: (i) either the pronoun *his* refers back to John, this is the STRICT READING, or (ii) it refers to the sentence's own subject, Bill. This is called the SLOPPY READING.

(58) a. John scratched his arm
     b. and Bill did Δ, too.

The deictic/deictic-reading is, of course, unproblematic. What is surprising is the fact that the single anaphoric reading of (58a) gives rise – besides the strict/strict-reading – to yet another reading, the strict/sloppy-reading. But how can that be, given our assumption that we are talking about two identical copies of VP, and our generalization that VP ellipsis requires parallelism? The solution to this puzzle – due to Sag (1976) and Williams (1977), though I will follow Heim & Kratzer's (1998) reinterpretation here – is the insight that (58a) allows, in principle, for two semantically equivalent syntactic (logical) analyses; cf. (59).

(59) a. John$_1$ did [scratch his$_1$ arm]
     b. John λ1 did [scratch his$_1$ arm]

Either there is simply coindexation of *John* and *his*, cf. (59a), resulting in an (accidental) coreferent interpretation. This corresponds to the (only) analysis available in cross-sentential anaphora as in *John$_1$ didn't make it. He$_1$ missed the bus.* Or there is binding of the pronoun triggered by short movement of *John*; cf. (59b). This corresponds to the (only) analysis available with quantificational DPs, as in *Nobody λ1 scratched his$_1$ arm*.

If we suppose that parallelism extends to the whole sentence, or alternatively, as Heim & Kratzer (1998: 254) suppose, that "no LF representation [...] must contain both bound occurences and free occurences of the same index", then we end up with the following two possible analyses of the sentence *Bill did* Δ:

(60) a. Bill$_2$ did [scratch his$_1$ arm]
 b. Bill λ1 did [scratch his$_1$ arm]

Indexation of *Bill* with a (non-binding) index other than 1 (that already points to *John*) results in the strict/strict-reading. The strict/sloppy-reading, then, turns out to be in fact a sloppy/sloppy- or bound/bound-reading: Given our assumptions, we are free to assign *Bill* the index 1, too, as long as we move both *John* in the antecedent clause, and *Bill* in the ellipsis clause. Here, we capitalize on the fact that (i) movement leads to binding (given certain circumstances), and (ii) after having bound an index, it doesn't matter from a semantical point of view which index we chose to start with, though it still matters, of course, from the point of view of syntax: If we had chosen to assign *Bill* as well as the pronoun *his* the index 2, we would have ended up with the same interpretation as in (60b), but the resulting VP wouldn't be identical to its antecedent VP, and thus VP ellipsis would be blocked. (As a side note let me mention that Sag (1976) and Williams (1977) originally proposed that the relevant movement takes place within VP, i.e., what is deleted in (60a) is the property λ$x.x$ *scratch his$_1$ arm*, whereas it is the property λ$x.x$ *scratch x's arm* in (60b). Note also that these two analyses are not fully equivalent, though this is not the place to go into details.)

There are, however, two general problems with this kind of approach (cf. the discussion in Fiengo & May 1994 and Lerner & Dünges 2003). Firstly, this approach predicts that sloppy readings are always bound to the subject of the target clause, simply because sloppiness is reduced to binding, and binding presupposes c-command. But, as Fiengo & May (1994) argue, (61) allows for another sloppy reading, one where Bill's coach thinks that Bill will win (in addition to the predicted reading that the two coaches think that they will win).

(61) John$_1$'s coach thinks that he$_1$ will win, and Bill's coach does Δ, too.

This reading, however, cannot be derived as long as we take it that the genitive can not be covertly moved out of its host DP, and there is quite good reason to do so, for this would constitute a violation of the so-called left branch condition. (Note, however, that we might be forced to do so, for, e.g., *Every boy's$_1$ coach thinks that he$_1$ will win* is just fine.)

Secondly, this approach also predicts that in a sequence of VP ellipses, each ellipsis site is resolved sloppily, if the first one is. This is because a sloppy pronoun requires binding, and, given our assumptions about indices, the bound index is thus no longer available for accidental coreference. Schiebe (1971) and Dahl (1973), however, discuss examples like (62), which show that a strict reading

(Bill's wife realizing that Bill is a fool; cf. the last conjunct) may in fact follow a sloppy reading (Bill not realizing that he himself is a fool).

(62) John $\lambda 1$ realizes that he_1 is a fool,
 but $Bill_2$ $\lambda 1$ does not Δ_j, even though his_2 wife does Δ_j.

Either we allow for an additional index 2 on Bill, and for Δ_j to be construed as *realize that he_2 is a fool*, thus weakening the identity conditions, or the pronoun will be bound to the subject his_2 *wife*. This data suggests that the relevant conditions on ellipsis must be weakened by doing away with c-command and/or by allowing for varying indices within the ellipsis site. Fiengo & May (1994) therefore develop a syntactic notion of parallelism that operates on sentences rather than on VPs, and Lerner & Dünges (2003) propose a sophisticated underspecification approach relying on the introduction and resolution of referential equations. Both approaches are, however, somewhat too complex to discuss them here in any further detail.

5 Information structure

What definitely needs to be discussed here, though, is the observation that – to the extent that a sloppy reading is available in (61) at all – this reading immediately vanishes if the DP *Bill* does not contrast with *John*; cf. example (63), discussed in Williams (1995).

(63) John's mother thinks that he will win, and Bill's FAther does Δ, too.

This strongly suggests that the sloppy reading in (61) is in fact not due to the pronoun being bound to *Bill* in the sense above, but by some mechanism of focus binding. This is also in accord with Tancredi's (1992) observation that the relevant strict/sloppy-ambiguity of pronouns is not restricted to ellipsis, but also occurs with deaccenting; cf. (64).

(64) John said he is brilliant, before $[BILL]_F$ *said he is a smart guy*.

The fact that the italicized pronoun *he* in (64) can be understood as either referring to John (strict) or to Bill (sloppy) therefore cannot be due to some ellipsis (or anaphora) specific mechanism, but needs to relate to focus structure. Rooth (1992a) comes to the same conclusion on the basis of similar data. Building on his alternative semantics for focus (cf. Rooth 1985; 1992b), he considers ellipsis to be ruled by two conditions, one syntactic, the other semantic: (i) the elided VP needs to be a copy of the antecedent VP; (ii) the target sentence needs to contrast with the antecedent sentence, where contrast is defined as follows (cf. also article 10 [this volume] (Hinterwimmer) *Information structure*): Suppose that focusing a constituent evokes alternatives to this constituent, and that alternatives to some given expression are computed on a level different from truth conditions. The second sentence S2 in (64), for example, evokes the set of propositions of the form "*x* said he is a smart guy", where *x* is some person. S2 now contrasts with S1 if the proposition *that John said he is brilliant* entails some proposition in the set of alternatives to S2. This is true in the case of (64), and it is *a fortiori* true in the case of (65).

(65) John said he is brilliant, before [BILL]$_F$ did Δ.

Construed in this way, VP ellipsis is, so to speak, simply deaccentuation plus the additional requirement that the relevant VPs be identical copies of each other. The syntactic requirement is of course indispensable, since the contrast relation is simply an entailment relation that cannot even guarantee semantic identity of the VP constituents in question.

However, if one accepts the notion of vehicle change as introduced above, one may want to drop the syntactic condition, and require the semantic value of the antecedent sentence to be *an element of* the set of alternatives to the target sentence in the case of ellipsis. This way, we implement a semantic identity condition which leaves some room for lexical variation within focused constituents (i.e., we end up with a semantic identity condition *modulo focus*). A variant of Rooth's analysis along these lines is applied to sluicing in Romero (1998), and to VP ellipsis in Tomioka (1997) and Fox (2000), the latter in particular showing that parallelism effects with quantifiers can be straightforwardly dealt with within this approach.

There are two (potential) problems though. If we suppose that the ellipsis site is all-focused (i.e., we have [Δ]$_F$), the above semantic identity condition completely ignores the lexical content within Δ. Therefore, it is necessary to stipulate that Δ and (virtually all of) its content remains unfocused. This, however, should follow from a theory of ellipsis. Secondly, to account for sloppy readings, the focused prenominal genitive in examples like (61) still needs to be raised out of the subject DP, thus violating the left branch condition.

For these and other reasons, Merchant (2001) proposes an essentially equivalent identity condition on ellipsis, one which makes the relation to deaccenting even more transparent. Schwarzschild (1999), building on previous work by von Stechow (1981), models deaccenting as an entailment relation modulo focus: Non-F-marked constituents never receive any accent, and need to be GIVEN in the context. They are GIVEN if they are entailed, modulo focus and modulo existential type-shifting, by some linguistic antecedent. In (66), for example, the verb *insulted* is deaccented, since the proposition *that someone insulted someone* is (mediated by implicature) entailed by the proposition *that Abby called Ben a Republican*.

(66) [Abby]$_F$ called [Ben]$_F$ a Republican, and then [Ben]$_F$ *insulted* [Abby]$_F$.

Entailment is, of course, not yet a sufficient condition for semantic equivalence – but mutual entailment is. Merchant (2001) therefore introduces the notion of e-GIVENness, which requires that not only the ellipsis clause needs to be GIVEN relative to the antecedent clause, but in addition the antecedent clause needs to be GIVEN relative to the ellipsis clause. According to this analysis, VP ellipsis is not licensed in (66), for *Ben insulted Abby* does not entail that *someone called someone a Republican*. In (67), however, ellipsis is licensed, for *Ben called Abby a Republican* does of course entail that *someone called someone a Republican*. Therefore mutual entailment modulo focus is ensured, and e-GIVENness is met.

(67) [Abby]$_F$ called [Ben]$_F$ a Republican, and then [Ben]$_F$ ~~called~~ [Abby]$_F$ ~~a Republican~~.

This analysis is proposed in Merchant (2001) with respect to Sluicing, and generalized to short answers and Gapping in Merchant (2004). If we try to generalize this analysis to also capture VP ellipsis, a weakness similar to that in Rooth's analysis reveals itself. In the case of VP ellipsis it is quite common that the antecedent clause is all-focused; cf. (68).

(68) *(What's going on here?)*
[Abby called Ben a Republican]$_F$, and then [Sue]$_F$ did ~~insult Ben~~.

In this situation, however, e-GIVENness reduces to GIVENness, for any proposition entails the antecedent's focus closure *that somebody did something*. Therefore, VP ellipsis is predicted to be fine in (68), contrary to fact (cf., e.g., Reich 2007 for details).

Despite the fact that none of the two approaches readily solves the problem of focus trivialization or the problem of focus movement out of islands (necessary to derive some sloppy readings), I still think that they lie, in one form or another, at the heart of any theory of ellipsis, for they reveal the central role of information structure in ellipsis. It seems plausibel to me that some notion of contrast along the lines of Rooth (1992a), or rather Rooth (1992b), may be a necessary condition for all kinds of a-ellipsis. In some cases this may already be sufficient, in other cases it may not be. VP ellipsis certainly is a good candidate that (at least in some cases) requires additional syntactic constraints on the elided constituent.

6 Discourse

The latter point is substantiated by the fact that, at least in some cases, VP ellipsis seems to be sensitive to a change in voice; cf. once more (69a), taken from Kehler (2002). Given that a change in voice has no relevant effect on the truth-conditions of a sentence, this suggests the presence of a syntactic condition on VP ellipsis. In other cases, like (69b) for example, a change in voice seems to be perfectly fine, however. By the same reasoning, the VP ellipsis in (69b) thus cannot be subject to any syntactic precondition.

(69) a. *This problem was looked into by Sue, and Bob did Δ, too.
   b. This was looked into by Sue, even though Bob already had Δ.

This is a puzzle we can hardly escape as long as we take it that there is always one and only one way to resolve VP ellipsis, either syntactically or semantically. However, if we allow VP ellipsis to be resolved semantically in some instances and syntactically in others, how can we decide, or better predict, in which cases which strategy is actually operative?

According to recent work by Dan Hardt (cf. Hardt 1993; 2003), Nick Asher (cf. Asher 1993; Asher, Hardt & Busquets 2001) and Andrew Kehler (cf. Kehler 2002; 2004), this is where pragmatics comes in. Let me illustrate this point with Kehler's analysis.

Given any two (adjacent) sentences S1 and S2 in a discourse, these sentences are typically related to each other by some contentful relation R like temporal succession, explanation, etc. so that we end up with a coherent text rather than just a sequence of sentences. Since in the case of a-ellipsis, there is always an antecedent clause and a target clause, there is also always some coherence relation R linking these two sentences. Kehler (2002) now suggests that there are (disregarding contiguity relations) essentially two kinds of coherence relations: those expressing resemblance relations, and those expressing cause/effect relations. Resemblance relations (like contrast) are defined as establishing some kind of parallelism between the two sentences, and thus have to be defined as operating on structured propositions like $\langle\langle b, p\rangle, \lambda\langle x, y\rangle. \textit{that x looked into y}\rangle$. Cause/effect relations (like explanation), on the other hand, do not need access to syntactic information and can, thus, be modeled as operating on unstructured propositions like *that Bill looked into the problem*. The claim, then, is that VP ellipsis is subject to an additional syntactic constraint if, and only if, the antecedent clause and the target clause are linked by some resemblance relation, for only in those cases does syntax matter (to some extent). In (69a), for example, the two sentences are linked by the resemblance relation "parallel". But since the relevant structured propositions are not parallel, the ellipsis is out. In (69b), the two sentences are linked by the cause/effect relation "denial of preventer". Since, however, this relation only operates on unstructured propositions, we do not need to care about the change in voice (for critical discussion, cf. Kennedy 2003).

Hendriks (2004) and Reich (2008; 2009b) argue that Kehler's approach does not directly carry over to the analysis of subject gaps in coordinate structures in German and Dutch (so-called SGF-coordination, cf. Höhle 1983); cf. (70).

(70) *Hoffentlich kommt   Hans nicht zum Umzug und hilft Δ uns beim Tragen*
hopefully shows-up Hans not at-the move and helps Δ us carry
I hope Hans doesn't show up at the move and help us carry.

This discussion, however, does not dispute the fact that, in principle, coherence relations do have an effect on the way ellipsis is resolved. It simply shows that the extent to which they do may vary from language to language, and from construction to construction.

7 Psycholinguistics

Besides a strong focus on information and discourse structural factors, recent years have also seen a substantial increase in psycholinguistic work on ellipsis. Even though I cannot go into details here, I'd nevertheless like to highlight some results which I think are relevant for any theory of ellipsis. Let me start with dynamic syntax. Phillips (2003) and Cann et al. (2005) develop, in different frameworks, incremental models for syntactic structures which mimic the left-to-right processing of utterances. They argue, quite convincingly, that the dynamic perspective on syntax may be the key to understanding the special status of LD. The crucial insight is that, from a dynamical perspective, the (italicized) 'first conjunct' in a LD structure like (71) is in fact a (temporary) constituent at some stage in the derivational process of building the syntactic structure; cf. (71a) to (71c).

(71) *Wallace will give* and Wendolene will send some crackers to Gromit
   a. Wallace (step 1)
   b. Wallace will (step 2)
   c. Wallace will give (step 3)

Thus, LD can be considered to be some kind of (unusual) constituent coordination. The appeal of this analysis is that it immediately predicts that LD is left-adjacent to the coordinating conjunction (though other explanations are conceivable; cf. Hartmann 2002).

As we saw in section 4, Sag (1976) and Williams (1977) proposed virtually identical syntactic (LF) constraints on VP ellipsis. This, however, is only part of the truth, for they crucially differ in the way the final structure of the ellipsis site is arrived at: Whereas Sag (1976) defends a deletion approach, Williams (1977) argues (essentially) that the ellipsis site starts out as a pronominal-like element Δ which requires that the syntactic (LF) representation of its antecedent be copied into Δ at some point.

Is there some way to decide which analysis is the more promising one? In fact, there may be. Frazier & Clifton (2001) report on several experiments which show that the processing time of VP ellipsis and Sluicing does not depend on the complexity of its antecedent. This, they argue, supports the view that there is in fact some copy mechanism (which they call "copy α") at work here (but cf. Steiner 2004 for discussion). However, in a questionnaire study, Carlson (2001; 2002) found good evidence that in Gapping, there is a strong bias towards an object construal of the first remnant, confirming findings of Kuno (1976) and Hankamer (1979). This is unexpected if there is in fact cost-free copying. Frazier & Clifton (2001) conclude from this data that copying is in fact only available if the syntactic scope of ellipsis is unambiguous. This is the case in Sluicing and VP ellipsis, but not in Gapping.

As Bryant (2006) shows in an acquisition study, the bias towards an object construal is not self-evident, but represents a syntactic strategy in resolving Gapping that is typical for adults. In contrast to adults, children up to the age of about 6 show a clear preference for a subject construal of the first remnant. Bryant (2006) argues that this indicates a semantic strategy in resolving Gapping, since coordinating sentences ($p \wedge q$) is, from a semantic point of view, less complex than coordinating VPs ($\lambda x.P(x) \wedge Q(x)$), and thus to be preferred.

Psycholinguistics thus may help us a great deal in understanding how ellipsis actually works, and it is one of the major challenges to bring together these different lines of research.

8 References

Asher, Nicholas 1993. *Reference to Abstract Objects in Discourse*. Dordrecht: Kluwer.
Asher, Nicholas, Daniel Hardt & Joan Busquets 2001. Discourse parallelism, ellipsis, and ambiguity. *Journal of Semantics* 18, 1–25.
Bachrach, Asaf & Roni Katzir 2007. Spelling out QR. In: E. Puig-Waldmüller (ed.). *Proceedings of Sinn und Bedeutung (= SuB) 11*. Barcelona: Universitat Pompeu Fabra, 63–75.
Baltin, Mark R. 1987. Do antecedent-contained deletions exist? *Linguistic Inquiry* 18, 127–145.
Barton, Ellen 1990. *Nonsentential Constituents*. Amsterdam: Benjamins.
Barton, Ellen & Ljiljana Progovac 2005. Nonsententials in minimalism. In: R. Elugardo & R. J. Stainton (eds.). *Ellipsis and Nonsentential Speech*. Dordrecht: Springer, 71–94.
Bayer, Samuel 1996. The coordination of unlike categories. *Language* 72, 579–616.
Bryant, Doreen 2006. *Koordinationsellipsen im Erstspracherwerb. Die Verarbeitung potentieller Gapping-Strukturen*. Berlin: Akademie Verlag.
Cann, Ronnie, Ruth Kempson, Lutz Marten & Masayuki Otsuka 2005. Right node raising, coordination and the dynamics of language processing. *Lingua* 115, 503–525.
Cardinaletti, Anna 1991. Subject/object asymmetries in German null-topic constructions and the status of SpecCP. In: J. Mascaró & M. Nespor (eds.). *Grammar in Progress. GLOW Essays for Henk van Riemsdijk*. Dordrecht: Foris, 75–84.
Carlson, Katy 2001. The effects of parallelism and prosody in the processing of gapping structures. *Language and Speech* 44, 1–26.
Carlson, Katy 2002. *Parallelism and Prosody in the Processing of Ellipsis Sentences*. London: Routledge.
Chao, Wynn 1987. *On Ellipsis*. Ph.D. dissertation. University of Massachusetts, Amherst, MA.
Chung, Sandra, William A. Ladusaw & James McCloskey 1995. Sluicing and logical form. *Natural Language Semantics* 3, 239–282.
Culicover, Peter W. & Ray Jackendoff 2005. *Simpler Syntax*. Oxford: Oxford University Press.
Dahl, Östen 1973. On so-called "sloppy identity". *Synthese* 26, 81–112.
Dalrymple, Mary, Stuart M. Shieber & Fernando C. N. Pereira 1991. Ellipsis and higher-order unification. *Linguistics & Philosophy* 14, 399–452.
Depiante, Marcela Andrea 2000. *The Syntax of Deep and Surface Anaphora. A Study of Null Complement Anaphora and Stripping/Bare Argument Ellipsis*. Ph.D. dissertation. University of Connecticut, Storrs, CT.
Eisenberg, Peter 1973. A note on "Identity of constituents". *Linguistic Inquiry* 4, 417–420.
Erteschik-Shir, Nomi 1987. Right node raising. In: M. A. Browning, E. Czaykoska-Higgins & E. Ritter (eds.). *The 25th Anniversary of MIT Linguistics* (MIT Working Papers in Linguistics 9). Cambridge, MA: MIT, 105–117.
Fiengo, Robert & Robert May 1994. *Indices and Identity*. Cambridge, MA: The MIT Press.
von Fintel, Kai 1993. Exceptive constructions. *Natural Language Semantics* 1, 123–148.

Fox, Danny 2000. *Economy and Semantic Interpretation*. Cambridge, MA: The MIT Press.
Frazier, Lyn & Charles Clifton 2001. Parsing coordinates and ellipsis. Copy alpha. *Syntax* 4, 1–22.
Fries, Norbert 1988. Über das Nulltopik im Deutschen. *Sprache & Pragmatik* 3, 19–49.
Goodall, Grant 1987. *Parallel Structures in Syntax: Coordination, Causatives, and Restructuring*. Cambridge: Cambridge University Press.
Grohmann, Kleanthes & Ricardo Etxepare 2003. Root infinitives. A comparative view. *Probus* 15, 201–236.
Hankamer, Jorge 1971. *Constraints on Deletion in Syntax*. Ph.D. dissertation. Yale University, New Haven, CT.
Hankamer, Jorge 1979. *Deletion in Coordinate Structures*. New York: Garland.
Hankamer, Jorge & Ivan Sag 1976. Deep and surface anaphora. *Linguistic Inquiry* 7, 391–426.
Hardt, Daniel 1993. *Verb Phrase Ellipsis. Form, Meaning and Processing*. Ph.D. dissertation. University of Pennsylvania, Philadelphia, PA.
Hardt, Daniel 1999. Dynamic interpretation of verb phrase ellipsis. *Linguistics & Philosophy* 22, 185–219.
Hardt, Daniel 2003. Ellipsis and the structure of discourse. In: K. Schwabe & S. Winkler (eds.). *The Interfaces. Deriving and Interpreting Omitted Structures*. Amsterdam: Benjamins, 251–262.
Hartmann, Katharina 2002. *Right Node Raising and Gapping. Interface Conditions on Prosodic Deletion*. Amsterdam: Benjamins.
Heim, Irene & Angelika Kratzer 1998. *Semantics in Generative Grammar*. Oxford: Blackwell.
Hendriks, Petra 2004. Coherence relations, ellipsis, and contrastive topics. *Journal of Semantics* 21, 133–153.
Höhle, Tilman N. 1982. Über Komposition und Derivation. Zur Konstituentenstruktur von Wortbildungsprodukten im Deutschen. *Zeitschrift für Sprachwissenschaft* 1, 76–112.
Höhle, Tilman N. 1983. *Subjektlücken in Koordinationen*. Ms. Tübingen, University of Tübingen.
Höhle, Tilman N. 1991. On reconstruction and coordination. In: H. Haider & K. Netter (eds.). *Representation and Derivation in the Theory of Grammar*. Dordrecht: Kluwer, 139–197.
Johnson, Kyle 1996. *In Search of the English Middle Field*. Ms. Amherst, MA, University of Massachusetts.
Johnson, Kyle 2000. Few dogs eat Whiskas or cats Alpo. In: K. Kusumoto & E. Villalta (eds.). *Issues in Semantics* (University of Massachusetts Occasional Papers in Linguistics 23). Amherst, MA: GLSA, 59–82.
Johnson, Kyle 2001. What VP ellipsis can do, and what it can't, but not why. In: M. Baltin & Ch. Collins (eds.). *The Handbook of Contemporary Syntactic Theory*. Oxford: Blackwell, 439–479.
Johnson, Kyle 2006. Gapping. In: M. Everaert & H. van Riemsdijk (eds.) *The Blackwell Companion to Syntax, vol. 1*. Oxford: Blackwell, 407–435.
Kehler, Andrew 1993. A discourse copying algorithm for ellipsis and anaphora resolution. In: *Proceedings of the Sixth Conference of the European Chapter of the Association for Computational Linguistics (EACL-93)*. Utrecht: Association for Computational Linguistics, 203–212.
Kehler, Andrew 2002. *Coherence, Reference, and the Theory of Grammar*. Stanford, CA: CSLI Publications.
Kehler, Andrew 2004. Discourse Coherence. In: L. R. Horn & G. N. Ward (eds.). *The Handbook of Pragmatics*. Oxford: Blackwell, 241–265.

Kennedy, Christopher 2003. Ellipsis and syntactic representation. In: K. Schwabe & S. Winkler (eds.). *The Interfaces. Deriving and Interpreting Omitted Structures*. Amsterdam: Benjamins, 29–53.

Klein, Wolfgang 1993. Ellipse. In: J. Jacobs et al. (eds.). *Syntax – Ein internationales Handbuch zeitgenössischer Forschung – An International Handbook of Contemporary Research* (HSK 9). Berlin: de Gruyter, 763–799.

Kuno, Susumu 1976. Gapping. A functional analysis. *Linguistic Inquiry* 7, 300–318.

Larson, Richard & Richard May 1990. Antecedent containment or vacuous movement. Reply to Baltin. *Linguistic Inquiry* 21, 103–122.

Lechner, Winfried 2004. *Ellipsis in Comparatives*. Berlin: Mouton de Gruyter.

Lerner, Jan & Petra Dünges 2003. *Anaphern, Quantoren und Parallelität*. Tübingen: Narr.

Lobeck, Anne 1995. *Ellipsis. Functional Heads. Licensing, and Identification*. Oxford: Oxford University Press.

May, Robert 1985. *Logical Form*. Cambridge, MA: The MIT Press.

McCloskey, James 1991. Clause structure, ellipsis and proper government in Irish. *Lingua* 85, 259–302.

Merchant, Jason 2001. *The Syntax of Silence – Sluicing, Islands, and the Theory of Ellipsis*. Oxford: Oxford University Press.

Merchant, Jason 2004. Fragments and ellipsis. *Linguistics & Philosophy* 27, 661–738.

Merchant, Jason 2006. Why no(t)? *Style* 20, 20–23.

Neijt, Anneke 1979. *Gapping*. Dordrecht: Foris.

van Oirsouw, Robert 1993. Coordination. In: J. Jacobs et al. (eds.). *Syntax – Ein internationales Handbuch zeitgenössischer Forschung – An International Handbook of Contemporary Research* (HSK 9). Berlin: de Gruyter, 748–763.

Pesetsky, David 1982. *Paths and Categories*. Ph.D. dissertation. MIT, Cambridge, MA.

Phillips, Colin 2003. Linear order and constituency. *Linguistic Inquiry* 34, 37–90.

Portner, Paul & Raffaella Zanuttini 2005. The semantics of nominal exclamatives. In: R. Elugardo & R. J. Stainton (eds.). *Ellipsis and Nonsentential Speech*. Dordrecht: Springer, 57–67.

Postal, Paul 1974. *On Raising*. Cambridge, MA: The MIT Press.

Pullum, Geoffrey 2001. Hankamer Was! In: S. Chung, J. McCloskey & N. Sanders (eds.). *The Jorge Hankamer WebFest*. Santa Cruz, CA: University of California. http://ling.ucsc.edu/Jorge/pullum.html. December 7, 2010.

Reich, Ingo 2007. Toward a uniform analysis of short answers and gapping. In: K. Schwabe & S. Winkler (eds.). *On Information Structure, Meaning and Form*. Amsterdam: Benjamins, 467–484.

Reich, Ingo 2008. From discourse to 'odd coordinations' – On asymmetric coordination and subject gaps in German. In: C. Fabricius-Hansen & W. Ramm (eds.). *'Subordination' vs. 'Coordination' in Sentence and Text*. Amsterdam: Benjamins, 281–303.

Reich, Ingo 2009a. From phases to 'across the board movement' – On asymmetric coordination and subject gaps in German. In: M. Elliott et al. (eds.). *Proceedings from the Annual Meeting of the Chicago Linguistic Society (= CLS)* 43(2). Chicago, IL: Chicago Linguistic Society, 217–232.

Reich, Ingo 2009b. *"Asymmetrische Koordination" im Deutschen*. Tübingen: Stauffenburg.

Reinhart, Tanya 1991. Elliptic conjunctions. Non-quantificational LF. In: A. Kasher (ed.). *The Chomskyan Turn*. Oxford: Blackwell, 360–384.

Reis, Marga 1995. Über infinite Nominativkonstruktionen im Deutschen. In: O. Önnerfors (ed.). *Festvorträge anläßlich des 60. Geburtstags von Inger Rosengren*. Lund: University of Lund, 114–156.
Reis, Marga 2003. On the form and interpretation of German *Wh*-infinitives. *Journal of Germanic Linguistics* 15, 155–201.
Repp, Sophie 2009. *Negation in Gapping*. Oxford: Oxford University Press.
Romero, Maribel 1998. *Focus and Reconstruction Effects in wh-Phrases*. Ph.D. dissertation. University of Massachusetts, Amherst, MA.
Rooth, Mats 1985. *Association with Focus*. Ph.D. dissertation. University of Massachusetts, Amherst, MA.
Rooth, Mats 1992a. Ellipsis redundancy and reduction redundancy. In: S. Berman & A. Hestvik (eds.). *Proceedings of the Stuttgarter Workshop on Ellipsis* (Arbeitspapiere des Sonderforschungsbereichs 340, Bericht Nr. 29). Stuttgart: University of Stuttgart.
Rooth, Mats 1992b. A theory of focus interpretation. *Natural Language Semantics* 1, 75–116.
Ross, John R. 1967. *Constraints on Variables in Syntax*. Ph.D. dissertation. MIT, Cambridge, MA.
Ross, John R. 1970. Gapping and the order of constituents. In: M. Bierwisch & M. Heidolph (eds.). *Progress in Linguistics*. The Hague: Mouton, 249–259.
Sag, Ivan A. 1976. *Deletion and Logical Form*. Ph.D. dissertation. MIT, Cambridge, MA.
Schein, Barry 1993. *Plurals and Events*. Cambridge, MA: The MIT Press.
Schiebe, T. 1971. Zum Problem der grammatisch relevanten Identität. In: F. Kiefer & N. Ruwet (eds.). *Generative Grammar in Europe*. Dordrecht: Reidel, 482–527.
Schwabe, Kerstin 1994. *Syntax und Semantik situativer Ellipsen*. Tübingen: Narr.
Schwarzschild, Roger 1999. Givenness, Avoid F, and other constraints on the placement of accent. *Natural Language Semantics* 7, 141–177.
Shieber, Stuart M., Fernando Pereira & Mary Dalrymple 1999. Interactions of scope and ellipsis. In: S. Lappin & E. Benmamoun (eds.). *Fragments. Studies in Ellipsis and Gapping*. Oxford: Oxford University Press, 8–31.
Stainton, Robert J. 2004. The pragmatics of non-sentences. In: L. R. Horn & G. N. Ward (eds.). *The Handbook of Pragmatics*. Oxford: Blackwell, 266–287.
Stanley, Jason 2000. Context and logical form. *Linguistics & Philosophy* 23, 391–434.
von Stechow, Arnim 1981. Topic, focus and local relevance. In: W. Klein & W. Levelt (eds.). *Crossing the Boundaries in Linguistics*. Dordrecht: Reidel, 95–130.
Steiner, Ilona 2004. The syntax of DP-coordination. Combining evidence from reading time studies and agrammatic comprehension. In: S. Kepser & M. Reis (eds.). *Pre-Proceedings of the International Conference on Linguistic Evidence 2004*. Tübingen: University of Tübingen, 126–130.
Sternefeld, Wolfgang 2006. *Syntax. Eine morphologisch motivierte generative Beschreibung des Deutschen, Bd. 2*. Tübingen: Stauffenburg.
Tancredi, Chris 1992. *Deletion, Deaccenting, and Presupposition*. Ph.D. dissertation. MIT, Cambridge, MA.
Tomioka, Satoshi 1997. *Focusing Effects in NP Interpretation and VP Ellipsis*. Ph.D. dissertation. University of Massachusetts, Amherst.
Wiese, Richard 1996. *The Phonology of German*. Oxford: Oxford University Press.
Wilder, Chris 1997. Some properties of ellipsis in coordination. In: A. Alexiadou & T. A. Hall (eds.). *Studies on Universal Grammar and Typological Variation*. Amsterdam: Benjamins, 59–107.
Wilder, Chris 2003. Antecedent-containment and ellipsis. In: K. Schwabe & S. Winkler (eds.). *The Interfaces. Deriving and Interpreting Omitted Structures*. Amsterdam: Benjamins, 79–119.

Wilder, Chris 2007. Shared constituents and linearization. In: K. Johnson (ed.). *Topics in Ellipsis*. Cambridge: Cambridge University Press, 229–258.
Williams, Edwin 1977. Discourse and logical form. *Linguistic Inquiry* 8, 101–139.
Williams, Edwin 1978. Across the board rule application. *Linguistic Inquiry* 9, 31–43.
Williams, Edwin 1995. *Ellipsis*. Ms. Princeton University, Princeton, NJ.
Winkler, Susanne 2005. *Ellipsis and Focus in Generative Grammar*. Berlin: Mouton de Gruyter.
Winkler, Susanne & Andreas Konietzko 2010. Contrastive ellipsis: mapping between syntax and information structure. *Lingua* 120, 1436–1457.
Zoerner, Ed & Brian Agbayani 2000. Unifying left-peripheral deletion, gapping and pseudo-gapping. In: K. Okrent & J. P. Boyle (eds.). *Papers from the Regional Meeting of the Chicago Linguistic Society (= CLS) 36–1*. Chicago, IL: Chicago Linguistic Society, 549–561.

Stefan Hinterwimmer
10 Information structure and truth conditional semantics

1   Introduction —— 340
2   Focus and background —— 341
3   Topic and comment —— 344
4   Givenness —— 352
5   Truth conditional effects of focus marking —— 355
6   Truth conditional effects of topic marking —— 364
7   Givenness and truth conditions —— 374
8   Conclusion —— 375
9   References —— 376

Abstract: I discuss the relation between information structure and truth conditional semantics, concentrating on the question of whether there is any direct interaction between the various information structural dimensions and operators such as quantified DPs and quantificational adverbs. Concerning the focus-background dimension, we will see that in most cases truth-conditional effects do not result from direct focus sensitivity of the involved operators, but rather come about as indirect effects of the need to resolve a free variable that is present in the denotation of these operators on the basis of contextual information – with the notable exception of exclusives such as *only*. Concerning the topic-comment dimension, in cases where a quantificational DP functions as the aboutness topic of a sentence, the need to interpret the comment as a predicate that can be applied to the topic has truth-conditional effects in the presence of either another quantificational DP, a quantificational adverb or generic tense. In cases where a quantificational DP is marked as a contrastive topic, on the other hand, truth-conditional effects come about indirectly. Finally, concerning the given-new dimension, there is also no evidence for a direct influence on the truth conditions of sentences, but only for indirect effects.

Stefan Hinterwimmer, Cologne, Germany

https://doi.org/10.1515/9783110589863-010

1 Introduction

The term *information structure* is meant to capture the different dimensions at which linguistic messages can be structured in accordance with requirements imposed by the linguistic and extralinguistic context as well as the communicative intentions of the speaker. At the first level, (the meanings of) sentences can be decomposed into *topic* and *comment*, where the term *topic* according to the most widely held view (but see below) intuitively stands for the entity about which the rest of the sentence – the comment – is felt to convey information. At the second level, sentences can be decomposed into *focus* and *background*, where the term *focus* intuitively stands for that part of the sentence that conveys the information the speaker wishes to represent as most prominent and onto which s/he wants to draw the hearer's attention. Finally, at the third level the distinction between *given* (i.e. already mentioned explicitly or implicitly) and *new* information applies. It is important to keep these levels apart, i.e. it is not necessarily the case that topics are given, while foci are new, or that the topic coincides with the background, while the focus coincides with the comment, although simple examples like (1b) seem to suggest this:

(1) a. Tell me something about John.
    b. John married BERTHA.

In the case of (1b), the subject noun phrase *John* is given, and furthermore has been made the aboutness topic (see below) by the preceding utterance (1a). On the other hand, the verb phrase *married Bertha* is not only new, but also focal, which is indicated by the main stress on the object noun phrase *Bertha* (see below). In addition to that, since *topic-comment* as well as *focus-background* are complementary notions, the background consists of the noun phrase *John*, while the comment consists of the verb phrase *married Bertha*. We thus have a perfect coincidence of topic, given information and background, on the one hand, and focus, new information and comment, on the other. However, one only needs to change the context in which the sentence in (1b) is uttered as minimally as shown in (2a) to see that this coincidence does not hold necessarily:

(2) a. Tell me something about John. Who did he marry?
    b. John married BERTHA.

Now, while *John* is still both given and topical, the focus does not coincide with the comment anymore: the focus consists only of the object noun phrase *Bertha*, but the whole VP *married Bertha* makes up the comment. Similarly, the topic neither coincides with the background nor with the given information anymore, since both consist not only of the subject noun phrase *John*, but also contain the verb *married*. Below, we will even see cases where topics introduce novel information, and where given items are focussed. Traditionally, truth conditional semantics is not concerned with differences of the kind exemplified by the contrast between (1) and (2): (1b)/(2b) denotes the same proposition, independently of whether it is uttered in a context like (1a) or (2a), and the same generally holds for sentences that (only) differ overtly with respect to which item has been marked as topical/focal/given etc. Therefore, information structure is usually seen as belonging to the realm of pragmatics, since it only seems to be concerned with the question of *how* something is said (cf. Chafe 1976, who coined the term *information packaging* to capture this fact), but not *what* is said. We will see, however, that there are many cases where information structure and truth conditional content cannot be separated so neatly, and where it actually makes a difference to truth conditions whether an item is topical/focal or not. As we will see below, however, this does not necessarily mean that there is a direct interaction between the semantic and the pragmatic component of the language faculty. Rather, the observed truth conditional effects may also be interpreted as resulting from the combination of the following facts: first, some operators are semantically underspecified in the sense of containing free variables that need to be resolved on the basis of contextual information. Second, the information structure of a sentence encodes certain properties of the context in which the sentence is uttered. It is thus only natural that information structural distinctions like the one between focus and background or the one between topic and comment are made use of to resolve the respective variables.

2 Focus and background

At an intuitive, pre-theoretical level, the focus of a sentence is that part which represents the information the speaker considers most important and to which s/he accordingly wants to draw the hearer's attention. In languages such as English and German and many others, focus is indicated by stress: the part of the sentence that is focussed must contain the syllable onto which the main stress falls. The exact conditions governing the decision of which word in a complex constituent must contain the syllable carrying the main accent are often assumed to be taken care of by rules of *focus projection* (Selkirk 1984). Such rules account for the fact that in many cases one and the same accent pattern can either indicate narrow focus on the word containing the syllable that receives highest stress, or wide focus on some larger constituent containing that word. The contrast between (1b) and (2b) above is a case in point, where main stress on the first syllable of the proper name *Bertha* may either indicate that it is just the object noun phrase that is focussed, or the whole VP. Note, however, that phonological focus marking is by no means universal: there are languages such as Hungarian where focus is marked by dedicated syntactic positions, and others (many African tone languages such as Buli, Guruntum and Bole are cases in point) where morphological means are chosen.

According to a very common and classical view, which goes back to Paul (1880) and was taken up by Halliday (1967), and which we already employed in our discussion of (2) above, the focus of a sentence is identified with that part of a sentence that replaces the *wh*-part of a constituent question. Accordingly, the request in (1a) ensured that in (1b) the whole VP was focussed, while the question in (2a) ensured that in (2b) only the object NP *Bertha* was focussed.

In truth conditional semantics it is commonly assumed, following Hamblin (1973), that a question denotes the set of its possible congruent answers, i.e. a question such as *What about John?* denotes the set {⟦John married Bertha⟧, ⟦John went to the movies yesterday⟧, ⟦John won the Nobel prize in literature⟧, … }, while a question such as *Who did John marry?* denotes the set {⟦John married Bertha⟧, ⟦John married Paula⟧, ⟦John married Jane⟧, … }. Rooth (1985, 1992) now developed a formal theory of focus interpretation that employs the same formal object in order to model the denotation of focussed constituents. Simplifying somewhat, Rooth assumes that the semantic effect of focus marking is the introduction of a (contextually restricted) set of alternatives to the (denotation of the) respective constituent, where the alternative set always includes the original denotation of the focus-marked constituent. These alternatives are then composed with the rest of the clause in pointwise fashion, resulting in a set of propositions which only differ from each other with respect to the chosen alternative. This set is called the *focus semantic value* (in addition to the *ordinary semantic value*) of the respective sentence. Accordingly, the focus semantic value (indicated by the superscript F, while the subscript F indicated focus marking) of the focussed constituent in (1b) is the set in (3a), while the focus semantic value of the whole sentence is the set in (3b). (4a, b) gives the same two objects for (2b).

(3) a. ⟦married Bertha⟧^{F} = {$\lambda x.\lambda s.$ married(x, Bertha)(s), $\lambda x.\lambda s.$ went_to_the_movies(x)(s), $\lambda x.\lambda s.$ won(x, Nobel prize)(s), … }

b. ⟦John [$_F$ married Bertha]⟧^{F} = {$\lambda s.$ married(John, Bertha)(s), $\lambda s.$ went_to_the_movies(John)(s), $\lambda s.$ won(John, Nobel prize)(s), … }

(4) a. ⟦Bertha⟧ᶠ =   {Bertha, Paula, Jane, ...}
    b. ⟦John married [_F Bertha]⟧ᶠ =   {λs. married(John, Bertha)(s),
                                        λs. married(John, Paula)(s),
                                        λs. married(John, Jane)(s), ... }

The set in (3b) is identical to the denotation of the question in (1a), while the set in (4b) is identical to the question denotation in (2a). The theory of Rooth (1985, 1992) can thus account for the observed correspondence between the *wh*-parts of questions and focus marking in a natural and elegant way by requiring the focus semantic value of a sentence to be a superset of the respective question denotation. In cases such as (5a, b), where this requirement is not met, infelicity ensues:

(5) a. Who did John marry?
    b. #John MARRIED Bertha.

The problem with (5a, b) is that while the question in (5a) denotes the already familiar set {⟦John married Bertha⟧, ⟦John married Paula⟧, ⟦John married Jane⟧, ...}, the answer in (5b) denotes the set {⟦John married Bertha⟧, ⟦John kissed Bertha⟧, ⟦John talked to Bertha⟧, ...}, which is clearly not a superset of the first set. Crucially for our purposes, however, while (5b) is pragmatically infelicitous as an answer to (5a), its truth conditions, which correspond to the ordinary semantic value of the sentence, do not differ from the truth conditions of the congruent answer *John married BERTHA*. In other words, the alternatives introduced by the focus do not play any role at the level of truth conditions. Note that it is not even clear what pragmatic function they have in such cases since the plausible function of highlighting the part of the respective answer that provides the requested information does not seem to require the introduction of alternatives in any obvious way (but see Krifka 2008, who speculates that question-answer congruence might help the hearer to accommodate the meaning of implicit questions). An alternative account, according to which focus does not introduce alternatives, but rather triggers the presupposition that there exists an entity of the same type as the focus marked expression (Geurts & van der Sandt 2004), can explain the observed necessity of question-answer congruence in the following way: in the case of (2), for example, the presupposition triggered by the focus marking in (2b) matches the presupposition of the question in (2a), namely that John married somebody. In the case of (5), in contrast, this is not the case: while the question presupposes that John married somebody, the answer presupposes that John stands in some relation to Bertha. The problem with cases such as (5) would thus be that the immediate context does not satisfy the presupposition triggered by focus marking.

In cases other than information focus, however, the pragmatic role of the alternatives introduced via focus-marking is more obvious, although they still do not influence the truth conditions: in both (6b) and (6c), the implicit introduction of the alternatives to the asserted proposition allows the speaker to express her conviction that among these alternatives the asserted proposition is the only one that is true. This leads to a *corrective* interpretation in the first case, and to a *confirmative* interpretation in the second case:

(6) a. John married Bertha.
    b. (No,) John married [$_F$ Jane].
    c. (Yes,) John married [$_F$ Bertha].

In section 5 we will discuss cases where the alternatives introduced via focus marking play a role at the level of the truth conditions. But let us first turn to the second important dimension, the one where sentences are decomposed into topic and comment.

3 Topic and comment

3.1 Aboutness topics

As already said in the introduction, according to the most popular view today, which goes back to ideas formulated in different terms by Gabelentz (1869) and Paul (1880), and was brought to the fore in modern linguistic thinking by Reinhart (1981), the topic of a sentence is the part about whose denotation the rest of the sentence – the comment – is intuitively felt to convey information. In the case of (1b) above, for example, the topic status of the entity referred to by the proper name *John* was made explicit by the preceding (1a). Often, however, this is not the case, and there is nevertheless a clear intuition as to which part of a given sentence is to be taken as the topic. As already noted by Hockett (1958), in the default case the topic coincides with the grammatical subject. This, however, does not have to be the case, as shown by the contrast between (7a) and (7b):

(7) a. Peter finished his new paper yesterday.
    b. The telephone is ringing.

While (7a) is naturally understood as conveying information about Peter, (7b) is not felt to convey information about some salient telephone, even though the DP *the telephone* is the grammatical subject in (7b). Rather, (7b) is most naturally understood as describing a particular spatiotemporal region or situation. The intuition that in sentences such as (7b) neither the grammatical subject nor any other overt constituent is the topic can be accounted for in two ways: either these sentences are analyzed as topicless or antitopical (Jacobs 2001), or they are analyzed as being about the respective salient spatiotemporal region/situation (Cohen & Erteshik-Shir 2002).

Furthermore, in many languages such as German, Japanese, Hungarian and Korean there exist explicit morphological and syntactic means to unambiguously mark a constituent as the topic of a sentence, and there is no requirement for the constituent marked as the topic to be the grammatical subject. The sentence in (8), which exemplifies *German Left Dislocation* (henceforth: GLD), is a case in point:

(8) (Den) Peter, den hab ich lange nicht gesehen.
 the-acc Peter RP-ACC.SING.MASC have I long not seen
 'I haven't seen Peter for a long time.'

GLD, whose first systematic description in modern terms is found in Altmann (1981), is characterized by the following configuration: a constituent that occupies the left-peripheral position of the respective sentence co-occurs with a resumptive pronoun in clause-initial position with which it agrees in case-, number-, and gender-features. According to Frey (2004), German left-dislocated phrases which are not understood contrastively (see below) are necessarily interpreted as topics. This is evidenced by the fact that (8) is fine as an answer to a question like *What about Peter?* or a command like *Tell me something about Peter*, while it is odd as an answer to a question like *Who haven't you seen for a long time?*, at least if it is not read with an intonational break after the fronted noun phrase and a strong accent on the resumptive pronoun. We can thus conclude that in (8), it is the left-dislocated object noun phrase *Peter* that is the aboutness topic of the sentence, not the subject noun phrase *ich*. Because of the prevalence of examples with proper names, definite descriptions and pronouns in the literature on topics, many linguists subscribe to the view that topics are necessarily at least weakly familiar, i.e. the existence of the respective entity must at least be inferable from the context/general world knowledge (cf. Hockett 1958; Kuno 1972; Gundel 1988; Portner & Yabushita 1998). It has, however, been observed by Reinhart (1981) (see also Molnár 1993 and Frey 2000, 2004) that familiarity cannot be a defining property of topics since not only individual-denoting noun phrases can be sentence topics, but also indefinite DPs (while other quantificational DPs are excluded from topic positions; more on this below), as shown by (9).

(9) | Einem | Freund | von Peter, | dem | hat |
|---|---|---|---|---|
| a/one-DAT.SING.MASC | friend | of Peter | RP-NOM.SING.MASC | has |
| Angela Merkel | gestern | die Hand | gegeben. | |
| Angela Merkel | yesterday | the hand | given. | |

'Angela Merkel yesterday shook the hand of a friend of Peter.'

Note that in all examples discussed so far, topic marking only serves the pragmatic function of structuring the information conveyed by the respective sentence in a certain way, while it does not have any influence on the truth conditions: the variants given in (10), where no special topic marking devices are employed and where (the entities denoted by) *his new paper*, *I* and *Angela Merkel* therefore are the default topics because of subjecthood, are true under exactly the same conditions as (7a), (8) and (9), respectively.

(10) a. His new paper was finished by Peter yesterday.
     b. Ich habe (den) Peter lange nicht gesehen.
        'I haven't seen Peter for a long time.'
     c. Angela Merkel hat gestern einem Freund von Peter die Hand geschüttelt.
        'Angela Merkel yesterday shook the hand of a friend of Peter.'

In addition to that, there are cases such as (11) where (the denotation of) a constituent that can plausibly be analysed as the topic stands only in a loose, underspecified relation to the proposition denoted by the rest of the sentence, and which have accordingly been classified as involving *hanging topics*:

(11) Concerning Schoenberg, I like *Moses und Aron*.

In section 6, we will discuss examples where topichood clearly has an effect on the truth conditions. But let us first go into a little more detail about the alleged pragmatic effect of topicality in examples like the ones discussed so far. According to Reinhart's (1981) very influential account – whose basic understanding of topichood goes back to Strawson (1964) – the topic corresponds to the address where the proposition denoted by the respective sentence is stored. Accordingly, Reinhart adopts a view of the *common ground* (CG), i.e. of the mutually shared knowledge of speaker and hearer, that is slightly more articulated than Stalnaker's (1974, 1978) in the following sense: According to Stalnaker, the CG just consists of a set of propositions whose intersection gives the set of worlds that are compatible with everything that both speaker and hearer(s) know. Reinhart (1981), in contrast, assumes that these propositions are stored under particular addresses which she conceives of as mental files, i.e. an assertion of (8) results in the proposition that the speaker has not seen Peter in a long time being added to the address where information concerning the individual *Peter* is stored. This basic idea has been developed in different directions by Vallduvi (1992), Lambrecht (1994), and Portner & Yabushita (1998), who propose a model-theoretic re-definition of the concept of a file where information is stored.

3.2 Frame-setting topics

The example in (12) is not easily captured by the notion of aboutness topicality introduced in the last section: it does not make much sense to conceive of the proposition that Maria is doing well as being added to a file where information about health is stored. Rather, the fronted adverb *gesundheitlich* ('healthwise') specifies the way in which the predicate *gut gehen* (be fine) is to be understood.

(12) Gesundheitlich   geht   es   Maria   gut.
      healthwise   goes   expl. Maria well.
      'Healthwise, Maria is fine.'

Nevertheless, researchers such as Chafe (1976) and many others have argued that the fronted constituents in examples of this type should be analyzed as topics, which is further confirmed by the observation that in languages such as Japanese where topics are marked morphologically, the corresponding constituents are marked as such. Jacobs (2001) therefore argues for a view according to which there is not one unified definition of topicality, but rather a cluster of distinct, but nevertheless related properties that together define the field of topic-comment structures: informational separation (of the topical constituent from the rest of the sentence), predication (i.e. the comment is interpreted as a predicate that applies to the topic), addressation (which corresponds to aboutness), and frame-setting. Crucially, a constituent does not have to satisfy all of these properties to count as a topic, but only a substantive subset thereof, and Jacobs accordingly analyses various topic marking constructions in German as being specified for different combinations. Jacobs defines frame-setting in informal terms as in (13) (Jacobs 2001: 656):

(13) In (X Y), X is the *frame* for Y iff X specifies a domain of (possible) reality to which the proposition expressed by Y is restricted.

Jacobs claims that in contrast to aboutness topicality, frame-setting topicality always has a direct influence on the truth conditions, since "the comment does not hold regardless of the topic, but only within the domain specified by the topic" (Jacobs 2001: 656). Here, Jacobs in my view confuses two different aspects, however: it is surely correct that marking a constituent as the aboutness topic in many cases does not have an influence on the truth conditions, either because the proposition denoted by the sentence remains the same regardless of which constituent is marked as the aboutness topic (examples (7a) and (8)–(10)), or because the aboutness topic stands only in an underspecified relevance relation to the respective proposition (example (11)). Concentrating on the latter case, it may seem that there is a general difference in the influence on truth conditions between frame-setting topicality and aboutness topicality, because dropping the hanging topic would not alter the truth conditions of the proposition functioning as the comment in examples like (11), while it would in examples like (12). This, however, only shows that the denotation of the topical adverb directly contributes to the meaning of the proposition – just as the meanings of the respective topical constituents in (7a) and (8)–(10) do. Its topic status as such does not alter the truth conditions, however. After all, the truth conditions of (14), where the adverb *gesundheitlich* ('healthwise') remains in clause-internal position, do not differ from the truth conditions of (12):

(14) Maria geht es gesundheitlich gut.
      'Healthwise, Maria is fine.'

There is, however, another aspect in which (12) and (14) differ, which we glossed over so far: in contrast to (14), (12) is intuitively contrasted with alternative propositions where *gesundheitlich* has been replaced with other framesetters like *finanziell* ('financially'), while *gut* has been replaced with other evaluative adverbs like *schlecht* ('bad') (cf. Krifka 2008: 46). Furthermore, observe that examples such as (12) are most natural if they are read with a rising accent on *gesundheitlich* in combination with a falling accent (which signals focus marking) on *gut*. As we will see in the following section, this combination is characteristic of *contrastive topics*. We therefore have another option to analyse examples such as (14): namely as not instantiating a special kind of topicality (namely frame-setting topicality), but as exemplifying ordinary contrastive topicality, with a frame-setting adverb as the contrastive topic. Consequently, frame-setting would be entirely independent of topicality.

3.3 Contrastive topics

As mentioned above, contrastive topics, which have been discussed extensively by Büring (1997a, 1999) and Jacobs (1997), are marked by a characteristic intonation pattern in German (cf. Jackendoff's 1972 discussion of the "B-accent" in English): a rising accent on the fronted constituent, which functions as the contrastive topic, is combined with a falling accent on some sentence-internal constituent, which is thus marked as focal. A typical example is given in (15):

(15) /SCHOENberg   MAG\   ich   (während ich Berg und Webern hasse).
     'Schoenberg   like   I
     'Schoenberg, I like (while I hate Berg and Webern).'

(15) is automatically understood as being implicitly contrasted with sentences involving alternatives to Schoenberg, and since the other two composers of the second Viennese School, Alban Berg and Anton Webern, are natural choices, the continuation in brackets would be entirely natural. Now, the introduction of alternatives via intonational prominence is certainly reminiscent of focus marking, so one might ask why examples such as (15) are not simply analysed as involving two instances of focus marking. There are mainly two reasons why this cannot be correct: first, in sentences like (16b), which clearly contain two focussed items (see section 2 above), both are marked by a falling accent:

(16) a. Peter hat gestern   auf der Party Maria geküsst (habe ich gehört).
        Peter has yesterday at the party Maria kissed have I heard
        'Yesterday at the party, Peter kissed Maria (so I have heard).'

   b. Nein, PAUL/ hat ClauDIne/ geküsst.
      no   Paul has Claudine kissed
      'No, Paul kissed Claudine.'

Second, in contrast to double focus, contrastive topicality in an answer to a question clearly indicates non-completeness, as can be shown by the contrast between (17b) and (17c): (17b) can only be understood as a partial answer, and therefore requires an interpretation of (17a) as a pair-list question. (17c), on the other hand, is naturally understood as an exhaustive answer, and thus requires (17a) to be understood as a single-pair question.

(17) a. Who kissed whom?
     b. /PAUL hat ClauDIne\geküsst.
     c. PAUL\ hat ClauDIne\geküsst.
        'Paul kissed Claudine.'

From this we can conclude that the alternatives introduced via contrastive topic marking differ from the ones introduced by focus marking insofar as they indicate non-completeness, i.e. contrastive topic-marking is only appropriate if there are other relevant propositions that are true in the respective context, and that differ from the one asserted in both the constituent marked as the contrastive topic and the one marked as the focus. Consequently, (17b) would not only be inappropriate if nobody kissed anyone else, but also if Paul kissed other people.

According to the very influential theory of Büring (1997a, 1999), contrastive topic marking similarly to focus marking results in the introduction of a set of alternatives to the (denotation of the) respective constituent, the so-called *topic semantic value*. The crucial difference between focus and topic semantic value is that the respective alternatives are structured in a different way: the double focus in (17c) introduces a set like the one in (18a), while the combination of contrastive topic- and focus marking in (17b) introduces a set (of sets) like the one in (18b):

(18) a. {[[Paul kissed Claudine]], [[Peter kissed Maria]], [[Eva kissed Maria]], ... }
 b. {{[[Paul kissed Claudine]], [[Paul kissed Maria]], ... }, {[[Peter kissed Maria]], [[Peter kissed Martina]], ... }, {[[Eva kissed Claudine]], [[Eva kissed Maria]], ... }, ... }

Thus, while (18a) simply lists all possible kisser-kissee combinations, (18b) is structured in a more complex way: for each possible kisser, the set of all possible kissees is listed. In other words, (18a) contains the set of all possible answers to (17a), i.e. the denotation of the question in (17a). (18b), in contrast, contains the set of all answers to a set of sub-questions of the form *Who did Paul kiss?*, *Who did Peter kiss?*, *Who did Eva kiss?*, i.e. the denotations of the respective sub-questions. Consequently, the above mentioned contrast between (17b) and (17c) can be interpreted as follows: (17c) is understood as picking out the unique true proposition from the set in (18a), while (17b) is only understood as picking out the unique true proposition from the first sub-set in (18b), giving rise to the expectation that the same will be done for the other sub-sets. The feeling of incompleteness that contrastive topic in contrast to focus-marking triggers can thus be explained in pragmatic terms along the following lines (Büring 2003: 9): since contrastive-topic marking generates a set of sub-questions, and since one of these sub-questions is already answered by the ordinary semantic value of the respective sentence, the principle of Informativity (Atlas & Levinson 1981) ensures that the hearer can assume the answers to the other sub-questions to differ with respect to the focus-marked constituent. Otherwise, i.e. if in a case like (17b) above someone besides Paul (say Peter) had kissed Claudine as well, the speaker should have said *Paul and Peter kissed Claudine* instead of (17b).

The theory just sketched informally, according to which contrastive topic marking generates a set of sets of propositions (i.e. a set of questions), while focus marking simply generates a set of propositions (i.e. a question), gives us a plausible and elegant account of the discourse-pragmatic effects of contrastive topicality, and in section 6 we will see that it can also account for some observed truth-conditional effects. However, it leaves open the question of what contrastive topicality has to do with other kinds of topicality, especially with aboutness topicality (recall from section 3.2 that there are reasons to doubt the existence of frame setting topicality as a distinct kind of topicality). Concerning the empirical basis of grouping aboutness topics and contrastive topics together, the following observations speak in favour of such a classification: first, languages like Japanese use the same device to mark contrastive topics and aboutness topic – namely the particle *wa*, and also in German contrastive topicality is at least compatible with GLD (but see below for a qualification). Second, just like aboutness topics, contrastive topics tend to be fronted (in German, for example, this is almost obligatory, while English is more liberal in this respect and allows foci to precede contrastive topics (see Jackendoff 1972)). Third, we have seen above that questions of the form *What about X?* serve to explicitly mark the constituent *X* as the aboutness topic of the sentence answering the respective question. As shown in (19), sentences containing contrastive topics can be used as partial answers to such questions:

(19) a. Who did the girls talk to at the party yesterday?
      b. /MarIa hat mit PAUL\geredet.
         'Maria talked to Paul.'

Consequently, one could make the following assumption: the object created via contrastive topic marking – the topic semantic value – always consists of propositions each of which contains a partial aboutness topic, i.e. a part of the complex object denoted by the respective (complete) aboutness topic. The special accent pattern indicating contrastive topicality would then simply result from the respective partial aboutness topic being contrasted with the other partial aboutness topics, which requires focus marking (cf. Krifka 1998).

This proposal works well in many cases, since it is often plausible to assume that the required sub-questions can be accommodated easily (see Roberts 1996, van Kuppevelt 1995 and Büring 2003 for the view that the topic-focus-articulation of sentences is best captured in terms of (answers to) explicit and implicit questions under discussion). Nevertheless it faces some serious problems. First, recall from section 3.1 that in GLD, which can plausibly be assumed to mark aboutness topicality, only a limited set of DPs is acceptable in left-dislocated position: the only quantifiers that are acceptable are indefinites with unmodified determiners, i.e. determiners such as *three* in contrast to *more than/less than/at least/at most*, as shown by the unacceptability of examples like (20a). In contrast to this, even downward entailing quantifiers like the one in (20b) are acceptable as contrastive topics (recall from above that while contrastive topicality is in principle compatible with GLD, contrastive topics do not need to be marked via GLD):

(20) a. ??Weniger als acht Jungen, die haben Fußball gespielt.
 less than eight boys RP-NOM.PL have soccer played
 b. Weniger als/ACHT Jungen haben FUßball\gespielt (und weniger als/ NEUN Jungen HANDball\).
 'Less than eight boys played soccer (and less than nine boys handball).'

To make things worse, the sentence in (20b) is even acceptable as a (partial) answer to a question like the one in (21):

(21) How many boys played which game?

Now in this case, even if we assume sub-questions such as *Which game did less than eight boys play?* to be accommodated, these can not plausibly be considered as establishing the respective DP as aboutness topic, since a variant like *What about less than eight boys? Which game did they play?* is extremely odd. I therefore conclude that at least for the time being we have to acknowledge the existence of (at least) two distinct kinds of topicality – aboutness topicality and contrastive topicality.

4 Givenness

The third information structural dimension that I will discuss in the present paper is the distinction between given and new information. As already alluded to in section 1, the given-new distinction cannot be reduced to the focus-background distinction, since it is both possible that material which has been explicitly mentioned in the preceding discourse is focus marked, and that focal material contains given sub-parts, as shown by (22) (see Schwarzschild 1999) and (23) (from Wagner 2006; see also Féry & Samek-Lodovici 2006):

(22) a. Who did John's mother praise?
 b. She praised HIM/JOHN.

(23) Mary sat at her desk. John walked in. What happened next?
   a. #She kissed JOHN.
   b. She KISSED John.

Now, as already discussed by Halliday (1967) and Chafe (1976), de-accentuation is a means that is very commonly employed by languages to indicate that (the denotation of) a constituent has either been introduced explicitly or implicitly (in the sense of its existence being entailed by the common ground) into the discourse. Nevertheless, in (22b) the need to ensure question-answer congruence via focus marking the constituent that replaces the *wh*-term in the question in (22a) overrides the need to indicate the givenness of the individual referred to by *John* or *him* via de-accentuation. Alternatively, the elaborate account of givenness developed by Schwarzschild (1999) can explain the accent pattern in (22b) along the following lines: first, constituents whose denotation is entailed by a salient antecedent in the preceding context count as given. Since entailment is only defined for propositions, Schwarzschild assumes a mechanism of existential closure, "which raises expressions to type *t*, by existentially binding unfilled arguments" (Schwarzschild 1999: 147), and which applies after F-marked parts have been removed. For our limited expository purposes, F-marking, which corresponds to an additional abstract level of marking that is meant to capture the above mentioned rules of focus projection, can be equated with focus marking. Second, non-F-marked constituents are given (*Givenness*). Third, F-marking is to be minimized (*AvoidF*). Applying these principles to the case of (22), the accent pattern of (22b) is correctly predicted: *She praised HIM* is given, since the proposition that we get by removing *HIM* and applying existential closure, namely that there is someone that John's mother praised, is entailed by the preceding question in (22a). *She praised him*, in contrast, is not given, since the context does not entail the proposition that John's mother praised John. *Him*, accordingly, has to be F-marked, while F-marking anything else would violate *AvoidF*.

In the case of (23), question-answer congruence ensures that the whole sentence is focal (and the same is true of Schwarzschild's system: the question in (23a) neither entails that Mary kissed somebody, nor that Mary did something to John, nor that Mary did something etc.). Nevertheless, the need to indicate the givenness of the individual referred to by *John* is strong enough to override the accentuation pattern that would normally be employed in such a case, and according to which the complement of the verb would receive the main accent (as shown in (22b)). Note, however, that given constituents (even if they do not need to be accented because of being focal for independent reasons, as in (22b)) are not always de-accented, as shown by Wagner (2006: 3) for examples like the following one:

(24) Mary's uncle, who produces high-end convertibles, is coming to her wedding. I wonder what he brought as a present.
a. He brought [a CHEAP convertible].
b. #He brought [a RED convertible].
c. He brought [a red CONVERTIBLE].

In the above context, the bracketed DP is always focal, and the noun *convertible* is always given. Nevertheless, it may only be de-accented in (24a), but not in (24b). Intuitively, the relevant contrast between the two is that *cheap* can naturally be contrasted with *high-end*, while *red* can't. Based on these and similar observations, Wagner (2006) argues that in order for a constituent x to be marked as given via de-accentuation, it has to be given relative to its sister, i.e. the context has to make available an alternative y' to its sister y such that [y' x] is given. Technically, this is accomplished by assuming that de-accentuation is regulated by an operator presupposing relative givenness in the sense just sketched (cf. Schwarzschild 1999 and Sauerland 2004 for earlier approaches that work with givenness operators).

Other means than de-accentuation to indicate givenness are deletion, pronominalization, the choice between the indefinite (for new discourse referents) and the definite (for given discourse referents) article (cf. Heim 1982) and word order. Concerning the latter aspect, there is a strong tendency for given material to precede new material, which may be overwritten if canonical word order is employed, but has to be strictly respected if non-canonical word order is chosen (see article 12 [this volume] (Ward & Birner) *Discourse and word order*, where this is shown in detail for English). The optional (re-)ordering of argument DPs in the German middle field which is known as *scrambling* is a case in point: while indefinite DPs may precede definite DPs as long as the canonical argument order (subject before indirect object, indirect object before direct object) is respected (as shown in (25a)), and while definite objects may be scrambled across indefinite subjects (as shown in (25b)), indefinite objects (at least if they are not marked as contrastive topics) may not be scrambled across definite subjects (as shown by (25c); see Büring 2001):

(25) a. (weil) ein Student den Dekan geohrfeigt hat.
(because) a-nom student the-ACC dean slapped-in-the-face has
'... (because) a student slapped the dean in the face.'
b. (weil) den Dekan ein Student geohrfeigt hat.
(because) the-ACC dean a-NOM student slapped-in-the-face has
c. ??(weil) einen Studenten der Dekan geohrfeigt hat.
(because) a-ACC student-acc the-NOM dean slapped-in-the-face has
'... (because) the dean slapped a student in the face.'

We have seen that the distinction between given and new material is linguistically relevant in the sense that languages employ a rich array of means to indicate givenness. It is also clear that the conditions under which the respective marking strategies apply have to be stated in semantic terms, since it is always identity of denotation that is relevant, not identity of form. This, however, still leaves open the question of whether givenness affects truth-conditions, i.e. whether there are, for example, any logical operators which associate exclusively with given material, or whether the means employed to mark givenness may also be used to achieve truth conditional effects.

5 Truth conditional effects of focus marking

5.1 Ex situ focus in Hungarian and exhaustivity

One of the prime examples that is often cited to show that focus marking can have truth conditional effects is the case of Hungarian ex situ focus, which is claimed to give rise to exhaustivity effects (Szabolcsi 1981) – in contrast to in situ focus, which behaves just like (intonational) focus in English insofar as it implicates, but does not entail exhaustivity:

(26) Nem PÉTER aludt a padlón, hanem PÉTER ÉS PÁL.
      not Peter slept the floor.on but Peter and Pal
      'It isn't Péter who slept on the floor; it's Péter and Pál.'

As argued for by Szabolcsi, examples like the one in (26) would be contradictory if it was not part of the truth conditions, but merely an implicature that the (denotation of the) focussed constituent was the only one among the salient alternatives that had the property in question. From the observation that they are perfectly coherent she thus concludes that the position to the immediate left of the tensed verb is a special focus position in Hungarian that is directly associated with exhaustivity. More concretely, she assumes that the focussed constituent occupies the specifier position of an exhaustivity operator whose meaning is given in DEF1:

DEF1 $\lambda x[\lambda P[P(x) \ \& \ \forall y[P(y) \rightarrow y = x]]]$

Applying the operator in DEF1 to the focus marked constituent to its left and to the rest of the first sentence in (26) in turn gives us (27), whose negation is indeed coherent with the continuation in (26). (Note that we have to assume that *Péter and Pál* denotes a sum individual in the sense of Link 1983.)

(27) slept_on_floor(peter) & ∀y[slept_on_floor(y) → y = peter]

There are, however, other facts which cast doubt on the assumption that the focus position in Hungarian is directly associated with exhaustivity. Consider the two sentences in (28), which were adapted by Wedgwood (2007) from an English example that Horn (1981) used to show that *it*-clefts do not encode exhaustivity ('VM' means *verbal modifier*).

(28) a. #Azt   tudtam,   hogy   Mari   megevett   egy   pizzát, de
       that   knew.1SG   that   Mari   VM.ate.3SG   a   pizza   but
       most   vettem észre,   hogy   egy   PIZZÀT   evett   meg.
       now   take   mind.to(VM) that   a   pizza.ACC   ate   VM
      #'I knew that Mari ate a pizza, but now I know that it was a pizza that she ate.'
   b. Azt   tudtam,   hogy   Mari   megevett   egy   pizzát, de most
       that   knew.1SG   that   Mari   VM.ate.3SG   a   pizza   but now
      vettem észre,   hogy   csak   egy   pizzát evett   meg.
      take   mind.to(VM) that   only   a   pizza.ACC   ate   VM
      'I knew that Mari ate pizza, but now I know that it was only pizza that she ate.'

In contrast to (28b), which contains the Hungarian equivalent of *only*, (28a) is infelicitous, which it should not be if *a pizza* in the second conjunct occupied the specifier position of the exhaustivity operator discussed above, i.e. if an exhaustive interpretation of *a pizza* was actually part of the asserted content. Now, Kenesei (1986) has argued for a modification of Szabolcsi's (1981) analysis according to which the operator into whose specifier the focus marked constituent is moved has the denotation in DEF2:

DEF2 $\lambda x[\lambda P[x = \iota y\,[P(y)]]]$

The crucial difference between (DEF1) and (DEF2) is that while in (DEF1) uniqueness of the (denotation of the) focus marked constituent is part of the truth conditional content, it is merely presupposed in (DEF2), since the application of the iota operator only yields a defined result if there is exactly one object that has the property denoted by the non-focal part of the clause. (28a) would thus be infelicitous for the same reason that (29) is: since the object that Mari ate has already been introduced under the description *pizza*, it is completely redundant to identify it with an object that is characterized by satisfying the same predicate.

(29) #I knew that Mari ate pizza, but now I know that the thing Mari ate was pizza.

Modifying the operator analysis in the way suggested by Kenesei (1986) thus captures the empirical facts quite well. Wedgwood (2007) nevertheless claims that the position occupied by the focus marked constituents in (26) and (27) cannot be a designated focus position, since in sentences with broad focus (i.e. in cases where the whole sentence is in focus) it is occupied either by the verbal modifier (if the main verb is marked for tense) or by the main verb. From this he concludes that the identificational interpretation sketched above comes about by inferential processes on the basis of an underspecified, incremental semantics. In a nutshell, he assumes that the position under discussion is reserved for the 'main predicate' of the respective clause, which in the default case is some verbal element. If it is a non-verbal element, however, this is only compatible with a situation where the (information provided by the) rest of the clause is presupposed, which leads to an identificational interpretation. The data discussed in this section thus at least do not have to be interpreted as showing that ex situ focus in Hungarian is directly associated with an exhaustive interpretation.

5.2 Focus sensitive operators

As already mentioned in section 2, in English, too, there are cases where focus marking has an effect on the truth conditions of sentences:

(30) a. Peter only goes to the BEACH with Mary.
     b. Peter only goes to the beach with MARY.

(31) a. Peter always goes to the BEACH with Mary.
     b. Peter always goes to the beach with MARY.

(30a) and (31a), are both false in a situation where Peter on nine of ten occasions where he goes somewhere with Mary goes to the beach with her, but takes her to the park on every tenth occasion. (30b) and (31b), in contrast, are true in such a scenario, as long as Peter never goes to the beach with anyone but Mary. In light of these and similar observations, which for the case of *only* and other degree particles such as *even*, *also* etc. have first been discussed by Dretske (1972), and for the case of adverbial quantifiers like *always*, *usually* etc. by Rooth (1985), it has been suggested by many researchers that the respective items are *focus sensitive operators*, i.e. operators whose denotations are directly sensitive to the structuring of the clauses they occur in into focus and background (Jacobs 1983, Rooth 1985, von Stechow 1989, Krifka 1992, Herburger 2000). A second line of research attempts to explain the observed truth conditional effects in a different way, namely as an optional association of the (underspecified) interpretation of the respective operators with the information provided by focus marking (von Fintel 1994, Roberts 1996, Geurts & van der Sandt 1997, Schwarzschild 1997; Rooth 1992 argues for an intermediate position). Finally, a third position is argued for by Beaver & Clark (2003, 2008): they present evidence for treating *only* as a focus sensitive operator, and *always* as an operator whose association with focus is only a pragmatically driven default option that can be overridden by other factors.

Concerning the first line of research, I will briefly sketch the analysis of Rooth (1985). He assumes that operators such as *only* and *always* take the focus semantic value of a sentence (minus the operator, that is) as their first argument, the *restrictor*, and the ordinary semantic value as their second argument, the *nuclear scope*. In the case of (30a) and (31a), for example, the focus semantic value (see section 2) is a set of propositions that only differ from each other with respect to the place where Peter goes with Mary, i.e. a set such as {⟦Peter goes to the beach with Mary⟧, ⟦Peter goes to the park with Mary⟧, ⟦Peter goes to the cinema with Mary⟧ ... }. Rooth (1985) now assumes that *only* is a propositional operator which yields the following truth conditions when it is applied to the ordinary semantic value p and the focus semantic value R of a sentence S:

(32) $\forall r \, [r \in R \land r \neq p \rightarrow \text{false}(r)]$

Both (30a) and (31a) are thus true if among the relevant alternatives no other proposition than 'Peter went to the beach with Mary' is true, where the difference in truth conditions comes about because the respective alternative sets R are different, due to focus marking: in the first case the propositions vary with respect to the location where Peter goes with Mary, while in the second case they vary with respect to the person that accompanies Peter to the beach. Concerning *always*, in contrast, Rooth assumes that it is a quantifier over situations. It can therefore not operate directly on the focus semantic value, which is a set of propositions. Rather, set union has to be applied, which in the case of (30b) for example gives us the proposition that Peter either went to the beach or to the park or to the cinema etc. with Mary, i.e. the proposition that Peter went somewhere with Mary. This proposition is now assumed to characterize the situations in the restrictor of *always*, while the ordinary semantic value is assumed to characterize the nuclear scope. The truth conditions of (30b), for example, can thus be paraphrased as follows: all situations where Peter goes somewhere with Mary are situations where he goes to the beach with Mary. Since the respective focus semantic value determines the situations quantified over, the truth conditions are correctly predicted to depend on focus marking.

Concerning the second line of research, which assumes association with focus to be not directly encoded in the lexical entries of the operators, but to come about via indirect pragmatic processes in the default case, I will briefly sketch the theory of von Fintel (1994), which essentially differs from Rooth's only in the following respect: the restrictor of the respective operators is filled by a free variable ranging over sets of propositions (in the case of *only*) or over situation predicates, i.e. propositions (in the case of *always* and other adverbs of quantification such as *usually*, *often* etc.). The respective variables now have to be resolved on the basis of contextually available information. Since the alternatives making up the focus semantic value have to be determined on the basis of contextual information, too, the value for the respective C-variable can in the default case be identified with the focus semantic value/the object generated by applying set union to the focus semantic value.

As already mentioned above, Beaver & Clark (2003, 2008) represent a third line of research insofar as they assume that a theory along the lines of Rooth (1985) is suitable for the case of *only*, while one along the lines of von Fintel (1994) is suitable for the case of *always* (and presumably other adverbs of quantification). This conclusion is based on a variety of tests which show that while association with focus can be overwritten by other factors in the case of *always*, it holds strictly and furthermore has to obey tighter constraints in the case of *only*. For reasons of space, I can only illustrate their case with a few examples. First, in contrast to *always*, *only* has to c-command the focus marked constituent it associates with:

(33) a. PETER always goes to the beach with Mary.
      b. *PETER only goes to the beach with Mary.

Second, while *always* can also associate with phonetically reduced (or extracted) material, this is impossible for *only*, as shown by the contrast between (34a) and (34b) (from Beaver & Clark 2003: 343), which are assumed to be uttered in a context where the speaker is asked how often the person he talked about with Sandy was Fred:

(34) a. I [always]$_F$ discussed 'im with Sandy.
      b. #I [only]$_F$ discussed 'im with Sandy.

Third, in contrast to *only*, the restrictor of *always* can sometimes be determined on the basis of lexical presuppositions instead of the focus, as shown by the fact that the preferred interpretation of (35) (from Beaver & Clark 2003: 235) is the one in (a.), not the one in (b.), while in the case of (36), the interpretation in (b.) is the only one available. The presupposition associated with *complete* thus overrides the effect of focus marking in the case of *always*, while it is unable to do so in the case of *only*:

(35) Mary always managed to complete her [exams]$_F$.
  a. 'Whenever Mary took exams, she completed them.'
  b. 'Whenever Mary completed something, it was invariably an exam.'

(36) Mary only managed to complete her [exams]$_F$.
  a. ''What Mary did when taking exams was complete them and nothing else.'
  b. 'What Mary completed was an exam and nothing else.'

5.3 Focus and determiner quantification

In the last section, we have discussed two operators whose arguments are not entirely determined by the syntax, and which therefore have to rely on other mechanisms to obtain their restrictor: either by direct association with focus, or by searching a suitable value that the free variable which initially makes up their restrictor can be resolved to, where the information provided by focus marking is made use of by default. Let us now turn to quantificational determiners such as *every*, *a*, *some*, *more than three* etc., which according to the by-now standard view take two expressions denoting sets of individuals as arguments and map them onto a proposition that is true if the respective sets stand in a certain lexically specified relation to each other (see Barwise & Cooper 1981). Here, matters are different: the first argument, i.e. the restrictor, is the denotation of the NP-complement of the quantificational determiner. The second argument, i.e. the nuclear scope, is the denotation of the syntactic sister of the entire DP if the DP is in subject position. Since the subject quantificational DP is the highest argument of the respective verbal predicate, its sister is guaranteed to be of the right type – namely a one-place predicate, i.e. (the characteristic function of) a set of individuals. Consider the examples in (37a, c):

(37) a. [$_{TP}$ [$_{DP}$ Every [$_{NP}$ dolphin]] [$_{T'}$ is smart]].
  b. {x: dolphin(x)} ⊆ {y: smart(y)}
  c. [$_{TP}$ [$_{DP}$ A [$_{NP}$ dog]] [$_{T'}$ bit my sister]].
  d. {x: dog(x)} ∩ {y: bit-my-sister(y)} ≠ ∅

In the case of (37a), the proposition is true if the set of dolphins is a subset of the set of smart entities (as shown in (37b)), while in the case of (37c), the proposition is true if the intersection between the set of dogs and the set of entities that bit my sister is non-empty (as shown in (37d)). With quantificational DPs in object position, the syntax-semantics mapping is less straightforward, since in these cases the sister of the respective DP is a transitive verb, i.e. (the characteristic function of) a set of pairs of individuals. One very popular solution to this problem is to assume that quantificational DPs can be moved away from their base position at LF and adjoin to the TP-node via *Quantifier Raising* (QR) (cf. May 1985). Under the additional assumptions that the trace left behind by the quantificational DP is interpreted as a variable of type *e*, and that a lambda-operator binding this variable is inserted directly beneath the moved DP, the sister of this DP is again of the right type for it to function as the second argument of the D-quantifier (cf. Heim & Kratzer 1998 for discussion), as shown below:

(38) a. Paul owns every book by John Updike.
 b. LF: [$_{TP}$ [Every book by John Updike]$_i$ [$_{TP}$ λ$_i$ [$_{TP}$ Paul owns t$_i$]]]
 c. {x: book-by-John-Updike(x)} ⊆ {y: owns(Paul, y)}

The important point for our current purposes is that in general the arguments of quantificational determiners are strictly determined by (LF-)syntax. While prosodic as well as contextual information might have an influence on the truth conditions of sentences containing two or more quantificational DPs (see below), there is no way for this kind of information to alter the order in which a quantificational determiner such as *every* is combined with its two arguments: the NP-complement of a quantificational determiner can never be interpreted as its nuclear scope, while the sister of the entire DP is interpreted as the restrictor. Consequently, even if we put a strong focal accent on *dolphin* in (37a) or on *book* in (38a), the sentences still do not mean that every smart being is a dolphin or that everything that John owns is a book by John Updike.

Nevertheless, there are two types of examples which at first sight seem to be problematic for the view that determiner quantification is not influenced by information structural notion such as focus marking. First, it has been observed by Krifka (1990) (see also Partee 1991, 1999) that in examples like (39a) the truth conditions are influenced by focus marking in the sense that the restrictor consists not only of the NP-complement of the quantificational determiner, but also of the non-focal material in the rest of the sentence, as shown by the paraphrase in (39b):

(39) a. Most ships passed through the lock [at NIGHT]$_F$.
 b. 'Most ships that passed through the lock passed through the lock at night.'

This, however, does not show that *most* is a focus sensitive operator, since it can easily be accounted for via assumptions about the influence of the context on the interpretation of quantificational DPs that are by now rather standard (cf. Beaver & Clark 2008). It is well known that the restrictor of quantificational determiners in many cases is not only determined by overtly given material (i.e. the respective NP), but also by contextually salient information: if I utter a sentence such as *Most students understood Lewis's theory of counterfactuals* in the context of a discussion of a class on conditionals that took place yesterday, it need not be the case that more than fifty percent of the students in the whole world understood Lewis's theory for the sentence to be true. Rather, it suffices that more than half of the students in my class got it. Observations such as these can easily be explained if it is assumed that quantificational determiners come with a free variable ranging over predicates that is intersected with the denotation of the NP they take as their first argument, and which is resolved on the basis of contextually salient information (von Fintel 1994; see also Stanley 2000 and Martí 2003 for additional discussion). Now, in the case of (39a), everything except the PP *at night* is de-accented, indicating its status as given information. From this, the hearer can conclude that the existence of ships passing through the lock is contextually salient information, and the free variable in the restrictor of *most* can accordingly be resolved to the predicate $\lambda x.\ passed\_through\_the\_lock(x)$, which gives us the desired result.

More problematic for the view that there is no direct influence of focus marking on the truth conditions of sentences with quantificational DPs is the existence of examples such as (40a, b) (from Herburger 1997, 2000; see Westerståhl 1985, Herburger 1992, Eckardt 1999 for the initial observations):

(40) a. Many ScandiNAvians won the Nobel prize in literature.
     b. Few COOKs applied.

According to Herburger (1997, 2000), focussing *Scandinavians* and *cooks*, respectively, makes available the readings paraphrased in (41a, b), where the argument order that is normally obligatory for quantificational determiners has apparently been switched: the VPs *won the Nobel Prize in literature* and *applied* are interpreted in the restrictor, while the NPs *Scandinavians* and *cooks* are interpreted in the nuclear scope.

(41) a. Many of the winners of the Nobel Prize in literature were Scandinavians.
     b. Few of the people that applied were cooks.

Crucially, such reversed readings are not available to strong quantifiers such as *all/most/all but four*: the sentences in (42) cannot be interpreted as saying that all/most/all but four of the people who won the Nobel Prize in literature are Scandinavians. Note that other than *many* and *few*, weak quantifiers (i.e. ones that can occur in *there*-insertion contexts such as *there were three/many/few/no Scandinavians*) cannot be tested this way, since they are all symmetrical: *three/no philosophers arrived* has the same truth conditions as *three/no people who arrived were philosophers*.

(42) All/Most/All but four SCANDINAVIANS won the Nobel Prize in literature.

From these observations Herburger (1997, 2000) concludes that in contrast to strong quantifiers, the arguments of weak quantifiers are determined on the basis of focus marking, but that this effect is only visible in the case of the weak proportional quantifiers *many* and *few*. Cohen (2001) argues for a different view, according to which it is not necessary to reverse the order of the arguments that *many* and *few* combine with. Nevertheless, he still assumes that the alternatives evoked by placing the main accent on some element within the respective NP directly enter the process whereby the truth conditions of the sentences are computed. He assumes that *many* and *few* both have *relative proportional readings* which are computed in the following way: the proportion of the individuals satisfying both restrictor and nuclear scope among those satisfying the restrictor is compared to the proportion of individuals satisfying both any of the alternatives to the restrictor and the nuclear scope among those satisfying any of the alternatives to the restrictor. In the case of *many*, the respective sentence is true if the first proportion is greater than the second, while in the case of *few*, the first proportion needs to be smaller than the second. Applying this method to our example (40a), we get truth conditions that can be paraphrased as follows: among the Scandinavians, the proportion of Nobel Prize winners in literature is greater than among people in general (i.e. among individuals who satisfy any of the relevant alternatives and are thus either Scandinavian or French or Chinese etc.).

According to Beaver & Clark (2008: 58ff.; see also Büring 1996), the relevant truth conditions can also be obtained without having to assume *direct* focus sensitivity of *many* and *few*. They assume that in order for a sentence with *many* to be true, either the proportion of people satisfying both restrictor and scope among those satisfying the restrictor or the number of people satisfying both restrictor and scope has to be higher than expected, while in the case of *few*, it has to be lower. What is expected is given in the form of either a proportion or an absolute number α that is determined by the context. Now, since focus on some part of the respective NP evokes a set of alternative propositions, it is natural for the hearer to assume that at least some of these alternatives are false, while the proposition actually uttered is true (see above). The value for α thus has to be chosen accordingly, i.e. in the case of (40a), for example, it has to be chosen in such a way that it allows the proportion of Nobel Prize winners in literature among the Scandinavians to exceed it, while the proportions of winners among the French, Chinese, etc. are below it. This gives us the desired result, since the alternatives evoked by focus marking play a decisive role in determining the value for α, and this creates the impression of direct focus sensitivity.

In section 5 we have discussed some cases where focus marking has an influence on the truth conditions of sentences. It has turned out that in most cases (exhaustive focus in Hungarian, adverbial quantifiers, and determiner quantification in general) the observed effects can be explained as indirect effects insofar as an underspecified element in the denotation of some operator is resolved on the basis of clues given by focus marking. On the other hand, we have seen that there are operators like *only* which are most plausibly analysed as directly focus sensitive (see Beaver & Clark 2008 for a thorough investigation of the class of focus sensitive operators). In the next section we will discuss truth conditional effects of topic marking.

6 Truth conditional effects of topic marking

6.1 Aboutness topicality

As already mentioned in section 3, in most cases marking a constituent as an aboutness topic does not have an observable truth conditional effect: first, there are no operators which seem to be topic sensitive in a sense comparable to focus sensitive operators such as *only*. While it has been claimed by Partee (1991, 1999) that adverbial quantifiers are sensitive to information structure insofar as topical material is interpreted in their restrictor while focal material is interpreted in their nuclear scope, we have already seen in section 5 that the observed effects can also be explained without having to assume such a direct sensitivity. Second, in most cases the constituent marked as the aboutness topic denotes an object of type e and is therefore unable to take scope anyway. But as soon as we turn our attention to indefinites headed by unmodified determiners – which are the only quantifiers that can appear in constructions marking aboutness topicality overtly such as GLD – , the picture changes: in contrast to the fronted indefinite in (43a), the left-dislocated one in (43b) can only be interpreted with scope over *jeder* ('everyone'). This is shown by the fact that while both the continuation in (43c) and the one in (43d) are possible for (43a), only the one in (43c) is possible for (43b).

(43) a. Einen   Song von Bob Dylan   kennt   jeder.
       a/one-ACC song   by   Bob Dylan   knows   everybody
       'Everybody knows a/one song by Bob Dylan.'
   b. Einen   Song von Bob Dylan, den   kennt jeder.
       a/one-ACC song   by   Bob Dylan RP-ACC.SING.MASC knows everybody
       'There is a/one song by Bob Dylan that everybody knows.'
   c. Nämlich   *Blowing in the Wind*.
       Namely   *Blowing in the Wind*.
   d. Maria kennt *Visions of Joanna*, Peter kennt *Everybody Must Get Stoned*, und
       Maria knows *Visions of Joanna* Peter knows *Everybody Must Get Stoned* and
       Paula kennt *Blowing in the Wind*.
       Paula knows *Blowing in the Wind*.

At first sight, examples such as (44a), where a pronoun contained within the left-dislocated indefinite can be interpreted as bound by a quantifier from within the matrix clause, seem to falsify the claim that left-dislocated indefinites have to be interpreted with widest scope. Endriss (2009) shows, however, that the indefinites do not really receive narrow scope, but rather functional wide scope. This is evidenced by the fact that the continuation in (44b), which names a function (namely the function that maps pupils onto a picture of their first day at school), is fine, while the one in (44c) is odd:

(44) a. Ein Bild   von sich,   das   hat jeder Schüler mitgebracht.
       A   picture of himself RP.NEUT.SING has every pupil   brought-with-him
       'Every pupil has brought a (certain) picture of himself.'
   b. Nämlich sein   Einschulungsfoto.
       Namely   his   picture-of-his-first-day-at-school.
       'Namely a picture of his first day at school.'
   c. #Paul   ein   Bild   von   sich   mit   seiner   Tante,
       Paul   a   picture of   himself   with his   aunt,
       Peter   ein   Bild   von   sich   mit   seiner   Katze, ...
       Peter   a   picture of   himself   with his   cat

Nevertheless, while being unable to be interpreted in the scope of other quantificational DPs, left-dislocated indefinites nevertheless do not always have to be interpreted with widest scope. As shown by (45a), they can be interpreted in the restrictor of adverbial quantifiers (but not in the nuclear scope): the sentence is most naturally interpreted in a way that can be paraphrased as "most dogs are smart". Finally, (45b) shows that left-dislocated indefinites are also capable of receiving generic readings: the sentence cannot only be interpreted as a statement about a particular dog, but also as a statement about dogs in general.

(45) a. Ein Hund, der   ist meistens schlau.
        a dog RP-NOM.SING.MASC   is usually smart
   b. Ein Hund, der   ist schlau.
        a dog RP-NOM.SING.MASC   is smart

In order to capture all these interpretative possibilities, Endriss & Hinterwimmer (2009) (see also Endriss 2009) argue for a formal implementation of the aboutness concept of Reinhart (1981) that can roughly be described as follows: first, the (denotation of the) left-dislocated constituent is established as the topic in a separate speech act (cf. Searle 1969 and Jacobs 1984), which corresponds to the creation of an address. This first speech act is then combined via speech act conjunction with a second speech act, in which it is asserted that the comment holds of the topic, and which corresponds to the storage of the information provided by the respective sentence under the address created for the topic. Now, in cases such as (46a), where the topic is an object of type e, i.e. an individual, this is completely unproblematic: assuming that the resumptive pronoun in the specifier of the matrix-clause CP behaves like a relative pronoun in a relative clause insofar as it triggers lambda abstraction (Heim & Kratzer 1998), the whole matrix clause can be interpreted as a predicate that applies to the topic. The resulting interpretation is given schematically in (46b). Note that with respect to the truth conditions, it does not differ from the interpretation of the corresponding sentence in (46c) where Peter is not explicitly marked as the aboutness topic receives, which is given in (46d):

(46) a. (Den) Peter, den mag ich.
       (the-ACC) Peter RP-ACC.SING.MASC like I
       'Peter, I like.'
   b. $\exists \alpha [\alpha = \text{Peter} \,\&\, \text{ASSERT} \,[\lambda s. \text{like}(I, \alpha)(s)]]$
   c. Ich mag (den) Peter.
       I like (the-ACC)
   d. like(I, peter)

In cases where an indefinite is marked as the aboutness topic, things are not so simple. First, Endriss & Hinterwimmer (2009) assume the generalized quantifiers, i.e. sets of sets of individuals, in contrast to individuals and sets are too complex objects to serve as addresses for storing information. Second, the predicate denoted by the matrix-CP cannot be applied to them, i.e. they cannot be interpreted as the logical subject of this predicate, which would have to be of type <<<e, t>, t>, t> for this to be possible. Therefore, the type of the generalized quantifiers has to be lowered via typeshifting. Let us first consider the case of (43a): in order to serve as an address for storing the information provided by the rest of the sentence, the indefinite has to be lowered to the type of sets at least. This can be done in the following way: a *representative* of the quantifier in the form of a *minimal witness set* (in the sense of Barwise & Cooper 1981; see also Szabolcsi 1997) is created, where a minimal witness set of a quantifier is an element of this quantifier that does not contain any "unwanted" elements. The formal definition is given in (47):

(47) Definition of a minimal (witness) set X of a generalized quantifier G:
min(X)(G) = [G(X) ∧ ∀Y [G(Y) → ¬(λx.Y(x)) ⊂ λx.X(x)]]

In the case of a quantifier like *three dogs*, for instance, a minimal witness set of this quantifier is a set that contains three dogs and nothing else. Such a minimal witness set can function as the address where the information conveyed by the comment is stored. In order for this to be possible, however, the denotation of the topic – which now is an object of type <e, t> – has to be combined with the denotation of the comment, which is of the same type. Furthermore, the intuition has to be respected that the topic is the logical subject of the predicate denoted by the comment. This can be achieved in the following way: an operator ⊓, which collects the elements of the minimal witness set and turns them into a (sum) individual is applied to the respective minimal witness set. Taking all this together, the sentence in (43a) is interpreted as shown in (48):

(48) ∃α[min(α)(⟦a song by Bob Dylan⟧]) &
ASSERT[λs.∀y[human(y) → know(y, ⊓{x: α(x)}(s)]]]

This is the correct result. It reflects the wide scope reading for the indefinite and at the same time respects the principle underlying the formalization proposed by Endriss & Hinterwimmer (2009): it allows the creation of an address corresponding to the minimal witness set where the information conveyed by the comment can be stored. Endriss (2009) argues that the need to create a representative in the form of a minimal witness set excludes all generalized quantifiers except indefinites headed by unmodified articles from functioning as aboutness topics, since it leads to unwanted results in all other cases. Furthermore, she argues that exceptional wide scope readings of these indefinites (Fodor & Sag 1982), i.e. readings where they take scope out of islands that generally cannot be crossed by quantifiers, also come about because the respective indefinite is interpreted as the (not overtly marked) aboutness topic.

Let us now turn to the case exemplified by (45a), where an indefinite marked as aboutness topic is interpreted in the restrictor of an adverbial quantifier. In a nutshell, Endriss & Hinterwimmer (2009) argue that the existence of such readings, where the quantificational force of the indefinite seems to vary with the force of the quantificational adverb and which accordingly exemplify a phenomenon dubbed *Quantificational Variability Effect* (QVE) (Berman 1987), can be reconciled with the need for the indefinite to function as the aboutness topic in the following way: first, the indefinite is applied to the dummy predicate λxλs. *in(x)(s)*, which turns it into a situation predicate – in the case of (45a), into the situation predicate λs. ∃x[*dog(x)* ∧ *in(x)(s)*]. Second, quantificational adverbs are systematically ambiguous between a variant whose restrictor is given in the form of a free variable (see section 5) and one that combines with its arguments in reverse order (from the perspective of determiner quantification), i.e. with the nuclear scope first and then with the restrictor. Note that something like this second variant is needed anyway in order to allow for a compositional derivation in cases where a left-adjoined *when*- or *if*-clause is interpreted in the restrictor of the Q-adverb (cf. Chierchia 1995). Third, the resumptive pronoun, which occupies the specifier of the matrix-CP at the surface, can optionally be reconstructed into its clause-internal base position, where it no longer triggers lambda-abstraction, but rather is interpreted as a free variable. As a free variable, it can be bound dynamically (Groenendijk & Stokhof 1991) by the indefinite ending up in the restrictor of the quantificational adverb. Taking all this together, we arrive at the following result: in a first step, the left-dislocated indefinite is shifted to a situation predicate which can function as an address for storing the information provided by the rest of the sentence. In a second step, it is asserted that the result of applying the Q-adverb to the situation predicate denoted by the matrix clause (i.e. its nuclear scope) is applied to the situation predicate denoted by the left-dislocated indefinite. This is shown schematically for (45a) in (49):

(49) ∃α[α = λs. ∃x [dog(x) ∧ in (x)(s)] &
       ASSERT [λP.λs. Most s´ [s´≤ s ∧ P(s´)] [∃s´´[s´≤s´´ ∧ smart(x)(s´´)]](α)]] =
       ∃α[α = λs. ∃x [dog(x) ∧ in(x)(s)] &
       ASSERT [λs. Most s´ [s´≤ s ∧ α(s´)] [∃s´´[s´≤s´´ ∧ smart(x)(s´´)]]]]

The result of combining the Q-adverb with its nuclear scope can be seen as a higher order predicate that specifies the degree to which the nuclear scope applies to its logical subject (the restrictor), i.e. the degree to which the set denoted by the restrictor is included in the set denoted by the nuclear scope. In our example, it is asserted that most elements of the set of situations containing a dog x is included in the set of situations where x is smart. By enforcing the situations quantified over to be minimal in the sense of containing nothing beyond what is necessary to make them a situation satisfying the respective predicate (the minimality conditions have been suppressed for ease of exposition), we get the desired result: since the situations vary with the dogs they contain, the illusion of direct quantification over dogs is created (Berman 1987; von Fintel 1994; Herburger 2000).

Concerning the generic reading exemplified by (44b), Endriss & Hinterwimmer (2009) assume that it is nothing but a special case of the reading exemplified by (45a), where the overt quantificational adverb has been replaced by a covert generic operator with quasi-universal force (see Krifka et al. 1995 and the references cited therein for discussion).

The analysis just sketched can also be applied to sentences with left-dislocated temporal clauses and conditional antecedents (see Iatridou 1994 and Bhatt & Pancheva 2001 for an analysis of *if-then*-sentences as instances of left-dislocation), since the set of situations/the closest world (Stalnaker 1968 and Schlenker 2004) characterized by the respective clause can be viewed as the aboutness topic in such cases (see Haiman 1978 and Bittner 2001 for the general idea that conditionals are topics). Based on the idea that the establishment of (aboutness) topicality involves a separate speech act, Ebert, Endriss & Hinterwimmer (2009) argue that the difference in truth conditions between regular conditionals such as (50a) and relevance conditionals such as (50b) can be phrased in terms of the difference between two kinds of aboutness topicality: the one discussed in this section, which in German is marked via GLD, and the one exemplified by the so-called *hanging topic* in (50c):

(50) a. If you are thirsty, (*then) there is beer in the refrigerator.
 b. If Kim was at the party, (then) it was fun.
 c. As for the pastor, the marriage sermon was wonderful.

Ebert, Endriss & Hinterwimmer (2009) show that what both types of aboutness topicality have in common is the relation of relevance: the information provided by the comment is presented as relevant with respect to the topic, which corresponds to the storage of this information under the address created for the topic. Now, while in the case exemplified by GLD relevance is trivially ensured via the relation of predication, an appropriate relation has to be inferred on the basis of contextual information, world knowledge, etc. in the second case. This accounts for the observed truth conditional difference between (50a) and (50b): while (50b) is automatically understood as conveying that the party's having been fun depends on the presence of Kim, the beer's being in the refrigerator is not understood as depending on the addressee's being thirsty in the case of (50a). Rather, the sentence is understood as conveying that the information that there is beer in the refrigerator is only relevant for the hearer in case s/he is thirsty. In other words, an address is created for the closest world where the addressee is thirsty (which might, or might not be the actual world), and the information that there is beer in the refrigerator in the actual world is stored under this address. In the case of (50a), in contrast, the information that the party was fun in the closest world where Kim was present is stored under the address created for the closest world where Kim was present.

Summarizing the main results of this section, aboutness topicality can have truth conditional effects if the aboutness topic is an indefinite since two requirements have to be met that necessitate typeshifting: first, an object has to be created from the original denotation of the indefinite as a generalized quantifier that can serve as an address for storing the information provided by the rest of the sentence. Furthermore, the rest of the sentence has to function as a (first- or higher-order predicate) that applies to this object. This either leads to an interpretation that is equivalent to one where the indefinite receives widest scope or (in the case of adverbially quantified and generic sentences) to an interpretation that is equivalent to one where the indefinite is interpreted in the restrictor of the quantificational adverb/the covert generic operator. Furthermore, we have seen that the truth-conditional difference between regular conditionals and relevance conditionals can be traced back to the difference between two types of aboutness topicality only one of which involves predication, while the other involves an (under-specified) relation of relevance. In the next section, I will deal with truth conditional effects of contrastive topicality. Concerning frame setting topics, we have already seen in section 3 that the alleged truth conditional effects does not have anything to do with the marking of the respective constituents as topics, since leaving them in sentence-internal position results in exactly the same truth conditions.

6.2 Contrastive topicality

In section 3, we saw that the restrictions that keep quantificational DPs other than indefinites headed by unmodified determiners from functioning as aboutness topics do not apply to contrastive topics. It is therefore not surprising that we find no evidence for the typeshifting operations discussed in the last section in sentences where quantificational DPs are marked as contrastive topics – they do not have to take widest scope in the presence of other quantificational DPs, and neither do they have to be interpreted in the restrictor of overt or covert quantificational adverbs. Nevertheless, there is evidence that contrastive topic marking has an influence on the interpretation of quantificational DPs. It has been observed that the rise-fall contour indicating contrastive topicality makes available scope-inversion in configurations where it would normally (i.e. without this contour) be excluded in German (Jacobs 1982, 1983, 1984; Höhle 1992; Büring 1997a, b; Krifka 1998), as evidenced by the examples in (51) (from Krifka 1998: 80, ex. (16a, b))

(51) a. /JEder   Student hat mindestens EINen\ Roman gelesen. ∃ (∀),∀ (∃)
        every-NOM student has at-least   one-ACC   novel read
     b. Mindestens /EIN   Student hat jEden\   Roman gelesen. ∃ (∀),∀ (∃)
        at-least   one-NOM student has   every-ACC novel read

As indicated, both sentences are ambiguous: (51b), for example, may either be true if there is one student that read every book, or if every book was read by, at least a student, where the students may vary with the books. This is exceptional for German, where the word order is freer than in English, and where accordingly only sentences where the canonical word order has been altered are scope-ambiguous. Frey (1993) accounts for this fact by assuming that in German (and other languages with relatively free word order such as Hungarian) an operator α may only be interpreted with scope over an operator β if α either c-commands β or a trace of β. Now, in (51a, b) the subject c-commands the object on the surface, which is the canonical word order. There should thus be no reading where the object has wider scope, contrary to fact. Krifka (1998) now assumes that the additional scope options brought into play by contrastive topic marking of the higher operator result from complex derivations involving several invisible movement operations. Consequently, the higher operator leaves behind traces that are c-commanded by the surface position of the lower operator, which allows the latter to take scope over the former, in accordance with Frey's assumptions. Let us have a closer look at the derivation Krifka assumes for (52b) (Krifka 1998: 11). The crucial steps are given in (52): first, after the finite auxiliary verb has moved to C^0 (as shown in (52b)), the direct object DP is scrambled across the subject DP (as shown in (52c)). Then, the subject DP receives focus marking in its derived verb adjacent position (as shown in (52d)) and is moved to the specifier of CP (as shown in (52e)). According to Krifka, the latter movement operation "has a specific discourse pragmatic function, contrastive topicalization" (Krifka 1998: 11). Finally, the object DP receives focus marking in its derived verb adjacent position (as shown in (52f)).

(52) a. [$_{CP}$ e [$_{C'}$ e [mindestens ein Student [jeden Roman [gelesen]] hat]]

   b. [$_{CP}$ e [$_{C'}$ hat$_1$ [mindestens ein Student [jeden Roman [gelesen]] t$_1$]]

   c. [$_{CP}$ e [$_{C'}$ hat$_1$ [jeden Roman$_2$ [mindestens ein Student [t$_2$ [gelesen]]] t$_1$]]

d. [$_{CP}$ e [$_{C'}$ hat$_1$ [jeden Roman$_2$ [[mindestens ein Student]$_F$ [t$_2$ [gelesen]]] t$_1$]]
e. [$_{CP}$ [mindestens ein Student]$_{F,3}$ [$_{C'}$ hat$_1$ [jeden Roman$_2$ [t$_3$ [t$_2$ [gelesen]]] t$_1$]]
f. [$_{CP}$ [mindestens ein Student]$_{F,3}$ [$_{C'}$ hat$_1$ [[jeden Roman]$_{2,F}$ [t$_3$ [t$_2$ [gelesen]]] t$_1$]]
g. [$_{CP}$ Mindestens/EIN   Student [$_{C'}$ hat [\JEden   Roman [gelesen]]]
   at least   one-NOM   student   has   every-ACC novel read

Now, the crucial movement operation is the one shown in (52c), which brings the object DP into a position from where it c-commands a trace left behind by the subject DP and thus allows it to take scope over the subject DP. According to Krifka, it is motivated as follows: first, as already mentioned in section 3, contrastive topicality is a combination of aboutness topicality and focus marking. Second, focus is preferably assigned to preverbal constituents in German. This forces the object DP to move across the subject DP, since otherwise the subject DP would not be in the right position for focus marking.

While we have seen that there are good reasons to doubt Krifka's assumption that contrastive topicality involves aboutness topicality, it is nevertheless reasonable to assume that it involves focus marking, since both contrastive topic marking and focus marking can fruitfully be analysed in terms of the introduction of alternatives, as we have seen above. Furthermore, Krifka (1998: 87–97) discusses a whole battery of empirical observations which support the assumption that focus is preferably assigned to constituents in preverbal position in German. His account of how contrastive topicality makes available scope options that otherwise would not exist in German is thus by and large well motivated, leaving only the "altruistic" scrambling of the object DP shown in (52c) as an assumption that is problematic from the point of view of the highly influential Minimalist Program inaugurated by Chomsky (1995), according to which all movement operations are feature-driven. Note, however, that the existence of scrambling is problematic for this view, anyway, since there does not seem to be any independent motivation for postulating a feature that all scrambled elements share and that needs to be checked. It is thus more promising to analyse scrambling as an option that is in principle freely available, but which is only employed if it has any payoffs at either of the interfaces (cf. Reinhart 2006), which is compatible with Krifka's account.

A related pattern, where contrastive topicality has an influence on the truth conditions of sentences containing scope taking elements, is discussed by Büring (1997b): as has been observed by Jacobs (1984) and Löbner (1990), the two sentences in (53) only have a reading according to which the lower operator takes scope over the higher one – i.e. (53a) can only be interpreted as saying that it is not the case that all politicians are corrupt, and (53b) as saying that the addressee does not have to smoke so much.

(53) a. /ALle   Politiker   sind   NICHT/   korrupt.
        All   politicians   are   not   corrupt
     b. Du   /MUSST   NICHT/   so   viel   rauchen
        you   must   not   so   much   smoke

Based on the theory of contrastive topicality proposed by Büring (1997a), Büring (1997b) offers a pragmatic account of this pattern. He starts from the assumption that the two sentences in (53) are structurally ambiguous at LF at latest, which is compatible with Frey's (1993) assumptions discussed above, since negation may in both cases have been base generated in a position where it c-commands the base position of the other operator. Now recall from section 3 that contrastive topic marking introduces a set of sets of propositions where both the denotation of the constituent marked as the contrastive topic and the one marked as the focus have been replaced by alternatives. If in the case of (53a), for example, the universally quantified DP is interpreted with scope above negation, we get the set shown in (54a), and if it is interpreted with scope beneath negation, we get the set in (54b):

(54) a. { {all(politicians)(λx. ¬corrupt(x)), all(politicians)(λx. corrupt(x))},
         {most(politicians)(λx. ¬corrupt(x)), most(politicians)(λx. corrupt(x))},
         {some(politicians)(λx. ¬corrupt(x)), some(politicians)(λx. corrupt(x))},
         {one(politician)(λx. ¬corrupt(x)), one(politicians)(λx. corrupt(x))},
         {no(politician)(λx. ¬corrupt(x)), no(politicians)(λx. corrupt(x))} }
     b. { {¬all(politicians)(λx. corrupt(x)), all(politicians)(λx. corrupt(x))},
         {¬most(politicians)(λx. corrupt(x)), most(politicians)(λx. corrupt(x))},
         {¬some(politicians)(λx. corrupt(x)), some(politicians)(λx. corrupt(x))},
         {¬one(politician)(λx. corrupt(x)), one(politicians)(λx. corrupt(x))},
         {¬no(politician)(λx. corrupt(x)), no(politicians)(λx. corrupt(x))} }

Now observe that there is a crucial contrast between the two sets. In the case of (54b), asserting the proposition corresponding to the first element of the first set only eliminates the second element of the first set as an option that is still open: while it cannot possibly be the case that all politicians are corrupt and that not all politicians are corrupt, we can neither conclude that it is the case that most politicians are corrupt nor that it is not the case that most politicians are corrupt from the fact that not all politicians are corrupt, and the same holds for all the other quantifiers listed above. In the case of (54a), in contrast, asserting the proposition corresponding to the first element of the first set automatically decides the question of which of the two elements in each set is true for all the other sets: as soon as we know that all politicians are not corrupt, we automatically know that most politicians are not corrupt, that some politicians are not corrupt and that it is not the case that no politician is not corrupt, i.e. that no politician is corrupt. As the reader can easily check for herself, the same reasoning applies to (53b). Büring (1997b) now assumes that contrastive topic marking is subject to the following pragmatic constraint: after a sentence *A* has been uttered, there must at least be one disputable element in the set corresponding to the topic semantic value of *A*, where a set of propositions *P* is disputable with respect to the common ground if it contains at least one element *p* such that both *p* and ¬*p* could informatively and coherently be added to the common ground. Since in the case of (53a) as well as (53b) the reading where the higher operator has scope above negation violates this constraint, it is correctly predicted that only the reading where negation takes higher scope is available.

This account is very attractive insofar as it comes at practically no cost at all: apart from the independently well-supported assumption that contrastive topic marking introduces a set of sets of alternative propositions, Büring only needs the disputability constraint. This constraint is extremely natural, however, since it simply formalizes the idea that there has to be a point in introducing such a complex semantic object as the topic semantic value of a sentence: if the truth value of all alternatives to the ordinary semantic value of the respective sentence is already decided on via entailments of the ordinary semantic value, there simply is no point in introducing these alternatives in the first place. Note, however, that in spite of its attractiveness Büring's account can not replace the one of Krifka (1998), since it only works for a limited set of data. We thus need both to account for the full range of facts.

In this section we have seen that while contrastive topic marking can have an influence on the truth conditions of sentences containing multiple scope taking elements, these effects do not show that truth conditional semantics is directly sensitive to contrastive topicality. Rather, they can naturally be explained as indirect effects of either formal requirements that contrastive topic marking is subject to, or of a pragmatic principle that requires the introduction of the topic semantic value of a sentence to fulfil some communicative purpose. In the next section we will briefly discuss the question of whether there is any interaction between givenness marking and truth conditional semantics.

7 Givenness and truth conditions

In section 3 we have seen that there are good reasons to reject the idea that adverbial quantifiers like *always* and quantificational determiners like *most*, *many* and *few* are directly focus sensitive. Rather, the observed effects can be better explained by assuming that all of these operators introduce a free variable as part of their denotation which needs to be resolved on the basis of contextually available information. Focus marking, which allows the reconstruction of implicit questions under discussion, is important in the task of finding suitable values for these variables insofar as it often gives a clue as to which part of the respective sentence counts as contextually available information. This does not show, however, that the operators which have been analysed as focus sensitive should be analysed as directly sensitive to givenness instead, since there is no reason to assume a grammaticalized dependency on constituents marked as given (by phonological, morphological, or syntactic means), as shown by the fact that in some instances (such as example (35) discussed in section 5) even focal material can be interpreted in the restrictor of an adverbial quantifier.

Apart from the operators just mentioned there is a whole class of expressions which depend on (directly or indirectly) given information insofar as they only yield a defined value if the context in which they are uttered satisfies certain conditions: namely all so-called presupposition triggers such as the definite article, factive verbs like *realize* and *regret*, implicative verbs like *manage* etc. (see article 14 [Semantics: Interfaces] (Beaver & Geurts) *Presupposition* for discussion). However, in these cases, too, there is no grammaticalized sensitivity to constituents that are explicitly marked as given: it does not matter whether the required information is given explicitly or implicitly in the discourse, is part of the shared background knowledge of the discourse participants, or can be accommodated. There is thus no evidence for a direct influence of givenness marking on the truth conditions of sentences.

8 Conclusion

In this paper I have discussed the relation between information structure and truth-conditional semantics, concentrating on the question of whether there is any direct interaction between the various information structural dimensions and operators such as quantified DPs and quantificational adverbs. Concerning the focus-background dimension, we have seen that in most cases truth-conditional effects do not result from direct focus sensitivity of the involved operators, but rather come about as indirect effects of the need to resolve a free variable that is present in the denotation of these operators on the basis of contextual information – with the notable exception of exclusives such as *only* (cf. Beaver & Clark 2008).

Concerning the topic-comment dimension, I have argued that in cases where a quantificational DP functions as the aboutness topic of a sentence, the need to interpret the comment as a predicate that can be applied to the topic has truth-conditional effects in the presence of either another quantificational DP, a quantificational adverb or generic tense (Endriss & Hinterwimmer 2009). In cases where a quantificational DP is marked as a contrastive topic, on the other hand, truth conditional effects come about indirectly – either because the alternatives thus introduced could not be put to use otherwise (Büring 1997b), or because contrastive topic marking results in a more complicated syntactic derivation that opens up additional scope possibilities (Krifka 1998).

Finally, concerning the given-new dimension, there is no evidence for a direct influence on the truth conditions of sentences, but only for indirect effects that come about in basically the same way as the above mentioned indirect effects of focus marking.

9 References

Altmann, Hans 1981. *Formen der „Herausstellung" im Deutschen: Rechtsversetzung, Linksversetzung, Freies Thema und verwandte Konstruktionen*. Tübingen: Niemeyer.
Atlas, Jay & Stephen Levinson 1981. It-clefts, informativeness, and Logical Form: Radical pragmatics (Revised standard version). In: P. Cole (ed.). *Radical Pragmatics*. New York: Academic Press, 1–61.
Barwise, Jon & Robin Cooper 1981. Generalized quantifiers and natural language. *Linguistics & Philosophy* 4,159–219.
Beaver, David & Brady Clark 2003. *Always* and *only*: Why not all focus sensitive operators are equal. *Natural Language Semantics* 11, 323–362.
Beaver, David & Brady Clark 2008. *Sense and Sensitivity*. Oxford: Blackwell.
Berman, Stephen 1987. Situation-based semantics for adverbs of quantification. In: J. Blevins & A. Vainikka (eds.). *Studies in Semantics* (University of Massachusetts Occasional Papers 12). Amherst, MA: GLSA, University of Massachusetts, 46–68.
Bhatt, Rajesh & Roumyana Pancheva 2001. The Syntax of Conditionals. Ms. Austin, TX/Los Angeles, CA, University of Texas / University of Southern California.
Bittner, Maria 2001. Topical referents for individuals and possibilities. In: R. Hastings et al. (eds). *Proceedings of Semantics and Linguistic Theory (=SALT) XI*. Ithaca, NY: Cornell University, 36–55.
Büring, Daniel 1996. A Weak Theory of Strong Readings. In: T. Galloway & J. Spence (eds.). *Proceedings of Semantics and Linguistic Theory (=SALT) VI*. Ithaca, NY: Cornell University, 17–34.
Büring, Daniel 1997a. *The Meaning of Topic and Focus – The 59th Street Bridge Accent*. London: Routledge.
Büring, Daniel 1997b. The great scope inversion conspiracy. *Linguistics & Philosophy* 20, 175–194.
Büring, Daniel 1999. Topic. In: P. Bosch & R. van der Sandt (eds.). *Focus – Linguistic, Cognitive, and Computational Perspectives*. Cambridge: Cambridge University Press, 142–165.
Büring, Daniel 2001. What do definites do that indefinites definitely don't? In: C. Féry & W. Sternefeld (eds.). *Audiatur Vox Sapentiae – A Festschrift for Arnim von Stechow*. Berlin: Akademie Verlag, 70–100.

Büring, Daniel 2003. On D-trees, beans, and B-accents. *Linguistics & Philosophy* 26, 511–545.
Chafe, Wallace 1976. Givenness, contrastiveness, definiteness, subjects, topics, and point of view. In: C.Li (ed.). *Subject and Topic*. New York: Academic Press, 25–55.
Chierchia, Gennaro 1995. *The Dynamics of Meaning: Anaphora, Presupposition, and the Theory of Grammar*. Chicago, IL: The University of Chicago Press.
Chomsky, Noam 1995. *The Minimalist Program*. Cambridge, MA: The MIT Press.
Cohen, Ariel 2001. Relative readings of *many*, *often*, and generics. *Natural Language Semantics* 9, 41–67.
Cohen, Ariel & Nomi Erteschik-Shir 2002. Topic, focus, and the interpretation of bare plurals. *Natural Language Semantics* 10, 125–165.
Dretske, Fred 1972. Contrastive statements. *Philosophical Review* 81, 411–437.
Ebert, Christian, Cornelia Endriss & Stefan Hinterwimmer 2009. A unified analysis of indicative and biscuit conditionals as topics. In: T. Friedman & S. Ito (eds.). *Proceedings of Semantics and Linguistic Theory (=SALT) XVIII*. Ithaca, NY: Cornell University, 266–283.
Eckardt, Regine 1999. Focus with nominal quantifiers. In: P. Bosch & R. van der Sandt (eds.). *Focus – Linguistic, Cognitive, and Computational Perspectives*. Cambridge: Cambridge University Press, 166–186.
Endriss, Cornelia 2009. *Quantificational Topics – A Scopal Treatment of Exceptional Wide Scope Phenomena*. Berlin: Springer.
Endriss, Cornelia & Stefan Hinterwimmer 2009. Indefinites as direct and indirect aboutness topics. In: C. Féry & M. Zimmermann (eds.). *Information Structure*. Oxford: Oxford University Press, 89–115.
Féry, Caroline & Vieri Samek-Lodovici 2006. Focus projection and prosodic prominence in nested foci. *Language* 82, 131–150.
von Fintel, Kai 1994. *Restrictions on Quantifier Domains*. Ph.D. dissertation. University of Massachusetts, Amherst, MA.
Fodor, Janet & Ivan Sag 1982. Referential and quantificational indefinites. *Linguistics & Philosophy* 5, 355–398.
Frey, Werner 1993. *Syntaktische Bedingungen für die semantische Interpretation*. Berlin: Akademie Verlag.
Frey, Werner 2000. Über die syntaktische Position der Satztopiks im Deutschen. In: K. Schwabe (ed.). *Issues on Topics*. Berlin: Zentrum für Allgemeine Sprachwissenschaft, 137–172.
Frey, Werner 2004. Notes on the syntax and the pragmatics of German left dislocation. In: H. Lohnstein & S. Trissler (eds.). *The Syntax and Semantics of the Left Periphery*. Berlin: Mouton de Gruyter, 203–233.
von der Gabelentz, Georg 1869. Ideen zu einer vergleichenden Syntax. Wort und Satzstellung. *Zeitschrift für Völkerpsychologie und Sprachwissenschaft* 6, 376–384.
Geurts, Bart & Rob van der Sandt 1997. Presuppositions and backgrounds. In: P. Dekker, M. Stokhof & Y. Venema (eds.). *Proceedings of the 11th Amsterdam Colloquium*. Amsterdam: ILLC, 37–42.
Geurts, Bart & Rob van der Sandt 2004. Interpreting focus. *Theoretical Linguistics* 30, 1–44.
Groenendijk, Jeroen & Martin Stokhof 1991. Dynamic predicate logic. *Linguistics & Philosophy* 14, 39–100.
Gundel, Jeannette 1988. Universals of topic-comment structure. In: M. Hammond & E. Moravcsik (eds.). *Studies in Syntactic Typology*. Amsterdam: Benjamins, 209–239.
Haiman, John 1978. Conditionals are topics. *Language* 54, 564–589.

Halliday, Michael A. K. 1967. Notes on transitivity and theme in English, part 2. *Journal of Linguistics* 2, 177–274.
Hamblin, Charles 1973. Questions in Montague English. *Foundations of Language* 10, 41–53.
Heim, Irene 1982. *The Semantics of Definite and Indefinite Noun Phrases*. Ph.D. dissertation. University of Massachusetts, Amherst, MA. Reprinted: Ann Arbor, MI: University Microfilms.
Heim, Irene & Angelika Kratzer 1998. *Semantics in Generative Grammar*. Oxford: Blackwell.
Herburger, Elena 1992. Focus and the LF of NP quantification. In: U. Lahiri & A. Wyner (eds.). *Proceedings of Semantics and Linguistic Theory (=SALT) III*. Ithaca, NY: Cornell University, 77–96.
Herburger, Elena 1997. Focus and weak noun phrases. *Natural Language Semantics* 5, 53–78.
Herburger, Elena 2000. *What Counts: Focus and Quantification*. Cambridge, MA: The MIT Press.
Hockett, Charles 1958. *A Course in Modern Linguistics*. New York: Macmillan.
Höhle, Tilman 1992. Über Verum-Fokus im Deutschen. In: J. Jacobs (ed.). *Informationsstruktur und Grammatik*. Opladen: Westdeutscher Verlag, 112–141.
Horn, Laurence R. 1981. Exhaustiveness and the semantics of clefts. In: V. Burke & J. Pustejovsky (eds.). *Proceedings of the North Eastern Linguistic Society (=NELS)* 11. Amherst, MA: GLSA, 125–142.
Iatridou, Sabine 1994. On the meaning of conditional *then*. *Natural Language Semantics* 2, 171–199.
Jackendoff, Ray 1972. *Semantic Interpretation in Generative Grammar*. Cambridge, MA: The MIT Press.
Jacobs, Joachim 1982. Neutraler und nicht-neutraler Satzakzent im Deutschen. In: T. Vennemann (ed.). *Silben, Segmente, Akzente. Referate zur Wort-, Satz- und Versphonologie anläßlich der vierten Jahrestagung der DGfS, Köln, 2. – 4. März 1982*. Tübingen: Niemeyer, 141–169.
Jacobs, Joachim 1983. *Fokus und Skalen. Zur Syntax und Semantik der Gradpartikeln im Deutschen*. Tübingen: Niemeyer.
Jacobs, Joachim 1984. Funktionale Satzperspektive und Illokutionssemantik. *Linguistische Berichte* 91, 25–58.
Jacobs, Joachim 1997. I-Topikalisierung. *Linguistische Berichte* 168, 91–133.
Jacobs, Joachim 2001. The dimensions of topic-comment. *Linguistics* 39, 641–681.
Kenesei, István 1986. On the logic of word order in Hungarian. In: W. Abraham & S. de Mey (eds.). *Topic, Focus and Configurationality*. Amsterdam: Benjamins, 143–159.
Krifka, Manfred 1990. Four thousand ships passed through the lock: Object-induced measure functions on events. *Linguistics & Philosophy* 13, 487–520.
Krifka, Manfred 1992. A framework for focus-sensitive quantification. In: C. Barker & D. Dowty (eds.). *Proceedings of Semantics and Linguistic Theory (=SALT) II*. Ithaca, NY: Cornell University, 215–236.
Krifka, Manfred 1998. Scope inversion under the rise-fall pattern in German. *Linguistic Inquiry* 29, 75–112.
Krifka, Manfred 2008. Basic notions of information structure. *Acta Linguistica Hungarica* 55, 243–276.
Krifka, Manfred, Francis J. Pelletier, Gregory N. Carlson, Gennaro Chierchia, Godehard Link & Alice ter Meulen 1995. Introduction to genericity. In: G. Carlson (ed.). *The Generic Book*. Chicago, IL: The University of Chicago Press, 1–124.

Kuno, Susumu 1972. Functional sentence perspective: A case study from Japanese and English. *Linguistic Inquiry* 3, 269–336.
van Kuppevelt, Jan 1995. Discourse structure, topicality and questioning. *Journal of Linguistics* 31, 109–147.
Lambrecht, Knud 1994. *Information Structure and Sentence Form*. Cambridge: Cambridge University Press.
Link, Godehard 1983. The logical analysis of plurals and mass terms. In: R. Bäuerle, Ch. Schwarze & A. von Stechow (eds.). *Meaning, Use and the Interpretation of Language*. Berlin: de Gruyter, 303–323.
Löbner, Sebastian 1990. *Wahr neben Falsch. Duale Operatoren als die Quantoren natürlicher Sprache*. Tübingen: Niemeyer.
Martí, Luisa 2003. *Contextual Variables*. Ph.D. dissertation. University of Connecticut, Storrs, CT.
May, Robert 1985. *Logical Form: Its Structure and Derivation*. Cambridge, MA: The MIT Press.
Molnár, Valéria 1993. Zur Pragmatik und Grammatik des Topik-Begriffes. In: M. Reis (ed.). *Wortstellung und Informationsstruktur*. Tübingen: Niemeyer, 155–202.
Partee, Barbara 1991. Topic, focus and quantification. In: S. Moore & A. Wyner (eds.). *Proceedings of Semantics and Linguistic Theory (=SALT) I*. Ithaca, NY: Cornell University, 257–280.
Partee, Barbara 1999. Focus, quantification, and semantics-pragmatics issues. In: P. Bosch & R. van der Sandt (eds.). *Focus – Linguistic, Cognitive, and Computational Perspectives*. Cambridge: Cambridge University Press, 213–231.
Paul, Hermann 1880. *Prinzipien der Sprachgeschichte*. Halle: Niemeyer.
Portner, Paul & Katsuko Yabushita 1998. The semantics and pragmatics of topic phrases. *Linguistics & Philosophy* 21, 117–157.
Reinhart, Tanya 1981. *Pragmatics and Linguistics: An Analysis of Sentence Topics*. Bloomington, IN: Indiana University.
Reinhart, Tanya 2006. *Interface Strategies: Optimal and Costly Computations*. Cambridge, MA: The MIT Press.
Roberts, Craige 1996. Information structure in discourse: Towards an integrated formal theory of pragmatics. In: J.-H. Yoon & A. Kathol (eds.). *Papers in Semantics* (OSU Working Papers in Linguistics 4). Columbus, OH: Ohio State University, 91–136.
Rooth, Mats 1985. *Association with Focus*. Ph.D. dissertation. University of Massachusetts, Amherst, MA.
Rooth, Mats 1992. A theory of focus interpretation. *Natural Language Semantics* 1, 75–116.
Sauerland, Uli 2004. Scalar implicatures in complex sentences. *Linguistics & Philosophy* 27, 367–391.
Schlenker, Philippe 2004. Conditionals as definite descriptions. A referential analysis. *Research on Language and Computation* 2, 417–462.
Schwarzschild, Roger 1997. *Why Some Foci Must Associate*. Ms. New Brunswick, NJ, Rutgers University.
Schwarzschild, Roger 1999. GIVENness, AvoidF and other constraints on the placement of accent. *Natural Language Semantics* 7, 141–177.
Searle, John 1969. *Speech Acts: An Essay in the Philosophy of Language*. Cambridge: Cambridge University Press.
Selkirk, Elisabeth O. 1984. *Phonology and Syntax: The Relation between Sound and Structure*. Cambridge, MA: The MIT Press.

Stalnaker, Robert 1968. A theory of conditionals. In: W. Harper, R. Stalnaker & G. Pearce (eds.). *Ifs*. Dordrecht: Reidel, 41–55.

Stalnaker, Robert 1974. Pragmatic presuppositions. *Journal of Philosophical Logic* 2, 447–457.

Stalnaker, Robert 1978. Assertion. In: P. Cole (ed.). *Syntax and Semantics 9: Pragmatics*. New York: Academic Press, 315–332.

Stanley, Jason 2000. Context and Logical Form. *Linguistics & Philosophy* 23, 391–434.

von Stechow, Arnim 1989. *Focusing and Backgrounding Operators* (Arbeitspapiere des Fachbereichs Sprachwissenschaft, Nr. 6). Konstanz: University of Konstanz.

Strawson, Peter 1964. Intention and convention in speech acts. *The Philosophical Review* 73, 439–460.

Szabolcsi, Anna 1981. The semantics of topic-focus-articulation. In: J. Groenendijk, T. Janssen & M. Stokhof (eds.). *Formal Methods in the Study of Language*. Amsterdam: Mathematical Centre, 513–541.

Szabolcsi, Anna 1997. Strategies for scope taking. In: A. Szabolcsi (ed.). *Ways of Scope Taking*. Dordrecht: Kluwer, 109–116.

Vallduví, Enric 1992. *The Informational Component*. New York: Garland.

Wagner, Michael 2006. Givenness and locality. In: M. Gibson & J. Howell (eds.). *Proceedings of Semantics and Linguistic Theory (=SALT) XVI*. Ithaca, NY: Cornell University, 295–312.

Wedgwood, Daniel 2007. Identifying inferences in focus. In: K. Schwabe & S. Winkler (eds.). *On Information Structure, Meaning and Form*. Amsterdam: Benjamins, 207–227.

Westerståhl, Dag 1985. Logical constants in quantifier languages. *Linguistics & Philosophy* 8, 387–413.

Craige Roberts
11 Topics

1   Two notions of topic in discourse —— 381
2   Proposed tests for Topicality —— 390
3   Topic-marking across languages —— 392
4   The universality of Topicality —— 405
5   References —— 409

Abstract: The term Topic is used for at least two different notions in the linguistic literature. Distinctions are proposed to help resolve the resulting terminological confusion. Several tests for Topicality from the earlier literature are considered, and it is demonstrated that they themselves probe for distinct, though closely related, functions in discourse. Based on the proposed tests, it is argued that though Topicality is reflected across a wide variety of the world's languages, it is realized rather differently from language to language, presumably in part as a function of the languages' inherent syntactic and semantic resources. The resulting picture argues for more careful methodology in selecting and analyzing the data on which theories of the role of Topicality in natural language are developed, with implications for syntax, semantics and pragmatics.

1 Two notions of topic in discourse

Quite often in making an utterance, a speaker in some way brings our attention to an entity that is relevant at that point in the discussion, in order to tell us something about it. The relevant entity may be an individual or it may be a situation or event. In any such case, we say that the entity to which our attention is drawn is the *Topic* of the utterance. Let us say that the constituent of the utterance which denotes or otherwise indicates the Topic is thereby *Topical*. Depending on the language in use, a Topical constituent may be an N(oun) P(hrase) or an adverbial element of some sort; a Yiddish Topic may even be indicated by preposing a verb stem, per Davis & Prince (1986). The adverbial PP *in any such case* in the third sentence of this paragraph is an interesting case in point. If the PP were removed from the sentence altogether, the passage would be a bit choppy: The first sentence is about circumstances where speakers bring their

Craige Roberts, Columbus, OH, USA

https://doi.org/10.1515/9783110589863-011

addressees' attention to such an entity as a prelude to telling us something about it. The second sentence enumerates a class of entities in the world – individuals, situations, events, etc. – which are typically attended to in those circumstances, while the third sentence is again about the circumstances themselves, discussing an arbitrary instance. The PP facilitates a shift in Topic, from the class of entities to the circumstances in which one of them is attended to. The PP could remain *in situ* in the matrix: *We say that the entity to which our attention is first drawn in any such case is the Topic*, but placing it utterance-initially arguably facilitates the smoothest transition from one utterance to the next: Recognizing what the entities are that the speaker is going to tell us about makes it clear how the new utterance is relevant to what comes before, and hence it is easier to readily grasp how the proposition uttered fits into the structure of the speaker's argument. If we take such smooth transitions to be a feature of a maximally cohesive text, then they are motivated by how they foster optimal comprehension.

A typical dictionary definition for *Topic* cites two rather different notions: that of the subject-matter of a discussion, and that of the subject of a text (e.g., of a sentence uttered). This is reflected in two uses of the term in the linguistic literature, which, albeit closely related, are different in important respects, leading to some confusion and conflation of the two notions. As Erdmann (1990) puts it, "The literature on *topic* (/*comment*) suffers from the confusion of grammatical ('the first constituent in the sentence') with narrative ('what a text is about') features." I will say something brief about each of these notions, and about how they might be related, then focus on the utterance/"sentence"-specific notion, the one illustrated and discussed in the first paragraph of this essay. In what follows, I take it that an utterance is the ordered pair of the sentence or other linguistic expression uttered (under a linguistic analysis) and the context in which it is uttered (Bar-Hillel 1971). The linguistic phenomena motivating theories of dynamic interpretation might be taken to argue that this characterization is not adequate, since context can change utterance-internal, but it will suffice for present purposes, especially as Topical constituents in the sense to be considered here typically are root phenomena, i.e. observed only in matrix sentences, at least in English.

With respect to what a discourse ("text", "narrative") is about, much recent work on formal pragmatics, drawing on older work by members of the Prague School and by Halliday and his colleagues, is based on the hypothesis that a central organizing factor in discourse is the *discourse topic*, also called the *issue* or *question under discussion*, or the *Theme* (Halliday 1985). (Note that this is *not* what the Prague School calls *Theme*, discussed below.) *Inter alia*, the topic in this sense is said to play an important role in determining the *prosodic focus* of an utterance (that portion of the utterance which is prosodically most prominent, in English marked by tonic stress) and in constraining the resolution of presuppositions, including those involved in discourse anaphora, domain restriction and ellipsis; in generating conversational implicatures; and in determining the speech act expressed in a given context. For more about the subject-matter of a discussion, see Ginzburg (1996, 2012), Roberts (1996, 2004), and article 10 [this volume] (Hinterwimmer) *Information structure*. In order to prevent confusion with the other sense of *Topic* in use in linguistics, I will refer to the discourse topic as the *Question Under Discussion (QUD)*.

The term *Theme* is similarly ambiguous, referring both to the discourse topic/QUD (whatever the discourse is about) and to that portion of a sentence which is congruent with the QUD in the context of utterance. I'll use the term *Theme* in the latter sense: the constituent or constituents of the uttered sentence which are congruent with the QUD in the context of utterance. In Halliday's (1985) terminology, the Theme is complementary to the *Rheme*, the portion of the sentence which correlates intuitively with the answer to the question being addressed. Those who use the term *Topic* for what I'm calling *Theme* generally use the term *Comment* instead of *Rheme*, as in the Erdmann quote above. But because of the ambiguity in the term *Topic*, there is also marked confusion about the meaning of *Comment*, so that it's sometimes taken to be the *Rheme*, in the sense defined just above, and others to be the complement of the Topical constituent. I'll avoid the term here, in the interest of clarity, but one could use it in a way consistent with the terminology I'm using to mean the complement of the Topic of an utterance, if any.

The Theme/Rheme distinction is illustrated by the following:

(1) Who saw the tornado?
 [Mary]$_{Rheme}$ [saw the tornado]$_{Theme}$

Here *Mary* corresponds to *who* in the preceding question, the QUD in this little discourse. The Theme in the answer is congruent to the QUD in that abstracting on the *wh*-word in the question yields the property 'seeing the tornado', which is the denotation of the Theme, as well. Note that a Theme need not be Topical; arguably, *saw the tornado* in (1) is not a Topical constituent in the intuitive sense discussed above – the speaker does not draw the addressee's attention to the denotation of the VP, then tell her something about it. Note also that (in English at least) a Rheme is prosodically focused: In (1) *Mary* would typically bear the nuclear accent in the utterance, with no accent on any words in the Theme. Hence, the Theme in the sense of interest here is often called the Ground of Focus, taken to be complementary to the Focus of the utterance. But this terminology is misleading because sometimes constituents in the Theme can be prosodically focused as well – Halliday's *rhematic themes*, as will be illustrated below. Theme/Rheme here is purely a functional characterization of a partitioning over the sentence uttered, relative to the QUD. E.g., it is not necessarily reflected in (any level of) the syntactic structure of the sentence uttered.

The other notion of *Topic* is embodied by a sentential constituent that plays the special pragmatic role in the discourse context sketched informally in the first paragraph, in some sense indicating what the sentence uttered is about. A Topical constituent seems to be more or less what Prague School authors mean by the *Theme* of a sentence. And this is quite close to Vallduví's (1992, 1993) notion of a *Link*, which he takes to be a constituent that indicates where the information conveyed by the sentence should be entered in the hearer's knowledge store. I'll use the adjective *Topical* to characterize a constituent with something like this special pragmatic role, thereby differentiating a Topical constituent from the Topic it introduces, and use *Topicality* to refer to the discourse functional role(s) associated with a Topic. Note that, as in the example discussed in the first paragraph, a Topical constituent sometimes does not directly denote the Topic: *in any such case* restricts the domain of circumstances to which the generic verb phrase *say that...* applies to those which are Topical; it involves quantification over those cases and a quasi-locative preposition *in*; thus it is the domain of the quantifier *any* which is the Topic here, not the whole Topical PP (see Portner & Yabushita 1998 for examples in Japanese).

In what follows, the terms *Topic* and *Topical(ity)* will consistently be used in these senses, and it should be understood that what I am attributing to other authors is not this terminology (since that is used quite differently from author to author), but ideas about the underlying notions.

Ward (1985) speculated that Topics correspond to the Backward Looking Centers (CB) of Centering Theory (Joshi & Weinstein 1981, Grosz, Joshi & Weinstein 1983, 1995, Walker, Joshi & Prince 1998), which attempts to explain what constitutes a felicitous transition between utterances, focusing on structurally or grammatically based prominence rankings of the NPs in the utterances in question. Vallduví (1992) hypothesized a similar correspondence for those Links expressed by NPs, and the Topic/CB correspondence has subsequently been assumed by Gundel (1998) and Beaver (2004), among others. But Poesio, Stevenson, di Eugenio & Hitzeman (2004), considering a variety of realizations of Centering Theory, argue that the identification of Topics with CBs is not strongly supported by the corpus data. And Gordon, Grosz & Gillion (1993) do not find experimental evidence for the claims of Centering Theory about preferences for certain types of transitions between utterances in discourse. This is not surprising if we take the core function of Topicality to be indicating what an utterance is intuitively about, since the most prominent Centering algorithms do not attempt to assess aboutness, tending to use features of the structure of the sentence uttered which can be automatically retrieved, without reflection on meaning. Hence, with CB as usually defined, the correspondence between Topic and CB seems questionable.

Topic is often confused with the grammatical notion of Theme illustrated in (1), the notion sometimes called the *Ground of Focus*. This conflation is fairly natural, since the Theme, corresponding to the QUD being addressed, is old information in one sense, the Topic is often old information in some sense (see below), and both are under discussion. In fact, von Fintel (1996) argued that the two notions of *Topic*, what I'm calling *QUD* and *Topic*, are one and the same, and captured the sense in which they are both (typically) old information by making them anaphoric. But Vallduví (1993) and Portner & Yabushita (1998) have argued against the conflation of the Topical constituent with the Theme, for a wide range of languages. Vallduví gives examples similar to the following, with the Topical constituent here (and below) marked with italics:

(2) a. What about Mary? What did she give to Harry?
 Mary gave [a shirt]$_{Rheme}$ to Harry.
 b. What about Harry? What did Mary give to him?
 To Harry Mary gave [a shirt]$_{Rheme}$.

In (2a) and (2b) we have the same Rheme, expressed by *a shirt*, and hence the same Theme, the remainder of the sentence: *Mary gave...to Harry* (in some order). (Note that Vallduví did not use the term *Rheme* in his original examples (2) and (6) below, but marked the NP *a shirt* (in (2)) or the VP (in (6b)) as Focus.) But there are distinct Topics, the denotations of *Mary* in (2a) and *Harry* in (2b). In both, the Rhematic portion of the answer is denoted by the constituent with the same grammatical role as that of *what* in the immediately preceding question (the QUD) *What did Mary/she give to Harry?* Hence, the Topical constituents are only a proper sub-part of the Theme. This argues against the conflation of QUD and Topic proposed by von Fintel (1996); see Portner & Yabushita (1998) for other arguments, especially as applied to the Japanese case.

Here is another thing Topics and Themes have in common: Both may be entirely absent from a given utterance. Poesio et al. (2004) found that the majority of the utterances in their corpus lacked a Backward Looking Center, providing empirical support for this contention. When the utterance has maximally broad focus, for example in response to a question like *What's happening?*, then it is all-Rheme. Similarly, when the rhetorical point of an utterance is not to tell us about a particular entity but to simply note a fact or noteworthy event, there is no Topical constituent. Kuroda (1972, 1992) distinguishes between cases where there is a Topic (and a Topical constituent) and those where there is none via the distinction between *Categorical* and *Thetic* judgments, drawing on the earlier work of Brentano (1874/1924). Ladusaw (1994) illustrates Kuroda's distinction with Japanese examples like the following (my proposed translations). Note that the Japanese nominal particles *ga* and *wa*, to be discussed further below, play a crucial role in signaling the two kinds of judgments in these examples:

(3) Neko ga   asoko de nemutte iru.   (Thetic)
    a/the cat there   sleeping is
    'A/the cat is sleeping.'

(4) *Neko wa* asoko de nemutte iru.   (Categorical)
    the cat   there   sleeping is
    'As for the cat, it is sleeping.'

(5) *Neko wa*   inu ga   oikakete iru.   (Categorical)
    the cat   dog   chasing is
    'As for the cat, a/the dog is chasing it.' (Ladusaw 1994: 222)

Ladusaw continues:

> [The thetic judgment (3)] ... simply affirms the existence of an eventuality of a certain type. [The categorical judgment (4)] might be used to describe the same situation, but in an essentially different way...: [I]t draws attention first to the cat, and then says of the cat that it is sleeping there. Correlated with this difference is the fact that in [(4)], the bare noun marked by *wa* cannot be taken as a nonspecific indefinite cat; it must be a particular cat. This follows from the presuppositional nature of the subject of a categorical judgment.
> (Ladusaw 1994: 222)

Similarly, in the categorical (5) the addressee's attention is first drawn to the cat, here denoted by the direct object, and then the rest of the utterance tells us about one of its properties.

Here is something else to note about the Topic in examples like (2a) and (2b): The first, *what about X?* question implies a contrast between the mentioned entity X and the other members of some implicit set of relevant entities. The second question is, then, about that individual, implying that the comparison is to be made via the property queried in this question. The answer given by the indicative then continues to be about the same individual, contrasted there with the other members of the implicit set with respect to the answer to the second question, the QUD. The denotation of the topical constituent in such a contrastive context (and often, by extension, the constituent itself) is called a *Contrastive Topic*. (I take it this is also what Kuno & Takami 1993: 112 call a *Sorting Key*: "In a multiple *wh* question, the leftmost *wh*-word represents the key for sorting relevant pieces of information in the answer." It is also what Jackendoff 1972 calls an *independent focus*.)

Contrastive Topics are generally realized by prosodically focused constituents (in English and German, at least; Jackendoff 1972, Roberts 1996, Büring 1997, 2003, Rooth 2005). They typically carry a special type of prosodic contour, the so-called *B-accent* of Jackendoff (1972); in ToBI transcription (Beckman & Ayers 1994), this is the contour L+H* LH%. This illustrates why it would not be desirable in general to conflate the notion of Topic (a constituent) with that of the Focal Ground: It is not generally the case that a Topical constituent is in that portion of the uttered sentence which contains no prosodic focus. To underline this, Vallduví also gives minimal pairs similar to the following, with the same Contrastive Topical NP but two different Rhemes, both Focused constituents:

(6) a. What about Mary? What did she give to Harry?
    Mary gave [a shirt]$_{Rheme}$ to Harry.
  b. What about Mary? What did she do?
    Mary [gave a shirt to Harry]$_{Rheme}$.

In fact, even non-Contrastive Topics are quite often prosodically focused (in English, at least), particularly those which are displaced to occur utterance-initial; for example, a realization in speech of the adverbial *in any such case* in the third sentence of this article bears focal prosody, constituting an entire phonological phrase in the sense of Beckman (1996). Since each phonological phrase includes a pitch accent, hence a nuclear accent, each such phrase has a Focus (Selkirk 1996). The fact that the Rheme in examples like those in (2) and (6) may be a proper part of the complement of the Topical constituent reflects one of Prince's (1998) observations about English examples like (2b) (see also Ward 1985): that the non-Topical tonically stressed constituent in the utterance should be replaced with a variable, the result representing an "open proposition" which is "saliently and appropriately on the hearer's mind at that point in the discourse, the tonically stressed constituent representing the instantiation of the variable and the new information in the discourse". E.g., in (2a, b) or (6a) we replace the tonically stressed *a shirt* with x to yield the open proposition *Mary gave x to Harry*; this is congruent with the QUD *What did Mary give Harry?*, which, as QUD, is on the mind of any attentive participant in the discourse.

Hence, examples with Contrastive Topics, like those in (6), illustrate a relationship between the two notions of topic in certain contexts, one which has been argued for in detail by Büring (2003). In such contexts, an entire section of a discourse reflects a strategy of inquiry (Roberts 1996) wherein the speaker singles out first one, then another member of some relevant set of entities, considering in turn which relevant property each of these entities has. Consider (7):

(7) [after a trip to the zoo] What about the African animals? Who saw which animal?
  a. *The zebra,* [Mary]$_{Rheme}$ saw.
  b. *The elephant* was seen by [Harry]$_{Rheme}$
  c. and [Zach]$_{Rheme}$ saw *the giraffe.*

In (7a), *the zebra* is Contrastive Topic, marked both by the B-accent typical of Contrastive Topics and by Topicalization – the English construction wherein the Topical NP occurs sentence-initial, serving as the filler for a gap in the matrix clause, there in the direct object position following the verb. In (7b) the Contrastive Topic is *the elephant*, made utterance-initial by passivization and bearing B-accent. And in (7c) *the giraffe* is marked as Contrastive Topic by bearing B accent, even though it remains *in situ*. The speaker is effectively answering one sub-question of the explicit QUD at a time: *who saw the zebra?, who saw the elephant?, who saw the giraffe?*, one question for each (relevant) African animal. This illustrates how the overt question being replied to (*Who saw which animal?*) needn't be the QUD implicitly assumed by the speaker of an utterance, as reflected in the utterance's Theme. The possibility of an implicit QUD is even clearer in the following:

(8) (No prior discourse, at least on a related subject)
  A: [When are you going to China]$_F$?
  B: Well, I'm going to *China* in [April]$_{Rheme}$.   (Roberts 1996: 38)

Here, B answers A's question, with A-accent on the Rheme *April*, but also uses B-accent on *China* to mark it as a Contrastive Topic, presupposing that there is a larger set of relevant entities (countries) for which one might pose the question of when B is going to visit them, and implicitly inviting A to inquire about those as well.

As illustrated by (7c) and (8), though Topical constituents are often utterance-initial, they need not be, at least not in English. So the notion of a Topical constituent should not be confused with that of a Topicalized constituent: Topical constituents needn't be Topicalized, and, as we will see below, Topicalized constituents are not always Topical. This is cautionary: We must be careful not to take *one way Topicality may be encoded* to be the *unique* way it is encoded or even to always encode topicality. In studying the relationship between Topicality and Topic-marking in a given language, we must carefully control for function, in order to determine Topicality, and then determine what expressive options exist, and conversely, for any given construction, determine what functional roles for a particular sub-constituent are consistent with use of the construction across a range of possible contexts of utterance.

Table. 11.1 summarizes the terminology and distinctions proposed here.

Tab. 11.1: Notions of Topic in discourse

Notions of Topic:	Discourse Topic: QUD	Utterance Topic
Linguistic correlates:	**Interrogative sentence;** in indicative sentences reflected by the *Theme* (portion of sentence congruent with QUD). Cf. the complement of the Theme: the *Rheme*(s): the answer portion, correlated with the *wh-* element(s) in a preceding interrogative	***Topical constituent*** (NP, AdjP, PP, adverbial phrase or clause, etc., sometimes *in situ*)
comparison:	Topical constituents, including those which are Topicalized or Left Dislocated, may be proper sub-parts of the Theme of an utterance. The traditional Topic/Comment distinction consists of the Topical constituent and its complement in the sentence uttered; this does not coincide with the distinction between Theme and Rheme. Every utterance has a Rheme, but Themes and Topical constituents are optional. When there is a Topical constituent, the utterance is *Categorical;* otherwise, it is *Thetic*. I.e., **Theme ≠ Topical constituent**	
Possible conventional indication(s) in an utterance:	Theme is generally unmarked, while Rheme is marked, e.g. by prosodic status and/or word order	Topicalized constituent (English) Left Dislocated constituent (English) Passive subject (English) *wa-* marked constituent (Japanese) *nun* -marked constituent (Korean)
comparison:	Thematic-status is the *unmarked case*, whereas Topicality tends to be *marked*, so the indications noted for Themes tend to be indirect, and may be over-ridden by other factors. E.g., English Rhemes are always prosodically focused, with Themes often unaccented; but some sub-constituents of Themes may be focused as well, e.g. Contrastive Topics. And while the Theme of an utterance tends to stay *in situ*, Topical sub-constituents of the Theme quite often do not.	
Pragmatic function:	establishing or confirming the current discourse goal determines what's relevant	*Topicality:* directing addressee attention to some relevant discourse referent
comparison:	Questions have a special status in the organization of discourse (Information Structure), and hence Theme/Rheme structure is generally associated with the Focus structure of an utterance. But we may wish to direct our addressees' attention to other relevant entities as well – individuals, events, situations, etc. – and these entities are thereby Topical. When the purpose is to contrast the Topical entity with others in a relevant set, we have a *Contrastive Topic*.	

2 Proposed tests for Topicality

The *what about* questions in (2) and (6) illustrate one of the tests proposed in the literature for identifying Topical constituents in English, the *what about* test of Gundel (1974, 1985). A similar test is due to Reinhart (1981): the *say about X that S* test. Two others due to Gundel are the *as for* and *speaking of* tests. These tests and the differences between them are illustrated in the following examples (see Ward 1985, Chapter 2 for consideration of other proposed tests in the literature):

(9) Then Tom Cruise went to work for Francis Ford Coppola, on this spring's semi-successful film version of "The Outsiders". *Coppola* he found to be "just like one of the guys. And he totally trusted me. He let me go anywhere I wanted to go with the character..." (*Philadelphia Inquirer*, p. 8-C, 9/1/83, "His star is rising, but his feet remain firmly on the ground.", cited in Ward 1985: 73)
Tests:
 (i) ABOUT COPPOLA, he said that he found him to be.....
 (ii) #WHAT ABOUT COPPOLA? He found him to be...
 (iii) #AS FOR COPPOLA, he found him to be.....
 (iv) #SPEAKING OF COPPOLA, he found him to be.....

The ABOUT test succeeds in (9), i.e. yields a felicitous, sense-preserving substitute for the target constituent *Coppola* in italics at the beginning of the second sentence. Arguably this is because the utterance including the target *is* about Coppola, i.e. Coppola is the Topic of the utterance. But the WHAT ABOUT and AS FOR tests seem to implicate a contrast between Coppola and some other salient entity or entities, a contrast which isn't drawn, explicitly or implicitly, in this discourse. That is, the denotation of *Coppola* in the original text is not a Contrastive Topic, nor is there some salient contrast set to which he is being compared, so these tests strike one as infelicitous in this context (as indicated by '#'). SPEAKING OF X does not necessarily contrast X with some other relevant entity. It does seem to presuppose that Coppola has been recently mentioned, but also that he was not under discussion at that point: Perhaps he was only mentioned in passing, in some other connection. Then the adverbial serves to signal a shift to talking about him. But in the context given, one might argue that at the end of the first sentence Coppola, or at least Coppola's relationship with Cruise, is as plausibly under discussion as is Cruise himself, so the implication of a shift seems unnecessary and infelicitous. (In terms of Centering Theory, SPEAKING OF X seems to indicate the establishment of a Backward Looking Center (CB) which was not in the set of Forward Looking Centers (CF) of the previous utterance. See Poesio et al. 2004. But Coppola *is* in the CF for the first sentence here.)

Consider how the tests work with another example. (10) uses the four test frames as ways that the indicative reply to the QUD in (6a) or (6b) might be continued, on the assumption that Sue and Mary are (merely) implicitly known by the interlocutors to both be members of some salient and relevant set of individuals:

(10) a. What about Mary? What did she give to Harry?
     Mary gave [a shirt]$_{Rheme}$ to Harry.
  b. What about Mary? What did she do?
     Mary [gave a shirt to Harry]$_{Rheme}$.

> Possible continuations of the indicative responses in (a) and (b):
> (i) #ABOUT SUE, (I would say that) she gave Harry a scarf.
> (ii) WHAT ABOUT SUE? (What did she do?)
> (iii) AS FOR SUE, she gave Harry a scarf.
> (iv) #SPEAKING OF SUE, she gave Harry a scarf.

ABOUT SUE seems to presuppose that Sue was already mentioned (as we saw in (9)); since this is not the case in the contexts given, it is infelicitous in these examples. This also leads to infelicity of SPEAKING OF SUE. But WHAT ABOUT SUE? (with or without repetition of the main question from (10a, b)) simply seems to extend the contrastive strategy begun with WHAT ABOUT MARY?, as does AS FOR SUE, so that both are felicitous so long as Sue and Mary are plausibly both members of the same relevant contrast set. (Ward 1985 has claimed that this should be a partially ordered set, but that doesn't seem to be necessary in general. Here, for example, a simple set of close friends would suffice.)

The following (constructed) discourse illustrates appropriate use of SPEAKING OF X:

(11) A: I was at the mall yesterday and I ran into Louise Clark, who was here visiting Sue Topping.
  B: Interesting. [interlude of talk about Clark, followed by:]
     (i) #ABOUT SUE, Louise said that...
     (ii) WHAT ABOUT SUE? {What's she up to?/I heard she was moving.}
     (iii) #(But) AS FOR SUE, did you know...
     (iv) But SPEAKING OF SUE, did you know she's engaged?

With SPEAKING OF, Sue is a non-contrastive Topic, because she isn't being compared with any other salient entities in some relevant respect – the speaker merely switches to talking about Sue and offers some interesting news about her. After WHAT ABOUT SUE? Sue is also the Topic, but she may also be Contrastive Topic, indicated by the fact that reference to Sue in the following utterance involves B-accent. This is the case in the follow-up question *What's she up to?*, where Sue is being contrasted with Louise in respect to what each is up to and *she* receives B-accent. In the alternative follow-up *I heard she was moving*, if *she* receives B-accent, Sue is contrasted with Louise Clark (who presumably has moved away), while if *she* is unaccented Sue is merely Topic, without implied contrast with respect to the predicate in question, *moving*. The example also shows that felicity conditions on use of WHAT ABOUT X differ from those for AS FOR X. WHAT ABOUT SUE? is felicitous in this context without prior indication that Sue and Louise were to be contrasted in this connection, even if Sue is the Contrastive Topic in the subsequent utterance. But AS FOR SUE seems to presuppose that the speaker is working her way through a salient contrast set, indicating a turn of attention to someone already understood to be a member of that set; the contrast in this example might be facilitated by the use of *but*. Since there is no such salient set in the context given, (iii) is infelicitous.

As we have seen, these four tests proposed for Topicality in English actually differ in the felicity conditions involved, though they all do seem to insure Topicality for the entity mentioned (Coppola or Sue in these examples). But given these subtle differences, we can readily imagine that any of these tests might not be available in direct translation in another language, or that that language might offer ways of testing for Topicality other than direct translations of these particular utterance frames. Keeping this in mind, we turn to consider how Topicality may be marked cross-linguistically.

3 Topic-marking across languages

Although most of the examples considered above are English, Topicality is, of course, marked in some way or other in most, if not all human languages. A first pass through the catalog of ways in which various languages encode Topicality leads one to observe that they frequently involve syntactic constructions which place the Topical constituent utterance-initial, or near-initial, whether these involve a filler-gap relationship (e.g. Topicalization) or not (e.g., so-called Left Dislocation, where the utterance-initial dislocated constituent is associated with a coreferential resumptive pronoun *in situ* in the root clause). As we will see, in some languages, Topicality is at least sometimes morphologically marked, this marking sometimes combined with placement of the Topical constituent at the left-periphery of the root clause. However, when we look carefully at the specifics of the relevant constructions and morphological markings, we find that they vary a great deal from language to language, in syntactic detail and/or in corresponding pragmatic function(s) and felicity conditions. So though there may be many common factors, in the end it appears that what these various conventions realize is a family of closely related notions, rather than a syntactic or pragmatic universal. Following are some examples very briefly illustrating this diversity across a range of language families. Topical constituents in the illustrative examples are in italics throughout.

Saeed (1984) claims that in *Somali* (Chadic) preposed Topical NPs are typically Left Dislocated, not corresponding to a syntactic gap in the root clause, as in his examples (12) and (13). (In Saeed's glosses *FOC* is a focus particle, which follows a focused NP. As he notes, the Topical NP in (13), *suuga*, is not grammatically locative.)

(12) *Shandadaha* kuwa birta   ah baa ka   culus kuwa santa ah.
     suitcases$_{def}$ those metal$_{def}$ are FOC more heavy those leather are
     'Suitcases, those which are metal are heavier than those which are leather.'

(13) *Suuga*   hilib geelku aad buu qaalisan yahay.
     market$_{def}$ meat camel very FOC expensive is
     'The market, camel's meat is very expensive.' (Saeed 1982: 31)

This differs from *Hungarian* (Kiss 1998), a Finno-Ugric VSO language which has distinguished preverbal positions for Topical constituents, quantificational NPs (or DPs), and Focused NPs/PPs, in that order. Left dislocated constituents occur before Topical NPs at the left periphery of the root clause. Topical NPs bind a gap in the root clause, as in her examples (14) and (15):

(14) *Zsuzsának* [[János]$_{Foc}$ mutatta   be   Imrét].
     Susan.DAT   John   introduced prev Imre.ACC
     'Susan was introduced to Imre by *János*.'

(15) *Imrét*   [[Zsuzsának]$_{Foc}$ mutatta   be   János].
     Imre.ACC   Susan.DAT   introduced prev John
     'Imre was introduced by John to *Susan*.' (Kiss 1998: 682)

Note that neither (14) nor (15) is a passive structure; the Case-marking of the NPs is the same in both, regardless of their position and role as (non)-Topic. See also Roberts (1998) for more discussion of the Hungarian left periphery and its relationship to Focus.

According to Sturgeon (2006) the Slavic language *Czech* has two kinds of Left Dislocation constructions which can mark Topicality, Contrastive Left Dislocation (CLD) and Hanging Topic Left Dislocation (HTLD). But these differ both syntactically – for example, only CLD displays connectivity effects between the left dislocated constituent and the resumptive pronoun in the main clause – and pragmatically: While HTLD "promotes the discourse referent of the left dislocate to topic status", CLD marks the left-dislocate as a Contrastive Topic.

All three of these languages display the tendency to place Topical constituents on the left-periphery of the root clause, as in the English examples (2) – (7) above. But we also saw that in English there are a variety of constructions which achieve this: Topical NPs may be preposed via Topicalization, as in (2b) or (7a) above, but may also be promoted to subject by Passivization, as in (7b), or even be left *in situ* in subject position, as in (2a), (6a) or (6b). Prince (1998) argues that Left Dislocation can also mark Topicality in English, as in (16), which involves the mixed use of Left Dislocation (*one* and *another*) and Topicalization (*the third*):

(16) She had an idea for a project. She's going to use three groups of mice$_{i,j,k}$. *One$_i$*, she'll feed them$_i$ mouse chow, just the regular stuff they make for mice. *Another$_j$* she'll feed them$_j$ veggies. And *the third$_k$* she'll feed e$_k$ junk food. (SH, 11/7/81, reported in Prince 1998: 287)

But occurrence on the left-periphery is neither necessary nor sufficient to mark a constituent as Topical in English. English Topical constituents may also remain *in situ* post-verbally, as in (7c) or (8), where the Contrastive Topics are prosodically marked with the B-accent. And Prince offers evidence that Left Dislocated NPs may play another role than that of (Contrastive) Topic. This non-Topical role is illustrated by her (17) (with the target constituent in small caps for ease of identification):

(17) My sister got stabbed. She died. Two of my sisters were living together on 18th Street. They had gone to bed, and this man, their girlfriend's husband, came in. He started fussing with my sister and she started to scream. THE LANDLADY$_k$, SHE$_k$ WENT UP, and he laid her$_k$ out. So sister went to get a wash cloth to put on her$_k$, he stabbed her in the back. But she saw her death. She went and told my mother when my brother was

buried, "Mother," she said, "your trouble is not over yet. You're going to have another death in the family. And it's going to be me." And sure enough, it was. (Prince 1981: 15)

In (17), the Left Dislocated NP *the landlady* has not been mentioned previously, i.e. in Prince's terms is Discourse New (although weakly familiar in the sense of Roberts 2004). Prince points out that the discourse is not about the landlady at this point, and in keeping with this, the example fails a number of the tests for Topicality considered above. None of the Topicality tests in (18i) – (iii) is felicitous in the context given:

(18) [Context] A: He started fussing with my sister and she started to scream.
  i. #She said he started fussing with her sister and she started to scream. She said ABOUT THE LANDLADY that she went up and he laid her out. So she said her sister went to get a washcloth to put on her, he stabbed her in the back.
  ii. B: #WHAT ABOUT THE LANDLADY?
      A: The landlady, she went up and he laid her out. So sister went to get a washcloth to put on her, he stabbed her in the back.
  iii. #He started fussing with my sister and she started to scream. AS FOR/ SPEAKING OF THE LANDLADY, she went up and he laid her out.

The ABOUT test fails in (18i) because the utterance in the original text is *not* about the landlady, but (still) about the occasion of the sister's murder. Nor is the landlady being contrasted in some relevant respect with other participants in the event, so that she isn't a Contrastive Topic. So switching to talk about her makes no sense in this context, yielding a discourse which is not optimally coherent. Similarly, because a WHAT ABOUT X question makes the denotation of *X* the Contrastive Topic in any felicitous reply, introducing this question in (18ii) also leads to discourse incoherence, and in any case to a discourse which seems to switch Topic in a way not displayed in (17). The AS FOR and SPEAKING OF tests also lead to infelicity in (18iii). Not only do they trigger the infelicitous Topic-switch, but both seem to have an additional presupposition, that the entity inquired about is already salient in the context. But the landlady in (18iii) is Discourse-new (Prince 1992) in this context, and so could not reasonably be taken to be relevant or salient in the discourse before her mention. Finally, the AS FOR test seems to presuppose that the Topic is being contrasted in some respect with another entity recently under discussion, hence infelicitously making it a Contrastive Topic.

Prince argues that Left Dislocation is used in (17) because subject positions are dispreferred for Discourse-new entities (Halliday 1967, Geluykens 1992), so *the landlady* is Left Dislocated to introduce that person into the discourse, thereafter referring to her pronominally. Prince calls this use an instance of "simplifying Left Dislocation", about which she says that it "serves to simplify the discourse processing of Discourse-new entities by removing the NPs evoking them from a syntactic position disfavored for NPs evoking Discourse-new entities and creating a separate processing unit for them. Once that unit is processed and they have become Discourse-old, they (or, rather, the pronouns which represent them) may comfortably occur in their canonical positions within the clause." This kind of careful consideration of the discourse function(s) of occurrence on the left periphery is lacking (so far as I can tell) in the discussions of Topicality in other languages cited above.

In *Japanese*, Topical NPs and sometimes other Topical constituent types as well, are said to be morphologically marked with the enclitic *-wa* (see Kuroda 1965, Kuno 1973, and a wealth of literature; see the useful overview in Heycock 2007). Something quite similar occurs in *Korean*, which marks Topicality with *-(n)un* (Choi 1997, 1999, Lee 2003). We get a feeling for their distribution from the following story fragment in the two languages modified from examples considered by Kubota & Lee (2007). (In these examples and those that follow, *NOM* is nominal case, *ACC* accusative case, *DECL* declarative; *HON* is honorific.)

(19) *Japanese*:
Gakusei-ga/#-wa   kyoozyu-to   menkaisi-te i-ta.
student-NOM/ TOP   professor-with   meet PROG-PAST
'A student was meeting with a professor'.
   Gakusei-wa   syukudai-nituite   situmon-o   si,
   student-TOP   homework-about   ask.questions-ACC do
   kyoozyu-wa   sore-ni   teineini   kotae-ta.
   professor-TOP   it-DAT   carefully   answer-PAST
   'The student asked questions about homework and the professor answered them carefully.'
   Hutari-wa   gakusei-no   taamu-purojekuto-nituite-mo hanasi-at-ta.
   two-TOP   student-GEN   term-project-about-also   discuss-PAST
   'They also talked about the student's term project.'
   Totuzen kyoozyu-ga/ ?-*wa*   yuka-ni   taore-ta.
   suddenly professor-NOM/ TOP floor-DAT fall-PAST
   'Suddenly, the professor fell on the floor.' (Yusuke Kubota p.c.)

(20) *Korean*:
Han haksayng-i/#-*nun*   han kyoswu-nim-kwa   manna-koiss-ess-ta.
one student-NOM/TOP   one professor-HON-with meet-PROG-PAST-DECL

'A student was meeting with a professor.'
Haksayng-un   swukcey-ey.tayhaye   mwul-ess-ko,
student-TOP   homework-about   ask-PAST-and
kyoswu-nim-un   chincelhakey   taytaphaycwu-si-ess-ta.
professor-HON-TOP   kindly   answer-HON-PAST-DECL
'The student asked him about the homework, and the professor answered the question kindly.'

Twu salam-un   kimal-puloceyktu-ey.tayhaye-to iyakiha-yess-ta.
Two people-TOP   term-project-about-also   talk-PAST-DECL
'They also talked about the term project.'

Kapcaki kyoswu-nim-i/?-*un*   patak-ey ssuleci-ess-ta.
suddenly professor-NOM/TOP   floor-on fall-PAST-DECL
'Suddenly, the professor fell on the floor.' (Jungmee Lee, p.c.)

In each, the first sentence introduces a pair of (discourse-new) participants, and use of the TOP-marker *-wa* or *-nun* is infelicitous. In the second and third clause in each language TOP-marker *-wa* or *-nun* is acceptable on the subject, denoting one of those participants; the same is the case for the subject of the fourth clause, denoting the pair. In these three central clauses, the NOM-marker *-i* is also acceptable on the subject in Korean and *-ga* is marginally acceptable in Japanese, though there seems to be a clear preference for a uniform choice of marking throughout the sequence: all TOP (preferably) or all NOM. Note that although there arguably are uses of *-wa/-nun* that are Contrastive Topics, the TOP-marked subjects in these examples would not be treated as Contrastive Topics if translated into English, e.g. associated with the B-accent or paraphrased with AS FOR THE STUDENT/AS FOR THE TWO OF THEM; they would not be the contrastive topics of Lee (2006a, 2006b). Nor is it clear that the ABOUT X test gives positive results here. The final utterance is of particular interest: In each language, although the subject is one of the same familiar entities TOP-marked previously, native speakers are clear that the nominative case-marker is preferable to *-wa* or *-nun*. Kubota & Lee (2007) hypothesize that the sharp shift marked by 'suddenly' is what makes the TOP-marking infelicitous. One might hypothesize, following Kuroda (1972), that unlike the preceding utterances reporting categorical judgments about the participants, the adverbial signals that what's of interest in the final utterance is the unexpectedness of the event, reported by a thetic judgment, and not what is said about the subject.

There are a number of other parallels between the uses of these particles in the two languages. For example, each language permits the use of the TOP-marker for a so-called "double subject" construction where the *-wa* or *-nun*-marked constituent does not correspond to a gap in the root clause, as in the following Japanese example (Kiss 1998) and its Korean counterpart (Jungmee Lee, p.c., omitted for reasons of space):

(21) Sakana wa tai ga   oisii.
      Fish   TOP red.snapper delicious
      'As for fish, red snapper is delicious.'

In this construction, as reflected in the gloss, the *wa*-marked NP does appear to function as a Topic, in the sense of what the utterance is about.

Also, each language admits of a second use of -*wa*/-*nun*, a non-Topical function indicating exclusivity (often called a "contrastive use" in the literature; see Kuno 1973, and more recent work on contrastive -*wa* by Noda 1991, Hara 2010, Oshima 2008 and Sawada 2008) – note that this is not always a Contrastive Topic in the sense defined above (and see Lee 2006a, 2006b). The non-Topical use is illustrated by this Korean example, where the second –*(n)un*-marked phrase is non-Topical:

(22) *Mary-nun* John-un   chohaha-n-ta.
      Mary-TOP John-TOP   like-PRES-DECL
      'As for Mary, she likes John (but not others).' (Jungmee Lee, p.c.)

(22) can serve as an answer to *What about Mary? Who does she like?* (or *Who likes her?*), but not to *What about John? Who does he like?/Who likes him?*, arguing that *Mary-nun* here is a Contrastive Topic, while *John-un* is not Topical but instead serves as the focused Rheme.

Besides NPs and predicates (Heycock 2007), Korean and Japanese can mark with -*nun*/-*wa* a variety of adverbial constituents, as with the temporal adverbial clause in the Korean (23):

(23) [Nay-ka ttena-l-ttay   -nun]   John-i   ca-koiss-ess-ta.
      I-NOM leave-REL-time-TOP   John-NOM   sleep-PROG-PAST-DECL
      'As for the time when I left, John was sleeping.' (Jungmee Lee, p.c.)

(23) also has a non-Topical exclusive interpretation: 'John was sleeping when I left (but not at other times)'. The temporal adverbial may instead follow the subject *John-i*, in which case it has the same two readings.

But for all these parallels, Japanese -*wa* and Korean -*nun* differ in at least one important respect: sensitivity to the familiarity, or Givenness of the constituent they mark. Portner & Yabushita (1998, 2001) provide evidence that non-contrastive -*wa* NPs usually presuppose definiteness, technically realized as a kind of familiarity. Kubota (2007) argues that this should be Weak Familiarity, in the sense of Roberts (2003). But Portner and Yabushita also observe that Japanese quantificational NPs can occur with -*wa* just in case they are presuppositional, which "indicates that [the] quantifier's domain is contextually given in some way or another." This is illustrated in their examples following:

(24) Heya wa subete sansetto biichi ni menshite-imasu.
 Room(s) TOP every Sunset Beach LOC facing-be
 'Every room faces Sunset Beach.'

(25) Sansetto biichi wa subete no heya kara miemasu.
 Sunset Beach TOP every of room(s) from seeable.
 'Sunset Beach can be seen from every room.'

(26) Taitee no kan'kookyku ga ∅ kin'itte-imasu.
 most of tourists NOM pro pleased-be
 'Most tourists like it/them/that.' (Portner & Yabushita 2001: 286)

(24) and (25) have "essentially the same propositional content" but establish distinct Topics, which lead to distinct possibilities for resolving subsequent anaphora. Following (24), the null object *pro* in (26) is understood to refer to either the rooms (the Topic and domain of *subete*) or the idea that every room faces the beach; while following (25), the *pro* can be taken to refer to either Sunset Beach (the Topic, denotation of the NP *Sansetto biichi*) or to the fact that the beach is seeable from every room.

In this vein, Kubota & Lee (2007) provide data arguing that -*wa* is only felicitous with those quantificational NPs which admit of a partitive interpretation, presupposing a familiar domain of quantification, and so presuppositional in Portner and Yabushita's sense. Hence the contrast between Kubota and Lee's (27), where the partitive interpretation is not available, and (28), where it is, as reflected in the gloss:

(27) #{San-nin/go-nin-izyoo/takusan/oozei/kazoekire-nai-hodo/nan-nin-mo}-no
 three-CL/five-CL-more/many/many/countless/numerous -GEN
 gakusei-wa siken-o uke-ta.
 student-TOP exam-ACC take-PAST
 'Three/more-than-five/many/countless/numerous students took the exam.'

(28) Ooku-no gakusei-wa/ga siken-o uke-ta
 many-GEN student-TOP/NOM exam-ACC take-PAST
 'Many of the students took the exam.' (Kubota & Lee 2007: 5)

(With *-ga* (28) can also mean non-partitive 'there were many students who took the exam'.)

But Korean does allow non-partitive quantificational NPs with *-nun*, so that the Korean counterpart of (27) in (29) (as well as that of (28)) is grammatical:

(29) {Sey-myeng-uy/tases-myeng-isang-uy/manhun}   haksayng-tul-un
      three-CL-GEN/five-Classifier-more_than-GEN/many   student-PL-TOP
      sihem-ul   chi-ess-ta.
      exam-ACC take-PAST-DECL
      'Three/more-than-five/many students took the exam.'   (Kubota & Lee 2007: 5)

The acceptability of (29) reflects that fact that, more generally, Korean contrastive *-nun* is acceptable with (non-specific) indefinites like *etten saram* 'some man', in contexts where Japanese *-wa* would result in infelicity (Kubota & Lee 2007).

Italian presents yet another range of options for indicating Topicality. According to Rizzi (1997), in Italian there is a sharp distinction between the Clitic Left Dislocation (CLLD) structure, involving an IP-internal resumptive clitic coreferential to an initial Topical NP, as in his (30), and contrastive focus preposing, involving a preposed NP linked to a matrix-internal gap, as in his (31):

(30) *Il tuo libro,* lo ho letto.
      the POSS.2sg book clitic perf read
      'Your book, I have read it.'

(31) [Il tuo libro]$_{Foc}$ ho letto (, non il suo).
      the POSS.2sg book   perf read   the POSS.3sg
      'Your book I read (, not his).'   (Rizzi 1997: 286)

Rizzi isn't clear about the contexts in which these utterances would be felicitous. About (30), Rizzi notes that "the English gloss...is somewhat misleading" (1997: 286). And about (31) he says that "It could not be felicitously uttered as conveying non-contrastive new information, i.e. as an answer to the question 'What did you read?'" But since the gloss (with Rizzi's labeling of the preposed constituent as *Foc*) makes it clear that the preposed direct object is contrastive, it may be a Contrastive Topic: Recall that in English topicalized NPs in general, and topicalized Contrastive Topics in particular are Foci.

Arregi (2003) argues that in Spanish CLLD the left dislocated phrase is a Contrastive Topic, in the sense defined above. But there are differences from the Italian case, where CLLD obligatorily involves a clitic: Spanish left dislocated phrases display an interesting semantic pattern wherein those with clitics must be reconstructed at LF (to capture the correct scope potential of Left Dislocated indefinites), while indefinites may undergo Left Dislocation without clitics, and in the latter case they do not undergo reconstruction.

In French, the sharp distinction Rizzi draws between the pragmatic functions of CLLD and constructions like (31) does not seem to obtain. Abeillé, Godard & Sabio (2008) argue that in French, as we saw earlier for English, there is more than one way to mark a constituent as Topical. French CLLD is one of these. But they consider two other types of French construction where an NP occurs on the left periphery of the clause without an overt clitic – one in which the filler-gap relationship is sensitive to islands, as in English Topicalization and Rizzi's (31), and the other in which it is not, as in CLLD. They give evidence that in each of these French constructions the initial NP may be Topical, though it need not be. Moreover, in both constructions the preposed NP may alternatively serve as the (narrowly Focused) Rheme, in marked contrast with Rizzi's claim about the Italian constructions.

There is another striking difference between the Italian and English constructions. In the Italian, CLLD is acceptable in embedded clauses, as in the relative clauses in Rizzi's (32) and (33), whereas English Topicalization and Left Dislocation are not, as we see in (34) and (35) (Rizzi 1997: 306):

(32) Un uomo a cui, il tuo libro$_i$, lo$_i$ potremmo dare.
 'A man to whom, your book, we could give it.'

(33) Un uomo che, il tuo libro$_i$, lo$_i$ potrebbe comprare.
 'A man who, your book, could buy it.'

(34) *A man to whom your book$_i$ we could give e$_i$/it$_i$.

(35) *A man who your book$_i$ could buy e$_i$/it$_i$.

The tests we considered in the preceding section all seem to treat Topicality as a function of the utterance, hence we would predict it to be appropriate only at the root level. Insofar as these constructions reflect Topicality, this prediction is borne out in English, but not in Italian, calling the pragmatic status of the Italian construction even more into question: Does *your book* in (32) or (33) stand in contrast to some other entity? Or is it what the whole utterance is about in some sense?

The unacceptability of Topicalization in most embedded clauses in English reflects what Emonds (1970, 1976) called the *Root Restriction*: English Topicalization is said to be a root phenomenon, and hence we only expect it in main clauses. There are, however, cases when it is acceptable (for some speakers) when embedded under certain predicates, namely in the complement clauses of verbs of saying (36), quasi-evidentials like *it appears* and *it seems* (37), factives and semi-factives (38), (39) (Hooper & Thompson 1973, Heycock 2005, Simons 2007, Dayal & Grimshaw 2009):

(36) Bill warned us that *flights to Chicago* we should try to avoid. (Bianchi & Frascarelli 2010: 45)

(37) It appears that *this book* he read thoroughly. (Hooper & Thompson 1973: 478)

(38) I am glad that *this unrewarding job,* she has finally decided to give up. (Bianchi & Frascarelli 2010: 69)

(39) He tried to conceal from his parents that *the math exam* he had not passed, and *the biology exam* he had not even taken. (Bianchi & Frascarelli 2010: 69)

Haegeman (2004) provides examples arguing that English Topicalization is sometimes possible in adversative clauses (40), (41), *because* clauses (42), and some conditional clauses (43), when these have "root like properties". Here are some of her examples:

(40) His face not many admired, while *his characte*r still fewer felt they could praise. (Quirk et al 1985: 1378)

(41) We don't look to his paintings for common place truths, though *truths* they contain none the less (*Guardian*, G2, 18.02.3, page 8, col1; cited in Haegeman 2004: 8).

(42) I think we have more or less solved the problem for donkeys here, because *those we haven't got*, we know about. (*Guardian*, G2, 18.2.3, page 3, col2; cited in Haegeman 2004: 3).

(43) If *anemonies* you don't like, why not plant roses instead? (Haegeman 2004: 4)

Simons (2005) and Dayal & Grimshaw (2009) consider the general phenomenon of root-like complement clauses. They argue that there is an irreducibly pragmatic aspect of these occurrences, and that they cannot be explained solely in terms of syntactic factors or of the lexical semantics of the predicates involved. Simons takes the matrix predicate in such uses to be "parenthetical" – typically serving an evidential function, and argues that the complement clause in such cases constitutes the main point of the utterance. For example, it is the complement which is the answer to the question under discussion in her (44) and (45), the latter displaying the non-canonical syntactic form possible in some (but not all) embedding verbs with parenthetical uses:

(44) A: Why didn't Louise come to the meeting yesterday?
 B: I heard that she's out of town.

(45) a. Louise, I hear(d), is out of town.
 b. Louise is out of town, I hear(d).   (Simons 2005: 2)

But the proposition expressed by the sentence as a whole is still asserted in these uses. This is supported by the fact that there are two ways a hearer might respond to B's utterance in (46):

(46) A: Why isn't Louise coming to our meetings these days?
 B: Henry thinks that she's left town.
 C: a. But she hasn't. I saw her yesterday in the supermarket.
   b. No he doesn't. He told me her saw her yesterday in the supermarket.
        (Simons 2005: 15)

(Ca) responds to the proposition embedded under the evidential *Henry thinks*; in this case, the embedded proposition is the main point because it is what is relevant to the question A asked. But (Cb) responds to the whole proposition expressed by B, arguing that it is asserted. Dayal & Grimshaw (2009) similarly argue that the complement clause is, indeed, syntactically embedded.

This main-point function of the complement clause embedded under parenthetical/evidential predicates provides an avenue for a pragmatic explanation for the root phenomena displayed in the complement, including Topicalization. Hence, there is some explanation for their violation of the Root Restriction, which is otherwise quite robust in English. It remains to be seen whether this type of account could naturally be extended to the adverbial clause examples in (40)–(43). But clearly one cannot plausibly attribute main point function to relative clauses:

(47) A: What did you do yesterday?
 B: #I want to introduce you to a woman who I went sky-diving with yesterday.

In (47), the proposition that B went sky-diving with a woman yesterday addresses A's question, but this cannot make B's utterance felicitous, since it cannot be taken to answer A's question, hence seems irrelevant. The fact that a relative clause cannot be the main point in Simon's sense predicts that we wouldn't expect to find such root phenomena as Topicalization in English relative clauses, and that is the case, as we saw in (34) and (35). This makes the acceptability of CLLD in Italian (32), (33) even more striking. In fact, Italian CLLD is acceptable in all finite subordinate clauses (Cinque 1990, Rizzi 1997, Frascarelli 2000, DeCat 2002).

However, Bianchi & Frascarelli (2010) argue that Italian embedded CLLDs are *not* Topical, but instead are "used to resume background information or for topic continuity." Unlike Topical CLLDs in main clauses in Italian, embedded CLLDs do not affect "the conversational dynamics". For example, consider the embedded CLLD *la torta* in (48B):

(48) A: Devo   guardare anche la torta?
         must.1sg watch   also the cake
         'Should I watch the cake too?'
     B: Sì, te   l'   ho   detto: resta   in cucina
         yes to-you.CL it.CL have.1sg said stay.IMP in kitchen
         finché *la torta* non la   vedi   pronta da sfornare.
         until the cake   not it.CL see.2sg ready to take out
         'Yes, I told you: stay in the kitchen until you see the cake is ready.'
         (Bianchi & Frascarelli 2010: 65)

The English translation of (48) would be quite odd with any of the diagnostics for Topicality: #*about the cake, stay in the kitchen until you see it is ready*, #*as for the cake...*, #*speaking of the cake...*, arguing that the CLLD *la torta* is not Topical.

Italian is not alone in permitting such embedded Topic-like constituents. For example, this is also observed in *Tz'utujil* (Mayan) according to Aissen (1992), and in Korean (Jungmee Lee, p.c.). But embedded non-contrastive *-wa* marked NPs are not acceptable in Japanese (Yusuke Kubota, p.c.). What the discussion of Italian brings to light is the importance of first establishing clear diagnostics for Topicality for the language in question, before attempting to determine the function of any particular construction which is Topic-like, and may in some cases be Topical. Topicalization doesn't always correlate with Topicality. Moreover, because Topicality is essentially a function of the constituent's role in context, in presenting examples one must be careful to present sufficient context to make it plausible that the target constituent has a Topical function *in that context*.

The above illustrate just a few of the ways that languages differ in expressing something taken by theorists to be Topic. Though space precludes elaborating further, we might mention briefly a couple of other interesting differences gleaned from the literature:

a) Many languages, including Catalan (Vallduví 1992: 48), Korean (Jungmee Lee, p.c.), Somali (Saeed 1984), Hungarian (Kiss 1998), and Yucatec Mayan (Judith Tonhauser, p.c.), permit multiple preposed NPs which are said to be Topical (in some sense), whereas Reinhart (1981) convincingly argues that English generally only permits one Topical NP, whether Topicalized or Left Dislocated, at least according to her tests.
b) Some languages treat *wh*-elements as non-Topical, while others treat (some of) them as Topical. For example, Hungarian *wh*-NPs are preposed between the distinguished pre-verbal position for Topical constituents and that for Foci. English Topical constituents and preposed *wh*-elements may co-occur, in that order (*As for Tom, who likes him?*), and given that the language does not permit multiple Topical constituents, this argues that they are in distinct syntactic positions, as well as functionally distinct. But Bulgarian (Jaeger 2001) allows Clitic Doubling of *wh*-phrases, in which case they behave like Topical constituents, occurring before other *wh*-expressions and often interpreted as an echo-question or Contrastive Topic; see also Grohmann (2006). Kubota & Lee (2007) show that in Japanese only D-linked (Pesetsky 1987) – and hence familiar – *wh*-expressions may be marked with -*wa*, and the same seems to hold in Korean.

All this underlines the importance of trying to develop clear pragmatic tests and/or criteria (contextual felicity conditions) for determining whether, in a given language, a particular construction or other (e.g. morphological) means is consistently used to mark a constituent as Topical, and to determine whether that notion of Topicality corresponds with the notion as reflected in other languages, like English. Until we do this, from a pragmatic (or functional) point of view we may well be comparing apples and oranges. And it raises a question that needs to be addressed in a rigorous way language-by-language: Just because a particular construction in a particular language serves as the best-translation for another construction in a distinct language, does that mean that the two have the same functional load from a semantico-pragmatic point of view?

4 The universality of Topicality

What can we say about Topicality in human language generally? Is it reflected in a universal at some level, e.g. syntactic or pragmatic? A number of authors offer extended discussions of these questions: Reinhart (1981), Ward (1985), Gundel (1988), von Fintel (1996), McNally (1998), Prince (1998), Portner & Yabushita (1998), Jacobs (2001), Portner (2002), and Ward & Birner (2004), among many others. There is not the space here to go through their proposals in detail. But we can mention two features of Topics that many of these authors agree on, although, again, the terminology they use often differs:

A Topic is familiar.
A Topic is must be something that is either familiar (or given) itself, or is an identifiable member of some familiar set of entities.

A Topic is what the utterance in which it occurs is about.

Of course, it has been noted by many that a Topical NP, in English for instance, need not be definite. But at least in Japanese, if a Topical NP is indefinite, it must be specific. Portner & Yabushita (1998, 2001) argue for a view of specificity in which the indefinite NP in question is taken to have a familiar (singleton) domain, unifying this case with that of the definites. Note that if the familiarity of Topics is taken to be the Weak Familiarity of Roberts (2003), which seems to be appropriate for both Japanese and English, it subsumes Portner and Yabushita's specificity.

Portner and Yabushita formally realize the *aboutness* criterion by taking the information conveyed by the utterance to update the discourse referent corresponding to its Topic, if it has one. This update procedure is an implementation of the notion of Linkhood of Vallduví (1992, 1993), quite similar to Reinhart's (1981) notion of *aboutness* or Jacob's (2001) *addressation*. In all its instantiations in the literature, the notion of *aboutness* remains relatively vague, and as we saw, the tests proposed to check for aboutness give slightly different results for different examples, even in the same language. Across languages, it is even less clear that the exact same notion is operative. For example, it may be that categorical judgment is what is relevant for Japanese or Korean, as we saw in (19) and (20); clearly many examples with *-wa/-(n)un* would not be Topical according to the tests proposed for English. But English certainly would not support Topicalization across the full range of categorical utterances. I strongly suspect that Topicality is really a family of closely-related notions, rather than one notion which can be defined with a single set of necessary and sufficient conditions.

It does seem fairly certain that all languages have some means of expressing the combination of familiarity and aboutness which I take to characterize Topicality in the general case. But we must exercise caution in drawing this conclusion, in view of the evidence that Korean *-nun* – so closely related to Japanese *-wa* in other respects – does not always presuppose familiarity (or specificity).

What does all this tell us about language universals? McNally (1998: 164) observed that in many accounts "the universality of such primitives [as Focus and Topic] is presupposed rather than hypothesized, [and] the fine-grained distinctions among constituents that roughly correspond to, for example, topic are not considered important." The prevalence cross-linguistically of dedicated structural positions and/or morphological or prosodic indications of something like Topicality has led many to argue, or simply to assume that Universal Grammar (in Chomsky's sense) contains a functional category Topic, heading a Topic Phrase in the phrase structural characterization of any given language. For example, Rizzi (1997) argues for the existence of a number of phrases between the root node of a syntactic tree, the CP ("Complementizer Phrase") and the IP (the constituent in which are located tense, aspect, etc.); one of these is a Topic Phrase, headed by a functional head Topic, with the Topical constituent located in the Spec(ifier) of this functional head, and the remainder of the sentence (its *Comment*) as its complement:

(49)   TopP

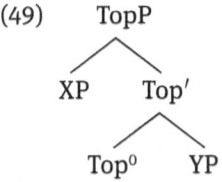

Top⁰:	a functional head belonging to the complementizer system
Spec(TopP) = XP:	the Topic
YP:	the Comment

(Rizzi 1997:286)

But the diversity observed in the languages briefly reviewed above argues that while this phrase structure may be appropriate to Italian, and perhaps for some other closely related Romance languages as well (though possibly not French), it is unlikely as a syntactic universal. Both structurally and in terms of function, those elements of the surveyed languages which are sometimes utilized to reflect Topicality include morphological and prosodic markers, as well as functionally distinguished syntactic positions (both with and without long distance dependencies) and scrambling, thus constituting a set of very diverse structural devices. Moreover, we often find multiple means utilized within a single language, even within a single discourse, as we saw in English and French.

I am reminded of a theme from Chomsky (1982). Talking about notions like *passive* and *relativization*, he points out that in early work in generative grammar, there were said to be universal syntactic rules, realized in all languages, that corresponded to those notions. Some of us can remember when people debated about the character of the presumed universal Passive transformation. But Chomsky argues:

> The notions "passive," "relativization", etc., can be reconstructed as processes of a more general nature, with a functional role in grammar, but they are not "rules of grammar".
>
> We need not expect, in general, to find a close correlation between the functional role of such general processes and their formal properties, though there will naturally be some correlation. Languages may select from among the devices [available to them] to provide for such general processes as those that were considered to be specific rules in earlier work. At the same time, phenomena that appear to be related may prove to arise from the interaction of several components, some shared, accounting for the similarity. The full range of properties of some construction may often result from interaction of several components, its apparent complexity reducible to simple principles of separate subsystems.
>
> (Chomsky 1982: 7; see also 120ff)

Similarly, I would argue that Topic is not a structural universal that we expect to find in the *grammar* of all human languages. Instead, what we have is a loose functional universal, Topicality, so useful in human discourse that we tend to find specialized means of indicating it across a broad variety of languages. This may be the kind of thing that Jacobs (2001) has in mind in talking about *prototypical Topics*. It is useful because it helps lend coherence to discourse to talk about a single entity, often over an extended set of utterances, and to indicate when we have switched what we're talking about. But even in languages as similar in many respects as Japanese and Korean, the realization of Topicality differs in subtle but interesting ways, depending in the brief data-set considered above on a difference in the presuppositions associated with the enclitics used *inter alia* to mark Topicality: whether they conventionally presuppose familiarity.

To resolve these questions requires careful, detailed work on a broader variety of languages, adopting a carefully defined terminology in order to facilitate comparison of results across those languages. It requires the development and refinement of tests which permit us to ferret out distinctions like those sketched so briefly above for English, so that for a given construction we have evidence of the functional role of any purported marker of Topicality. And in making claims about any essentially contextual function like this one, we must examine sentences not in isolation, but embedded in enough context to permit us to grasp the discourse dynamic in which the Topicality plays a part: The Topicality of a given constituent can only be assessed in context.

I am grateful to Yusuke Kubota, Jungmee Lee, Paul Portner, and Judith Tonhauser for useful discussion and comments, and to Luigi Rizzi for pointing out relevant literature on Italian.

5 References

Abeillé, Anne, Danièle Godard & Frédéric Sabio 2008. Two types of NP preposing in French. In: S. Müller (ed.) *Proceedings of the 15th HPSG Conference*. Stanford, CA: CSLI Publications, 306–324.

Aissen, Judith 1992. Topic and focus in Mayan. *Language* 68, 43–80.

Arregi, Karlos 2003. Clitic left dislocation is contrastive topicalization. In: E. Kaiser & S. Arunachalam (eds.). *Proceedings of the 26th Annual Penn Linguistics Colloquium* (Penn Working Papers in Linguistics 9.1). Philadelphia, PA: Penn Linguistics Club, 31–44.

Bar-Hillel, Yehoshua 1971. *Pragmatics of Natural Language*. Dordrecht: Reidel.

Beaver, David 2004. The optimization of discourse anaphora. *Linguistics & Philosophy* 27, 3–56.

Beckman, Mary E. 1996. The parsing of prosody. *Language and Cognitive Processes* II (1/2), 17–67.

Beckman, Mary E. & Gayle M. Ayers 1994. *Guidelines for ToBI labeling guide, ver. 2.0*. www.ling.ohio-state.edu/~tobi/. April 3, 2011.

Bianchi, Valentina & Mara Frascarelli 2010. Is Topic a root phenomenon? *Iberia* 2, 43–88.

Brentano, Franz 1874/1924. *Psychologie vom empirischen Standpunkt*. English translation in: A.C. Rancurello, D.B. Terrell, & L. McAlister (eds.). *Psychology from an Empirical Standpoint*. London: Routledge, 1973, 137–207.

Büring, Daniel 1997. *The Meaning of Topic and Focus: The 59th Street Bridge Accent*. London: Routledge.

Büring, Daniel 2003. On D-Trees, beans, and B-Accents. *Linguistics & Philosophy* 26, 511–545.

Choi, Hye-Won 1997. Topic and focus in Korean: The information partition by phrase structure and morphology. In: H.-M. Sohn & J. Haig (eds.). *Japanese and Korean Linguistics, vol. 6*. Stanford, CA: CSLI Publications, 545–561.

Choi, Hye-Won 1999. *Optimizing Structure in Context: Scrambling and Information Structure*. Stanford, CA: CSLI Publications.

Chomsky, Noam 1982. *Lectures on Government and Binding*. Dordrecht: Foris.

Cinque, Guglielmo 1990. *Types of A9-Dependencies*. Cambridge, MA: The MIT Press.

Davis, Lori J. & Ellen F. Prince 1986. Yiddish verb-topicalization and the notion "Lexical Integrity". In: A. Farley, P. Farley & K.-E. McCullough (eds.). *Papers from the 22nd Regional Meeting of the Chicago Linguistic Society*. Chicago, IL: Chicago Linguistic Society, 90–97.

Dayal, Veneeta & Jane Grimshaw 2009. *Subordination at the Interface: The Quasi-Subordination Hypothesis*. Ms. New Brunswick, NJ, Rutgers University.

DeCat, Cécile 2002. *French Dislocation*. Ph.D. dissertation. University of York.

Emonds, Joseph 1970. *Root and Structure-Preserving Transformations*. Ph.D. dissertation. MIT, Cambridge, MA.

Emonds, Joseph 1976. *A Transformational Approach to English Syntax: Root, Structure-Preserving and Local Transformations*. New York: Academic Press.

Erdmann, Peter 1990. *Discourse and Grammar: Focusing and Defocusing in English*. Tübingen: Niemeyer.

von Fintel, Kai 1996. *Restrictions on Quantifier Domains*. Ph.D. dissertation. University of Massachusetts, Amherst, MA.

Frascarelli, Mara 2000. *The Syntax-Phonology Interface in Focus and Topic Constructions in Italian*. Dordrecht: Kluwer.

Geluykens, Ronald 1992. *From Discourse Process to Grammatical Construction: On Left-Dislocation in English*. Amsterdam: Benjamins.

Ginzburg, Jonathan 1996. Dynamics and the semantics of dialogue. In: J. Seligman & D. Westerstahl (eds.). *Language, Logic and Computation*. Stanford, CA: CSLI Publications, 221–237.

Ginzburg, Jonathan 2012. *The Interactive Stance: Meaning for Conversation*. Oxford: Oxford University Press.

Gordon, Peter C., Barbara J. Grosz & Laura A. Gillion 1993. Pronouns, names and the centering of attention in discourse. *Cognitive Science* 17, 311–348.

Grohmann, Kleanthes K. 2006. Top issues in questions: Topics – Topicalization – Topicalizability. In: L. Cheng & N. Corver (eds.). *Wh-movement: Moving on*. Cambridge, MA: The MIT Press, 249–288.

Grosz, Barbara, Aravind Joshi & Scott Weinstein 1983. Providing a unified account of definite noun phrases in discourse. In: *Proceedings of the 21st Annual Meeting of the Association for Computation Linguistics*. Cambridge, MA: Association for Computational Linguistics, 44–50.

Grosz, Barbara, Aravind Joshi & Scott Weinstein 1995. Centering: A framework for modeling the local coherence of discourse. *Computational Linguistics* 21, 202–225.

Gundel, Jeannette K. 1974. *The role of Topic and Comment in Linguistic Theory*. Ph.D. dissertation. University of Texas, Austin, TX.

Gundel, Jeannette K. 1985. "Shared knowledge" and topicality. *Journal of Pragmatics* 9, 83–107.

Gundel, Jeannette K. 1988. Universals of topic-comment structure. In: M. Hammond, E. Moravcsik & J. Wirth (eds.). *Studies in Syntactic Typology*. Amsterdam: Benjamins, 209–239.

Gundel, Jeannette K. 1998. Centering theory and the givenness hierarchy: Towards a synthesis. In: M. Walker, A. Joshi & E. Prince (eds.). *Centering Theory in Discourse*. Oxford: Oxford University Press, 183–198.

Haegeman, Liliane 2004. Topicalization, CLLD and the left periphery. In: C. Maienborn, W. Frey & B. Shaer (eds.). *ZAS Papers in Linguistics 35: Proceedings of the Dislocated Elements Workshop 1*. Berlin: ZAS, 157–192.

Halliday, Michael 1967. Notes on transitivity and theme in English: Parts 1 and 2. *Journal of Linguistics* 3, 37–81, 199–244.

Halliday, Michael 1985. *An Introduction to Functional Grammar*. Baltimore, MD: Edward Arnold.

Hara, Yurie 2010. Implicature unsuspendable: Japanese contrastive *wa*. In: P. Denis et al. (eds.). *Proceedings of the 2004 Texas Linguistics Society Conference*. Somerville, MA: Cascadilla Press, 35–45.

Heycock, Caroline 2005. Embedded root phenomena. In: M. Everaert & H. van Riemsdijk (eds.). *The Blackwell Companion to Syntax Vol. II*. Oxford: Blackwell, 174–209.

Heycock, Caroline 2007. Japanese *-wa*, *-ga*, and information structure. In: S. Miyagawa & M. Saito (eds.). *The Oxford Handbook of Japanese Linguistics*. Oxford: Oxford University Press, 54–83.

Hooper, Joan & Sandra Thompson 1973. On the applicability of root transformations. *Linguistic Inquiry* 4, 465–497.

Jackendoff, Ray 1972. *Semantic Interpretation in Generative Grammar*. Cambridge, MA: The MIT Press.

Jacobs, Joachim 2001. The dimensions of topic-comment. *Linguistics* 39, 641–681.

Jaeger, T. Florian 2004. Topicality and superiority in Bulgarian *wh*-questions. In: O. Arnaudova et al. (eds.) *Proceedings of FASL-12: The Ottawa Meeting 2003*. Ann Arbor, MI: University of Michigan Slavic Publications, 207–228.

Joshi, Aravind & Scott Weinstein 1981. Control of inference: Role of some aspects of discourse structure – centering. In: P. Hayes (ed.). *Proceedings of the 7th International Joint Conference on Artificial Intelligence*. Vancouver, BC: University of British Columbia, 435–439.

Kiss, Katalin É. 1998. Discourse-configurationality in the languages of Europe. In: A. Siewierska (ed.). *Constituent Order in the Languages of Europe*. Berlin: de Gruyter, 681–727.

Kubota, Yusuke 2007. *The Japanese Topic Marker 'wa'*. Ms. Columbus, OH, The Ohio State University.

Kubota, Yusuke & Jungmee Lee 2007. *Topic Marking in Japanese and Korean*. Ms. Columbus, OH, The Ohio State University.

Kuno, Susumu 1973. *The Structure of the Japanese Language*. Cambridge, MA: The MIT Press.

Kuno, Susumu & Ken-Ichi Takami 1993. *Grammar and Discourse Principles: Functional Syntax and GB Theory*. Chicago, IL: The University of Chicago Press.

Kuroda, Sige-Yuki 1965. *Generative Grammatical Studies in the Japanese Language*. Ph.D. dissertation. MIT, Cambridge, MA.

Kuroda, Sige-Yuki 1972. The categorical and the thetic judgment. *Foundations of Language* 9, 153–185.

Kuroda, Sige-Yuki 1992. *Japanese Syntax and Semantics*. Dordrecht: Kluwer.

Ladusaw, William 1994. Thetic and categorical, stage and individual, weak and strong. In: M. Harvey & L. Santelmann (eds.). *Proceedings of Semantics and Linguistic Theory (= SALT) IV*. Ithaca, NY: Cornell University, 220–229.

Lee, Chungmin 2003. Contrastive topic and/or contrastive focus. In: W. McClure (ed.). *Japanese/Korean Linguistics Vol. 12*, Stanford, CA: CSLI Publications, 352–364.

Lee, Chungmin 2006a. Contrastive topic/focus and polarity in discourse. In: K. von Heusinger & K. Turner (eds.). *Where Semantics Meets Pragmatics*. Amsterdam: Elsevier, 381–420.

Lee, Chungmin 2006b. Contrastive (predicate) topic, intonation, and scalar meanings. In: C. Lee, M. Gordon & D. Büring (eds.). *Topic and Focus: Crosslinguistic Perspectives on Meaning and Intonation*. Dordrecht: Springer, 151–175.

McNally, Louise 1998. On recent formal analyses of 'topic'. In: J. Ginzburg et al. (eds.). *The Tbilisi Symposium on Language, Logic and Computation*. Stanford, CA: CSLI Publications, 147–160.

McNally, Louise 1998. Encoding of information packaging instructions. In: P. Culicover & L. McNally (eds.) *The Limits of Syntax*. New York: Academic Press, 161–183.

Noda, Hisashi 1991. *Wa to ga (Wa and ga)*. Tokyo: Kurosio Publishers.

Oshima, David Y. 2008. Morphological vs. phonological contrastive topic marking. In: R. Edwards et al. (eds.). *Papers from the Regional Meeting of the Chicago Linguistic Society (= CLS) 41*. Chicago, IL: Chicago Linguistic Society, 371–384.

Pesetsky, David 1987. Wh-in situ: Movement and unselective binding. In: E. Reuland & A. ter Meulen (eds.). *The Representation of (In)definiteness*. Cambridge, MA: The MIT Press, 98–129.

Poesio, Massimo, Rosemary Stevenson, Barbara di Eugenio & Janet Hitzeman 2004. *Centering: A Parametric Theory and Its Instantiations*. NLE Technical Note TN-02-01, CS Technical Report CSM-369, http://cswww.essex.ac.uk/staff/poesio/publications/CL04TN.pdf. April 8, 2011. Abridged in: *Computational Linguistics* 30, 309–363.

Portner, Paul 2002. Topicality and (non-)specificity in Mandarin. *Journal of Semantics* 19, 275–287.

Portner, Paul & Katsuhiko Yabushita 1998. The semantics and pragmatics of topic phrases. *Linguistics & Philosophy* 21, 117–157.

Portner, Paul & Katsuhiko Yabushita 2001. Specific indefinites and the information structure theory of topics. *Journal of Semantics* 18, 271–297.

Prince, Ellen F. 1981. Topicalization, focus-movement, and Yiddish-movement: A pragmatic differentiation. In: D. Alford et al. (eds.). *Proceedings of the Seventh Annual Meeting of the Berkeley Linguistics Society*. Berkeley, CA: Berkeley Linguistics Society, 249–264.

Prince, Ellen F. 1992. The ZPG letter: Subjects, definiteness and information status. In: S. Thompson & W. Mann (eds.). *Discourse Description: Diverse Analyses of a Fund-Raising Text*, Amsterdam: Benjamins, 295–325.

Prince, Ellen 1998. On the limits of syntax, with reference to left-dislocation and topicalization. In: P. Culicover & L. McNally (eds.). *The Limits of Syntax*. New York: Academic Press, 281–302.

Quirk, Randolph, Joseph Greenbaum, Geoffrey Leech & Jan Svartvik 1985. *A Comprehensive Grammar of the English Language*. London: Longman.

Reinhart, Tanya 1981. Pragmatics and linguistics: An analysis of sentence topics. *Philosophica* 27, 53–94.

Rizzi, Luigi 1997. The fine structure of the left periphery. In: L. Haegeman (ed.). *Elements of Grammar: Handbook of Generative Syntax*. Dordrecht: Kluwer, 281–337.

Roberts, Craige 1996. Information structure in discourse: Towards an integrated formal theory of pragmatics. In: J. H. Yoon & A. Kathol (eds.). *Ohio State University Working Papers in Linguistics 49*. Columbus, OH: The Ohio State University, 91–136.

Roberts, Craige 1998. Focus, the flow of information, and universal grammar. In: P. Culicover & L. McNally (eds.). *The Limits of Syntax*. New York: Academic Press, 109–160.

Roberts, Craige 2003. Uniqueness in definite noun phrases. *Linguistics & Philosophy* 26, 287–350.

Roberts, Craige 2004. Context in dynamic interpretation. In: L. R. Horn & G. Ward (eds.). *Handbook of Pragmatics*. Oxford: Blackwell, 197–220.

Rooth, Mats 2005. Topic accents on quantifiers. In: G. Carlson & J. Pelletier (eds.). *Reference and Quantification: The Partee Effect*. Stanford, CA: CSLI Publications, 303–328.

Saeed, John 1984. *The Syntax of Focus and Topic in Somali*. Hamburg: Helmut Buske Verlag.

Sawada, Osamu (2008). The Japanese contrastive wa: A mirror image of EVEN. In: *Proceedings of the Annual Meeting of the Berkeley Linguistics Society (= BLS) 33*. Berkeley, CA: Berkeley Linguistics Society.

Selkirk, Elisabeth O. 1996. Sentence prosody: Intonation, stress and phrasing. In: J. Goldsmith (ed.). *The Handbook of Phonological Theory*. London: Blackwell, 550–569.

Simons, Mandy 2007. Observations on embedding verbs, evidentiality, and presupposition. *Lingua* 117, 1034–1056.

Sturgeon, Anne 2006. *The Syntax and Pragmatics of Contrastive Topic in Czech*. Ph.D. dissertation. University of California, Santa Cruz, CA.

Vallduví, Enric 1992. *The Informational Component*. New York: Garland.

Vallduví, Enric 1993. *Information Packaging: A Survey*. Research paper HCRC/RP-44. Human Communication Centre, Edinburgh, University of Edinburgh.

Walker, Marilyn A., Aravind K. Joshi & Ellen F. Prince (eds). 1998. *Centering Theory in Discourse*. Oxford: Clarendon Press.

Ward, Gregory L. 1985. *The Semantics and Pragmatics of Preposing*. Ph.D. dissertation. University of Pennsylvania, Philadelphia, PA. Reprinted: New York: Garland, 1988.

Ward, Gregory & Betty J. Birner 2004. Information structure and noncanonical syntax. In: L. R. Horn & G. Ward (eds.). *The Handbook of Pragmatics*. Oxford: Blackwell, 153–174.

Gregory Ward and Betty J. Birner
12 Discourse effects of word order variation

1   Introduction —— 413
2   Information structure: Constituents —— 418
3   Information structure: Open propositions —— 432
4   Conclusion —— 446
5   References —— 447

Abstract: The influence of information status on word order is widely recognized. Both canonical and noncanonical word orderings share a general preference for positioning old information before new information, although there is much disagreement regarding how to characterize "old" and "new" information. Among the key factors that determine the structuring of information in English are the information's discourse-status and hearer-status (Prince 1992) and the salience of particular open propositions in the discourse. Because noncanonical constructions are used in consistent ways to structure information, formal features of a particular construction make it possible to infer the status of its constituents; thus, the choice of construction for information-packaging purposes simultaneously marks that information's information status. The type of information status to which a particular English construction is sensitive is partly predictable from its form.

1 Introduction

One of the primary factors contributing to the coherence of a discourse is the existence of informational links between the current utterance and the prior context. These links facilitate discourse processing by allowing the hearer to establish and track relationships such as coreference between discourse entities. A variety of linguistic forms, in turn, mark these relationships. For example, the use of the definite article marks the referent of a noun phrase as being unique or individuable within the discourse model (Russell 1905; see also Birner & Ward 1994; Abbott 2004; and Roberts 2003; *inter alia*), and thereby cues the listener to the likelihood that the entity in question has been previously evoked and individuated;

Gregory Ward, Evanston, IL, USA
Betty J. Birner, DeKalb, IL, USA

thus, the listener will look for an appropriate referent in his or her store of already evoked information rather than constructing a new discourse entity. The ordering of elements within the sentence can also reflect informational links and facilitate processing. Chafe (1976) notes that speakers "package" information so as to accommodate their beliefs regarding their addressees' state of mind, and Vallduví (1992) similarly observes that information packaging can help to "optimize the entry of data into the hearer's knowledge-store."

Many languages package information on the basis of an "old/new" principle – that is, information that is assumed to be previously known tends to be placed before that which is assumed to be new to the hearer (although it's possible that this principle may apply only to SV languages; at least some languages with VS ordering have been argued to display the reverse order, as discussed by Tomlin & Rhodes 1979, 1992; Creider & Creider 1983; Siewierska 1988, *inter alia*). The tendency toward a given-before-new ordering of information was codified by Prague School linguists in terms of Communicative Dynamism, or CD. According to the principle of CD, a speaker tends to order a sentence so that its CD (roughly speaking, its informativeness, or the extent to which it presents new information) increases from the beginning to the end of the sentence. This results in a general tendency toward a given-before-new ordering of information within an utterance, a tendency discussed by Gundel (1988) and many others. Consider, for example, the beginning of *Alice's Adventures in Wonderland:*

(1) Alice was beginning to get very tired of sitting by her sister on the bank, and of having nothing to do: once or twice she had peeped into the book her sister was reading, but it had no pictures or conversations in it, 'and what is the use of a book,' thought Alice 'without pictures or conversation?'
[Lewis Carroll, *Alice's Adventures in Wonderland*]

Here, the first clause introduces Alice, who then constitutes given information and is therefore appropriate for early mention in the next clause (*once or twice she....*). This second clause then introduces a book, which in turn now constitutes given information, and is therefore appropriate for early mention in the next clause (*but it had no pictures....*).

The nature of the givenness and newness in question has been the subject of investigation by various authors, who have invoked notions such as topic/comment, focus/presupposition, open proposition/focus, and centering to clarify the nature of various types of information status. Others have noted the effects of both informational weight (what the Prague School called Communicative Dynamism) and formal weight (the length of a linguistic element in terms of words or constituents), both of which tend to rise toward the end of the sentence. As noted by Hawkins (1994) and others, informational weight and formal weight are related: Since less information is required to identify an already-known entity, noun phrases for such entities will tend to be shorter, with pronouns constituting the shortest and least informative type of noun phrase – and also the overwhelming majority of subjects in English (Lambrecht 1994: 132). This close correlation between informational and formal weight thus leaves open the question of whether the crucial factor in sentence position is informational weight, formal weight, or both. Wasow (2002), however, shows that both factors are relevant, and that in at least some cases they exert distinct influences on word order within a sentence.

Thus, the influence of information status on word order is widely recognized, and distinguishable from the contribution of formal weight. Nonetheless, canonical word order in English is unmarked with respect to information structure (Lambrecht 1994); that is, while there is a strong tendency for given information to precede new information in an SVO sentence in English, there is no sense of infelicity invoked by violating this ordering, as in (2):

(2) Alice was beginning to get very tired of sitting by her sister on the bank, and of having nothing to do: once or twice the book her sister was reading had caught her attention, but no pictures or conversations appeared in it, 'and what is the use of a book,' thought Alice 'without pictures or conversation?'

While this version is intuitively more difficult to process, there is no apparent infelicity in its ordering of information. Thus, a canonical-word-order sentence in English discourse prefers, but does not require, its constituents to be ordered with given information preceding new information.

In the case of noncanonical word order, however, the situation is somewhat different. A variety of noncanonical-word-order constructions serve to mark the information status of their constituents, and at the same time facilitate processing through the positioning of various units of information. The speaker's choice of construction, then, serves to structure the informational flow of the discourse. This dual function of structuring and marking the information in a discourse is illustrated in (3):

(3) Beds ringed the room, their iron feet sinking into thick *shirdiks* woven in colorful patterns of birds and flowers. *At the foot of each bed rested a stocky wooden chest*, festooned with designs of cranes and sheep, horses and leaves.
　　　　　　　　[Wilson, D.L. *I Rode a Horse of Milk White Jade*. 1998: 133]

Here, the NP *each bed* in the underlined clause has as its referent the set of beds already evoked in the first sentence; *the foot of each bed*, in turn, can be inferred on the basis of the generally known fact that a bed has a head and a foot. The inversion italicized here serves the dual function of on the one hand structuring the information so as to link up *the foot of each bed* with the previously mentioned *beds* for ease of processing and on the other hand marking the NP *the foot of each bed* as linked in this way, via its sentence-initial placement, so that the hearer knows to search for a previously evoked or inferrable entity rather than constructing a new entity.

In such cases, the purpose of the noncanonical construction is precisely to enable the speaker to place information with a particular information status in a particular syntactic position, and the use of the construction therefore marks that information as having that status. For this reason, such constructions require these constituents to have the appropriate information status, and if they do not, the use of the construction will be infelicitous. For example, notice, in contrast to (2) above, that if the information structure of the inversion in (3) is altered so that the initial PP represents new information while the postverbal NP represents previously evoked, salient information, the use of the inversion becomes infelicitous:

(4) Two chairs sat in the room, their iron feet sinking into thick *shirdiks* woven in colorful patterns of birds and flowers. #*At the foot of a bed rested the chairs, their backs festooned with designs of cranes and sheep, horses and leaves.*

Thus, noncanonical-word-order constructions that serve to mark information status differ from canonical word orders in that, although both are subject to a preferred ordering of information, only the former impose such an ordering as a requirement for the felicity of the utterance.

As we will see below, canonical and noncanonical orderings share a general preference for positioning old information before new information. Extensive research, however, has failed to identify a unitary notion of 'oldness' or 'givenness' at work in all of the noncanonical constructions that are sensitive to givenness. Rather, some constructions are sensitive to the status that the information has in the discourse – whether it has been previously evoked or can plausibly be inferred from something that has been previously evoked – whereas others are sensitive to the status that the information has for the hearer – i.e., whether the speaker believes it is already known to the hearer (not in the sense of 'known to be true', but rather present in the hearer's knowledge store). Moreover, certain constructions are sensitive to the status of a single constituent (in an absolute sense), whereas others are sensitive to the relative status of two constituents.

Among the key factors that determine the structuring of information in English are the information's discourse-status and hearer-status (Prince 1992), and the salience of particular 'open propositions' (i.e., propositions containing an underspecified element) in the discourse. (All of these factors will be discussed below.) Because noncanonical constructions are used in consistent and characteristic ways to structure such information, formal features of a particular construction make it possible to infer the status of the constituents of the construction; in this way the choice of construction for information-packaging purposes simultaneously marks the information so packaged as to, e.g., its discourse- and hearer-status. Thus, the use of a particular construction tells the hearer something about the status of the constituents, due to the hearer's knowledge of the constraints on the use of that construction. In turn, the constraints on the construction are partly predictable from its form. We will show below how a range of noncanonical syntactic constructions in English show broad regularities with respect to the constraints on the information status of their constituents. (For extension of the information-theoretic principles discussed here to other SV languages, see Birner & Ward 1998, *inter alia*.) In particular, we will show that PREPOSING constructions (that is, those that place canonically postverbal constituents in preverbal position) mark the preposed information as familiar within the discourse, while POSTPOSING constructions (those that place canonically preverbal constituents in postverbal position) mark the postposed information as new, either to the discourse or to the hearer. Constructions that reverse the canonical ordering of two constituents (placing a canonically preverbal constituent in postverbal position while placing a canonically postverbal constituent in preverbal position) mark the preposed information as being at least as familiar within the discourse as is the postposed information. In addition, non-locative constructions incorporating a preposed constituent (i.e., preposings and inversion) require the presence of a particular type of salient OPEN PROPOSITION for their felicitous use, as do a number of other syntactic constructions. (See articles 10 [this volume] (Hinterwimmer) *Information structure* and 11 [this volume] (Roberts) *Topics* for more extensive treatments of the focus/presupposition distinction that are essentially compatible with the open-proposition formulation.)

We will illustrate all of these regularities using naturally-occurring linguistic data wherever possible, avoiding the use of constructed examples except to illustrate infelicitous usages (for which, of course, natural examples are generally unavailable) or in the construction of paradigms illustrating variants on a single example (also typically unavailable in natural discourse). Since the field of pragmatics deals centrally with the influence of contextual factors on individual utterances – and that is certainly the case with respect to issues of information status – little can be said about linguistic usages without making reference to the natural-language contexts in which they appear.

2 Information structure: Constituents

The first dimension of information structure we will discuss is the so-called given/new articulation of information at the constituent level. That is to say, we will begin with a discussion of those noncanonical-word-order constructions that are sensitive to the information status of their component constituents.

2.1 Preposing

Our survey of constructions displaying noncanonical word order begins with preposing. Following Ward (1988) and Birner & Ward (1998), we define a preposing as a sentence in which a lexically governed, or subcategorized, phrasal constituent appears to the left of its canonical position, specifically pre-verbally and typically sentence-initially. Preposing is not restricted to any particular phrasal category, as illustrated by the examples of a preposed NP, PP, VP, and AP in (5) through (8), respectively:

(5) NP To illustrate with a simple analogy, consider a person who knows arithmetic, who has mastered the concept of number. In principle, he is now capable of carrying out or determining the accuracy of any computation. *Some computations he may not be able to carry out in his head.* Paper and pencil are required to extend his memory.

[Chomsky, N. *Rules and Representations*. 1980: 221]

(6) PP But keep in mind that no matter which type of equipment you choose, a weight-training regimen isn't likely to provide a cardiovascular workout as well. *For that, you'll have to look elsewhere.*

[*Philadelphia Inquirer*, 8/28/83]

(7) VP They certainly had a lot to talk about *and talk they did.*

[*The New Republic*, 4/23/84]

(8) AP Interrogative *do* should then be classed as a popular idiom. *Popular it may indeed have been*, but I doubt the different origin.

[Ellegård, A. *The Auxiliary* do, *the Establishment and Regulation of its Use in English*. 1953: 168]

In each case, a single argument appears in preposed position and thus, following the generalization we outlined earlier, that argument is constrained to represent old information. More specifically, felicitous preposing in English requires that the information conveyed by the preposed constituent constitute a discourse-old anaphoric link to the preceding discourse (see Reinhart 1981, Horn 1986, Vallduví 1992).

This information can be related to the preceding discourse in a number of ways, including such relations as type/subtype, entity/attribute, part/whole, identity, etc. These relations can all be defined as set relationships. The notion of a set subsumes both coreferential links, where the linking relation between the preposed constituent link and the corresponding set is one of simple identity, and non-coreferential links, where the relation is more complex. To see the difference with respect to preposing, consider (9):

(9) Customer: Can I get a bagel?
    Waitress: No, sorry. We're out of bagels. *A bran muffin I can give you.*
    [customer to waitress in service encounter]

Here, the link (*a bran muffin*) and the previously evoked *bagels* stand in a set relation as alternate members of the inferred set {breakfast baked goods}. However, note that the link could also have been explicitly mentioned in the prior discourse, as in (10):

(10) A: Can I get a bagel?
     B: Sorry – all out.
     A: How about a bran muffin?
     B: *A bran muffin I can give you.*

Although the link *a bran muffin* in this example is coreferential with the entity explicitly evoked in A's second query, the most salient linking relation here is not one of identity. Rather, this link is related via a type/subtype relation to the evoked set {breakfast baked goods}, of which both bagels and bran muffins are members. Thus, the discourse-old link need not itself have been explicitly evoked within the prior discourse; as long as it stands in an appropriate relationship with previously evoked information, it is treated by speakers as discourse-old. (Note also that there are important prosodic differences between the two renditions of *A bran muffin I can give you* in (9) and (10); however, these differences are not relevant to the point at hand.)

Thus, both (9) and (10) illustrate preposings whose links are related to previously evoked sets containing multiple set members. However, some types of preposing also permit links to sets containing only a single member. Consider (11):

(11) Facts about the world thus come in twice on the road from meaning to truth: once to determine the interpretation, given the meaning, and then again to determine the truth value, given the interpretation. *This insight we owe to David Kaplan's important work on indexicals and demonstratives, and we believe it is absolutely crucial to semantics.*

[Barwise, J. & J. Perry. *Situations and Attitudes*. 1983: 11]

Here, the link *this insight* stands in a relation of identity to the evoked set, consisting of a single member. By virtue of this set relation, the link serves as the point of connection to the prior discourse.

Another case of an identity link to the prior discourse is a type of preposing called PROPOSITION AFFIRMATION, illustrated in (12) (see Ward 1990; Birner & Ward 1998; Ward, Birner & Huddleston 2002):

(12) With her new movie, called "Truth or Dare" in America, and "In Bed with Madonna" in Europe, Madonna provides pundits with another excuse to pontificate. *And, on both sides of the Atlantic, pontificate they have – in reviews, essays, magazine features and on television chat shows.*

[*The Economist*, July 27th 1991]

Here, the link *pontificate* is evoked in the immediately preceding sentence. Thus, as in (11), the relevant set in (12) consists of a single member, evoked in the prior context and repeated in the link.

2.2 Left-dislocation

Before we leave preposing, it is important to distinguish it from a superficially similar – but functionally distinct – construction with which preposing is often confused. Left-dislocation (LD) is superficially similar to preposing in that a nonsubject appears in sentence-initial position, but in left-dislocation a coreferential pronoun appears in that constituent's canonical position. Consider (13):

(13) One of the guys I work with, he said he bought over $100 in Powerball tickets.

[JM to WL, in conversation]

Here, a subject pronoun *he* – coreferential with the sentence-initial constituent – appears in canonical subject position; therefore, unlike preposing, there is no 'empty' argument position. It is the presence of this coreferential pronoun that distinguishes LD from preposing in terms of sentence structure, and it is also what distinguishes the two constructions in terms of information structure. As we have seen, the preposed constituent of preposing uniformly represents discourse-old information in context. In the case of LD, however, it is possible for the initial constituent to be not only discourse-new, but even hearer-new, as in (13), where the guy in question is being mentioned for the very first time and is presumably unknown to the hearer.

Prince (1997) argues that there are three types of left-dislocation (LD), distinguishable on functional grounds. Type I LD is what Prince calls SIMPLIFYING LDs:

> A 'simplifying' Left-Dislocation serves to simplify the discourse processing of Discourse-new entities by removing them from a syntactic position disfavored for Discourse-new entities and creating a separate processing unit for them. Once that unit is processed and they have become Discourse-old, they may comfortably occur in their positions within the clause as pronouns. (Prince 1997: 124)

That is, LDs of this type involve entities that are new to the discourse and would otherwise be introduced in a non-favored (i.e. subject) position. Contrast (14a) with (14b–c):

(14) a. Two of my sisters were living together on 18th Street. They had gone to bed, and this man, their girlfriend's husband, came in. He started fussing with my sister and she started to scream. *The landlady, she went up and he laid her out.*

[*Welcomat*, 12/2/81]

b. She had an idea for a project. She's going to use three groups of mice. *One she'll feed them mouse chow.* Just the regular stuff they make for mice. *Another she'll feed them veggies.* And the third she'll feed junk food.

[SH in conversation, 11/7/81 (=Prince 1997, ex. (9e))]

c. That woman you were just talking to, I don't know where she went.

In (14a), the landlady is new to the discourse (and presumably to the hearer as well); however, the speaker is introducing her via an NP in subject position – a position disfavored for introducing new information. The dislocated NP creates a new information unit and thus, according to Prince, eases processing (see also Halliday 1967, Rodman 1974, and Gundel 1974, 1985 for similar proposals). The other two types of LD – triggering a set inference (14b) and amnestying an island violation (14c) – typically do, according to Prince, involve discourse-old information. The fact that not all left-dislocated constituents involve old information stands in stark contrast to true preposing constructions, in which the preposed constituent must always represent a discourse-old link to the prior discourse.

2.3 Postposing

Whereas preposing constructions serve to place relatively familiar information in preverbal position (via the preposing of a discourse-old link), postposing constructions preserve the old-before-new information-structure paradigm by presenting relatively unfamiliar information in postverbal position. That is, when canonical word order would result in the placement of new information in subject position, postposing offers a way of placing it instead toward the end of the clause, in the expected position for new information. Nonetheless, different postposing constructions serve this function in slightly different ways. In this section we will discuss existential *there*, presentational *there*, and extraposition. These postposing constructions will then be contrasted with right-dislocation, which is structurally and functionally distinct.

Two postposing constructions in English place nonreferential *there* in subject position while placing what would be the canonical subject into postverbal position. These constructions are illustrated in (15):

(15) a. In Ireland's County Limerick, near the River Shannon, *there is a quiet little suburb by the name of Garryowen, which means "Garden of Owen"*.
[Brown Corpus]

b. After they had travelled on for weeks and weeks past more bays and headlands and rivers and villages than Shasta could remember, *there came a moonlit night when they started their journey at evening, having slept during the day.*
[C.S. Lewis, *The Horse and His Boy*]

Example (15a) presents an instance of existential *there*, defined by the presence of nonreferential *there* occurring in subject position while the NP that would canonically appear in subject position instead appears postverbally, and finally by the presence of *be* as the main verb. Presentational *there*, as in (15b), is similar in that nonreferential *there* appears in subject position while the NP that would canonically appear in that position instead appears postverbally; it differs, however, in having a main verb other than *be* (here, *came*). Note that (15a) also admits a second reading, in which *there* is referential; under this reading *there* receives an H* pitch accent (see Pierrehumbert 1980) and is coreferential with the previously evoked location in County Limerick. It is only the nonreferential reading that concerns us here.

Both constructions constrain the postverbal NP (PVNP) to represent new information; in this way, both offer a way to preserve the given-before-new ordering of information in cases where canonical word order would violate this ordering. The specifics of the constraint, however, differ slightly in the two constructions: Existential *there* requires that the PVNP represent information that is hearer-new, while presentational *there* requires only that the PVNP represent information that is discourse-new. Thus, the constraint on presentational *there* is weaker than that on existential *there*, since it is possible for information to be new to the discourse while still being known to the hearer, and such information may felicitously occur in clauses containing presentational *there*. To see this, consider (16):

(16) a. As soon as he laughed, he began to move forward in a deliberate way, jiggling a tin cup in one hand and tapping a white cane in front of him with the other. *Just behind him there came a child, handing out leaflets.*
[Flannery O'Connor, *Wise Blood*]

b. [...] Just behind him there came the mayor, handing out leaflets.

Here we see that both the variant with a hearer-new PVNP (16a) and the variant with a hearer-old PVNP ((16b), where towns are known to have mayors) are acceptable, because in both cases the PVNP represents an entity that is new to the discourse. If we alter the discourse so that the PVNP is discourse-old, presentational *there* becomes infelicitous:

(17) As they laughed, John and the mayor began to move forward in a deliberate way. John jiggled a tin cup in one hand and tapped a white cane in front of him with the other. #*Just behind him there came the mayor, handing out leaflets.*

Existential *there* is likewise felicitous with a hearer-new, discourse-new PVNP, as in (15a) above; however, consider the hearer-old, discourse-new PVNP in (18), modeled after the corresponding presentational-*there* variant in (16b):

(18) As soon as he laughed, he began to move forward in a deliberate way, jiggling a tin cup in one hand and tapping a white cane in front of him with the other. #*Just behind him there was the mayor, handing out leaflets.*

In this case, *the mayor* still represents hearer-old information, but unlike presentational *there*, existential *there* in this sentence is infelicitous. That is, both constructions require a new PVNP, but the type of newness differs: Presentational *there* requires only discourse-new status, whereas existential *there* also requires hearer-new status.

Notice that we cannot simply phrase the constraint in terms of definiteness; that is, the difference is not merely in whether the PVNP may be definite. Many authors (Milsark 1974; Safir 1985; Reuland & ter Meulen 1987; Lasnik 1992 *inter alia*) have assumed that there is a 'definiteness effect' that prevents definite NPs from appearing in postverbal position in these sentences. However, as shown in Ward & Birner 1995 and Birner & Ward 1998, this illusion arises from the close relationship between the constraint on definiteness and that on the PVNP in a *there*-sentence. While the PVNP is constrained to be either discourse-new or hearer-new (depending on the construction), a definite NP in general is constrained to be, loosely speaking, identifiable; more specifically, it must be individuable within the discourse model (Birner & Ward 1994, 1998; cf. Gundel, Hedberg & Zacharski 1990, 1993; Abbott 1993). While most referents satisfying the newness criterion for PVNP status will fail to meet the criterion for definiteness, this is not invariably the case; there are a number of contexts in which a definite NP may appear in a *there*-sentence, as in for example hearer-new tokens of hearer-old (hence identifiable) types (19a), hearer-new entities with fully identifying descriptions that render them individuable (19b), and FALSE DEFINITES, which represent discourse-new, hearer-new information that does not in fact satisfy the usual criteria for definiteness (19c):

(19) a. The Woody Allen-Mia Farrow breakup, and Woody's declaration of love for one of Mia's adopted daughters, seems to have everyone's attention. *There are the usual sleazy reasons for that, of course* – the visceral thrill of seeing the extremely private couple's dirt in the street, etc.
[*San Francisco Chronicle*, 8/24/92]

b. In addition, as the review continues, there is always the chance that we'll uncover something additional that is significant.
[Challenger Commission transcripts, 3/18/86]

c. There once was this sharp Chicago alderman who also happened to be a crook. [*Chicago Tribune*; cited in Birner & Ward 1998: 139]

In (19a), the current set of sleazy reasons is hearer-new, but it represents an instance of a hearer-old type – the "usual" sleazy reasons for being interested in the troubles of celebrity couples. The hearer-new status of the current set of reasons justifies its postverbal placement in the existential, while the identifiability of the hearer-old type justifies the definite. In (19b), the definite is justified by the fact that the PVNP fully and uniquely individuates the chance in question, while its position in the existential is justified by the fact that this represents hearer-new information. Finally, in (19c), the NP *this sharp Chicago alderman* constitutes hearer-new information and hence is felicitous as a PVNP; in fact, this NP does not in any way represent identifiable or individuable information within the discourse model and hence is a 'false definite' (Prince 1981b; Wald 1983; Ward & Birner 1995).

Notice that because the PVNPs in (19) are also discourse-new, they are equally felicitous in presentational *there* clauses:

(20) a. The Woody Allen-Mia Farrow breakup, and Woody's declaration of love for one of Mia's adopted daughters, seems to have everyone's attention. *There exist the usual sleazy reasons for that, of course* – the visceral thrill of seeing the extremely private couple's dirt in the street, etc.
   b. In addition, as the review continues, there always exists the chance that we'll uncover something additional that is significant.
   c. There once lived this sharp Chicago alderman who also happened to be a crook.

In each case in (20), presentational *there* is licensed by the discourse-new status of the PVNP. Other cases in which a definite PVNP may occur in an existential or presentational *there*-sentence include hearer-old information treated as hearer-new, as with certain types of reminders, and hearer-old information newly instantiating the variable in an OP; see Ward & Birner (1995) for details.

The last type of postposing construction to be discussed is extraposition. In extraposition, a subordinate clause is postposed from subject position, while its canonical position is filled by nonreferential *it*. Consider the canonical sentences in (21) and their variants with extraposition in (22):

(21) a. That a bloodthirsty, cruel capitalist should be such a graceful fellow was a shock to me.
    [Davis, *The Iron Puddler*; token courtesy of Philip Miller]

   b. Yet to determine precisely to what extent and exactly in what ways any individual showed the effects of Christianity would be impossible.
    [Brown Corpus; token courtesy of Philip Miller]

(22) a. It was a shock to me that a bloodthirsty, cruel capitalist should be such a graceful fellow.
b. Yet it would be impossible to determine precisely to what extent and exactly in what ways any individual showed the effects of Christianity.

In both examples in (22), the clause appearing as an embedded subject in the canonical version is instead extraposed to the end of the matrix clause. As shown by Miller (2001), extraposition, like the other postposing constructions discussed above, serves to preserve an old-before-new ordering in the discourse. In particular, Miller shows that the canonical variant is felicitous only if the embedded subject clause represents familiar information; if it represents new information, it must be extraposed (cf. Horn 1986).

To see this, consider the constructed examples in (23–24):

(23) a. A: Jeffrey didn't turn in his term paper until a week after the deadline.
B: It's a miracle that he turned in a term paper at all.
b. A: Jeffrey didn't turn in his term paper until a week after the deadline.
B: That he turned in a term paper at all is a miracle.

(24) a. A: Jeffrey isn't a very good student.
B: Yeah; #that he turned in a term paper at all is a miracle.
b. A: Jeffrey isn't a very good student.
B: Yeah, it's a miracle that he turned in a term paper at all.

In (23), the fact that Jeffrey turned in a term paper is discourse-old, having been presupposed in A's utterance, and both variants are felicitous. In (24), on the other hand, this fact is new to the discourse, and only the extraposed variant is felicitous. Notice that unlike each of the other constructions we have dealt with, in which the noncanonical version is subject to some constraint on its felicity, in the case of extraposition it is the canonical variant that is constrained; that is, the canonical variant is infelicitous when the embedded subject represents new information, and in such cases extraposition becomes obligatory.

Although Miller frames this constraint in terms of discourse-old vs. discourse-new status, it appears that in fact it is hearer-status that is relevant – i.e., that non-extraposed subject clauses are felicitous when they represent hearer-old information (Ward, Birner, & Huddleston 2002). Consider (25):

(25) His act takes on lunatic proportions as he challenges female audience members to wrestling matches, falling in love with one while grappling it out on the canvas. *How he and feminist Lynne Margulies (Courtney Love) became life partners is anyone's guess.*
[*Man on the Moon* movie review (=Ward, Birner & Huddleston 2002, sec. 7, ex. 3.iii)]

Here the fact that the referent of *he* (comedian Andy Kaufman) and Lynn Margulies became life partners is treated as shared background knowledge, despite not having been evoked in the prior discourse. Hence it is hearer-old but not discourse-old, yet the utterance is nonetheless felicitous. Thus, extraposition is required only when the embedded clause represents hearer-new information, and the extraposition in that case serves once again to preserve the ordering of old before new information within the utterance.

2.4 Right-dislocation

Just as left-dislocation is functionally distinct from preposing, so is right-dislocation functionally distinct from postposing, despite the fact that both constructions involve the rightward placement of information that would canonically appear earlier in the clause. In existential and presentational *there*-sentences, for example, the PVNP is required to represent information that is new, either to the discourse (for presentational *there*) or to the hearer (for existential *there*). For right-dislocation, no such requirement holds:

(26) Below the waterfall (and this was the most astonishing sight of all), a whole mass of enormous glass pipes were dangling down into the river from somewhere high up in the ceiling! *They really were* ENORMOUS, *those pipes*. There must have been a dozen of them at least, and they were sucking up the brownish muddy water from the river and carrying it away to goodness knows where.
[R. Dahl, *Charlie and the Chocolate Factory*. 1964: 74–75]

Here, the pipes in question have been explicitly evoked in the previous sentence and therefore are both hearer-old and discourse-old; in fact, discourse-old status is not only permitted but indeed required:

(27) Below the waterfall (and this was the most astonishing sight of all), a whole mass of enormous glass pipes were dangling down into the river from somewhere high up in the ceiling! #*They really were* ENORMOUS, *some of the boulders in the river.*

Here we see that when the right-dislocated NP represents discourse-new information, the utterance is infelicitous; thus, none of the requirements placed on postposing constructions (all of which permit or in fact require discourse-new information in postposed position) hold for right-dislocation. Notice, however, that the two are structurally distinct as well, paralleling the structural distinction seen above to hold between preposing and left-dislocation; specifically, whereas all of the above postposing constructions place a semantically empty element (*there* or *it*) in subject position while placing the canonical subject in postverbal position, right-dislocation instead places a coreferential pronoun in the right-dislocated NP's canonical position. That is, instead of nonreferential *there* or *it*, we get the referential pronoun *they* in subject position in (26). This pronoun, like anaphoric pronouns in general, represents familiar (indeed, discourse-old and highly salient) information – and because the pronoun is coreferential with the dislocated constituent, that constituent too will therefore represent familiar (discourse-old) information. In this way, the form of the right-dislocation – specifically, the presence of an anaphoric pronoun – constrains its information-packaging function.

2.5 Argument reversal

We have seen how preposing places a single constituent to the left of its canonical position, where it is constrained to represent old information. We have also seen how postposing places a single constituent to the right of its canonical position, where it is constrained to represent new information. In this section, we examine argument reversal, a process that involves the displacement of *two* arguments and thus, we claim, imposes a relative rather than absolute constraint on the information status of the displaced constituents. Specifically, we have found that the preposed constituent must represent information that is at least as familiar as that represented by the postposed constituent (Birner 1994, 1996; Birner & Ward 1998).

The English argument-reversing constructions we will consider are inversion and *by*-phrase passives, which we discuss in turn.

Inversion
In inversion, the logical subject appears in postverbal position while some other, canonically postverbal, constituent appears in preverbal position (Birner 1994). Thus, the order of the two major arguments is reversed. As with preposing, any phrasal constituent can be preposed via inversion:

(28) PP   He, the publisher, is twenty-six. Born in Hungary, he emigrated to Canada after the revolution. He is as informal as the others. *On his lapel is a large "Jesus Loves You" button*; on his feet, sneakers. His dog scrounges about on a blanket in this inner office.
[Terkel, *Working*, 1974: 583]

(29) AdjP   Along U.S. Route 6, overscale motels run by the national chains have started to supplant the quaint, traditional transients' cottages. *Typical of these new giants is the Sheraton Ocean Park at Eastham, which boasts an indoor swimming pool with cabanas in a tropic-like setting.*
[*Philadelphia Inquirer*, p. 2-A, 9/6/83, article "On Cape Cod, charm ebbs as numbers grow"]

(30) NP   She's a nice woman, isn't she? *Also a nice woman is our next guest.*
[David Letterman, 5/31/90]

(31) VP   Discussion of the strategy began during this year's General Assembly and will conclude next year. *Dropped from consideration so far are the approaches of the past, which The Economist recently described as "based on the idea that the rules of orthodox economics do not hold in developing countries."*
[*New York Times Week in Review*, November 5, 1989, p. 2]

Note in particular that although the linear word order in (30) (NP – *be* – NP) is the same as that of a canonical-word-order sentence, it is nonetheless an inversion, given that the postverbal NP (*our next guest*) represents the logical subject, of which the information represented by the preverbal NP (*a nice woman*) is being predicated. (See Birner 1994 for discussion.)

Felicitous inversion in English depends on the relative discourse-status of the information represented by the preposed and postposed constituents. As noted in Birner 1994, the most common distribution of information is for the preposed constituent to represent discourse-old information while the postposed constituent represents discourse-new information, as in (32):

(32)   We have complimentary soft drinks, coffee, Sanka, tea, and milk. *Also complimentary is red and white wine.* We have cocktails available for $2.00.
[Flight attendant on Midway Airlines]

Here, the preposed AdjP *also complimentary* represents information previously evoked in the discourse, while the postposed *red and white wine* is new to the discourse. In a corpus study of over 1700 tokens, 78% of the tokens exhibited this distribution of information, while not a single example was found in which the situation was reversed – i.e., in which a preposed discourse-new element combined with a postposed discourse-old element. Moreover, information that was merely inferrable (Prince 1981a) behaved as discourse-old, occurring in the same range of contexts as explicitly evoked information.

It is not the case, however, that the preposed constituent need always be discourse-old, or that the postposed constituent need always be discourse-new. The pragmatic constraint on argument reversal disallows only a preposed constituent being *less* familiar in the discourse than the postposed constituent. Felicity is possible, for example, when both constituents represent discourse-old information; however, in these cases the preposed element is consistently the more recently mentioned of the two, as in (33):

(33) Each of the characters is the centerpiece of a book, doll and clothing collection. The story of each character is told in a series of six slim books, each $12.95 hardcover and $5.95 in paperback, and in bookstores and libraries across the country. More than 1 million copies have been sold; and in late 1989 a series of activity kits was introduced for retail sale. *Complementing the relatively affordable books are the dolls, one for each fictional heroine and each with a comparably pricey historically accurate wardrobe and accessories....*

[*Chicago Tribune* story on "American Girl" dolls]

Here, although the dolls have been evoked in the prior discourse, they have been evoked less recently than the books. Reversing the preposed and postposed constituents in the inversion results in infelicity:

(34) Each of the characters is the centerpiece of a book, doll and clothing collection. The story of each character is told in a series of six slim books, each $12.95 hardcover and $5.95 in paperback, and in bookstores and libraries across the country. More than 1 million copies have been sold; and in late 1989 a series of activity kits was introduced for retail sale. #*Complementing the relatively affordable dolls are the books, one for each fictional heroine....*

Thus, even in cases where both constituents have been previously evoked, the postposed constituent nonetheless represents less familiar information, where familiarity is defined by prior evocation, inferrability, and recency of mention. Therefore, what is relevant for the felicity of inversion in discourse is the relative discourse-familiarity of the information represented by these two constituents.

Passives
By-phrase passives are passive constructions with a *by*-phrase containing the logical subject, as in (35):

(35) Connaught said it was advised that the Ciba-Geigy/Chiron offer would be increased to $26.51 a share from $25.23 a share if the company adopted a shareholder-rights plan that facilitated the Swiss and U.S. firms' offer. *That offer was rejected by Connaught, which cited its existing pact with Institut Merieux.*
[*Wall Street Journal*, 9/12/89]

Note that in this construction the canonical order of the two major NP constituents is reversed.

In referring to the preverbal NP in a *by*-phrase passive (e.g., *that offer* in (35)) as the syntactic subject, and to the postverbal NP (e.g., *Connaught*) as the *by*-phrase NP, we break with the tradition of calling the *by*-phrase NP an 'agent' and the construction itself an 'agentive passive' (e.g., Siewierska 1984). Such terminology is misleading given that in many cases the *by*-phrase NP does not act as a semantic agent (in the sense of Fillmore 1968). In (36), for example, *Ivan Allen Jr.* is not an agent:

(36) The mayor's present term of office expires January 1. *He will be succeeded by Ivan Allen Jr....*
[Brown Corpus]

As an argument-reversing construction, this type of passivization requires that its syntactic subject represent information that is at least as familiar within the discourse as that represented by the *by*-phrase NP (Birner 1996). Thus, when the information status of the relevant NPs is reversed, infelicity results. Compare (36) with (37):

(37) Ivan Allen Jr. will take office January 1. #*The mayor will be succeeded by him.*

The subject *he* in (36) represents discourse-old information, while the *by*-phrase NP, *Ivan Allen Jr.*, represents discourse-new information, and the token is felicitous. In (37), on the other hand, the syntactic subject, *the mayor*, represents discourse-new information while the NP in the *by*-phrase, *him*, represents discourse-old information, and the passive is infelicitous. Note that, as with inversion, it is not the absolute status of the constituents that is relevant, but rather their relative status; in (35), for example, both constituents represent discourse-old information, yet the passive is felicitous.

Thus, *by*-phrase passives share with inversion the property of requiring the preposed constituent to represent information that is at least as familiar in the discourse as that represented by the postposed constituent. The relative (vs. absolute) information status to which argument reversal in general is sensitive is, in turn, a direct consequence of there being a displacement of two constituents. The transposition of arguments found in both passivization and inversion imposes a relative constraint on the information status of those constituents, unlike the absolute constraint found for the noncanonical constructions that displace only a single constituent.

3 Information structure: Open propositions

The other major dimension of information structure is the so-called focus/focus-frame articulation of information at the propositional level. While in the previous section we looked at constructions sensitive to the information status of their component constituents, in this section we will be examining those noncanonical word order constructions that are sensitive to information status at the propositional level. We begin once again with preposing.

3.1 Preposing

In addition to marking its preposed constituent as old information, preposing is a focus/focus-frame construction in that it marks as salient or inferrable an open proposition (OP) in the discourse. Preposings can be classified into two major types based on their focus structure: FOCUS PREPOSING (or FOCUS MOVEMENT, as it is often referred to in the literature) and TOPICALIZATION. The preposed constituent of focus preposing contains the focus of the utterance and bears nuclear accent (i.e., INTONATIONAL PROMINENCE in the sense of Terken & Hirschberg 1994; see also Pierrehumbert 1980); the rest of the clause is typically deaccented. Topicalization, on the other hand, involves a preposed constituent *other than the focus* and bears multiple pitch accents: at least one on the preposed constituent and at least one on the (non-preposed) focus. Nonetheless, both types of preposing require a salient or inferrable OP at the time of utterance for felicity, except in the case of semantically locative preposed constituents (see below).

Consider first the focus preposing in (38), in which the focus is contained within, and indeed exhausts, the preposed constituent:

(38) Colonel Kadafy, you said you were planning on sending planes – *M-16s I believe they were* – to Sudan.
[Peter Jennings on ABC's "World News Tonight"]

The preposed constituent in this example, *M-16s*, contains the nuclear accent, which identifies it as the focus of the utterance. To construct the OP, the preposed constituent containing the focus is first placed in its canonical argument position. The focus is replaced with a variable, whose instantiation is being presupposed by the speaker to represent a member of some contextually licensed set, as informally represented in (39a). (A rough gloss of the OP is provided in (39b).) The focus, provided in (39c), instantiates the variable in the OP (see, for example, Rooth 1992; articles 10 [this volume] (Hinterwimmer) *Information structure* and 11 [this volume] (Roberts) *Topics*).

(39) a. OP = The planes were of type X, where X is a member of the set {types-of-military-aircraft}.
b. The planes were of some type.
c. Focus = M-16s

Here, *M-16s* serves as the link to the preceding discourse. It is a member of the set {military aircraft}, which is rendered salient by the mention of *planes* in the speaker's prior utterance. From *planes*, we can infer that the planes were of some type, as in (39a). While the set {military aircraft} is discourse-old, the preposed constituent itself represents information that has not been explicitly evoked in the prior discourse. In the case of focus preposing, then, the set must be discourse-old while the link – as focus – is new. Thus, it follows that the set must contain at least one other member in addition to the link.

The (primary) focus in a topicalization, on the other hand, is not contained in the preposed constituent but occurs elsewhere in the utterance. Intonationally, preposings of this type contain multiple accented syllables: (at least) one occurs within the constituent that contains the (obligatory) primary focus and (at least) one occurs within the preposed constituent. Consider (40):

(40) G: Do you watch football?
E: Yeah. *Baseball I like a lot* BETTER.
[Conversation]

Here, it is the postverbal adverb *better* – and not the preposed NP *baseball* – that serves as the primary focus of the utterance, and thus bears nuclear accent. What *baseball* does is serve as the link to the set {sports}, inferrable on the basis of the evoked set member *football*. Although *baseball* in (40) does not receive nuclear accent, it is nonetheless accented because it serves as a secondary focus, contrasting with *football* and occurring in a separate intonational phrase. (See article 10 [this volume] (Hinterwimmer) *Information structure* for more detailed elaboration of focus.)

The OP is formed in much the same way as for focus preposing, except that the set member represented by the preposed constituent is replaced in the OP by the relevant set:

(41) a. OP = I like-to-X-degree {sports}, where X is a member of the set {degrees}.
b. I like sports to some degree.
c. Focus = better

In (41a), the OP includes the variable corresponding to the primary focus, but the link *baseball* has been replaced by the set {sports}, i.e. the set that includes both the previously evoked set member and the link. In other words, the OP that is salient in (40) is not that the speaker likes baseball *per se*, but rather that he likes sports to some degree.

As noted by Birner & Ward (1998), however, the OP requirement for preposing does not seem to hold in cases in which the preposed constituent represents a semantically locative element. Consider (42):

(42) In the VIP section of the commissary at 20th Century-Fox, the studio's elite gather for lunch and gossip. The prized table is reserved for Mel Brooks, *and from it he dispenses advice, jokes and invitations to passers-by.*
[Philadelphia Inquirer, 2/19/84]
OP = He dispenses X from {places}, where X is a member of the set {types of banter}.

Here, the proposition that Mel Brooks dispenses something from some location is not salient, yet the preposing is felicitous. Note that only semantically locative preposed constituents are exempt from the OP requirement; other semantic types of PPs, for example, are infelicitous in the absence of a salient OP. Consider the preposed instrumental in (43a), the preposed goal in (43b), and the preposed benefactive in (43c):

(43) a. Ah, there's a knife. #*With it, I'll cut the bread.*
b. We have a new mail carrier. #*To him, the dog runs every day.*
c. It's my brother's birthday tomorrow. #*For him, I'll bake a cake.*

What these examples show is that preposings whose preposed constituents are non-locative are subject to the general requirement that there be a salient or inferrable OP in context.

3.2 Inversion

Like preposing, inversion also generally requires a salient open proposition for its felicity. Consider the example in (44):

(44) Two CBS crewmen were wounded by shrapnel yesterday in Souk el Gharb during a Druse rocket attack on Lebanese troops. They were the 5th and 6th television-news crewmen to be wounded in Lebanon this month. One television reporter, Clark Todd of Canada, was killed earlier this month. *Wounded yesterday were cameraman Alain Debos, 45, and soundman Nick Follows, 24.*
[Philadelphia Inquirer, 9/24/83]

Here, the link *wounded yesterday* is related to the set {injury times}, ordered by a relation of temporal precedence. This set is readily inferrable on the basis of the phrases *wounded by shrapnel yesterday*, *wounded in Lebanon this month*, and *killed earlier this month* in the preceding discourse. The OP associated with this inversion is formed in the same way as with the preposing discussed above in (41). The link is replaced with the relevant set and the focused item (the postposed NP) is replaced with a variable, as illustrated in (45):

(45) a. OP = X was wounded at {injury times}, where X is a member of the set {television-news crewmen}.
 b. Focus = cameraman Alain Debos, 45, and soundman Nick Follows, 24

Once again, we see that the OP includes the set of which the link is a member. Thus, the OP is not simply that X was wounded yesterday, but rather the more abstract proposition that X was wounded at some time. It is this OP that must be salient or inferrable in context for the inversion to be felicitous. Consider the same utterance in a context where the OP is not licensed:

(46) Several CBS crewmen arrived in Souk el Gharb last week to cover the latest peace talks. #*Wounded yesterday were cameraman Alain Debos, 45, and soundman Nick Follows, 24.*

Here, the relevant OP is neither salient nor inferrable, and the inversion is consequently infelicitous. Thus, it appears that inversion involves the same sorts of OPs that have been shown to be relevant for preposing.

However, as we saw in the case of preposing, this OP requirement for inversion is also relaxed in cases where the preposed constituent represents a locative element:

(47) There are three ways to look at East State Street Village, a low-income apartment complex in Camden. None of them are pretty views. *To the west of the 23 brightly colored buildings flows the Cooper River, a fetid waterway considered one of the most polluted in New Jersey.*
[Philadelphia Inquirer, 5/7/84]
OP = X flows to {locations}, where X is a member of the set {waterways}.

And again, it is the semantically locative nature of the PP that exempts the inversion containing it from the OP requirement; thus, while the preposed locative PP in (48a) is felicitous, the preposed benefactive PP in (48b), in the absence of an appropriate salient OP, is not:

(48) a. Yesterday, I was sitting on the patio when into the yard came a neighbor.
b. Yesterday, I was sitting on the patio when #for my roommate came a package.

Thus, for both preposing and inversion, a salient OP is required except in the case of semantically locative preposed constituents.

3.3 Gapping

Gapping is another noncanonical construction that is sensitive to the information status of its component constituents. A gapping is a sentence whose main verb (and possible additional elements within the VP) is elided under identity with a prior occurrence of that verb in a pragmatically appropriate context. Thus, a 'gapped' sentence cannot appear in isolation; its felicity depends upon the prior occurrence of a non-gapped sentence (to serve as the 'source' sentence) which licenses the elision (or 'gapping') of the main verb in the subsequent clause (the 'target' sentence). Consider the (constructed) example in (49):

(49) John talked to Jeff about linguistics, and to Mary about politics.

Here, we see that the source clause in (49) 'JOHN TALKED TO JEFF ABOUT LINGUISTICS' contains the main verb *talk*, which licenses the elision of this verb in the target clause *and to Mary about politics*. (See article 9 [this volume] (Reich) *Ellipsis*.)

As noted by previous researchers (Prince & Levin 1986; Kehler 1995, 2002), gapped sentences, unlike their canonical counterparts, are pragmatically restricted in that they may not receive 'asymmetrical' interpretations. As an illustration, consider the non-gapped sentence in (50a) with its gapped counterpart in (50b):

(50) a. Sue and Nan had worked long and hard for Carter. When Reagan was declared the winner, *Sue became upset and Nan became downright angry.*
[=Levin & Prince 1986, ex. (4a)]

b. Sue and Nan had worked long and hard for Carter. When Reagan was declared the winner, *Sue became upset and Nan downright angry.*

Here, the two events described in the prior context are understood to be causally independent of one other; they could have been reported in the opposite order with equal felicity. This symmetrical interpretation is available in both the gapped and non-gapped versions.

Gapped sentences, however, do not permit the asymmetric interpretation, in which the event described in the source clause is taken to be the cause or reason for the event described in the target clause. Consider the contrast between (51a) and (51b):

(51) a. Sue's histrionics in public have always gotten on Nan's nerves, but it's getting worse. Yesterday, when she couldn't have her daily Egg McMuffin because they were all out, *Sue became upset and Nan became downright angry.*
b. Sue's histrionics in public have always gotten on Nan's nerves, but it's getting worse. Yesterday, when she couldn't have her daily Egg McMuffin because they were all out, #*Sue became upset and Nan downright angry.*
[=Levin & Prince 1986, ex. (5a)]

Here, in a context that strongly favors the asymmetric interpretation – in which Sue's histrionics are what leads to Nan's anger – the non-gapped variant in (51a) is felicitous while the gapped variant in (51b) is not.

As further evidence that gapping is restricted to symmetrical interpretations, Kehler (2002) observes that gapping is felicitous only with coordinators that denote a PARALLEL RELATION between the target and source clauses. As an illustration of this restriction, consider the various coordinators in (52):

(52) a. #Pat voted for a Democrat but Tom a Republican.
 b. #Pat voted for a Democrat although Tom a Republican.
 c. #Pat voted for a Democrat so Tom a Republican.
 d. #Pat voted for a Democrat with greater confidence than Tom a Republican.
 e. #Pat voted for a Democrat because Tom a Republican.

Note that this restriction on gapping to the coordination of parallel events is inherently semantic, not syntactic; the conjunction *but* in (52a) involves syntactic coordination, but nonetheless induces a non-parallel interpretation.

In terms of its information structure, gapping, like preposing and inversion, depends on a salient or inferrable OP to ensure felicity. However, gapping is more restricted, in that one of the gapped elements must be a tensed verb. Furthermore, gapping requires that there be a source sentence containing an instance of the verb that is elided in the target sentence; when the elided verb does not explicitly appear in the source sentence, as in (53), infelicity results:

(53) I have a serious hangover. Way too much wine! #*And my partner, beer.*
 [cf. And my partner drank way too much beer.]

In this example, the preceding context licenses the inference that the speaker drank "way too much" wine. However, unless the verb *drank* is explicitly evoked, gapping in this context is infelicitous.

As with other noncanonical constructions, the constituents of gapping that bear nuclear accent represent instantiations of variables in the OP and, as such, constitute the foci of the utterance. What distinguishes gapping from other noncanonical constructions is that there are necessarily multiple foci. Consider the following example:

(54) a. John's mother voted for a Democrat and his father voted for a Republican.
 b. John's mother voted for a Democrat and his father a Republican.
 c. X voted for Y, where X is a member of the set {parents} and Y is a member of the set {U.S. political parties}.

The open proposition in (54c) may be paraphrased informally as 'One of John's parents voted for a member of a political party'. This OP is clearly salient, and therefore discourse-old, in the context of the preceding sentence *John's mother voted for a Democrat*. Although the two foci in this example, 'John's father' and 'a Republican', are not explicitly evoked in the prior discourse and are therefore not part of the OP, they nonetheless stand in a salient set relationship with the previously evoked 'John's mother' and 'a Democrat', respectively.

As evidence that the sets in question must be salient or inferrable in context for the gapping to be felicitous, consider (55), in which the sets do not have this information status:

(55) #Mr. Brown likes apricots and my neighbor London.

The infelicity of (55) can be attributed to the real-world implausibility of sets that comprise Mr. Brown and my neighbor, on the one hand, and apricots and London on the other.

In sum, we see that while gapping is not alone among noncanonical constructions in requiring that an open proposition be salient or inferrable in discourse, it is significantly more constrained than other such constructions in requiring both semantic parallelism and an occurrence of the elided verb in the source sentence.

3.4 OPs and canonical word order

Thus far, we've been focusing on constructions that employ noncanonical word order to indicate a marked information structure. However, as is well known, word order is not the only indicator of a marked construction. In this section, we discuss two copular constructions in English whose noncanonical status does not derive from word order variation: DEFERRED EQUATIVES (Ward 2004) and EPISTEMIC *would* EQUATIVES (Birner, Kaplan & Ward 2007). We begin with an analysis of epistemic *would* equatives.

Epistemic would *equatives*
The epistemic *would* equative construction consists of two NPs linked by the copula *be*. Consider the examples in (56), taken from Birner, Kaplan & Ward (2007):

(56) a. Dad: Uh... Who's that boy hanging out in our front yard, Danae?
  Danae: *That would be Jeffrey,* my not-so-secret admirer.
   ["Non Sequitur" comic, *Chicago Tribune*, Sunday, 3/3/02, sec. 9, p. 3]

  b. Q: Can you tell us if you recognize this clothing?
  A: *That would be our standard attire,* correct.
   [Simpson transcripts, 2/7]

c. I need to talk to Andy to see if he's interested in going to a departure lunch for a Zenith employee this Friday at Little Villa – *the employee would be myself.*

[Answering machine message, 9/21/00]

Crucial to the analysis is the epistemic modal *would*, whose presence in this construction requires that an OP be salient in context for felicity. Note that this requirement is specific to the modal itself, not to the demonstrative and copula that frequently, but not necessarily, cooccur with it in what we have in past work called the TWBX ('that would be X') construction (Ward, Birner & Kaplan 2003). That is, all clauses with epistemic *would* – with or without a copula and with or without a pronominal subject – share the OP requirement, as illustrated in (57):

(57) Recently I saw a photo of a protestor at the Federal Building in Westwood carrying a sign that read, "CIA, what assets are we going to war for?" I believe *those assets would be life, liberty, and the pursuit of happiness.* [letter to the editor, *LA Times*, 10/13/01 (=Birner, Kaplan & Ward 2007, ex. (17b))]

In this context, the OP 'The assets we are going to war for are X' is clearly salient; if it were not, the utterance would be infelicitous.

Interestingly, when a deictic subject appears in an equative in the context of an appropriate salient OP, the cooccurrence of these three elements gives rise to the possibility of using the demonstrative to refer to the instantiation of the variable in the OP, and in turn using the equative to equate this entity with the postcopular focus. We see this illustrated in (58):

(58) a. A [holding cup]: Whose is this?
B: *That would be my son.* My youngest son, to be exact.
[conversation, 2/4/01]
OP = 'This cup belongs to X'

b. GW: What is the per minute charge to Italy?
Operator: Do you have the one-rate plan?
GW: I'm not sure – can I find out through you?
Operator: No, *that would be... 1-800-466-3728.*
[conversation with AT&T operator, 6/23/01]
OP = 'You can find out through X'

c. Villager [in reference to an ogre]: He'll grind your bones for his bread!
Shrek: *Actually, that would be a giant.*

[movie "Shrek"]
OP = 'The creature that grinds your bones for his bread is X'
[=Birner, Kaplan & Ward 2007, ex. (18a)–(18c)]

As argued in Birner, Kaplan & Ward (2007), the most plausible referent for the demonstrative in each of these examples is the instantiation of the variable in the OP – in (58a), the person to whom the cup belongs; in (58b), the entity from whom one can find the desired information; and in (58c), the creature that actually does grind your bones for his bread. In each of these cases, the context provides no other obvious candidate for the referent of the deictic; for example, the salient ogre in (58c) is not the intended referent of the deictic.

Due to the possibility of using a demonstrative subject to refer to the instantiation of the OP variable, examples such as those in (58) are systematically ambiguous between the reading on which the demonstrative is used to refer to the instantiation of the variable and a reading on which it is used to refer anaphorically or deictically to a discourse entity. Thus, the *that* of *That would be my son* in (58a) could, in a context in which the son in question has just entered the room, be taken deictically. Although context typically disambiguates, this isn't always the case; thus, in a context that provides a plausible discourse referent, the demonstrative remains ambiguous in its reference:

(59) [King dips his finger in a bowl held by a servant and then licks the food off his finger and proclaims it delicious.]
King: What do you call this dish?
Servant: *That would be the dog's breakfast.*
[movie "Shrek 2"]
OP = 'You call this dish X'
[=Birner, Kaplan & Ward 2007, ex. (21a)]

Here, the demonstrative subject in the epistemic *would* equative can be used to refer either to the instantiation of the variable in the salient OP 'YOU CALL THIS DISH X' or to the salient dish itself. In the first case, the sentence is paraphraseable as *We call this dish the dog's breakfast*, whereas in the second it is paraphraseable as *That dish is the dog's breakfast*.

Because the demonstrative may be used to refer to the instantiation of the OP variable, we occasionally find what appears to be a case of number disagreement. This, however, can be explained in terms of the referent being the instantiation of the variable. Consider the examples in (60):

(60) a. One of the best mulches is composted leaves, so good for the garden, the flower bed, and a wonderful amendment to the soil. Also, here's hoping you won't burn your leaves, wasting them, despite the fact that burning them is illegal in most Illinois counties – *that would be the populated ones, like Cook, DuPage, Lake, e.g.* [email, 4/24/01]
OP = 'The Illinois counties in which burning leaves is illegal are X'

b. By the way, I heard your names (*that would be you and Andy*) on NPR yesterday … happy anniversary!
[email, 6/26/02]
OP = 'I heard the names of X'
[=Birner, Kaplan & Ward 2007, ex. (22a)–(22b)]

In both of these cases, the most salient entity in the discourse immediately preceding the equative is plural – *most Illinois counties* in (60a) and *your names* in (60b). However, instead of the plural distal demonstrative *those*, we find the demonstratives in (60a–b) appearing in the singular. Birner, Kaplan & Ward (2007) account for the apparent mismatch by arguing that the demonstrative is not being used to refer to the plural entity evoked in the prior discourse, but rather to the (singular) instantiation of the variable in the OP. For example, associated with the italicized clause in (60a) is the OP 'The Illinois counties in which burning leaves is illegal are X'. The epistemic *would* equative, then, serves to instantiate the variable, equating X with the set of populated counties. Since what is being instantiated is a singular variable, the demonstrative agrees with it in number.

In the same way, we frequently find what at first appears to be a temporal clash in cases of the TWBX ('that would be X') construction. Note that in reference to a past event, the verb complex frequently reflects this past time through the use of *have* (as in (61a)), but sometimes it does not (as in (61b)):

(61) a. "Where'd you get the new shingles? They're a perfect match." He examined the shingles in his hands, as if noticing this for the first time, and then called back, "Well, they ought to be, they're all from the same lot. I bought two hundred extras when I put this roof on."
"When was that?" I asked.
He looked up at the clouds. I don't know whether he was divining the weather or the past. "Right after the war," he said. *"That would have been forty-six."*
[Barbara Kingsolver, *Animal Dreams*, Harper Collins, 1990: 275]
OP = 'I put this roof on at time X'

b. Sabrina: Do you remember a rainy afternoon we spent together? My father had driven your mother and David into town for a music lesson.
Linus Larrabee: How old was he?
S: I don't know... Fourteen, fifteen.
L: *That would be the oboe.*
[movie "Sabrina"]
OP = 'David was taking lessons in X at that time'
[=Birner, Kaplan & Ward 2007, ex. (24a)–(24b)]

In (61a), the subject demonstrative is coreferential with the earlier demonstrative *that*; both are used to refer to the time when the roof was put on. Because the event in question occurred in the past, it is referenced in the verb complex with *have been*. In (61b), however, despite the fact that the speakers are discussing a past-time event, the final clause contains *be* rather than *have been*.

The explanation, however, mirrors the explanation provided for the apparent number mismatch discussed above. Because the demonstrative can be used to refer either to a previously evoked constituent or to the instantiation of the OP variable, the equative as a whole can be taken to be making an assertion either about the past event or about the present instantiation of the variable. Thus, the demonstrative in (61b) is being used to refer to the instantiation of the variable in the salient OP 'David was taking lessons in X at that time', and the clause may then be interpreted as conveying 'X is the oboe' (Birner, Kaplan & Ward 2007).

In sum, epistemic *would* equatives require the presence of a salient OP for felicity. Moreover, the possibility of reference to the instantiation of the variable of that OP accounts for a number of otherwise mysterious properties associated with this construction: systematic referential ambiguity, apparent number mismatch, and apparent tense mismatch.

Deferred equatives
The second canonical-word-order construction we will discuss is the deferred equative construction. Like epistemic *would* equatives, deferred equatives are canonical-word-order copular sentences consisting of two NPs linked by the copula *be*. (In using the term 'equative' for identity copular sentences of the form NP-*be*-NP, we are following the terminology and analysis of Heycock & Kroch 1997 and Mikkelsen 2004 (but cf. Higgins 1979), yet nothing in what follows depends on this particular syntactic analysis.) What is of particular interest is that this construction seems to involve a type of DEFERRED REFERENCE (Nunberg 1977, 1979, 1995; Ward 2004): the metonymic use of an expression to refer to an entity related to, but not denoted by, the conventional meaning of that expression.

Examples of deferred equatives are provided in (62):

(62) a. [customer to server holding tray full of dinner orders at a Thai restaurant]
I'm the Pad Thai.
[Conversation, 8/10/02]

b. [request to unplug out-of-reach laptop power cable]
A: Hi, can you unplug me?
B: Sure, which one are you?
A: *I'm the one on the end.*
[Conversation, 12/12/06; token courtesy of Robert Daland]

By means of such equatives, the speaker conveys that a particular correspondence (other than strict identity) holds between the two NPs of the equative. What makes these equatives "deferred" is that they are not being understood as literal identity statements. In (62a), for example, the speaker is associating himself with his dinner order – rather than asserting that he is literally coextensive with it – in order to convey that he is the person who ordered the Pad Thai.

To account for the sort of linguistic metonymy illustrated in (62), Nunberg (1995) introduces the notion of MEANING TRANSFER: "[t]he name of a property that applies to something in one domain can sometimes be used as the name of a property in another domain, provided the two properties correspond in a certain ("NOTEWORTHY") way" (Nunberg 1995: 111). One of the linguistic mechanisms for meaning transfer that Nunberg identifies is nominal or 'common noun' transfer, illustrated in (63):

(63) COMMON NOUN TRANSFER
The ham sandwich is at table 7. ⇒ 'The ham sandwich orderer is at table 7.'
[=Nunberg 1995, ex. (19)]

With nominal transfer, the relevant common noun – *ham sandwich* in (63) – supplies a property which then undergoes a meaning transfer to the property of 'being the person who ordered a ham sandwich'. Such a transfer would be relevant in, e.g., the context of a server referring to one of his customers. A crucial consequence of Nunberg's account is that the relevant relationship of meaning transfer is between predicates and properties and not between (sets of) discourse entities. Thus, according to Nunberg, the NP *the ham sandwich* in (63) does not serve to evoke an entity in the discourse model corresponding to an actual ham sandwich. Rather, this NP is merely the source of the relevant property which provides the basis of the meaning transfer. In other words, Nunberg's meaning 'transfer' is one of SENSE and not REFERENCE.

However, as argued in Ward (2004), in the case of equatives like those in (62), neither NP undergoes any transfer of sense **or** reference; rather, the two NPs retain their literal meanings, with the copula being interpreted non-literally as expressing a noteworthy correspondence between their referents. This correspondence crucially involves a salient mapping between sets of discourse entities; in the case of the Pad Thai example in (62a), for example, the relevant sets are {Thai lunch orders} and {customers}.

The use of a deferred equative to convey a particular correspondence between set members requires that the general correspondence itself be salient in the discourse at the time of utterance. We can represent this correspondence by means of an open proposition. Consider (62a), repeated in (64a):

(64) a. I'm the Pad Thai.
      b. OP = X corresponds to Y (where X is a member of the set {customers} and Y is a member of the set {orders}).
      c. FOCI: I, the Pad Thai

The equative in (64a) presupposes an OP sketched informally in (64b). It is formed in the usual way by replacing the two foci (*I, the Pad Thai*) with variables, whose instantiations must be drawn from the two sets involved in the mapping. For this example, we might gloss the instantiation informally as: 'I, a member of the set of customers, correspond to the Pad Thai, a member of the set of orders'. What makes the utterance in (64a) 'deferred', therefore, is not (*contra* Nunberg) a transfer of sense or reference from either of the equative NPs; rather, it is the shift in the interpretation of *be* to *correspond to* as represented in the OP.

As evidence of the OP requirement, consider the deferred equative in (65a) in a context in which the OP in (64b) is *not* salient:

(65) A: [on cell phone] Sorry to interrupt your lunch. How is it?
      B: Delicious! #*I'm the Pad Thai.*

Here, the OP in (64b) – that various lunch orders correspond to various customers – is not salient, and the deferred equative is consequently infelicitous. In contrast, note that the corresponding utterance without deferred reference is felicitous, as illustrated in (66):

(66) A: Sorry to interrupt your lunch. How is it?
      B: Delicious! I ordered the Pad Thai.

Thus, we can attribute the infelicity of the deferred equative in (65) to the absence of a salient double-variable OP. Note that equatives that do not involve deferred reference, as in (67), are *not* subject to this constraint:

(67)   a. The guy that you were just talking to is my neighbor Sam Miller.
       b. That building on your left is the Sears Tower.
       c. This painting is the same as the one hanging in the Louvre.

These identity clauses are felicitous in the absence of any particular OP, from which we can conclude that the OP requirement does not apply to equatives as a class, but rather only to those that receive a deferred interpretation.

In sum, deferred equatives are interpreted as assertions of correspondences – rather than literal identity statements – and involve no transfers of sense **or** reference. Moreover, deferred equatives require that an OP be salient in the discourse at the time of utterance.

4 Conclusion

The structuring of information in English is a complex issue, but as we have shown, broad generalizations can nonetheless be made regarding both the types of givenness and newness to which particular constructions may be sensitive, and the specific constraints that are likely to apply to a particular construction type. We have surveyed a range of syntactic constructions that require an open proposition to be salient in the discourse at the time of utterance, as well as a range of constructions that are sensitive to either the hearer-status or the discourse-status of some subpropositional constituent. In some cases, as with preposing, both types of constraint may apply; that is, a felicitous preposing requires not only that the appropriate open proposition be salient in the discourse context, but also that the preposed constituent represent discourse-old information (whether or not it is the focus of the open proposition). We have moreover shown that functions are not randomly correlated with forms in English; while the correlation of form and function in English is not entirely predictable, it is nonetheless subject to strong and reliable generalizations that hold across a wide range of construction types. Finally, we have compared noncanonical constructions in English with a pair of marked canonical-word-order constructions in which discourse-functional constraints are correlated with properties other than word order variation.

This chapter represents a revised and expanded version of Ward & Birner (2004). We are grateful to the publishers of the volume in which that paper appeared for granting us permission to reproduce it here.

5 References

Abbott, Barbara 1993. A pragmatic account of the definiteness effect in existential sentences. *Journal of Pragmatics* 19, 39–55.
Abbott, Barbara 2004. Definiteness and indefiniteness. In: L.R. Horn & G. Ward (eds.). *Handbook of Pragmatics*. Oxford: Blackwell, 122–149.
Birner, Betty J. 1994. Information status and word order: An analysis of English inversion. *Language* 70, 233–259.
Birner, Betty J., Jeffrey Kaplan & Gregory Ward 2007. Functional compositionality and the interaction of discourse constraints. *Language* 83, 317–343.
Birner, Betty J. & Gregory Ward 1994. Uniqueness, familiarity, and the definite article in English. In: S. Gahl, C. Johnson & A. Dolbey (eds.). *Proceedings of the Annual Meeting of the Berkeley Linguistics Society (= BLS) 20*. Berkeley, CA: Berkeley Linguistics Society, 93–102.
Birner, Betty J. & Gregory Ward 1998. *Information Status and Noncanonical Word Order in English*. Amsterdam: Benjamins.
Birner, Betty J. 1996. Form and function in English *by*-phrase passives. In: L. Dobrin, K. Singer & L. McNair (eds.). *Papers from the Regional Meeting of the Chicago Linguistic Society (= CLS) 32*, Chicago, IL: Chicago Linguistic Society, 23–31.
Chafe, Wallace 1976. Givenness, contrastiveness, definiteness, subjects, topics, and point of view. In: C. Li (ed.). *Subject and Topic*. New York: Academic Press, 25–55.
Creider, Chet A. & Jane T. Creider 1983. Topic-comment relations in a verb-initial language. *Journal of African Languages and Linguistics* 5, 1–15.
Fillmore, Charles 1968. The case for case. In: E. Bach & R.T. Harms (eds.). *Universals in Linguistic Theory*. New York: Holt, Rinehart & Winston, 1–88.
Gundel, Jeanette 1974. *The Role of Topic and Comment in Linguistic Theory*. Ph.D. dissertation. University of Texas, Austin, TX.
Gundel, Jeanette 1985. 'Shared knowledge' and topicality. *Journal of Pragmatics* 9, 83–107.
Gundel, Jeanette 1988. *The Role of Topic and Comment in Linguistic Theory*. New York: Garland.
Gundel, Jeanette, Nancy Hedberg & Ron Zacharski 1990. Givenness, implicature, and the form of referring expressions in discourse. In: D. Costa (ed.). *Proceedings of the Annual Meeting of the Berkeley Linguistics Society (= BLS) 16*. Berkeley, CA: Berkeley Linguistics Society, 442–453.
Gundel, Jeanette, Nancy Hedberg & Ron Zacharski 1993. Cognitive status and the form of referring expressions in discourse. *Language* 69, 274–307.
Halliday, Michael A.K. 1967. Notes on transitivity and theme in English, part 2. *Journal of Linguistics* 3, 199–244.
Hawkins, John A. 1994. *A Performance Theory of Order and Constituency*. Cambridge: Cambridge University Press.
Heycock, Caroline & Anthony Kroch 1997. Inversion and equation in copular sentences. In: *Papers on Syntax of Clefts, Pseudo-clefts, Relative Clauses, and the Semantics of Present Perfect ZAS Papers in Linguistics 10*. Berlin: Zentrum für Allgemeine Sprachwissenschaft, 71–87.
Higgins, Roger F. 1979. *The Pseudo-cleft Construction in English*. New York: Garland.
Horn, Laurence R. 1986. Presupposition, theme and variations. In: A. Farley, P. Farley & K.-E. McCullough (eds.). *Papers from the Regional Meeting of the Chicago Linguistic Society (= CLS) 22*. Chicago, IL: Chicago Linguistic Society, 168–192.

Kehler, Andrew 1995. *Interpreting Cohesive Forms in the Context of Discourse Inference*. Ph.D. dissertation. Harvard University, Cambridge, MA.

Kehler, Andrew 2002. *Coherence, Reference, and the Theory of Grammar*. Stanford, CA: CSLI Publications.

Lambrecht, Knud 1994. *Information Structure and Sentence Form*. Cambridge: Cambridge University Press.

Lasnik, Howard 1992. Case and expletives: Notes toward a parametric account. *Linguistic Inquiry* 23, 381–405.

Mikkelsen, Line 2004. *Specifying Who: On the Structure, Meaning, and Use of Specificational Copular Clauses*. Ph.D. dissertation. University of California, Santa Cruz, CA.

Miller, Philip 2001. Discourse constraints on (non)extraposition from subject in English. *Linguistics* 39, 683–701.

Milsark, Gary 1974. *Existential Sentences in English*. Ph.D. dissertation. MIT, Cambridge, MA.

Nunberg, Geoffrey 1977. *The Pragmatics of Reference*. Ph.D. dissertation. City University of New York, New York.

Nunberg, Geoffrey 1979. The non-uniqueness of semantic solutions: Polysemy. *Linguistics & Philosophy* 3, 143–184.

Nunberg, Geoffrey 1995. Transfers of meaning. *Journal of Semantics* 12, 109–132.

Pierrehumbert, Janet 1980. *The Phonology and Phonetics of English Intonation*. Ph.D. dissertation. MIT, Cambridge, MA.

Prince, Ellen F. 1981a. Toward a taxonomy of given/new information. In: P. Cole (ed.). *Radical Pragmatics*. New York: Academic Press, 223–254.

Prince, Ellen F. 1981b. On the inferencing of indefinite-*this* NPs. In: A. Joshi, B. Webber & I. Sag (eds.). *Elements of Discourse Understanding*. Cambridge: Cambridge University Press, 231–250.

Prince, Ellen F. 1992. The ZPG Letter: Subjects, definiteness, and information-status. In: S. Thompson & W. Mann (eds.). *Discourse Description: Diverse Analyses of a Fundraising Text*. Amsterdam: Benjamins, 295–325.

Prince, Ellen F. 1997. On the functions of left-dislocation in English discourse. In: A. Kamio (ed.). *Directions in Functional Linguistics*. Amsterdam: Benjamins, 117–144.

Prince, Ellen F. & Nancy Levin 1986. Gapping and causal implicature. *Papers in Linguistics* 19, 351–364.

Reinhart, Tanya 1981. Pragmatics and linguistics: An analysis of sentence topics. *Philosophica* 27, 53–94.

Reuland, Eric & Alice ter Meulen (eds.) 1987. *The Representation of (In)definiteness*. Cambridge, MA: The MIT Press.

Roberts, Craige 2003. Uniqueness in definite noun phrases. *Linguistics & Philosophy* 26, 287–350.

Rodman, Robert 1974. On left dislocation. *Papers in Linguistics* 7, 437–466.

Rooth, Mats E. 1992. A theory of focus interpretation. *Natural Language Semantics* 1, 75–117.

Russell, Bertrand 1905. On denoting. *Mind* 14, 479–493.

Safir, Kenneth 1985. *Syntactic Chains*. Cambridge: Cambridge University Press.

Siewierska, Anna 1984. *The Passive: A Comparative Linguistic Analysis*. London: Croom Helm.

Siewierska, Anna 1988. *Word Order Rules*. London: Croom Helm.

Terken, Jacques & Julia Hirschberg 1994. Deaccentuation and words representing 'given' information: Effects of persistence of grammatical function and surface position. *Language and Speech* 37, 125–145.

Tomlin, Russell S. & Richard Rhodes 1979. The distribution of information in Ojibwa texts. In: P. Cline, W. Hanks & C. Hofbauer (eds.). *Papers from the Regional Meeting of the Chicago Linguistic Society (= CLS) 15*. Chicago, IL: Chicago Linguistic Society, 307–320.

Tomlin, Russell S. & Richard Rhodes 1992. Information distribution in Ojibwa. In: D. L. Payne (ed.). *Pragmatics of Word Order Flexibility*. Amsterdam: Benjamins, 117–135.

Vallduví, Enric 1992. *The Informational Component*. New York: Garland.

Wald, Benji 1983. Referents and topic within and across discourse units: Observations from current vernacular English. In: F. Klein-Andreu (ed.). *Discourse Perspectives of Syntax*. New York: Academic Press, 91–116.

Ward, Gregory 1990. The discourse functions of VP Preposing. *Language* 66, 742–763.

Ward, Gregory 1988. *The Semantics and Pragmatics of Preposing*. New York: Garland.

Ward, Gregory 2004. Equatives and deferred reference. *Language* 80, 262–289.

Ward, Gregory & Betty J. Birner 1995. Definiteness and the English existential. *Language* 71, 722–742.

Ward, Gregory & Betty J. Birner 2004. Information structure and noncanonical syntax. In: L. R. Horn & G. Ward (eds.). *The Handbook of Pragmatics*. Oxford: Blackwell, 153–174.

Ward, Gregory, Betty J. Birner & Rodney Huddleston 2002. Information packaging. In: G. K. Pullum & R. Huddleston (eds.). *The Cambridge Grammar of the English Language*. Chapter 16. Cambridge: Cambridge University Press, 1363–1447.

Ward, Gregory, Betty J. Birner & Jeffrey Kaplan 2003. A pragmatic analysis of the epistemic *would* construction in English. In: R. Facchinetti, M. Krug & F. Palmer (eds.). *Modality in Contemporary English*. Berlin: Mouton de Gruyter, 71–79.

Wasow, Thomas 2002. *Postverbal Behavior*. Stanford, CA: CSLI Publications.

Andrew Kehler
13 Cohesion and coherence

1   Introduction —— 450
2   Desiderata for a theory of coherence —— 454
3   Coherence begets cohesion —— 460
4   Other 'cohesive' phenomena —— 466
5   Question-under-discussion models —— 473
6   Conclusion —— 476
7   References —— 477

Abstract: Although both are commonly invoked as constraints on discourse well-formedness, cohesion and coherence are very different things. Cohesion regards the existence and distribution of particular discourse-dependent linguistic phenomena (pronouns, ellipsis, and so forth), whereas coherence is defined in terms of the underlying semantic relationships that characterize and structure the transitions between utterances. In this article, the cohesion and coherence analyses of discourse well-formedness are described and compared. Consideration of the evidence will support the coherence view, and a coherence analysis is offered that sees the space of possible discourse continuations as characterizable within the three types of "connections among ideas" put forth by David Hume in his Inquiry Concerning Human Understanding. Nonetheless, it is only natural that there would be an empirical correlation between coherence in discourses and correspondingly high degrees of cohesiveness: Utterances in coherent discourses will tend to talk about the same entities, relationships, and events, which will in turn license the use of linguistically reduced forms to refer to them. This article surveys a variety of so-called cohesive forms – including pronouns, ellipsis, conjunction, and deaccentuation – and argues that they are not only in part the products of the coherence properties of discourse, but their felicity is dependent on these properties in highly specific ways.

1 Introduction

To begin their landmark volume *Cohesion in English*, Halliday & Hasan (1976) make the central observation that is the focus of this paper as well:

Andrew Kehler, San Diego, CA, USA

> If a speaker of English hears or reads a passage of the language which is more than one sentence in length, he can normally decide without difficulty whether it forms a unified whole or is just a collection of unrelated sentences. (Halliday & Hasan 1976: 1)

The goal of their book is to describe what makes the difference between the two.

Their answer – as suggested by their book's title – is that discourses exhibit COHESION. Cohesion is created by the existence of cohesively related items called TIES. These 'ties' are pairs of items that participate in various types of dependency relations, such as an anaphoric pronoun and its antecedent expression, an instance of ellipsis and the expression that licenses it, pairs of identical content words (giving rise to lexical repetition), connectives (e.g., *but, so, then*) and the clauses or sentences they relate, and even the intonational properties of an utterance (e.g., anaphoric deaccenting) and the expression that licenses those properties. These examples all involve situations in which the interpretation of an element in the discourse is dependent on that of another. These are precisely the situations in which cohesion is said to occur, giving rise to the defining property of TEXTURE that Halliday and Hasan claim distinguishes texts from non-texts.

Three years later, however, Hobbs (1979) began his classic paper *Coherence and Coreference* with a rejection of the cohesion hypothesis:

> Successive utterances in coherent discourse refer to the same entities. The common explanation for this is that the discourse is coherent *because* successive utterances are "about" the same entities. But this does not seem to stand up. The text
>
> (1) John took a train from Paris to Istanbul. He likes spinach.
>
> is not coherent, even though "he" can refer only to John. At this point the reader may object, "Well, maybe the French spinach crop failed and Turkey is the only country..." But the very fact that one is driven to such explanations indicates that some desire for coherence is operating, which is deeper than the notion of a discourse just being "about" some set of entities. (Hobbs 1979: 68)

The end of this passage introduces an idea to compete with the cohesion hypothesis: That COHERENCE is the defining property of discourses. Coherence, Hobbs argues, is the product of establishing that one of a small set of possible COHERENCE RELATIONS relate successive utterances (or collections of utterances) to one another. An example coherence relation is Explanation:

> EXPLANATION: Infer P from the assertion of S_1 and Q from the assertion of S_2, where normally $Q \rightarrow P$.

Each such relation is associated with constraints that must be met in order for them to be established for a particular set of utterances. In the case of Explanation, the hearer must be able to determine how the eventuality described by the second clause contributes to the cause of the eventuality described in the first clause. It is precisely this constraint that caused Hobbs's hypothetical hearer to invent a scenario under which the second clause of example (1) could be understood as explaining the first.

In many cases establishing these constraints requires the ACCOMMODATION of unstated information, which explains why the information that a hearer carries away from a coherent discourse is typically greater than the information encoded by what was explicitly said. To illustrate, consider the variant of (1) given in (2):

(2) John took a train from Paris to Istanbul. He has family there.

In an unexceptional context, a hearer will infer an Explanation relationship between the clauses, and hence would normally be licensed to draw the inference that John's reason for taking the trip is to visit his family. The inference comes so effortlessly that the hearer may not notice that this explanation is not explicitly expressed. Indeed, our hypothetical hearer might felicitously respond *But I thought John hated his family!* Here, the *but* does not indicate contrast with anything that was actually said (after all, the speaker never claimed otherwise), but instead with information that needs to be accommodated in order to establish the coherence of the passage.

This view thus offers quite a different explanation for the 'textuality' of (2) than the cohesion view, which relies only on the fact that the second clause contains a cohesive tie in the form of a pronominal reference to John. And in light of this, the cohesion view is immediately confronted with several problems. First, the cohesion analysis offers no explanation for why the aforementioned inferences are required to make the passage coherent, that is, why hearers go beyond assuming that they are simply being offered two facts about John that are otherwise unrelated to one another. Second, as Hobbs pointed out, it offers no explanation for why (2) is coherent and (1) is not, given that the both have the same sole tie between the pronoun *he* and John. Lastly, one might expect under the cohesion view that an explicit cohesive tie that signals an Explanation relationship – such as the connective *because* – would remedy the incoherence of (1). It in fact does not; consider the variants of (1) and (2) given in (3) and (4) respectively:

(3) John took a train from Paris to Istanbul, because he likes spinach.

(4) John took a train from Paris to Istanbul, because he has family there.

Example (3) is just as incoherent as (1): Adding the connective *because* does nothing to make it more coherent. Although such 'cohesion-forming' connectives can serve to constrain the set of coherence relations that can hold between two or more utterances, connectives in and of themselves do not *create* coherence. Any coherence relation indicated by a connective must still be established using the same inferential processes and world knowledge as required in the case in which the coherence relation is not explicitly signalled. The establishment of Explanation in both (1) and (3) fails because of the lack of causal knowledge that would explain why liking spinach would cause someone to travel to Istanbul.

Indeed, it is not hard to construct an extended, highly cohesive collection of sentences that is nonetheless utterly incoherent as a unit, and thus not what one would call a 'discourse'. Consider the following passage about the Senate:

(5) The Senate of the United States was named after the ancient Roman Senate. Next year, Senator Dick Durbin will be responsible for counting votes and monitoring legislation on the Senate floor. Recently, Senator Norm Coleman applauded the Senate's unanimous passage of the Postal Accountability and Enhancement Act conference report. The Senate is currently in recess, and thus neither Durbin nor Coleman are in Washington. The Senate has several exclusive powers enumerated in Article One of the United States Constitution not granted to the House of Representatives.

Despite the sense of 'aboutness' engendered by the repeated references to the Senate, Senators Durbin and Coleman, etc, the passage lacks true coherence, for the same sorts of reasons that (1) does.

The natural question to ask in turn is whether cohesion is dispensable as a concept of interest, that is, whether one can have coherence without cohesion. The answer is affirmative; consider (6):

(6) The country is eagerly awaiting news of impending changes in the government's power structure. The mid-term elections are being held today. The Democrats are outwardly optimistic, whereas the Republicans are trying to exhibit a quieter strength and confidence. No one expects the results to be known until late in the evening, if not tomorrow or even longer.

This passage is rich in coherence relationships but lacks cohesion: There are no pronouns, no ellipses, no repeated content words, and contains but one connective. Of course, constructing such a passage takes a little work: It is only natural that typical coherent discourses will be about the same entities, and thus license cohesive elements. But as the foregoing discussion suggests, the latter is strictly a side-effect of the former (see also Hobbs 1979: 67 and Brown & Yule 1983: 196 for similar arguments).

Despite arguments against treating cohesion as an interesting property of discourse (let alone a defining one), a subdiscipline of linguistics built around the notion continues to exist. In addition to theoretical lines of discourse analysis research, cohesion is also appealed to in certain areas of applied quantitative linguistics, such as second language learning and assessment (Crossley et al. 2007, Crossley & McNamara 2008, inter alia), automatic essay evaluation (Graesser et al. 2004, McNamara et al. 2006, inter alia), and evaluation of linguistic competence of populations with language disorders (Baltaxe & D'Angiola 1992, Fine et al. 1994, inter alia), among others. The appeal of employing cohesion in these latter areas is understandable: It is easier to calculate statistics over things that we can see before us, whereas assessing coherence requires trained analysis, and is hindered by the fact that our understanding of coherence remains in a state of relative infancy. But it must always be borne in mind that cohesion is a side-effect, and as such a rather imperfect measurement, of true discourse coherence. Any research that measures cohesion with the *intent* of measuring coherence bears the burden of demonstrating (rather than assuming) the degree of empirical correlation between the two.

2 Desiderata for a theory of coherence

Whereas I will now assume that we have settled on coherence as the central concept of interest, this leaves us with the task of producing a theory of it. Where do these so-called coherence relations come from? And what compels us as language comprehenders to use them to connect successive utterances in a discourse?

Perhaps surprisingly, much of the previous literature on the topic is not overly concerned with such questions, but instead looks to achieve, in the terminology of Sanders et al. (1992), DESCRIPTIVE ADEQUACY. Descriptive adequacy is an understandable criterion if one's primary goal is to provide a tool to allow a text analyst to characterize arbitrary examples of naturally-occurring data. The Rhetorical Structure Theory (RST) of Mann & Thompson (1987), for instance, is an example of such a framework. RST posits a set of 23 relations that can hold between two adjacent spans of text, termed the NUCLEUS (the more central text span) and SATELLITE (the span containing less central, supportive information). (A small set of relations – e.g. JOINT, SEQUENCE, CONTRAST – are multi-nuclear, in that they may relate more than two spans of text.) RST relation definitions are made up of five fields: CONSTRAINTS ON NUCLEUS, CONSTRAINTS ON SATELLITE, CONSTRAINTS ON THE COMBINATION OF NUCLEUS AND SATELLITE, THE EFFECT, and LOCUS OF THE EFFECT. The fields in RST relations generally contain only informal descriptions of the constraints, however, as in their definition of the EVIDENCE relation:

RELATION NAME: EVIDENCE
> CONSTRAINTS ON NUCLEUS: The hearer might not believe nucleus to a degree satisfactory to the Speaker.
> CONSTRAINTS ON SATELLITE: The hearer believes the satellite or will find it credible.
> CONSTRAINTS ON THE COMBINATION OF NUCLEUS AND SATELLITE: The hearer's comprehending the satellite increases the hearer's belief of the nucleus.
> EFFECT: The hearer's belief of the nucleus is increased.

Mann & Thompson claim that their relations are suitable for describing a large and varied assortment of texts, but ultimately suggest that the set is open to extension:

> There are no doubt other relations which might be reasonable constructs in a theory of text structure; on our list are those which have proven most useful for the analysis of the data we have examined. (Mann & Thompson 1987: 8, fn. 5)

As Knott & Dale (1994) point out, however, such an approach is inherently unsatisfactory. They note, for instance, that without *a priori* constraints on relation definitions one could just as easily define relations that describe incoherent texts, such as positing an INFORM-ACCIDENT-AND-MENTION-FRUIT relation that would cover example (7).

(7) ? John broke his leg. I like plums.

If one can add relations to the theory when necessary, the claim that the theory is sufficient for analyzing a large and varied set of texts is not particularly meaningful, especially if there is nothing in the theory to prevent the analogous description of arbitrary incoherent texts. As such, if we are to have an explanatory theory of coherence, it cannot be up to us to concoct a set of relations for our own purposes – our job instead is to uncover the pre-existing ground truth. On scientific grounds, it is difficult to see how an unconstrained and potentially unbounded catalog of relations could give rise to an explanatory account of coherence.

While descriptive adequacy remains an important objective, the foregoing discussion highlights the importance of a second criterion for evaluating a theory of coherence, specifically PSYCHOLOGICAL PLAUSIBILITY (Sanders, Spooren & Noordman 1992). We expect that there are fundamental cognitive principles at work which will serve both to constrain the set of possible relations and to provide an explanation for why a particular set of relations is to be preferred to one containing more, fewer, or different relations. What are these principles? Once again, we can see what Hobbs has to say:

> It is tempting to speculate that these coherence relations are instantiations in discourse comprehension of more general principles of coherence that we apply in attempting to make sense out of the world we find ourselves in, principles that rest ultimately on some notion of cognitive economy. [...] Recognizing coherence relations may thus be just one way of using certain very general principles for simplifying our view of the world. (Hobbs 1990: 101)

Taking my cue from Hobbs, I argued in Kehler (2002) for a classification of coherence relations in which these more general principles of coherence are to be found in three types of "connection among ideas" first articulated by David Hume in his *Inquiry Concerning Human Understanding*:

> Though it be too obvious to escape observation that different ideas are connected together, I do not find that any philosopher has attempted to enumerate or class all the principles of association – a subject, however, that seems worthy of curiosity. To me there appear to be only three principles of connection among ideas, namely *Resemblance*, *Contiguity* in time or place, and *Cause* or *Effect*. (Hume 1748/1955: 32)

I will now briefly describe how a set of previously proposed relations – most either taken or adopted from Hobbs (1990) – can be seen as emerging from these three general principles. First, the relations in the Cause-Effect category include Result, Explanation, Violated Expectation, and Denial of Preventer:

RESULT: Infer P from the assertion of S_1 and Q from the assertion of S_2, where normally $P \rightarrow Q$.

(8) Joe Biden is by far the most experienced in foreign policy of all the presidential candidates. He will probably win the election.

EXPLANATION: Infer P from the assertion of S_1 and Q from the assertion of S_2, where normally $Q \rightarrow P$.

(9) Joe Biden will probably win the election. He is by far the most experienced in foreign policy of all the presidential candidates.

VIOLATED EXPECTATION: Infer P from the assertion of S_1 and Q from the assertion of S_2, where normally $P \rightarrow \neg Q$.

(10) Joe Biden is by far the most experienced in foreign policy of all the presidential candidates, but he will probably not win the election.

DENIAL OF PREVENTER: Infer P from the assertion of S_1 and Q from the assertion of S_2, where normally $Q \to \neg P$.

(11) Joe Biden will probably not win the election, even though he is by far the most experienced in foreign policy of all the presidential candidates.

In each of these definitions, the variables S_1 and S_2 represent the first and second sentences being related, and P and Q their meanings, respectively. The hearer's task is then to identify a causal chain between P and Q, drawing inferences and accommodating information as necessary. It should be noted that the single arrow ($\to$) used here is not material implication in the standard sense found in classical logic, but instead is used more loosely, to mean roughly "could plausibly follow from". For instance, when understanding a passage such as *John pushed Bill, and Bill fell*, comprehenders utilize the causal relationship between someone being pushed and their subsequent falling, even though it is not the case that pushing someone always causes them to fall: If someone falls, having been pushed is a *possible* explanation for it, unlike, say, having red hair or being a political independent (assuming unexceptional circumstances). As such, the applicability of the implication relation to particular examples might be contingent on other things being true of the world, and inferences that utilize such causal relations will necessarily be defeasible.

With this in mind, we can see that examples (8)–(11) all presuppose the same thing – *if a candidate is the most experienced in foreign policy, then it plausibly follows that that candidate would win the presidential election* – even the examples that explicitly deny this relationship for the particular case of Joe Biden (10)–(11). As such, all of these relations can be seen as instantiations of a single and more general principle of coherence. With this observation, we begin to get away from the 'laundry list' complaint commonly made against unconstrained theories of coherence such as RST.

In contrast to the Cause-Effect relations, establishing Resemblance relations is a fundamentally different process. Resemblance requires that commonalities and contrasts among corresponding sets of parallel relations and entities be recognized. As such, the process of establishing Resemblance is more analogically-based. The canonical case of a Resemblance relation is Parallel, which is exemplified in passage (12). (Note that this definition treats Parallel as if it can relate only two clauses, when it in fact can relate longer sequences. See also Section 5.)

PARALLEL: Infer $p(a_1 a_2, ...)$ from the assertion of S_1 and $p(b_1, b_2, ...)$ from the assertion of S_2, for a common p and similar a_i and b_i.

(12) Biden has been touting his years of experience on the Senate foreign relations committee. Giuliani has been reminding everyone about September 11th at every conceivable opportunity.

Example (12) is characterized by a pair of parallel entities a_1 and b_1 – Biden and Giuliani – and a pair of parallel predications that together can be analyzed in terms of a more general COMMON TOPIC, e.g., *the things X has been doing to advertise X's leadership skills*.

Other relations in the Resemblance category follow this general pattern. For instance, the EXEMPLIFICATION relation requires that the same type of parallelism be established, in this case between a general statement and an instantiation of it.

EXEMPLIFICATION: Infer $p(a_1, a_2, ...)$ from the assertion of S_1 and $p(b_1, b_2, ...)$ from the assertion of S_2, where b_i is a member or subset of a_i for some i.

(13) Presidential candidates stand much to gain by touting examples of their leadership skills. Indeed, Giuliani has been reminding everyone about September 11th at every conceivable opportunity.

Other relations in this class include CONTRAST, GENERALIZATION, EXCEPTION, and ELABORATION; see Kehler (2002) for further details.

Finally, the third class of relation is Contiguity, into which only one relation is placed, specifically OCCASION.

OCCASION: Infer a change of state for a system of entities from the assertion of S_2, establishing the initial state for this system from the final state of the assertion of S_1.

(14) A flashy-looking campaign bus arrived in Iowa yesterday. Mitt Romney then gave his first speech of the primary season. (adapted from Hobbs 1990)

Occasion allows a speaker to express a situation centered around a system of entities by using intermediate states of affairs as points of connection between partial descriptions of that situation. As such, the inference process that underlies Occasion attempts to equate the initial state of the eventuality denoted by the second utterance with the final state of the first. Additional inferences that result from establishing Occasion in (14) come effortlessly, e.g., that Romney was on the bus, and that he gave his speech in Iowa. It is therefore worth noting that merely establishing temporal progression between events is not enough (pace Halliday & Hasan 1976, Longacre 1983, inter alia).

Having articulated a set of relationships that can hold between pairs of utterances, we are naturally led to the question of how they can be used to offer a coherence criterion on larger discourses. This question remains an ever present topic of debate; one that currently centers around the data structures required: in particular, whether discourse structure can be represented as a tree or requires the expressive power of graphs. On the tree-based view, the coherence criterion is straightforward to state: Starting with the assumption that sentences are discourse segments, larger segments (all the way up to the entire discourse) result by relating two smaller segments by a coherence relation. In contrast to sentential structures, the 'syntactic' component for building discourse structures is therefore trivial; the real work is lies in the process of establishing coherence relations. Hobbs et al. (1993) posit a mechanism for doing this, based on a cost-based notion of logical abduction. A different approach based on nonmonotonic deduction is utilized by Asher & Lascarides (2003, inter alia). The reader is referred to these works for further detail.

The tree-based conception has been argued by various researchers to be too simplistic, however; Wolf & Gibson (2006), for instance, argue that the full power of a graph structure is necessary. On this analysis the coherence criterion is less restrictive, requiring only that discourses be characterizable as a connected graph; this constraint, unlike the case for tree-based structures, allows for nodes with multiple parents and for crossing dependencies. Webber et al. (2003) offer a third view, arguing that while multiple parents are permissible, the evidence for crossing dependencies is eliminated when one distinguishes between discourse relationships that are STRUCTURAL versus those that are ANAPHORIC, the latter of which are not represented in the discourse structure. A full exploration of the issues is beyond the scope of this chapter; suffice it to say that future work is necessary to resolve these questions and many others regarding theories of discourse structure.

To summarize this section, Hume addressed the ways in which ideas in the mind are associated with each other by identifying three: Cause-Effect, Resemblance, and Contiguity. The analysis of discourse coherence here identifies coherence relations as instantiations of these categories. It therefore constitutes an attempt to satisfy the psychological plausibility criterion on theories of coherence, in which the relations are seen only as convenient labels for certain types of cognitively primitive operations. This analysis is but one of many possible, of course, and many questions remain concerning the proper inventory of coherence relations and the way in which they are utilized to describe the coherence of larger discourses.

3 Coherence begets cohesion

In Section 1 we examined the properties that define a text by pitting the cohesion view against the coherence view. Whereas we sided with the coherence view, we noted that coherent discourses do tend to be cohesive. The work surveyed in this section and the next will suggest that this is no accident; indeed, coherence begets cohesion.

We begin by observing that the coherence property of discourses makes the content of ensuing discourse easier to predict. In normal circumstances, when a speaker says:

(15)   John admires Bill.

the hearer knows that there is a good chance that the following sentence will explain the source of this admiration, e.g.:

(16)   He knows a lot about foreign politics.

Although never directly stated, John is presumably the kind of person who is impressed by such people. These expectations would simply not exist if standard practice was to run together sentences that were irrelevant to one another.

Zipf (1935) famously noted that language has a tendency to reduce expressions that refer to the familiar and predictable. And we just saw an example: The speaker's expectations about the knowledge state of the hearer allowed her to reduce the mention of Bill to a pronoun, despite the existence of another male referent in the discourse (in the subject position no less, a preferred position for pronominal antecedence on many theories). I thus submit that cohesion is the natural result of the predictive properties of coherent discourses, giving rise to the (mistaken) impression that cohesion is what *makes* discourses coherent, rather than a natural consequence of, but nonetheless an epiphenomenon of, a set of deeper semantic factors that determine discourse coherence.

In the remainder of this section, I work through a case study of a particular so-called cohesive form: the third person personal pronoun. I begin with Hobbs's proposal concerning the relationship between coherence and coreference, and then move on to the role of prediction in a coherence-driven theory. Section 4 will then more briefly address three other forms Halliday and Hasan consider to be cohesive. In all of these cases, the coherence properties of a discourse are argued to play a role in determining when the use of these forms is licensed.

3.1 Coherence and coreference

Pronouns are the cohesive forms *par excellence*, and indeed, appropriate use of them appears to facilitate discourse comprehension. And yet this very fact makes their existence seem paradoxical. After all, in choosing to use a pronoun, a speaker is electing to use a potentially ambiguous expression that, at least on most theories, requires effort to resolve, rather than a less ambiguous or even unambiguous one that would presumably not (such as a uniquely-identifying definite description, or a proper name). The intuition that pronouns can have a facilitating effect has been confirmed in the experiments of Gordon et al. (1993, inter alia), for instance, which showed that certain discourses tend to be read more slowly if a proper name is used to refer to a focused entity instead of a pronoun.

To my knowledge, Hobbs (1979) was the first to develop a theory of pronoun interpretation specifically based on the establishment of coherence relations. In fact, in his analysis pronoun interpretation is not an independent process at all, but instead results as a by-product of more general reasoning about the most likely interpretation of an utterance. Pronouns are modeled as free variables in logical representations which become bound during these inference processes; potential referents of pronouns are therefore those which result in valid proofs of coherence.

Let us illustrate with passages (17a) and (17b), adapted from an example from Winograd (1972).

(17) The city council denied the demonstrators a permit because…
   a. …they *feared* violence.
   b. …they *advocated* violence.

In Hobbs's account, the correct assignment for the pronoun in each case falls out as a side-effect of the process of establishing Explanation (here signalled by *because*), the definition of which is repeated below.

> EXPLANATION: Infer P from the assertion of S_1 and Q from the assertion of S_2, where normally $Q \rightarrow P$.

Oversimplifying considerably, I will code the world knowledge necessary to establish Explanation for (17) within a single axiom, given in (18). (See Hobbs et al. 1993: 111 for a more detailed analysis of a similar example.)

(18) $fear(X, V) \wedge advocate(Y, V) \wedge enable\_to\_cause(Z, Y, V) \supset deny(X, Y, Z)$

Instantiating it for the current example, the axiom says that if the city council fears violence, the demonstrators advocate violence, and a permit would enable the demonstrators to bring about violence, then this might cause the city council to deny the demonstrators a permit.

The first sentence in (17) can be represented with the predication given in (19).

(19) $deny(city\_council, demonstrators, permit)$

This representation matches the consequent of axiom (18), triggering an inference process that can be used to establish Explanation. At this point, X will become bound to *city_council*, Y to *demonstrators*, and Z to *permit*.

Each of the follow-ons (17a–b) provides information that can be used to help 'prove' the predications in the antecedent of the axiom, thereby establishing a connection between the clauses. Clause (17a) can be represented with predicate (20), in which the unbound variable T represents the pronoun *they*.

(20) $fear(T, violence)$

When this predicate is used to match the antecedent of axiom (18), the variables T and X are necessarily unified. Since X is already bound to *city_council*, the variable T representing *they* also receives this binding, and the pronoun is therefore resolved.

Likewise, clause (17b) can be represented as predicate (21).

(21) $advocate(T, violence)$

This predicate also matches a predicate within the antecedent of axiom (18), but in this case, the variables T and Y are unified. Since Y is already bound to *demonstrators*, the representation of *they* also receives this binding.

Thus, the correct referent for the pronoun is identified as a by-product of establishing Explanation in each case. The crucial information determining the choice of referent is semantic in nature, based on the establishment of the relationship between the predication containing the pronoun and the predication containing the potential referents. The fact that coreference came "for free" captures the effortlessness with which people appear to be able to interpret pronouns, offering a potential explanation for how the choice to use of pronoun can actually facilitate, rather than hinder, the process of discourse comprehension.

3.2 Toward a processing model

The true picture is almost certainly not this simple, however. Pronoun interpretation research in psycholinguistics has been rich source of on-line evidence that language interpretation proceeds in a highly incremental fashion (Caramazza et al. 1977, Gordon & Scearce 1995, Stewart, Pickering & Sanford 1998, Koornneef & van Berkum 2006, and many others). In the Hobbsian conception outlined in the last section, however, the inference process operates on complete logical forms of clauses and sentences, leaving unresolved the question of how inferencing can begin mid-utterance. We thus need to ask how coherence establishment can influence pronoun interpretation in cases in which the pronoun is encountered before the coherence relation is known.

Recent work (Rohde, Kehler & Elman 2006, Rohde, Kehler & Elman 2007, Kehler et al. 2008) has addressed this question, demonstrating that hearers encode probabilistic expectations about how passages are likely to be followed with respect to coherence. (See Arnold 2001 for a similar proposal, as well as recent work in sentence processing that contends that on-line measurements of interpretation difficulty can be successfully predicted by probabilistic, expectation-driven models, e.g., Hale 2001 and Levy 2008.) The central insight of the model is that any discourse context will give rise to expectations about two types of probabilistic information that are naturally combined: (i) how the discourse is likely to be continued with respect to the ensuing coherence relation, and (ii) the likelihood that a certain referent will get mentioned by a pronoun which, crucially, is *conditioned on those coherence relations*. These come together in the following equation (in which *referent* stands for a possible referent in a particular grammatical or thematic position, and *CR* stands for coherence relation):

(22) $P(pronoun = referent) = \sum_{CR \in CRs} P(CR) * P(pronoun = referent \mid CR)$

For example, to compute the likelihood that a pronoun will corefer with the subject of the previous sentence, we simply sum, over all coherence relations, the likelihood of seeing that coherence relation multiplied by the likelihood of a subject reference given that coherence relation. The equation makes explicit the idea that at any point during comprehension the hearer will have expectations about how the discourse will be continued with respect to coherence, and that the difficulty in interpreting the linguistic material to follow will be conditioned in part on those expectations. These expectations will then evolve based on subsequent linguistic input that influences the probabilities represented.

Values for these terms need to be estimated in order to make predictions about on-line interpretation. Sentence completion tasks have become a standard way to estimate biases of this sort (Caramazza et al. 1977; McKoon, Greene & Ratcliff 1993; Stewart, Pickering & Sanford 1998; Koornneef & van Berkum 2006, inter alia). Stevenson et al. (1994), for instance, report on a series of such story completion experiments that included passages with a transfer-of-possession context sentence followed by an ambiguous pronoun prompt, as in (23):

(23) John handed a book to Bob. He _____

In such cases, the subject fills the Source thematic role and the object of the preposition fills the Goal role. Participants were asked to provide a natural completion to the pronoun prompt provided in the second sentence, and the pronoun was then categorized by judges as referring to the Source or the Goal. Stevenson et al. (1994) found that Goal continuations occurred about as frequently (49%) as Source continuations (51%), an unexpected result in light of the commonly-cited grammatical subject and grammatical role parallelism preferences, since both point to John as the preferred referent.

Rohde, Kehler & Elman (2006) ran a similar experiment, but had judges also categorize the continuations by coherence relation. The results are shown in Tab. 13.1; the second and third columns provide estimates of $P(CR)$ and $P(pronoun = source|CR)$ respectively. When applied to equation (22), these numbers result in an average 56.7% bias toward the Source at the time that a subject pronoun is encountered. While these overall results are similar to the near 50–50 split found by Stevenson et al. (1994), they show that there is nothing 50–50 about the pattern once coherence is taken into account. Each of the coherence relations encodes a considerably stronger bias one way or the other about who will be mentioned next; it is only after the frequencies of coherence continuation are factored in that the biases have a cancelling effect.

Tab. 13.1: Probabilities from Rohde, Kehler & Elman (2006)

Coherence Relation	Percentage of Corpus	Source Bias
Occasion (171)	.38	.18
Elaboration (126)	.28	.98
Explanation (82)	.18	.80
Violated Expectation (38)	.08	.76
Result (25)	.06	.08

Equation (22) predicts that contextual factors that influence the distribution $P(CR)$ will in turn influence pronoun interpretation biases. Rohde, Kehler & Elman (2007) report on another study that elicited passage completions with the same stimuli as Rohde, Kehler & Elman (2006), but added an additional condition that bore only on the instructions. In one version, the participants were asked to have their completion answer the question *What happened next?*, whereas in the other they were to answer the question *Why?*. The idea was that this difference should give rise to different distributions of coherence relations; specifically, more Occasion relations (which, per Tab. 13.1, are Goal-biased) in the first case, and more Explanation relations (which are Source-biased) in the second.

The outcome was as predicted. On the one hand, the biases toward particular pronoun referents conditioned on coherence relation (i.e., the probabilities $P(pronoun = referent \mid CR)$) were consistent between the two conditions as well as with Rohde et al. (2006). The distribution of coherence relations varied, however, and in the way predicted by equation (22), the overall pattern of pronoun interpretations shifted dramatically: there were significantly more source interpretations in the *Why?* condition than the *What next?* condition. This result is surprising on any theory of pronoun interpretation that is driven by morphosyntactic 'cues', since the stimuli themselves were identical between conditions.

Since the foregoing experiments were run only with stimuli that contained pronoun prompts, these results are not sufficient to establish that pronoun interpretation preferences are solely attributable to coherence establishment. Indeed, other results from Stevenson et al. (1994) are hard to reconcile with such an assumption. Stevenson et al. (1994) paired passages with a pronoun prompt as in (23) with variants that had no pronoun as in (24), in which participants chose their own forms of referring expressions.

(24) John handed a book to Bob. _____

Across their stimulus types, they found that the choice of reference was heavily biased towards a pronoun when the referent was the previous subject, and likewise towards a name when the referent was a non-subject. (Arnold 2001 found similarly strong biases.) The data therefore suggest that the context sentence in (23) and (24) gives rise to a strong *next mention* bias toward the Goal, but that this bias is counteracted somewhat by a subject-oriented bias introduced by the pronoun in (23).

If pronoun interpretation is associated with a subject bias, this bias would be predicted to have repercussions for coherence establishment: Because the mere presence of a pronoun – even one whose reference is ambiguous as in (23) – would bias interpretation towards the subject of the last clause, encountering a pronoun would be expected to cause a shift in comprehenders' expectations in favor of the Source-biased coherence relations in Table 13.1, as compared to the completions for no-pronoun passages like (24) in which participants choose their own referring expressions. This prediction was confirmed in a study by Rohde & Kehler (2008): significantly more instances of Source-biased coherence relations resulted in continuations with pronoun-prompt contexts like (23) as compared to no-pronoun contexts like (24).

These results demonstrate not only that coherence establishment biases influence pronoun interpretation expectancies, but conversely that independent biases in pronoun production influence expectations about ensuing coherence relations. As such, whereas these experiments support the claim that coherence establishment is a critical factor for pronoun interpretation, the situation appears to be more complicated than the model proposed by Hobbs, in which pronouns are represented as variables that are ultimately bound solely as a by-product of semantic and discourse reasoning.

To sum, these experiments provide evidence that hearers implicitly track expectations about how the current discourse will be continued with respect to coherence. Although these expectations exist independently of the existence of cohesive phenomena like pronouns, they nonetheless have considerable impact on how these forms are interpreted. It is difficult to see how a model of pronoun interpretation could be formulated to account for this data without appealing to a sufficiently rich notion of discourse coherence.

4 Other 'cohesive' phenomena

Of course, pronouns are only one of a variety of forms that Halliday and Hasan treat as cohesive. In this section I give a briefer consideration of three other such phenomena: ellipsis, conjunction reduction, and deaccentuation. In all cases, the coherence properties of a discourse are argued to influence when the use of reduced forms is licensed.

4.1 Ellipsis

Verb phrase ellipsis (VPE) is exemplified by sentence (25):

(25) John voted for Al Gore, and Bill did too.

The stranded auxiliary in the second clause (henceforth, the *target* clause) marks a vestigial verb phrase (VP), a meaning for which is to be recovered from another clause (henceforth, the *source* clause), in this case, the first clause.

In their discussion of different cohesive forms, Halliday and Hasan make a fundamental distinction between SUBSTITUTION phenomena, which involve reference to elements of the text itself, and REFERENCE phenomena, which involve reference to semantic objects. They claim that ellipsis falls into the substitution category, with the main proviso being that it involves a substitution of something with nothing, that is, that 'ellipsis is simply substitution by zero' (Halliday & Hasan 1976: 142). VPE receives a similar treatment in Hankamer & Sag's (1976) well-known dichotomy between SURFACE and DEEP anaphora (see also Sag & Hankamer 1984); their categorization of VPE as a surface anaphor predicts that a suitable syntactic verb phrase must be available as an antecedent for the ellipsis to be felicitous.

There is certainly evidence for this position; consider (26a–c).

(26) a. #The aardvark was given a nut by Wendy, and Bruce did too. [gave the aardvark a nut] (Webber 1978, ch. 4, ex. 40)
b. #Al_i blamed $himself_i$, and George did too. [blamed Al]
c. #James defended $George_i$ and he_i did too. [defended George]

The unacceptability of sentence (26a) is predicted by the surface anaphoric account: Because the source clause is in the passive voice, the active voice VP needed at the ellipsis site – *gave the aardvark a nut* – is not available. Whereas a syntactically parallel VP does occur in (26b), on the other hand, it is not one that could have occurred in the ellipsis site due to the Condition A violation that would result. Likewise for (26c), in which Condition C is the principle violated.

However, as discussed by many authors (Dalrymple, Shieber & Pereira 1991, Hardt 1992, Kehler 1993, inter alia), felicitous examples of VPE that violate these constraints are well-attested:

(27) a. In November, the citizens of Florida asked that the election results be overturned, but the election commission refused to. [overturn the election results] (adapted from Dalrymple 1991, ex. 15a)
b. Al_i defended $himself_i$ because Bill wouldn't. [defend Al] (adapted from Dalrymple 1991, ex. 75a)
c. George expected Al_i to win the election even when he_i didn't. [expect Al to win the election] (adapted from Dalrymple 1991, ex. 75c)

Examples (27a–c) display patterns opposite to those in (26a–c): Example (27a) is acceptable despite a passive-active voice mismatch, and examples (27b–c) are felicitous despite the same expectation for Condition A and C violations that we saw in (26b–c) respectively.

In Kehler (2000; 2002), I argued that the cause for the diverging judgments between (26a–c) and (27a–c) lies in the fact that the two clauses in each of (26a–c) are related by the Resemblance relation Parallel, whereas (27a–c) are related by Cause-effect relations (Violated Expectation, Explanation, and Denial of Preventer respectively). The theory I advocated claims that VPE is anaphoric (and therefore not syntactically mediated), which, if otherwise left unconstrained, would predict that (26a–c) should be as acceptable as (27a–c). However, an additional constraint comes from the process of establishing coherence itself: The establishment of Resemblance relations, but not others, requires that a syntactic VP be accessed in order to identify and align the parallel elements to the relation. Thus, unlike surface anaphoric theories, syntactic reconstruction is *not* performed to recover the meaning of the missing VP, but instead is done only in service of the establishment of those coherence relations that require it. See Kehler (2000; 2002) for arguments that this theory predicts a variety of facts about the gapping construction as well, and Section 4.3 for a discussion of the influence of coherence on the focus/background partition assigned to utterances. The latter influence is particularly salient in that it raises the question of whether the constraints on ellipsis, like those on deaccentuation, are actually information structural (Tancredi 1992; Rooth 1992; Hendriks 2004; Kertz 2010), with coherence playing a indirect role.

In sum, VPE provides another example of how coherence begets cohesion. According to the theory summarized here, VPE is licensed when discourse interpretation can recover the information it needs to establish coherence. In addition to the meaning of the elided VP, this information also includes the syntactic structure when a Resemblance relation is operative.

4.2 Conjunction reduction

Another example of a cohesive form cited by Halliday and Hasan is conjunction. We have already made the point (in Section 1, with respect to examples (3)–(4)) that conjunctions – or more generally, connectives – do not themselves create discourse coherence. Passages that contain connectives will remain incoherent if the coherence relations associated with the connectives cannot be established using the same inferential mechanisms that apply to passages without connectives.

In this section I address a more specific 'cohesive' phenomenon pertaining to conjunction, particularly so-called CONJUNCTION REDUCTION, illustrated by the difference between the conjoined sentential clauses in (28a) and the conjoined VPs in (28b).

(28) a. He went to the coffee cart and he bought some whiskey.
b. He went to the coffee cart and bought some whiskey.

There is a variety of evidence that conjunction reduction correlates with some notion of 'conceptual distance' between the elements being related (Haimon 1985, inter alia). Consider, for instance, (28a) and (28b) as answers to the question *What did John do today?*. Informants commonly (although not universally) report that response (28b) surprises them in a way that (28a) does not, in that (28b), unlike (28a), more strongly implicates that the whiskey was bought at the coffee cart. That there would be such an implicature difference is surprising, since both answers express the same propositions: John went to the coffee cart, and John bought some whiskey. It seems as if bundling the verb phrases together in (28b) implies a tighter coherence relationship between the two. As a result, conjunction reduction is not merely about reducing clauses when the subjects are coreferential – the reduction to conjoined VPs may carry additional implicatures.

There is reason to believe that the operative notion of 'conceptual distance' in such examples and the implicatures that result are driven by a difference in coherence relationship. That is, informants report that (28a) is tilted more toward a Parallel relationship, in that it offers two things that John did today: They need not have occurred at the same time or place. On the other hand, they report that (28b) is biased more to an OCCASION construal: Not only did both events occur today, but they are more strongly connected with respect to time, space, and enablement. Importantly, these effects are only pragmatic, and perhaps somewhat weak at that: (28b) *could* still denote two independent events, and (28a) *could* still denote connected events.

The effect becomes must stronger when extraction is involved, however. Let us first consider examples (29a–b):

(29) a. #This is the whiskey that John bought and he stole the vodka.
b. #This is the whiskey that John bought and stole the vodka.

These illustrate the types of examples that Ross (1967) cited in arguing for a Coordinate Structure Constraint (CSC) in language grammar, which states that any NP that is extracted from a coordinate structure must be extracted from all of the conjuncts (i.e., "across-the-board"). The unacceptability of (29a–b) is therefore captured by the constraint, since these cases involve extraction from only the first conjunct. (Note that Ross would therefore have starred ('*') these examples to indicate ungrammaticality. Below I will claim that such sentences are ruled out by pragmatic principles, hence the use of the pound sign ('#').)

Examples (29a–b) can be contrasted with the variants of (28a–b) shown in (30a–b):

(30) a. #This is the snack that John went to the coffee cart and he stole.
b. This is the snack that John went to the coffee cart and stole.

Whereas (30a) is unacceptable as predicted, example (30b) is felicitous; an unanticipated result for the constraint. What is to account for the difference?

Building on insights of Lakoff (1986) and others, in Kehler (2002) I argued that the constraints responsible for licensing extraction from coordinate structures are not grammatical, but instead result from an information-structural constraint on extraction – in particular, the TOPICHOOD CONDITION of Kuno (1976; 1987) – and the manner in which these interact with different coherence relationships. The unextracted correlates of examples (29a–b) and (30a) – e.g., *John bought the whiskey and stole the vodka* for (29b) – are most readily understood as Parallel relations. In these cases extraction from all clauses is necessary, since an entity in a Parallel relation, which by definition means that the utterances are bound by a common topic, can only be part of the topic if it is mentioned in each clause. The clauses in example (30b), on the other hand, are related by Occasion. Occasion relations do not require that a topical entity be mentioned in every clause; the first clause of passage (30b) merely 'sets the scene', and thus the topic of the passage can still include the snack. Note that while (28b) merely favors an Occasion interpretation, the topichood constraint correctly predicts that the acceptability of (30b) is contingent on it receiving an Occasion interpretation, that is, it *has* to be the case that the snack was stolen from the coffee cart.

In accordance with this observation, an assortment of counterexamples to the CSC that have been discussed in the literature are unified by the fact that they all involve coherence relations in categories other than Resemblance:

(31) a. How much can you drink and still stay sober? [Violated Expectation] (Goldsmith 1985)
b. That's the stuff that the guys in the Caucasus drink and live to be a hundred. [Result] (Lakoff 1986, attributed to Peter Farley)
c. What did Harry buy, come home, and devour in thirty seconds? [Occasion] (Adapted from Ross 1967)

Thus, extraction from coordinate clauses provides another example that illustrates the theme of this section. It is not the occurrence of reduced linguistic forms that determines the felicity of a passage. Instead, it works the other way around: It is the coherence properties of a passage that determine when linguistic reduction can felicitously take place.

4.3 Accent placement

In Section 5.9 of *Cohesion in English*, Halliday and Hasan consider the cohesive properties of intonation (cf. article 10 [this volume] (Hinterwimmer) *Information structure* and article 5 [this volume] (Krifka) *Questions*). Perhaps the most basic insight in the literature is the anaphoric (and/or presuppositional) nature of deaccented material, generally taken to be licensed by the previous mention of a coreferential element. Example (32) provides an illustration; the accent on *praised* in (32b) reflects the fact that it contributes new information into the discourse, whereas the lack of accent on *she* and *him* accords with the fact that they denote information that is old, or GIVEN, since their referents were both mentioned in (32a).

(32) a. {What did John's mother do?}
  b. She [[PRAISED]$_F$him]$_F$.   (Schwarzschild 1999, ex. 9)

The association between Givenness and deaccentuation becomes more complicated in examples like (33) and (34), however, in which accent is placed on *John* and *him* respectively, despite the fact that they refer to information that was previously introduced:

(33) a. {John's mother voted for Bill.}
  b. No, she voted for JOHN$_F$.   (Schwarzschild 1999, ex. 2)

(34) a. { Who did John$_i$'s mother praise?}
  b. She praised [HIM$_j$]$_F$.   (Schwarzschild 1999, ex. 11)

In the face of such complexities, Halliday (1967) offers three definitions of New, specifically "textually and situationally non-derivable information", "contrary to some predicted or stated alternative", and "replacing the WH-element in a presupposed question". These definitions cover examples (32–34) respectively.

As successfully argued by Schwarzschild (1999) and others, these complications result in part from the fact that accent in English is used not only to avoid the presupposition that the meanings of particular words are Given, but also to avoid the presupposition that the meanings of larger constituents that contain those words are Given. Consider the clause *she voted for John* in (33b), for instance. Whereas the meaning of every word in this clause is Given, the meaning of the VP *voted for John* is not. The rules of accent placement in English thereby necessitate that accent appear somewhere in the VP, in this case on *John*.

In Kehler (2005) I argued that the operative coherence relations in a discourse influence when a constituent can be felicitously deaccented. A brief (and highly incomplete) synopsis of Schwarzschild's analysis should suffice to understand the argument. The *F* subscripts shown in (32b–34b) are examples of F-MARKING, which in his system serves as the interface between semantics and phonology. On the semantics side, felicitous utterances are entailed by the prior discourse (that is, *Given*), with the proviso that F-marking a phrase effectively turns it into a 'wildcard' (or 'F-variable') when matching against an antecedent. For instance, in a context that mentions *a red apple*, the NP *a [green]F apple* will be considered Given. On the phonology side, there is a constraint that FOC-marked nodes – F-marked nodes that are not immediately dominated by another F-marked node – must contain an accent. As such, the word *green* in *a [green]F apple* will require accent.

FOC-marked nodes are assigned discourse antecedents by a function h for establishing Givenness; in the example just given, h will map the denotation of *green* to that of *red*. An optimality-theoretic optimization procedure solely determines h. It is this aspect of the analysis that I argued against in Kehler (2005), where I claimed that it cannot predict the difference in accent patterns for examples like (35b) and (36b).

(35) {John cited Mary, but}
　　a. he DISSED$_F$ SUE$_F$.
　　b. #he [dissed$_F$ SUE$_F$]$_F$.　(Schwarzschild 1999, ex. 60)

(36) {Fred read the menu and then}
　　a. #he ORDERED$_F$ [a HAMBURGER]$_F$.
　　b. he [ordered$_F$ [a HAMBURGER]$_F$]$_F$.

The follow-on clause in each case contains a subject that denotes given information and a verb and object that denote new information, and as such, the factors that determine F-marking in Schwarzschild's system are identical. Nonetheless, whereas it is infelicitous to accent the verb in addition to the object NP in (36b), such accent is required in (35b).

This difference, I argued, results from the fact that different coherence relations create different partitions with respect to background and focus. In the case of Contrast – the operative relation in (35) – h uses the same mapping that results from the identification of parallel elements (i.e., the a_i and b_i) for establishing coherence. In Schwarzschild's system, this entails that both *dissed* and *Sue* must be F-marked (and ultimately, accented), since these are not coreferential with the antecedents that *h* maps them to, specifically *cited* and *Mary* respectively. No such mapping is used to establish non-Resemblance relations like Occasion – the operative relation in (36) – and thus they enforce no such constraint on the mapping established by *h*. In this case only the VP needs to be marked as new, and thus accent (rather than F-marking) can be economized by placing intonational prominence on only the direct object.

Lest there be any doubt that these different interpretation patterns are due to the difference in coherence type, we can ask whether passages that are ambiguous between multiple coherence construals enforce different constraints on the interpretation of unaccented expressions. This is indeed the case; consider (37):

(37) Powell defied Cheney, and Bush punished him. (Kehler 2002)

On the Parallel construal of (37) (paraphrase *and* as *and similarly*), *him* can only refer to Cheney if unaccented (i.e., it can refer to Powell only if it receives accent). On the other hand, on the Result construal (paraphrase *and* as *and as a result*), *him* can refer to Powell if it is unaccented. This difference can only be attributed to the coherence construal, since the example is morphosyntactically identical on the two interpretations.

The crucial fact to be taken away from this brief discussion is that Resemblance relations like Parallel and Contrast, by way of establishing a mapping between parallel elements, give rise to a particular focus/background partition. A side-effect of this partition is that an expression that does not corefer with its parallel element will require accent *regardless of its Givenness status in the remainder of the discourse*. Non-Resemblance relations such as Occasion and Result are not similarly restricted, and as such, the optimal focus/accent distribution may result in a distinct placement of accent. As such, the operative coherence relations play an important role in determining what constituents can be felicitously (if not 'cohesively') deaccented.

To summarize this section, three types of linguistic expressions that Halliday and Hasan include in their catalog of cohesive forms – ellipses, conjunction, and deaccentuation – are not only in part the products of the coherence properties of the discourse, but their felicity is dependent on them in highly specific ways.

5 Question-under-discussion models

The coherence relation analysis is not the only approach to discourse coherence in the literature. Another type is the QUESTION UNDER DISCUSSION (QUD) analysis, proposed by Carlson (1983) and considerably extended and formalized by Roberts (1998). (See also van Kuppevelt 1995, Ginzburg 1996, and article 5 [this volume] (Krifka) *Questions.*) In QUD analyses, discourses are structured by question/answer relationships rather than coherence relationships. Roughly speaking, an utterance is coherent insofar as it provides an answer to a (generally implicit) question that is relevant to the preceeding discourse.

Unlike the informational relations that characterize the coherence relation view, discourses in Roberts' analysis are organized around the conversational goals that interlocutors have and the STRATEGIES OF INQUIRY they employ to satisfy them. In this regard the analysis shares many properties of the intentional approach of Grosz & Sidner (1986) and related works, although intentions in her analysis appear to be more narrowly restricted to providing full or partial answers to QUDs. She suggests, following Stalnaker (1979), that discourse is to be viewed as an attempt by conversational participants to discover and share "the ways things are" (or, to phrase it another way, to answer the question *What is the way things are?*). Thus, by engaging in a conversation, the interlocutors agree to jointly adopt goals that center around finding the answers to this question. This in turn will generally necessitate the adoption and satisfaction of subgoals centered on answering sub-questions, giving rise to a hierarchical discourse structure. Understanding a discourse therefore requires that hearers not only understand the particular utterances in the discourse, but also situate them within the underlying strategy of inquiry.

As Roberts briefly notes, the coherence relation and QUD analyses are related, in that coherence relations can often be characterized in terms of implicit questions that intervene among utterances. For example, whereas in Section 2 we analyzed example (38) as related by Explanation on its most accessible interpretation, a QUD analysis would posit the implicit question *Why?* as intervening between (38a–b).

(38) a. Joe Biden will probably win the election.
 b. He is by far the most experienced in foreign policy of all the presidential candidates.

Note that the constraints on recognizing the coherence of this discourse are similar on the two analyses: Recovering the implicit Explanation relation or the implicit QUD *Why?* both require that the hearer use world knowledge to infer that (38b) describes the *reason* for the event described in (38a). Other corresponding relationships between coherence relations and questions readily come to mind: *How come?* and *What for?* also correspond to Explanation, *What happened next?* corresponds to Occasion or Result, and *Where/when/how?* correspond to Elaboration.

The Parallel relation also receives a natural treatment within the QUD analysis, and is worth considering separately because of its configurational properties. In Section 2 we characterized utterances that participate in a Parallel relation as being related by a common topic that each utterance instantiates; in the case of (12), repeated below in (39a–b), this topic was *the things X has been doing to advertise X's leadership skills*. These utterances are equally naturally characterized as providing partial answers to an implicit QUD as shown in (39). In this case the QUD sits above both utterances rather than intervening between them as in the previous example.

(39) *What have presidential candidates been doing to advertise their leadership skills?*
    a. Biden has been touting his years of experience on the Senate foreign relations committee.
    b. Giuliani has been reminding everyone about September 11th at every conceivable opportunity.

This treatment captures the oft-cited intuition that the Parallel relation is paratactic, or using the terminology of RST, 'multi-nuclear'. It also captures the reason why Parallel can relate more than two utterances at once, unlike the other relations. Finally, Roberts (1998) and Büring (2003) demonstrate that the intonational properties of such passages follow predicted patterns of question-answer congruence under this model.

The experiments of Rohde, Kehler & Elman (2007) discussed in Section 3 also bear on the relationship between coherence relations and QUDs with respect to incremental interpretation. Recall that Rohde, Kehler and Elman argued that experimentally-observed biases in pronoun interpretation can be predicted only with a model that captures comprehenders' contextually-driven probabilistic expectations about what coherence relation will ensue. Interestingly, they demonstrated this using what could be characterized as a QUD-based manipulation: Participants were asked to complete passages with pronoun prompts in a way that answered either the question *Why?* or *What happened next?*. The choice of QUD changed the distribution of coherence relations employed in the passage completions, which in turn resulted in a significantly different distribution of pronoun interpretations, despite the fact that the stimuli themselves were identical across conditions. Whereas Rohde, Kehler and Elman posited an equation (shown in (22)) that captured hearer's expectations regarding the likelihood that different coherence relations might ensue, these expectations could similarly be cast in terms of

QUDs, that is, as a distribution over implicit questions that the hearer expects the next utterance to answer.

One could therefore potentially argue that the QUD analysis might ultimately prove more general than the coherence relation view, in that it addresses the role of questioning in dialog in addition to implicit questions in monologue. Further work will be required, however, for a fuller understanding of the relationship between them.

6 Conclusion

COHESION and COHERENCE are two very different things. Cohesion is defined in terms of particular linguistic phenomena that exist in a discourse, whereas coherence is defined in terms of the underlying semantic relationships that characterize and structure the transitions between utterances. In this article, I compared the cohesion and coherence analyses of discourse well-formedness, arguing that the evidence lands squarely on the side of the coherence view. On the one hand, coherent discourses may not display much cohesion, and yet be perfectly felicitous. On the other hand, a 'discourse' can be rich in cohesive phenomena and yet be utterly infelicitous.

It is nonetheless natural that there would be an empirical correlation between coherence in discourses and correspondingly high degrees of cohesiveness. Coherent discourses will tend to talk about the same entities, relationships, and events, which will in turn license linguistically reduced forms to refer to them. As Zipf would have it, speakers have motivation to economize on form when there is enough contextual information to allow them to get away with it. In this chapter, we have seen that the properties of coherence establishment processes play a large role in dictating when a speaker can get away with it.

I have described the coherence relation view in terms of an analysis that sees the space of possible discourse continuations as characterizable within Hume's three types of "connections among ideas". A variety of other approaches are possible and have indeed been put forth. While the details of different analyses will no doubt continue to be debated, it is nonetheless clear that a variety of semantic and inferential constraints govern the production and interpretation of felicitous discourses. As such, it can hardly be surprising that coherence-driven constraints play a role in determining the contexts in which various discourse-sensitive linguistic phenomena can be felicitously employed.

The author thanks Paul Portner for comments on an earlier draft.

7 References

Arnold, Jennifer 2001. The effect of thematic roles on pronoun use and frequency of reference continuation. *Discourse Processes* 21, 137–162.
Asher, Nicholas & Alex Lascarides 2003. *Logics of Conversation*. Cambridge: Cambridge University Press.
Baltaxe, Christiane A. M. & Nora D'Angiola 1992. Cohesion in the discourse interaction of autistic, specifically language-impaired, and normal children. *Journal of Autism and Developmental Disorders* 22, 1–21.
Brown, Gillian & George Yule 1983. *Discourse Analysis*. Cambridge: Cambridge University Press.
Büring, Daniel 2003. On D-trees, beans, and B-accents. *Linguistics & Philosophy* 26, 511–545.
Caramazza, Alfonso, Ellen H. Grober, Catherine Garvey & Jack B. Yates 1977. Comprehension of anaphoric pronouns. *Journal of Verbal Learning and Verbal Behaviour* 16, 601–609.
Carlson, Lauri 1983. *Dialogue Games. An Approach to Discourse Analysis*. Dordrecht: Reidel.
Crossley, Scott A., Max M. Louwerse, Philip M. McCarthy & Danielle S. McNamara 2007. A linguistic analysis of simplified and authentic texts. *Modern Language Journal* 91, 15–30.
Crossley, Scott A. & Danielle S. McNamara 2008. Assessing second language reading texts at the intermediate level. An approximate replication of Crossley, Louwerse, McCarthy & McNamara (2007). *Language Teaching* 41, 409–429.
Dalrymple, Mary 1991. *Against Reconstruction in Ellipsis*. Technical Report SSL-91-114. Palo Alto, CA, Xerox PARC.
Dalrymple, Mary, Stuart M. Shieber & Fernando Pereira 1991. Ellipsis and higher-order unification. *Linguistics & Philosophy* 14, 399–452.
Fine, Jonathan, Giampiero Bartolucci, Peter Szatmari & Gary Ginsberg 1994. Cohesive discourse in pervasive developmental disorders. *Journal of Autism and Developmental Disorders* 24, 315–329.
Ginzburg, Jonathan 1996. Dynamics and the semantics of dialog. In: J. Seligman & D. Westerståhl (eds.). *Logic, Language and Computation, vol. 1*. Stanford, CA: CSLI Publications, 221–257.
Goldsmith, John 1985. A principled exception to the coordinate structure constraint. In: *Papers from the Twenty-First Regional Meeting of the Chicago Linguistic Society*. Chicago, IL: Chicago Linguistic Society, 133–143.
Gordon, Peter C., Barbara J. Grosz & Laura A. Gilliom 1993. Pronouns, names, and the centering of attention in discourse. *Cognitive Science* 17, 311–347.
Gordon, Peter C. & Kimberly A. Scearce 1995. Pronominalization and discourse coherence, discourse structure and pronoun interpretation. *Memory and Cognition* 23, 313–323.
Graesser, Arthur C., Danielle S. McNamara, Max M. Louwerse & Zhiqiang Cai 2004. Coh-metrix: Analysis of text on cohesion and language. *Behavior Research Methods, Instruments, and Computers* 36, 193–202.
Grosz, Barbara J. & Candace L. Sidner 1986. Attention, intentions, and the structure of discourse. *Computational Linguistics* 12, 175–204.
Haimon, John 1985. *Natural Syntax*. Cambridge: Cambridge University Press.
Hale, John 2001. A probabilistic early parser as a psycholinguistic model. In: *Proceedings of the Second Meeting of the North American Chapter of the Association for Computational Linguistics*. Pittsburgh, PA: Association for Computational Linguistics, 159–166.
Halliday, Michael A. K. 1967. Notes on transitivity and theme in English (part 2). *Journal of Linguistics* 3, 199–244.

Halliday, Michael A. K. & Ruqaiya Hasan 1976. *Cohesion in English*. London: Longman.
Hankamer, Jorge & Ivan Sag 1976. Deep and surface anaphora. *Linguistic Inquiry* 7, 391–426.
Hardt, Daniel 1992. VP ellipsis and contextual interpretation. In: *Proceedings of the 15th International Conference on Computational Linguistics (= COLING-92)*. Nantes: ICCL, 303–309.
Hendriks, Petra 2004. Coherence relations, ellipsis and contrastive topics. *Journal of Semantics* 21, 133–153.
Hobbs, Jerry R. 1979. Coherence and coreference. *Cognitive Science* 3, 67–90.
Hobbs, Jerry R. 1990. *Literature and Cognition*. Stanford, CA: CSLI Publications.
Hobbs, Jerry R., Mark E. Stickel, Douglas E. Appelt & Paul Martin 1993. Interpretation as abduction. *Artificial Intelligence* 63, 69–142.
Hume, David 1748/1955. *An Inquiry Concerning Human Understanding*. Reprinted: C. W. Hendel (ed.). New York: The Liberal Arts Press, 1955.
Kehler, Andrew 1993. A discourse copying algorithm for ellipsis and anaphora resolution. In: *Proceedings of the Sixth Conference of the European Chapter of the Association for Computational Linguistics (EACL-93)*. Utrecht: Association for Computational Linguistics, 203–212.
Kehler, Andrew 2000. Coherence and the resolution of ellipsis. *Linguistics & Philosophy* 23, 533–575.
Kehler, Andrew 2002. *Coherence, Reference, and the Theory of Grammar*. Stanford, CA: CSLI Publications.
Kehler, Andrew 2005. Coherence-driven constraints on the placement of accent. In: E. Georgala & J. Howell (eds.). *Proceedings of Semantics and Linguistic Theory (= SALT) XV*. Ithaca, NY: Cornell University, 98–115.
Kehler, Andrew, Laura Kertz, Hannah Rohde & Jeffrey L. Elman 2008. Coherence and coreference revisited. *Journal of Semantics* 25, 1–44.
Kertz Laura 2010. *Ellipsis Reconsidered*. PhD Thesis, University of California, San Diego.
Knott, Alistair & Robert Dale 1994. Using linguistic phenomena to motivate a set of coherence relations. *Discourse Processes* 18, 35–62.
Koornneef, Arnout W. & Jos J. A. van Berkum 2006. On the use of verb-based implicit causality in sentence comprehension: Evidence from self-paced reading and eye-tracking. *Journal of Memory and Language* 54, 445–465.
Kuno, Susumu 1976. Subject, theme, and the speaker's empathy – A reexamination of the relativization phenomena. In: C. N. Li (ed.). *Subject and Topic*. New York: Academic Press, 419–444.
Kuno, Susumu 1987. *Functional Syntax – Anaphora, Discourse and Empathy*. Chicago, IL: The University of Chicago Press.
van Kuppevelt, Jan 1995. Discourse structure, topicality, and questioning. *Journal of Linguistics* 31, 109–147.
Lakoff, George 1986. Frame semantic control of the coordinate structure constraint. In: A. Farley et al. (eds.). *Papers from the Twenty-Second Regional Meeting of the Chicago Linguistic Society, part 2: Papers from the Parasession on Pragmatics and Grammatical Theory*. Chicago, IL: Chicago Linguistic Society, 152–167.
Levy, Roger 2008. Expectation-based syntactic comprehension. *Cognition* 106, 1126–1177.
Longacre, Robert E. 1983. *The Grammar of Discourse*. New York: Plenum Press.
Mann, William C. & Sandra A. Thompson 1987. *Rhetorical Structure Theory: A Theory of Text Organization*. Technical Report RS-87-190. Marina del Rey, CA: Information Sciences Institute, University of Southern California.

McKoon, Gail, Steven B. Greene & Roger Ratcliff 1993. Discourse models, pronoun resolution, and the implicit causality of verbs. *Journal of Experimental Psychology: Learning, Memory, and Cognition* 18, 266–283.

McNamara, Danielle S., Yasuhiro Ozuru, Arthur C. Graesser & Max Louwerse 2006. Validating coh-metrix. In: R. Sun (ed.). *Proceedings of the 28th Annual Conference of the Cognitive Science Society*. Austin, TX: Cognitive Science Society, 573–578.

Roberts, Craige 1998. Information structure in discourse: Towards an integrated formal theory of pragmatics. http://semanticsarchive.net/Archive/WYzOTRkO/InfoStructure.pdf. December 7, 2010. (Revised version of: Roberts, Craige 1996. Information structure in discourse: Towards an integrated formal theory of pragmatics. In: J. H. Yoon & A. Kathol (eds.). *Papers in Semantics* (OSU Working Papers in Linguistics 49). Columbus, OH: The Ohio State University, 91–136.)

Rohde, Hannah & Andrew Kehler 2008. The bidirectional influence between coherence establishment and pronoun interpretation. Poster presented at the *21st Annual CUNY conference on Human Sentence Processing*. University of North Carolina, Chapel Hill, NC, 13–15.

Rohde, Hannah, Andrew Kehler & Jeffrey L. Elman 2006. Event structure and discourse coherence biases in pronoun interpretation. In: R. Sun (ed.). *Proceedings of the 28th Annual Conference of the Cognitive Science Society*. Austin, TX: Cognitive Science Society, 697–702.

Rohde, Hannah, Andrew Kehler & Jeffrey L. Elman 2007. Pronoun interpretation as a side effect of discourse coherence. In: D. McNamara & J. Trafton (eds.). *Proceedings of the 29th Annual Conference of the Cognitive Science Society*. Austin, TX: Cognitive Science Society, 617–622.

Rooth, Mats 1992. Ellipsis redundancy and reduction redundancy. In: S. Berman & A. Hestvik (eds.). *Proceedings of the Stuttgart Workshop on Ellipsis* (Arbeitspapiere des Sonderforschungsbereichs 340, Bericht Nr. 29). Stuttgart: University of Stuttgart.

Ross, John Robert 1967. *Constraints on Variables in Syntax*. Ph.D. dissertation. MIT, Cambridge, MA.

Sag, Ivan & Jorge Hankamer 1984. Toward a theory of anaphoric processing. *Linguistics & Philosophy* 7, 325–345.

Sanders, Ted J. M., Wilbert P. M. Spooren & Leo G. M. Noordman 1992. Toward a taxonomy of coherence relations. *Discourse Processes* 15, 1–35.

Schwarzschild, Roger 1999. GIVENness, AVOID F, and other constraints on the placement of accent. *Natural Language Semantics* 7, 141–177.

Stalnaker, Robert 1979. Assertion. In: P. Cole (ed.). *Syntax and Semantics 9: Pragmatics*. New York: Academic Press, 315–332.

Stevenson, Rosemary J., Rosalind A. Crawley & David Kleinman 1994. Thematic roles, focus, and the representation of events. *Language and Cognitive Processes* 9, 519–548.

Stewart, Andrew J., Martin J. Pickering & Anthony J. Sanford 1998. Implicit consequentiality. In: M. Gernsbacher & S. Derry (eds.). *Proceedings of the 20th Annual Conference of the Cognitive Science Society*. Mahwah, NJ: Lawrence Erlbaum Associates, 1031–1036.

Tancredi, Christopher 1992. *Deletion, Deaccenting, and Presupposition*. Ph.D. dissertation. MIT, Cambridge, MA.

Webber, Bonnie Lynn 1978. *A Formal Approach to Discourse Anaphora*. Ph.D. dissertation. Harvard University, Cambridge, MA. Reprinted: New York: Garland, 1979.

Webber, Bonnie Lynn, Matthew Stone, Aravind Joshi & Alistair Knott 2003. Anaphora and discourse structure. *Computational Linguistics* 29, 545–587.
Winograd, Terry 1972. *Understanding Natural Language*. New York: Academic Press.
Wolf, Florian & Edward Gibson 2006. *Coherence in Natural Language. Data Structures and Applications*. Cambridge, MA: The MIT Press.
Zipf, George Kingsley 1935. *The Psycho-Biology of Language*. New York: Houghton-Mifflin.

Bart Geurts
14 Accessibility and anaphora

1 Discourse referents —— 481
2 Neo-Russellian revisionism —— 485
3 Discourse representation theory —— 487
4 Accessibility, givenness, and bridging —— 494
5 Piggyback anaphora again —— 497
6 Piggyback anaphora and bridging —— 501
7 Rethinking accessibility —— 505
8 Conclusion —— 507
9 References —— 509

Abstract: Dynamic theories of discourse interpretation seek to describe and explain antecedent-anaphor relations with the help of discourse referents. In a dynamic framework, it is the function of indefinite expressions to introduce new discourse referents, whilst anaphoric expressions serve to retrieve them. Dynamic theories provide a simple and intuitively appealing solution to a variety of problems. For instance, they explain how it is possible for an indefinite expression to bind a pronoun that isn't c-commanded by it, and they impose accessibility constraints on the interpretation of pronouns that, by large, seem to be adequate. However, it has been known for a long time that dynamic theories encounter problems with what I call "piggyback anaphora": anaphoric links that are enabled by the fact that the anaphoric expression sits in the scope of an expression that quantifies over the same range of entities as the expression whose scope contains the intended antecedent. I argue that the key to solving this problem lies in the fact that this type of anaphora involves a form of bridging.

1 Discourse referents

Classical logic provides us with two candidate models for analysing anaphoric pronouns. One is the bound variable: in (1), "she" may be construed as a variable bound by "every contestant":

Bart Geurts, Nijmegen, The Netherlands

https://doi.org/10.1515/9783110589863-014

(1) Every contestant is convinced that she will win the prize.

This captures one possible construal of the sentence, but there is another, in which the pronoun targets one particular individual. For this reading, the model of the free variable is more suitable: the value of "she" is fixed by a preselected assignment function, to be thought of as part of the context in which the sentence is uttered.

Unfortunately, there are plenty of pronoun occurrences that fit neither model; perhaps the simplest type of example is the following:

(2) Our vicar owns a Toyota$_i$. It$_i$ is grey.

We would like to say that "a Toyota" is the most natural antecedent for "it", but as long as we are sticking with classical logic we can say no such thing. On the one hand, the pronoun isn't bound by its intended antecedent, for this would entail that the scope of "a Toyota" extends beyond the sentence in which it occurs. On the other hand, "it" doesn't seem to function as a free variable, either: somehow or other the pronoun owes its referent to the indefinite, though without being bound by it.

Using a notion introduced by Karttunen in his trailblazing 1971 paper, the most intuitive way of describing what goes on in (2) is that the indefinite "a Toyota" serves to introduce a *discourse referent*, which is subsequently picked up by the pronoun. The purpose of this article is to trace how this notion developed since the 1970s, and then present and perhaps solve some of the problems it is up against, with emphasis on what I will call "piggyback anaphora".

One of the truly impressive achievements of Karttunen's paper is that although at the time he didn't have anything like a theory of discourse referents, his discussion evinces a clear sense of what such a theory would be able to do, and where it might run into trouble. Karttunen begins by showing how a discourse like (2) contrasts with:

(3) Our vicar doesn't own a Toyota$_i$. *It$_i$ is grey.

In a first stab at capturing this contrast, Karttunen suggests that, whereas in (2) the indefinite introduces a discourse referent for the pronoun to pick up, in (3) no such discourse referent is established. However, later in the paper he refines the notion of discourse referent to accommodate examples like the following:

(4) a. John wants to catch a fish$_i$ and eat it$_i$ for supper. *Do you see the fish$_i$ over there?
   b. I don't believe that Mary had a baby$_i$ and named her$_i$ Sue. *The baby$_i$ has mumps.

In the face of these data, Karttunen settles for the idea that discourse referents have "lifespans" of varying lengths. In (4a) the lifespan of the discourse referent introduced by way of "a fish" is bounded by the scope of "wants", while in (4b) it is coterminous with the scope of "believe". However, as Karttunen (1971, 11) points out, "the lifespan of a short-term [discourse] referent is not always so neatly bound as the above examples suggest." To illustrate the lack of neatness, Karttunen offers the following observations:

(5) a. You must write a letter$_i$ to your parents. It$_i$ has to be sent by email. The letter$_i$ must get there by tomorrow.
 b. Harvey courts a girl$_i$ at every convention. She$_i$ always comes to the banquet with him. The girl$_i$ is usually also very pretty.
 c. If Mary had a car$_i$, she would take me to work in it$_i$. I could drive the car$_i$ too.
 d. I wish Mary had a car$_i$. She would take me to work in it$_i$. I could drive the car$_i$ too.

In each of these discourses, a pronoun and then a definite NP unexpectedly manage to "refer back" to a narrow-scope indefinite in the opening sentence. What makes this possible, apparently, is that the anaphors are in the scope of an expression that somehow extends the mode of quantification (over worlds, events, or what have you) of the first sentence. For example, the first sentence of (5a) quantifies over worlds, and the subsequent sentences quantify over the same worlds. Similarly, the first sentence of (5b) quantifies over events of a certain kind, and the following sentences quantify over the same events. Similarly, mutatis mutandis, for the other discourses in (5). So, although the details of the process are very much unclear, it seems obvious enough that the anaphors in (5) are piggybacking on the interpretation of the expressions in whose scope they occur; I will therefore call them "piggyback anaphora".

I'm proposing "piggyback anaphora" as a name for a natural kind that, to the best of knowledge, has not been named before. To my mind, the examples in (5) are so similar that we should expect them to admit of a unified explanation. However, the post-Karttunen literature suggests a different picture, with authors usually focusing on one class of facts to the exclusion of others. An important factor in this development may have been Roberts's (1987, 1989) influential work on "modal subordination". Concentrating her attention on data like Karttunen's (5a) and (5c), Roberts had very little to say about the others, and thus may have fostered the impression that the modal cases are special. Be this as it may, I see no reason to believe that this impression is correct, and as far as I know, it has never even been argued that it is, either. Hence, I will proceed on the assumption that the data in (5) exemplify a single phenomenon, and are therefore entitled to a unified explanation.

The following examples are evidently related to the ones in (5), but create further problems of their own:

(6) a. Suppose Mary had a car$_i$. She takes me to work in it$_i$. I drive the car$_i$ too. (Karttunen 1971)
b. In each room there was a cat$_i$ and a goldfish$_j$. The cat$_i$ was eyeing the goldfish$_j$. (Stenning 1978)
c. Every chess set comes with a spare pawn$_i$. It$_i$ is taped to the top of the box. (Sells 1985)
d. Every director gave a present$_i$ to [a child from the orphanage]$_j$. They$_j$ opened them$_i$ rightaway. (Kamp & Reyle 1993)

Although the anaphoric expressions in these examples are perfectly felicitous, none of them are in the scope of an overt quantifier that could bind them. However, in all of these cases, it is plausible to assume that piggyback anaphora is enabled by *implicit* quantification. For example, the intended interpretation of the second sentence in (6c) is something like, "*In every chess set* the spare pawn is taped to the top of the box". The other examples in (6) are similar. The problem, then, is to explain where the implicit quantifiers come from. In the case of (6d) this is fairly clear (though the plural morphology of "them" raises some hairy problems): it is the distributive reading of "they" that calls for a universal quantifier (Kamp & Reyle 1993, Krifka 1996). The examples in (6a–c) are considerably less straightforward, but as the special problems caused by such examples will have to be addressed anyhow, we will leave them aside here (the problems as well as the examples), and confine our attention to those cases where piggyback anaphora are enabled by overt quantification over individuals, worlds, and so on.

Another point that should be mentioned but will not be addressed is that piggybacking is not confined to pronouns and definite descriptions, but manifests itself with presuppositional expressions generally. As far as I know, this was first pointed out by Roberts (1995) and Geurts (1995) (though see McCawley 1981), but the relevant examples have been around since the early seventies:

(7) a. I wish Mary had a car. She would take me to work in it. I could drive the car too. (= (5d); Karttunen 1971)
b. Bill believed that Fred had been beating his wife and hoped that Fred would *stop* beating her. (Karttunen 1973)
c. Possibly Boris killed Louis and possibly Boris *regrets* killing Louis. (Gazdar 1979)

The factive verb "regret" in (7c) triggers the presupposition that Boris killed Louis. This presupposition is satisfied in the possible worlds selected by the first conjunct, and if we may assume that the second modal sentence resumes these possibilities, the construction is essentially the same as what we saw in (5). The same, mutatis mutandis, for (7a, b). (Sequenced attitude reports like (7b) are discussed at length by Heim 1992 and Geurts 1995, 1999.)

In the remainder of this paper we will focus our attention on the facts illustrated by the discourses in (5).

2 Neo-Russellian revisionism

Some people will say that the very idea of piggyback anaphora is completely off the track, as is the concept of discourse referent, for that matter. What we need instead, according to such people, is just the quantifiers and variables of classical logic, plus Russell's (1905) theory of descriptions. Pronouns are either bound variables or else go proxy for definite descriptions à la Russell. Hence, in (7a) "it" is a kind of shorthand for "Mary's car"; it is an "E-type pronoun" (Evans 1977, Heim 1990, Neale 1990, Elbourne 2005).

This sort of theory comes in a great many varieties, all of which come with their own epicycles, and I have neither the space nor the inclination to argue against all of them. The main purpose of this section is to bring out the signal differences between descriptivist theories and discourse-based theories of anaphora inspired by Karttunen's work.

Russell's theory of descriptions famously construes "The cup is empty" as "There is one and only one cup, and it is empty". That is to say, it claims that the semantics of the definite article entails descriptive uniqueness. This claim is either false or vacuous. Consider the following state of affairs:

In this situation, "the square with the dot" is a perfectly felicitous and unequivocal means of referring to the square on the right (Haddock 1987). But, prima facie at least, this is *not* the unique square with the unique dot; for there are two dots. So if we take the uniqueness claim at face value, it is false.

Needless to say, various kinds of repair strategies are on offer. One is to claim that the occurrence of "the dot" in "the square with the dot" is actually short for a more elaborate description that does meet the uniqueness requirement. For example, if "the dot" abbreviates "the dot in the square on the right", then "the square with the dot" comes out meaning "the square with the dot in the square on the right", and everything is hunky dory. (I know this sounds preposterous, but I didn't make it up.) Another strategy is to slice situations so finely that, within some narrowly circumscribed situation, "the dot" will refer uniquely, after all (cf. Heim 1990, Elbourne 2005). The idea is that one of the minimal constituents of the situation pictured above is a situation containing just the square on the right, and in this situation there is only one dot.

The two strategies are obviously related, and they equally render the Russellian analysis vacuous: since all things are unique, it is *always* possible to find, for any given individual, some description that fits, and some situation that contains, that individual and nothing else.

It is somewhat of a mystery why one should want to insists on *making* definite descriptions uniquely referring when it is perfectly obvious that they don't have to be. It is never a problem if several individuals match a definite description as long as there is something – anything – that sets apart the intended referent from its detractors. In the example above, the rightmost dot is the right one because the referent of "the dot" is to help selecting between the three squares, so the one in the middle is so much as irrelevant – and that's all there is to it.

Given that Russell's theory of descriptions is seriously problematic, there is every reason to be suspicious of the notion that some pronouns go proxy for Russellian definite descriptions. Still, let us briefly consider how the story goes, using the following example:

(8) Last week a student$_i$ came to my office. She$_i$ is German but her Dutch is impeccable.

On the neo-Russellian view defended by Neale, for example, the pronoun "she" in the second sentence goes proxy for, say, "the student who came to my office last week". To begin with, it should be obvious that this proposals inherits all the problems attendant on Russell's treatment of definite description; in this case, the problem is how to avoid the entailment that only one student came to my office last week. But in addition the descriptivist view on pronouns gives rise to the question of how pronouns manage to select suitable descriptions, in the first place. As the discussion in the last part of Heim's 1990 paper makes abundantly clear, this is a very tough question indeed, and as far as I know there isn't even the beginning of a viable answer.

Ever since Evans (1977), the notion that some pronouns are definite descriptions in disguise has proved to be strangely appealing. The reason for this, I suspect, is that for *practical* purposes there may be no harm in saying that, for example, the pronoun "she" in (8) means "the student who came to my office last week";

a speaker may do this to clarify his meaning. But this practice should not be mistaken for the seed of a theory of pronouns.

Finally, I should like to note that, from a psychological point of view, the descriptivist approach has a pronounced cart-before-the-horse flavour. Once it has been linked to its antecedent it may indeed be possible to paraphrase a pronoun by means of a definite description. But since by then we have the antecedent, what point is there in doing so? Small wonder, therefore, that processing theories invariably adopt a Karttunen-style approach to anaphora.

3 Discourse representation theory

The theory prefigured in Karttunen's 1971 paper saw the light ten years later in the work of Kamp (1981) and Heim (1982). Kamp's Discourse Representation Theory and Heim's File Change Semantics were the first of a long and successful line of so-called "dynamic" theories of semantics developed since by Groenendijk & Stokhof (1990, 1991), Muskens (1996), Veltman (1996), Beaver (2001), and many others (cf. also article 11 [Semantics: Theories] (Kamp & Reyle) *Discourse Representation Theory*). In this article I will gloss over the differences between these various theories, and DRT will be my framework of choice. By and large, this will not matter much, though one caveat is in order. As is well known, DRT is a representational theory of discourse interpretation, which is to say that it postulates a level of semantic representations, called "discourse representation structures", which other dynamic theories prefer to do without. There has been a somewhat tedious debate over this issue (see Geurts & Beaver 2007 for recent discussion), which I will pass over here, but it should be noted that in a non-representational framework it may be difficult to implement some of the ideas to be discussed in the following, especially Sections 6 and 7.

A discourse representation structure (DRS) is a mental representation built up by the hearer as the discourse unfolds. A DRS consists of two parts: a universe of discourse referents and a set of DRS-conditions which encode the information that has accumulated on these discourse referents. The following DRS represents the information that there are two individuals, one of which is a farmer, the other a donkey, and that the former chased the latter:

(9) [x, y: farmer(x), donkey(y), x chased y]

The universe of this DRS contains two discourse referents, x and y, and its condition set is {farmer(x), donkey(y), x chased y}.

A DRS like the one in (9) can be given a straightforward model-theoretic interpretation. In DRT this is done by means of embedding functions, which are partial functions from discourse referents to individuals in a given model M. An embedding function f verifies (9) in M iff the domain of f includes at least x and y, and according to M it is the case that f(x) is a farmer, f(y) is a donkey, and f(x) chased f(y).

The DRS in (9) is designed to reflect the intuitive meaning of:

(10) A farmer chased a donkey.

In the absence of any information about the context in which this sentence is uttered, the semantic representation of (10) is (9). So the indefinite expressions "a farmer" and "a donkey" are not treated as regular quantifiers; rather, they prompt the introduction of two new discourse referents, x and y, and contribute the information that x is a farmer and y a donkey; the verb adds to this that the former chased the latter.

If a discourse opens with an utterance of (10), the DRS in (9) is constructed, and this DRS forms the background against which the next utterance is interpreted, which might be (11a), for example:

(11) a. He caught it.
     b. [v, w: v caught w]

(11b) is the DRS that reflects the semantic content of (11a) before the pronouns are resolved. In this DRS, the anaphoric pronouns "he" and "it" in (11a) are represented by the discourse referents v and w, respectively, which are underlined to indicate that they want to be identified with discourse referents that are given already. (The double underlining merely serves to distinguish between anaphors.) (11a) is uttered in the context of (9), so the next step in the interpretation of this sentence is to merge the DRS in (11b) with that in (9), the result of which is (12a):

(12) a. [x, y, v, w: farmer(x), donkey(y), x chased y, v caught w]
     b. [x, y, v, w: v = x, w = y,
         farmer(x), donkey(y), x chased y, v caught w]
     c. [x, y: farmer(x), donkey(y), x chased y, x caught y]

Since (11a) is immediately preceded by (10), the most likely antecedents of "he" and "it" are "a farmer" and "a donkey", respectively. At DRS level, this is represented by equating v with x and w with y. These equations yield (12b), which is equivalent to (12c). Either DRS is verified in any model featuring a farmer who chased and caught a donkey.

Thus far, we have only considered DRSs with simple conditions, but in order to account for negated and conditional sentences, say, complex conditions are required.

(13) a. Pedro doesn't have a donkey.
 b. [x: Pedro(x), ¬[y: donkey(y), x owns y]]

(13b) is the sentence DRS corresponding to (13a). This DRS contains a condition that consists of a DRS prefixed by a negation sign. An embedding function f verifies (13b) in a model M iff f maps x onto an individual in M which "is a Pedro", i.e. which is called "Pedro", and f cannot be extended to a function g which verifies the embedded DRS; that is to say, no such g should map y onto a donkey owned by Pedro.

The negated DRS in (13b) contains a token of the discourse referent x which is introduced in the main DRS. Apart from that, the embedded DRS also introduces a discourse referent of its own, i.e. y, which is associated with the indefinite NP "a donkey", and whose lifespan is delimited by the sub-DRS in which it is introduced. This explains Karttunen's observation that if (13a) were followed by (14a), for example, the pronoun could not be linked to the indefinite:

(14) a. It is grey.
 b. [z: grey(z)]
 c. [x, z: Pedro(x), ¬[y: donkey(y), x owns y], grey(z)]

If we merge (13b) and (14b), which is the sentence DRS associated with (14a), we obtain (14c). In this representation, the discourse referent z does not have access to y, because y is introduced in a DRS that is not accessible to the DRS in which z is introduced, and therefore it is not possible to bind z to y. Thus, Karttunen's notion that a discourse referent may have a limited lifespan is explained in terms of accessibility. And as we will see in the next section, accessibility boils down to the standard notion of scope, albeit that the DRT logic is non-standard.

Like negated sentences, conditionals give rise to complex DRS-conditions, too:

(15) a. If Pedro owns a donkey, he beats it.
 b. [x: Pedro(x), [y: donkey(y), x owns y] ⇒ [v, w: v beats w]]

c. [x, v: Pedro(x), v = x,
      [y, w: w = y, donkey(y), x owns y] ⇒ [: v beats w]]
   d. [x: Pedro(x), [: [y: donkey(y), x owns y] ⇒ [: x beats y]]

(15b) is the sentence DRS associated with (15a), and assuming for convenience that this sentence is uttered in an empty context, it is also the initial DRS of the discourse. The complex condition in this structure is interpreted as follows: if f is to verify (15b) in the current model, then f(x) must be an individual called "Pedro", and every extension of f which verifies the antecedent-DRS must itself be extendable to a function that verifies the consequent-DRS. It follows from this that the main DRS in (15b) is accessible to the antecedent-DRS, which in its turn is accessible to the consequent-DRS, and therefore v may be linked to x (accessibility being a transitive relation) and w to y. The result is (15c), which is equivalent to (15d), with both DRSs expressing that Pedro beats every donkey he owns.

The interpretation of quantified sentences is very similar to what we have just seen:

(16) a. Every farmer who owns a donkey$_i$ beats it$_i$.
   b. [: [x, y: farmer(x), donkey(y), x owns y]⟨∀x⟩[u: x beats u]]
   c. [: [x, y: farmer(x), donkey(y), x owns y]⟨∀x⟩[: x beats y]]

There are various ways of spelling out the interpretation of so-called duplex conditions of the form K⟨∀x⟩K′. Here we will settle for the weak interpretation, on which (16a) comes out meaning that every farmer who owns a donkey beats at least one of his donkeys.

It is still a matter of debate what the exact truth conditions of donkey sentences are. It is traditionally assumed that a sentence like (16a) is standardly interpreted as implying that every farmer beats every donkey he owns, so the sentence's truth conditions would be strong by default, though this assumption is not borne out by experimental data (see Geurts 2002 for further discussion). But whether weak or strong, the interpretation of a condition of the form K⟨Qx⟩K′, where Q may be any quantifier, makes K accessible to K′, and in this respect conditionals and quantified sentences are alike. Consequently, the discourse referent y in (16b) is accessible to u, and the latter may be equated to the former. The resulting representation is equivalent to (16c).

The DRT analysis of quantified expressions like "all" or "most" is fairly standard. A quantifier binds a variable and delivers the truth conditions one should expect. Indefinites are different. An indefinite like "a donkey" is treated not as a quantifier but as a device for introducing a discourse referent and some descriptive material in the form of DRS-conditions; on the DRT account, indefinites have no quantifying force of their own. What quantifying force they seem to have is not theirs, but derives from the environment in which they occur (see also Lewis 1975). If the semantic material associated with "a donkey" is introduced in the main DRS, as in (12), the quantifying effect will be existential, owing to the fact that this DRS is verified in a model M iff *there is* a way of verifying it in M. If the semantic material associated with "a donkey" is introduced in the antecedent of a conditional, as in (15), the quantifying effect will be universal, owing to the fact that a condition $K \Rightarrow K'$ is verified in M iff *every* way of verifying K can be extended to a way of verifying K'. This context-dependent force is a consequence of the way DRT fleshes out Karttunen's idea that indefinites serve to introduce discourse referents. What Karttunen called the "lifespan" of a discourse referent is modeled by treating discourse referents as bound variables and extending the notion of scope in two ways: across sentence boundaries and within quantifying and conditional structures.

In order to make these ideas a bit more precise, we define the DRS language as follows:

DRSs and DRS-conditions
– A DRS K is a pair $\langle U_K, Con_K \rangle$, where U_K is a set of discourse referents, and Con_K is a set of DRS-conditions.
– If P is an n-place predicate, and $x_1, ..., x_n$ are discourse referents, then $P(x_1, ..., x_n)$ is a DRS-condition.
– If x and y are discourse referents, then $x = y$ is a DRS-condition.
– If K and K' are DRSs, then $\neg K$, $K \Rightarrow K'$, and $K \vee K'$ are DRS-conditions.
– If K and K' are DRSs and x is a discourse referent, then $K \langle \forall x \rangle K'$ is a DRS-condition.

The truth-conditional semantics of the DRS language is given by defining when an embedding function verifies a DRS in a given model. An embedding function is a partial mapping from discourse referents to individuals. Given two embedding functions f and g and a DRS K, we say that g extends f with respect to K, or f[K]g for short, iff $Dom(g) = Dom(f) \cup U_K$, and for all x in Dom(f): $f(x) = g(x)$. Viewing functions as sets of pairs, this can be formulated more succinctly as follows:

f[K]g iff $f \subseteq g$ and $Dom(g) = Dom(f) \cup U_K$

We now proceed to define what it takes for an embedding function to verify a DRS or DRS-condition in a given model. As usual, a model M is a pair $\langle D, I \rangle$, where D is a set of individuals and I is an interpretation function that assigns sets of individuals to one-place predicates, sets of pairs of individuals to two-place predicates, and so on. To enhance the legibility of the definition somewhat the qualification "in M" is omitted throughout:

Verifying embeddings
- f verifies a DRS K iff f verifies all conditions in Con_K.
- f verifies $P(x_1, ..., x_n)$ iff $\langle f(x_1), ..., f(x_n)\rangle \in I(P)$.
- f verifies $x = y$ iff $f(x) = f(y)$.
- f verifies $\neg K$ iff there is no g such that f[K]g and g verifies K.
- f verifies $K \vee K'$ iff f there is a g such that f[K]g and g verifies K or f[K']g and g verifies K'.
- f verifies $K \Rightarrow K'$ iff, for all g such that f[K]g and g verifies K, there is an h such that g[K']h and h verifies K'.
- f verifies $K\langle\forall x\rangle K'$ iff, for all individuals $d \in D$, if there is a g such that f[K]g, $g(x) = d$, and g verifies K, then there is an h such that g[K']h and h verifies K'.

A DRS is true in a model iff we can find a verifying embedding for it:

Truth
A DRS K is true in a model M iff there is an embedding function f such that $Dom(f) = U_K$ and f verifies K in M.

Let us now have a closer look at the notion of accessibility, in terms of which we will formulate DRT's central claim about the interpretation of anaphoric expressions. Accessibility is a relation between DRSs that is transitive and reflexive, i.e. it is a preorder. More precisely, it is the smallest preorder for which the following holds, for all DRSs K, K', and K":

Accessibility
If Con_K contains a condition of the form ...
- $\neg K'$ then K is accessible to K'
- $K' \vee K''$ then K is accessible to K' and K"
- $K' \Rightarrow K''$ then K is accessible to K' and K' is accessible to K"
- $K'\langle\forall x\rangle K''$ then K is accessible to K' and K' is accessible to K"

The "accessible domain" of a DRS K contains all and only those discourse referents that are introduced in DRSs accessible to K:

Accessible domains
$A_K = \{x \mid$ there is a K' such that K' is accessible to K and $x \in U_{K'}\}$

Note that, since accessibility is a reflexive relation, it always holds that $U_K \subseteq A_K$. If x is a discourse referent introduced in K, i.e. $x \in U_K$, then we will say that all and only the members of A_K are accessible to x.

Consider now the following, somewhat abstract example:

(17) a. If there is an A, it is a B.
 b. [: [x: A(x)] ⇒ [y: B(y), y = x]]
 c. [: [x: A(x)] ⇒ [: B(x)]]

(17b) is the DRS for (17a), where x and y are the discourse referents associated with "an A" and "it", respectively. The model-theoretic interpretation of the DRS language guarantees that the occurrences of x in [x: A(x)] and [y: B(y), y = x] are "the same", in the sense that the range of possible values of x in [y: B(y), y = x] is fixed by [x: A(x)]; for the meaning of "⇒" entails that no g is eligible as a verifying embedding of [y: B(y), y = x] unless there is some f ⊆ g such that f is a verifying embedding of [x: A(x)]. It is for this reason that (17b) and (17c) are equivalent.

As it turns out, two occurrences of any discourse referent x are guaranteed to covary in their values iff one of them is accessible to the other. Hence, the semantics of DRT entails the following constraint on the interpretation of anaphoric expressions:

Accessibility constraint
Let x be the discourse referent associated with a given anaphoric expression: then x must be equated with a discourse referent that is accessible to it.

Thus the following contrast, observed already by Karttunen (Section 1.), is explained by the fact that, unlike (18a), (18b) cannot be interpreted in such a way that the accessibility constraint is satisfied:

(18) a. Our vicar owns a Toyota$_i$. It$_i$ is grey. (= (2))
 b. Our vicar doesn't own a Toyota$_i$. *It$_i$ is grey. (= (3))

From a logical point of view, DRT construes anaphoric expressions as bound variables. But its apparatus of variable binding is heterodox: indefinites aren't treated as quantifiers, though in a sense they are variable binders, and anaphors may be bound across a quantifier, across "if", and even across a sentence boundary. Such is the logic of DRT and other dynamic theories of interpretation.

Compared to syntax-based theories, theories of the DRT family extend the binding domain of an indefinite in two ways. First, DRT makes it possible for an indefinite sitting in the restrictor of a quantifying expression Q, like "all" or "if ... then", to bind an anaphor in Q's scope. Secondly, DRT enables indefinites to bind anaphors across a conjunctive expression or a sentence boundary (the latter may be seen as a special instance of conjunction). Empirically speaking, these are the defining features of DRT and its kin.

4 Accessibility, givenness, and bridging

The accessibility constraint imposes restrictions on the interpretation of anaphoric expressions. But what are anaphoric expressions? In the foregoing I assumed as a matter of course that personal pronouns and definite descriptions fall under this rubric, without even trying to define it. The accessibility constraint may be seen as a first shot at doing just this: we can define an anaphoric expression as any expression that is represented by a discourse referent x which must be equated to some accessible discourse referent $y \in A_K$, where K is the DRS in which x is introduced. The intuitive idea is that A_K contains the discourse entities that are *given* at the point where x enters the discourse representation. Hence, the function of an anaphoric expression is to anchor an utterance in given information. This is, of course, a view with a long pedigree, but note that the traditional view is extended by taking it below the sentence level. For example, in (17a) the information contained in the antecedent of the conditional is accessible, and therefore given, from the vantage point of the consequent.

In order to make this more precise, a lot more has to be said about how information comes to be given. Thus far, we have restricted our attention to anaphoric expressions that serve to retrieve a discourse referent previously introduced by an indefinite NP. But there are other ways in which discourse referent may become given. For example, "the chandelier" may be used to refer to a fixture in the room where the discourse takes place, and "the moon" is generally used to refer to the Earth's only natural satellite. In cases like these the intended referent need not have been mentioned in the previous discourse, and they are accounted for quite naturally by assuming that common knowledge is *ipso facto* given, i.e. represented in the main DRS.

Things become considerably murkier when definite descriptions are used to refer to entities that are not given in the strict sense of the word:

(19) I was at a wedding last week.
 a. The bride was pregnant.
 b. The mock turtle soup was a dream.

These are instances of "bridging" (Haviland & Clark 1974), in which a definite NP is used for identifying a referent that wasn't given previously, and that may be more (19a) or less (19b) expectable under the circumstances. However, even such data may be brought in line with the notion that anaphoric expressions serve to pick up discourse referents that are given, as follows. For examples like (19a) it may be argued that, although the existence of a bride is not entailed by the given information (after all, it could have been a gay wedding), the fact that there was a marriage makes it quite likely that there was a bride, so she counts as given.

Whatever the merits of this argument, it surely does not apply to (19b): although mock turtle soup may be served at a wedding, it is doubtful that, in general, the mere mention of a wedding will raise mock-turtle-soup expectations to any significant degree. But even such cases may be consistent with the view that definite descriptions are anaphoric in the sense that their function is to select discourse referents that are given. For it may be argued that examples like (19b) involve *accommodation* in the sense of Lewis (1979). Accommodation occurs if a speaker chooses to present new information *as if* it were given already. Here, the speaker uses the expression "the mock turtle soup" because a proper introduction of the dish would have been too much of a hassle, and he reckons that his audience won't mind if he treats it as given. In effect, the speaker expects his audience to update their DRSs with a discourse referent for the mock turtle soup before they go on interpreting the definite description. So on this view of how examples like (19b) work, we can say that "the mock turtle soup" refers to a given entity, after all, even if the whole thing is a bit of a charade.

All this is more or less common lore. What is less widely realised is that these observations hold for anaphoric pronouns just as much as they do for definite descriptions. To begin with, the intended referent of a pronoun need not be given by the previous discourse. If Jill, who has just left the house, returns, and Jack guesses that she forgot her car keys, he may help her out by saying:

(20) They're on the kitchen table.

Similarly, if a friend of Jill's calls and Jack answers the phone, he may utter (21) without previous mention of Jill:

(21) I'm sorry, she just left for work.

In these examples, it is the situational context that furnishes the pronouns' referents, but otherwise they are no different from cases in which the intended referent is introduced by way of an indefinite NP. Nor do there seem to be any qualitative differences between the kind of pronominal reference witnessed in (20)–(21) and the "situational uses" of definite descriptions discussed earlier. The main difference is that the descriptive content of a personal pronoun is much paltrier than that of a definite description like "the chandelier" or "the moon", as a consequence of which the context is even more important in these cases (and therefore this use of personal pronouns will be rarer), but this is a quantitative difference, not one in kind (Bosch 1983).

Basically, anaphoric pronouns are just semantically attenuate definite descriptions, and not very different from non-lexical definites like "the man" or "the thing". Most importantly, for the purposes of this paper, pronouns can be interpreted by way of bridging just as full definite NPs can, though again the possibilities are somewhat reduced due to the fact that the descriptive content of a pronoun is relatively poor:

(22) a. When the doorbell rang I thought *it* was Vernon.
 b. What's that shadow creeping up the wall? Could *it* be a burglar?
 c. The Jones's had been happily married for six years when *he* became unemployed.
 d. A car's coming up to the junction and *he* starts to turn right. (Yule 1982)
 e. John bled so much *it* soaked through his bandage and stained his shirt. (Tic Douloureux 1971)
 f. When Little Johnny threw up, was there any pencil-eraser in *it*? (ibid.)
 g. Maxine was kidnapped but *they* didn't hurt her. (Bolinger 1977)

In each of these examples, the italicised pronoun has to be interpreted by way of bridging, since there is no antecedent expression introducing a suitable discourse referent. For example, the neuter pronoun in (22a) must be construed as referring to the person who rang the doorbell, and similarly for the other examples.

Some of the readers of an earlier version of this paper have suggested to me that the neuter pronouns in (22a) and (22b) are expletive rather than referential. Note, however, that in both cases we can exchange "it" for a demonstrative pronoun:

(23) a. When the doorbell rang I thought that was Vernon.
 b. What's that shadow creeping up the wall? Could that be a burglar?

These are perhaps more marked than the original examples, but that may be attributed to the fact that "that" is marked vis-à-vis "it".

One of the stock-in-trade examples of the DRT literature is due to Barbara Partee:

(24) a. Exactly one of the ten marbles is not in the bag. *It* is under the couch.
 b. Exactly nine of the ten marbles are in the bag. ?*It* is under the couch.

As observed by Kamp, van Genabith & Reyle (2011), among many others, this minimal pair shows that anaphora is contingent on more than truth-conditional content alone: the first sentence in (24a) expresses the same propositional content as its counterpart in (24b), yet anaphora is possible in the former case but not in the latter. It is often suggested that this is because the first sentence in (24a) introduces a discourse referent for the missing marble, whilst its counterpart in (24b) does not. In my view, this is a misleading, or at the very least incomplete way of describing what goes on in these examples. Note, to begin with, that it is perfectly possible to retrieve the missing marble in (24b) by means of an anaphoric expression:

(24) b'. Exactly nine of the ten marbles are in the bag. *The missing marble* is under the couch.

Furthermore, the acceptability of examples like (24b) can be improved by changing the context. Suppose that last night there was a breakout from the local prison. With 150 inmates to be accounted for, it is reported to the governor that:

(25) 138 of the prisoners are safe in their cells.

In this situation, the governor might very well exclaim, "I want them back before noon!", referring to the 12 escapees. The trick of this scenario is that it makes the missing prisoners so important that they become sufficiently salient to be retrieved by pronominal means. The same trick will work to improve (24b). Suppose that the marbles in question are pure gold and owned by the addressee. Then the first sentence of (24b) will raise the salience of the missing marble to such a degree that the speaker can reassure its owner by saying: "Don't you worry: it's under the couch."

I agree with Kamp et al. that the opening sentence of (24b) does not introduce a discourse referent for the missing marble, and that this is why the anaphor in the second sentence is odd – at first. However, the opening sentence entails that there is a missing marble, and with some help from the context this may prompt the introduction of a discourse referent, after all. The concept of bridging will reappear in Section 6, where it will figure prominently in an account of piggyback anaphora.

5 Piggyback anaphora again

All in all, the vanilla version of DRT outlined in Section 3. captures Karttunen's ideas about discourse referents quite well: an indefinite introduces a discourse referent that may be picked up by an anaphoric expression, and whose "lifespan" is bounded by any operator that has the indefinite in its scope. More accurately: if an indefinite occurs in the scope of one or more operators, the lifespan of its discourse referent is the scope of the innermost operator. This is what Karttunen had in mind, with one important exception: it doesn't give us an account of piggyback anaphora. To see what causes the problem, let us have another look at Karttunen's example (5b), repeated here as (26a):

(26) a. Harvey courts a girl$_i$ at every convention. She$_i$ always comes to the banquet with him.
b. [x: Harvey(x), [e: convention(e)]⟨∀e⟩[y: girl(y), x courts y at e]]

As pointed out by Karttunen, "a girl" in (26a) allows for a specific and a non-specific reading. On the specific construal, the first sentence entails that there is a particular girl who is courted by Harvey at every convention; this reading is unproblematic, so we can set it aside. On its non-specific construal, the indefinite is in the scope of the universal quantifier, which we may represent as in (26b). The problem with this reading is that the lifespan of the discourse referent y is bounded by the scope of "every convention", so there is no way the anaphoric pronoun in the second sentence could have access to it. Sometimes, this is what we want:

(27) Harvey courts a girl$_i$ at every convention. She$_i$ is called "Jackie".

Our current version of DRT predicts that this can only be read with a specific construal of "a girl", which is correct, but by the same token it prohibits a non-specific construal of the indefinite in (26a), which is not correct.

The same problem arises with other scope-bearing expressions, like modals, for example:

(28) a. Wilma may have bought a car.
b. [x: Wilma(x), ◊[y: car(y), x bought y]]

In order to account for sentences like (28a), we have to modalise the DRS language. The simplest way of doing this is by introducing the standard one-place modal operators, as illustrated by (28b). Extending the DRS semantics so as to interpret these structures is straightforward, too: we add to our models sets of worlds and accessibility relations, and interpret DRSs relative to embedding functions and worlds. The semantics is just as one would expect; the clause for ◊-conditions comes out as follows:

f verifies ◇K at world w iff, for some world w' accessible from w, there is an embedding function g such that f[K]g and g verifies K at w'.

This predicts that modals constrain anaphora just like negation does: a discourse referent introduced within the scope of a modal α can only be picked up by a pronoun if the pronoun occurs in the scope of α, too. As we saw in Section 1, this is only partly right:

(29) Wilma may have bought a car$_i$.
    a. *It$_i$'s a Volkswagen.
    b. It$_i$ may be a Volkswagen.

Assuming that, in this case, a specific construal of "a car" is not feasible, anaphora is possible in (29b) but not in (29a). As it stands, DRT doesn't account for this contrast, nor does any other dynamic theory of interpretation, for that matter.

Broadly speaking, there are three ways of dealing with the problems posed by piggyback pronouns. I call them the "inferential" model, the "resumption" model, and the "mixed" model. Between these, the resumption model is no doubt predominant, while the mixed model is probably the least known. In the following I will discuss each of these models in turn, and argue that the mixed model deserves to be taken more seriously than it has been thus far.

The clearest example of the inferential approach to piggyback anaphora is Roberts's (1987, 1989) work on what she calls "modal subordination", i.e. piggyback anaphora in modal environments. On Roberts's view, modal subordination is enabled by pragmatic inferences that constrain the domain of possible worlds a modal expression quantifies over. In the case of (30a), pragmatic inferences constrain the domain of the second modal, as shown in the transition from (30b) to (30c), as a result of which the neuter pronoun gets access to a suitable antecedent. (Here and in the following inferred material is marked in boldface.)

(30) a. Wilma may have bought a car$_i$. It$_i$ may be a Volkswagen.
    b. [x: Wilma(x),
        ◇[y: car(y), x bought y],
        ◇[z: VW(z)]]
    c. [x: Wilma(x),
        ◇[y: car(y), x bought y],
        ◇[z, **y: car(y), x bought y,** VW(z), z = y]]

The main problem with Roberts's account is that, in a sense, it is too pragmatic: by leaving essentially everything to pragmatics, Roberts ends up with an analysis that is insufficiently constrained. For example, there is nothing in Roberts's theory that rules out sequences like the following:

(31) Wilma may have bought a car$_i$. *Fred can drive it$_i$, too.

For further discussion of Roberts's take on modal subordination, see Geurts (1995, 1999) and Frank (1997).

As observed in Section 1, the problematic anaphor in (30a) and similar examples would seem to be enabled by the circumstance that the anaphoric expression occurs in the scope of an expression that somehow extends the mode of quantification of the first sentence (whence the term "piggyback anaphora"). This at any rate is the intuitive idea underlying the resumption model, which is instantiated in a range of otherwise very different theories proposed since the mid-1990s by Kibble (1994), Geurts (1995, 1999), Krifka (1996), Frank (1997), Frank & Kamp (1997), van Rooij (2005), Asher & McCready (2007), and others. (The first exponent of this view may have been a pre-publication version of Groenendijk & Stokhof's 1990 paper, discussed by Roberts (1995), which presents an analysis of piggyback anaphora in modal contexts that is very similar to later proposals by Kibble, Geurts, and others. However, this analysis didn't make it into the published article.)

Consider the discourse in (30a), and suppose that the first sentence introduces a set of possible worlds in which Wilma bought a Volkswagen. Suppose, furthermore, that the modal in the second sentence quantifies over the same worlds. Then each of the worlds at which the pronoun is evaluated contains a suitable object for "it" to refer to. The same, mutatis mutandis, for piggyback anaphora generally. Unfortunately, things aren't quite as simple as this: in order for the resumption scheme to work, track will have to be kept of which VWs Wilma bought in which worlds: the discourse referent standing in for the neuter pronoun will have to find a discourse referent introduced by the indefinite NP in the scope of the first modal. Typically, though not invariably, this is done by pairing worlds with embedding functions. The same holds for other forms of quantification:

(32) Last week, all employees received a letter$_i$. Most of them read it$_i$ rightaway.

On a resumption theory, we have to make sure that, by the time the second sentence is being interpreted, we still know which employee received which letter; which usually is done by pairing individuals in the domain of quantification with embedding functions. The upshot of all this is that the resumption theories of piggyback anaphora invariably run into considerable technical rigmaroles: without exception, the theories listed above are tremendously complex. For example, Krifka's (1996) definition of what he calls "parametrised sum individuals", which are pairs of ordinary individuals and assignment functions (i.e. embedding functions), takes up no fewer than eight clauses, and while other theories may be very different from Krifka's, all of them involve technical apparatus that is at least as complex. And, crucially, none of these complexities is justified on independent grounds; they are needed solely for dealing with piggyback anaphora. It seems safe to conclude, therefore, that even if the core intuition underlying the resumption model is quite straightforward, its implementation is anything but.

Another problem with the resumption model is empirical rather than methodological; it is illustrated by the following discourse:

(33) Last week, all employees received a letter$_i$. Most of them read it$_i$ rightaway, except for Jones, who lost it$_i$.

Intuitively, the two occurrences of "it" in (33) should be interpreted analogously, but the resumption approach entails that they are fundamentally different: whereas the first occurrence of "it" is a run-of-the-mill piggyback anaphor licensed by the quantifier "most", there is no overt expression to license the second occurrence of "it", and unlike some of the cases discussed in Section 1, there doesn't seem to be a covert quantifier, either (cf. the examples in (6)). Hence, whatever the true story about the second "it" may be, the resumption view entails that the only thing the second "it" has in common with the first is that they share the same antecedent; otherwise they are bound to function in entirely different ways. Which doesn't seem very likely.

6 Piggyback anaphora and bridging

Even if these problems aren't fatal, they are serious enough not to be too happy with the resumption model. Still, I believe the basic intuition that drives this approach is sound. What causes the trouble, in my view, is an assumption that is never made explicit, let alone defended. To explain, consider the constellation in which piggyback anaphora arise:

$$Q[... \text{Indefinite}_i ...] \ ... \ Q'[... \text{Anaphor}_i ...]$$

(Where Q and Q' are expressions that quantify over individuals, worlds, and so on.) The tacit assumption is that giving Q' the right sort of interpretation is *sufficient* for enabling the anaphoric link into the scope of Q. In DRT terms, it is presupposed that once Q' has been linked to Q, the discourse referent introduced by Indefinite$_i$

is *ipso facto* accessible to the discourse referent associated with Anaphor$_i$, and therefore the two can be equated. This is the reason why embedding functions are being incorporated into the semantic values of plurals, modals, and so on.

Once the assumption has been exposed it is evident, I trust, that there are no compelling reasons for sticking to it. So let's give it up and see what our options are. What I would like to suggest in its stead, revamping a proposal by Kamp & Reyle (1993), is that piggyback anaphora always involves a *bridging inference*, which is licensed by the interpretation of Q' in the scheme above. In fact, once Q' has received the right interpretation, the bridging inference is a *logical* one; it is an entailment. I call this a "mixed" model, because it supposes that piggyback anaphora requires resumption as well as an inferential element.

To show how this will work, I'm going to discuss (33) sentence by sentence:

(34) a. All employees received a letter.
 b. [X, Y: all(X, Y),
    employees(X), Y = X ∩ x̂[x, y: letter(y), x received y]]

X and Y are discourse referents representing groups of individuals, which we will model as sets. Alternatively, we might interpret them in terms of mereological sums, for example, as long as it is understood that they don't contain embedding functions. So "all" in "all(X, Y)" is a perfectly ordinary quantifier, whose interpretation is as simple as it gets:

- f verifies all(X, Y) iff f(X) ⊆ f(Y)
- f verifies some(X, Y) iff f(X) ∩ f(Y) ≠ ∅
  etc.

The condition "employees(X)" in (34b) is to mean that all individuals in X are employees, and "Y = X ∩ x̂K" defines Y as that subgroup of X whose members have the property of being an x such that K. This condition contains two complex discourse referents, which may be interpreted by extending embedding functions as follows:

  For any embedding function f:
  - f(X ∩ Y) = f(X) ∩ f(Y)
  - f(x̂K) = {d ∈ D | there is a g such that f[K]g, g(x) = d, and g verifies K}

(It will not be hard to see that this analysis of quantification preempts the standard DRT treatment of quantified donkey sentences; we will come to that in the next section.) Finally, "all" being a quantifier, it presupposes its domain, but as (34a) just serves to get our example discourse started, we will ignore that for now.

The first conjunct of the second sentence in (33) is represented thus:

(35) a. Most of them read it rightaway.
  b. [Y̲′, Z: most(Y′, Z), Z = Y′ ∩ ẑ[z, u̲: z read u]]

(35b) contains two discourse referents that are presuppositional (or anaphoric, if you prefer): Y′ and u. If we merge the DRSs (34b) and (35b), bind Y′ to Y, and simplify the result, we get:

(36) [X, Y, Z:
  all(X, Y), employees(X), Y = X ∩ x̂[x, y: letter(y), x received y],
  most(Y, Z), Z = Y ∩ ẑ[z, u̲: z read u]]

In this DRS, u does not as yet have access to a suitable antecedent. However, since any eligible value of Z is a subset of some value of Y, (36) *entails* (37), where the difference between the two DRSs is marked in boldface:

(37) [X, Y, Z:
  all(X, Y), employees(X), Y = X ∩ x̂[x, y: letter(y), x received y],
  most(Y, Z), Z = Y ∩ ẑ[z, u̲, **y: letter(y), z received y**, z read u]]

Now u can be bound to its intended referent, and we end up with the DRS in (38), which gives us the reading we were looking for:

(38) [X, Y, Z:
  all(X, Y), employees(X), Y = X ∩ x̂[x, y: letter(y), x received y],
  most(Y, Z), Z = Y ∩ ẑ[z, y: letter(y), z received y, z read y]]

In prose: there is a set of employees X (which is presupposed and therefore determined by the context) all of whom received a letter, there is a set Y which consists of those individuals in X that read the letter in question, and Y contains most individuals in X.

The key feature of this analysis, which generalises in a straightforward way to other cases of piggyback anaphora, is that it treats the problematic pronoun in terms of bridging: once the quantifier in (35a) has been interpreted, we are entitled to infer within the scope of "most" (so to speak) that there is a letter, which then may be picked up by the pronoun. The interpretation of the quantifier plays a crucial role, but it is not the whole story.

This proposal has all the virtues and none of the vices of previous accounts. First, it is very simple, both in terms of the representational machinery it requires and the procedures needed to associate a discourse with an adequate representation. Secondly, it has no need for esoteric semantic types: plural discourse referents denote sets of individuals, propositional discourse referents denote sets of possibilities, and so on. Thirdly, the proposed account brings out the family resemblance between piggyback anaphora and other cases of anaphoric reference. The last sentence in (33), that is

(39) Jones lost it.

is a patent instance of bridging: assuming that Jones is one of the employees, the preceding discourse entails that he received a letter, which is the intended referent of "it". The difference with (35a) is merely that the bridging inference isn't enabled by a quantifying expression, but by an implicit premiss.

This bridging account of piggyback anaphora is based on the observation that Kamp & Reyle's (1993) treatment of their orphanage examples (see (6d), Section 1) generalises to all kinds of piggyback anapora. This type of treatment has provoked harsh criticisms, which typically fasten on the fact that information gets copied from one part of a DRS to another:

> A more principled objection to the illustrated treatment of plural anaphora concerns the power of the rules involved. The DRS construction rules are virtually unconstrained re-writing rule. [...] There is nothing that would restrict the type of copying operations that are possible. (Krifka 1996, 560)

Although it has to be said that the way Kamp and Reyle present their analysis may have fostered such misgivings, they are beside the point. For, as I have been at pains to emphasise in my own presentation, the copy-and-paste "construction rules" used by this theory are in fact rules of inference that are sound, in the logical sense of the word, with respect to the semantics of the DRS language. They are, in other words, *highly* constrained.

Finally, it may be noted that Krifka's copy-and-paste objection does apply, and has been applied, to Roberts's (1987, 1989) theory of modal subordination. As we saw in the last section, Roberts holds that piggyback anaphora is chiefly dependent on pragmatic inferences, and this is precisely why it is insufficiently constrained. The mixed model of piggyback anaphora doesn't suffer from this defect.

7 Rethinking accessibility

The potential ramifications of this theory go beyond the analysis of piggyback anaphora. For, if my proposal is on the right track, there are reasons for fearing that, in some respects at least, DRT's treatment of accessibility may not be. Consider the standard semantic clause for universal quantification, as given in Section 3:

f verifies $K\langle\forall x\rangle K'$ iff, for all individuals $d \in D$, if there is a g such that $f[K]g$, $g(x) = d$, and g verifies K, then there is an h such that $g[K']h$ and h verifies K'.

On reflection, this definition is not as unproblematic as it may seem to be at first. For one thing, considering how simple the intuitive notion of universal quantification is, the standard DRT treatment is alarmingly complex. For another, this definition *stipulates* that the restrictor of the universal quantifier is accessible to its nuclear scope. Hence, the keystone of DRT's celebrated account of donkey sentences like (40) is arguably ad hoc.

(40) Every farmer who owns a donkey$_i$ beats it$_i$. (= (16a))

In other words, classical DRT suffers from the same problems that theories of piggy-back anaphora run into (Section 5); the same goes for other members of the dynamic semantics family (cf. Schlenker's 2007 recent critique).

In the last section I proposed the following definition of universal quantification:

f verifies all(X, Y) iff $f(X) \subseteq f(Y)$

This is very simple and intuitive and as far as I can tell it is not stipulative in any way. However, if we adopt it the standard account of donkey sentences goes by the board, because the restrictor of the universal quantifier (or any other quantifier) is no longer accessible from its nuclear scope; so the indefinite in (40) cannot bind the pronoun, as it can in DRT and other dynamic theories.

In the version of DRT presented in the last section, (40) is represented as follows (ignoring the domain presupposition associated with the quantifier):

(41) [X, Y: all(X, Y),
    X = $\hat{x}$[x, y: farmer(x), donkey(y), x owns y],
    Y = X ∩ $\hat{x}$[x, u: x beats u]]

In this representation, the anaphoric discourse referent u does not have access to its "target" y. However, using the same reasoning as before, (41) entails:

(42) [X, Y: all(X, Y),
   X = x̂[x, y: farmer(x), donkey(y), x owns y],
   Y = X ∩ x̂[x, u, y: **farmer(x), donkey(y), x owns y**, x beats u]]

Now u can be equated to y and we obtain:

(43) [X, Y: all(X, Y),
   X = x̂[x, y: farmer(x), donkey(y), x owns y],
   Y = X ∩ x̂[x, y: farmer(x), donkey(y), x owns y, x beats y]]

This says that every farmer who owns a donkey is a farmer who owns and beats a donkey; which is the reading to be accounted for. Hence, it is natural, and more economical, to explain anaphora in sentences like (40) in terms of bridging, and jettison what has become the standard account in DRT and related theories.

It is clear that the analysis I envisage for (40) will apply to any form of quantification, be it over individuals, worlds, or times; so it extends to nominal, adverbial, and modal quantification, as well as conditionals. More precisely, what I have outlined is a general explanation of anaphora from the nuclear scope of a quantifying expression into its restrictor.

As noted at the end of Section 3, there are two features that distinguish DRT from syntax-based theories of binding. One is that DRT enables indefinites sitting in the restrictor of a quantifying expression to bind anaphors in its scope. The other is that DRT makes it possible for an indefinite to bind an anaphor across "and" or a sentence boundary. If we adopt a bridging account of donkey anaphora, we lose the first feature. What about the second?

Sad to say, with the advent of dynamic theories of interpretation, the semantics of "and" has become undeservedly moot, and in this point my own views go against the dynamic current, but since I don't have much space left, the following remarks will have to be brief. First, it is not too difficult to incorporate sentential conjunction in DRT. We simply introduce conjoined DRSs of the form $K \wedge K'$, as follows:

$K \wedge K'$ is a DRS, where

- $U_{K \wedge K'} = U_K \cup U_{K'}$
- $Con_{K \wedge K'} = Con_K \cup Con_{K'}$

So (44a) is represented as (44b), which (save for the fact that the possessive pronoun gets glossed over) has the right meaning. Most importantly, for our purposes, the anaphoric link between "a Toyota" in the first conjunct and "it" in the second is nicely accounted for:

(44) a. Our vicar owns a Toyota$_i$ and it$_i$ is grey.
 b. [x, y: vicar(x), car(y), x owns y] ∧ [: grey(y)]

This result is obtained by inserting an old-fashioned form of conjunction into a dynamic framework. It is equivalent to treating conjunction by merging DRSs, as it is usually done (though this clear and simple idea has unfortunately been muddied, but I'm coming to that), for (44b) has the same truth conditions as:

(44) b.' [x, y: vicar(x), car(y), x owns y, grey(y)]

What this analysis doesn't provide is an explanation of the contrast between (44a) and (45):

(45) *It$_i$ is grey and our vicar owns a Toyota$_i$.

It has become de rigueur, in dynamic circles, to claim that this contrast must be accounted for by hard-wiring it into the lexical entry of "and". Against this view, I have argued that the observed contrast is purely pragmatic, and that there is no good reason for doubting the conventional wisdom that "and" is commutative (Geurts 1999). So I'm going to be brazenly conservative and assume that the definition of conjunction given above is correct.

Now my point is, quite simply, that this treatment of conjunction is as frugal as it can be and that it seems most unlikely that we could come up with an alternative story in terms of bridging that explains cross-conjunct anaphora and is more economical than the conservative account given above. In brief, the second feature of the dynamic analysis of discourse referents stands unchallenged: if there is a distinctive feature of DRT and related theories, it is this.

8 Conclusion

It has long since been recognised that the interpretation of non-lexical definites, like "the president" or "the carburetor", may involve so-called bridging inferences, which anchor the newly introduced president or carburetor to a suitable object in the preceding discourse. Although, to the best of my knowledge, it has never been denied that the same holds for anaphoric pronouns, I believe it has been widely assumed that bridging interpretations of pronouns are of marginal relevance, at best. I have argued that that this assumption is mistaken. It may be the case that pronouns are harder to interpret by way of bridging than non-lexical definites, but bridging construals of pronouns aren't hard to find, either. Once this is appreciated, there is no reason why bridging shouldn't play a key role in piggyback and donkey anaphora.

The paramount advantage of introducing bridging into the analysis pronominal anaphors is that it simplifies the dynamic treatment of anaphora, and simplifies it hugely, especially in the case of piggyback anaphora. However, there are empirical and conceptual benefits as well. On the empirical side, the bridging analysis captures the similarity between the two neuter pronouns in examples like (46):

(46) Last week, all employees received a letter$_i$. Most of them read it$_i$ rightaway, except for Jones, who lost it$_i$. (= (33))

On the conceptual side, bridging allows us to stick to a repertoire of semantic entities that are more faithful to people's semantic intuitions: instead of having to assume that modal expressions quantify over pairs of possible worlds and embedding functions, we can revert to the simpler, and intuitively more palatable, view that they quantify over worlds. Similarly, there is no need to suppose that nominal quantifiers range over pairs of individuals and embedding functions: they range over individuals, as they should. In sum, the advantages of the bridging analysis, simple as it is, are considerable.

My final remark concerns the portability of the analysis presented in the foregoing pages. One of the reasons why I have used DRT is that it is rather easy to incorporate bridging into a DRT framework, and it will be obvious that a framework that cannot accommodate bridging inferences would have been unsuitable for my purposes. Now, it is not unlikely that some dynamic theories of interpretation will run into considerable technical trouble when they try to incorporate bridging inferences, and for this reason may find it hard, if not impossible, to accommodate a bridging analysis of pronouns. But surely, it cannot be held against the proposed analysis that such theories exist.

Portions of the material in this article were presented to audiences in Amsterdam, Cambridge (the transatlantic one), Paris, and Seoul, to all of whom I am indebted for discussion. I'm especially grateful to Paul Portner for his extensive comments on an earlier version of this paper.

9 References

Asher, Nicholas & Eric McCready 2007. *Were, would, might* and a compositional account of counterfactuals. *Journal of Semantics* 24, 93–129.
Beaver, David 2001. *Presupposition and Assertion in Dynamic Semantics*. Stanford, CA: CSLI Publications.
Bolinger, Dwight 1977. *Pronouns and Repeated Nouns*. Bloomington, IL: Indiana University Linguistics Club.
Bosch, Peter 1983. *Agreement and Anaphora*. New York: Academic Press.
Elbourne, Paul D. 2005. *Situations and Individuals*. Cambridge, MA: The MIT Press.
Evans, Gareth 1977. Pronouns, quantifiers, and relative clauses (I). *Canadian Journal of Philosophy* 7, 467–536.
Frank, Annette 1997. *Context Dependence in Modal Constructions*. Doctoral dissertation, University of Stuttgart.
Frank, Annette & Hans Kamp 1997. On context dependence in modal constructions. In: A. Lawson (ed.). *Proceedings of Semantics and Linguistic Theory (=SALT) VII*. Ithaca, NY: Cornell University, 151–168.
Gazdar, Gerald 1979. *Pragmatics: Implicature, Presupposition, and Logical Form*. New York: Academic Press.
Geurts, Bart 1995. *Presupposing*. Doctoral dissertation, University of Stuttgart.
Geurts, Bart 1999. *Presuppositions and Pronouns*. Amsterdam: Elsevier.
Geurts, Bart 2002. Donkey business. *Linguistics & Philosophy* 25, 129–156.
Geurts, Bart & David Beaver 2007. Discourse representation theory. In: E.N. Zalta (ed.). *The Stanford Encyclopedia of Philosophy (Winter 2008 Edition)*. http://plato.stanford.edu/archives/win2008/entries/discourse-representation-theory/, March 16, 2011.
Groenendijk, Jeroen & Martin Stokhof 1990. Dynamic Montague Grammar. In: L. Kálmán & L. Pólos (eds.) *Papers from the Second Symposium on Logic and Language*. Budapest: Akadémiai Kiadó, 3–48.
Groenendijk, Jeroen & Martin Stokhof 1991. Dynamic predicate logic. *Linguistics & Philosophy* 14, 39–100.
Haddock, Nicholas J. 1987. Incremental interpretation and combinatory categorial grammar. In: J.P. McDermott (ed.). *Proceedings of the 10th International Joint Conference on Artificial Intelligence IJCAI'87, Milan. Volume 2*. Burlington, MA: Morgan Kaufmann, 661–663.
Haviland, Susan E. & Herbert H. Clark 1974. What's new? Acquiring new information as a process in comprehension. *Journal of Verbal Learning and Verbal Behavior* 13, 512–521.
Heim, Irene 1982. *The Semantics of Definite and Indefinite Noun Phrases*. Ph.D. dissertation. University of Massachusetts, Amherst, MA. Reprinted: Ann Arbor, MI: University Microfilms.
Heim, Irene 1990. E-type pronouns and donkey anaphora. *Linguistics & Philosophy* 13, 137–178.
Heim, Irene 1992. Presupposition projection and the semantics of attitude verbs. *Journal of Semantics* 9, 183–221.
Kamp, Hans 1981. A theory of truth and semantic representation. In: J. Groenendijk, T. Janssen & M. Stokhof (eds.). *Formal Methods in the Study of Language*. Amsterdam: Mathematical Centre, 277–322.
Kamp, Hans, Josef van Genabith & Uwe Reyle 2011. Discourse Representation Theory. In: D. M. Gabbay & F. Guenthner (eds.). *Handbook of Philosophical Logic. 2nd edition. Vol. 15*. Dordrecht: Springer, 125–394.

Kamp, Hans & Uwe Reyle 1993. *From Discourse to Logic*. Dordrecht: Kluwer.
Karttunen, Lauri 1971. *Discourse Referents*. Bloomington, IL: Indiana University Linguistics Club. Reprinted in J.D. McCawley (ed.) *Syntax and Semantics 7: Notes from the Linguistic Underground*. New York: Academic Press, 1976, 363–385.
Karttunen, Lauri 1973. Presuppositions of compound sentences. *Linguistic Inquiry* 4, 167–193.
Kibble, Rodger 1994. Dynamics of epistemic modality and anaphora. In: H. Bunt, R. Muskens & G. Rentier (eds.). *Proceedings of the 1st International Workshop on Computational Semantics*. Tilburg: ITK, Tilburg University, 121–130.
Krifka, Manfred 1996. Parametrized sum individuals for plural anaphora. *Linguistics & Philosophy* 19, 555–598.
Lewis, David K. 1975. Adverbs of quantification. In: E. L. Keenan (ed.). *Formal Semantics of Natural Language*. Cambridge: Cambridge University Press, 3–15.
Lewis, David K. 1979. Scorekeeping in a language game. *Journal of Philosophical Logic* 8, 339–359.
McCawley, James D. 1981. *Everything that Linguists have Always Wanted to Know about Logic but were Ashamed to Ask*. Oxford: Blackwell.
Muskens, Reinhard 1996. Combining Montague semantics and discourse representation. *Linguistics & Philosophy* 19, 143–186.
Neale, Stephen 1990. *Descriptions*. Cambridge, MA: The MIT Press.
Roberts, Craige 1987. *Modal Subordination, Anaphora and Distributivity*. Ph.D. dissertation. University of Massachusetts, Amherst, MA.
Roberts, Craige 1989. Modal subordination and pronominal anaphora in discourse. *Linguistics & Philosophy* 12, 683–721.
Roberts, Craige 1995. Domain restriction in dynamic semantics. In: E. Bach et al. (eds.). *Quantification in Natural Languages, vol. 2*. Dordrecht: Kluwer, 661–700.
van Rooij, Robert 2005. A modal analysis of presupposition and modal subordination. *Journal of Semantics* 22, 281–305.
Russell, Bertrand 1905. On denoting. *Mind* 14, 479–493.
Schlenker, Philippe 2007. Anti-dynamics: Presupposition projection without dynamic semantics. *Journal of Logic, Language and Information* 16, 325–356.
Sells, Peter 1985. *Restrictive and Non-Restrictive Modification*. Technical Report 85–28. Stanford, CA, Stanford University.
Stenning, Keith 1978. Anaphora as an approach to pragmatics. In: M. Halle, J. Bresnan & G. A. Miller (eds.). *Linguistic Theory and Psychological Reality*. Cambridge, MA.: The MIT Press, 162–200.
Tic Douloureux, P.R.N. 1971. A note on one's privates. In A. Zwicky, P. Salus, R. Binnick, and A. Vanek (Eds.), *Studies out in left field: defamatory essays presented to James D. McCawley on the occasion of his 33rd or 34th birthday*. Indiana University Linguistics Club, 45–51.
Veltman, Frank 1996. Defaults in update semantics. *Journal of Philosophical Logic* 25, 221–261.
Yule, George 1982. Interpreting anaphora without identifying reference. *Journal of Semantics* 1, 315–322.

Malte Zimmermann
15 Discourse particles

1 Introduction —— 511
2 The meaning of discourse particles —— 515
3 Interaction with sentence types —— 526
4 Secondary interpretive effects —— 529
5 Syntax and compositionality —— 532
6 Cross-linguistic survey —— 535
7 Open issues —— 540
8 References —— 541

Abstract: The article gives an overview of the distribution and interpretation of discourse particles. Semantically, these expressions contribute only to the expressive content of an utterance, and not to its core propositional content. The expressive nature of discourse particles accounts for their taking scope over question and imperative operators and over structured propositions, setting them apart from modal auxiliaries and adverbs. Discourse particles are distinguished from other discourse-structuring elements by their specific semantic function of conveying information concerning the epistemic states of discourse participants. A discussion of German discourse particles identifies three semantic core functions: (i.) the proposition expressed is marked as part of the Common Ground (*ja*); (ii.) it is marked as not activated with one of the discourse participants (*doch*); (iii.) the commitment to the proposition expressed is weakened (*wohl*). Further topics discussed are the interaction of discourse-particles with sentence types, secondary pragmatic effects (politeness, surprise, indirect speech acts), and the feasibility of a surface-compositional analysis and its problems. The article concludes with a brief cross-linguistic survey that shows that discourse particles are attested in languages across the world.

1 Introduction

Discourse particles form a closed class of invariable natural language expressions. They help to organize a discourse by conveying information concerning the epistemic states of the speaker, or her interlocutors, or both, with respect to

Malte Zimmermann, Potsdam, Germany

the descriptive, or propositional, content of an utterance. This article discusses their semantic contribution to the meaning of an utterance.

The structure of the article is as follows: The remainder of the introduction gives a first approximation to the meaning of discourse particles in general. This is followed by a brief overview of the existing literature. Finally, the class of discourse particles is set off from the larger class of discourse markers, i.e. elements with a more general discourse-structuring function. Section 2 discusses the semantic contribution of discourse particles by concentrating on three discourse particles from German. Section 3 turns to the interaction of discourse particles with sentences types. Section 4 shows how the presence of discourse particles can trigger illocutionary effects in certain contexts. Section 5 discusses issues of compositionality. Section 6 provides a brief cross-linguistic comparison. Section 7 concludes with a list of open problems. Due to the often elusive or ineffable (cf. article 17 [Semantics: Interfaces] (Potts) *Conventional implicature and expressive content*; Potts 2007) quality of the semantic contribution of discourse particles, the discussion is mainly restricted to discourse particles in German, but it nonetheless provides the necessary tools for the analysis of parallel phenomena in other languages.

1.1 The general meaning of discourse particles

Discourse particles in the narrow sense are used in order to organize the discourse by expressing the speaker's epistemic attitude towards the propositional content of an utterance, or to express a speaker's assumptions about the epistemic states of his or her interlocutors concerning a particular proposition. More generally, discourse particles have the function of fitting the propositional content of a sentence to the context of speech by giving an utterance its specific 'shade' (Hartmann 1998: 660), or alternatively, by imposing restrictions on appropriate contexts for a given utterance (cf. articles 12 [Semantics: Interfaces] (Zimmermann) *Context dependency* and 17 [Semantics: Interfaces] (Potts) *Conventional implicature and expressive content*). For this reason, they are sometimes also called *shading* or *modal particles* (Weydt 1969, Hartmann 1998). Discourse particles thus play a role at the semantic level of *discourse maintenance* in the sense of Krifka (2008). Alternatively, they can be seen as contributing to the *procedural meaning* component of Blakemore's (2002) relevance-theoretic approach. Discourse particles provide the discourse participants not with descriptions of particular states of affairs, but rather with clues as to which propositions count as mutually accepted, as controversial, or as uncertain. That is, they establish a link between the proposition expressed by an utterance and the knowledge and belief systems of the discourse participants. This semantic characterization of discourse particles brings them in close connection to evidential markers (cf. article 11 [Semantics: Noun Phrases and Verb Phrases] (Portner) *Verbal mood*) in other languages, as the two kinds of expressions operate on overlapping semantic domains; see section 6.4.

To illustrate, the sentences in (1a–c) do not differ in propositional content: They all have the same truth-conditions (cf. article 7 [Semantics: Theories] (Zimmermann) *Model-theoretic semantics*). A difference in the choice of the particle (*ja, doch, wohl*) leads to a difference in felicity conditions, however, such that each sentence will be appropriate in a different context.

(1) a. Max ist *ja* auf See.
 b. Max ist *doch* auf See.
 c. Max ist *wohl* auf See.
 Max is PRT at sea

As a first approximation, (1a) indicates that the speaker takes the hearer to be aware of the fact that Max is at sea. In contrast, (1b) signals that the speaker takes the hearer not to be aware of this fact at the time of utterance. (1c), finally, indicates a degree of speaker uncertainty concerning the truth of the proposition expressed. In each case, the discourse particle does not contribute to the descriptive, or propositional, content of the utterance, but to its expressive content, where expressive content refers to the more elusive or ineffable aspects of semanto-pragmatic meaning that link the proposition expressed to the context of utterance (cf. article 17 [Semantics: Interfaces] (Potts) *Conventional implicature and expressive content*). In the case of discourse particles, they do so by introducing felicity conditions on the knowledge states of the discourse participants concerning the situations or events described by the propositional content of the utterance.

1.2 Literature overview

There is quite a large body of literature on discourse particles in languages that have them (see, e.g., Zeevat 2000, 2005 on Dutch; Karlsson 1999 and Abraham & Wuite 1984 on Finnish; Holton, Mackridge & Philippaki-Warburton 1997 on Greek; Li 2006 on Chinese; Hara 2006 on Japanese), and in particular on discourse particles in German. The existing accounts differ in empirical coverage and analytical depth. At one extreme, we find mainly descriptive accounts that more or less list the various uses of discourse particles in various contexts and give paraphrases of their semantic contribution (e.g. Weydt 1969, Kriwonossow 1977, Helbig & Kötz 1981). Next, we find contrastive studies that compare the particle system of one language (often German) with that of another (e.g. Nekula 1996;

Péteri 2002; Rinas 2006). Finally, there is also an increasing number of formal semantic studies of the meaning of individual particles, which try to derive their different uses and their syntactic distribution on principled semantic grounds, see e.g. the case studies in Abraham (1991a), Kratzer (1999), and Zimmermann (2008), among others. Doherty's (1985) formal study of various discourse particles constitutes a promising first attempt at a compromise between descriptive adequacy and formal rigour, which is taken up in Karagjosova (2004a).

Owing in part to the elusive semantic nature of discourse particles, formal semantic studies of them are a relatively recent development, dating back no longer than 20 years ago or so. As a result, there is to date no generally accepted formal analysis of the meaning of discourse particles and other expressive elements, but see Kaplan (1999) for a promising line of research on expressives in general. Discourse particles have been treated alternatively (i.) as modifiers on illocutionary operators, cf. Jacobs (1991) and Lindner (1991), or as speech act modifiers (Waltereit 2001, Karagjosova 2004a); (ii.) as speech act markers of non-standard discourse contexts (Zeevat 2000, 2005); (iii.) as adding felicity conditions on appropriate utterance situations, which combine with the standard truth-conditional meaning of the clause, cf. Kratzer (1999); (iv.) as epistemic functors over propositions or facts, which sometimes come with additional implicatures, cf. Doherty (1985) and Ormelius-Sandblom (1997); (v.) as modifiers on sentence type operators in the C-domain of the clause, cf. Zimmermann (2008); or (vi.) as contributing to the procedural meaning in a relevance-theoretic framework, cf. König & Requardt (1991).

Further controversy arises from the fact that discourse particles are polyfunctional in that many members of this class also belong to other lexical classes, such as focus particles, adverbials, and discourse markers. In particular, the relation of the unstressed discourse-particles *ja* and *wohl* with their stressed, discourse-structuring counterparts in German has raised some interest, see section 1.3. While some authors hold the *maximalist* position that the meanings of the two kinds of expressions are synchronically unrelated, others subscribe to a *minimalist* position on which one interpretation can be derived from the other, see Abraham (1991b) for relevant discussion.

1.3 Discourse markers

The term *discourse particle* or *discourser marker* is often used to refer to a wider class of discourse-structuring expressions that act as *'discourse glue'* (Fraser 1990: 385). Discourse markers in this general sense establish discourse coherence (cf. article 13 [this volume] (Kehler) *Cohesion and coherence*) in a variety of ways: Some are used to express acceptance or rejection of a previous utterance (2a, b); some indicate turn-taking (3a), or a change of topic (3b); and some can be used to conclude a discourse sequence (4).

(2) a. A: Peter has gone home.
    B: *Uhuh*. → *acceptance*
  b. A: Peter didn't go home.
    B: *Yes*, he did. → *rejection*

(3) a. *By the way*, Peter has won.
  b. A: What a funny game!
    B: Let's go on all night long!
    C: *Well*, I am tired.

(4) A: I can't stand Herman.
  B: He's *just* an idiot.

Cross-linguistically, such discourse-structuring particles are more widespread than discourse particles in the narrow sense, as all languages seem to exhibit the former, but not the latter. In addition, some discourse-structuring expressions in German, such as accented *já* and *wóhl*, are the stressed counterparts of otherwise identical discourse particles, suggesting that the two classes of elements may have a common origin (Abraham 1991b). Finally, the existence of discourse-structuring elements raises interesting issues concerning the link(s) between sentence meaning and discourse meaning, and about the cognitive nature of linguistic meaning in general, cf. Blakemore (2002) for an overview. Nonetheless, we will ignore discourse-structuring elements in what follows, as our main interest lies in giving a good analysis of the narrower class of discourse particles defined in 1.1.

2 The meaning of discourse particles

German has a particularly rich inventory of some 20 or more discourse particles; see Hartmann (1998) for a comprehensive list. As mentioned above, many of these elements belong to more than one lexical class. The present discussion of the meaning of discourse particles focuses on three core cases, namely on the particles *ja*, *doch*, and *wohl*. Capturing the meanings of these particles in more formal terms than we did below (1), these elements will be analysed (i.) as indicating the existence of (potential) mutual knowledge in the *Common Ground* (Stalnaker 1978) (= *ja*); (ii.) as indicating an adversative attitude to certain background assumptions (= *doch*); and (iii.) as indicating a weakened commitment to the descriptive content of an utterance (= *wohl*), respectively; see section 2.1. Given that such functions are associated with discourse particles cross-linguistically (see section 6), the semantic behaviour of the three German particles is taken as representative of the phenomenon of discourse particles at large even though this assumption should be corroborated by more cross-linguistic study.

Section 2.2 presents two empirical arguments to the effect that discourse particles contribute exclusively to the expressive meaning component. This property would set them aside from epistemic adverbs and modal auxiliaries (cf. article 14 [Semantics: Noun Phrases and Verb Phrases] (Hacquard) *Modality*), which are shown to contribute to the propositional descriptive content in section 2.3, supporting analyses by Kratzer (1977, 1981), Papafragou (2006) and von Fintel & Gillies (2007), among others, pace Lyons (1977). Section 2.4 shows that different discourse particles contribute to the expressive meaning of an utterance in different ways. While some discourse particles add extra meaning to the descriptive content in form of a presupposition or conventional implicature (cf. articles 14 [Semantics: Interfaces] (Beaver & Geurts) *Presupposition* and 17 [Semantics: Interfaces] (Potts) *Conventional implicature and expressive content*), others operate more directly on the descriptive and illocutionary meaning, e.g. by changing the strength of speaker or hearer commitment towards the proposition expressed.

2.1 Characteristics and basic meaning

The meaning of ja: The particle *ja* is presumably the best researched of all German discourse particles, with formal treatments found in Doherty (1985), König & Requardt (1991), Jacobs (1991), Lindner (1991), Kratzer (1999), Karagjosova (2003, 2004a), and Kaufmann (2004). Informally, there is agreement on the basic semantic function of *ja*, which consists in establishing or reconfirming a proposition *p* as part of the Common Ground, often based on perceivable contextual evidence: By adding *ja* to an utterance with propositional content *p*, a speaker indicates that he thinks *p* to be uncontroversial at the time of utterance t_u, i.e. that there is no proposition *q* activated at t_u that would contradict *p* (Lindner 1991: 173):

(5) ⟦ja⟧(p) = p is true and speaker believes p uncontroversial.

A proposition *p* will be uncontroversial if a speaker assumes its content to be shared by the addressee, i.e. to be part of the Common Ground, or if the speaker considers the addressee to be in the possession of sufficient evidence for judging *p* to be true. The latter condition brings out the intimate connection between *ja* and evidentials in other languages, and gets us close to the felicity conditions on the use of *ja* in Kratzer (1999). Kratzer combines the descriptive and the expressive content of utterances containing *ja* to a *meaning⁺* (Kaplan 1999) by introducing the respective meaning components in form of appropriateness conditions on possible utterance situations. According to (6), *ja* takes a proposition p as argument and maps it to the set of situations in which p is true and in which p might – for all the speaker knows – already be known to the addressee (Kratzer 1999: 4):

(6) 〚ja〛 = $\lambda p.\lambda s.(p(w_s)$ & $\text{might}(s)(\lambda s'(\text{know}(s')(p)(\iota x(\text{addressee}(s)(x)))))$

Kratzer's formal treatment is the first step in an attempt to formally integrate the expressive meaning with the descriptive meaning. This program is taken up in Potts (2005), who treats the meaning of expressive elements in terms of partially defined identity functions. Such functions give a sentence its ordinary semantic value if and only if the contextual restrictions introduced by the expressive element are satisfied, thus mimicking the semantic effects of presuppositions (cf. article 14 [Semantics: Interfaces] (Beaver & Geurts) *Presupposition*) or conventional implicatures (cf. article 17 [Semantics: Interfaces] (Potts) *Conventional implicature and expressive content*).

The semantics of *ja* in (5) and (6) correctly predict the particle to be felicitous in contexts where the speaker can safely assume the addressee to be aware of the truth of the proposition expressed:

(7) *First brother to second brother:*
Morgen wird Mama ja siebzig.
Tomorrow turns mum PRT seventy
'Mum turns 70 tomorrow, y'know.'

In contrast, *ja* is illicit whenever the truth of the propositional content of an utterance is not known to be shared by the addressee, or even known to be controversial. This is typically the case in breaking news (8a); in answers to questions, which denote a set of controversial alternatives to be resolved by the addressee (8b); or in corrections of previous assertions (8c):

(8) a. *Happy young dad to passer-by:*
   #Ich habe ja eine Tochter.
   I have PRT a daughter
   'I've got a daughter, y'know.'
 b. Q: Who won?
   A: #Peter hat ja gewonnen.
    Peter has PRT won
    'Peter has won, y'know.'

c. A: That's a rabbit.
   B: #Nein, das   ist ja   ein Hase.
      No   that   is   PRT a   hare
      'No, it's a hare, y'know.'

While the contextual restrictions on *ja* brought about by the expressive addition in (5) and (6) are quite clear, the formal status of this additional meaning component is debated. For Jacobs (1991) and Lindner (1991), *ja* operates on the illocutionary operator *ASSERT*, forming a new illocutionary operator *J-ASSERT*. This operation introduces the expressive meaning component as a meaning postulate. For Doherty (1985), the insertion of *ja* triggers a conventional implicature. And for Kratzer (1999), *ja* restricts the set of appropriate utterance situations at the integrated semantic level *meaning*⁺. We will return to this problem in 2.4.

The meaning of doch: The particle *doch* adds expressive meaning to the descriptive content, too. Its presence in utterances with descriptive content *p* indicates that *p* is not under discussion or entertained at the time of utterance (Lindner 1991):

(9) 〚doch〛(p) = p is true and speaker assumes p not to be activated at the current stage in the discourse.

In the typical case, an utterance of *doch* a with propositional content *p* is used in order to express the speaker's assumption that the addressee is not aware of *p* (Karagjosova 2003). For instance, the addressee may have (temporarily) forgotten about *p* (10), or she may think *p* false (11):

(10) Du   gehst? Es gibt   *doch* Bier!
     You go   there.is   PRT   beer
     'You're off? But there's beer.'

(11) A: Mary went to the club.
     B: Nein, Maria ist *doch* zu Hause.
        No   Mary is PRT   at home
        'But Mary is at home.'

The fact that *doch* indicates non-activation of the proposition expressed, typically with the addressee, also explains its affinity to concessive clauses with adversative interpretations, such as (12); cf. Lerner (1987):

(12) Er   fährt, und doch trinkt   er.
      He   drives and PRT   drinks   he
      'He drives, but he drinks.'

The first clause in (12) implicates pragmatically that ¬p, where $p = \lambda s.\ drink'(x)(s)$. The non-activation of p in (12) is correctly indicated by the presence of *doch* in the second clause. Notice that *doch* in (11) and (12) is felicitous even though the sentences can be taken to convey information that is new to the addressee. This is in line with claims in Karagjosova (2004b) that frequently observed givenness effects with *doch* do not follow from its lexical meaning per se, but from independent information-structural factors that interact with the basic meaning of *doch* (indicating a contrast in the activation status of p).

The analysis of *doch* in (9) also makes a prediction concerning illicit contexts of use: *doch* is illicit whenever the context states or implies that the addressee actively entertains p. Compare (10), (11), and (12) with their infelicitous counterparts in (13) to (15), respectively:

(13) A: I'm off, even if there's beer.
      B: #Du   gehst? Es gibt   doch Bier.
         you   go   there.is   PRT   beer

(14) A: Mary is at home.
      B: #Nein, Maria ist doch zu Hause.
         no   Mary   is   PRT   at home

(15) #Er fährt,   doch er trinkt nicht.
       he drives,   PRT   he drinks not
      'He drives, but he doesn't drink.'

The meaning of wohl: The presence of *wohl* effects a weakened commitment towards the truth of the proposition expressed, such that the descriptive content of the clause is not presented as secure knowledge, but rather as an assumption or a conjecture (Doherty 1985, Abraham 1991b, Green 2000, Zimmermann 2008):

(16) $[\![wohl_x]\!](p) =$ ASSUME (x, p)

The right-hand side of (16) can be read as 'x is weakly committed to the truth of p', where x's weakened commitment towards p is expressed by the operator ASSUME. The variable nature of x indicates that the uncertainty can be on the side of the speaker (in declaratives), the addressee (in interrogatives), or both, see 3.1.

It follows that *wohl* in declaratives will be infelicitous in contexts where the speaker is strongly committed to the propositional content of a declarative clause:

(17) A: I know for sure:
   #Hein ist *wohl* auf See.
   Hein is PRT at sea

In contrast, *wohl* in declaratives is felicitous whenever the context suggests that the speaker is not 100% sure about *p*:

(18) A: I can't see Hein.
   Er ist *wohl* auf See.
   'He may be at sea.'

An alternative analysis, based on ideas in Davis, Potts & Speas (2007) would establish a more direct link between discourse particles like *wohl* and evidentials. On this analysis, the semantic contribution of *wohl* lies solely in its context-change potential. In an utterance with descriptive content *p*, *wohl* temporarily lowers the quality threshold (C_T), i.e. the degree of epistemic certainty required for a felicitous utterance of *p*, as indicated in (19):

(19) $C + [\![wohl]\!](p) = C' + [\![p]\!]$
   where $C' = C$, except $C_T > C'_T$

2.2 Evidence for the expressive nature of discourse particles

We have argued that discourse particles do not contribute to the descriptive, or propositional, content of an utterance, but rather to its expressive content. This difference is hard to detect in simple declarative clauses, for which it is difficult to decide empirically if discourse particles contribute to their descriptive content, e.g. by mapping propositions to more complex propositions, or to an integrated *meaning*[+] (Kratzer 1999). Alternatively, they could form part of the expressive content, e.g. by modifying illocutionary operators like *ASSERT* (Jacobs 1991) or sentence-type operators, such as *DECL* and *INT* (Zimmermann 2008).

Zimmermann (2008) discusses two kinds of empirical evidence supporting the claim that discourse particles do not contribute to the descriptive content. The first is based on their behaviour in sentence types other than declaratives. The second involves their interaction with the focus-background structure of a clause (cf. article 10 [this volume] (Hinterwimmer) *Information structure*). See also Jacobs (1991).

In imperative and interrogative clauses (cf. articles 5 [this volume] (Krifka) *Questions* and 6 [this volume] (Han) *Imperatives*), the meaning of discourse particles does not contribute to the proposition expressed: Discourse particles are invisible to the sentence-type operators *IMP* and *INT*, which take propositions as arguments and map them to semanto-pragmatic objects with a particular illocutionary force. That is, the meaning of *doch* in (20) does not enter the content of the command itself, unlike all propositional material.

(20) Gib mir *doch* das Buch!
    give me PRT the book
    'Give me the book, do!'

If the meaning of *doch* formed part of the proposition, we would expect the imperative in (20) to express the speaker's desire that the addressee have the proposition of her giving the book to the speaker deactivated, contrary to fact. Instead, (20) expresses the speaker's wish that the addressee bring about the state of affairs described by the proposition $p = \lambda s. \textit{give'}(addressee, speaker, \iota x.book(x), s)$, and in addition the speaker expresses her assumption that the addressee does not have this proposition p ($\approx \lambda s.$ addressee gives speaker the book in s) activated in the sense that p is, or will be made true. This holds, for instance, when the addressee does not intend to make p true. Imperatives like (20) are thus commonly used when the speaker has reason to suspect that the addressee is unwilling to obey the command, or that she has forgotten about it altogether.

In parallel fashion, the meaning of *wohl* in (21) does not find its way into the alternative propositions formed by the interrogative operator *INT*, which operates on the basic proposition of the clause (Hamblin 1973, Karttunen 1977) (cf. article 5 [this volume] (Krifka) *Questions*):

(21) Hat Hans *wohl* Maria eingeladen?
    has Hans PRT Mary invited
    'What do you reckon: Has Hans invited Mary?'

The question in (21) is not about whether or not the addressee is lacking in commitment towards the proposition $p = \lambda s. \textit{invite'}(Hans, Mary, s)$. Rather, the question is about whether or not Hans has invited Mary, but by using *wohl* the speaker indicates her awareness that the addressee may not be fully committed to her answer. Crucially, the semantic contribution of *wohl* takes scope over the alternative answers invoked by the interrogative operator. Adopting an analysis in Truckenbrodt (2004, 2006) of interrogative questions as expressing a hidden command for the addressee to contribute to the Common Ground by giving an answer, the meaning of (21) can be roughly represented as in (22), where S and A stand for speaker and addressee respectively:

(22) WANT (S, A, know (S & A, ASSUME {Hans invited Mary, Hans did not invite Mary}))

What S wants A to do in case of *wohl*-interrogatives is to contribute to the Common Ground (= A&S's mutual knowledge) by speculating on the questioned proposition. This can be stated more informally as 'Tell me your best guess concerning the following set of alternatives: Hans invited Mary, or he didn't.' The meaning contribution of *wohl* in (22) is indicated by the operator ASSUME, which operates on the set of propositions that are created by the interrogative operator INT, and which jointly constitute the set of possible answers. The operator lowers the degree of epistemic certainty required for uttering any of these propositions as a felicitous answer; see the end of section 2.1 for a possible technical implementation of this weakening effect. Interrogative questions with *wohl*, then, function as requests for best guesses, or plausible assumptions, rather than for absolute certainties on the side of the addressee (Asbach-Schnittger 1977, Zimmermann 2008). This aside, they do not differ in meaning from their *wohl*-less counterparts.

Turning to the interaction of discourse particles with the focus-background structure of the clause (cf. article 10 [this volume] (Hinterwimmer) *Information structure*), it shows that the semantic contribution of discourse particles affects only the meaning of the focus constituent, rather than the entire proposition. The meaning of (23a, b) differs depending on which constituent is in focus:

(23) a. MAX$_F$ fährt *wohl* nach Ulm.
    b. Max fährt *wohl* nach ULM$_F$.
       Max goes PRT to Ulm

In (23a), with focus accent on *Max*, the speaker presupposes that somebody is going to Ulm and adds the assumption that this somebody is Max. In (23b), with focus accent on *Ulm*, the speaker presupposes that Max is going somewhere and adds the assumption that this somewhere is Ulm. Parallel effects – modulo the meaning contribution of the particle – can be observed when the particle *wohl* in (23a, b) is replaced by *ja* or *doch*. Crucially, the semantic contribution of the discourse particles in (23a, b) is not mapped to the background of the clause, as is typical of unfocused propositional material. This can be seen from the fact that it is impossible to cast doubt on, let alone cancel the non-focused part of (23a) in the sub-sequent discourse. One would expect such a discourse move to be licit if the presence of *wohl* turned the background presupposition into an assumption (Zimmermann 2008):

(24) #MAX_F fährt wohl nach Ulm,
vielleicht fährt aber auch niemand dorthin.
#'I assume it is Max that is going to Ulm, but maybe nobody is going there.'

Discourse particles thus scope over the entire focus-background structure of the clause (Jacobs 1991), which shows once again that they do not contribute to the descriptive, propositional content of the clause.

2.3 Modal auxiliaries and adverbs

At first sight, the meaning of at least some discourse particles, e.g. *wohl*, seems very close to the meaning of epistemic modal auxiliaries or modal adverbs, such as *must* and *presumably/probably* (cf. article 14 [Semantics: Noun Phrases and Verb Phrases] (Hacquard) *Modality*):

(25) a. Max *must* be at sea now.
b. Max is *presumably* at sea now.

On closer inspection, though, these expressions behave differently in the contexts discussed in section 2.2, as do their German counterparts *muss* and *vielleicht/ vermutlich*. First, modal auxiliaries and adverbs are visible to the interrogative operator INT, as shown in (26a, b):

(26) a. 〚Must Max be at sea?〛 = ?{Max must be at sea, ¬(Max must be at sea)}
b. 〚Is Max presumably at sea?〛 = ?{ASSUME(x, Max at sea), ¬ASSUME(x, Max at sea)}

The question (26a) asks whether or not Max must necessarily be at sea (NEG > *must*). The slightly odd (26b) asks whether or not there is reason to suspect that Max is at sea (NEG > *presumably*). Since the meaning of these modal elements forms part of the alternatives under discussion, we take them to contribute to the propositional content.

In a similar vein, the meaning of modal auxiliaries and modal adverbs is mapped to the background when not in focus. (27) presupposes that someone presumably went to Ulm, and asserts that this someone is Max. Crucially, it does not presuppose that someone went to Ulm for sure, cf. Zimmermann (2008):

(27) MAX_F presumably went to Ulm.
<λx.x presumably went to Ulm, MAX>

For additional differences between discourse particles and modal auxiliaries and adverbials see Zimmermann (2008). More generally, the behaviour of modal auxiliaries and modal adverbs in questions and focus structures supports their analysis as contributing, at least in part, to the propositional content; see, e.g., Kratzer (1977, 1981), Papafragou (2006), and von Fintel & Gillies (2007) for analyses along these lines; Lyons (1977) and Groenendijk, Stokhof & Veltman (1996) for non-propositional analyses of modal expressions; and Portner (2009) for an overview of the different proposals.

2.4 Semantic differences

In spite of their semantic similarities, discourse particles also differ in two important respects. First, some discourse particles do not *add* information on top of the descriptive meaning of a clause, e.g. by adding a presupposition or a conventional implicature. This becomes clear by looking again at the sentence triple *Max ist ja / doch / wohl auf See* 'Max is PRT at sea' from (1a–c). Here, the particles *ja* and *doch* do not affect the basic assertion of the clause, namely that Max is at sea. Moreover, they add information to the effect that the addressee is taken to entertain this proposition as well (*ja*), or not (*doch*). (1c) with *wohl* differs in that it does not assert that Max is at sea. In fact, the presence of *wohl* weakens the degree of commitment to the asserted proposition from strong to only relatively certain. As a result, (1c), but not (1a) or (1b), is consistent with Max's not being at sea at all:

(28) A: Max ist wohl auf See. (= (1c))
      Oder er ist zuhause.
      'Or he is at home.'

Rather than adding to the descriptive meaning of the declarative, *wohl* thus weakens it, similar to the effects observed with certain evidentials; see 2.1 and 6.4.

The second difference between different kinds of discourse particles concerns their embeddability. Kratzer (1999) argues, based on examples like (29), that the particle *ja* cannot occur in embedded contexts when it intervenes between a quantifier (here: *jeder*) and a bound pronoun:

(29) Jeder$_1$ von den Arbeitern   hat   seinen$_1$ Job verloren, weil er$_1$
      each   of   the   workers   has   his   job   lost   since he
      (*ja)   in   der   Gewerkschaft   war.
      PRT   in   the   union   was
      'Each of the workers lost his job because he was in the union.'

According to Kaufmann (2004), however, *ja* in (29) will be felicitous 'if it is common knowledge that all workers were in the union'. At the same time, *ja* is generally impossible in complement clauses (30a), except under *verba dicendi* (often with subjunctive mood, cf. article 11 [Semantics: Noun Phrases and Verb Phrases] (Portner) *Verbal mood*) (30b). Notice that the embedding of *ja* in (30a) is blocked in the absence of any binding relation:

(30) a. Tom bedauert/glaubt, dass es (*ja) Erdbeeren gibt.
       Tom regrets/thinks   that it PRT strawberries give
       'Tom regrets/thinks that there will be strawberries.'
    b. Tom erinnerte Ulf, dass es *ja* Erdbeeren gäbe.
       Tom reminded Ulf that it PRT Strawberries give.subj
       'Tom reminded Ulf that there would be strawberries.'

Importantly, (30a) is bad even though there is a sensible interpretation, according to which Tom regrets or believes something that is common knowledge either to the participants of the situation described, or else to speaker and addressee of (30a). The particles *doch* and *wohl*, in contrast, can occur embedded under appropriate matrix predicates:

(31) a. Tom hat vergessen, dass es *doch* Erdbeeren gibt.
       Tom has forgotten   that it PRT   strawberries gives
       'Tom forgot that there will be strawberries after all.'
    b. Tom bedauert/glaubt, dass es *wohl* Erdbeeren gibt.
       Tom regrets/thinks   that it PRT   strawberries gives
       'Tom regrets/thinks that presumably there will be strawberries.'

Notice that *doch* and *wohl* in (31a, b) are interpreted in embedded position as they refer to the information state of the matrix subject, not to that of speaker or addressee. In contrast, *ja* is always evaluated with respect to the utterance context. Hence, it cannot be embedded, unless it forms part of a reported speech act under a *verb of saying* (Kratzer 1999). In sum, these findings argue for an analysis of *ja* as a modifier on illocutionary operators, as proposed in Jacobs (1991). As such operators are typically restricted to matrix clauses and reported speech acts, the distribution and interpretation of *ja* will fall out immediately. By the same token, *wohl* and *doch* do not function as modifiers on illocutionary operators, as these elements are interpretable in embedded position. In fact, the embeddability of *wohl* has been taken as an additional argument for its analysis as a modifier on sentence types in Zimmermann (2008); see Döring (2007) for a more extensive survey of the embeddability of German discourse particles.

The semantic differences observed thus cut across the three particles in different ways: First, both *ja* and *doch* add to the descriptive meaning of a clause, to the exclusion of *wohl*, which does not add extra meaning, but weakens the speaker's/addressee's commitment to a given proposition by modifying the sentence-type operator. Second, *doch* and *wohl* can be syntactically and semantically embedded, to the exclusion of *ja*, which cannot.

These findings suggest that the quest for a unified semantic analysis of all discourse particles, or even for a set of necessary properties apart from the general characteristics discussed in section 1, may be in vain. Rather, it seems that although the three discourse particles discussed all contribute to the expressive content of an utterance, they do so in different ways.

3 Interaction with sentence types

Discourse particles interact with sentence types in two different ways. First, the identification of the epistemic reference point of some discourse particles may depend on the sentence type (section 3.1). Second, discourse particles often display an incompatibility with, or a specific affinity to particular sentence types (section 3.2).

3.1 Identification of reference point

As shown in section 2, the semantic effect of a discourse particle always depends on a particular *epistemic reference point* (speaker, addressee, both), also known as *epistemic judge* (Lasersohn 2005, Stephenson 2007), relative to whose knowledge base the whole utterance is evaluated.

The effects of sentence type on a discourse particle's epistemic reference point are particularly apparent with *wohl*. Section 2.1 showed that *wohl* in declaratives is always evaluated with respect to the knowledge base of the speaker, making utterances of *wohl* a infelicitous in contexts where the speaker knows for sure that a, cf. (17). With interrogatives, however, the epistemic reference point of *wohl* is shifted to the addressee. As shown in section 2.2, interrogative questions containing *wohl* indicate that the addressee may not know the answer for sure (cf. Asbach-Schnitker 1977). This conclusion gets further support from the fact that *wohl* is infelicitous in interrogatives whenever the addressee can be taken to know the answer for sure. This typically happens in so-called *expert contexts*, where the addressee is considered an expert concerning the question under discussion, and which license rising declarative questions (Gunlogson 2003). Consider the infelicity of the rising declarative with *wohl* in the airport context from Gunlogson (2003) in (32):

(32) *A to an airline official:*
Geht der Flug (#*wohl*) um 7.00h?
leaves the flight PRT at 7am
'Does the plane leave at 7am?'

In contrast to (32), interrogatives with *wohl* are felicitous whenever the addressee is likely not to know the answer for sure, for instance, in the school test situation in (33):

(33) *Teacher to student:*
Was ist *wohl* die Wurzel aus 9?
What is PRT the square root of 9
'What'd be the square root of 9?'

The felicity of (33) is in line with the analysis of *wohl* in (22). By using *wohl*, the teacher asks the student for what she *assumes* to be the correct answer, rather than for what she knows the correct answer to be. This triggers a conversational implicature (cf. article 15 [Semantics: Interfaces] (Simons) *Implicature*) to the effect that the student does not know the full answer, thus adding a touch of rudeness to the question, see section 4 for more discussion of conversational implicatures.

As for what determines the choice of the reference point of *wohl*, we assume that the particle inherits it from the sentence type, such that it is the speaker in the case of declaratives, and the hearer in the case of interrogative and rising declarative questions (Doherty 1985; Gunlogson 2003).

Finally, the following examples with *doch* demonstrate that *wohl* is not alone in displaying sentence-type sensitivity when choosing its epistemic reference point. In the declarative (34a), *doch* signals that it is the addressee that has not activated the proposition expressed. In contrast, in the interrogative (34b), *doch* signals that it is the speaker that does not actively entertain the propositional core of the question (notice that *doch* is accented in this case):

(34) a. Es gibt doch Bier.
There is PRT beer
'But there will be beer! (Have you forgotten about it?)'

b. Gibt es DOCH Bier?
   Is there PRT beer
   'Is there beer, after all? (I didn't know!)'

Doch thus differs from *wohl* in requiring an epistemic reference point that is opposite to the one of its clause, which is again reminiscent of evidentials.

3.2 Incompatibilities and affinities

The second kind of sentence-type sensitivity shows up in form of an incompatibility between certain particles and particular sentence types, or alternatively in form of an affinity of certain particles to particular sentence types. The literature makes repeated mention of this phenomenon (e.g. Doherty 1985). An in-depth discussion of which particles can occur in interrogative clauses, and which ones cannot, is found in König (1977). A well-known observation in this connection is that *ja* cannot occur in interrogative questions, cf. (35). Further incompatibilities are observed between *wohl* and rising declarative questions (36) and imperatives (37a, b), respectively.

(35) *Ist Peter ja gekommen?
     Is Peter PRT come
     'Has Peter PRT come?'

(36) *Der Flug geht wohl um 9 Uhr/?
     the flight goes PRT at 9am
     'The plane leaves PRT at 9am?'

(37) a. *Gib mir wohl das Buch!
        give me PRT the book
        'Give me PRT the book!'
     b. *Nimm wohl Platz!
        take PRT seat
        'Take PRT a seat!'

As for affinities, the particle *wohl* shows a strong tendency to occur in verb-final questions introduced by the complementizer *ob* 'if':

(38) Ob Peter wohl kommt?
     If Peter PRT comes
     'Do you think Peter will come?'

In most cases, the observed incompatibilities seem to follow from an incompatibility between the meaning of the particle and the meaning of the sentence type, see Lindner (1991). Concerning the ill-formedness of (35), we have seen that the presence of the particle *ja* marks the proposition expressed by (35) as uncontroversial. This is in direct conflict with the semantic contribution of the interrogative clause, which denotes a set of alternative, and hence potentially controversial propositions that qualify as possible answers (cf. articles 5 [this volume] (Krifka) *Questions*). That is, the very semantic nature of the interrogative in (35) as opening up a set of alternatives counteracts the semantic nature of *ja* as indicating unanimity.

In a similar vein, the particle *wohl* is banned from occurring in the rising declarative question in (36). The semantic function of this question type consists in singling out the addressee, which also functions as its epistemic reference point, as being in the possession of the required expert knowledge for answering the question (Gunlogson 2003). It is precisely this meaning component of rising declaratives that clashes with the meaning of *wohl*, which expresses a degree of uncertainty on the side of the addressee when used in questions. The result is the uninterpretability of (36).

Finally, consider the impossibility of *wohl* in the imperative sentences in (37a, b). Unlike declaratives and interrogatives, imperatives are not proposals or requests for enlarging the Common Ground, i.e. the set of mutually known propositions, but they express a command or permission to *bring about* a state of affairs described by the propositional content *p*. Unlike with epistemic attitudes, which can come with a greater or lesser degree of certainty, it would make no sense for the speaker to put herself in a relation of weakened commitment to the propositional content *p* that she wants (or permits) the addressee to bring about if she is serious about the command or permission in question. In other words, unlike (requests for) information about the world, the speaker's commitment to the propositional content of the speech-acts COMMAND and PERMISSION must be absolute for these to succeed, and thus cannot be weakened by *wohl*.

As for the affinity of the particle *wohl* to verb-final questions with *ob*, Thurmair (1989: 63) and Truckenbrodt (2004: 334) show that this specific subtype of question is restricted to contexts in which the speaker has reason to believe that the addressee does not know the answer with certainty. Obviously, this particular contextual requirement of verb-final questions is in line with the semantic contribution of *wohl* in questions, which likewise indicates a degree of uncertainty on the part of the addressee.

4 Secondary interpretive effects

In addition to their basic meaning, most discourse particles serve a couple of additional interpretive functions: (i.) they support the expression of paralinguistic categories, such as emotion and politeness (Gussenhoven 2004); (ii.) in certain linguistic environments, they trigger indirect speech acts. These additional interpretive effects do not follow from a lexical ambiguity, but are best analysed as secondary effects that arise from a combination of a discourse particle's basic meaning and general semantic properties of the embedding utterance, sometimes accompanied by some Gricean pragmatic reasoning (cf. also article 15 [Semantics: Interfaces] (Simons) *Implicature*).

4.1 Expressing emotion and politeness

Discourse particles play a role in the expression of emotion and politeness in (39) to (41):

(39) Du bist ja wieder zurück!
you are PRT again back
'You're back!'

(40) Gib mir doch (mal) das Buch!
give me PRT (time) the book
'Give me the book, will you?'

(41) Haben Sie wohl etwas Kleingeld?
Have you PRT some change
'Could you spare some change?'

In (39), the particle *ja* seems to add a moment of surprise to the declarative utterance. In (40), the presence of *doch* seems to add a moment of exasperation, at least in certain contexts. Due to this fact some authors (e.g. Helbig & Kötz 1981) have treated the respective particles as polysemous. This is problematic, however, given that the same interpretive effect can be achieved by the use of different particles: *ja* and *doch* are often found in utterances with a surprise interpretation, while the particles *doch* and *halt* are frequently found with exasperation. Notice, too, that the expression of emotions in (39) and (40) is contingent on particular intonational patterns of the respective clauses, which will trigger the respective emotive readings even in the absence of the particles (cf. article 1 [Semantics: Interfaces] (Truckenbrodt) *Semantics of intonation*): (39) must be realized with an exclamative intonation, for the surprise reading to arise, cf. Lindner (1991); and (40) must be realized with heavy stress on the initial verb for the exasperation reading to arise.

We can thus conclude that the presence of the particles in (39) and (40) only assists in the derivation of the relevant paralinguistic meaning, instead of triggering it by virtue of its lexical meaning. For instance, as was shown in connection with (20), the imperative *doch(p)!* encodes the assumption that *p* is not activated (with the addressee) as part of its linguistic meaning. As a result, such structures lend themselves to being used in contexts in which the speaker is exasperated at the addressee's (repeated) unwillingness to obey the command and therefore to activate *p* by bringing its content about and thus making *p* true.

The politeness effect observed with *wohl* in (41) follows directly from its basic interpretation in interrogative clauses. As pointed out repeatedly, the use of *wohl* in interrogatives allows the addressee a certain degree of uncertainty concerning the correct answer. Uttering (41) thus puts the addressee in a position, where he is not required to answer with a blunt *yes* or *no*, where a *yes* would portray the speaker as presumptuous, while a *no* would portray the addressee as tight-fisted. Rather, the presence of *wohl* in the question presents the addressee with the opportunity of giving a less direct answer, which leaves her with enough room to handle this potentially awkward social situation without losing face. Crucially, there is no need for postulating a specific meaning component of politeness for *wohl*, in particular as the politeness effects arise only in few, well-defined contexts.

4.2 Indirect speech acts

In certain cases, the presence of a discourse particle, e.g. *wohl*, will facilitate the secondary interpretation of an utterance by means of an indirect speech act. This happens when the direct interpretation of an utterance makes no sense, because the respective meanings of the particle and the rest of the clause clash, as in the interrogative command in (42a). Or it can happen when the presence of the particle leads to an unusually weak statement, as in the falling declarative question in (42b):

(42) a. Bist Du *wohl* still!
        are you PRT quiet
        'Will you be quiet!'
    b. Das ist wohl deine Mutter?
        that is PRT your mother
        'That would be your mother?'

On its direct interpretation, the interrogative clause in (42a) asks for the addressee's assumption concerning her own being quiet or not. As one is normally perfectly aware of one's being quiet or not, it would have been more economical for the speaker to leave out the particle. From the fact that he did not, the cooperative addressee can deduce – by way of a Gricean conversational implicature – that the speaker had another reason for uttering (42a). This will lead the addressee to reconstruct the secondary speech act of an interrogative command. Of course, this only works when the direct question meaning is such that the addressee can be safely assumed to know the answer with certainty, as e.g. in questions about the immediate physical or personal circumstances of the addressee.

(42b) can get a secondary question interpretation, i.e. as a request for information, in contexts where the addressee is taken to have an information advantage over the speaker, such that she knows that the person accompanying her is her mother. In such circumstances, interpreting the declarative in (42b) as a weakened assertion will be of no informative value to the addressee whatsoever, and thus violate the Gricean maxim of quantity. When the speaker signals her uncertainty by using *wohl*, the cooperative addressee can rescue (42b) by assigning it the secondary meaning of a question; see Zimmermann (2008) for more detailed discussion.

5 Syntax and compositionality

This section investigates to what extent the expressive nature of discourse particles has an effect on their syntactic distribution, and whether their relative ordering with respect to one another follows from a compositionality requirement on semantic interpretation (cf. articles 6 [Semantics: Foundations, History and Methods] (Pagin & Westerståhl) *Compositionality* and 6 [Semantics: Interfaces] (von Stechow) *Syntax and semantics*).

5.1 Syntactic distribution

The syntactic distribution of German discourse particles can be captured in terms of the following generalizations: (i.) they must not occur sentence-initially in the pre-field, as they cannot be stressed; (ii.) in the middle-field, they occupy a position typical of adverbial elements, namely at the left edge of VP (Jacobs 1991); (iii.) being located at the edge of vP/VP, they precede all focused material and follow all background material that has scrambled out of the VP, cf. (43) (Diesing 1992):

(43) ..., weil   wir   die   Kinder$_1$ *ja/wohl/doch* [$_{VP}$ in Hamburg t$_1$ treffen].
       since   we   the   children   PRT PRT PRT   in Hamburg   meet
       'since we will JA/WOHL/DOCH meet the children in Hamburg.'

Crucially, discourse particles are generated in a higher position than the constituent denoting the propositional core of the clause, namely the verbal projection containing the verb and all its arguments (VP or vP). This syntactic finding matches with the fact that all discourse particles take semantic scope over the (structured) proposition denoted by the clause. However, the surface position of discourse particles is not in line with the assumption that at least some of them function as modifiers on speech-act operators (*ja*) or sentence-types (*wohl*), at least if surface compositionality (cf. articles 6 [Semantics: Foundations, History and Methods] (Pagin & Westerståhl) *Compositionality* and 6 [Semantics: Interfaces] (von Stechow) *Syntax and semantics*) is assumed to hold. On common assumptions, sentence type and speech act are coded (if at all) in the C-system of the clause in the left periphery (Rizzi 1997), but German discourse particles are blocked from occurring there because of their inability to take stress. The non-occurrence of German discourse particles in the left periphery is thus unexpected from the perspective of surface compositional semantics. It also sets them apart from discourse particles in many other languages, which do occur as overt functional heads in the left periphery; see section 6. A promising way of dealing with the two-fold task of meeting the semantic needs of compositionality, on the one hand, and ensuring a uniform cross-linguistic treatment of discourse particles, on the other, would therefore be to assume that German discourse particles raise into the left periphery at LF. In this structurally high position, they can associate with sentence-type and speech act operators; see Zimmermann (2008).

5.2 Particle combinations

Surface compositionality seems to play a more direct role when it comes to the relative ordering of several co-occurring discourse particles. This can be seen in (44) with combinations of two particles, and in (45) with three particles (attempts at paraphrases can be found in the discussion below (47)):

(44) Kathrina hat *ja doch / ja wohl / doch wohl*   St. Louis verschont.
     Kathrina has PRT PRT / PRT PRT / PRT   PRT   St. Louis spared
     'Kathrina has JA WOHL/ JA DOCH/ DOCH WOHL spared St. Louis.'

(45) Kathrina hat *ja   doch   wohl* St. Louis verschont.
     Kathrina has PRT PRT   PRT   St. Louis spared
     'Kathrina has JA DOCH WOHL spared St. Louis'

As shown by the ungrammaticality of (46), the linear order of the particles is subject to strict licensing conditions. Both *ja* and *doch* must precede *wohl*, and *ja* must precede *doch*. This yields the relative ordering in (47) (Doherty 1985: 83):

(46) *Kathrina hat *doch ja* / *wohl ja* / *wohl doch* St. Louis verschont.
    Kathrina has PRT PRT / PRT PRT / PRT PRT St. Louis spared

(47) ja > doch > wohl

Abstracting away from discussions of particle combinations in more traditional terms (see, e.g., Thurmair 1989; Rinas 2006), there are few formal semantic analyses of particle combinations. Noteworthy exceptions are Doherty (1985) and Lindner's (1991) discussion of the interpretation of the combination of *ja* and *doch*. As neither particle seems to take semantic scope over the other, Lindner (1991: 196) tentatively concludes that their linear order is conditioned by phonological factors, and that the meaning of both particles applies simultaneously. For instance, (44) with *ja doch* expresses the two (speaker) assumptions that (i.) it is uncontroversial that the storm spared St. Louis, but that (ii.) this proposition is currently not activated with the addressee. However, the assumption of simultaneous interpretation is problematic in view of the fact that the combinations *ja wohl* and *doch wohl* in (44) do receive compositional interpretations, as shown in (48) and (49), respectively:

(48) JA(WOHL(Kathrina spared St. Louis.)) =
    Speaker assumes the weakened proposition that it is relatively certain that St. Louis was spared to be uncontroversial, cf. (5).

(49) DOCH (WOHL(Kathrina spared St. Louis.)) =
    Speaker assumes the weakened proposition that it is relatively certain that St. Louis was spared not to be activated at the current discourse stage, cf. (9).

While the compositional procedure yields correct results for the combinations *ja wohl* and *doch wohl*, it fails to rule out the non-attested inverse combinations in (46), which would give rise to meaningful compositional interpretations as well, as the reader may verify for herself. A possible way out of this dilemma would be to view the observable surface orders between particles as reflecting their attachment at different syntactic and semantic levels. On this view, *ja* would come first in the linear sequence because it operates on illocutionary operators and takes a speech act as its semantic argument, see section 2.4. In contrast, *wohl* would come last because it functions as a sentence-type modifier and takes a proposition (or a set of propositions) as its semantic complement.

Obviously, such an approach is itself not without problems, not the least of them being the identification of the proper attachment site of *doch*, which sometimes patterns with *ja* and sometimes with *wohl*. Another problem arises from the assumption put forward in 5.1 that German discourse particles raise covertly at LF. Given this, their surface order would be of only limited interest for semantic purposes anyway. In order to account for the observable sequencing effects, we would be forced to assume an isomorphism requirement between the surface order of particles and their order at LF. Whatever the reason behind such an isomorphism (e.g. intervention effects), let us note that the alternative of interpreting the particles in situ, e.g. as partially defined identity functions (Potts 2005) or as adding secondary speech acts, gives no satisfactory account for the observable restrictions on linear order either. Clearly, this issue is in need of more research. This notwithstanding, the sketched approach offers a promising line of research into the combinatorial possibilities of discourse particles: It is backed up by independent evidence, discussed in section 2.4, and similar sequencing effects are found with the focus particles *even*, *also*, and *only* (see section 7).

6 Cross-linguistic survey

Cross-linguistically, the realm of discourse particles is subject to two kinds of variation. First, discourse particles are realized in different structural positions in different languages (section 6.1). Second, the meaning contribution of discourse particles can be realized by alternative grammatical means in languages such as English, which do not have them (section 6.2). The empirical findings of sections 6.1 and 6.2 will lead to the formulation of a tentative universal concerning the grammatical realization of discourse particles in section 6.3. Section 6.4 adds some tentative comments on similarities and differences between discourse particles and evidential markers.

6.1 Discourse particles in other languages

Discourse particles are not restricted to German, but are found in a range of historically and typologically unrelated languages. Perhaps not surprisingly, they are attested in the closely related West Germanic languages Dutch (Zeevat 2000, 2005), and Afrikaans. The particle *immers* in the Dutch example (50) corresponds to German *ja*:

(50) Hij is *immers* in Paris.
     He is PRT in Paris
     'Uncontroversial: He is in Paris'

Even though the lexical source of the particles may differ from case to case, their range of interpretation and syntactic distribution appears to be by and large the same.

Ancient and Modern Greek are other Indo-European languages that are known for their inventory of discourse particles or adverbs, which 'express[es] the speaker's evaluation of the meaning of the whole clause or sentence' (Holton, Mackridge & Philippaki-Warburton 1997: 363). The following example from Modern Greek features the particles *vévea* and *málon*, respectively (Skopeteas, p.c.):

(51) O jánis ine *vévea* / *málon* s-ti thálasa.
 the John is PRT PRT at-the sea
 'Janis is PRT at sea.'

Using *vévea*, the speaker takes the hearer to be aware of the fact that Janis is at sea (≈ *ja*). Using *málon*, the speaker expresses a degree of uncertainty concerning the truth of the proposition expressed (≈ *wohl*).

Discourse particles are also attested in Slavic languages, such as Czech (Nekula 1996; Rinas 2006). According to Rinas (2006), the three Czech particles *přece*, *vždyt*, and *však* span a semantic continuum that covers the meanings of the German particles *doch* and *ja*, where *přece* is associated more closely with *doch*, *však* corresponds more closely to *ja*, and *vždyt* is somewhere in between. Syntactically, the three particles are restricted to occur either in sentence-initial position (*vždyt*, *však*) or in the Wackernagel position (*přece*); see Gast (2008).

The Finno-Ugric languages Finnish and Hungarian feature several counterparts to German-style discourse particles, too. The Finnish counterparts occur as free forms and as bound suffixes (-*han*/-*hän*, -*pa*/-*pä*) in the highest functional projection of the clause. Depending on their clause-type, they give rise to different semantic effects (Karlsson 1999). The suffix -*han*/-*hän*, for instance, is more or less identical in meaning to German *wohl* in the question (52a), and to *ja* or *doch* in the assertive declarative in (52b) from Abraham & Wuite (1984):

(52) a. On-ko-*han* Sylvi kotona?
 is-Q-PRT Sylvi home
 'Would Sylvi be at home?'

 b. Olet-*han* sinä vielä nuori.
 are-PRT you still young
 'You are still young after all.'

In Hungarian, the particle *ugye* behaves like the German particle *ja* in marking a proposition as (having the potential) to be in the Common Ground (Péteri 2002; Gyuris 2009):

(53) Mary *ugye* elolvasta a könyvet.
    Mary PRT VM.read.past the book
    'Mary has read the book, as you know.'

Turning to non-European languages, discourse particles are found in the East Asian languages Mandarin Chinese (Li 2006) and Japanese (Hara 2006), as well as in Singapore English (Kim & Wee 2009). Mandarin Chinese has a number of sentence-final particles (*ne, ba, ma*), which are syntactically restricted to matrix clauses and which serve to express 'the speaker's attitude towards the propositional content of the clause' (Li 2006: 12). The particles *ba* and *ma* in (54) express different degrees of speaker commitment to the proposition 'Hongjian is at the office'. While *ba* marks a low degree of commitment, corresponding to German *wohl*, *ma* expresses a high degree of commitment (Li 2006: 32):

(54) Hóngjiàn zài bàngōngshì ∅/*ba*/*ma*
    Hongjian at office PRT PRT
    'Hongjian is at the office'

In Japanese, the presence of the particle *darou* indicates that the speaker 'has an epistemic bias for *p* derived from reasoning and not from observable (direct or indirect) evidence' (Hara 2006: 9). Example (55) from Morimoto (1994) is felicitous in a context in which the speaker has broken up with his ex-girlfriend a long time ago.

(55) Kanojo-wa mou kekkon-shita *darou*.
    she-TOP already marriage-did PRT
    'She will be married by now.'

Furthermore, Hara (2006) shows that *darou* does not form part of the proposition by applying the question test from section 2.2. As for Singapore English, Kim & Wee (2009) provide a detailed semantic analysis of the particle *hor* as a general marker of speaker-addressee asymmetry (Zeevat 2000) in the epistemic (knowledge) or deontic (authority) domain.

Even though detailed semantic descriptions are frequently lacking, discourse particles are attested in a range of African languages. For instance, the particle *ni* in the Central Chadic language Mandara marks a subsequent statement as unexpected relative to the Common Ground (Pohlig & Pohlig 1994: 217):

(56) Iya   ya   egzdere   ni   ka   ɓela   iya.
     1s   1sg   child   PRT   2s   send   1s
     'I, a child. You are sending me?'

Likewise, a particle *má* is used to reinforce speaker-hearer shared expectations or assumptions (Fluckiger & Whaley 1983: 281), somewhat comparable to German *ja*.

The above list is far from complete. Other languages, e.g. Papago (Uzo-Aztecan) have been reported to contain discourse particles in their inventory of formative elements (Kratzer 1999), and many more languages may be expected to do so. For instance, other plausible candidates for discourse particles may be presuppositional negations in Romance (Zanuttini 1997). More comparative work is required in particular on plausible candidates for discourse particles in the semantically under-researched languages of Africa, Asia and the Americas.

6.2 Alternative ways of expressing the meaning of discourse particles

English is a good example of a language without a lexical inventory of discourse particles. In the absence of particles, English resorts to other grammatical means for expressing speaker and/or hearer attitudes towards a proposition (see also Waltereit (2001) for a discussion of alternative strategies in Romance languages). These alternative means comprise intonation (cf. article 1 [Semantics: Interfaces] (Truckenbrodt) *Semantics of intonation*), cf. (57) from Ward & Hirschberg (1985) and Pierrehumbert & Hirschberg (1990), and sentence-final tags, cf. (58).

(57) A: Harry's such a klutz.
     B: He's a good BADMINTON player.
                 L*+H   LH%
     → The proposition that H is good at playing badminton not activated with A
     ≈ *doch*

(58) Q: Where is John?
     A: He's at home, *isn't he*?
     → weakened commitment ≈ *wohl*

It is interesting to note that both tags and intonation apply at the edge of the syntactic clause, which they modify semantically.

6.3 A tentative universal

The empirical survey in 6.1 and 6.2 has shown that – with the exception of some Indo-European languages (German, Dutch, Greek) and Hungarian – discourse particles and comparable grammatical formatives are frequently located in a sentence-peripheral position. Similarly, intonation and tags in English can be considered to be located in the periphery of their clause. Based on these findings, we can thus formulate the tentative universal in (59) concerning the structural realization of speaker or hearer knowledge in the grammatical system:

(59) The grammatical means used for relating to the knowledge states of discourse participants with respect to the proposition expressed by an utterance tend to be realized at the periphery of a clause.

This cross-linguistic tendency seems to be grounded in semantic considerations of compositionality: Discourse particles operate at least at the level of propositions, but in most cases on semantic categories (sentence-type operators, speech-act operators) that are structurally and semantically associated with the periphery of the clause (Rizzi 1997).

6.4 Discourse particles and evidentials

The discussion has made repeated mention of similarities between discourse particles and evidential markers. This gives rise to the question of whether *discourse particle* and *evidential* are but two different labels for the same phenomenon, or whether these notions refer to different semantic categories? If one assumes with Matthewson, Davis & Rullmann (2007) that evidentials contribute to the truth-conditional, i.e. descriptive, content, they will be different from discourse particles, which do not, as was shown for modal auxiliaries in 2.3. However, even if one adopts the position that evidentials behave like discourse particles in contributing only to the expressive content of a sentence (Faller 2002; Davis, Potts & Speas 2007), the two kinds of objects should still be kept apart as they relate to the knowledge states of the interlocutors in different ways. While discourse particles register and sometimes compare these knowledge states as they are, evidential markers provide information concerning the *source* of this knowledge in form of particular kinds of evidence. Although in part related, these are quite different kinds of information, for which reason the two notions should be kept apart (see also Hara's discussion of the Japanese data above (55)).

This being said, it may of course be possible to achieve some of the typical interpretive effects of discourse particles by means of an evidential marker as well. For instance, if the evidence for the validity of a given proposition *p* is only indirect, say through hearsay, the speaker need not be fully committed to its truth (≈ *wohl*). In contrast, if a speaker uses an evidential marker for direct perceptual evidence, say for visual perception, and if the addressee is known to have the same visual input, the use of the evidential may come close to the use of the Common Ground marker *ja*. We may therefore expect languages with evidential markers to do just fine without an additional category of discourse particles in their lexical inventory. Does this mean that the two expression types form complementary sets from which a language may choose one over the other? Or are there also languages that allow for both expression types in their inventory of functional elements, as predicted by the assumption that discourse particles and evidential markers are semantically different? Further cross-linguistic study must show whether languages with both expression types are indeed attested.

7 Open issues

Even though our knowledge of the semantics of discourse particles has considerably increased over the past two decades, the following problems are left largely unresolved. First of all, it is still not completely clear in what sense discourse particles constitute a natural semantic class by themselves. As shown in section 2, different particles combine with different semantic constituents to different interpretive ends. At the same time, at least some discourse particles share important properties with other expressive elements (Potts 2007). This stresses the need for a list of reliable – albeit negative – criteria that would single out discourse particles from other expressives; see, for instance, the discussion of evidentials in 6.4.

A second, related question is whether the additional semantic contribution of the discourse particles *ja* and *doch* should be analysed as a presupposition or as a conventional implicature. Standard instances of semantic presuppositions enrich the descriptive content by giving additional information on the situation *described* by the clause. For instance, the uniqueness presupposition of the definite requires that there be one and only one individual with the relevant property. Discourse particles, in contrast, relate to epistemic attitudes of the discourse participants towards these descriptions. For this reason, it may be more adequate to analyse their semantic contribution as a conventional implicature in the sense of Potts (2005). Such implicatures leave the basic descriptive meaning unaffected and add information at an independent level of interpretation.

The final question concerns the relationship between discourse particles and focus particles (*only, also, even*), which are also focus-sensitive and sometimes double as discourse particles. Most interestingly, focus particles also exhibit curious restrictions on their relative word order (*Peter even also only drank water* vs. **Peter only also even drank water*), which cannot be explained in terms of an implausible reading for the unattested order. It is possible, then, that different focus particles combine with different semantic constituents, too.

It is hoped that the foregoing remarks will open up new lines of research towards a better understanding of the semantic nature of discourse particles in the languages of the world.

8 References

Abraham, Werner (ed.) 1991a. *Discourse Particles*. Amsterdam: Benjamins.
Abraham, Werner 1991b. Discourse particles in German: How does their illocutive force come about? In: W. Abraham (ed.). *Discourse Particles*. Amsterdam: Benjamins, 203–252.
Abraham, Werner & Eva Wuite 1984. Kontrastive Partikelforschung unter lexikographischem Gesichtspunkt: Exempel am Deutsch-Finnischen. *Folia Linguistica Europaea* 18, 155–193.
Asbach-Schnitker, Brigitte 1977. Die Satzpartikel 'wohl'. In: H. Weydt (ed.) *Aspekte der Modalpartikeln*. Tübingen: Narr, 38–62.
Blakemore, Diane 2002. *Relevance and Linguistic Meaning. The Semantics and Pragmatics of Discourse Markers*. Cambridge: Cambridge University Press.
Davis, Christopher, Christopher Potts & Margaret Speas 2007. The pragmatic values of evidential sentences. In: T. Friedman & M. Gibson (eds.). *Proceedings of Semantics and Linguistic Theory (=SALT) XVII*. Ithaca, NY: Cornell University, 71–88.
Diesing, Molly 1992. *Indefinites*. Cambridge, MA.: The MIT Press.
Döring, Sophia 2007. *Zur Kontextverschiebung bei deutschen Diskurspartikeln*. BA thesis. Humboldt University, Berlin.
Doherty, Monica 1985. *Epistemische Bedeutung*. Berlin: Akademie Verlag.
Faller, Martina 2002. *Semantics and Pragmatics of Evidentials in Cuzco Quechua*. Ph.D. dissertation. Stanford University, Stanford, CA.
von Fintel, Kai & Anthony S. Gillies 2007. An opinionated guide to epistemic modality. In: T. S. Gendler & J. Hawthorne (eds.). *Oxford Studies in Epistemology, vol. 2*. Oxford: Oxford University Press, 32–62.
Fluckiger, Cheryl A. & Annie H. Whaley 1983. Four discourse particles in Mandara. In: E. Wolff & H. Meyer-Bahlburg (eds.). *Studies in Chadic and Afroasiatic Linguistics*. Hamburg: Buske, 277–286.
Fraser, Bruce 1990. An approach to discourse markers. *Journal of Pragmatics* 14, 383–395.
Gast, Volker 2008. Review of K. Rinas. Die Abtönungspartikeln 'doch' und 'ja'. Semantik, Idiomatisierung, Kombinationen, tschechische Äquivalente (Frankfurt, 2006). *Languages in Contrast* 8, 134–141.
Green, Mitchell 2000. Illocutionary force and semantic content. *Linguistics & Philosophy* 23, 435–473.

Groenendijk, Jeroen, Martin Stokhof & Frank Veltman 1996. Coreference and modality. In: S. Lappin (ed.). *The Handbook of Contemporary Semantic Theory*. Oxford: Blackwell, 179–213.

Gunlogson, Christine 2003. *True to Form: Rising and Falling Declaratives as Questions in English*. New York: Routledge.

Gussenhoven, Carlos 2004. *The Phonology of Tone and Intonation*. Cambridge: Cambridge University Press.

Gyuris, Beáta 2009. Sentence-types, discourse particles and intonation in Hungarian. In: A. Riester & T. Solstad (eds.). *Proceedings of Sinn und Bedeutung (= SuB)13*. Stuttgart: University of Stuttgart, 157–170.

Hamblin, Charles L. 1973. Questions in Montague English. *Foundations of Language* 10, 41–53.

Hara, Yuri 2006. *Non-Propositional Modal Meaning*. Ms. Newark, DE, University of Delaware.

Hartmann, Dietrich 1998. Particles. In: J.L. Mey (ed.). *Concise Encyclopedia of Pragmatics*. Amsterdam: Elsevier, 657–663.

Helbig, Gerhard & Werner Kötz 1981. *Die Partikeln. Zur Theorie und Praxis des Deutschunterrichts für Ausländer*. Leipzig: Enzyklopädie.

Holton, David, Peter Mackridge & Irene Philippaki-Warburton 1997. *Greek: A Comprehensive Grammar of the Modern Language*. New York: Routledge.

Jacobs, Joachim 1991. On the semantics of modal particles. In: W. Abraham (ed.). *Discourse Particles*. Amsterdam: Benjamins, 141–162.

Kaplan, David 1999. *The Meaning of "ouch" and "oops". Explorations of the Theory of Meaning as Use*. MS. Los Angeles, CA, University of California.

Karagjosova, Elena 2003. Modal particles and the Common Ground: Meaning and function of German 'ja', 'doch', 'eben'/'halt' and 'auch'. In: P. Kühnlein, H. Rieser & H. Zeevat (eds.). *Perspectives on Dialogue in the New Millenium*. Amsterdam: Benjamins, 335–349.

Karagjosova, Elena 2004a. *The Meaning and Function of German Modal Particles*. Doctoral dissertation. Universität des Saarlandes, Saarbrücken.

Karagjosova, Elena. 2004b. German 'doch' as a marker of given information. *Sprache und Datenverarbeitung* 28, 71–78.

Karlsson, Fred 1999. *Finnish. An Essential Grammar*. New York: Routlegde.

Karttunen, Lauri 1977. Syntax and semantics of questions. *Linguistics & Philosophy* 1, 3–44.

Kaufmann, Stefan 2004. A Modal Analysis of Expressive Meaning: German *ja* under quantifiers. Paper presented at Kobe Shoin University, Kyoto, 2004.

Kim Chonghyuck & Lianel Wee 2009. Resolving the paradox of Singapore English *hor*. *English World-Wide* 30, 241–261

König, Ekkehard 1977. Modalpartikeln in Fragesätzen. In: H. Weydt (ed.). *Aspekte der Modalpartikeln. Studien zur deutschen Abtönung*. Tübingen: Niemeyer,115–130.

König, Ekkehard & Susanne Requardt 1991. A relevance-theoretic approach to the analysis of modal particles in German. *Multilingua* 10, 63–77.

Kratzer, Angelika 1977. What "must" and "can" must and can mean. *Linguistics & Philosophy* 1, 377–355.

Kratzer, Angelika 1981. The notional category of modality. In: H.-J. Eikmeyer & H. Rieser (eds.). *Words, Worlds, and Contexts: New Approaches in Word Semantics* Berlin: Walter de Gruyter, 38–74.

Kratzer, Angelika 1999. *Beyond 'ouch' and 'oops' How Descriptive and Expressive Meaning Interact*. Ms. Amherst, MA, University of Massachusetts.

Krifka, Manfred 2008. Basic notions of information structure. *Acta Linguistica Hungarica* 55, 243–276.

Kriwonossow, Alexej 1977. *Die modalen Partikeln in der deutschen Gegenwartssprache* (Göppinger Arbeiten zur germanistischen Linguistik 214). Göppingen: Kümmerle.
Lasersohn, Peter 2005. Context dependence, disagreement, and predicates of personal taste. *Linguistics & Philosophy* 28, 643–686.
Lerner, Jean-Yves 1987. Bedeutung und Struktursensitivität der Modalpartikel *doch*. *Linguistische Berichte* 109, 203–229.
Li, Boya 2006. *Chinese Final Particles and the Syntax of the Periphery*. Ph.D. dissertation. University of Leiden.
Lindner, Katrin 1991. 'Wir sind ja doch alte Bekannte' – The use of German *ja* and *doch* as modal particles. In: W. Abraham (ed.). *Discourse Particles*. Amsterdam: Benjamins, 303–328.
Lyons, John 1977. *Semantics*. Cambridge: Cambridge University Press.
Matthewson, Lisa, Henry Davis & Hotze Rullmann 2007. Evidentials as epistemic modals. In: J. Craenenbroeck (ed.). *The Linguistic Variation Yearbook 7*. Amsterdam: Benjamins, 201–254.
Morimoto, J. 1994. *Hanashite no shukan o Arawasu Fukushi ni Tusite* (On Adverbs that Represent the Speaker's Subjectivity). Tokyo: Kuroshio.
Nekula, Marek 1996. *System der Partikeln im Deutschen und Tschechischen. Unter besonderer Berücksichtigung der Abtönungspartikeln*. Tübingen: Niemeyer.
Ormelius-Sandblom, Elisabet 1997. *Die Modalpartikeln "ja", "doch" und "schon". Zu ihrer Syntax, Semantik und Pragmatik* Ph.D. dissertation. Lund University.
Papafragou, Anna 2006. Epistemic modality and truth conditions. *Lingua* 116, 1688–1702.
Péteri, Attila 2002. *Abtönungspartikeln im deutsch-ungarischen Sprachvergleich*. Budapest: ELTE.
Pierrehumbert, Janet & Julia Hirschberg 1990. The meaning of intonational contours in the interpretation of discourse. In: P. R. Cohen, J. Morgan & M. E. Pollack (eds.). *Intentions in Communication*. Cambridge, MA: The MIT Press, 271–311.
Pohlig, A. Whaley & James N. Pohlig 1994. Further thoughts on four discourse particles in Mandara. In: S. H. Levinsohn (ed.). *Discourse Features of Ten Languages of West-Central Africa* (SIL Publications 119). Arlington, TX: University of Texas, 211–221.
Portner, Paul 2009. *Modality*. Oxford: Oxford University Press.
Potts, Christopher 2005. *The Logic of Conventional Implicatures*. Oxford: Oxford University Press.
Potts, Christopher 2007. The expressive dimension. *Theoretical Linguistics* 33, 165–198.
Rinas, Karsten 2006. *Die Abtönungspartikeln 'doch' und 'ja'. Semantik, Idiomatisierung, Kombinationen, tschechische Äquivalente*. Frankfurt: Lang.
Rizzi. Luigi 1997. The fine structure of the left periphery. In: L. Haegeman (ed.). *Elements of Grammar*. Dordrecht: Kluwer, 281–337.
Stalnaker, Robert 1978. Assertion. In: P. Cole (ed.). *Syntax and Semantics 9: Pragmatics*. New York: Academic Press, 315–332.
Stephenson, Tamina C. 2007. *Towards a Theory of Subjective Meaning*. Ph.D. dissertation. MIT, Cambridge, MA.
Thurmair, Maria 1989. *Modalpartikeln und ihre Kombinationen*. Tübingen: Niemeyer.
Truckenbrodt, Hubert 2004. Zur Strukturbedeutung von Interrogativsätzen. *Linguistische Berichte* 199, 313–350.
Truckenbrodt, Hubert 2006. On the semantic motivation of syntactic verb movement to C in German. *Theoretical Linguistics* 32, 275–306.
Waltereit, Richard 2001. Modal particles and their functional equivalents: A speech-act theoretic approach. *Journal of Pragmatics* 33, 1391–1417.

Ward, Gregory & Julia Hirschberg 1985. Implicating uncertainty: The pragmatics of fall-rise intonation. *Language* 61, 747–776.
Ward, Gregory & Julia Hirschberg 1990.
Weydt, Harald 1969. *Abtönungspartikeln*. Bad Homburg: Gehlen.
Zanuttini, Raffaela 1997. *Negation and Clausal Structure: A Comparative Study of Romance Languages*. Oxford: Oxford University Press.
Zeevat, Henk 2000. Discourse particles as speech act markers. *LDV-Forum* 17, 74–91.
Zeevat, Henk 2005. A dynamic approach to discourse particles. In: K. Fischer (ed.). *Discourse Particles. Studies in Pragmatics 1*. Amsterdam: Elsevier, 133–148.
Zimmermann, Malte 2008. Discourse particles in the left periphery. In: B. Shaer et al. (eds.). *Dislocated Elements in Discourse: Syntactic, Semantic, and Pragmatic Perspectives*. London: Routledge, 200–231.

Index

accent placement 471–473
accessibility 88, 481, 489–494, 498, 505
alternative questions 173, 179, 180, 186, 191, 193, 198, 201–204, 218
anaphora 25–33, 38–41, 208, 309, 311–314, 322–328, 383, 467, 481–487, 496–508
– piggyback 481–485, 497–505, 508
answer congruence 171, 181–185, 188–196, 343, 353, 475
argument reversal 428–432

biased questions 216, 217
binding 1–42, 78, 115, 138, 232, 244, 265–272, 276–278, 312, 323–328, 353, 361, 462, 493, 506, 525
– variable-free 15, 18–23, 271
– variable-ful 18–23
bridging 481, 494–497, 501–508

categorical 286, 386, 389, 397, 406
coherence 42, 183, 331, 332, 408, 413, 450–476, 514
– and coreference 451, 460–462
cohesion 450–454, 460, 468, 471, 476, 514
comment 339–341, 344, 347, 348, 366–369, 375, 382, 383, 389, 407, 414
conjunction 85, 135–168, 189–192, 215, 314–317, 333, 366, 438, 450, 466–469, 473, 493, 506, 507
– reduction 136, 137, 148–152, 157, 160, 161, 164, 168, 466–471
connectivity 23, 250–253, 258, 265–277, 394
constituent ellipsis 313, 321–325
constituent questions 173–180, 204, 209, 212, 213, 342
contradiction 46–54, 61, 69, 78, 106, 107, 122
contrast 138–143, 165, 216, 236, 289, 329–331, 348–360, 370–376, 386–401, 422, 454, 457–459, 472, 473, 519
coordinate ellipsis 314–321
Coordinate Structure Constraint 135, 137, 140, 141, 148–150, 159, 469, 470
coordination 17, 135–156, 162–168, 201, 203, 254, 314, 315, 318, 332, 333, 438

coordination vs. Subordination 137–143
coordinator 135–145, 153, 154, 158, 437
copular clauses 250–255, 259–265, 271, 277, 278, 284
copular sentences 33, 284, 288, 290, 301, 302, 443
copula 23, 33, 146, 150, 250–278, 281, 284, 288, 290, 301, 302, 439, 440, 443, 445
counting quantifiers 25, 31, 34–36
covert subject 225–227, 232, 236, 244–246

definiteness effect 107, 424
definiteness restriction 281, 285, 288, 291–301
dependent indefinites 93, 113–115
directive operator 227
discourse
– coherence 454, 459, 460, 466, 468, 473, 514
– cohesion 451–454, 460, 476
– interpretation 234, 235, 466, 468, 476, 481, 487
– markers 512, 514, 515
– organization 382, 389, 474, 511, 512
– particles 310, 511–541
– particles and evidentials 520, 539, 540
– referents 71, 113–115, 126, 151, 286, 287, 354, 389, 394, 406, 441, 481–507
Discourse Representation Theory 39, 166, 487–493, 496–502, 505–508
disjunction 6, 57–59, 85, 135–138, 142, 143, 153–156, 165–167, 198, 201, 209
dislocation
– left 287, 345, 351, 364–369, 392–396, 400, 420–422, 427
– right 422, 427, 428
distributive scope 1, 25–39
domain widening 63, 73, 104–112
downward entailment 59, 79–81, 87, 125

ellipsis 4, 17, 22, 97, 135–141, 150–152, 164–166, 255, 266–269, 277, 306–334, 383, 436, 450–453, 466–468, 473

546 — Index

ellipsis
- A- 308, 313–325, 331
- constituent 313, 321–325
- coordinate 314–321
- S- 309–313
embedded coordinations 137, 162–164
embedding 56, 87, 114, 171, 189–193, 198, 209–216, 253–255, 264, 403, 488–493, 498–502, 508, 525, 530
epistemic states 511, 512, 529
equative clauses 253, 261–264
equatives 252–254, 257, 258, 261–263, 268, 439, 443–446
existential construction 283, 298, 422–425
expletive subject 282, 285
expressing emotion and politeness 530, 531
expressive meaning 19, 513–518, 520

focus 52, 53, 175, 182, 183, 188, 191–194, 200, 205, 218, 251, 258, 316, 328–330, 340–344, 349–364, 371, 372, 375, 382–387, 414, 432–434, 473, 522, 541
- and background 340–344, 358
- and NPIs in questions 72, 76, 218–219
- marking 104, 183, 355–364
- sensitive operators 291, 357–360, 364, 375
force 58, 85, 108, 160, 168, 177, 217, 225–227, 234–238, 242–247, 291, 368, 369, 491, 521
frame-setting topic 347, 348, 351, 370
free choice items 73, 74, 84–86, 90–93, 107–112

gapping 137, 140, 152, 153, 167, 313–322, 330, 333, 436–439, 468
generalized quantifiers 4–6, 36, 146, 156, 208, 296, 366, 367
given and new information 340, 352, 414–416, 418, 423, 471, 495
givenness 330, 352–355, 374, 375, 398, 414, 416, 446, 471–473, 494, 519

identificational clauses 252, 255, 259–263, 357
identification of reference point 526, 528
illocutionary forces of imperatives 228, 234

imperatives 84, 86, 90, 93, 110, 147, 225–247, 521, 528, 529
imperative subject 232, 233, 236, 238, 244–247
implicature 46, 54–65, 77, 102–106, 116, 126, 145, 155, 163, 167, 220, 235, 330, 355, 383, 469, 512–518, 524–531, 540
indefinites and interrogatives 171, 207–209
indeterminacy 310, 311
indirect speech acts 235, 236, 511, 530, 531, 532
information
- status 413–418, 428, 431, 432, 436, 439
- structure 221, 257, 260, 287, 298, 328–330, 339–341, 364, 375, 383, 389, 415–418, 421, 432–434, 438–439, 471, 520, 522
inquisitive semantics 184, 201–209, 219
inversion 257, 258, 371, 416, 417, 428–432, 435–438

logical entailment 54–66, 154

minimizers 69, 71, 76, 94–103, 125
modal auxiliaries 511, 516, 523, 524, 539
modality 99, 125, 225–227, 238–244, 247
multiple questions 175, 186, 197, 204, 212, 386

negation 2, 46–67, 69–127, 142, 155, 164–167, 186, 191, 203, 205, 258, 271, 291, 300, 321, 355, 373, 374, 489, 499, 538
- and contradiction 46–54
- and logical entailment 54–67
non-deictic indefinites 93, 116, 120
NPI-licensing/-licensers (see also *polarity*) 37, 60, 66, 76–104, 125, 267
NPIs in veridical contexts 99–103

occasion 458, 459, 464, 469, 470, 473

parallel 325, 332, 437, 457, 458, 467–475, 512
parallelism 143–152, 325–331, 458
- and conjunction reduction 150–152
particle combinations 533–535
partitional approach 195–200, 206

Plan Set 234–236, 247
polarity
– negative 37, 69–73, 79, 112, 218, 251, 265
– negative polarity item (NPI) 37, 46, 59–120, 125–127, 218, 219, 251, 265–267, 270, 271, 275, 278
  strong NPIs 60–63, 71, 81, 84, 93–100, 118
– positive 69, 70, 74, 75, 116–125
– positive polarity item (PPI) 64, 69, 70, 74–76, 116–125
– questions 173, 177–180, 186, 188, 191, 193, 198, 216
polymorphic *be* 264, 265, 274
postposing 417, 422, 425–428
predicate restriction 300–302
predicates
– individual-level 285, 286, 300
– stage-level 285, 286, 300
predicational clauses 252–256, 261–264
preposing 381, 400, 417–422, 427, 428, 432–438, 446
presupposition 40, 48–54, 77, 82, 143, 187, 197, 212, 297, 343, 360, 375, 383, 395, 408, 414, 417, 471, 485, 505, 516, 522, 540
processing model 463
pronouns 8, 15–25, 38–41, 174, 190, 207, 208, 245, 251, 256, 267, 271, 285, 293–300, 307, 311, 328, 345, 396, 415, 421, 428, 450, 453, 461–466, 481–499, 508
– as definite descriptions 38–41
– that start out as free variables 18
propositional coordination 153–155

quantificational 38, 39, 48–54, 104, 157, 254, 272, 281–300, 324, 326, 339, 345, 360–362, 365, 368–376, 393, 399, 400
quantification 40, 52, 53, 62, 63, 71, 115, 185, 215, 288, 359–364, 368–369, 384, 399, 483, 484, 500–506
Quantifier Raising 37, 159, 294, 361
quantifiers 4, 15, 35, 50, 82, 146, 215, 296, 361
quantifying into questions 214, 215
question/answer relation 22, 171, 181, 188, 343, 474

question-embedding predicates 198, 209–212
questions 76–78, 83, 108–111, 123, 171–220, 237, 251, 268, 277, 309, 342, 343, 350–353, 383–388, 459, 473–476, 521, 527–532
– and text structure 219, 220
Question under Discussion 219, 351, 375, 382–389, 403, 473–476

referential deficiency 70, 93, 104, 112–116
referential variation 30, 31

scalar implicature 54–62, 65, 116, 167
scalarity 69, 70, 74, 76, 93, 103–112, 116, 117, 124–126
scope 1–42, 49–54, 61–66, 71–79, 102, 112–126, 151, 162–167, 215, 289–292, 300, 325, 333, 358–376, 481–484, 491, 493, 498–506, 533
– judgments 26, 27
Skolem functions 31–33
some indefinites 30, 117–121, 207–209
specificational clauses 252–258, 261–277
specificity 31–33, 113, 121, 406
speech acts 171–173, 182, 209, 215, 218, 235, 310, 366, 514, 535
strong NPIs 60–63, 71, 81, 84, 93–100, 118
Syntactic and semantic relations among coordinands 143–153
syntax/semantics interface 3, 42, 66, 324

theme 286, 312, 382–385, 388, 389, 407, 470
thetic 286, 386, 389, 397
topicality 346–352, 364, 369–374, 381, 384, 388–396, 400, 401, 404–408
– tests for 390–392, 395, 406
– universality of 405–408
topic marking 346–351, 364–374, 392–405
topic 286, 339, 340, 344–352, 364–374, 381–408, 470
– and comment 286, 340–352, 366, 375, 389, 407
– in discourse 145, 351, 381–389, 394–397, 406–408
– aboutness 339, 340, 345, 348, 351, 352, 364–370, 375
– contrastive 339, 348–351, 370–376, 386–395, 398, 400, 405

variable 8, 11, 15–23, 32, 112–116, 126, 236, 271, 273, 441, 443, 462
– -free binding 15, 18–23, 271
– -ful binding 18–23
veridicality 76, 85–92, 120
– non- 76, 86–90, 92, 93, 99, 101–103, 125, 126, 219
– anti- 90, 93–99

widening 62, 63, 73, 74, 104–112, 125, 126
word order 36, 37, 137, 178, 315, 319, 354, 371, 389, 413–418, 422–423, 429, 432, 439, 443, 446, 541

www.ingramcontent.com/pod-product-compliance
Lightning Source LLC
Chambersburg PA
CBHW031539300426
44111CB00006BA/107